MORE CREATIVE

USES OF

CHILDREN'S LITERATURE

Volume I

MORE CREATIVE
USES OF
CHILDREN'S LITERATURE

Volume I
Introducing Books in All Kinds of Ways

Mary Ann Paulin

Library Professional Publications
1992

First published as a Library Professional Publication,
an imprint of The Shoe String Press, Inc.
Hamden, Connecticut 06514

Printed in the United States of America

Library of Congress Cataloging-in-Publication Data

Paulin, Mary Ann, 1943–
More creative uses of children's literature/
Mary Ann Paulin
p.   cm.
Includes bibliographical references and indexes.
Contents: v. 1. Introducing books in all kinds of ways
1. School libraries—Activity programs.
2. Children's literature—Study and teaching.
3. Libraries, Children's—Activity programs.
4. Activity programs in education.
5. Children—Books and reading.
I. Title.
Z675.S3P247   1992   92-8916
027.8—dc20
ISBN 0-208-02202-3 (cloth)
ISBN 0-208-02203-1 (paper)

The paper used in this publication meets the
minimum requirements of American National Standard
for Information Sciences-Permanence of Paper for
Library Printed Materials, ANSI Z39.48-1984 ∞

*To my husband, Ken; my parents, Bertha and
the late Ervin Strieter; and to all children
everywhere, especially my nieces and nephews:
Jeanne and John Rose, Heidi and Marisa Strieter,
and Mike and John Strieter.*

CONTENTS

Preface

This book has been written to answer the question posed to me by teachers, librarians, and school library/media specialists—"When are you going to write another book that will introduce the new books published since 1982?" *More Creative Uses of Children's Literature* is the answer to that question.

More Creative Uses of Children's Literature is divided into two volumes, and this is *Volume 1*. It is organized in much the same manner as chapter one of *Creative Uses of Children's Literature,* as it introduces books in all kinds of ways—this time covering those titles published from the early 1980s right up to 1990. The objectives are the same as those of *Creative Uses,* too, but the techniques vary depending upon the books or other media being introduced. Because there is carryover in topics from one book to another, each section of text incorporates page references to *Creative Uses of Children's Literature.* This is indicated as [CU + page numbers]. These page numbers in turn lead to previously published books and other media, to expand the user's web of possibilities in introducing books to children.

More Creative Uses of Children's Literature, Volume 2, concentrates on specific marriages of literature with other enrichments: experiencing art through picture books; enhancing books through music; enjoying poetry; and having fun with storytelling, puppets, creative dramatics, riddles, read-alouds, and thinking skill exercise. It, too, cross-references to *Creative Uses,* and connects to *Volume 1* of *More Creative Uses* by its dual subject index. Both volumes of *More Creative Uses of Children's Literature* can therefore be used independently, together, and in conjunction with the parent volume.

More Creative Uses of Children's Literature is based on the same premise as *Creative Uses of Children's Literature*: introduce as many books as possible to children in as many creative ways as possible; every book or topic should be enhanced by a dozen related books or media; and there are fascinating books out there for everyone—they just have to be identified and shared. This whole premise has been the keystone of my career as a school library/media specialist. Within the last few years, these ideas have gained nationwide popularity and have been incorporated into the "Whole Language Approach" and "Literature-Based Reading." I applaud this effort to share children's literature with children and will continue to practice these techniques and encourage other teachers and librarians to do so.

During the study of books and multimedia about children's literature during the last seven years, I have perceived several interesting trends:

1. A number of studies of our educational system have placed emphasis on reading or the lack of reading skills in the United States. Searches for improved methods of teaching reading have been one result. Also "reading" and "literacy" have become household words and the awareness has had some positive effects.

2. The introduction of literature-based reading and the resurgence of the whole language approach are just two developments. The "discovery" that children can learn to read by reading "real books" is an extension of the individualized reading approach of the 1960s.

3. New approaches in the teaching of reading have produced basal readers with more selections from quality children's literature.

4. Favorite books about reading aloud are in new editions and other authors are also preparing lists of books to read aloud to children at various ages. Many of these books are aimed at parents.

5. Emphasis has been placed on the importance of books and the authors and illustrators who create them, and on writing as a companion to reading comprehension. More students are becoming involved in *writing* projects which produce class or individual publications.

6. The emphasis on creativity and thinking skills has made quality children's literature more attractive as a source of involving children in thinking and feeling.

7. Books are available in a variety of formats. Two formats which have burgeoned in large numbers are board books and "big" books. Neither is new but their rebirth is the reaction to the philosophy that reading to children should begin soon after they are born. Working professional parents with two incomes may account for the success of these books because they can afford to buy them. In our search for information about the "Whole Language Approach," we turned to Australia and New Zealand where this approach has long been used. In doing so we found the "big book" which has been employed in both countries for decades. Although the concept of the big book has been used by teachers using the "language experience" technique, the commercial publication of those books is new in our country.

8. An ever-increasing number of multimedia spin-offs include recordings, 16mm films, and sound filmstrips are now joined by videos, dolls, rubber stamps, and more exposure to books on network, instructional, and cable television.

9. For years the library profession has been asserting that the publishing life of books needs to be extended. A new trend is the reissuing of favorite books, some published as long ago as 40 years or more.

10. Related to #7 is that old favorites are being expanded into a never-ending list of sequels. Whenever a character is a success, that person, as well as family members, are introduced into other books. Maybe this idea was borrowed from the television spin off idea.

11. Books are being packaged and marketed for a new audience—parents and children. The library is no longer the main purchaser of books for children. This trend has contributed to the increase in the number of books in series because the recognition factor is so important in advertising.

12. In a number of books, several authors and illustrators have combined talents and contributed segments or chapters of a whole book. Some of these books have been sold for charity purposes. Some books have also been illustrated with paintings and art objects from museums.

13. More poetry anthologies, especially attractively illustrated ones, have entered the market. We already had picture books based on individual songs. There are more of these, as well as individual picture books of single poems. Classic poems and songs that are in the public domain provide illustrators with text by deceased writers who do not ask to split royalty payments.

14. More books are aimed at the preschool child. Again the concern about education and more discretionary income has helped these books to sell.

15. Books in the contemporary realism category have gained in popularity. Books about divorce, varying family patterns, and child abuse are popular. Books about death are now being joined by ones about grandparents and aging people. There are more books with adult main characters.

16. More books are being published with multicultural themes. Many of these books are in the folklore category. Illustrations in picture books show children of many cultures to reflect our changing census.

17. Unfortunately books, just like everything else, are suffering from inflation. It is not uncommon to find picture books as well as other children's titles priced at $17.00. Increased costs have helped the ever-popular paperback and have also resulted in more original paperbacks.

18. While we give lip service to the importance of providing quality literature to children, we are allowing increasing cuts in library/reading services to children: decreased budgets for materials which have become more expensive; elimination of local branch libraries or children's departments; cuts in professional staffing of school library/media centers and public li-

braries; and the closing of departments in institutions of higher learning that train these professionals.

Despite all these changes, there are many professionals dedicated to helping children to listen, look, research, think, plan, create, and above all to read. This book is for them.

Acknowledgments

Special thanks go to the following libraries and librarians for opening their collections to me: Bay County Library, Bay City, MI; Boys and Girls Haus of the Toronto Public Library, Toronto, Ontario, Canada; The Cairns Public Library, Cairns, Queensland, Australia; The Canadian Children's Book Center, Toronto; The Carnegie Public Library, Ishpeming, MI; The Cooperative Children's Book Center, University of Wisconsin, Madison, WI; Dallas Public Library, Dallas, TX; Library of Congress, Washington, D.C.; Library of Michigan, Escanaba, MI; school libraries in the Marquette Area Public Schools, Marquette, MI; Martin Luther King Public Library, Washington, D.C.; school library/media centers in the Negaunee Public Schools, Negaunee, MI; Negaunee Public Library, Negaunee, MI; Peter White Public Library, Marquette, MI; New Orleans Public Library, New Orleans, LA; school library/media centers and central media center, Newport News Public Schools, Newport News, VA; Olivera Library, Texas Southmost College/Pan American University, Brownsville, TX; Olson Library, Northern Michigan University, Marquette, MI; Salt Lake City Public Library, Salt Lake City, UT; San Antonio Public Library, San Antonio, TX; San Francisco Public Library, San Francisco, CA; Superiorland Library Cooperative, Marquette, MI; Sylvia Ashton-Warner Library, Auckland College of Education, Auckland, New Zealand; Thomas Hughes Children's Library, Chicago Public Library/Cultural Center, Chicago, IL; University of Wisconsin-Madison, School of Library and Information Studies Library, Madison, WI; and the Whitebridge Primary School Library, Newcastle, New South Wales, Australia. And as late additions, the Atlanta Public Library, Atlanta, GA, and REMC 21, Regional Educational Media Center in Marquette, MI.

List of Abbreviations

The following abbreviations are used in the text to designate publishers of textbook series. All individual volumes and editions are cited by author in the book index, and by title in the title index at the back of this book.

Ginn: Ginn Press (a division of Simon & Schuster, Inc.)
HBJ: Harcourt Brace Jovanovich, Inc.
HM: Houghton Mifflin Co.
Mac: Macmillan Publishing
SF: Scott, Foresman Co.
SB/Ginn: Silver Burdett & Ginn (a division of Simon & Schuster, Inc.)

The Objectives of This Book and How to Make the Most of Them

A LIST OF OBJECTIVES

1. To introduce students to a variety of books from which they can make selections for educational or recreational reading.

2. To furnish teachers, public librarians, and school library/media specialists with techniques and samples of ways to present books to children in an interesting manner.

3. To inspire adults who work with children to read more widely and share what they read with children.

4. To emphasize the importance of promoting reading through bulletin boards and displays, booktalks and panels.

5. To suggest books that have been successfully shared with students to teachers, public librarians, school library/media specialists, and parents.

6. To employ such media as sound filmstrips, recordings, 16mm films, and videos, to stimulate the use of print materials.

7. To capitalize on movies or network and cable television to stimulate reading.

8. To utilize instructional television to promote reading.

9. To help students to distinguish between fiction and nonfiction.

10. To introduce children to various literature genres: fantasy, science fiction, biography, historical fiction, survival stories, and mystery and detective stories.

11. To expand the vocabulary of students to include such terms as sequel, series, editor, author, pseudonym, title, publisher, copyright date, title page, table of contents, and index.

12. To enhance the basal reading program of the school by providing supplementary reading.

13. To enrich the reading and writing of students using the whole language approach.

14. To discover the wealth of materials for use in literature-based reading programs.

MAKING THE MOST OF MEDIA INTRODUCED HERE

1. Use booktalks to give group reading guidance.

2. Involve students in booktalks by referring to special interests or experiences of particular students.

3. Share personal experiences during booktalks, especially reading experiences.

4. Establish rapport and common ground during a booktalk by reading or referring to clippings from magazines and newspapers that relate to subjects found in books that are being discussed.

5. Introduce the universal instinct for survival to students through a booktalk on survival books.

6. Investigate and understand other periods in history or contemplate the future through a booktalk on books about time travel.

7. Utilize objects as vehicles for entering the past in time travel books.

8. Give a booktalk about the Holocaust to teach students the value of learning history to avoid repeating the mistakes of the past.

9. Motivate students to read by sharing popular books that are winners of state awards chosen by children.

10. Utilize the enthusiasm of student readers in peer book panels.

11. Examine parallels between situations in literature and the real lives of people.

12. Provide bibliographies to follow up booktalks.

13. Utilize computer databases to register books and their many subjects so students can locate them easily or pull them for subject bibliographies.

14. Employ commercial computer games and databases to introduce books to students.

15. Teach students to identify and locate books which contain the elements of: plot, theme, style, characterization, and setting through multimedia and children's books.

16. Explain phrases in book titles to introduce theme and plot of a book with students.

17. Identify the settings (time or place) of books to students and discuss the relevance of setting to a story.

18. Introduce characterization through the following types of book characters: humans, nonhumans, animals, and inanimate objects.

19. Compare literary characters to each other.

20. Help students to understand the style of an author in one or more books by that author.

21. Encourage beginning readers by providing easy-to-read books for practice and fun.

22. Expand basal readers by providing poems, books, and multimedia on subjects found in basal readers.

23. Correlate library instruction to basal reader topics or subjects from literature-based studies.

24. Suggest books and sequels or books in series to stimulate students to read an entire book from which a selection appears in a basal reader.

25. Provide students with books by an author whose article or fiction selection appears in a basal reader.

26. Teach students to locate information about authors and discuss the connection between their experiences and their writing, to enrich the reading of their books.

27. Introduce books about animals to students through a booktalk which includes titles with animal characters.

28. Use book titles as mnemonic devices to introduce books through plot, theme, style, characterization, and setting.

29. Introduce time settings in book titles to reinforce the concepts of minutes, hours, days, nights, weeks, months, and years.

30. Discuss the differences between fiction and nonfiction through a variety of subjects found in books, magazines, and multimedia.

31. Locate nonfiction materials to corroborate information found in fiction.

32. Teach students to use *The National Geographic Index, 1888–1988*; *The Abridged Readers' Guide to Periodical Literature*; and *The Children's Magazine Guide* to locate magazine articles.

33. Capitalize on the natural interests of students by introducing books about the *Titanic*, robots, trucks, cars, boats, airplanes, and space flight.

34. Use multimedia to introduce a variety of subjects in fiction and nonfiction including: whales, dolphins, sharks, dinosaurs, snakes, mice, foxes, owls, pigs, and penguins.

35. Learn more about the following world areas from fiction and nonfiction: the Antarctic, the Everglades, and prairies.

36. Interpret relationships with siblings, grandparents, parents, and friends through books.

37. Share books about interpersonal relationships which include manners, bullies, handicaps, and personal problems found in nonfiction and realistic fiction.

38. Capture the past in fiction and nonfiction through fascinating time periods such as Ancient Egypt, the Middle Ages, the American Civil War, and frontier and pioneer life.

39. Expand the reading of students through related books, magazines, and multimedia.

40. Research a topic like spiders to locate related folklore, fiction, nonfiction, or poetry in books, magazines, and multimedia.

41. Increase the reading and writing abilities of students through the whole language approach to reading or through literature-based reading.

42. Introduce favorite book characters through sequels and series.

43. Reintroduce children's literature classics through paperbacks, new editions, adaptations, author background information, sound recordings, television, filmstrips, 16mm films, and videos.

44. Share nonfiction through magazines, books, reference materials, and a variety of multimedia.

45. Teach students to use the table of contents and indexes of books to find information in nonfiction books. Also teach the use of indexes to reference sets.

46. Expand teaching about biography by introducing the following types: individual biography, collective biography, autobiography, fictionalized biography, and biographical fiction.

47. Remind students of the benefits of democracy through books about the U.S. Constitution.

48. Emphasize our multicultural heritage through reading about the Statue of Liberty, Ellis Island, and immigrants.

49. Incorporate reading, writing, speaking, listening, and researching projects into the study of immigration and family history.

50. Encourage students to explore family history through stories of family experiences in books or real life and to interpret them through writing, speaking, and other forms of expression.

51. Celebrate the birthdays or anniversaries of favorite book characters or new editions of their books.

52. Provide books about birthdays to students when they have birthdays, and have birthday students choose the books to be read on their birthdays.

53. Display or read books by authors on their birthdays. Send authors a birthday card.

54. Increase the ability of students to locate many books by an author.

55. Discuss authors by showing sound filmstrips, 16mm films, or videos about them and their books; by relating firsthand information gleaned from conferences and workshops; by reading information taken from book jackets, biographies, and collective biographies from the reference section of the library. Teach students to locate this information also.

56. Review the information found on the book's title page and its reverse side: author or editor; title; subtitle; place of publication; publisher; and copyright date.

57. Identify the following parts of a book: title page; table of contents; index; and glossary while students are studying nonfiction.

58. Stimulate discussion of many topics after reading related books.

59. Help students adjust to real-life situations through fiction and nonfiction.

60. Encourage an appreciation of senior citizens through characters found in literature.

61. Stimulate an interest in fantasy and science fiction while defining the genres.

62. Furnish realistic fiction to students to help them understand themselves and cope with situations they face in real life.

63. Use historical fiction to enhance the study of any period in the history of the world.

64. Capitalize on instructional television programs to introduce books on many subjects to students.

65. Stimulate reading by advertising or following up on programs from network television through displays of related materials.

66. Allow television programs which introduce books and characters from children's literature to motivate students to read those books.

67. Capitalize on television and movie viewing by providing books and other media to further related interests.

68. Introduce the techniques of television viewing through books which include television in the plot.

69. Enjoy mysteries with students through displays or individual and group reading guidance.

70. Learn more about history through biography, nonfiction, and historical fiction, especially the following periods: the American Civil War and frontier and pioneer life.

CHAPTER ONE

Booktalks

Booktalks [CU 17–30; 711] are an important means of introducing books to students. In formal booktalks, school and public librarians, school library/media specialists, and teachers introduce books by sharing a group of books with a class as a whole. Students can also give compelling booktalks because they have credibility with their peers. When four or five students appear together on a peer book panel, it's more fun and less threatening for the students giving the booktalks. Choose students from a variety of backgrounds so there will be someone on the panel with whom listeners can identify. Each student can talk about a different genre, one which he or she especially identifies with and can discuss enthusiastically. If five students talk about five books, then 25 books are shared.

There are professional books which can help in giving booktalks. Bodart-Talbot's *Booktalk! 3* contains 500 booktalks, contributed by 80 booktalkers from all over the United States which range from two to seven minutes in length. More booktalks supplement *Booktalk! 3* and are included in special pull-out sections of the *Wilson Library Bulletin* called "The Booktalker." Bodart's *Booktalk! 2: Booktalking for All Ages and Audiences* shares hundreds of books and ways to introduce them to students and replaces her first book *Booktalk! Booktalking and School Visiting for Young Audiences*. A videocassette, *Booktalking with Joni Bodart*, shares the following categories of booktalks: plot summaries; anecdotes, episodes and short stories; characterization; and mood-based booktalks.

The newest in the Juniorplots series is Gillespie and Naden's *Juniorplots 3: A Book Talk Guide for Use with Readers Ages 12–16*. This book also includes biographies of the authors whose titles are included in the book. Earlier books include Gillespie and Lembo's *Introducing Books: A Guide for the Middle Grades* and *Juniorplots: A Book Talk Manual for Teachers and Librarians*, and Gillespie's *More Juniorplots: A Guide for Teachers and Librarians*.

Spirt's *Introducing Bookplots 3: A Book Talk Guide for Use with Readers Ages 8–12* is a recent sequel to her *Introducing More Books: A Guide for the Middle Grades*. Professionals will find *Primaryplots: A Book Talk Guide for Use with Readers Ages 4–8* by Thomas to be helpful.

Nine rules for booktalks appear on pages 23–24 of Kimball's *Children's Caravan*. Ten easy and painless steps to booktalking appear on pages 11–13 of Freeman's *Books Kids Will Sit Still For*. Types of booktalks appear on pages 13–19. Check pages 6–7 of DeBruyne and Sherman's *The Handbook for the 1988 Young Readers' Choice Award Nominees* for eight "Helpful Hints for Booktalkers." These annual booklets are for teachers, librarians, and school library/media specialists who are getting students ready to vote on the Young Readers' Choice Award in Alaska, Alberta, British Columbia, Idaho, Montana, Oregon, and Washington. Information for two booktalks is included with each of the 15 nominees. Check the most recent handbook for more booktalks.

Although Rochman's *Tales of Love and Terror: Booktalking the Classics, Old and New* is aimed at professionals who work with students in grades 7 through 12, the techniques cited can be used with intermediate and middle school students. Rochman covers such topics as selection, preparation, style, themes, and techniques. Rochman appears on a video of the same title in which she demonstrates techniques for preparing a booktalk and for choosing the right excerpt to read aloud.

Chapter 3, "Booktalks" of Bauer's *This Way to Books*, pages 147–92, contains information about traditional and unusual booktalks. Some creative booktalks include the use of mailboxes, banners, slides, and letters. Other booktalk topics are food, cats, growing things, and cities. Methods include the personal approach, author approach, theme approach, and the use of intriguing first sentences.

STEPS FOR PREPARING AND PRESENTING BOOKTALKS [CU 20–22].

Booktalks allow adults to share books with a whole group of students while reading guidance is done with students on an individual basis. However, the means for remembering titles and information for sharing the plot and characters in booktalks and reading guidance are often very similar. Ideas for introducing books through their titles appear in the chapter, "Introducing Books by Titles," with various subthemes.

The following guidelines can be helpful when preparing and presenting booktalks.

1. DEFINE THE OBJECTIVES FOR THE BOOKTALK. The purpose may be to present many books on a topic being studied by a class so that students can pick one book to read and report on. Public librarians or school library/media specialists may use booktalks to introduce themselves as persons who know about books and can help students choose from a a wide variety. Booktalks provide an excellent vehicle for sharpening listening skills. Another purpose might be to introduce new fiction or unfamiliar authors to students. Students in clubs and special interest groups can learn about fiction or nonfiction pertaining to their hobby or interest. The purpose of a booktalk might be to introduce a specific genre to students.

2. DECIDE ON A THEME OR SUBTHEME. The theme of the booktalk is tied closely to its objectives. If the purpose of a booktalk is to introduce a specific genre of books to students, then the theme is specific to that genre—fantasy, science fiction, mystery, biography, historical fiction, realistic fiction, etc. Each of the booktalks included in this chapter has a

theme. The time travel booktalk highlights books from one type of fantasy. The Holocaust booktalk introduces students to a period in history when unspeakable horrors took place and the theme can be how to keep this from happening again and/or to show how humans can overcome adversity. The survival booktalk also shows how humans overcome adversity in disasters such as plane crashes, boating accidents, earthquakes, or tornadoes. A broader booktalk could relate to overcoming adversities caused by disasters, war, or handicaps. Books about frontier and pioneer life can be introduced to students via a booktalk. Books on a particular historical period can include nonfiction, biography, and historical fiction. Books that have won state awards in contests in which students pick the winners have special appeal. Books on all these topics are found in TIME TRAVEL: A BOOKTALK; SURVIVAL BOOKS: A LITERATURE-BASED UNIT OR BOOKTALK TOPIC; THE HOLOCAUST: A BOOKTALK; BOOKTALK-ING: 118 AWARD-WINNING TITLES, all in Chapter 1; and "If You Like the 'Little House' Books" in Chapter 10.

3. READ MANY BOOKS. In order to find books to share successfully, you have to read many books. Don't use books that you didn't enjoy yourself and don't try to talk about books you haven't read. Discard any books that are not suitable to the objectives and theme you have selected.

4. MAKE A NOTE CARD FOR EACH BOOK. Include basic bibliographic information: author; title; place of publication; publisher; copyright date; call number; reading level; and the library where the book is located. Also include: an annotation; pages from which quotes or descriptions are taken; sequels; similar books; and ways to introduce the book. It is helpful to attach any paragraphs or pages to be read to the card. When planning the booktalk, arrange the note cards in the order of presentation. Rereading the card just prior to booktalk time refreshes the memory about the book.

5. CHOOSE THE BOOKS TO BE DISCUSSED. Be sure to include more books than there are students if students are to choose a book for a report. This is especially important when students are to present oral reports on their books. If the purpose is just to introduce books to read for fun, more than one copy of a book could be made available. Decide which books will be explained in depth and which will be mentioned briefly as sequels or series titles, or as books with a similar theme.

6. PREPARE AN ANNOTATED BIBLIOGRAPHY. Use the note cards to prepare an annotated bibliography which is in alphabetical order by the author. The list should include all books whether discussed in depth or just mentioned briefly. Some booktalkers give the bibliography to the students so books of interest can be checked as the booktalk progresses. Others find the rattling of papers distracting. If the bibliography is not provided to students, tell them at the beginning of the booktalk where to

find it at a later time. Students often ask months later for a booktalk book and the bibliography will be helpful to them at that time. After the booktalk, place the bibliography on a bulletin board, in a booktalk notebook, or attach it to a cart with some of the books from the booktalk. As books are returned, place them on the cart. Students appreciate having them together in one place for some time after the booktalk so they can find more than one book.

7. DECIDE METHODS FOR INTRODUCING EACH BOOK. Booktalkers can introduce books in a variety of ways: by introducing main characters (humans, nonhumans, animals, inanimate objects); by giving part of the plot (but never the ending); by explaining the title; by describing or providing background for the setting which may include either time or place; by reading an excerpt; by comparing it with a similar book; by making a connection between the book and that particular group of listeners; by sharing a personal experience connected with the book; by providing anecdotes and information about the author; by explaining the author's purpose for writing the book, or the circumstances under which the book was written.

8. ARRANGE THE BOOKS IN THE ORDER OF PRESENTATION. When organizing the booktalk, arrange the books on a booktruck or on tables in the order in which they are to be introduced. Booktrucks are essential if the booktalk is not held in the library/media center. Place all books which are alike together, then determine how they are to be linked. Put the note cards with the books if you need to use them again.

9. ESTABLISH TRANSITION BOOKS. In order to effect a smooth transition from one title to another, link them with a common thread. Common elements could be authors, setting, plot similarities, characters, style, theme, or genre. Sometimes chronological order determines when books are introduced. Fiction can be separated from nonfiction unless the books are linked by theme or time period.

10. HOLD UP EACH BOOK AS YOU SPEAK ABOUT IT. Be sure to mention the author and title clearly so students can write them down or check them on their bibliographies. The book cover or jacket can help interest students in the book.

11. DISCUSS BOOKS IN A CONVERSATIONAL MANNER. Remember that you are sharing books with friends, not lecturing to an audience.

12. PLACE THE BOOKS SO LISTENERS CAN SEE THEM. If you have enough space available, books can be set up with the front cover showing. If many books are introduced, pile them on top of each other with the spines facing the listeners.

13. INVITE STUDENTS TO CHECK OUT THE BOOKS. After all, the chief purpose of sharing the books is so that students will read them.

14. STAND ASIDE FROM THE RUSH TO CHECK OUT THE BOOKS. If the booktalk has been successful, you will have to step aside quickly so students can grab the books that especially appeal to them. Stay nearby to help locate a particular title that the listener wants. If a student wants to read a book and the book has been chosen by someone else, prepare a reserve slip for that student.

TIME TRAVEL: A BOOKTALK [CU 109–18; 728].   Books about time travel can be introduced to all students through booktalks and there are several ways to introduce them. However, they are especially appropriate for gifted students because of the frequent use of flashbacks, the stimulus for investigating another period in history, and understanding the significance of a future event. Books about time travel can be a separate category of any booktalk which includes fantasy or science fiction books. Because of shades of difference in the definitions of fantasy and science fiction, a space and time book can appear in either category and sometimes in both. When a booktalk is composed of only time travel books, they can be organized into groups by how the main character(s) enter(s) the new time; when that other time (past or future) occurs; similar themes in the books; sequels; and authors who write in the genre.

The most common method of introducing time travel books is to describe the means of entering the other time. This could be through a watch or sundial, fog, harp, tombstone, stone, garden, house, game, painting, thimble, sword, coin, boat, ship, or a cupboard.

One of the most famous series of books about time travel is the Narnia series, beginning with *The Lion, the Witch, and the Wardrobe*, written by C. S. Lewis [CU 117–18]. Share these books in a booktalk by explaining that the children travel to the magic land through a wardrobe (which may have to be defined as a closetlike cupboard). Then introduce the 7 books with a sentence about each one. Students may wish to read Barratt's *C. S. Lewis and His World*.

Several stories transport characters into another time using a watch or sundial. A watch transports Audrey and Nathan into New York during the American Revolution in Chew's *Trapped in Time*. Read the Latin inscription on the sundial in Cresswell's *Moondial*: "Light and shadow by turns, but always Love" (see the introduction and page 159). The meaning of the statues on the sundial is that Chronos means time and Eros means love. Araminta (Minty) Kane has come to stay at an old stone cottage opposite Beeton House, part of the National Trust which is open to visitors from April to October. While her mother is in a coma because of an accident, Minty tapes her search for the two children from the past and the time travel experiences with the sundial or moondial. The children that Minty meets are Tom, a Victorian kitchen boy, and

Sarah, an abused child with a birthmark. Tom is also trying to free his sister Dorrie. In Lindbergh's *The Shadow on the Dial*, ten-year-old Dawn and her younger brother, Marcus, time travel with the help of a moving van and a sundial. The contemporary siblings travel to the early twentieth century to help their uncle achieve his heart's desire.

In Pearson's *A Handful of Time*, Patricia, a 12-year-old Canadian girl, winds an old watch and finds herself in the past when her mother was her own age. Seeing her mother's relationship with her family, Patricia is better able to understand her. A family mystery and the divorce of her parents are also part of the story.

Fog is often a way of entering another time. One of the most famous of the space and time fog stories is Sauer's *Fog Magic*, a Newbery Honor Book, in which 12-year-old Greta of Nova Scotia finds a village that has been lost for 100 years. An English boy in Houghton's *Steps Out of Time* is lonely and rejected by his classmates, but whenever Jonathan comes back to his home in a mist or fog he finds himself in the future with a family that accepts him. Ten-year-old Nina from Levy's *Running Out of Time* is the youngest girl in her state to complete a marathon. One day when she and her friends Francie and Bill are running in a fog, they find themselves on the Appian Way in 73 B.C. during the days of the Roman Empire. The three children are taken with slaves to the arena where gladiators are practicing and are befriended by Spartacus and his wife. When Francie is harassed, Spartacus is angered and the slave revolt begins. When the children return to their proper time, they read about Spartacus in an encyclopedia to see if he escaped. Did he? In Levy's *Running Out of Magic with Houdini*, the same children run in a fog in New York and find themselves in 1912 with Houdini.

Boats are featured in Adkins's *A Storm Without Rain*, Wibberley's *The Crime of Martin Coverly*, Chew's *The Magic Coin*, and Westall's *The Wind Eye*. In the first book, 15-year-old Jack Stone goes off in a boat to explore Penikese Island off the coast of Massachusetts. Chapter 2 is good for reading aloud. In Wibberley's book 15-year-old Nick lives in Key West with his uncle who owns a bookshop. One day Nick comes across an old notebook with entries from the 1720s, including coldblooded descriptions of sea battles, stolen cargo, and the deaths of men. When Nick and his uncle go out in a sailboat, Nick falls into the 1700s and comes back wondering if the pirate sentenced to death at Newgate is really his uncle. Chew's *The Magic Coin* is another book about pirates in which two children go back to the 1600s. In *The Wind Eye*, children find a boat which is really a time ship. It maroons Sally in the medieval times of St. Cuthbert, and Beth and Bertrand in the middle of a Viking raid.

Games are vehicles for taking children into the past in Park's *Playing Beatie Bow* and Cresswell's *A Game of Catch*. One day, while watching younger children play a game called "Beatie Bow," Abigail follows a shadow child who has been watching the game into a poor section of Sydney in the 1870s. In Cresswell's *A Game of Catch*, 10-year-old Kate and her brother Hugh see an 18th-century painting of Lady Katherine and her brother Charles in a museum gallery. If the book is read aloud to students, ask them if they think the ball in the picture changes hands. In *Rembrandt Takes a Walk* by Strand, the famous artist steps out of a painting and takes a walk with a modern boy. Rachel and Scott buy "The Build Anything Kit" on sale in Chew's *Do-It-Yourself Magic*. Leaders of the planet Gann kidnap a football team in the middle of a game in Higdon's *The Team That Played in the Space Bowl*, thinking that the Elston University team is a professional team that can win the Space Bowl for them. The rival planet has videos of great football games of the past and future and the team Elston U. plays against is made up of robot players reenacting the best of football history. The names of players from which Coach Stark can choose include such running backs as Red Grange, O. J. Simpson, and Jim Brown. Have students make up their own team from football greats. With cheerleader Deedle Murphy as their coach, the team confuses the pros by running sandlot and high school football plays because the robots aren't programmed for them. Can the Elston University team beat a team made up of the best players from the past and future?

Catherine Aitken from Wiseman's *Thimbles* discovers a trunk in her grandmother's sewing room with a thimble which transports her back 100 years into the time of Kate, a working girl, and Sophie, the daughter of wealthy parents. A key event in the story is the march on St. Peter's Fields in Manchester on August 16, 1819. The rights of 19th-century workers are also important in Mooney's *The Stove Haunting*. The stove transports 11-year-old Daniel into the past where he has the same name as a stove boy in a rector's manse. The protest here involves farmers who want the local landowners to pay liveable wages.

In Palin's *The Mirrorstone: A Ghost Story with Holograms*, a boy in a mirror beckons Paul into a medieval world. There he is to help Salaman perfect a mirror that will show people what they are really like inside. Bond's Caldecott Honor Book, *A String on the Harp*, has been reprinted in paperback format. Twelve-year-old Peter, 10-year-old Becky, and 15-year-old Jen leave Massachusetts to live with their recently widowed father who is teaching at the University of Wales. Peter finds a tuning key for the harp of Taliesin, the great Welsh bard, and is drawn back into the sixth century. Finn blows a magic whistle and lures 11-year-old Fiona and her 8-year-old brother Bran into Celtic Ireland in Tannen's *The Wizard Children of Finn*. A map shows the legendary journey on which Finn has to outsmart the Sons of Marna who have killed his father and also want him. The story is based on an ancient legend. In the sequel, *The Lost Legend of Finn*, Fiona and Bran try to return to the time of Finn but travel instead to Ireland of 839 A.D. There Druids turn them into ravens so they can find out the secret of their past. A small carving of a knight on horseback transports Eddie into the time of King Richard III in *Knight on Horseback* by Rabinowitz. A sword takes a boy into medieval times in Hunter's *The Three-Day Enchantment*.

Books provide the entrée into other times and places for a contemporary girl in Wood's *The Secret Life of Hilary Thorne*. Hilary visits ancient Greece, the Middle Ages, and 19th-century Missouri. In Dunlop's *The Valley of Deer,* a charm stone takes Anne from a Scottish archaeological dig in 1954 to the 17th century, where she becomes Alice, a girl accused of witchcraft. Anne learns more about Alice from a Bible entry and historical records.

In *The Indian in the Cupboard* by Banks, 9-year-old Omri receives a plastic Indian from his best friend Patrick. When Omri puts the statue in an old cupboard (described on page 3), the Indian comes alive and demands food, fire, a wife, and weapons. More problems arise when Patrick wants to turn his toy cowboy into a real person also. Omri names his Indian Little Bear and finds an Iroquois longhouse for him, but Little Bear and the cowboy, Boone, fight. When Little Bear fights in the French and Indian War, Tommy, an English soldier and Red Cross medical orderly from World War I, is brought to life to provide medical help for the small figures. In the sequel, *The Return of the Indian*, it is one year later and Omri brings Little Bear and his wife, Bright Stars, back to life so he can share the news that he has won 300 pounds sterling in a creative writing contest for a story called "The Plastic Indian." When Omri brings Little Bear back to life, he gives him modern weapons to fight his 1700s war, and Omri goes back to the Algonquin raid of the village. A third title is *The Secret of the Indian.*

A cat expedites travel back in time in *Cat's Magic* by Greaves. Orphan Louise Genevieve Higgs goes to live on her Aunt Harriet's farm where she saves the kitten Casca from drowning. Ashley, a contemporary girl, follows a white cat through a hedge in a forbidden garden of the early 1900s in Hahn's *The Doll in the Garden*. Other time travel books involving cats are Stolz's *Cat in the Mirror* and Alexander's *Time Cat*. Erin, a modern American girl, and Irun, a girl of Egypt 3,000 years ago, meet in Stolz's book. Alexander's cat has several lives.

Magic is involved in Bedard's *A Darker Magic*. Mrs. Potts, a teacher, went to a magic show on August 8, 1936, and is haunted by the memory. Something strange happens when August 8th falls on a Saturday again. In Levy's *Running Out of Magic with Houdini*, while in New York City for a marathon, Nina, Francie, and Bill are running in a fog and find themselves in 1912 when they come across some men shoving a handcuffed man bound by a ball and chain into a packing case. Later the children discover that the man is Houdini, and he takes them home with him. With Houdini's help they expose a crooked medium and foil a plot to kill the great magician. When the children come back to their own time, they go to the library and get two biographies of Houdini to see if he escaped from his jump from a tugboat in the East River. Levy's book is for intermediate students, while another time travel book featuring Houdini includes 18-year-old heroes born in 1958. In Bethancourt's *The Tomorrow Connection*, two teenage jazz musicians and nostalgia buffs, Richie Gilroy and Marty Owen from the book *Tune in Yesterday,* are stranded in 1906. The boys ask Houdini to locate San Francisco's Golden Gate Park for them and they arrive just in time for the earthquake. Racial prejudice, encountered by one of the boys while they are assistants to Manfred the Great traveling the vaudeville circuit, is one of the themes in the story.

In Wiseman's *Jeremy Visick*, 12-year-old Matthew Clemens from Cornwall is asked by his teacher to investigate old tombstones to find out more about local history. Matthew is drawn to the tombstone of the Visick family, which records the deaths of Reuben Visick and his two sons, killed in the Wheal Maid mining accident on July 21, 1852. Read about the inscription that haunts Matthew: "And to Jeremy Visick, his son, aged twelve years, whose body still lies in Wheal Maid." Matthew and readers learn much about the copper mining of that day because Matthew time travels with Jeremy down into the mine on that fateful day. Although this ALA Notable Book is easy to booktalk, it is an even better book to read aloud. When two children from Anderson's *In the Circle of Time* see someone near an ancient Scottish stone circle, they realize that three of the 12-foot stones are missing. When Robert and Jennifer investigate, they fall into the future.

Elizabeth, 9-year-old daughter of the Duke of Umberland, travels from 1600 to an Iowa pig farm in 1988 with her doll and music box in *The Princess in the Pigpen* by Thomas. Elizabeth is stunned by electricity, gasoline engines, modern plumbing, penicillin, black female doctors, and women in pantaloons. She must also convince her modern counterpart that she is really a visitor from Elizabethan England.

Tom's Midnight Garden by Pearce has long been considered a classic of time and space books and has been reissued. In the Carnegie Medal winning book, Tom is bored until one night he hears the clock strike 13 and goes outside to find a beautiful garden where he meets Hatty and other children. If the book is read aloud to students, stop before reading Chapter 14, "The Pursuit of Knowledge," and ask students to figure out the time period from which Hatty comes. Then read the chapter, which tells how Tom uses subject headings, indexes, books, and an encyclopedia to place Hatty in the Victorian era. *Tom's Midnight Garden* is a program in the instructional television series *More Books from Cover to Cover.*

In Hahn's *The Doll in the Garden*, 10-year-old Ashley goes through a hedge in a forbidden rose garden to discover the owner of the china doll she found in a wooden box. Although she has been dead for 80 years, Louisa, the owner of the doll, is distraught because her doll has been stolen. Ashley learns who is responsible for taking the doll, but is unable to prevent Louisa's death.

In St. George's *The Mysterious Girl in the Garden*, 10-year-old Terrie Wright, an American, goes with her parents to a place near London, England. While Terrie's father conducts business, her mother takes courses at the 300-acre Kew Botanic Gardens. One day Terrie follows the dog Lioni into the garden, where she meets another girl who is bored and has nothing to do. The girl is Princess Charlotte Augusta of Windsor Castle, Carlton House, and Kew

Palace and granddaughter of King George III. The year is 1805. Have students investigate Charlotte and King George III.

The relation between the garden grotto completed in 1759 and the modern garden that Tim's grandfather likes to putter in provides the time connection in Lively's *The Revenge of Samuel Stokes*. Stokes does not want the new sub-division to be built on the site of his old home and garden. Ten-year-old August Brown is unhappy in Lindbergh's *The People of Pineapple Place* because of his parents' divorce and having to leave Vermont for Washington, D.C., where his lawyer mother has a new job. Then one day August, outside alone, is intrigued by a bag lady in a scarlet coat and follows her into a narrow alley to a pink house that says "Pineapple Place, NW" on it. The children he meets there have remained the same age for 43 years and are invisible to everyone except August. They have exciting adventures together in the present and the past. Check pages 26–28, 42–43, 50–53, 57–59, 117, and 133–36 of *The People in Pineapple Place* for descriptions of these unusual people. *The Prisoner of Pineapple Place* is the sequel. In it the children have moved to Athens where Jeremiah meets Ruby and becomes visible for a while.

After students have chosen and read several space and time books, have them compare the alley in Lindbergh's *The People in Pineapple Place* with the street in Park's *Playing Beatie Bow*.

Setting is also important to Lunn's *The Root Cellar*, which is a Canadian Library Association Children's Book of the Year as well as an ALA Notable Book. After her grandmother dies, 12-year-old Rose is sent from New York State to Ontario, Canada, to live with her Aunt Nan, with four children and one on the way, in a 160-year-old house. When the unhappy Rose goes into the root cellar she meets Susan, once the hired girl at the farmhouse, and Will, who goes off to fight in the American Civil War. When Will doesn't return, Rose and Susan set out to find him. Host John Robbins of the instructional television program *More Books from Cover to Cover* entices fifth graders into reading *The Root Cellar*, Program #14.

Old houses are also featured in Uttley's *Traveler in Time* and McDonald's *The Ghosts of Austwick Manor*. In the first book, Penelope Taberner Cameron is sent to live in an old manor house, Thackers, with her great-aunt Tissie and her great-uncle Barnabus. Penelope becomes involved in a plot to save Mary Queen of Scots in 1582. It is at this time that tunnels were built to rescue the queen from a neighboring manor. There are lots of interesting sidelights to mention to listeners in a booktalk: "Greensleeves" is a modern song in Eliza-bethan England; mummers perform at Christmas; and people sing the "Was-sailing Song" and "The Ballad of Robin Hood." Check page 224 for the historical background of the nursery rhyme "Hark! Hark! The Dogs Do Bark." The fore-word to Uttley's book can be used to introduce this book and other fantasies: "Many of the incidents in this story are based on my dreams, for in sleep I went through secret hidden doorways in the house wall and found myself in another century." Hillary McDonald, the narrator of *The Ghosts of Austwick*

Manor, tells how her 15-year-old brother Don is approached by their father's great-uncle (who has the same name) to keep the family records. Don, Hillary, and Heather live with their mother and stepfather and Don is the last of his line because his own father has died under mysterious circumstances. Don's legacy includes the records and household accounts as well as a model of a Scottish manor house from 1540. Several sets of dolls are also part of the legacy. Read the description of the house on page 17 as well as the warning on pages 15 and 16 that they are not to handle the dolls. Ask the listeners if they would have obeyed or ignored the warning. Through the dolls, Heather and Hillary meet Margaret and learn of the curse on the family that took their father as a victim and could affect their brother. Can the sisters make anybody believe them? Can they save their brother from the curse? For a review of their trips into 16th-century Scotland, check pages 114–18. One of the trips is during Cromwell's time when Roundhead soldiers invade the manor.

Another miniature building appears in Winthrop's *The Castle in the Attic.* Ten-year-old William has a busy father and a mother who is not only a physician but a school board member. William relies on his nanny, Mrs. Phillips, for help in his gymnastics practice as well as moral support and love. Mrs. Phillips's parting gift to William before she returns to England is a toy castle and a silver knight. During the booktalk, it would be interesting to read some of the rules for knights listed on page 98. Teachers and librarians wishing to use *The Castle in the Attic* to develop thinking skills can consult Kruise's *Those Blooming Books: A Handbook for Extending Thinking Skills. The Castle in the Attic* is Program #8 on the instructional television series *More Books from Cover to Cover* for fifth graders. Winthrop's book was chosen best book of 1987 by children in Vermont.

There are several books by Boston in the Green Knowe series. In *Children of Green Knowe,* Tolly is staying at Green Knowe with his great-grandmother, who tells him stories of three 17th-century children, Toby, Linnet, and Alexander. After finding their toys, Tolly sees them. In *Treasure of Green Knowe,* Granny tells stories while working on a patchwork quilt. Tolly meets Susan and Jacob and discovers the treasure. In *River at Green Knowe,* Ida Oskar, a Polish refugee, and her aunt rent Green Knowe for the summer. Characters include a displaced boy named Ping, an old hermit, a winged horse, and a giant. In *Stranger at Green Knowe,* Ping, spending the summer at Green Knowe with Mrs. Oldknow, has sympathy for Hanno, a giant gorilla, who escapes from the zoo. This book is a Carnegie Medal winner. In *Enemy at Green Knowe,* Tolly and Ping become involved in activities of a mad alchemist from 1630 when Miss Powers comes to search out old alchemists' books.

In Lively's *The House in Norham Gardens,* Clare lives with two maiden aunts in a Victorian house. A shield brought back from New Guinea by a great-grandfather causes dreams. Naylor's *Shadow on the Wall* is the first book of the York Trilogy. Chapter 1 is good to read aloud to introduce the story. Also, use pictures in the prologue to explain about the walled city of Roman times that has four gates or bars into the city. While in England, Dan can get credit for the semester if he writes a 20-page essay on the history of an English city. Dan chooses York and becomes further interested when a cab driver tells him about an 18-year-old named Martindale who has also seen Roman soldiers coming out of the wall and has heard a trumpet at Michlegate Bar (Gate). The reason for their trip to England supposedly is to research father's family ties, but is really to see if Dan and his father have Huntington's disease. Teachers and librarians can read pages 62, 63, 85, and 127 to get a sense of the story.

In Cameron's *Beyond Silence*, a 15-year-old American boy, Andrew Cames, and his father go to Scotland to Cames Castle, now a hotel but formerly the family home. Alexander dreams about the death of his older brother Hoagy, a Vietnam veteran, and Hoagy seems to blame Alexander for something. A letter from the past (Boer War days) comes from someone named Dierdre, who appears several times to Andrew. Through his experience in Scotland Andrew is able to come to terms with his brother's death. Questions of quarks, relativity, and the Quantum Theory are possible pursuits after reading this book.

Sometimes characters stumble into another time period because they are lost or because they have wandered into unknown territory. In Hurmence's *A Girl Called Boy*, 11-year-old Blanche Overtha Yancey, Boy for short, hates the fact that her ancestors have been slaves. On page 4 Boy says "They deserved to be slaves . . . the way they let themselves be pushed around and never tried to fight back or anything. I wouldn't stand for it. They couldn't make me a slave." While lost in the South Carolina mountains, the modern black girl is transported into the 1850s and is caught by slavers. Chapters 1 and 2 are excellent for reading aloud. In *Here Abide Monsters* by Norton, Nick shows Linda a shortcut to her friend's house on the lake and they fall into King Arthur's Avalon. Stewart's *Walk in Wolf Wood: A Tale of Fantasy and Magic* takes the characters to medieval Germany. While John and Margaret are exploring the forest they meet Lord Mardian, who is cursed to roam the woods at night as a werewolf because the evil sorcerer Alaric has assumed his identity. However, in trying to help Lord Mardian, the children find themselves caught in the 14th century.

When 14-year-old Peggy Donovan in Wiseman's *Adam's Common* moves to the drab industrial town of Traverton, England, she sees Adam's Common as the only redeeming feature. It seems more beautiful to her than her beloved Boston Common and the public gardens combined because it is wild and unspoiled. When developers decide to build on the site, Peggy, her mother, a lawyer, and a teacher work together to keep this from happening. William Trafford of Trafford Court reaches across time from the mid-1800s to help them. Peggy verifies the manor house of the past with a picture in a book published in 1862 called *The Story of Traverton*, and her curiosity about why it is called "Adam's Common" helps her to save the area. Pages of special interest for review are 3, 118–27, 135–42, 75–76, and 84–92. In the book, Mr. Richard's class is working on a project in order to win the Trafford Award, a prize for a pupil or pupils who make the best contribution to the well-being of the community. Any class that is researching local history or studying community affairs should read the Wiseman books, *Adam's Common* and *Jeremy Visick*.

The Mother Goose rhyme beginning "How many miles to Babylon?" from the introduction can be used to introduce Doty's *Can I Get There by Candlelight?* because of the significance of candlelight in the title. Gail Simmons, her family, and a Welsh pony Candlelight, Candy for short, move one summer. In an old carriage house Gail finds a broken two-wheeled pony cart and a trunk containing an old riding habit, sidesaddle, and a dark green felt hat. Show the picture opposite page 3 of Gail taking the items out of the trunk. Developers have changed the old estate, but Gail opens the latch on a gate in a stone wall and enters Babylon of 100 years ago. That Babylon is a world of gazebos, summer estates, servants, finishing schools, and riding sidesaddle. There Gail and Candy meet Hillary, who lives in New York but spends her summers at Babylon. Special pages to review are 3–5, 60–61, and 96–101.

Several of the characters in space and time books have to travel outside of their own time to appreciate members of their family. Twelve-year-old Brann in Voigt's *Building Blocks* is ashamed of his father because he doesn't stick up for things and has a lousy job. Falling asleep, Brann is transported back to a time during the Depression when his father is 10 years old and learns not only that his father Kevin is the oldest child but is also beaten by *his* father. Brann also learns why he was named Brann and, after becoming friends with his father as a boy, Brann learns to appreciate him. Lynnie Kirk from Park's *Playing Beatie Bow* is only 10 when her father leaves them for his secretary. To disassociate herself from her father she asks to be called Abigail but now her father wants a reconciliation and Abigail is unhappy. While watching children play a game called Beatie Bow in the park (description on page 10), Abigail follows the waif who has been watching the game into the colony of New South Wales in Victorian Australia. The story is so vivid that anyone who stands in "Argyle Cut" or "The Rocks" area of Sydney can picture the conditions of the late 1800s in that area. To meet the family that takes Abigail in, read page 61. Second sight, a prophecy, and an injury are all involved in "The Prophecy," which is explained on pages 106–8, and Abigail is the "Mysterious Stranger." It is not until Abigail falls in love with the sailor son of the family that she begins to understand the love between her parents. A crochet piece from her experiences in the past becomes a link to Abigail's happy future. *Playing Beatie Bow* is an ALA Notable Book and an Australian Book of the Year. When Patricia in Pearson's *A Handful of Time* is disturbed about her parents' pending divorce, she finds herself in the time when her mother is 12 years old. When she learns about her mother's relationship with her brothers, she understands her mother better. In Pascal's *Hangin' Out With Cici*, 14-year-old Victoria bumps her head while riding on a train and travels back to 1944, where she meets Cici, who is really her own mother. Knowing Cici helps Victoria to understand her mother. A film based on the book is called *My Mother Never Was a Kid*. Eddie clarifies his feelings toward his father after his adventures in Rabinowitz's *Knight on Horseback*. In Yolen's *The Devil's Arithmetic*, a modern-day 14-year-old girl isn't interested in the family stories about surviving the Holocaust until she becomes a girl in Nazi Germany who is sent to a Polish death camp in 1942.

Jacqueline Raven goes to visit her father, his second wife, and children (Lewis and Dora) in Mahy's *Aliens in the Family*. Like Abigail in *Playing Beatie Bow*, 12-year-old Jacqueline asks to be called another name, Jake, and tries to project a tough, self-reliant image, which includes being an expert rider when she doesn't even know how to ride. The three children come together when they protect Bond, an alien from Galonqaua, who is on earth completing a time-travel project called an assessment. The alteration in time is effected by a teleport. Although Bond is the alien from another planet, Jake is an alien to her family. References to Jake's alienation are found on pages 18 and 23.

Twelve-year-old Kenny Huldorf moves back to slavery days in Avi's *Something Upstairs: A Tale of Ghosts*. Fifteen-year-old Jack sails away to Penikese Island off the coast of Cape Cod because he doesn't want to give a speech at his grandfather's 93rd birthday party and he isn't interested in family trees or family parties in *A Storm Without Rain* by Adkins. Caught in a storm, Jack finds himself in 1904 and is befriended by his grandfather, as a boy. Chapter 3 contains a good description of Jack's noticing that he is not in his own time. In Houghton's *Steps Out of Time*, 13-year-old Jonathan gains confidence in himself when he goes to the future and finds his grandchildren at the same age he is now. An orphan girl learns the truth about her past when she travels back in time to Ireland in Melling's *The Singing Stone*.

Sixteen-year-old Chris Davenport and his 15-year-old sister Gail are in the attic getting out the Christmas tree trimmings when they see some old photographs and their mother's diary in Payne's *Trapped in Time*. The hardback title is *It's About Time*. When they find the picture of their parents trimming the tree together on the night they met, they wonder what their parents were like as teenagers. When they teleport themselves back to December 24, 1955, they find that father is a hotrodder and that mother dislikes him. The two almost keep their parents from meeting; if it hadn't turned out the way it did, Chris and Gail might never have been born. The priest helps them bring their parents together, and the two siblings also meet their grandparents.

In *The Green Futures of Tycho* by Sleator, Tycho is the youngest of four children. Sixteen-year-old Ludwig Tithonus, named after Ludwig von Beethoven, has already written numerous compositions and is working on an opera. Fifteen-year-old Tamara Tithonus is named after the Russian dancer Tamara Karsavina and plans to dance "Giselle" before she is 20. Thirteen-year-old Leonardo Tithonus is named after the Italian artist and inventor and has filled many notebooks with sketches and inventions. And then there is 11-year-old Tycho who is named after Tycho Brahe, a Danish astronomer. However, Tycho is a disgrace to his family; he never sticks with projects and won't take lessons after school like the others. Then one day, digging in his garden, Tycho finds an egglike object with dials on it that takes him into the future. Tycho doesn't like what he finds, but there are opportunities and choices to make to change the future. It would be fun for students to locate information about the famous people named in the book and make a list of five talents that children named after these people share. Then ask students to add other children to the family and describe them.

In *Cave Beyond Time* by Bosse, 15-year-old Ben goes to live with his archaeologist uncle in Arizona after his father and brother are killed in an accident. An unhappy Ben goes out into the desert, falls while chasing wild pigs, is bitten by a rattlesnake, and follows a jackrabbit into an ancient time. Hunters who kill a mammoth, a new friend who is killed by a tiger, capture and initiation into the Bison Clan, and a woman of his own are all part of his experiences. Most of the incidents in Ben's visits to those other times have some relationship to his family and his loss. When Ben returns to the dig, he has a new appreciation for archaeology and stops feeling sorry for himself.

There are several books containing short stories about space and time that would be good for students in middle school and above. Fenner's *Wide-Angle Lens: Stories in Time and Space* contains 10 stories by writers such as Bradbury, Heinlein, E. B. White, and Asimov. *Time Warps*, edited by Asimov, Greenberg, and Waugh, includes five short stories. Finney's *About Time* contains a dozen stories. *Tales Out of Time* contains 14 stories including an excerpt from H. G. Wells's *Time Machine*.

Several books besides *The Time Machine* deal with taking people into other times via a machine. Sadler's *Alistair's Time Machine* is the only easy picture book among the space and time books. Alistair builds a time machine for a science fair. In Greer's *Max and Me and the Time Machine*, Steve's friend Max becomes his horse and he becomes Sir Robert Marshall, and they travel around medieval England in the 13th century. Steve buys the time machine called Flybender's Fantastic Hunk of Junk at a garage sale. They encounter bloodletting, leeches, jousting, magic potions, and a beautiful lady. The medieval manners described on pages 80–81 are interesting. Einstein Anderson earns his nickname for being clever, in Simon's *Einstein Anderson Tells a Comet's Tale*. When his friend Stanley finds an ad for plans for a time machine that uses a camera, Einstein wants proof that the time machine really works. The proof he is sent are photos taken during Roman times. Readers have to figure out how Einstein knows that the picture is a fake in Chapter 8, "The Time Machine," pages 54–58.

Computers can become modern time machines. In Landsman's *Gadget Factor*, 13-year-old genius Michael Goldman learns to time travel through a computer game. Freshmen at Franklin College, Mike and his roommate Worm create a computer game called Universe Prime in which they program a universe with galaxies, planets, and laws. The boys become so caught up that they work at it day and night for two months and miss classes and eating. Michael wants to preserve the game and Worm wants to destroy it. Who wins? Who should win? In Curry's *Me, Myself and I*, the main character is an electronics genius who begins college at age 12. To meet JJ and his girlfriend read pages 3 and 4. JJ is curious about the big machine that Professor Poplov calls "Pandora's Box" when he sees a holographic image of himself. When the professor is away, JJ gets into the time machine and meets himself in several pasts to become Me, Myself and I. JJ meets himself as Mutt or "me" at age 8 and as Jacko or "myself" at age 12. Teachers and librarians should read pages 48–49, 56–59, 64–65, and 182–83 to refresh their memories about JJ's selves. While they are fooling around with their father's computer, Sandy and Dennys Murray are thrown back into the time of Noah in L'Engle's *Many Waters*. This book is the fourth book in L'Engle's famous Time Quartet. When Blossom Culp from Peck's *The Dreadful Future of Blossom Culp* comes from 1914 to the 1980s, she meets a modern boy, Jeremy, who thinks she is part of his Atari game.

Luke Crantock is another very intelligent boy who becomes involved with a time machine. Luke wins the prized Grainger Scholarship to Caius College, Cambridge. Read the newspaper article about Thomas Humboldt on pages 49–50 of Huddy's *The Time Piper* that Luke's father reads aloud to him. Luke meets a new girl named Hare who seems to follow him to London when he gets a summer job working for Tom Humboldt. Hare and the children with vacant eyes that come from all over the world to Tom Humboldt have some connection with Germany and the time machine experiments. In a sequel, *The Humboldt Effect*, Luke is invited by Tom Humboldt to be in charge of the crew on a submarine in the Mediterranean while Humboldt controls the time machine at the Institute in London. During the experiment, Luke's best friend falls into the water at the same time they take aboard a man from 4th-century Joppa. In order to repeat the Humboldt Effect and switch the men, Luke has to go back in time. The central question is whether or not the experiment can be repeated. It will be interesting to see who recognizes the identities of the two men from the past who are part of the stories. The man from 12th-century Germany is the Pied Piper and the man from the 4th century is Jonah.

Some space and time books are concerned with parallel worlds, new dimensions, and future worlds. In Johnson's *The Danger Quotient*, 18-year-old Casey, also called K/C 4 (SCI), is a supergenius who lives in an underground colony after a nuclear world war. Casey is faced with a mysterious disease that begins to kill off members of the colony, and the only way to solve the mystery is to go into the past. In Anderson's *In the Circle of Time*, the children fall into the year 2179 where Kartan helps save Robert and Jennifer from the Barbaric Ones. In *Steps Out of Time* by Houghton, Jonathan moves into a time when his grandchildren are the same age as he is now—13. When an egglike object transports Tycho, from Sleator's *The Green Futures of Tycho*, into the future, he meets several of his own selves that he doesn't like—a boring braggart and a selfish hated monster. Tycho eventually learns that there are coincidences, opportunities, and choices that can be made to change the future.

Michael in Landman's *Gadget Factor* goes to the University of Ohio on a bus to check out his theories with those of a 31-year-old professor, Terry Miller. Prof. Miller thinks they have the makings of a Nobel Prize, but when Michael won't go public with their information because of the time travel aspect, Terry steals the information to present to a national scientific conference. Michael doesn't want to make the information public because it would give humans the capability of being able to rob the past to save the future until all ends in nothingness. The past and future find their counterparts in the present in Anderson's *In the Keep of Time*.

A Tale of Time City by Jones is about a place outside time where the past and future flow through time locks and it is possible to go into a past time (like the unstable 20th century) and make changes to balance the era. The book is full of fixed and unstable eras, times when history has gone critical, time patrols, time ghosts, and the Perpetuum or library. The information about Elio the Android on pages 91–94 is interesting to read aloud. Vivian Smith is being evacuated from London to the English countryside because London is being bombed in 1939, when she is kidnapped and taken to Time City.

Parallel time periods exist in the Fireball Trilogy by Christopher. In *Fireball*, Brad, an American boy, visits an English cousin, Simon. Brad's encyclopedic fund of knowledge, picked up from reading, helps when he and Simon get into parallel worlds because of the fireball, a description of which appears on pages 12–13. The cousins are thrown into a place where the Roman Empire has survived into the late 20th century but without social, technological, or religious changes. When the revolution occurs, the dictatorship that follows is even worse than the empire, so Brad, Simon, and two Romans (Bos and Curtius) travel by ship to the new world. A summary of *The Fireball* appears on pages 3 and 4 of the sequel, *The New Found Land*, which takes place in the new world during the rule of the Algonquin Indians who want to take the boy's possessions and starve them. The Danish Vikings think they are fulfilling a prophecy that Romans would come to the island again so they plan a ritual killing. Winning an athletic contest and almost becoming a human sacrifice is part of their experience with the Aztecs before they arrive on the West Coast. Brad and Simon are in California living with Indians in the concluding book, *Dragon Dance*. After trouble with the Indians, the boys are captured by slavers and taken to China in a Chinese junk to meet Li Mei and Bei-Kun. Teachers and librarians will never tell students, but might wish to know, that Bei-Kun is Roger Bacon. The trilogy ends with a chance to learn about the fireball and get home again. The Fireball Trilogy can be introduced to students who like Christopher's Tripod (or White Mountain) Trilogy, which includes *The White Mountains*, *The Pool of Fire*, and *The City of Gold and Lead*. The prequel to the trilogy is *When the Tripods Came*. *The Homeward Bounders* by Jones is a space and time book that reminds readers of the Tripod Trilogy. Twelve-year-old Jamie Hamilton is trying to get home and so are others who are controlled by "THEM." Jamie is an ordinary boy who lives in a grocery store in a city and likes football, but his life changes when he climbs over a wall and becomes involved in another dimension.

Four books by Richard Peck about Blossom Culp, who is a teenager in the early 1900s, take her into the future through her gift of second sight: *Ghosts I Have Been, The Ghost Belonged to Me, The Dreadful Future of Blossom Culp, and Blossom Culp and the Sleep of Death.* A 15-minute episode of *Ghosts I Have Been* from Program 4 of the instructional television series, *Storybound,* for sixth graders can be used to introduce the books about Blossom. In the first book, Blossom's ability allows her to see the sinking of the *Titanic* but she is powerless to help. In the second book, Blossom appears only as a neighbor of the narrator, Alexander Armsworth, who notices a ghost in his barn. In the third book, Blossom enters high school and is involved in getting a "haunted house" ready for a freshman project. While in the house, Blossom leaves 1914 for the 1980s and meets eighth grader Jeremy, who speaks a jargon she can't understand. Read pages 98–99. There is a contrast between Blossom's silent movies and Jeremy's life of Pac-Man fever, Sears Toughskins, and Adidas. In the fourth book, Blossom becomes involved in helping a suffragette teacher to keep her job and an Egyptian princess to regain her tomb.

In Cresswell's *The Secret World of Polly Flint,* Polly's father is hurt in a mining accident so she and her mother and father have to live with Aunt Em for a while. Polly is fascinated with the Maypole and the tale that hundreds of years ago a village called Grimstone was located on that very spot until it vanished off the face of the earth. Polly not only hears the church bells of Grimstone but she sees the Time Gypsies. Four of them (Gil, Sam, Granny Porter, and Baby Porter) have slipped the net of time and are trying to return to Grimstone. Their dog Baggins becomes Polly's dog because anyone from Grimstone who eats food on earth will be caught forever beyond his time. For the Time Gypsies to return to Grimstone they must have a human go with them willingly between May Day and Midsummer's Eve. Will Polly go with them, even if there is a danger that she might never return?

Virginia Hamilton's Dustland Trilogy includes *Justice and Her Brothers, Dustland,* and *The Gathering.* In the first book, Justice and her twin brothers are just learning a form of telepathic tracing through which they can enter each other's minds. Eleven-year-old Justice, "The Watcher," is the strongest character. Thomas, nicknamed Tom Tom because he plays kettle drums and the oldest of the identicals, is jealous and mean and often takes over his twin brother Levi's mind. Thomas is also called "The Magician." Thirteen-year-old Levi, the other twin, is kind and caring. A neighbor, Leona Jefferson, is known as "The Sensitive" and her son Dorian is known as "The Healer." In *Dustland,* the four children, through a telepathic network, go to the future to a place called Dustland. To get there, they have to "crossover" between the future and the past. There they meet a blind bearlike dog named Miacis, and other creatures called the Rollers, Slakers, Terri, and Bamburra. While on Dustland, Thomas tries to get away from the others. The disturbing part of *The Gathering* is that it sounds prophetic. After reading pages 101–110, students can compare current problems on earth with the causes of destruction on Dustland. Deserts cover the area, machines have taken over, and human beings are reduced in importance. Read the paragraphs which surround the following quotes: "Final time of danger to humanity" on page 102, "Ultimate catastrophe" on page 102, and "dust to end everything" on page 106. Pages 116–20 tell about the Starters, superior beings. Students will be interested in Duster, Siv, Glass, Miacis, Mal, and the Slakers. The Colossus in this book reminds readers of the robot Orvis's refusing to make himself obsolete in Hooper's *Orvis*. The crossover reminds readers of Mahy's *The Changeover*. The trilogy ends with Justice's 12th birthday party and resolution of the mind war between the twins. Two other space and time books involving twins include Sleator's *Singularity* and L'Engle's *Many Waters*.

The most famous of the books about the fourth dimension are Madeleine L'Engle's Time Quartet. In the Newbery winner *A Wrinkle in Time*, Meg and her younger brother Charles Wallace search for their father, a scientist, who has disappeared while working on a secret project involving the tesseract, or "wrinkle in time." In *A Wind in the Door*, the bright Charles Wallace is not adapting to school and sees dragons in the garden of his twin brothers Sandy and Dennys. In *A Swiftly Tilting Planet*, Meg has become a mother and 15-year-old Charles Wallace goes back in time with the unicorn Gaudior to keep a dictator, Madog Branzillo, from destroying the world. While fooling around with their parents' computer in *Many Waters*, Sandy and Dennys are thrown back in time to a desert where there are mammoths and unicorns. There the twins meet Grandfather Lemech who is 777 years old, Noah who is 600 years old, and Noah's sons Ham, Shem, Japheth, and Japheth's daughter Yalith. When El (God) tells Noah to build a boat, the twins are worried about Yalith and whether or not she will be saved from the flood because her name does not appear in the Bible. The conversation about whether it would be better to be drowned or nuked appears at the bottom of page 178 and the top of 179.

Another L'Engle book about space and time is *An Acceptable Time*. Polly O'Keefe from *Arm of the Starfish* enters a door in time at the home of her grandparents and meets the ancient druids and warriors Tav, Anaral, and Karalys.

Sleator's *The Boy Who Reversed Himself* is about Lana, who, though her mother asks her to be nice to the strange boy Omar, is more interested in Pete, a popular basketball star. When Lana finds out that Omar can go into the fourth dimension, she pesters him until he takes her there. Nixon's *Astropilots* is also about the fourth dimension.

Students can be introduced to space and time books by the time period into which the main characters escape. Several books which deal with prehistoric times are: Senn's *The Double Disappearance of Walter Fozbek*; Collier's *Planet Out of the Past*; Bosse's *Cave Beyond Time*; and Mazer's *Saturday, the Twelfth of October*. In Collier's book, Weddy, Nuell, their father, a famous scientist, and his research assistant, Char, travel from earth to the planet Pleisto to study life of two million years ago during the Pleistocene age. The three become separated from the professor. Char, a poor boy who has been taken under the professor's wing, earns praise from his mentor, learns to accept the friendly rivalry between himself and Nuell, and hopes that someday Weddy will accept his kiss. Scenes featuring the attempt of the youngsters to communicate with Handy, a hominid or *Homo habilis*, are especially interesting. In Senn's book, Walter wakes up one day in his cousin Ralph's room and discovers that Ralph and everyone else have become dinosaurs. When Walter goes to Professor Krebnickel to see if he can help him, he learns that the human Walter and the dinosaur Walter are mirror images of matching universes that have switched because of a warp or crimp in space. Walter has to travel through a black hole to get back home in *The Double Disappearance of Walter Fozbek*.

Several other space and time books mention black holes. A black hole is featured in Sleator's *Singularity*, in which 16-year-old twins, Harry and Barry, go to live on an isolated farm in the Illinois cornfields, which their mother inherited from an uncle. With the parents away on a trip, the twins learn from a neighbor, Lucy, that Uncle Ambrose has been accused of making his neighbor's animals old before their time. There are skeletons of unusual animals and an old metal shed (description on page 21) that contains unusual items. When the twins learn the secret of the old shed, they learn about the theories of singularity, black holes, and time contraction. These phenomena are described on pages 62–65. Tapp's *The Scorpio Ghosts and the Black Hole Gang* is about a family that tries to renovate an old schoolhouse. The children go on a trip back to 1927 when ghosts drive a bookmobile past the intersection where an accident killing two people has occurred.

Students can also be introduced to space and time books by geography and history. Many of the books in this genre come from the British Isles. The Narnia series by C. S. Lewis and the Green Knowe series by Lucy Boston all take place in England. *The Children of Green Knowe* is one of two books which explain the importance of setting in the filmstrip *Setting* in the series *Literature for Children, Series 9*. Houghton's *Steps Out of Time* and Pearce's *Tom's Midnight Garden* also take place in England. Wiseman's *Adam's Common* takes place in the Cornwall England of the 1840s, *Thimbles* in 1819, and *Jeremy Visick* in Cornwall in 1852. Anderson's *To Nowhere and Back* has an American girl visiting England and experiencing peasant life of the 1800s. Mooney's *The Stove Haunting* takes place in England in the mid 1800s. Naylor's *The Shadow on the Wall* is set in York in the times of Roman Britain. Several books incorporate famous people into the story: Curry's *Poor Tom's Ghost* takes place in Shakespeare's England; Uttley's *Traveler in Time* concerns Mary Queen of Scots; Rabinowitz's *Knight on Horseback* involves Richard III; and St. George's *The Mysterious Girl in the Garden* is about George III's granddaughter, Princess Charlotte Augusta. Lively's *The House in Norham Garden*, Greaves's *Cat's Magic*, and Cresswell's *Moondial* are set in Victorian England, while

Park's *Playing Beatie Bow* is set in the British colony of New South Wales in Victorian Australia.

Books with a Scottish connection are: Anderson's *In the Circle of Time*, McDonald's *Ghosts of Austwick Manor,* Cameron's *Beyond Silence,* Dunlop's *Clementina* and *The Valley of Deer,* and Uttley's *A Traveler in Time.* Daisy's summer vacation is ruined by her good friend, Bridget, and a strange girl, Clementina, whom Bridget's mother invites to share the vacation. Clementina is linked with another girl from Scotland two centuries ago. Tanne's *The Wizard Children of Finn* and *The Lost Legend of Finn*, and Melling's *The Singing Stone,* are set in ancient Ireland. Melling's book takes place during the Bronze Age. *The Singing Stone* is about an 18-year-old orphan girl who thinks that the key to her dreams is the ancient Irish legends of the time of the Druids. Bond's *A String on the Harp* takes children to sixth-century Wales.

Palin's *The Mirrorstone* and Westall's *The Wind Eye* take place in medieval times, as does Stewart's *Walk in Wolf Wood*, which is set in Germany. Norton's *Here Abide Monsters*, Winthrop's *Castle in the Attic*, Rabinowitz's *Knight on Horseback*, and Hunter's *The Knight of the Golden Plain* and *The Three-Day Enchantment*, all involve knights. Hunter's *The Knight of the Golden Plain* is about a boy who becomes a knight on Saturdays. Sir Dauntless and his great black horse Midnight are followed by the dark and lurking demon magician Arriman to Crag Castle where Princess Dorabell lives. Dorabell's voice has flown out of her mouth in the shape of a bird and gone straight to Arriman in the Dark Forest beyond Rapid River. While a captive in a silver cage, the little bird sings every time it sees itself in the mirror and is about to sing itself to death. After Dorabell gives Sir Dauntless her blue silk handkerchief, off he goes to rescue her voice. *The Three-Day Enchantment* is a sequel. In *Knight on Horseback* Eddie Newby is visiting England when he finds a small carving of a knight on horseback that takes him back to the time of Richard III.

Although Mahy's *Aliens in the Family* takes place in New Zealand, it could have happened anywhere.

Third and fourth grade readers as well as older remedial readers will enjoy traveling back in time to 1492, when the reader is aboard the *Santa Maria* with Columbus in Reit's *Voyage with Columbus*. The mystery in the book involves students by having them choose alternatives. The second book in this Time Traveler series is *The Legend of Hiawatha*, about the founding of the Iroquois league. Other books in the series are: Gaskin's *First Settlers*, Lerangis's *Amazing Ben Franklin*, Kornblatt's *Paul Revere and the Boston Tea Party*, and Frankel's *George Washington and the Constitution.*

In another series called "Time Traveler," twins Diana and Tom Morris have a magic ring which allows them to return to an earlier time in *Gift of Fire, In Search of the Ruby Sword, In the Time of the Pharaohs,* and *Liberty for All,* all by Spirn.

In the Time Machine series, the reader travels to another time and place in search of a famous person, object, or event. Choices made by the reader determine whether or not the person will be sent to the place in the title or more dangerous locations. Titles in this series are: *American Revolutionary, Blade of the Guillotine*, and *Rings of Saturn*, Cover; *Bound for Australia*, Bailey; *Civil War Secret Agent*, Perry; *Death Mask of Pancho Villa*, Kornblatt; *Flame of the Inquisition*, Kornblatt; *Mission to World War II*, Naus; *Mystery of Atlantis, Secret of the Knights*, and *Sail With Pirates*, Gasperini; *Quest for the Cities of Gold*, Glazer; *Scotland Yard Detective*, Reit; *Search for Dinosaurs*, Bischaff; *Search for the Nile*, Walker; *Secret of the Royal Treasure*, Gaskin; *Sword of Caesar*, Stevenson; *Sword of the Samurai*, Reaves; and *Wild West Rider*, Olverholser.

Readers can also plot their own stories in Wandelmaier's *Secret of the Old Museum*. The choice involves the following situation. The reader is in the Cragmore Museum of Natural History to finish a term paper due the next morning and only two topics are left. If the reader chooses to taste the liquid in the bottle he or she is transported into ancient Egypt. In the other choice, the reader goes into the 23rd century on a spacecraft as well as back to prehistoric times. Three other books which include ancient Egypt are Alexander's *Time Cat*, Stolz's *Cat in the Mirror*, and Peck's *Blossom Culp and the Sleep of Death*. A class studying ancient Egypt could read these books as a model for writing a space and time book of their own.

Several of the time and space books have American settings. In Stein's *Time Raider*, Twistaplot #1, the Time Raider is a time machine owned by the reader's Uncle Edgar. Readers must make the decision to go into the past or the future. Some of the places to visit include slave ships, space ships, or the times of George Armstrong Custer or Daniel Boone. Students can be asked to locate on a map all the places mentioned in Lindbergh's *The People of Pineapple Place* and *The Prisoner of Pineapple Place*: Vermont, Washington, D.C., Phoenix, Missoula, Atlanta, New Orleans, Kalamazoo, and Chicago. A modern boy leaves Arizona for prehistoric times in Bosse's *Cave Beyond Time*. An Elizabethan girl of privilege finds herself in a 20th-century pigpen in Iowa in *The Princess in the Pigpen* by Thomas. Chew's *Summer Magic* takes place in the 1600s when the Dutch settle New York. Wibberley's *The Crime of Martin Coverly* takes place off Key West, Florida in the 1720s. New York during the American Revolution is the setting for Chew's *Trapped in Time*. Lucy Griffin sees her ancestor's silver stolen during the American Revolution in *Griffin Legacy* by Klaveness. An American Indian of the 1700s and a cowboy of the 1800s are main characters in *The Indian in the Cupboard* and *The Return of the Indian* by Banks. Slavery days of South Carolina in the 1850s provide the setting for *A Girl Called Boy* by Hurmence, while the same time period provides the setting for Avi's *Something Upstairs: A Tale of Ghosts*. The 1860s and the American Civil War is the time for Lunn's *The Root Cellar*. A *Storm Without Rain* by Adkins takes place off Cape Cod, Massachusetts in 1904. A boy returns to the Depression of the 1930s in Voigt's *Building Blocks*, and the children in Tapp's *The Scorpio Ghosts and the Black Hole Gang* go back to 1927. A girl is transported to 1944 in Pascal's *Hangin' Out With Cici.* Lindbergh's *The Shadow on the Dial* takes place in Florida and Massachusetts during this century.

Several space and time books have Canadian settings. Sauer's *Fog Magic* takes place in Nova Scotia, parts of Lunn's *The Root Cellar* take place in Ontario, McDonald's *The Ghosts of Austwick Manor* concerns a family that lives on Vancouver Island, and in Pearson's *A Handful of Time* the heroine goes from Ontario to Alberta to visit unknown cousins.

Several authors have written more than one time travel book. Students can be led back and forth from Christopher's White Mountain Trilogy to his Fireball Trilogy depending upon which they have read first.

After reading several books by one author, students are apt to be curious about that author, and information about him or her follows naturally. Some authors to investigate are Lucy Boston, Eleanor Cameron, John Christopher, Madeleine L'Engle, C. S. Lewis, Richard Peck, Virginia Hamilton, and William Sleator. Check page 62 of Asher's *Where Do You Get Your Ideas?* for information about the writing of Lee's *Timequake.*

Silverberg's "Absolutely Inflexible" is a story about Mahler, the inflexible bureau chief of moon prisons who investigates a two-way rig and finds himself in trouble. The story is from *Voyagers in Time: Twelve Stories of Science Fiction* and appears on pages 288–302 of Cullinan's seventh grade HBJ basal reader, *Patterns.* A profile of Silverberg appears on pages 286–87 of *Patterns.* A booktalk composed of any of the time travel books in this section could be given to students who have read this story.

Use information from a student-created database to make charts of parallels between books. If the major topic is setting, then time period and location can be subheadings. Several of the main characters suffer from the same problems: loneliness, being different because they have superintelligence, divorce of parents, and death of a parent or sibling. Social issues like strikes and protests, slavery, child abuse, and racial prejudice are addressed in the books. Using the space and time database, students can pull out time travel books on these subjects or by location and time period.

After reading to students the questions about Mahy's *Aliens in the Family* (from the section THINKING SKILLS from Volume 2 of this book), have students make up questions about the books they have read. Whenever two or more students have read the same book, have them go over the questions together.

A number of space and time titles have appeared in the computer game *BookBrain* (grades 4–6). Titles include: *Aliens in the Family* by Mahy, *The Boy Who Reversed Himself* by Sleator, *Castle in the Attic* by Winthrop, *Cat in the Mirror* by Stolz, *Conrad's War* by Davies, *The Double Disappearance of Walter Fozbek* by Senn, *Fog Magic* by Sauer, *The Green Futures of Tycho* by Sleator, *Hangin' Out With Cici* by Pascal, *The Indian in the Cupboard* by

Banks, *The Lion, the Witch and the Wardrobe* by Lewis, *Many Waters* by L'Engle, *Ralph Fozbek and the Amazing Black Hole Patrol* by Senn, *The Return of the Indian* by Banks, *The Root Cellar* by Lunn, *Running Out of Time* by Levy, *Saturday, the Twelfth of October* by Mazer, *A Swiftly Tilting Planet* by L'Engle, *Time at the Top* by Ormondroyd, *Time Cat* by Alexander, *The Time Garden* by Eager, *Tom's Midnight Garden* by Pearce, *The Wizard Children of Finn* by Tannen, and *A Wrinkle in Time* by L'Engle. Several of the books mentioned in this section are mentioned by series: the Blossom Culp series by Peck, the Chronicles of Narnia series by Lewis, the Fireball Trilogy by Christopher, and the White Mountain (Tripod) Trilogy by Christopher.

Some book titles which are mentioned within other entries in *BookBrain* include: *Cave Beyond Time* by Bosse, *Dragon Dance* by Christopher, *A Girl Called Boy* by Hurmence, *Locked in Time* by Duncan, *The People of Pineapple Place* by Lindbergh, *The String on the Harp* by Bond, and *The Time Machine* by Wells.

Eighteen space and time titles and 36 questions about them appear in Greenson and Taha's *Name That Book! Questions and Answers on Outstanding Children's Books.* Check the index on pages 241–42 for titles.

SURVIVAL BOOKS: A LITERATURE-BASED UNIT OR BOOKTALK TOPIC [CU 139–48, 727].

Because the instinct for survival is so important to humans, the subject appears in numerous books. A unit of study built around survival books would be appropriate for students in grades five through eight. Remedial students in grades 9 and 10 would also enjoy reading these selections. A literature-based unit could be built around Blackwood's *Wild Timothy,* Paulsen's Newbery Honor Book, *Hatchet,* George's *My Side of the Mountain,* or any of the other survival books mentioned in this section. Check pages 414–15 of Norton's *Through the Eyes of a Child: An Introduction to Children's Literature* for an example of a web or story map for "Survival on Islands" for a literature-based unit using O'Dell's *Island of the Blue Dolphins.* A guide for teaching O'Dell's book also appears on pages 80–84 of Somers and Worthington's *Response Guides for Teaching Children's Books.* The descriptions of the survival books can also be used in booktalks. Whenever basal readers carry selections from a survival book, these books can be used to extend those selections.

In Blackwood's *Wild Timothy,* 13-year-old Timothy Martin is pudgy, wears glasses, has few friends, and reads constantly. Tim doesn't like the out-of-doors, isn't athletically inclined like his brother Kevin, and is easily bored. While on a camping trip with his father, Tim becomes lost after dark while cutting firewood. Knowledge gained from his reading helps Tim to survive alone for three weeks. The following questions that can be asked about Tim's adventures are listed according to Bloom's Taxonomy of levels of thinking and Bloom's numbers from 1–6 precede the questions. 1—Describe what Tim eats and drinks and how he catches and cooks his food; 2—Name some items Tim uses for fish hooks; 5—Create another type of wilderness fishhook; 2—Describe Tim's relationship with his brother Kevin; 4—Compare Kevin and his dad; 4—Compare Tim and his mother; 1—List some blunders Tim makes while he is lost; 1—List some of the things Tim does right while on his own in the woods; 6—Examine your own knowledge of the woods and decide what you would have done in that situation; 4—Analyze how reading helps Tim; 1—Describe Tim's two injuries; 4—What effect did Tim's two injuries have on his survival?; 4—Compare the hunters with Tim's dad; 1 & 4—List names of books and short stories as well as a poem, magazine, and catalog that are mentioned in the book and compare them with Tim's interests; 2 & 5—Explain why "bewilderment" is a good term to use and change another verb, appropriate to the story, to a noun; 2—Why is Tim still afraid he will be called "Wrong Way Tim"?; 5—Predict what will happen to Tim after he meets the two men; 5—Predict what will happen to Tim before he goes back to school; 5—Write a news article for Tim's hometown newspaper about his adventures; 5—Write a TV news story about Tim's adventures; 1 & 6—Explain how Tim changes because of his adventure; would you have changed in the same way if you had had Tim's experiences?; 4—Compare and contrast Tim and his experiences with Sam Gridley from George's *My Side of the Mountain*; Brian from Paulsen's *Hatchet*; or Ralph, Piggy, Simon, and Jack from Golding's *Lord of the Flies*; 6—Evaluate your own knowledge of the wilderness and assess your chances for survival if you had been in Tim's situation; 6—Read two other survival books, decide which book is your favorite, and justify your choice; 6—Find at least one other person in the class who has chosen the same book and debate two or more other people who have chosen another survival book as their favorite.

Because Timothy Martin is a reader, he mentions Twain's *The Adventures of Tom Sawyer* and *The Adventures of Huckleberry Finn*; Golding's *Lord of the Flies*; Crane's *The Red Badge of Courage*; Dumas's *The Man in the Iron Mask*; Kipling's *The Jungle Book*; Frost's poem "The Road Not Taken"; *Field and Stream* magazine; *The L. L. Bean Catalog*; as well as Sherlock Holmes and Steinbeck.

Paulsen's *Hatchet* is about 13-year-old Brian Robeson, who survives 54 days alone in the Canadian wilderness while contemplating his parents' divorce. Show the sound filmstrip *Literature to Enjoy and Write About, Series 1* to students because just enough of *Hatchet* is shared so students will either want to finish the book to find out what happens or can write their own ending to it. A review of Taylor's *The Cay* also appears on that filmstrip. Philip Enright is being evacuated from the Dutch island of Curacao because of World War II when his ship is torpedoed by the Germans. Philip ends up on a cay or island and survives blindness and the death of Timothy, the black man on the island.

Encourage students to read other survival books by sharing brief information about them. In George's *My Side of the Mountain*, Sam Gridley winters alone in a hollow tree in the Catskill Mountains of New York State. *On the Far Side of the Mountain* is a sequel to the Newbery Honor Book. A selection from

My Side of the Mountain appears in the fifth grade HBJ basal reader, *Skylines*, in the Laureate edition collected by Cullinan, et al. School library/media specialists in schools which use that basal reader series can provide survival booktalks to students, and teachers can assign one extra survival book to students for individual reading. Students can organize the books by type of survival book and can present them to the class with panels or individual presentations.

In Reader's *Coming Back Alive*, Bridget and Dylan escape to the wilderness of the Trinity Mountains in northern California to run away from death and divorce. In Peck's *Jo Silver*, 16-year-old Kenny Matson reads a book called *My Sky* by a part Indian, Jo Silver Fox. To test his manhood, Kenny leaves his private school and goes backpacking in the Adirondack Mountains to find the author at Lost Pond, a place that isn't even listed on a map. After reading the book aloud, ask the students to answer this question: Has any book affected your life as this one affected Kenny's life? Two boys take a last wilderness canoe trip in the lakes of Minnesota in Dygard's *Wilderness Peril* before they go off on their separate ways to college. The boys find a hidden cache of money, buried by a hijacker who has parachuted into the wilderness with it, and have to get the money safely back to civilization.

In Cole's *The Goats*, Howie and Laura, outsiders, are stranded on an island without any clothes by their fellow campers as a prank. Their survival is a matter both physical and psychological. In *Game of Survival* by Regan, Nicky is disappointed that he is paired with Marta instead of another girl on their school camp weekend. Marta's experience and reading about outdoor survival change Nicky's mind when they are lost in the snow during a scavenger hunt. Have middle school students decide if they would rather be stranded with Tim (*Wild Timothy*) or with Marta. Fourteen-year-old Jimmy's year with an escaped convict on a deserted island in Lake Superior is also involuntary. In Hyde's *Island of the Loons* an orphan who has been adopted by the Upper Peninsula town of Munising, Michigan, Jimmy is abducted by Riggs Burkey, a stowaway on an ore freighter which capsizes in a storm. When Jimmy picks up Riggs in his boat, Riggs takes over and keeps him captive on the island where they weather the storm. Several of Jimmy's escape attempts are foiled. After surviving the winter, Riggs learns to read and to appreciate the flora and fauna of the island, especially the loons. A handcarving of a loon would be an appropriate prop to share with students before introducing this book because Riggs becomes a woodcarver. In Lindberg's *The Worry Week*, 11-year-old Allegra Sloane, her 13-year-old sister Alice, and 7-year-old sister Edith (Minnow) are spending July on an island in Maine when their parents are called home because of a death. When the aunt who was to care for them has to go away unexpectedly, the sisters don't tell their parents, but stay on the island alone for a week. Obtaining food is a major and time-consuming activity and is left mostly to Allegra. Literary references abound in this book, especially about their father's connection to Longfellow. Mr. Sloane has even named his three daughters after the girls in Longfellow's poem "The Children's Hour." Brian and Gary are suspicious about the death of Gary's grandfather in Wallace's *Trapped in Death Cave*. The boys set off with a map and a letter and experience kidnapping, starvation, and near drowning. Gina and Justin are first cousins who do not like each other in Skurzynski's *Trapped in the Slickrock Canyon*. The 12-year-old cousins learn to overcome their antipathy when they have to survive against the Colorado canyon wilderness, dangerous criminals, and a flash flood.

Speare's Newbery Honor Book *Sign of the Beaver* is a survival tale which takes place in the 18th-century Maine wilderness. Thirteen-year-old Matt is left behind at their new cabin while his dad goes back to get the family. After his gun is stolen, Matt has to learn how to find food in the forest and learns much from an Indian boy, Attean of the Beaver Clan, who is his own age. Check pages 660–61 of Huck's *Children's Literature in the Elementary School* for an example of webbing for a literature-based unit. The sound filmstrip *Literature to Enjoy and Write About, Series 1* contains a review of Speare's book. Speare is a winner of the Newbery Medal and the Laura Ingalls Wilder Award. "The Survival Story," an interesting article by Speare, appears on pages 163–72 of the March/April 1988 issue of *Horn Book Magazine* magazine. Books mentioned in the article are Speare's *Sign of the Beaver*, Taylor's *The Cay*, O'Dell's *Island of the Blue Dolphins*, Roth's *Iceberg Hermit*, and Callahan's *Adrift*. All the books are fiction except the last one.

Ullman's *Banner in the Sky*, a 1955 Newbery Honor Book, has been reprinted. A recording is also available. Rudy wants to conquer the Swiss mountain, the Matterhorn, even though his mother is afraid that the mountain will take him, as it did her husband.

An aboriginal boy helps 13-year-old Mary and 8-year-old Peter survive a plane crash in the Australian desert in Marshall's *Walkabout*. The book ends in tragedy because of a cultural misunderstanding.

Several survival stories deal with living through hurricanes and tornadoes. McNulty's *Hurricane* is a short book about John and his family, who discuss causes of hurricanes as they prepare for one at the end of a New England summer. A 200-year-old tree is a casualty of the storm. In Winthrop's *Belinda's Hurricane*, Belinda is on Fox Island with her grandmother when the hurricane hits. A 1900 hurricane that kills 6,000 people in Galveston, Texas, is the setting for Nelson's *Devil Storm*. Thirteen-year-old Walter Carroll, his little sister Alice, and his mother are saved by Old Tom the tramp, a black man. Walter has been punished previously for listening to Old Tom's stories. In Ruckman's *Night of the Twisters*, 12-year-old Dan Hatch resents his new baby brother until he has to save him during a tornado that hits their small town. Keeton's *Second-Best Friend* is about a seventh grader who loses her clothes in a Minnesota tornado in 1933. The dress she borrows is stolen. In Milton's *Tornado*, Paul tries to get help on an old CB radio when his mother's car goes off the road in a storm, mother sprains her ankle, and his 7-year-old sister is bitten by a snake. In Paulsen's *The Voyage of the Frog*, 14-year-old David Alspeth is caught in a freak storm at sea while scattering the ashes of his uncle, who has given him the boat. Fifteen-year-old Billie Wind survives a hurricane and a fire in the Florida Everglades in George's *The Talking Earth*. Butler's *My Sister's Keeper* is about two sisters who survive the Peshtigo Fire in Wisconsin that occurred October 8, 1871, at the same time as the Chicago fire. Use all of these survival stories in conjunction with a science selection by Sullivan, "Twister!" from pages 52–59 of the sixth grade HM basal reader, *Celebrations*, edited by Durr, et al.

Several books are about surviving earthquakes. Tarrian is trapped in a train during an earthquake in Hardcastle's *Quake*. Sullivan's *Earthquake* is a survival book in a science fiction setting. Eleven-year-old Philip is separated from his parents during an earthquake and saved by a girl cousin's knowledge.

Several survival books concern personal quests. Perhaps the most famous of these quests is found in Sperry's Newbery Medal winner *Call It Courage*, which set a standard for survival books. The book is available on a recording, a sound filmstrip, video, and television segment. Program #5 of the instructional television series *Storybound*, which targets sixth graders, is Sperry's *Call It Courage*. A selection from *Call It Courage* appears on pages 322–33 of the 6th grade SB/Ginn basal reader, *Wind by the Sea*, edited by Pearson, et al. Mafatu goes off in a canoe with his dog, Uri, and an albatross, Kivi, to prove that he is not a coward and is worthy of his name which means Stout Heart. A storm lands Mafatu on a tropical island where he survives hunger, a shark, and a wild boar. The multimedia cited above can provide an introductory or culminating activity for a literature-based unit using survival books. Ideas for teaching *Call It Courage* appear on pages 85–89 of Somers and Worthington's *Response Guides for Teaching Children's Books*.

One of the newest of the quest books is Paulsen's *Dogsong*. Fourteen-year-old Russell Susskit, a modern Eskimo boy, is not happy with himself, so an older Eskimo, Oogruk, tells him to go off and find his own song. Russell goes on a 1400 mile journey into the Arctic with Oogruk's dog sled. The dogs haven't been run for years, and the boy and dogs learn together. Lost in the Arctic wilderness, Russell lets the dogs take him home by instinct. Some of the challenges he survives are a floating ice pack, open water, a polar bear, fog, an abandoned pregnant girl, and the death of Oogruk. Read this book aloud to students and then ask them to write a personal song. Some books of Eskimo poetry to share with students are: *I Breathe a New Song* and *Out of the Earth I Sing: Poetry and Songs of Primitive Peoples of the World*, both by Lewis; *Songs of the Dream People: Chants and Images from the Indians and Eskimos of North America* and *Eskimo Songs and Stories* found in Knud Rasmussen's expedition journals but translated by Field; and *Beyond the High Hills* also collected by Rasmussen. *Dogsong* is available as a sound filmstrip and video.

Anyone who is interested in the dogs and dogsledding in *Dogsong* would like to read Calvert's *The Hour of the Wolf*, in which Jake Mathiessen survives the Iditarod, the famous 1,049-mile dogsled race from Anchorage to Nome which commemorates the teams that took the serum against diphtheria to Nome in

1925. Seventeen-year-old Jake has already survived a self-inflicted gunshot wound, which caused him to be sent from Minnesota to Alaska to stay with a veterinarian friend of his father. When his friend Danny commits suicide, Jake and Danny's sister, Kamina, each enter the Iditarod in Danny's memory. *The Hour of the Wolf* is a great dog story, a great adventure story, a great problem novel, and a great survival story. In O'Dell's *Black Star, Bright Dawn*, a 17-year-old Eskimo girl takes her father's place in the Iditarod race. A description of the sled dog Black Star appears on pages 2–3, and an explanation of why the girl was called Bright Dawn appears on page 10. The drama and excitement of the race is made clear in O'Dell's book.

Three programs from the instructional television series *Book Bird* are excellent companions to Paulsen's *Dogsong* and Calvert's *The Hour of the Wolf*. The 15-minute segments, narrated by John Robbins, are geared to fourth graders. Program #12, *Race Against Death*, is about how antitoxin for a diphtheria epidemic reaches Nome, Alaska, in 1925. The antitoxin is sent to Nenana by rail and then comes by dog sled through Arctic blizzards. Mowat's *Lost in the Barrens* is Program #16. While deer hunting, Jamie MacNair and Awasin, a Cree Indian, are separated from the others. When their canoe is wrecked and their supplies are lost, the boys are stranded above the subarctic forests of northern Canada, the Barren Lands, and spend six months in the wilderness before they are found by an Eskimo. Program #5 is Houston's *Frozen Fire*. Matthew Morgan and his father go to the Canadian Arctic, where Mr. Morgan takes off in a helicopter looking for copper deposits. When Mr. Morgan doesn't return, Matthew and an Eskimo friend, Kayak, go out in a snowmobile to find him and become lost when they return on foot after running out of gas. Kayak's knowledge helps the boys to survive until their rescue. The videos of these television programs can be viewed by a whole class or individually in the school library/media center and the reading/listening/viewing center in individual classrooms. *Race Across Alaska: First Woman to Win the Iditarod Tells Her Story* contains notes in the margin that make quick informational reading about the Iditerod. This autobiography by Riddles can accompany the cassette *Women of Courage: Libby Riddles*.

George's *The Talking Earth*, like her *Julie of the Wolves*, is about a girl who survives. The council of Seminoles in the Florida Everglades agrees that Billie Wind should be punished for doubting the existence of little people who live underground and the Everglades Serpent that punishes bad Seminoles. Billie Wind's self-inflicted punishment is to go into the swamp until she hears the animals talk and sees the serpent and the people who live underground. The 15-year-old girl lives in the Everglades for 12 weeks and survives a hurricane and a fire. Billie lives with the otter (Petang), adopts a baby panther (Cootchobee), and survives the hurricane with a boy on a name-seeking quest for his puberty rites. A selection from *The Talking Earth* appears in the eighth grade HBJ basal reader, *Panoramas* collected by Cullinan, et al. Check pages 103–09 of Somers and Worthington's *Response Guides for Teaching Children's*

Books for a literature-based study of *Julie of the Wolves*. In order to introduce *Julie of the Wolves*, show the sound filmstrip *Literature to Enjoy and Write About*, which shares the book but stops so that students can either read the story to find out how it ends or write an ending to it. A study guide for the filmstrip is available.

Karana is another strong female heroine. Program #13 of *Storybound*, an instructional television series geared for sixth graders, is O'Dell's Newbery winner, *Island of the Blue Dolphins*. Karana lives alone on an island for 18 years and is rescued in O'Dell's sequel, *Zia*. A selection from *Island of the Blue Dolphins* appears on pages 344–53 of the SB/Ginn fifth grade basal reader *Dream Chasers*, edited by Pearson, et al. That same anthology includes part of Bridbill's *Snow Shoe Trek at Otter River* on pages 310–21. A guide for a literature-based study of *Island of the Blue Dolphins* appears on pages 80–84 of Somers and Worthington's *Response Guides for Teaching Children's Books*.

Thiele's *Shadow Shark* also has a heroine, and both Meg and her orphan cousin Joe turn 13 at the end of the book. Students can be asked to locate on a map as many as possible of the places named: The Great Australian Bight, Ceduna, Melbourne, Port Lincoln, Cape Catastrophe, and the Eyre Peninsula. There are several places in the book where students can be asked to predict what will happen: after the first sentence of Chapter 5, on page 62, "The first task, of course, was to find Scarface"; lines 2 and 3 on page 77 of Chapter 6, "We'll get Scarface this time for sure"; Chapter 8, page 115, "The Shark's pulled George overboard"; Chapter 9, page 123, "Uncle Harry had a theory that accidents always come in pairs." Thiele's *Shadow Shark* is excellent for asking discussion questions based on Bloom's Taxonomy. Each of the questions is preceded by a number indicating the level of thinking. 4—How are Joe and Mophead the mutt alike?; 2—Describe old Scarface; 3—How does Joe feel when he learns he is swimming with the shark?; 4—How would you feel if you had been in Joe's place?; 4—How does Meg feel when she thinks her father is dying?; 5—Role play the experiences when Old Scarface gets away; 4—Could you have solved any of the problems Meg did because of her prior knowledge? A number of "What if" situations fit into the synthesis category, number 5. Have students think of alternatives: What if Mophead hadn't been killed in the explosion? What if Uncle Harry hadn't make a mistake in refueling the boat? What if Joe hadn't been a city boy? What if Meg hadn't been knowledgeable and resourceful? What if Uncle Harry hadn't saved George? What if the mortgage payment hadn't been made? What if the bolts to the fishing chair had been bolted down? What if old Scarface had been killed? What if Meg had continued in the story the way she was described earlier in the book? Books about sharks to read appear in a section of Chapter 5 called WHALES, DOLPHINS, SHARKS.

Once a student has read one book by an author, it is logical to introduce other titles by that author. Students who enjoyed Theile's *Shadow Shark* will like other adventure/survival books by Theile. *Blue Fin* is a Hans Christian

Andersen Honor Book and an Australian Book of the Year. Fourteen-year-old Snook Pascoe wants to impress his father, but every time he is aboard his father's tuna boat, the *Blue Fin*, he makes blunders. Finally, Snook redeems himself when the boat is caught in a storm. Thiele's *Fire in the Stone* is about 14-year-old Ernie who lives with a shiftless father in a crude dugout in Australian opal mining country. After thieves steal his opals, Ernie and an aboriginal friend, Willie, track them.

A variety of media about survival stories are available. Students can locate them in the school library/media center and bring them to the classroom reading/listening/viewing corner. A filmstrip and a sound recording are available for Defoe's classic, *Robinson Crusoe*. Excerpts from his journal are read on the recording. The book is a classic among stories of surviving a shipwreck. The other media mentioned in this section can be shown to a whole group or organized for individual use. Groups of students can be assigned to read a survival book which they present to the class through a peer book panel or a combination of testimonials and selections from various media. Students can vote on the favorite book based on the presentations. Show the testimonials by children from the television series *Reading Rainbow* as samples of how to share a book briefly and enthusiastically.

Whereas Robinson Crusoe is shipwrecked, many modern characters survive plane crashes. Three survival stories are part of the 15-minute reading motivational television series *Storybound* geared for sixth graders. Program #1 is *Pilot Down, Presumed Dead* by Phleger. Because of a tropical storm, pilot Steve Ferris lands his plane somewhere off the coast of Baja California. Steve lives off the land and the ocean and makes friends with a wild coyote. A selection from Elwood and Raht's *Walking Out* appears on pages 90–103 of the HBJ seventh grade basal reader *Patterns*, collected by Cullinan and others. A 16-year-old girl is on her way to Alaska to backpack with her father when she has to parachute from her charter plane into the wilderness in *Walking Out*.

Students can look up the authors of the survival books in the multi-volume set edited by Commire, *Something About the Author* (SATA) or can access all five titles in the Wilson series by consulting the index to Holtze's *The Sixth Book of Junior Authors and Illustrators* (6-JA). Although many of the authors listed in *Something About the Author* can also be found in *Authors in the News* (AITN) and all the revisions of *Contemporary Authors* (CA), those reference books are not referred to here, because most elementary and middle schools do not own the *Contemporary Authors* series. However, that set can be found at most public libraries. Some authors located in volumes of these author biography sets are: William Bell, AITN-1 and CA-4R; Beverly Butler, SATA-7 and 6-JA; Patricia Calvert, SATA-45 and 6-JA; Daniel Defoe, SATA-22; Thomas Dygard, SATA-24 and 6-JA; Jean George, SATA-2 and *More Junior Authors* (MJA); Michael Hardcastle, SATA-38 and 47; James Houston, SATA-13 and *Fourth Book of Junior Authors* (4-JA); Dayton Hyde, SATA-9; William Judson, CANR-12 and 105; Elizabeth Keeton, CA-29–32R; Alexander Key,

SATA-8; Anne Lindbergh (Sapieyevski), SATA-35 and 6-JA; Hilary Milton, SATA-23; Harry Mazer, SATA-31 and *Fifth Book of Junior Authors and Illustrators* (5JA); Farley Mowat, SATA-3; Scott O'Dell, MJA; Gary Paulsen, SATA-22 and 6-JA; Robert N. Peck, SATA 21 and 5-JA; Marjorie Phleger, SATA-1 and 47; Dennis Reader, CA-106; Ivy Ruckman, SATA-37 and 6-JA; Arthur Roth, SATA-28 and 43; Gloria Skurzynski, SATA-8 and 5-JA; Elizabeth Speare, SATA-5 and MJA; Armstrong Sperry, SATA-1 and 27, *Junior Authors*; Theodore Taylor, SATA-4 and 5 and 4-JA; Colin Thiele, SATA-14 and 5-JA; James Uhlman, 4-JA; Bill Wallace, SATA-47; Elizabeth Winthrop (Mahony), SATA-8; and J. D. Wyss, SATA-27 and 29.

Twenty-five titles and 50 questions about survival books appear in Greenson and Taha's *Name That Book! Questions and Answers on Outstanding Children's Books*. Check the index on page 246 for a listing. Have students make their own computer database listing the survival books, and have them retrieve the titles by particular type of survival books, i.e., shipwrecks, floods, fires, tornadoes, airplane crashes, locations, female protagonists, etc. The following survival books have annotated entries in the computer program *BookBrain* for students in grades four to six: *Call It Courage* by Sperry; *The Cay* by Taylor; *Escape to Witch Mountain* by Key; *Island of the Blue Dolphins* by O'Dell; *Julie of the Wolves* by George; *Lost in the Barrens* by Mowat; *My Side of the Mountain* by George; *Night of the Twisters* by Ruckman; *Pilot Down, Presumed Dead* by Phleger; *Robinson Crusoe* by Defoe; *The Sign of the Beaver* by Speare; *Snow Bound* by Mazer; *Snow Shoe Trek to Otter River* by Bridbill; *Swiss Family Robinson* by Wyss; and *Two for Survival* by Roth.

It is possible to extend the scope of a booktalk by the selection of a few books that are related. For example, Orlev's *Island on Bird Street* is about how 11-year-old Alex survives by himself in a Polish ghetto during the Holocaust while he is waiting for his father to return. Similar books from a section of this chapter called THE HOLOCAUST: A BOOKTALK can be used in a general booktalk about survival because surviving war is a legitimate theme among survival stories. Key's *Escape to Witch Mountain* could be added to the booktalk because it approaches survival from a different angle. Tony and Tia are in an orphanage for problem children and communicate with each other without words. The two have special powers which make them desirable to others, so they need to escape.

It is possible to change a booktalk used for intermediate or middle school students to one suitable for high school students by dropping the lowest reading level and adding adult books. Some young adult books have already been included in this selection of books to stretch students at the upper end of the scale. Some books to add for high school students include: Belle's *Crabbe's Journey*; Dickey's *Deliverance*; Golding's *Lord of the Flies*; Reed's *Freefall*; Reid's *Alive*; Robertson's *Survive the Savage Sea*; White's *Deathwatch*. These books are not included in the middle school booklist for various reasons such as the difficulty of the vocabulary or the maturity of the subject.

An example of an annotated bibliography of survival tales that includes a broader interpretation which goes beyond survival after plane crashes and shipwrecks appears in Chapter 14, "Survival Tales: A Focus Unit for Grades Five and Six" on pages 172–90 of *Focus Units in Literature: A Handbook for Elementary School Teachers* by Moss.

THE HOLOCAUST: A BOOKTALK [CU 91–96; 718]. Television programs about the Holocaust, although intended primarily for adults, which have been seen by many children, include *Shoah* in 1985 and the mini-series *War and Remembrance* in 1988–89. Whenever programs such as this appear on television, they can be followed by discussions and book sharing. Many schools have a place in the curriculum for study of the Holocaust in conjunction with history or with literature in reading the book by and about Anne Frank, *The Diary of a Young Girl*, or the play by Goodrich and Hackett, *The Diary of Anne Frank*.

Adults may wish to consult Posner's *Jewish Children's Books: How to Choose Them; How to Use Them*. This book includes information for booktalks for four Holocaust books: *The Children We Remember* by Abells; *In Kindling Flame* by Atkinson; *The Island on Bird Street* by Orlev; and *Upon the Head of a Goat* by Siegal. Other books for adults include *Plays of the Holocaust: An International Collection* by Fuchs; *Shadows of the Holocaust: Plays, Readings, and Program Resources* by Steinhorn; *The Holocaust: An Annotated Bibliography*; and *The Holocaust in Books and Films: A Selected Annotated List* by Muffs and Klein. Check my own list "The Holocaust: A Bibliography for Grades 6–9" on pages 284–87 of the Spring 1986 issue of *Top of the News*. The list includes recommended Holocaust books that were in print during that publication year. Unfortunately, some favorite books were not on the list because they were not included in the 1985–86 *Books in Print*. Favorites that were not on the list but are now back in print include *Friedrich* and *I Was There* by Richter and *I Am Rosemarie* by Moskin.

Most of the Holocaust books are written for intermediate and middle school students. Some of the books can be used in high school programs. However, Adler's *The Number on My Grandfather's Arm* is for primary students. A young girl notices the tattooed number on her grandfather's arm, asks him what it means, so he tells her of persecutions which include Auschwitz.

The booktalk described here is intended for students who need to choose a book to read after reading the play, *The Diary of Anne Frank*, and is best suited for grades eight or nine. The inclusion of adult books and the exclusion of some of the easiest children's books make the booktalk framework suitable for tenth grade. There are books on many reading levels because of varying ability levels of students in the classes. This booktalk is different from others I give because it includes a history lesson. The questions and answers to "How did this happen?" and "How can we keep it from happening again?" are woven throughout the booktalk in a variety of ways through the descriptions of the books. The booktalk is structured so that, while sharing the books, I can weave in history, personal experiences as a tourist visiting Dachau, and seeing the attic where Anne Frank lived in Amsterdam. Incidents of prejudice in our own school are cited also to show that bigotry can be stopped if people have the courage not to go along with the crowd. A brief history of anti-Semitism and conditions in Europe which allowed Hitler to win elections in Germany are part of the introduction. The need for a scapegoat for the economic and social instability is also discussed in the introduction. The similarity of economic conditions then and now is noted. After introducing the books, stand out of the way while students rush to make their selections.

The books are arranged chronologically by categories: Jews who escaped early from Germany; Jews losing rights, businesses, property; ghettos; concentration camps; survival; resistance; after the war; and companion books. Many people escaped from Germany at the beginning of Hitler's power because they knew their beliefs could not mesh with Hitler's ideology. Kerr's *When Hitler Stole Pink Rabbit* fits into this category because the father in that story was a newspaperman who knew his professional integrity would be compromised, so he left the country. The three children left later with their mother, pretending they were going on a weekend vacation. Each was allowed to take a personal possession and 9-year-old Ann, the youngest, regretted leaving her old pink rabbit in favor of a newer toy. On the other end of the reading scale is *The Story of the Trapp Family Singers* by Maria von Trapp, in which the heroine of the musical *The Sound of Music* told how her husband, an Austrian naval officer, could not in good conscience work for Hitler. Maria, her husband, and stepchildren left Austria for the United States. Levitin's *Journey to America* is about leaving Germany for Switzerland and then America. Murray's *The Crystal Nights* is about 15-year-old Elly's cousin Margot and her aunt and uncle who came to Connecticut to escape the Nazis. The Crystal Nights, named because there was so much broken glass from smashed Jewish-owned storefronts, happened on November 9 and 10, 1938. Rose's *Refugee* is about 12-year-old Elke who was sent from Belgium to the United States. The book ends when Elke is 18.

The first step in Hitler's plan was to take away businesses owned by Jews and a good example of that appears in Baer's *A Frost in the Night*, about a family that owned a department store. Sommerfeldt's *Miriam* gives an example of a Jewish home that was given to supporters of Hitler as a reward. In it, 16-year-old Hanne came to live in a house in Oslo where a girl named Miriam had lived. Richter's *Friedrich* describes how Jews had to wear stars symbolizing stars of David, neighbors often did nothing to help, and homes were destroyed. In this fiction book, a German boy tells about Friedrich Schneider, the boy who lived upstairs, who couldn't join the Jungvolk, and who lost his parents and his home. In Richter's *I Was There*, one of three teenagers tells what it was like to be a member of the Hitler youth movement.

Jews had to obey a whole list of regulations called the Nuremberg Laws, which went into effect in 1935. Hecht used these laws as headings for chapters for her book *Invisible Walls: A German Family Under the Nuremberg Laws*, because the laws affected her life when she was 14. Because her father was Jewish and her mother a titled Aryan, they were divorced. The children were stripped of their rights, denied the opportunity to study for a profession, and forbidden to marry.

After businesses and homes were taken away, the next step was to confine the Jews in ghettos. Many people were packed into space intended for a few. Suhl's *On the Other Side of the Gate* shows the dichotomy of Hitler's thinking. On one hand Hitler said that Jews were not good for anything, but on the other hand skilled workers were let out of the ghetto by day to work. A young couple, Hershel and Lena Bregman, decide whether or not to have their child even though the Nazis outlawed pregnancies. Smuggling the child out of the Warsaw ghetto with workers was one possibility. Will they take the chance? Ziemian, a member of the Jewish underground in Poland, wrote *The Cigarette Sellers of Three Crosses Square*, which is about Jewish children who escaped from the Warsaw ghetto and sold cigarettes to keep alive. Readers learn how to get out of the Warsaw ghetto using secret passages in Orlev's *The Island on Bird Street*. After an entire ghetto group was selected to leave for concentration camps, 11-year-old Alex slipped away and was on his own in the Warsaw ghetto for months. Alex compared his survival with that of Robinson Crusoe. Details of Alex's survival are fascinating. Zyskind's autobiography, *Stolen Years*, takes her from age 11 through 17. Sara Plager survives the Lodz ghetto, deportation, Auschwitz, and Mittelstein labor camp. Portrayal of life in the ghetto is especially vivid. Aaron's *Gideon* is a first person fictionalized account of a Polish Jew who survived because he forged papers and looked Aryan. After escaping from the Warsaw ghetto, Gideon went back to try to save his sister but he was caught and sent to Treblinka. Six true incidents in *Lost Childhood* by Pack and Weis include "The Potato Sack" on pages 21–37. A child named Hershl was hidden in a potato sack while the Nazis were making a "selection" of persons to be sent to extermination camps from Lodz ghetto in Poland. Kaplan's *Scroll of Agony: The Warsaw Diary of Chiam A. Kaplan* was found 20 years after the ghetto was destroyed. The diary, for adults, records from September 1, 1939 to August 1942.

There are many examples of survival stories. In Joffo's *A Bag of Marbles*, 10-year-old Joseph and 12-year-old Maurice hid from the Nazis after the invasion of Paris in 1941. *A Pocket Full of Seeds* by Sachs is about five years in the life of Nicole, a French girl, from age 8 to 13. Nicole Nieman was not taken with her family when her home was invaded because she was spending the night with a friend. Rubinowicz's *Diary of David Rubinowicz* is about a boy who was 12 years old at the time of the German occupation of Poland in 1940 and covers 1940–42. Kohn's autobiography, *Mischling, Second Degree: My Childhood in Nazi Germany* explains the terms used by the Nazis to determine "degrees of Jewishness." Ilsa had one Jewish grandparent, which made her a Mischling, Second Degree. A 9-year-old Polish boy posed as a Christian to escape Nazi persecution in Kuper's *Child of the Holocaust*. The last words spoken to her by her mother constitute the title of Wolf's book, *Take Care of Josette*. Jacqueline Wolf had to take care of her 4-year-old sister after their parents were arrested by the Gestapo in France. Rose Zar, a Polish Jew, wrote an autobiography *In the Mouth of the Wolf*, in which she tells how she used false papers to escape from the Nazis. In *Clara's Story* by Isaacman, Clara, a Romanian Jew living in Belgium, was one of the 5,000 out of 60,000 Jews from that country who remained alive. The book shows what it was like to stay alive under the Nazi occupation by being hidden and sent from place to place for two and a half years.

The "final solution" was the euphemism for Hitler's murder of the Jews. In Staden's *Darkness Over the Valley*, the niece of Hitler's first foreign minister shared her rural adolescence in Nazi Germany during the time when they learned of the death camp built in their family-owned valley.

There are numerous personal experiences about surviving concentration camps. Auerbacher's *I Am a Star: Child of the Holocaust* is an autobiographical account of only one of 100 children who survived Terezin concentration camp in Czechoslovakia, where the family went in 1941 when she was 7. Poems by the author are interspersed throughout the story. Drawings are by Bernbaum whose oil paintings in *My Brother's Keeper: The Holocaust Through the Eyes of an Artist* are noteworthy. Oberski's *Childhood*, a first person narrative, begins when Jona is 5 and ends when he is 7. Jona's parents want to go to Palestine but end up in Bergen-Belsen instead. Epstein's *Children of the Holocaust* is about surviving Auschwitz and Terezin. In Vegh's *I Didn't Say Goodbye*, 28 adults tell about their childhood in France during the Holocaust. Day-to-day life in Auschwitz is explained in Hart's *Return to Auschwitz: The Remarkable Story of a Girl Who Survived the Holocaust*. Leitner's *Fragments of Isabella: A Memory of Auschwitz* shares the story of members of a Hungarian family who were taken from their home and sent to Auschwitz. In *Three Children of the Holocaust* by Chanels, three children ranging in ages from 6 to 12 years old survived Auschwitz and were adopted by an American couple. Four Polish sisters, Mania, Pola, Anna, and Ruth, survived Auschwitz by helping each other and were sent to other work camps before being liberated by the Americans in Rubinstein's *The Survivor in Us All: Four Young Sisters in the Holocaust*. Bergen-Belsen is the concentration camp where the fictional Dutch girl, Rosemarie Brenner, was sent in Moskin's *I Am Rosemarie*. In Yolen's *The Devil's Arithmetic*, 12-year-old Hannah travels back in time to become Chaya, who was sent to a Nazi death camp in Poland in 1942. In Forman's *Survivor*, David Uhlman survived Auschwitz and went to Palestine. In *Gizelle, Save the Children* by Hersh, a 16-year-old girl tells how she and her three sisters managed to stay together and survive a concentration camp in Hungary. *Escape or Die* by Friedman contains a dozen stories of young people under the age of 20 who survived the Holocaust. Siegal's *Upon the Head of a Goat: A Childhood in Hungary, 1939–1944*, based on the author's experiences, begins when Piri is 9 years old and ends with the trip to Auschwitz. The sequel, *Grace in the Wilderness: After the Liberation 1945–1948* begins when Piri is 15 years old and liberated from Bergen-Belsen. Explain the term scapegoat in the title of the book as it was used during Hitler's Germany after reading a quote from Leviticus 16 at the front of the book. *Upon the Head of the Goat*, a Newbery Honor Book, is an excellent account of the events leading up to the final solution.

Not all Germans agreed with Hitler. In Horgan's *The Edge of War*, Anna's German Catholic parents weren't members of the Nazi party so her father was sent to be a POW commandant on the Eastern front and her mother was given a remote teaching job. Anna, who is 13 at the beginning of the story and 17 at the end, was responsible for 8-year-old Katie and 6-year-old Nikki. At one time Anna hid an uncle and a friend from the Nazis. The American occupation comes at the end of the book. In *Don't Say a Word* by Gehrts, Anna's father, a Luftwaffe colonel, secretly did not support the Nazis so his children had to learn to keep secrets. Hans and Anna pretended to be loyal members of the Hitler Youth, while having secret Jewish friendships, but Anna was ultimately executed for treason. Butterworth's autobiographical novel *As the Waltz Was Ending* begins in Vienna when Emma is eight years old. Emma's father hated the Nazis so she was an outsider because she did not join the Bund Deutscher Model, the Hitler Youth group for girls. Emma's grand passion was ballet. Thirteen-year-old girls remain friends although Inge is Jewish and Lieselotte is a member of Hitler youth in 1938 in Orgel's novel *The Devil in Vienna*. Gallaz and Innocenti's *Rose Blanche* is about a young girl, caught up in the excitement of Hitler's Germany, who decided to help Jews. In von der Grün's autobiography *Howl Like the Wolves*, Max's father's advice was to howl like the wolves so no one would know he wasn't one of them. The book shows post World War I life in Nazi Germany between 1926 and 1945. At age 17, Max was drafted into the labor camps and at 18 he was conscripted into the army. Later he became a POW and was sent to Louisiana.

There are books about real people who were involved in the resistance. Hannah Senesh (or Szenes) was British-trained and sent to Yugoslovia as a spy; she was captured and killed in 1944. Atkinson's *In Kindling Flame: The Story of Hannah Senesh, 1921–44* is the winner of the 1986 National Jewish Book Award for Literature. A shorter biography of her is Schur's *Hannah Szenes: A Song of Light*. Hans and Sophie Scholl, university students, were part of "The White Rose," an anti-Nazi group. They were arrested, tried, and executed in 1943. Their diaries and letters appear in *At the Heart of the White Rose*, edited by Jens. Vinke's *The Short Life of Sophie Scholl* won the Jane Addams Children's Book Award for a book "promoting the cause of peace, social justice, and world community." The Scholls's story in fiction is Forman's *Ceremony of Innocence*. Dumach and Newborn's *The Story of the White Rose: Shattering the German Night* is nonfiction and makes use of the Scholl diaries. The book begins with Hans and Sophie's involvement and later disillusionment with Hitler

Youth. Hans was actually a leader, distributing leaflets in Munich while he was a student. *Walls: Resisting the Third Reich—One Woman's Story* by Zassenhaus is about how a 17-year-old girl smuggled food from the Swedish Red Cross to prisoners. Meltzer's *Rescue: The Story of How Gentiles Saved Jews in the Holocaust* tells of the Resistance and how ordinary people risked their lives to make a difference. The first chapter is an excellent overview of the Holocaust. The origin of the word Holocaust is defined on page 2. Although it is written for adults, many good readers will enjoy *Anne Frank Remembered: The Story of the Woman Who Helped to Hide the Frank Family* by Meip Gies (who was Mr. Frank's secretary) and Alison Gold. Praeger's *World War II Resistance Stories* includes six stories about civilians. Cowan's *Children of the Resistance* tells how teenagers from France, Denmark, Italy, Norway, Yugoslavia, Holland, Czechoslovakia, and Germany sabotaged the Germans. Nine-year-old Renee Roth and her family left Alsace for Paris and defied the Germans. In 1940, Renee and her two sisters were hidden in a Catholic convent in Normandy where they converted to Catholicism to save their lives in the autobiography *Touch Wood: A Girlhood in Occupied France.* A similar autobiography, Weinstein's *The Hidden Childhood: A Jewish Girl's Sanctuary in a French Convent, 1942–1945,* tells of how a 7-year-old girl survived the Holocaust in a convent. Bernheim's *Father of the Orphans: The Life of Janusz Korczak* has a foreword by Katherine Paterson. Korczak, a Polish doctor and educator, was running orphanages when Hitler invaded Poland and he stayed with his children through the Warsaw ghetto and Treblinka. The biography is based on Korczak's diary. Levine's *Secret Missions: Four True Life Stories* contains information on pages 89–116 about a Dutch nurse who hid over 200 Jews from the Nazis in "Leesha Bos: Nazi Fighter." Suhl's *They Fought Back: The Story of the Jewish Resistance in Nazi Europe* contains 32 accounts of the resistance of Jews in ghettos, concentration camps, and in partisan groups including the one led by Uncle Misha.

Some of the books about the resistance are fiction. Suhl's *Uncle Misha's Partisans* and Samuels's *Motelle* tell about how 12-year-old Motelle, a Ukrainian Jew, spies for Uncle Misha's partisans after his parents are killed by the Nazis. Although both books are fiction, they are based on the life of a real boy named Motelle. Benchley's *Bright Candles: A Novel of the Danish Resistance* is about 16-year-old Jens Hansen who kept his resistance work a secret from his family. Ten-year-old Anne Marie Johansen and her family help her Jewish friend, Ellen Rosen, and her family leave Denmark for Sweden during World War II. This story of the Danish Resistance, Lowry's *Number the Stars*, is a Newbery Award winner. In Pelgrom's *The Winter When Time Was Frozen*, a Dutch farmer and his family take in a 12-year-old Jewish girl and her father. Reiss's *The Upstairs Room*, about a 10-year-old girl hidden from the Nazis by Dutch farmers, is available on a sound filmstrip or video. In the sequel, *The Journey Back*, Annie is reunited with her family after the war. In Haugaard's *Chase Me, Catch Nobody!*, a 14-year-old Danish boy is given a package by a man soon arrested by the Gestapo. Not only does Erik deliver the package in Hamburg, but he also rescues a girl who is hidden in an attic for a year. *Dark Hour of Noon* by Szambelan-Strevinsky begins in 1939 when Trina is 7 years old and Poland is invaded. Much of the story is about Trina's involvement in the underground with other children. The easiest story of the Resistance is McSwigan's *Snow Treasure*, which is fiction but based on a real event in which Norwegian children smuggle gold out of Norway on their sleds in 1940.

Some of the books cover events that occurred after the war. In Lisle's *Sirens and Spies*, 14-year-old Elsie accidentally discovers that her music teacher collaborated with the Germans during the occupation of France. Kate reads the diary of another Kate, her Aunt Sylvia's younger sister, written during the time they were at a Nazi girls' camp. Sylvia's behavior during the war causes Kate to change her feelings for her aunt in *The Visit* by Degens.

Levoy's *Alan and Naomi* is about a boy from the Bronx who is asked to make friends with the girl in the apartment upstairs. Naomi hasn't been able to forget her experiences during the Holocaust, including seeing the Nazis kill her father. David's grandfather, Max, consoles him when a puppy drowns by taking him to an art gallery where Max sees a painting that could be by a boyhood friend he thinks died in the Holocaust. Max and David search for Bernie Bauer but Max dies before Bernie is located in Provost's *David and Max*. Kerr's *Gentlehands* is difficult to share in a booktalk because the grandfather's involvement with Nazis does not come out until the end of the story and telling it would spoil the story. How the remnants of the Holocaust cloud life after the war can be the description of the book and fans of Kerr will choose it for her sake. Uhlman's *Reunion* is an example of irony. When he is invited back to Stuttgart, Germany, for a class reunion, Hans Schwartz reflects that he was asked to leave the school during the Nazi regime because he is Jewish. Hans also remembers his friendship with a German officer's son. Lang's *A Backward Look: Germans Remember* contains memories of Germans who were teenagers during Hitler's time. *Transport 7–41-R* by Degens is about a 13-year-old German girl with forged papers who leaves the Russian sector of Germany via cattle car so she can live in the areas controlled by England, France, or the United States. The girl in this first person narrative meets an old man who is trying to take his wife's body home to Cologne without the the authorities realizing that she died on the journey. A cassette of *Transport 7–41-R* is available.

In Sender's *The Cage*, Riva Minsky and her seven brothers and sisters are leading a normal life in Poland with their widowed mother. The book begins with Mama getting ready for Passover (or Petach) by making new clothes for her own family as well as Mrs. Gruber's Harry, a gentile. After the German invasion of Poland in 1939, the Gruber family turns on them, Mama is taken away, and older brothers and sisters escape to Russia. At 16, Riva works making military uniforms and has custody of her younger brothers until they are deported to Auschwitz. Life in the Lodz ghetto is portrayed well. After Auschwitz,

Riva is sent to a slave labor camp in Germany, escaping a death camp because her poetry, written on paper bags, is good for morale. Camp Grafenort is liberated by the Russians in 1945 at the end of the book. *To Life* is the sequel to *The Cage*. Riva is 19 years old when the Russians liberate the labor camp. Riva's search to find out if any of her family is alive is typical of what survivors faced after the war. During this time Riva meets Moniek, they marry and have two children before they finally receive papers to come to America. Introduce the books by reading the poem at the beginning of *The Cage*.

Another book for teenagers is Fink's *A Scrap of Time: Other Stories*. Fink, a survivor of the Holocaust, writes from the viewpoints of those who are living the Holocaust and those who have survived and are reminiscing. In Orenstein's *I Shall Live: Surviving Against All Odds, 1939–1945*, Henry tells how he and his parents, three brothers, and a sister lived under the Russians in Poland until 1942 and then under the Nazis. Orenstein's experiences included five concentration camps.

Greene's *Elie Wiesel: Messenger from the Holocaust* is about the 1986 Nobel Peace Prize winner, whose his acceptance speech is included. Wiesel's own Hungarian family's experiences of being sent to Auschwitz and Buchenwald appear in *Night*. Noble's *Nazi Hunter: Simon Wiesenthal*, is about a man who survived a concentration camp to become the Nazi hunter who searched out and brought to justice SS officers who disappeared at the end of the war. Two famous Nazis that Wiesenthal captured were Adolf Eichmann and Hermione Ryan.

Multimedia about World War II are suitable for a unit on the Holocaust. Serraillier's *Escape from Warsaw* is Program #16 of *Storybound*, a reading motivation series for sixth graders. The theme of the story is reuniting the family, which is accomplished through a silver sword or letter opener, all that was left in the rubble of the Balicki home in Warsaw. The book was originally called *The Silver Sword*. Program #14 of the instructional television program, *Readit!*, is *Twenty and Ten*, based on a book by Bishop. A group of 20 fifth graders who lived in the mountains during the occupation of France in 1944 hid 10 Jewish orphans from the Nazis. *Holocaust* is a set of two sound filmstrips in which Elie Wiesel gives the conclusion. *The Rise of Nazism: Terror and Tragedy* contains two filmstrips, a guide, and ditto master. A set of two filmstrips or a video, *Anne Frank: A Legacy for Our Time* consists of *The Story of Anne Frank* and *The Lesson of Anne Frank*. The filmstrips were developed in conjunction with the Anne Frank Center in Amsterdam and lead to a discussion of whether or not this tragedy could happen again. *The Life of Anne Frank* is a video.

Biographies of Anne Frank include Bull's *Anne Frank*, which describes living in the attic and is appropriate for fifth and sixth graders. Leigh's *Anne Frank* can be used by third graders because the information is so easily and attractively accessible. Leigh's book should be part of any unit about Anne Frank, regardless of grade level, because of the large print, illustrations, and photos. Leigh's slim volume is a perfect companion to the diary commenting on all the essentials: an explanation of the diary; Anne's childhood; Jewish life in 1940; school; hiding; other annexed occupants; life in the annex; how Anne spent her days; friendship between Anne and Peter, the world outside the annex; and discovery. A brief chronology, glossary, and bibliography are included. Also consult Tridenti's *Anne Frank*, Tames's *Anne Frank*, and Hurwitz's *Anne Frank: Life in Hiding*. Check Fradin's *Remarkable Children: Twenty Who Made History* for an article about Anne Frank. *Anne Frank's Tales from the Secret Annex* includes short stories, fables, essays, and reminiscences written by Anne Frank that were not published originally with her diary because Anne's father did not think some of the materials were suitable.

Meltzer's classic *Never to Forget: The Jews of the Holocaust* is still available in hardback and paperback. Check pages 84–91 for chapters "Under the Terror of the Swastika" and "The Holocaust" in Shamir's *The Young Reader's Encyclopedia of Jewish History*. Three recent Holocaust histories are Adler's *We Remember the Holocaust*; Chaikin's *A Nightmare in History*; and Rossell's *The Holocaust: The Fire That Raged.*

There are other nonfiction books about the Holocaust that are not biographies, autobiographies, or personal narratives. Bernbaum's *My Brother's Keeper: The Holocaust Through the Eyes of an Artist* is a book as well as a sound filmstrip. The oil paintings show Warsaw at the time of the Holocaust. Although the book itself has a picture-book format, it is not a young child's picture book and explanations and discussion of the symbolic illustrations and the commentary are necessary. *The Children We Remember* by Abells contains about 40 pages of haunting pictures of children under the Holocaust. It has a picture-book format and few words, and can be used with primary children or with adults. Hyett's *In Evidence: Poems of the Liberation of Nazi Concentration Camps* includes 150 poems by Allied soldiers. Chaikin's *A Nightmare in History: The Holocaust 1933–45* gives a history of anti-Semitism from biblical times through the Nazi era and includes excerpts from diaries and eyewitness reports. The uprising in the Warsaw ghetto is covered. How Hitler's plan to exterminate the Jews is accomplished is also part of Chaikin's book. Rogasky's *Smoke and Ashes: The Story of the Holocaust* is a very thorough coverage of the Holocaust and uses personal narratives and records by the Nazis to discuss the Nuremberg Laws, the Crystal Nights, ghetto life, deportations, trains, camps, and the Resistance. Many of the photos were taken by the Nazis. There is a chapter on the lack of interference by the U.S. and British governments and on Nazi war criminals.

Marrin's new book, *Hitler,* tells of the German dictator's experiences during World War I, his rise to power, and the effects of his reign. Other biographies of Hitler include Bullock's *Hitler: A Study in Tyranny,* Rubenstein's *Adolf Hitler,* and Shirer's *The Rise and Fall of Adolf Hitler.* A chapter about Hitler appears in Archer's *The Dictators.* Books about Nazis include Goldston's *The Life and Death of Nazi Germany* and Rubin's *Hitler and the Nazis.*

Snyder's *Encyclopedia of the Third Reich* is helpful for understanding specific events and people. Arnold and Silverstein's *Anti-Semitism: A Modern Perspective* defines anti-Semitism and discusses it historically and in the United States today. Chapter 3, "The Holocaust," appears on pages 42–62. Zeman's *Nazi Propaganda* emphasizes the propaganda techniques used by the Nazis to mold public opinion. Thalmann and Feinermann's *Crystal Night* is about the pogrom of November 9–10, 1938. Gallo's *The Night of the Long Knives* tells about Hitler's purge of the SA (Brown Shirts), on June 29–30, 1934. Gray's slim book *Hitler and the Germans* can be background reading for children and adults because it tells about the fall of Imperial Germany, the rise of the Weimar Republic, economic crisis and the Nazi takeover, the Third Reich, and the new order in Europe after the war. Brief sketches of eight leaders of the Third Reich are given. Key dates appear on page 32 and Anne Frank is mentioned on page 27.

There are several companion books to the Holocaust that could be part of a booktalk on World War II. In Taylor's *The Cay*, the ship Philip is on is torpedoed by the Germans and he and the black man Timothy are stranded on a Caribbean island. Hautzig's *The Endless Steppe: Growing Up in Siberia* is about Esther Rudomin and her parents who are exiled to Siberia when the Russians invade Poland during World War II. When 12-year-old Patty Bergen helps a German prisoner of war in Arkansas, her whole life changes in Greene's *Summer of My German Soldier.* The sequel, *Morning Is a Long Time Coming* takes place when Patty is 18 and her grandmother gives her money to go to college but she uses it to go to Paris. The sequel is more suitable for high school age than younger students. Walsh's *Fireweed* is about Bill and Julie, two strangers who were to be evacuated from London during the bombing, but who return and survive in the rubble.

Other companion books include books about the internment of Americans of Japanese ancestry in the United States during World War II. Their homes and businesses were taken away and they were placed in enemy alien camps. In *Farewell to Manzanar* by Houston, a young woman tells how her father lost his dignity and his fishing boats when the family was placed in Manzanar when she was 7 years old. Yoshiko Uchida, compiler of the classic folklore collections *The Magic Listening Cap* and *The Dancing Kettle and Other Japanese Folktales,* based her book *Desert Exile: The Uprooting of a Japanese American Family* on family accounts of life in an internment camp in Utah. *Journey to Topaz* is about how her mother and brother were sent to Topaz, a desert concentration camp. A nonfiction book is *Behind the Barbed Wire: The Imprisonment of Japanese Americans During World War II* by Davis. Garrigue's *The Eternal Spring of Mr. Ito* is fiction about the internment of Japanese-Canadians during World War II.

BOOK AWARDS CHOSEN BY CHILDREN. Numerous states conduct reading contests in which school children choose the outstanding book for the year. Although some states have several categories ranging from primary to high school, most of the states have an award for grades 4–6. Children's book awards are sponsored by combinations of the following organizations: State Reading Councils; State School Library/Media Associations; State Library Associations; State Departments of Educations; State Universities; State Libraries; State Parents and Teachers Associations; Co-Operative Extension Services; State Divisions of the American Association of University Women; State Associations for Childhood Education International; State Associations of Elementary School Principals; State Councils of Teachers of English.

Plan a display or a booktalk to introduce these books to children and call it "Books Kids Like" or "Winners!" Include the multimedia when preparing a display center in the school library/media center or classroom. Use the books in the following bibliography for your booktalk and remind students that the books being introduced are winners of state contests in which students their age have chosen the books. Most of the books are winners between 1980 and 1988. However, if an author has had previous winners, those books are also listed. After the basic bibliographic information, the year of the award and the abbreviation for the state or states which honor the book are given. The books on this list are representative of the following book awards: Arizona Young Readers Award; Arkansas—Charlie May Simon Award; California Young Reader's Medal; Florida—Sunshine State Young Reader's Award; Georgia Children's Book Award; Hawaii Nene Award; Indiana Young Hoosier Book Award; Iowa Children's Choice Award; Kansas—William Allen White Children's Book Award; Massachusetts Children's Book Awards; Michigan Young Readers' Awards; Minnesota—Maude Hart Lovelace Book Award; Missouri—Mark Twain Book Award; Nebraska—Golden Sower Award; New Hampshire—Great Stone Face Award; New Jersey—Garden State Children's Book Award; New Mexico—Land of Enchantment Children's Book Award; Ohio—Buckeye Children's Book Award; Oklahoma—Sequoyah Children's Book Award; Pacific Northwest—Young Reader's Choice Award (Alaska, Alberta, British Columbia, Idaho, Montana, Oregon, and Washington); South Carolina Children's Book Award; Texas Bluebonnet Award; Tennessee Children's Choice Book Award; Utah Children's Book Award; Vermont—Dorothy Canfield Fisher Award; Virginia Young Readers Program; Wisconsin—Golden Archer Award; Wyoming—Indian Paintbrush Award. After the abbreviation for the name of the state giving the award, a list of acronyms for adult reviewing sources which recommended the book are given. The list of places where the book has been reviewed are: *Children's Catalog,* ChCat; *Junior High School Library Catalog,* JHSC, *Elementary School Library Collection,* ESLC; National Council for the Social Studies annual list, NCSS; "Teacher's Choices," National Council of Teachers of English, NCTE; ALA Notable Book, ALANB; Newbery Medal or Newbery Honor Book, N, NH; *School Library Journal* Best Books, SLJBB; Sutherland's *Best in Children's Books,* S-79–86; *Books for Children,* Children's Literature Center, Library of Congress, LC. Also included is recognition that the book appeared on the International Reading Association's Children's Choice list, IR-ACC. SATA, JA, MJA, 3-JA, 4-JA, 5-JA, and 6-JA indicate that information about the author appears in the set *Something About the Author,* edited by Commire; *Junior Authors,* edited by Kunitz and Haycraft; *More Junior Authors,* edited by Fuller; *The Third Book of Junior Authors,* edited by DeMontreville and Hill; *The Fourth Book of Junior Authors and Illustrators,* edited by De-Montreville and Crawford; *The Fifth Book of Junior Authors and Illustrators*; and *The Sixth Book of Junior Authors and Illustrators,* both edited by Holtze. Multimedia materials such as filmstrips, FS; videos, 16mm films, cassettes, and TV programs are also listed.

BOOKTALKING 118 AWARD-WINNING TITLES

Adler, Carole. *The Magic of the Glits.* Macmillan, 1979. Avon Camelot pb, Scholastic pb. 1982-KS, ChCat, ESLC, S-79–86, IRACC, SATA-26, 6-JA. Twelve-year-old Jeremy, who has a broken leg, is spending the summer on Cape Cod with his mother. Jeremy befriends lonely 7-year-old Lynette by sharing the fantasy of imaginary creatures, Glits, with her.

Banks, Lynne Reid. *The Indian in the Cupboard.* Doubleday, 1980. Avon Camelot pb. 1984-PNW, 1985-CA, (intermed.), 1987/88-VA, ESLC, 6-JA. Sequel: *The Return of the Indian.* Doubleday, 1986.
Nine-year-old Omri receives a plastic Indian from his best friend. When he puts it in an old cupboard, the toy Indian comes to life. Patrick's toy cowboy also comes to life. Other toy figures become involved in this space and time book.

Banks, Lynne Reid. *The Return of the Indian.* Doubleday, 1986. Avon Camelot, Scholastic pb. 1989-WY. ChCat, 6-JA. Sequel: *The Secret of the Indian.* Doubleday, 1989.
Omri brings back his Indians to tell them that he has won a creative writing contest for his story "The Plastic Indian." Although he does not believe any more, Patrick contributes Boone so he can be brought to life. Modern weaponry in the hands of people of the past brings disaster to historical situations.

Bellairs, John. *The Letter, the Witch and the Ring.* Dial, 1976. Dell pb. 1981-UT. ChCat, ESLC, SATA-2, 5-JA. Sequel to *The House With a Clock on Its Walls* and *The Figure in the Shadows.* Both books are Dial hardback and Dell pb.
Thirteen-year-old Rose Rita Pottinger's best friend Lewis, who lives with his warlock uncle, Jonathan, goes off to camp and leaves her alone. However, Rose Rita's witch friend, Mrs. Zimmermann, receives a deathbed letter from her own uncle about a magic ring and takes Rose Rita on a trip with her to investigate. During their trip through the Upper Peninsula of

Michigan in the 1950s, Rose Rita and Mrs. Zimmermann are stalked by an evil force which tries to kill them.

Blume, Judy. *Are You There, God? It's Me, Margaret.* Bradbury, 1970. Dell pb. 1975-HI, 1980-NH, ChCat, ESLC, SATA-2 & 31, 4-JA. Spanish edition: *Estas Ahi, Dios? Soy Yo, Margaret.* Cliffhanger cassette: Listening Library, n.d. 3 cassettes: Listening Library, 1988.
Eleven-year-old Margaret has a Jewish father and a Catholic mother, so her sixth grade project is to find out about religion. Margaret also has moved to the New Jersey suburbs from New York City.

Blume, Judy. *Blubber.* Bradbury, 1974. Dell pb. 1977-PNW, ESLC, SATA-2 & 31, 4-JA. Spanish edition: *La Ballena.* Filmstrip: Pied Piper, 1984. Cliffhanger cassette: Listening Library, n.d.
When Linda is giving a report on whale blubber in fifth grade, Wendy passes a note to Caroline and then on to Jill which says "Blubber is a good name for her!" This is the beginning of their tormenting of Linda. When Jill finally decides to help Linda, the group turns on her.

Blume, Judy. *Otherwise Known as Sheila the Great.* Dutton, 1972. Dell pb. 1978–79-SC, ChCat, ESLC, SATA-2 & 31, 4-JA. Film or video: Barr Films, 1987.
Ten-year-old Sheila Tubman would rather walk up 10 flights of stairs than go on an elevator with a dog, is also afraid of spiders, storms, the dark, getting her face wet in the pool, and admitting that she doesn't know something. Sheila, who knows Peter Hatcher from *Tales of a Fourth Grade Nothing* and *Superfudge,* spends all her time outside the city for the summer.

Blume, Judy. *Superfudge.* Dutton, 1980. Dell pb. 1981, 1984, 1985, 1986-NH, 1981-OH, 1982-HI, 1982-TN, 1982-TX, 1982-UT, 1983-GA, l983-IA, 1983-IN, 1983-NE, intermed., 1983-NJ, 1983-PNW, 1984-NM, 1985-FL; 1985/86-VA, ChCat, ESLC, S-79–86, IRACC, SATA-2 & 31, 4-JA. Large print edition: ABC-CLIO, 1987. Filmstrip: *Superfudge.* Pied Piper, 1984. FS: *Literature to Enjoy and Write About, Series 1.* Pied Piper, 1989. Sequel to *Tales of a Fourth Grade Nothing.*
Four-year-old Fudge and his sixth grade brother Peter move from New York City to suburban New Jersey while their father writes a book. Fudge embarrasses Peter, Peter's old and new friends meet, Peter kisses his first girl, and Peter's mother is pregnant. Read aloud!

Blume, Judy. *Tales of a Fourth Grade Nothing.* Dutton, 1972. 1974/5-AR, 1975-OK, 1975-PNW, 1976–77-SC, 1977 & 1983-MA, 1982-NH. ChCat, ESLC, SATA-2 & 31, 4-JA. Large print edition: ABC-CLIO, 1987. Prequel to *Superfudge.*
Fourth grader Peter Hatcher's 2-year-old brother Farley Drexel (Fudge)

swallows Peter's pet turtle, Dribble. Peter is upset when everyone worries about Fudge and not Dribble.

Blume, Judy. *Tiger Eyes.* Bradbury, 1981. Dell pb. 1983-CA, JH; 1983-OH 4–6; 1983-VT, JHSC, SATA-2 & 31, 4-JA.
Tenth grader Davey, her seven-year-old brother, and mother move to Los Alamos to be near her dad's sister and her husband, Walter, after the dad is killed in his store by a robber. Davey has trouble coming to terms with her dad's death, has a girl friend who drinks, dislikes her mother's boyfriend, and quarrels with Walter. While a Candy Striper, Davey meets a dying man and his son Wolf, a young man she has met previously in a canyon. The two young people grapple with death together. Explain title.

Brittain, Bill. *All the Money in the World.* Harper, 1979. Trophy pb. 1981/82-AR, ChCat, ESLC, 5-JA.
Quentin Stone catches a leprechaun who grants him three wishes. Quentin wishes for all the money in the world but the results are different from what he expected.

Bulla, Clyde Robert. *Shoeshine Girl.* Crowell, 1975. 1977/78-AR, 1978-OK, 1979/80-SC, ChCat, ESLC, SATA-2 & 41, MJA.
Ten-year-old Sarah Idah is sent to spend the summer with Aunt Claudia to keep her away from unsuitable friends. Sarah learns about money and friendship as a shoeshine girl.

Bunting, Eve. *Karen Kepplewhite Is the World's Best Kisser.* Clarion, 1983. Archway pb. Scholastic pb. 1987-HI, ChCat. JHSC, SATA-18, 5-JA.
Seventh grade Karen's best friend gives her a book on kissing so they can be prepared for kissing games at Karen's birthday party. Even though the class know-it-all makes fun of the book in a bookstore window, it is obvious during the party that he has read it. The book is humorous and sensitive, especially when Karen and the boy she likes are out in the hall for their kiss.

Byars, Betsy. *The Computer Nut.* Viking, 1984. Puffin pb. 1986/87-AR, ESLC, SATA-4 & 46, 3-JA.
Ten-year-old Kate completes her self-portrait of a computer nut and her project on the computer appears on page 6. Kate receives a message from people who say they are from outer space and she carries on an exchange with them. The first message appears on page 7.

Byars, Betsy. *Cracker Jackson.* Viking, 1985. Penguin pb. 1986/87-SC, 1987-NE Honor, 1988-KS, ChCat, ESLC, NCSS, LC, IRACC, SATA-4 & 46, 3-JA.
Eleven-year-old Cracker learns that Alma, his former baby sitter, is being abused by her husband. Only after the husband harms their child does

Alma accept help. The humor in the book offsets the weighty subject matter.

Byars, Betsy. *The Cybil War.* Viking, 1981. Apple pb. 1983-NE Honor, 1983-TN, 1984-OK, ChCat, ESLC, ALANB, SLJBB, S-79–86, IRACC, SATA-4 & 46, 3-JA.
Simon and Tony, fifth graders, both like Cybil Ackerman. Tony is a pathological liar.

Byars, Betsy. *The Eighteenth Emergency.* Viking, 1973. Camelot pb. 1975-VT, ChCat, ESLC, SATA-4 & 46, 3-JA. Large Print: G. K. Hall, 1988.
Benjie Fawley, better known as Mouse, is afraid of the bully Marv Hammerman. It is an unwritten rule that it is OK to fight anyone in the same grade, but Marv is at least two grades behind, which puts them both in the sixth grade. While Mouse waits for Marv to beat him to a pulp he thinks of all the emergencies he can.

Byars, Betsy. *Night Swimmers.* Delacorte, 1980, Dell pb. ChCat, JHSC, ESLC, SLJBB, S-79–86, IRACC, SATA-4 & 46, 3-JA, American Book Award.
Because her father is busy with his career as a country-western singer, Loretta Anderson (Retta) has to take care of her two younger brothers. Swimming in someone else's pool is one of their activities.

Byars, Betsy. *Pinballs.* Harper, 1977. Dell pb. 1979/80-AR, 1980-CA JH, 1980-MO, 1981-MN, 1981-NE Honor, ChCat, ESLC, SATA-4 & 46, 3-JA. ITV *Storybound* #8.
Three foster children call themselves pinballs because they have no place to rest. Harvey, Carlie, and Thomas J. all come to live with the Masons.

Carris, Joan. *When the Boys Ran the House.* Lippincott, 1982. 1985-TN, 1986-IA, 1986-IN, ESLC, SATA-42 & 44.
Twelve-year-old Jut Howard is in charge of the three brothers, the youngest of whom is two years old, while father is in Europe on business and mother is ill. Numerous disasters befall, such as bees in the kitchen and an unexplainable smell in the living room. Jut also tries out for the eighth grade basketball team.

Catling, Patrick. *The Chocolate Touch.* Morrow, 1952. Bantam pb. 1983-UT, ESLC. Sequel: *John Midas in the Dreamtime.* Morrow, 1987. Bantam pb.
After John Midas finds a coin and buys chocolate with it, all he touches turns to chocolate. Compare this story with versions of "King Midas and the Golden Touch."

Cleary, Beverly. *Dear Mr. Henshaw.* Morrow, 1983. Dell pb. Scholastic pb, 1985-VT, 1986-MA, 1986-OK, 1989-HI. Ch Cat, ESLC, ALANB, N, SLJBB, S-79–86, SATA-2 & 43, MJA. Large print edition: ABC-CLIO,

1987. FS: Random/Miller-Brody, 1984. FS: *Literature to Enjoy and Write About, Series 1*. Pied Piper, 1989.
Ten-year-old Leigh Botts writes to an author and tells about his parents' divorce and his new school. The letters turn into a journal. Consider showing the filmstrip *Meet the Newbery Author: Beverly Cleary*. Random House, 1979. Read parts of Cleary's biography *A Girl from Yamhill: A Memoir*, Morrow, 1988.

Cleary, Beverly. *The Mouse and the Motorcycle*. Morrow, 1965. Dell pb. Scholastic pb. 1968-PNW, 1969-HI, 1983-NJ. ChCat, ESLC, SATA-2 & 43, MJA. 16mm, video: Churchill Films, 1986. Sequels: *Runaway Ralph* and *Ralph S. Mouse*. Companion book: Hewett's *On Camera: The Story of a Child Actor*. Clarion, 1987.
A mouse meets the boy Keith, who is staying at the Mountain View Inn. Keith gives Ralph a toy motorcycle.

Cleary, Beverly. *Ralph S. Mouse*. Morrow, 1982. Dell pb. 1985-IA. ChCat, SLJBB, S-78–86, IRACC, SATA-2 & 43, MJA, Golden Kite Award. Sequel to *Mouse and the Motorcycle* and *Runaway Ralph*.
Ralph S. Mouse goes to fifth grade with Ryan, the son of the new innkeeper at Mountain View Inn in California, and becomes the basis of a class project on mice. Ryan contends with Brad, who ruins Ralph's motorcycle.

Cleary, Beverly. *Ramona and Her Father*. Morrow, 1977. Dell pb. 1979-HI, 1980-TN, 1980-UT, 1981-NM, 1981-TX, ChCat, ESLC, NH, SATA-2 & 43, MJA. Recording: *Ramona and Her Father*. Random House, 1978. Sequel to *Ramona the Brave*.
Ramona is in second grade. Father loses his job and Ramona tries to get him to quit smoking. Ramona wants to get a job making TV commercials.

Cleary, Beverly. *Ramona and Her Mother*. Morrow, 1979. Dell pb. PNW-1980, 1982-NJ, 1985-NE Honor, ChCat, ESLC, ALANB, SLJBB, IRACC, SATA-2 & 43, MJA. Cassette: Random House, 1980. Sequel to *Ramona and Her Father*. Companion book: Scott's *Ramona: Behind the Scenes of a Television Show*. Morrow, 1988.
Father finally gets a job but doesn't like it. Mother likes her job and Ramona dislikes the babysitter. Mr. and Mrs. Quimby quarrel and the girls become upset. Beezus and her mother have a falling out over Beezus's hair. Ramona is in second grade and Beezus is in seventh grade.

Cleary, Beverly. *Ramona Forever*. Morrow, 1984. Dell pb. 1986-NE Honor, 1987-IA, ChCat, ESLC, ALANB, SLJBB, S-79–85, LC, IRACC, SATA-2 & 43, MJA. Filmstrip set: Random House, 1987.
Ramona is in third grade. Aunt Beatrice marries Howie's Uncle Hobart, who is a tease. Ramona and Beezus become latchkey children. Ramona is not excited about the expected new baby. Father is studying for a new job. Grandfather dies.

Cleary, Beverly. *Ramona Quimby, Age 8*. Morrow, 1981. Dell pb. 1983/84-AR, 1984-MI, 1984-NJ, 1985-OH, ChCat, ESLC, ALANB, NH, SLJBB, S-79–85, IRACC, SATA-2 & 43, MJA. Large print: ABC-CLIO, 1987. Cassette: Random House/Miller Brody, 1981. 10 TV shows: *Ramona*. Atlantis/Lancit Media and Revcon TV and Churchill Films, 1988. Taken from *Ramona and Her Mother*; *Ramona Quimby, Age 8*; and *Ramona Forever*.
Ramona is in third grade, mother has a job, Dad is in college studying to be a teacher.

Cleary, Beverly. *Ramona the Brave*. Morrow, 1975. Dell pb. 1978-MO, ChCat, ESLC, SATA-2 & 43, MJA. Sequel to *Ramona the Pest*.
Ramona is in first grade and has a teacher who doesn't like her imagination.

Cleary, Beverly. *Ramona the Pest*. Morrow, 1968. Dell pb. 1970-GA, 1971-NE, 1971-OK, 1971-PNW, ChCat, ESLC, SATA-2 & 43, MJA. Spanish edition: *Ramona La Chinche*. Morrow, 1988. Cassette recording, Random House, 1980. Sequel to *Beezus and Ramona*.
Ramona enters kindergarten. Ramona does not appreciate that the little boy who is a pest reminds adults of herself at that same age.

Cleary, Beverly. *Ribsy*. Morrow, 1964. Dell pb. 1966-VT, 1968-HI, ChCat, ESLC, SATA-2 & 43, MJA.
Henry Huggins's dog Ribsy gets lost from the car at a shopping center and has numerous adventures before he gets home.

Cleary, Beverly. *Runaway Ralph*. Morrow, 1970. Dell pb. 1972-HI, 1972/3-AR, ChCat, ESLC, SATA-2 & 43, MJA. 16mm film or video: Churchill Films, n.d. Preceded by *Mouse and the Motorcycle*, followed by *Ralph S. Mouse*.
Ralph runs away from the Mountain View Inn to the Happy Acres Camp in search of peanut butter sandwiches. Ralph is caught and placed in a cage with a hamster for a companion. Garfield Jernigan (Garf) is unhappy at camp but becomes Ralph's friend.

Clifford, Eth. *Help! I'm a Prisoner in the Library*. Houghton, 1979. Scholastic pb. Apple pb. 1982-IN, 1984-NE Honor, (intermed.), ESLC, SATA-3, 6-JA.
Ten-year-old Mary Rose and 7-year-old Jo-Beth are driving with their father during a blizzard when the car runs out of gas. While father goes off to get some gas, the girls go to a children's library in an old house to use the bathroom. The girls are locked in the library where displays come to life.

Clifford, Eth. *Just Tell Me When We're Dead*. Houghton, 1983. Scholastic pb, Apple pb. 1986-OK, SATA-3, 6-JA.
Nine-year-old Jeffrey, cousin to Mary Rose and Jo-Beth, runs away rather than have to live with the girls and their parents while his grandmother

goes to the hospital for an operation. Jeffrey runs to an island where two robbers are trying to locate money they had buried there. When the cousins follow, they become involved with the amusement park on the island.

Clymer, Eleanor. *The Get-Away Car.* Dutton, 1978. 1981-OK. ESLC, SATA-9, 4-JA.
Maggie's Aunt Ruby wants to take her away from her grandmother with whom she has lived since she was five years old and put Grandmother in an old folks home. So Grandmother, Maggie, Laurie (who loves cats and whose mother doesn't love her), Marcus (who loves dogs and takes on a stray), and Pedro (who can fix things and wants to go to school) all leave New York City for a country town to visit Cousin Esther who owns a big beautiful house. The surprise is that the house is a wreck and Mr. Ramon's car, which they have borrowed, is wanted by the police.

Conford, Ellen. *Hail, Hail Camp Timberwood.* Little, 1978. Archway pb. Bantam Starfire pb. 1981-CA (JH), 1981-PNW, JHSC, ESLC, SATA-6, 5-JA.
Melanie, an only child, is sent to summer camp. Melanie learns to stand up for herself against a bully in her cabin, gets a boyfriend, learns to swim, and earns the most improved rider award.

Coville, Bruce. *The Monster's Ring.* Pantheon, 1982. Minstrel pb. 1984/85-SC, ESLC, SATA-32.
Fifth grader Russell Crannaker wants to scare the bully, Eddie, at Halloween time. The magic ring that he buys from a little old man at Elves' Magic Supplies turns Russell into a monster several times. Turning himself back into a boy then becomes Russell's problem.

Dana, Barbara. *Zucchini.* Harper, 1982. Bantam pb. 1986-MN, 1987-NM, ChCat, ESLC.
When a ferret in the Bronx Zoo receives a letter from a third grader about his prairie origins, Zucchini runs away. Zucchini meets shy Billy at the ASPCA. Billy is unhappy because of a divorce and a recent move.

Danziger, Paula. *The Cat Ate My Gymsuit.* Delacorte, 1974. Dell pb. 1979-MA (7–9), 1980-HI. ChCat, JHSC, SATA-22, 5-JA. FS: Random, n.d. Sequel: *There's a Bat in Bunk 5.* Delacorte, 1980. Dell pb.
Thirteen-year-old Marcy Lewis is a chubby ninth grader who makes up excuses for not changing into her gym clothes. Marcy has troubles with her father and helps to reinstate her favorite English teacher, Ms. Finney, who has been fired.

DeClements, Barthe. *Nothing's Fair in Fifth Grade.* Viking, 1981. Scholastic pb. 1984-GA, 1984-HI, 1984-IA, 1984-MN, 1984-NE, 1984-NJ, 1984-OH, 1984-TX, 1985-MA, 1985-NM, 1986-CA (intermed.), SATA-35, 6-JA. Sequel: *Sixth Grade Can Really Kill You.*

Elsie Edwards, the new girl, is good in math, steals lunch money to buy candy, is overweight, and has parents who don't care. Jenny helps her by paying her for tutoring in fractions so Elsie can pay back the money she has stolen.

DeClements, Barthe. *Sixth Grade Can Really Kill You*. Viking, 1985. Scholastic pb and Teaching Guide. 1988-FL, 1989-NM, 1989-OH, ChCat, JHSC, IRACC, SATA-35, 6-JA.
Helen causes trouble and memorizes passages so no one will know she can't read. Helen's mother does not want her to attend the learning disabled room for help although her father does.

Duncan, Lois. *Locked in Time*. Little, 1985. Dell pb. 1987/88-SC, JHSC, IRACC, SATA-1 & 36, 5-JA.
Seventeen-year-old Nore Robbins and her father go to Shadow Grove, an old plantation in Louisiana, to be with the father's new family. Nore's dead mother warns her that their life is in danger from the new stepfamily, which has a sinister secret.

Duncan, Lois. *Stranger With My Face*. Little, 1981. Dell pb. 1983-MA (7–9), 1984-CA (HS), 1986-IN (6–8), JHSC, SATA-1 & 36, 5-JA.
Seventeen-year-old Laurie's astral twin, Lisa, wants to enter her body.

Duncan, Lois. *Summer of Fear*. Little, 1976. Dell pb. 1978-VT, 1983-NM, 1983-CA (HS), JHSC, SATA-1 & 36, 5-JA.
Rachel Bryant's 17-year-old cousin, Julia, comes to live with them after her parents die. Only Rachel realizes Julia is a witch who beguiles everyone but Rachel and the dog.

Duncan, Lois. *Third Eye*. Little, 1984. Dell pb. 1987-IN (6–8), JHSC, SHSC, ESLC, SATA-1 & 36, 5-JA.
Karen Connors has the psychic ability to locate missing children.

Fitzgerald, John D. *The Great Brain Does It Again*. Dial, 1975. Dell pb. 1980-GA, ChCat, ESLC, SATA-20 & 56, 5-JA. Books in series: *Great Brain*, Dial, 1967, Dell pb; *The Great Brain at the Academy*, Dial, 1972, Dell pb; *The Great Brain Reforms*, Dial, 1973, Dell pb; *Me and My Little Brain*, Dial, 1971, Dell pb; *More Adventures of the Great Brain*, Dial, 1969, Dell pb; and *Return of the Great Brain*, Dial, 1974, Dell pb. Cassettes: *The Great Brain*. The Great Brain Enterprise, 1987. Cassette/pb. Cliffhanger/Listening Library, 1986. FS: *The Great Brain Returns* appears in *Literature to Enjoy and Write About, Series 1*. Pied Piper, 1989.
Ten-year-old Tom Dennis Fitzgerald lived in Utah in 1896. His escapades remind readers of Twain's Tom Sawyer and Peck's Soup.

Fleischman, Sid. *The Whipping Boy*. Greenwillow, 1986. Troll pb. 1988/89-

AR. ChCat, ESLC, N, ALANB, SLJBB, SATA-8, 5-JA. ITV: Program #15 of *More Books From Cover to Cover*. FS: Pied Piper, 1988.
Because it is against the law to spank the heir to the throne, Prince Brat has an orphan boy, Jemmy, take his punishments for him. When Cutwater and Hold-Your-Nose kidnap Prince Brat, Jemmy is with him. The kidnappers believe Prince Brat's story that Jemmy is the prince because Jemmy can read and the Prince cannot.

Gardiner, John. *Stone Fox*. Crowell, 1980. Trophy pb. 1985-UT, 1987-MN, ChCat, ESLC, 6-JA. Cassette: Listening Library, n.d. ITV: #5 of *More Books From Cover to Cover*.
Ten-year-old Willy enters the dogsled race to win the prize so he can save his grandfather's farm in Idaho. Stone Fox is the formidable Indian contestant, based on a Rocky Mountain legend.

Gilson, Jamie. *Thirteen Ways to Sink a Sub*. Lothrop, 1982. Archway pb. Minstrel pb. 1985-OK, 1985-PNW, 1986-NE (intermed.), 1986-NM, 1987-FL, (6–8), 1987-OH, (6–8). ChCat, SATA-34 & 37, 6-JA. Sequels: *4-B Goes Wild*. Lothrop, 1983. Archway pb. Minstrel pb. ITV: #2 of *Books From Cover to Cover*. *Hobie Hanson, You're Weird*. Lothrop, 1987. Minstrel pb.
Hobie Hanson and friends like their unusual substitute teacher, but play tricks on her anyway. In *4-B Goes Wild*, fourth graders go on a three day camping trip.

Hahn, Mary Downing. *Daphne's Book*. Clarion, 1983. Bantam pb. 1986-KS, ChCat, JHSC, SLJBB, SATA-44 & 50, 6-JA.
When Jessica and Daphne collaborate on a picture book for children as a seventh grade English project, Jessica learns about Daphne's home life and problems. Daphne, the artist, is called Daffy by her schoolmates.

Hahn, Mary Downing. *Wait Till Helen Comes: A Ghost Story*. Clarion, 1986. Avon Camelot pb. 1988-UT, 1988-VT, 1989-IN, 1989-TX, 1989-PNW, ChCat, SATA-44 & 50, 6-JA.
Ten-year-old Michael and 12-year-old Molly don't like their 7-year-old stepsister Heather, who lies about them and gets them in trouble. The family moves into the country to a converted church which has a graveyard near it. A ghost child with the same initials as Heather tries to lure her into the pond.

Hall, Lynn. *Shadows*. Follett, 1977. 1981-TN, ESLC, SATA-4 & 47, 5-JA.
Audrey Schultz's mother dies just after Audrey tells her she hates her and wishes she were dead because she wouldn't let Audrey have one of her uncle's puppies. Then Audrey sees a mysterious collie near the gravel pit. It becomes her friend, the only one to whom she tells her terrible secret. But is the dog real or imaginary?

Haywood, Carolyn. *Eddie's Menagerie*. Morrow, 1978. Troll pb. 1981-UT, ChCat, SATA-1 & 29, JA. Other titles in the *Eddie* series are *Eddie and the Fire Engine*; *Eddie and Gardenia*; *Eddie and His Big Deals*; *Eddie and Louella*; *Eddie the Dog Holder*; *Eddie's Green Thumb*; *Eddie's Happenings*; *Eddie's Pay Dirt*; *Eddie's Valuable Property*; *Ever-Ready Eddie*; and *Little Eddie*.
Ten-year-old Eddie Wilson loves his job working in a pet shop for Mr. Cornball. Eddie helps his friends with their animal problems and helps out during and after the fire at the shop. Eddie also makes friends with a college baseball player.

Heide, Florence Perry. *Banana Twist*. Holiday, 1978. Bantam pb. 1980/81-AR, ChCat, ESLC, ALABB, SATA-32, 4-JA. Sequel: *Banana Blitz*. Holiday, 1983. Bantam pb.
Jonah, who is addicted to TV and junk food, wants to go to an exclusive private school because they have a TV and refrigerator in every room and his parents restrict his viewing and make him eat health foods. Jonah also tries to avoid his neighbor Goober, who surprises him at the end of the book with a "twist" in the plot. Each boy thinks the other has a "banana" fetish.

Hermes, Patricia. *You Shouldn't Have to Say Goodbye*. Harcourt, 1982. Apple pb. ChCat, SATA-31, 6-JA.
After 12-year-old Sarah's mother dies of cancer, she leaves a book she has written to her daughter.

Holland, Barbara. *Prisoners at the Kitchen Table or Run for Your Life*. Clarion/Houghton, 1979. 82/83-SC, ChCat, ESLC.
Quiet Josh and lively Polly reverse roles when they are kidnapped and spend a week's captivity at a kitchen table in an old cottage. The children regret believing the kidnappers' story that they are Polly's long lost aunt and uncle. Josh uses ingenuity to get away from the kidnappers and the stars to help them find their way home.

Howe, Barbara and James. *Bunnicula: A Rabbit-Tale of Mystery*. Atheneum, 1979. Avon Camelot pb. 1981-NE (intermed.), 1980/81-SC, 1981-VT, 1982-IA, 1982-NM, 1982-OK, 1982-PNW, 1983-HI, 1984-FL; ChCat, ESLC, ALANB, S-79–86, IRACC. Abridged recording: Caedmon, 1982. FS: *Mapping Mysteries*, Pied Piper, 1989. Sequel: *Howliday Inn*.
The Monroe's dog, Harold, writes about Chester the cat and the new bunny Bunnicula, a vampire who sucks the life out of vegetables.

Howe, James. *The Celery Stalks at Midnight*. Atheneum, 1983. Scholastic pb. 1986-NE Honor (intermed.), ChCat, ESLC, SATA-29, 6-JA. Sequel to *Howliday Inn*. Prequel to *Nighty-Nightmare*, Bk. 4. Atheneum, 1987. Avon Camelot pb. Cassette: Caedmon, 1987.

Chester reads books about vampires and decides that vegetables, once attacked, become monsters and zombie-vampires. Harold wrecks a carrot cake and "saves" Mr. Monroe from the water in the "Dunk-the-Teacher" booth. Bunnicula, the vampire bunny, wins first prize for being the most unusual pet in Centerville.

Howe, James. *The Day the Teacher Went Bananas*. Dutton, 1984. Unicorn pb. 1978-NE Honor (K–3). ChCat, ESLC, SATA-29, 6-JA.
The new teacher shows the class how to count on their toes in arithmetic, to write in a new way, to swing from trees, to work with clay, and to eat bananas. It seems a gorilla has been sent to school and Mr. Quackerbottom has been sent to the zoo by mistake.

Howe, James. *Howliday Inn*. Atheneum, 1982. Avon Camelot pb. 1984-TN, ESLC, SATA-29, 6-JA. Sequel to *Bunnicula*. Prequel to *Celery Stalks at Midnight*. Cassette: Caedmon, n.d.
When the Monroe family goes on vacation, they leave Harold the dog and Chester the cat at an animal hotel called Chateau Bow-Wow. Chester does not like any place that does not have cats in the title, calls the place Howliday Inn, and investigates the unusual happenings. Readers learn how the Monroe family comes to own the wire-haired dachshund Howie.

Hurwitz, Johanna. *Aldo Ice Cream*, Morrow, 1981. Archway pb. 1982. ChCat, ESLC, IRACC, SATA-20, 6-JA. Sequel to *Aldo Applesauce*. Morrow, 1979. Apple pb. and *Much Ado About Aldo*. Morrow, 1987. Soosi family appears in: *DeDe Takes Charge*, Apple pb; *Hurricane Elaine*. Morrow, 1986, Apple pb; and *Tough-Luck Karen*. Morrow, 1981, Apple pb.
Aldo helps his mother deliver meals on wheels and wins a dirty sneaker contest.

Hurwitz, Johanna. *Baseball Fever.* Morrow, 1981. Dell pb. 1984-NE Honor (intermed.), ChCat, ESLC, S-79–86, SATA-20, 6-JA.
Nine-year-old Ezra loves baseball but his father, a professor who was raised in Europe, thinks baseball is a waste of time. When another professor talks baseball with Ezra, his father agrees that he will go to a game with Ezra if Ezra beats him at chess. Use this one in a booktalk about baseball or sports books.

Hurwitz, Johanna. *Hot and Cold Summer.* Morrow, 1984. Apple pb. 1987-TX, 1987-WY, ChCat, ESLC, SATA-20, 6-JA. Sequel: *Cold and Hot Winter.* Morrow, 1988.
Ten-year-old best friends, Rory and Derek, live on either side of the Goldings. The Goldings great-niece Bolivia comes to stay for the summer and Derek goes off to summer camp, so Rory is stuck with Bolivia.

Kalb, Jonah. *The Goof That Won the Pennant*. Houghton, 1976. 1981-IN, ESLC, SATA-23.

Coach Venuti takes a losing team of misfit boys, the Blazers, and turns them around by giving them confidence. This is based on the true incident of September 23, 1908 when the Cubs won the pennant from the Giants, the greatest goof in the history of baseball.

King-Smith, Dick. *Babe, the Gallant Pig.* Crown, 1985. Dell pb. 1988-CA (intermed.), ESLC, NCTE, LC, IRACC, SATA-38 & 47, 6-JA. 1984 Guardian Award (England). Published in Great Britain under the title *The Sheep Pig.*
Farmer Hogget wins a pig by guessing its weight at the fair. Fly, the black and white collie who guards the sheep, calls the pig Babe. Fly takes the pig under her wing and teaches Babe to be a sheep pig. Eventually Hogget takes Babe to the dog trials. Read aloud.

Lowry, Lois. *Anastasia Krupnik.* Houghton, 1979. Bantam Skylark pb. 1983-MI, ChCat, ESLC, ALANB, IRACC, SATA-23, 5-JA. FS: *Character: Literature for Children, Series 9.* Pied Piper, 1989. Others in series: *Anastasia Again!* Houghton, 1981, Dell pb; *Anastasia at Your Service,* Houghton, 1982 Dell pb; *Anastasia, Ask Your Analyst,* Houghton, 1984, Dell pb; *Anastasia Has the Answers,* Houghton, 1986, Dell pb; *Anastasia on Her Own,* Houghton, 1986, Dell pb; *Anastasia's Chosen Career,* Houghton, 1987, Dell pb.
Ten-year-old Anastasia Krupnik gets a new baby brother, loses her grandmother, and has her first crush on a boy in this humorous book which is the first of many.

MacLachlan, Patricia. *Sarah, Plain and Tall.* Harper, 1985. Trophy pb. 1987/88-AR, 1988-NJ, ChCat, ESLC, N, ALANB, LC, IRACC, SATA-42, 6-JA. Recording: Caedmon, 1986. FS: Random, 1986.
Caleb and his sister, who live on the prairie, correspond with Sarah, who leaves Maine and comes to live with them to see if she will be their mother and a wife to their father. Good for focal book in literature-based study or pioneer unit.

Manes, Stephen. *Be a Perfect Person in Just Three Days!* Houghton, 1982. Scholastic pb. 1984/85-AR, 1987-GA, 1986-HI, 1986-FL; 1986-NE Honor, (intermed.), SATA-40 & 42. ITV: Program #12 of *Books from Cover to Cover.* TV: *Wonderworks.*
Milo finds a book in the library that will help him overcome all his problems with parents, siblings, and classmates. The cure includes wearing broccoli around his neck at school. This book fills the bill for a "funny book." Read aloud!

Mauser, Pat Rhodes. *A Bundle of Sticks.* Atheneum, 1982. 1984-VT, 1985-MO, ESLC, SATA-37.
Eleven-year-old Ben is plagued by a bully, so his parents enroll him in a

martial arts class. Ben also learns a philosophy for handling conflict in a new way.

Miles, Betty. *The Secret Life of the Underwear Champ*. Knopf, 1981. Bullseye pb. 1984-MO, 1986-GA, IRACC, SATA-8, 5-JA.
When 10-year-old Larry goes to New York City to visit the dentist, he is discovered by the Zigmund Model Agency and is signed to make TV commercials for Champ Win Knitting Mills. Then Larry finds out that making commercials may interfere with baseball practice and he has to wear blue underwear in the commercials.

Nhuong, Huyah Quang. *The Land I Lost: Adventures of a Boy in Vietnam*. Harper, 1982. Trophy pb. 1985-KS. ChCat, ESLC, S-79–86.
A description of life in a small Vietnamese village before the war.

O'Brien, Robert. *Mrs. Frisby and the Rats of NIMH*. Atheneum, 1971. Aladdin pb. 1974-PNW, 1978-MA, ChCat, ESLC, N, S-66–72. Recording, FS, and video: Random House, n.d. Sequel: Conly, Jane Leslie. *Rasco and the Rats of NIMH*. Harper, 1986, Trophy pb. ChCat, IRACC, SATA-23, 4-JA.
Mrs. Frisby, a mouse, accepts help from the rats when Farmer Fitzgibbon plows his fields and destroys her home. The super rats are from an experimental laboratory—NIMH, National Institute of Mental Health, where they have learned to read and write. The rats help with Timothy Mouse who is ill.

O'Connor, Jane. *Yours Till Niagara Falls, Abby*. Hastings, 1979. Scholastic pb. 1981-NE, ChCat, ESLC, SATA-47.
Ten-year-old Abby and Merle are best friends. Merle's family wants her to go to Camp Pinecrest and talks Abby's family into letting her go also. When Merle breaks her ankle and can't go, Abby has to go alone. Abby sends long letters to Merle and signs them "Yours Till Niagara Falls" but Merle doesn't write back. Abby's short letters to her parents turn into longer ones as she begins to enjoy camp.

O'Dell, Scott. *Island of the Blue Dolphins*. Houghton, 1960. Dell pb. 1981/82-VA, ChCat, JHSC, ESLC, N, ALANB, SATA-12, MJA. Large print: ABC-CLIO, 1987. Sequel: *Zia*. Houghton, 1976. Dell pb.
Twelve-year-old Karana and her younger brother Ramo are alone on a California island. After Ramo is killed by wild dogs, Karana lives alone on the island for 18 years; her only companions are the tamed wild dog (Rontu or "Fox Eyes") and an otter (Mon-a-nee or "Little Boy With Big Eyes"). In *Zia*, Karana is rescued from the island and gets to know her niece. Good to stimulate discussion.

Park, Barbara. *Operation: Dump the Chump*. Knopf, 1982. Avon Camelot pb. 1985-IN, 1986-TN, SATA-35 & 40, 6-JA.

Eleven-year-old Oscar Winkle has an eight-step plan to dump his younger brother Robert. The plan backfires.

Park, Barbara. *Skinnybones*. Knopf, 1982. 1985-GA, 1985-MN, 1985-TX, 1986-TN, 1987-UT, SATA-35 & 40, 6-JA. Sequel: *Almost Starring Skinnybones*. Knopf, 1988. ChCat.
Sixth grader Alex Frankovitch compensates for not being good at anything by making people laugh. Alex has been the Little League's most improved player for six years. Teachers do not always appreciate Alex's sense of humor. Alex wins the Kitty Fritters cat food contest and will be making a TV commercial. In *Almost Starring Skinnybones*, Alex's friends laugh at him because he plays a 6-year-old in a cat commercial.

Pascal, Francine. *Hand-Me-Down Kid*. Viking, 1980. Dell pb. 1982-VT, JHSC, ESLC, IRACC, SATA-37 & 51, 5-JA.
Eleven-year-old Ari Jacobs is the youngest in the family. Ari's sister has a new Peugeot bike which Ari is not allowed to touch. When Rhona Finkelstein, the bully, "borrows" the bike for a race, it is stolen.

Paterson, Katherine. *Bridge to Terabithia*. Harper, 1977. Trophy pb. Scholastic pb. 1980/1981-VA, ChCat, ESLC, N, ALANB, SATA-13 & 53, 5-JA. Large print edition: ABC-CLIO, 1987. Spanish: *Un Puente Hasta Terebithia*. Recording: Random House. TV: *Wonderworks*.
Fifth graders Jess and Leslie are best friends and create a secret place like Narnia in the woods. When Leslie drowns, Jess has to come to terms with her death.

Paterson, Katherine. *The Great Gilly Hopkins*. Crowell, 1978. Large print edition: ABC-CLIO, 1987. 1981-GA, 1981-IA, 1981-MA, ChCat, ESLC, NH, SATA-13 & 53, 5-JA.
Eleven-year-old Gilly has been abandoned by her mother and lives in a foster home. Gilly finds it difficult to learn to love.

Peck, Robert Newton. *Soup*. Knopf, 1974. 1984-MI (4–8), SATA-21, 5-JA. Other books in the series: *Soup in the Saddle*, Knopf, 1983; *Soup on Fire*, Knopf, 1987; *Soup on Ice*, Knopf, 1985; *Soup on Wheels*, Knopf, 1981; *Soup's Drum*, Knopf, 1980; *Soup's Goat*, Knopf, 1984; *Soup's Uncle*, Delacorte, 1988. All except the last one are available in Dell pb.

Peck, Robert Newton. *Soup and Me*. Knopf, 1975. Dell pb. 1981-Honor (intermed.), ChCat, ESLC, SATA-21, 5-JA.
The narrator, Rob Peck, gets taken advantage of by his friend Soup, Luther Wesley Vinson, who is a combination of Tom Sawyer and the Great Brain. Soup and Rob go swimming in the nude in Putt's Pond, and Janice Riker takes their clothes so they have to "borrow" women's clothes from a church rummage sale.

Peck, Robert Newton. *Soup for President.* Knopf, 1978. Dell pb. 1981-MO, ChCat, ESLC, SATA-21, 5-JA. Video: Coronet/MTI, n.d.
It's 1936 and Republican Vermont is gearing up to vote against FDR. Miss Kelly, the teacher in the one-room schoolhouse, suggests they hold an election. Rob is torn between voting for his best friend, Soup, or his girlfriend, Norma Jean Bissell.

Pfeffer, Susan. *Kid Power.* Watts, 1977. Apple pb. 1980-OK. SATA-4, 6-JA. Sequel: *Kid Power Strikes Back.* Watts, 1984. Apple pb.
Eleven-year-old Janie Golden and her sister are given half the money for a new bike and they need to pay the other half. Janie's older sister already has saved most of her half but Janie needs to find a way to make money. So Janie formulates Kid Power, an agency that takes on large and small jobs. When she gets too many jobs to handle, Janie hires other kids to help her.

Place, Marian. *The Boy Who Saw Bigfoot.* Dodd, 1978. 1981-MO. SATA-3.
Ten-year-old foster child, Joey Wilson, lives with Sara and Mike in the woods of western Washington State. A field trip is organized to look for Bigfoot. Television coverage adds an unusual twist to the story.

Rawls, Wilson. *Summer of the Monkeys.* Doubleday, 1977. Dell pb. 1979-OK, 1981-CA, ESLC, LC, SATA-22, 6-JA.
Fourteen-year-old Jay Berry finds monkeys that have escaped from the zoo in the Ozark Mountains of Oklahoma in the 1800s. Jay's plan to catch the monkeys and collect the reward is easier said than done.

Rawls, Wilson. *Where the Red Fern Grows.* Doubleday, 1961. Bantam pb. 1980-MN, 1987-MA. ChCat, ESLC, SATA-22, 6-JA. FS: *Literature to Enjoy and Write About, Series 1,* Pied Piper, 1989.
Ten-year-old Billy Colman scrimps to buy two coon hound dogs, Old Dan and Little Ann. Tragedy comes after the dogs win a coon hunt contest. Billy lives in the Cherokee country of the Oklahoma Ozarks. Read aloud!

Roberts, Willo Davis. *Baby-Sitting Is a Dangerous Job.* Atheneum, 1985. Fawcett pb. 1988-IN. ESLC, LC, SATA-21, 5-JA. ITV: #9 of *More Books from Cover to Cover.*
While Darcy Stevens is baby-sitting the three wealthy and spoiled Foster children, who are 6 years and younger, a series of strange events culminates in their being kidnapped. Darcy has to outwit two Doberman pinscher guard dogs if they are to escape.

Roberts, Willo Davis. *Don't Hurt Laurie.* Atheneum, 1977. Aladdin pb. 1980-IN, 1982-GA, SATA-21, 5-JA.
Eleven-year-old Laurie reminds her mother of the husband who has deserted her, so she abuses Laurie. They move frequently so people don't

ask questions. When her mother remarries, Laurie gets an ally in a new sibling.

Roberts, Willo Davis. *The Girl with the Silver Eyes*. Atheneum, 1980. Apple pb. 1983-MO, 1986-CA (JH), ChCat, ESLC, SATA-21, 5-JA.
Katie has silver eyes and psychokinetic powers. When Katie learns that there are other children with silver eyes whose mothers all have taken an experimental drug during pregnancy, she no longer feels alone.

Robinson, Barbara. *The Best Christmas Pageant Ever*. Harper, 1972. Avon Camelot pb, Trophy pb, Tyndale pb. 1982-MN, ChCat, ESLC, SATA-8, 5-JA.
Although the six Herdman children have terrible manners, they capture the essence of the Christmas spirit when they take part in the Sunday School Christmas pageant. Read this humorous book aloud.

Rockwell, Thomas. *How to Eat Fried Worms*. Watts, 1973. Dell pb. 1975-CA, 1975-TX, 1975/76-SC, 1976-HI, 1976-MA, 1976-OK, 1977-CA, 1979-TN, 1980-IA, ChCat, ESLC, LC, IRACC, SATA-7, 5-JA. 3 FS: Random, n.d. FS: *Plot: Literature for Children, Series 9*. Pied Piper, 1985. *How to Eat Fried Worms and Other Plays*. Delacorte, 1980. Sequel: *How to Fight a Girl*. Watts, 1987. Dell pb.
Ten-year-old Billy eats a worm a day for 15 days and wins 50 dollars. Everyone helps Billy by creating innovative ways to cook the worms.

Roos, Stephen. *My Horrible Secret*. Delacorte, 1983. Dell pb. 1985/86-AR, SATA-42 & 47, 6-JA.
Eleven-year-old Warren Fingler faces a challenge when he dares Claire Van Kemp to see which one can raise the most money to purchase a new head for the statue of Matthew Bumkis, a local hero. Warren receives unexpected help from his super jock brother and the girl who has a crush on Roger. Those who like or dislike baseball will like this book.

Ruckman, Ivy. *Night of the Twisters*. Crowell, 1984. Trophy pb. 1986-NE, 1987-OK, ChCat, JHSC, ESLC, S-79–86, IRACC, SATA-37, 6-JA.
Twelve-year-old Dan Hatch describes the night several tornadoes hit the fictional town of Grand Island, NE, where he lives with his baby brother and parents. While Dad is with his grandparents and Mom is with a neighbor, Dan has to survive the storm with Ryan and his friend Arthur. Dan's resentment of baby Ryan turns to love and appreciation. Use in a booktalk of survival books.

Schwartz, Alvin. *In a Dark, Dark Room and Other Scary Stories*. Harper, 1984. Trophy pb. 1987-OH (K–2), ChCat, ESLC, ALANB, SLJBB, SATA-4 & 56, 5-JA.
This easy reader contains seven spooky stories including the title story, which is excellent for reading aloud.

Schwartz, Alvin. *More Scary Stories to Tell in the Dark.* Lippincott, 1984. Trophy pb. 1989-OH, ChCat, S-79–87, LC, SATA-4 & 56. 5-JA. Cassette: Cliffhanger/LL, n.d.
See annotation for *Scary Stories to Tell in the Dark.*

Schwartz, Alvin. *Scary Stories to Tell in the Dark.* Lippincott, 1981. Harper Trophy pb. 1987-OH (3–5), 1987-UT, ChCat, ESLC, S-79–86, SATA-4 & 56, 5-JA. Record or cassette: Caedmon, n.d.
Excellent source notes appear at the end of these short scary stories from American Folklore.

Showell, Ellen. *The Ghost of Tillie Jean Cassaway.* Four Winds, 1978. 1981/82-SC, ESLC, SATA-33.
Twelve-year-old Willie Barbour and his 11-year-old sister Hilary separately try to learn more about the ghost of a girl who was playing by the river with her doll and drowned. Willie goes into the woods near Craig's Island and sees strange things happen. A mysterious trunk holds secrets. Willie hears voices and Hilary sees the ghost girl. Use this book to teach foreshadowing.

Silverstein, Shel. *A Light in the Attic.* Harper, 1981. 1984-KS, 1984-NJ (non-fiction), 1985-OH (6–8), ChCat, ESLC, S-79–86, SATA-27 & 33, 5-JA.
Over 100 humorous poems delight students who think they don't like poetry.

Silverstein, Shel. *Where the Sidewalk Ends.* Harper, 1984. 1981-MI, ChCat, ESLC, SATA-27 & 33, 5-JA. Recording: Columbia, 1984.
Choose any of the over 100 humorous poems to read aloud.

Singer, Marilyn. *It Can't Hurt Forever.* Harper, 1978. 1983-MN, SATA-38 & 48, 6-JA.
Eleven-year-old Ellie has a heart defect, patent ductus arteriosus, that requires an operation. Readers share Ellie's anxiety of the unknown and her fear of death. The people Ellie meets in the hospital, both on the staff as well as patients, provide readers with information about hospital procedures.

Skurzynski, Gloria. *Lost in the Devil's Desert.* Lothrop, 1982. 1984-UT, SATA-8, 5-JA.
While visiting his grandmother in Spriggs, Utah, 11-year-old Kevin Hoffman gets left in the desert by escaped convicts and no longer fears his father's new assignment in the Middle East. Use this book with survival books.

Slote, Alfred. *My Robot Buddy.* Lippincott, 1975. 1981-HI, ESLC, SATA-8, 5-JA. ITV: #2 of *Readit.* Sequels: *C.O.L.A.R.,* and *The Trouble with Janus.* Lippincott, 1981 and 1985.

Ten-year-old Jack Jameson wants a robot to play with so after a trip to the Atkins Robot factory, a robot is made to Jack's specifications. Jack learns the 5 P's of robots: Production; Programming; Psysiognomy (face); Personality; and Power. Teach foreshadowing through the robotnapper incident. The robot is Danny I.

Smith, Robert Kimmel. *Chocolate Fever.* Peter Smith, 1978. Dell pb. 1980-MA, SATA-12, 6-JA. Cassette: Cliffhanger/LL, n.d.
Henry Green loves chocolate—bitter, sweet, dark, light, and daily. Chocolate loves Henry and doesn't make him fat, hurt his teeth, stunt his growth, harm his skin, or give him a bellyache. Then one day, bumps the size of chocolate chips break out all over Henry's body—Chocolate fever. When Henry runs away, he is picked up by a semitruck that becomes hijacked.

Smith, Robert Kimmel. *Jelly Belly.* Delacorte, 1981. Dell Yearling pb. 1983/84-SC, 1984-IN, 1985-HI, SATA-12, 6-JA. Cassette: Cliffhanger, LL/n.d.
Eleven-year-old Nathaniel Robbins is 4′ 8″ and weighs 109 pounds. Phil Steinkraus, the bully, calls him Jelly Belly. The description of Nat's summer at Camp Lean-Too is filled with the desire for food and plans to get it. Introduce Nat (Ned) by reading page 1.

Smith, Robert Kimmel. *The War with Grandpa.* Delacorte, 1984. Dell pb. 1984–85-SC, 1986-VT, 1987-IN, 1987-NE, 1987-PNW, 1987-MO, ChCat, IRACC, SATA-12, 6-JA. Cassette: Cliffhanger/LL, n.d.
Peter Stokes is writing the story of how he went to war with Grandpa as a project for his fifth grade English teacher. Peter and his grandfather are at war because Peter has to give up his room to him now that grandfather lives with them. Even though he loves his Grandpa, peer pressure causes the feud to continue even after Grandpa takes him fishing.

Sommer-Bodenburg, Angela. *My Friend the Vampire.* Dial, 1984. Minstrel pb. 1986/87-VA. ESLC. Other books in series: *The Vampire Moves In.* Dial, 1984. Minstrel pb. *The Vampire on the Farm.* Dial, 1989. *The Vampire Takes a Trip.* Dial, 1985. Minstrel pb.
Tony reads vampire books and watches vampire movies. One night a vampire named Rudolph flies into Tony's window and takes him to the cemetery and invites him into a coffin. Rudolph's sister Anna has a crush on Tony.

Sutton, Jane. *Me and the Weirdos.* Houghton, 1981. 1986-UT, SATA-43 & 52.
Ten-year-old Cindy Krinkle becomes embarrassed by her family when the paper boy says they are weird. Cindy's mother wears red sneakers all year round, jogs in the house, and calls herself Squirrel because Crystal does not sound good with Krinkle. Cindy's father plants weeds in his garden and rides a bicycle to work that has an umbrella and a musical horn. Cindy's sister Sarah counts baked bean labels for a hobby and the family pet is

Gomer, a sea urchin. The Krinkles have a gumball machine and a drinking fountain in the living room.

Taylor, Theodore. *The Trouble with Tuck*. Doubleday, 1981. Avon pb. Doubleday pb. 1984-CA, 1984-NE Honor (intermed.), ESLC, S-79–86, LC, SATA-5 & 54, 4-JA. Filmstrip: Pied Piper, 1986. ITV: #10 of *Books from Cover to Cover.*
When Helen's dog Tuck goes blind at a young age, she tries to find a guide dog for him and finally gets an old retired dog named Daisy to help Tuck. Helen's persistence saves Tuck's life. Excellent core book for a literature-based study or animal booktalk.

Thomasma, Ken. *Naya Nuki: Girl Who Ran*. Illus. by Eunice Hundley. Baker/Voyager, 1983. 1986-WY.
An 11-year-old Shoshoni girl and her friend Sacajawea are taken prisoners by the Minnetares. One of the girls escapes and spends over a month finding her way home so she is renamed Naya Nuki, the girl who ran. In the epilogue, readers learn of a diary entry by Capt. Lewis, of the Lewis and Clark expedition, who wrote of the reunion of Sacajawea and a friend who had been taken captive with her.

Van Leeuwin, Jean. *The Great Christmas Kidnapping Caper*. Dial, 1975. 1978/79-SC, ChCat, ESLC, SATA-6, 5-JA. Series: *The Great Cheese Conspiracy*. Random, 1969. Dell pb. *The Great Rescue Operation*. Dial, 1982. Dell pb.
Marvin the Magnificent and his mice friends live in the toy department of Macy's. When Santa disappears, the mice rescue him. In *The Great Rescue Operation*, Fats is sold with a doll buggy and two other mice look for him.

Wallace, Barbara Brooks. *Peppermints in the Parlor*. Atheneum, 1980. 1983-KS, ESLC, SATA-4.
Emily, an orphan, goes to live with an aunt and uncle in San Francisco in the 1890s and finds that their mansion is run as a nursing home, her aunt is a maligned servant, and her uncle is missing. How Emily restores the home to her relatives makes a good story for mystery fans.

Wallace, Bill. *A Dog Called Kitty*. Holiday, 1980. Archway pb. 1983-OK, 1983-TX, 1985-NE (intermed.), ChCat, SATA-53.
Ricky's memories of a dog attack during infancy has resulted in a fear of dogs. When a stray pup comes to their Oklahoma farm, Ricky is won over little by little by the dog. When Kitty is killed suddenly, Ricky is crushed.

Wallace, Bill. *Trapped in Death Cave*. Holiday, 1984. Archway pb. 1989-UT, SATA-53.
Gary believes that his grandfather has been murdered for a map which tells where stolen gold is buried. Despite a curse on the gold because it is

on a tribal meeting place, Gary and his friend Brian locate the cave with the help of an unexpected ally but all three of them are trapped in the cave.

White, E. B. *Charlotte's Web*. Harper, 1952. Trophy pb. Scholastic pb. 1980-MI, 1984-MA, ChCat, NH, ESLC, SATA-2, 29, & 43. Large print: G K Hall, 1986. FS: *Meet the Newbery Author: E. B. White*. Random, 1987. Eight-year-old Fern can talk with animals in this classic that includes Wilbur the pig and Charlotte the spider. Friendship and death are themes in this classic.

White, E. B. *Trumpet of the Swan*. Harper, 1970. Trophy pb, Scholastic pb. 1973-OK, ChCat, ESLC, S-79–86, SATA-2, 29, & 43. FS: *Meet the Newbery Author: E. B. White*. Random, 1987. Eleven-year-old Sam Beaver meets Louis the cygnet on a Canadian camping trip and later at home in Montana where Sam lives and the swans have their winter home. Louis has no voice or trumpet with which to attract the attention of the female swan, Serena, so Sam's father tries to help Louis out.

Winthrop, Elizabeth. *The Castle in the Attic*. Holiday, 1985. Bantam pb. Scholastic pb. 1987-VT, 1989-CA, ChCat, LC, IRACC, SATA-8, 5-JA. ITV: Program #8 of *More Books from Cover to Cover*. Ten-year-old William's parents are too busy for him so his best friend is his nanny, Mrs. Phillips. Mrs. Phillips returns to England and gives William a toy castle with a silver knight that comes alive.

Wright, Betty. *Christina's Ghost*. Holiday, 1985. Scholastic pb. 1988-TX, 1989-IN. ESLC, IRACC, SATA-43, 6-JA. Christina is unhappy that she has to spend the summer with a grouchy uncle in a Victorian mansion in rural Wisconsin. The ghost of a boy makes the time more enjoyable and helps Christina's relationship with her uncle.

Wright, Betty. *The Dollhouse Murders*. Holiday, 1983. Scholastic pb. 1986-MO, 1986-PNW, 1986-TX, 1987-CA, 1988-GA, 1988-NM, 1988-WY, ChCat, JHSC, ESLC, SATA-48, 6-JA. Amy resents taking her retarded sister Louann everywhere with her. When Aunt Clare realizes that Amy needs time away from Louann, she invites her to stay. A dollhouse in an old family mansion contains a box of dolls that represent Grandma and Grandpa and Aunt Clare. The dolls come to life and help solve a family murder.

CHAPTER TWO

Introducing Books by Titles

It is not always possible to remember every detail about a book to recommend it to a reader. However, there are several ways to remember what books are about by remembering key issues from the titles. Some titles of books contain reminders about the plot of the book while others name the setting, which could be either time or place. Some book titles name the main character of the book, which can be a single human, a group of humans, animals, inanimate objects or nonhuman creatures. Remembering something about the title can lead to remembering enough about the book to interest someone in it. Any genre can be introduced by the title of the book. Books can be introduced in groups in formal booktalks or with one person during individual reading guidance.

In order to keep track of information about a book, make a card which includes the bibliographic details and the call number and name of the library where the book is located. This is especially important if school and public libraries as well as home and other libraries are used. Write down specific pages where descriptions of the main character are located as well as names and ages of characters. List any pages which contain quotations or paragraphs that are suitable for reading aloud. List genres and specific subjects on the card. List similar titles so that you know which books to share with a student who likes them. Other books by that author, especially sequels or those in series, can be recorded. If you have a computer, use a database to record this information so that it can be pulled for subject lists. However, the information triggered by remembering something about the title should go into your own computer, your brain, so information about the book can be retrieved during individual reading guidance or during an impromptu booktalk. Being able to give the right book to the right child at the right time often depends upon being able to recall and briefly describe a book title.

INTRODUCING BOOKS BY TITLES: PLOT [CU 25–26]. The books in this section are suitable for students in grades four through six. Share these books during a booktalk by using the title as a mnemonic device to remember the plot.

Taylor's title, *The Friendship*, gets right to the heart of the plot. A respected elder in the black community, Tom Bee, was responsible for saving the life of a white storekeeper, John Wallace, when he was young. John promised they would always be friends. Now years later, John insists on being called "Mister" as any white person in rural Mississippi during the Depression expected. John shoots Tom for publicly calling him by his first name. Witnesses to the incident are Cassie Logan and her brothers from Taylor's Newbery Award winner, *Roll of Thunder, Hear My Cry* and *Song of the Trees*. *The Friendship* is based on a true incident that happened to a former slave in Mississippi in 1933.

Chetwin's fantasy *The Riddle of the Rune* is book two in a series about *Gom on Windy Mountain*. Gom guards his rune while searching to find his mother, Harga the Wizard. The rune had been given to him by his mother. Lyrics to songs are included.

Jump Ship to Freedom by the Colliers is an example of one of their excellent historical fiction books. The book takes place in 1787 when Daniel Arabus is a slave. However, Daniel should be free because his father served in the Revolutionary War and earned money for Dan and his mother to be free. However, Jack is dead and Captain Ivers has the money. How can Daniel prove his freedom?

Morrison's *Whisper Goodbye* is about 13-year-old Katie McNeill who lives with her grandparents in a little town in Oregon where her Granddad owns a drug store. When the town is evacuated before the new dam floods the area, Granddad makes plans to buy a self-contained store and move to Portland. Katie has a dilemma. She can't find a place near Portland to board her horse Whisper where she could work to earn his keep so she thinks of living with her best friend Allison in the country in order to keep her horse. However, then she would have to leave her grandparents who have taken care of her since her parents died in a boating accident. Sometimes it is helpful to know where the author has gotten the background information for his or her book so that the information can be passed on to potential readers. Check page 181 for an author's note giving information about how the Columbia River system did displace farms and towns. The Introduction is dedicated "with love to Ann and Jenny who introduced me to the real Whisper Please." *Whisper Again* is the sequel.

Naylor's *Beetles, Lightly Toasted* is about Andy, a fifth grader, who enters an essay contest where the theme is conservation. Andy then combines the information that insects are edible with the contest theme. Those who liked Rockwell's *How to Eat Fried Worms* will enjoy reading about Andy's fried worms and beetle brownies.

Bulla's *The Chalk Box Kid* is about Gregory who draws a fantastic garden out of chalk on the walls of an abandoned chalk factory. Gregory draws to rid himself of his problems—a move, his father's lost job, and sharing his room with an uncle. *Two Under Par* by Henkes is about 10-year-old Wedge who lives with a stepfather who owns a miniature golf course.

In Snyder's *And Condors Danced*, 11-year-old Carly Hartwick lives on a California ranch in 1907. Although many condors are already dead by 1907, Carly and her friend Arthur go by donkey to Carlton Spring, formerly Condor Spring, to see the condors. Carly loves her dog Tiger, enjoys her neighbor and friend Arthur, feuds with Henry Quigley Babcock and his family, tries to make herself invisible, loves her Great Aunt M and her Chinese servant Woo Ying, and has an invalid mother. When her mother dies, Carly feels guilty because she felt worse when her dog Tiger recently died of hydrophobia from a rabid coyote.

Introduce George's *Water Sky* by explaining what that means. A description of a "water sky" appears on pages 27, 74–75,121. Lincoln Noah Stonewright's Uncle Jack has gone to the Arctic to educate the Eskimos about killing the whales. Now Lincoln, great-great-grandson of Whaler Amos Stonewright, is going to Barrow, Alaska, to live with Vincent Ologak and learn about whaling firsthand. The importance of whaling to the Eskimo culture is shown. Lincoln learns that it is not the Eskimos who are destroying the whales but those who use old-time methods. Learn how Lincoln gets his Eskimo name, Karok "Hit-on-the-head," and read on page 159 how Lincoln becomes captain of a whaling expedition. The book can be used in conservation units or in a historical study of whaling.

Ten-year-old Mary Rose and 7-year-old Jo Beth are trapped in the public library during a blizzard in Clifford's *Help! I'm a Prisoner in the Library.* The girls are on a two-hour trip with their father to Indianapolis to stay with their aunt until the new baby is born. On the way, their father, who does everything at the last minute, runs out of gas. When he leaves the car to get gas he tells them to keep the doors locked and not let anyone in the car. The girls have to go to the bathroom so they leave the car and enter a children's library located in an old house just after the librarian has checked the rest rooms before closing time. The girls become locked in the library and the lights go out. The title comes from Jo Beth's idea to put a sign in the window, "Help! I'm a prisoner in the library." Check page 61 of Clifford's *Just Tell Me When We're Dead*, also about Mary Rose and Jo Beth, to find out the meaning of that title.

Turn the title into a question during a booktalk. How can a Japanese high school baseball team called the Atami Dragons help Jerry adjust to his mother's death, to his father, and to the Japanese culture? Read *The Atami Dragons* by Klass and find out. Giff's *The Left Handed Shortstop* is about Walter Moles, who is picked to be a shortstop for the big game between the fourth and fifth graders. Walter isn't a very good player and would rather be working on science projects, so his friend Casey helps him make a papier-mâché cast to wear so he can get out of playing. Does the ploy work? Before reading Chapter 7, pages 45–49, have students think up ways Walter can get out of playing. In contrast, 10-year-old Ezra loves baseball but his father wants him to be interested in chess in Hurwitz's *Baseball Fever.* The compromise they work out is part of the plot. A whole booktalk of baseball books could be shared with students in a section called SHARING BASEBALL in Volume 2 of this book.

A group of unathletic seventh graders at South Orange River Middle School appear in Avi's *S.O.R. Losers* because they are assigned to a soccer team because everyone in the school has to be part of something athletic. The boys and their coach do not know and do not care about sports and consistently lose matches. The book becomes interesting when parents, classmates, and teachers expect them to uphold the tradition of their school.

Green's *Eating Ice Cream with a Werewolf* is about 12-year-old Brad Gowan who lives in Madison, Wisconsin. Brad's father is a retired football star, his mom is a freelance writer, and his sister is 4 years old. Brad has a babysitter, Phoebe Hadley, who always has a hobby. The story takes place while Brad's parents are gone and Phoebe and Dr. Curmudgeon's *Book of Magic* are in charge. What do two quarts of missing vanilla ice cream have to do with a werewolf? Read Green's book and find out.

Nine-year-old Austin is not interested in going to his grandparents' place in the country this summer because his grandfather, who had been going to teach him to fly-fish, has died. However, during the summer Austin and his grandmother come to terms with their loss and form a new friendship. *Blackberries in the Dark* by Jukes can be introduced by the following quotation: "'I was thinking,' he said after a moment, 'about last summer.' He paused. 'About when Grandpa took me fishing. We stayed out late. We picked blackberries in the dark. We brought them home and you made that pie—and we ate it, in the middle of the night.'"

Twelve-year-old Sam Mott has a learning disability and can only read at the second grade level, a fact which he covers up by making jokes in class. While at the orthodontist, Sam meets Mrs. Glass who hires Sam to take care of her two boys after school. Sam tries to keep his reading problem from her but she finds out and helps him. Sam also receives help from a teacher whose sister has had the same problem and from the smartest girl in the class, Alicia Bliss, who sees one of his papers. Sam becomes motivated to read when a tornado overturns a tree that yields artifacts that interest Sam, who would like to be an archaeologist but thinks he is too dumb to be one. Check pages 142–44 and 152 for information about Gilson's title *Do Bananas Chew Gum?*

Cricket Kaufman in Hurwitz's *Teacher's Pet* can't wait for school to start so she can impress her fourth grade teacher. However, Cricket gets off on the wrong foot with her new teacher. Furthermore, even if Cricket were the teacher's pet this year, Mrs. Schradenburg doesn't let the pet run all the errands but allows everyone a turn to be special. Cricket's life is also complicated by the new girl, Zoe Mitchell, who wins the spelling bee that Cricket plans to win. Finally, a Halloween party at Zoe's, where Cricket arrives early by mistake, breaks the ice and the two girls become friends.

Have you ever wished someone else's mom was your mom? Two seventh graders, Scotti Wheeler and Lorna Markham, not only get along better with each other's mothers but the mothers always seem to be comparing them unfavorably with each other. So the girls swap homes and also have to deal with their new families in *The Great Mom Swap* by Haynes.

Ten-year-old Ariel and her grandmother make a quilt for the new baby in Kinsey-Warnack's *The Canada Geese Quilt*. Megan buys an old cup at an auction and she and her grandmother fill it with change in Patterson's *The*

Christmas Cup. At Christmas time they buy a present to be given anonymously to a person who has been good to them.

Sixth grader Sara records her homesickness when she moves to Hawaii for five months in Slepian's *The Broccoli Tapes*. Events take a turn for the better when she and her brother rescue and adopt a wild cat named Broccoli and make friends with Eddie.

The Secret Window in Wright's book is Meg Korshak's precognition. Meg's whole life is coming apart: her father is leaving to write books off by himself, her brother may not accept his science scholarship to college, and her friend Gracie finds a new friend and almost gets her in trouble with drugs and the police. Meg writes about her precognition in a notebook because her parents don't want to know about it. Only Grandma Korshak seems to understand Meg's gift.

Siegal's *Upon the Head of a Goat: A Childhood in Hungary, 1939–1944* is a Newbery Honor Book about the Holocaust. Seigal's book contains an introduction from Leviticus 16 which talks about scapegoats. Also check page 176 for a scapegoat reference useful for introducing the book. The sequel is *Grace in the Wilderness: After the Liberation, 1945–1948*.

Check pages 113, 135, 146, and 168 for an explanation of Yolen's title for *The Devil's Arithmetic* which is about a modern Jewish girl, Hannah, who is bored with spending the Jewish holidays with relatives and who dislikes her grandfather's reactions to any mention of the Holocaust. When Hannah goes out the door into the 1940s to becomes Chaya, she understands what her grandfather has suffered as well as why it is important to remember. The days that Chaya remains alive in the concentration camp are "One plus one plus one. The Devil's Arithmetic . . ." Those in the camp soon learn "that as long as others were processed, THEY would not be. A simple bit of mathematics, like subtraction, where one taken away from the top line becomes one added on to the bottom. The Devil's arithmetic."

Eight-year-old Renee's mother would touch wood or knock on wood as a superstitious protection against evil and assure her that Hitler's persecutions of the Jews would not increase in Roth-Hana's *Touch Wood: A Girlhood in Occupied France*. The book is written as a diary.

In *Sidewalk Story* by Mathis, Lilly Etta, a black girl, is upset because her best friend Tanya and her family are evicted and all their belongings are placed on the sidewalk. When her own mother does not want to become involved, Lilly Etta phones the police and the newspaper.

Everyone has some secret fear. During a booktalk, ask students to stop and reflect on their own secret fear or fears for a minute. Then introduce Ben from Little's *Different Dragons* and Ricky from Wallace's *A Dog Called Kitty*.

Introduce Herzig and Mali's *The Ten-Speed Babysitter* with a rhetorical question. How would you like to be 14 years old and arrive at your summer live-in baby-sitting job to find out that you and Duncan, the child for whom you are baby-sitting, are going to be left alone while Duncan's mother visits the Bahamas? This is what happens to Tony. The title comes from Tony's five-mile back and forth biking expeditions to the beach with Duncan on the child's seat Some of the problems Tony faces are bedwetting, burglaries, sunburn, crank phone calls, and a hurricane blackout. *The Ten-Speed Babysitter* could also be part of a booktalk which introduces survival books. When two or more books have a connection such as this title and the next one, link the books together with the baby-sitting theme.

Books that can be explained by the title can also be introduced through multimedia. *Baby-Sitting Is a Dangerous Job* by Roberts is a suspense book that is also Program #9 on the instructional television program *More Books from Cover to Cover*. Darcy Stevens is baby-sitter to the wealthy Foster family that includes 6-year-old Jeremy and two younger sisters. After a series of strange events, Darcy and the children are kidnapped and taken to an isolated house where they are guarded by two Doberman pinschers. How can they escape?

Different Dragons by Little is Program #6 of the television series *Books from Cover to Cover*. While visiting his Aunt Rose, Ben Tucker is given a surprise. Ben is not happy because he is afraid of the dark and of dogs. The surprise is a Labrador retriever named Gully. When Ben hides under the bed during a thunder and lightning storm, he finds Gully there and comforts the dog. Later the dog lets Aunt Rose know where Ben and Hana are trapped in the attic.

Top Secret by Gardiner is Program #9 of the television series *Books from Cover to Cover*. Nine-year-old Allen Brewster is conducting his fourth grade science project on human photosynthesis. After much experimenting Allen drinks his concoction, turns green, is attracted to the sun, and loses the desire to eat. When the president of the United States speaks to a group called Stop World Starvation, Allen sends him a letter telling him how his discovery could prevent world hunger. Allen is asked to meet with a presidential advisor who says that Allen's project has to be kept "Top Secret" for various reasons. Students need to read the book to find out those reasons and how Allen does in the science fair.

A book from the library called *Be a Perfect Person in Just Three Days!* promises Milo that he will become a perfect person if he follows the directions given which include wearing a piece of broccoli hanging around his neck to school for a day. *Be a Perfect Person in Just Three Days!* is Program #12 of the television series *Books from Cover to Cover*.

Books for primary students can also be introduced by explaining the title. Macaulay's humorous story *Why the Chicken Crossed the Road* is a circular story which begins and ends with a chicken. Brighton's *Five Secrets in a Box* is a biography of Galileo which is explained by five items belonging to Galileo. Long's *Gone Fishing* is about a boy and his father who go out before dawn and catch two fish. In Purdy's *Least of All*, 6-year-old Raven Hannah teaches her grandmother to read and learns humility in the process. In Turkle's *Do Not Open!*, Miss Moody lives with her cat near a beach where she salvages items for her home, including a clock that doesn't work. When Miss Moody finds a purple bottle that says DO NOT OPEN, a voice offers her anything in the world she wants to open it but she doesn't give in until a child's voice begs to be let out of the bottle. The monster that escapes causes much trouble.

INTRODUCING BOOKS BY TITLES: SETTING (TIME) [CU 24–25]. When most people think of setting, they think of the place where a story occurs. However, setting can also refer to the time when the story happens. Many books set the time for readers in the title by naming days or times of the day, nights, weeks, seasons, or years. Books for primary students could be gathered together and used as a springboard for discussion about segments of time. Students could put the books in order by the length of time mentioned from shortest to longest. If only the titles are used, longer fiction can be included in this book timeline. Books on the level of the students could be explained by their titles and students could check out the books that they wish to read to themselves or have someone at home read to them. Books for intermediate students can be introduced in booktalks by explaining the significance of time in the title in relationship to the plot.

Several books which include time in the title are nonfiction. Lerner's *A Forest Year* is arranged by season and tells how various plants and animals live in a forest in the eastern half of the United States. Wolf's book, *In the Year of the Tiger*, depicts rural family life in China. A Papago Indian girl, Bird Wing, learns about the Sonora Desert in Arizona and the bats, lizards, woodpeckers, elf owls, and coyotes who live there in George's *One Day in the Desert*. George's *One Day in the Woods* shares a day with Rebecca as she learns about skunks, wood ducks, flying squirrels, gypsy moths, caterpillars and other creatures in a forest in New York State. Some of the animals might have lived in the forest in George's fiction book, *My Side of the Mountain*, which also takes place in a New York forest. Aronsky's *Sketching Outdoors in Spring* shows how the famous artist records the months from March to May. Aronsky also links art and nature in *Sketching Outdoors in Winter*. Langstaff's *What a Morning: The Christmas Story in Black Spirituals* celebrates the morning of Christ's birth with African-American spirituals. Readers can participate in a Chinese New Year's celebration in San Francisco in the photo essay *Chinese New Year* by Brown. These books are not appropriate for a booktalk in which students are introduced to fiction to be read for reports. However, they are included here because they could be part of a display of books featured in a library, school library/media center, or classroom. One excellent caption for such a display is the huge word "TIME" made up of collage pictures of clocks, calendars, or the words "Day," "Night," "Morning," "Afternoon," "Week," "Year," "Spring," "Summer," "Fall," and "Winter."

Some other books about time to include in the display are about holidays and events. Coerr's *The Big Balloon Race*, Page's *The Great Bullocky Race*, and Pomerantz's *The Half-Birthday Party* are about events. *Mousekin's*

Thanksgiving by Miller, *Cobweb Christmas* by Climo, *Apple Tree Christmas* by Noble and *The Twelve Days of Christmas* are about holidays. Reading the holiday Mousekin book can serve to introduce all of the other books about that woodland mouse that are listed in Chapter 5 in the section MICE ARE NICE.

In Murphy's *Five Minutes' Peace*, all Mother Elephant wants is a few moments to herself. A minute is too long for Eva in *The Very Last First Time*. In this Canadian book by Andrews, Eva has to walk under the sea ice to collect mussels and she is afraid. Rabbit explores a meadow full of beavers, deer, mice, pheasants and other animals in Tafuri's almost wordless book, *Rabbit's Morning*. *Breakfast Time, Ernest and Celestine* by Vincent is about a mouse and a bear and can be used to introduce the other books about these two. Domanska's *Busy Monday Morning* is a Polish folk song. Ernst's *The Colorful Adventures of the Bee Who Left Home One Monday Morning and What He Found Along the Way* shares the colors a bee sees before going back to its hive: a yellow hive; blue sky; purple flowers; black dog; green clover; brown shoes; red flowers; pink sleeve; gray sky; orange flower; and a white cloud. Ryder's *Mockingbird Morning* is about a poetic morning walk. Motyka's *An Ordinary Day* is a day in the life of a young boy who experiences outdoor pleasures as well as a storm and a rainbow. *Bonny's Big Day* is one of the incidents shared by veterinarian James Herriot. After the veterinarian sees two retired horses, he talks the owner into entering Bonny in the Darrowby Pet Show. The other horse does not enter because it is recuperating. Winning the pet show makes Bonny's day. What kind of teacher eats bananas and swings from trees? Read Howe's *The Day the Teacher Went Bananas* to find out. *Jam Day* by Josse is about Ben and Mama who visit Ben's grandparents for the annual berrypicking, jam-making day. Anno's *All in a Day* is what it is like on January 1st for children at nine places around the world. Nine other famous artists besides Anno each portray one place in the world. Prater's *The Perfect Day* consists of family fun at the beach, an amusement park, and the zoo for everyone in the family except Kevin. Viorst's classic *Alexander and the Terrible, Horrible, No Good, Very Bad Day* is now a 16mm film or video and appears on pages 238–44 of the SB/Ginn third grade basal reader, *Castles in the Sand*, edited by Pearson, et al. Lillie's *One Very, Very Quiet Afternoon* is about a tea party in which each person's three names are letters of the alphabet, such as in Anabelle Barbara Cavendish and Daniel Ezra Fiddleson. Ormerod's wordless books *Sunshine* and *Moonlight* show how a small girl wakes up and gets ready to leave in the morning and eats supper, bathes and gets ready for bed at night.

There are books for primary students about night. *An Evening at Alfie's* by Hughes portrays a hectic evening with Alfie and the baby-sitter. Aliki's *Overnight at Mary Bloom's* is about a child who stays overnight with a friend of her mother. In Rockwell's *The Night We Slept Outside*, sleeping on the deck is O.K. until it thunders. Hurd's *A Night in the Swamp: A Movable Book* introduces animals in a swamp at night and shows them in action. Use this book with Hurd's *Pea Patch Jig*. In Bunting's *Ghost's Hour, Spook's Hour*, Jake wakes up to a dark house where the lights won't go on and his parents aren't in their room. Mohr's *Silent Night* is about a special night in which a song is born. Compare with hers the illustrations by Jeffers in Lindberg's *Midnight Farm* in which a mother and child view animals settling for the night. *Midnight Farm* appears on pages 186–97 of the SB/Ginn primer *A New Day*, edited by Pearson, et al. A little girl also feels the mood of the night and the creatures out there in Ryder's *Step into the Night*. A father, mother, and child go for a walk to a street fair in Rice's *City Night*. Rylant's *Night in the Country* shares the sounds of an apple falling from a tree, a screen door opening, a dog's chain rattling, and the noises of owls and frogs. *Harry's Night Out* by Pizer is about the nocturnal adventures of Harry the cat, who looks for mice in an old barn and is frightened by an owl who has similar intentions. Hest's *The Midnight Eaters* is an intergenerational story.

There are primary books which contain days of the week or references to weeks in the titles. Every Wednesday night Anna and Grandma work on a surprise for Daddy's birthday in Bunting's *The Wednesday Surprise*. Girard's Katie visits her father *At Daddy's on Saturdays*. The first week after Daddy leaves is especially difficult for Katie. *Friday Night Is Papa Night* by Sonneborn shares the delight of having Papa home. Barney spends Sunday with his grandparents in Cazet's *Sunday*. *A Weekend with Wendell* by Henkes is available as a sound filmstrip and hardcover/cassette or paperback/cassette. Wendell, an ill-mannered mouse, comes to spend the weekend with Sophie. Whelan's *A Week with Raccoons* tells of the trouble they cause. In Sharmat's *The Seven Sloppy Days of Phineas Pig*, Phineas's parents and his friends think he is too neat, so they send him off to Cousin Humble's for seven days to learn to be piggish.

Three titles which have appeared on the television series *Reading Rainbow* are: *Tight Times* by Hazen, *The Three Hat Day* by Geringer, and *Three Days on a River in a Red Canoe* by Williams.

A booktalk for intermediate students which shares titles with times in them can include the books in this paragraph. Sometimes a single night can be significant as it is in Ruckman's *Night of the Twisters* when 12-year-old Dan Hatch survives a tornado in Nebraska. *The Story for a Black Night* by Bess is the story a Liberian father tells his children about a baby left at their home and the resulting tragedy when the baby has smallpox and baby sister Meatta dies. After Momo (the father who is telling the story) and the baby survive the smallpox, the child's grandmother comes to claim the child, but the new mother refuses to give her up. Hamilton's *Willie Bea and the Time the Martians Landed* is about a black family and what happens to them on the night in October, 1938 when the radio program by Orson Welles, "War of the Worlds," terrifies people. Calhoun's *The Night the Monster Came* is about Andy, who sees footprints and later thinks he sees Bigfoot. *The Night of the Solstice* by Smith is a mystery/fantasy of how Alys, Charles, Janie, and Claudia search for Morgana Shee, the guardian of the gates between the worlds, who has been captured by the evil sorcerer, Cadel Forge. *This Time of Darkness* by Hoover is a science fiction novel set in a future time when people must live inside a domed city because of the pollution outside. Eleven-year-old Amy is tired of the restricted life and agrees to leave with Axel, a boy who has been captured and who tells her that it is possible to live "Outside." Ancient Greek myths come alive for 13-year-old Carla in Fenton's *Morning of the Gods*. Carla is spending the summer in Greece during the early 1970s with a great-aunt and great-uncle because her mother is suddenly killed. Hillary is fascinated with the elf village in Sara-Kate's backyard and is drawn into her troubled life in Lisle's *Afternoon of the Elves*.

There are some books that can be added to the booktalk about the seasons. In Whelan's *Next Spring an Oriole*, a family goes by covered wagon to Michigan in 1837. The title refers to the fact that when they leave Virginia, the orioles and thrushes are singing. After arriving in Michigan, Papa finds an empty oriole nest and assures 10-year-old Libby that "Next spring they will surely return." The story can be read by second through intermediate grades. In Dixon's *The Summer of the White Goat*, Gordon Mohlen goes to Glacier National Park in Montana to observe mountain goats for a school research project. In Hurwitz's *Hot and Cold Summer*, 10-year-old Rory is stuck with a visiting girl when his best friend goes away for the summer. The sequel is *Cold and Hot Winter*. In Doren's *Borrowed Summer*, 10-year-old Jan's great-grandmother goes to live in a nursing home because Jan's pregnant mother can no longer care for Grand-mother, who has broken her hip. Then, Jan and some friends organize a Sun-shine Club to help out at the nursing home and later "kidnap" several of the patients. McDonnell's *Just for the Summer* is about Lydia, who goes to visit her Aunt May and Aunt Connie, college teachers, because her father is in the hospital. During that summer Lydia has fun with friends she has met during previous visits, plays with a dollhouse, wins a blue ribbon on her project for the fair, writes letters to her father, and looks forward to her mother's visit. Twelve-year-old Elvira Preston and "Doctor Bill," a German refugee, are the main characters in McCutcheon's *Summer of the Zeppelin*, which takes place in 1918 during World War I. Information about the role of Zeppelins during that war could be used in introducing this book. World War II is the setting for Richardson's *The July Plot*. On July 20, 1944, a plot to assassinate Adolph Hitler failed. This book describes the plot and tells what happened to those who were unsuccessful. In *Summer of the Monkeys* by Rawls, 14-year-old Jay Berry Lee and his dog Rowdy find a tree full of monkeys on their farm in rural Oklahoma. Jay Berry learns that the monkeys have escaped and that there is a reward for catching them. Determined to earn the reward and buy himself a gun and a pony, Jay Berry sets off on his adventure. A plague of grasshoppers threatens the prairie in the Dakota Territory in Turner's *Grasshopper Summer*. In Doty's *Summer Pony*, Ginny rents a pony named Mokey for the summer. In *Winter Pony*, Mokey pulls a sleigh, and by spring she delivers a foal. *The Winter When Time Was Frozen* by Pelgrom is about a 12-year-old girl and her father who are taken in by a farm family in Holland during World War II. In Hahn's *December Stillness*, Kelley's school project about the homeless backfires when she involves a Vietnam veteran.

There are books with seasons in the titles for primary students. Lindgren's *Springtime in Noisy Village* is about a classic Swedish village. Goodall's *An Edwardian Summer* is a wordless history of a special time in England's history. McPhail's *Emma's Vacation* is set in the summer when Emma and her parents go to a cabin for a vacation. While her parents are interested in taking various side trips, all Emma wants to do is wade in the stream, catch fish, and lie in the sun. *Julian's Glorious Summer* by Cameron is a sequel to *The Stories Julian Tells*. At the beginning of the summer, Gloria gets a new two-wheeler but 7-year-old Julian is afraid of falling and covers up his fear by avoiding her so he won't have to learn to ride a bike too. *Blanche and Smitty's Summer Vacation* by Malkin is about a girl named Blanche who plans her vacation without her mischievous cat but finds him when she unpacks. "How Summer Came to Canada" can be read aloud from pages 129–33 of *Maid of the North* by Phelps. Singer's *Turtle in July* contains poems month by month to complete the yearly cycle. Lionel uses a Tom Sawyer–like trick to get out of raking leaves in Krensky's *Lionel in the Fall*, an easy reader. Parnall's *Winter Barn* is about an old red barn in Maine and the various animals who shelter there for the winter: porcupines, skunks, cats, snakes, and mice. Woodchucks prepare for a long winter in Watson's *Has Winter Come?* Florian's *A Winter Day* shows a family enjoying a winter day while Gomi's *Spring Is Here* celebrates another season.

Primary students can also learn about a year. Rylant's *This Year's Garden* contains activities connected with planting a garden. In Bjork's *Linnea's Almanac*, Linnea records her indoor and outdoor activities each month and shares details of her projects such as learning about the Big Dipper and flying a kite. Houston's *The Year of the Perfect Christmas Tree* is about the commitment Ruthie's father has made to provide the Christmas tree for their church one year. With her father off to war, Ruthie and her mother fulfill the pledge. Snyder's *The Boy of the Three-Year Nap*, a Caldecott Honor Book, is a Japanese folktale about a clever but lazy boy. Taro is called "The boy of the three-year nap" because he sometimes sleeps for three years at a stretch.

A year in any given grade can be a significant time in anyone's life. Books with the grade level in the title can help children to learn for themselves the audience for which the book is intended. Pinkwater's *I Was a Second Grade Werewolf* is about Lawrence Talbot, who turns into a werewolf one morning and no one even notices. Lawlor's *How to Survive Third Grade* is about a boy who doesn't have any friends until a boy from Kenya, Jomo Mugwana, defends him from bullies. Ernest invites Jomo to share the pizza he has won as a prize in the school's balloon release contest. Kline's *Horrible Harry in Room 2B* plays tricks on others and learns what the receiving end is like when one of his jokes backfires. Gilson's *4-B Goes Wild* is a sequel to *Thirteen Ways to Sink a Sub* and is even funnier. The same fourth graders have a school carnival, Dinosaur Delight, to make money for the three-day Outdoor Education program at Camp Trotter in Wisconsin. Miss Ivanovich and Grandma Bosco go along as chaperones. In the first book, the boys and girls in the class have a contest to see which group can make the substitute teacher more miserable. In *The Fourth Grade Wizards* by DeClements, Marianne can't concentrate on her school work since the death of her mother, so her friend Jack helps her, and she in turn helps him to keep out of trouble. Casey Valentine wants to get herself elected president of her class so she can compete favorably with her older sister in Giff's *Fourth Grade Celebrity*. Casey is in fifth grade in Giff's *Love from the Fifth Grade Celebrity*. Casey Valentine meets Tracy Matson for the first time since Giff's *The Girl Who Knew It All*. Tracy moves to town and Casey is glad she is in the same grade until Tracy steals her friends and tells them embarrassing stories about Casey. In *Nothing's Fair in Fifth Grade* by DeClements, a new girl with a poor self-image is unwanted by her mother and her father's girlfriend. Elsie is on a special diet and steals money from her classmates to buy food. Her mother plans to send her to a boarding school. Ask students if they think Elsie should be sent to boarding school. When Jenny has trouble with fractions, she hires Elsie to help her and the earnings are used to pay back the stolen money. DeClements is also the author of *Sixth Grade Can Really Kill You*. Elsie and Jenny are in this book too, but the central character is Helen who causes trouble and memorizes passages so no one will know that she can't read. Eventually her father gives permission, over his wife's protests, for Helen to attend the learning disabled room for reading help. Although the word dyslexia isn't used, all of Helen's symptoms of mixing up *b*'s and *d*'s point to it. Bunting's *Sixth Grade Sleepover* is about sixth grader Janey, who wants to attend the sleepover in her school cafeteria for any girl in the Reading Club who has read and reported on a certain number of books. However, Janey is afraid to attend because of her embarrassing problem. Don't name the problem in the booktalk and create suspense for the readers. The boys in Sachar's *Sixth Grade Secrets* have a club, so Laura starts a secret club called Pig City. Nathanson's *The Trouble with Wednesdays* is about Becky, a sixth grader, who is excited about getting braces but comes to dread her Wednesday appointments because of the actions of her dentist. Convincing her family that something is wrong is not easy.

Lord's *In the Year of the Boar and Jackie Robinson* is an outstanding and humorous book to read aloud or for children to read for themselves. A Chinese girl adapts to the United States by learning about the Dodgers and Jackie Robinson and by playing baseball herself. Deciding to take an American name before moving to the United States, she first selects "Uncle Sam" but her grandfather doesn't care for that name so she chooses Shirley Temple Wong. Shirley and her mother go to their new home by boat and train during the Year of the Boar (1947 by the Julian calendar) to join Shirley's engineer father. Her mother tells her that the reputation of all Chinese rests upon her shoulders and she is "China's little ambassador." At PS 8, Shirley is bullied by Mabel, the strongest, tallest, and scariest girl in fifth grade but when Shirley does not squeal on her, Mabel becomes Shirley's protector. Shirley listens to the Dodgers on the radio while baby-sitting and becomes a true fan. Readers know 14-year-old Michael only from his conversation with his sister Jody on the first three pages of Pfeffer's *The Year Without Michael*. The first year after Michael runs away is told from the point of view of Jody. On Saturday, September 14 the family has a birthday cake for Michael's birthday but he doesn't come home; they forget Jody's birthday until the last minute.

The Newbery winner, *A Gathering of Days* by Blos, is the diary or journal between 1830 and 1832 of 13-year-old Catherine Cabot Hall of New Hampshire.

INTRODUCING BOOKS BY TITLES: SETTING (PLACE) [CU 24]. The focus of the setting can be a room, a building, a street, a farm, a garden, a river, a bay, an island, a town, a state, or a planet. A booktalk for intermediate students can introduce or reinforce the concept of setting and a wide variety of places. The books shared are as diverse as the audience. In Paulsen's Newbery Honor Book, *The Winter Room*, readers learn about 11-year-old Eldon, a Minnesota boy, and his family. During winter evenings, Great-uncle David tells stories about his youth in Norway. Eleven-year-old Alex is on his own in a Polish ghetto in Orlev's *The Island on Bird Street*. The ghetto may as well be an island. Twelve-year-old Rose uses a root cellar in Ontario as her access from modern times to Civil War times in Lunn's *The Root Cellar*. In Hamilton's *The House of Dies Drear*, 13-year-old Thomas Small lives in a house in Ohio that has an Underground Railroad history. The sequel is *Mystery of Drear House: The Conclusion of the Dies Drear Chronicle*. Loeper's *The House on Spruce Street* is about the people who live in a Philadelphia house from 1772 to the 1980s. *The Treasure of Plunderell Manor* by Clements takes place in house in England where Laurel is a maid during Victorian times. *Midnight Is a Place* by Aiken is a run-down mansion near Midnight Mill, a carpet factory. Thirteen-year-old Lucas is being groomed to take his dead father's place as Sir Randolph's partner, but learns that the Murgatroyds may have been gypped out of their part of the mill. *Midnight Is a Place* is Program #13 of the instructional television series *More Books from Cover to Cover* for fifth graders. Elsenberg's *Mystery at Snowshoe Mountain Lodge* takes place in a ski lodge in Utah. A student who is working on a thesis about the person who built a decaying mansion, Roscoe's Leap, is the catalyst for unraveling the mystery in *Roscoe's Leap* by Cross. *Redwall* by Jacques will probably become a classic fantasy. Redwall Abbey in Mossflower Forest is the home of a group of mice who form the Order of Redwall dedicated to kindness to all living creatures. Into their peaceful setting comes Cluny the Scourge, a rat who wants to take over the abbey. All the animals fight back including a young mouse, Matthias, who is inspired by the ancient hero, Martin the Warrior. The sequel is *Mossflower*. Sophie is the housekeeper for Wizard Howl, who lives in a castle with four turrets that moves around the countryside scaring people in *Howl's Moving Castle* by Jones. In *Pig-Out Inn* by Ruby, 14-year-old Dovi's mother buys a truck-stop in Kansas which is called the Klondike Cafe and Cottages, but which Dovi calls the Pig-Out Inn. A custody battle surrounding 9-year-old Tag is part of the action.

Hilary finds a doll buried in a garden and becomes involved with a ghost cat, a dying girl, and a grouchy landlady in Hahn's mystery, *The Doll in the Garden*. A new edition of *The Secret Garden* by Burnett is illustrated by Michael Hague. This classic about Mary, Dickon, and Colin and their secret place is excellent for reading aloud. Carroll's *Alice in Wonderland* is another good read-aloud classic. The Carnegie Medal winning *Watership Down* by Adams, about a family of rabbits who find a safe home on an English down, is excellent for reading aloud. Booktalkers should explain that a down is a treeless upland which is rolling and grassy like those found near the south coast of England. Townsend's *Tom Tiddler's Ground* is a patch of land near canals where five children find an old rotted canal boat with a treasure and a 50-year-old mystery. Selden's *The Old Meadow* is the place from which Chester Cricket in *The Cricket in Times Square* comes. Because the meadow has been designated a historical landmark, Abner Budd, a hermit, faces eviction. Wiseman's *Adam's Common* is a wild and unspoiled common in England that is in danger of being destroyed. Peggy Donovan searches for the deed given and William Trafford reaches across time to save his beloved common. In Tate's *The Secret of Gumbo Grove*, 11-year-old Raisin Stackhouse learns about black history while helping Miz Effie clean up the New Africa No. 1 Missionary Baptist Cemetery. *The Golden Pasture* by Thomas is about black cowboys in Oklahoma. Twelve-year-old Carl (who is part Cherokee) spends the summer at Gold Pasture, the ranch of his grandfather, a former rodeo star. An appaloosa horse and conflict among three generations provide the plot. *Pretty Penny Farm* by Hoppe is also a horse story. Fifteen-year-old Beth Bridgewater does not want to spend the summer on a New England farm nor does she want a girl invited by her mother to stay there either. A small Appalachian town in the early 1950s is the setting for White's *Sweet Creek Holler*. Wolkstein has retold Irving's classic ghost story in *The Legend of Sleepy Hollow*.

McKinley's *The Outlaws of Sherwood* is a retelling of the Robin Hood story. Chapter 1 gives background about those who work in the King's Forest of Nottingham. Readers learn about the death of Robin's father and why the chief forester doesn't like Robin. Chapter 2 explains how Robin is talked into hiding out in Sherwood Forest and providing a rallying point for the Saxons against the Normans. Read these two chapters aloud or retell them during a booktalk to interest students in reading the book.

Fourteen-year-old Plummey tries to catch an elusive trout called the Virgin Queen in Hyde's *The Major, the Poacher, and the Wonderful One-Trout River*. The trout is stocked in the pool of Major George Quillaine, the king of the flycatchers. Lunn's *The Shadow in Hawthorn Bay* is about 15-year-old Scottish

Mary Urquhart who has second sight and hears her cousin Duncan call to her from Canada. When she arrives at Hawthorn Bay, Ontario, she finds trouble of several kinds, including death. A boy is kidnapped by an escaped prisoner in Hyde's *Island of the Loons*, a fictional island based on one in Lake Superior off the shoreline of Michigan's Upper Peninsula. *The Halcyon Island* by Knowles is about 12-year-old Ken, who is afraid of the water. Another boy, Giles, is more sympathetic and helpful than Ken's own father. Then in another book, why did mother pack up 11-year-old Megan and her brother, 10-year-old Sandy, and drive all night to a remote cottage on a lake in Minnesota where their grandfather was recuperating from a leg injury? In *Megan's Island* by Roberts, Megan finds a psychological haven on an island close to the shore where she, Sandy, and the boy in the next cabin build a treehouse. The island becomes a physical haven too, from a pair of men who are looking for them. A school teacher and his 10-year-old son start a new life in Van Raven's *Harpoon Island*. *Castaways on Chimp Island* by Landsman is about Danny, a chimp who pretends that he has forgotten what he has learned in a language lab, so he is sent with three other chimps to an island to return to nature. Fox's *Village by the Sea* is about 10-year-old Emma who goes to visit her alcoholic Aunt Bea while her father is in the hospital for open heart surgery. Emma meets Alberta (Bertie) and they create a village by the bay.

Huxley and Zaza Hammond are sent to the Unexpected School where they study magic under Heathcliff Warlock in Mahy's *The Blood-and-Thunder Adventure on Hurricane Peak*. Twelve-year-old Ance stays at his grandparents' home while his mother is on an archaeological dig in Gabhart's *Discovery at Coyote Point*.

Talbot's *Orphan for Nebraska* is about Kevin O'Rourke, sent to Nebraska by the Children's Aid Society in the 1870s. *The Guardian of Isis* by Hughes is a sequel to *Keeper of the Isis Light*. Jody N'Komo lives on the backward planet of Isis during the year 2136, meets the Guardian and the Keeper and learns the connection between the history and mythology of the planet. *The Dark Secret of Weatherend* by Bellairs tells of a confrontation with a wizard who wants to turn the world to ice. Alexander's *Westmark* is a dangerous kingdom for Theo when his printing press is destroyed and he becomes a fugitive because of the wicked Cabbarus.

There are several books about places that overlap primary and intermediate grades. *No One Is Going to Nashville* by Jukes is about Sonia, who wants to be a veterinarian. While staying with her father and stepmother Annette, Sonia finds a stray dog named Max, but knows her mother won't allow her to keep it and her father says she isn't with him enough to take care of it. Max reminds Annette of her own dog Maxine, who went off one day and didn't come back. The title is derived from the idea that Maxine might have hopped a freight train to Nashville to be a country western singer. Will Sonia get to keep the dog? *What Happened in Hamelin?* by Skurzynski is about the events surrounding rats, children, and the Pied Piper in Hamelin, Germany in 1284. *Shaker*

Lane by the Provensens is about land sold off by two elderly sisters to poorer families who built homes there. The conflict occurs when a reservoir is built on the property and homeowners are forced to relocate. Gerstein's *The Mountains of Tibet* is about the death and reincarnation of a Tibetan woodcutter. Although he has always wanted to travel and see the world, when given a choice the woodcutter chooses circumstances similar to those of his former life and comes full circle and returns to the same place as a girl. Tejima's *Owl Lake* can be enjoyed by anyone who appreciates the woodcuts of the owls that come out at night and fish in the lake among the mountains.

Use the video of *Abel's Island* by Steig to introduce the idea of setting to primary students. Abelard and Amanda, mice, are swept away to a deserted island by a storm. In Cooney's *Island Boy*, Matthias is one of 12 children born on the island. Though he goes away to sea, Matthias comes back later to Tibbetts Island with his own family. Lessac's *My Little Island* is a featured book on the television series *Reading Rainbow*. *The Secret of Foghorn Island* by Hayes is an easy-to-read detective story involving shipwrecks. There have been too many shipwrecks so Captain Poopdeck and a mermaid go to Foghorn Island to outwit Sid Rat and his henchmen. Kellogg's *The Island of the Skog* is available as a cassette with either a hardback or a paperback, sound filmstrip, 16mm film, or video. Lent's *Bayberry Bluff* is an island community based on a real one on Martha's Vineyard, an island off Massachusetts. Rockwell's *At the Beach* is for preschoolers. *Beside the Bay* by Samton shares colors in rhyme. Raffi's *Down by the Bay* is a picture book of the rollicking song. In Say's *Lost Lake* a boy and his dad go to find a lake the dad remembers from long ago only to find that it is no longer isolated but full of holiday seekers. *Lily Pad Pond* by Lavies is about the animals and insects that live near a lily pond.

Several books are about gardens. Carter's *Bella's Secret Garden* is an easy book about how Bella Rabbit's meadow is disappearing. *Murgatroyd's Garden* by Zavos is really Murgatroyd's hair, which is so messy that a variety of animals make their home in the tangle. In *In Abigail's Garden* by Williams, there are a dozen poems about gardens, flowers, and trees. Bjork's *Linnea in Monet's Garden* is about a girl who visits the garden of impressionist artist Claude Monet. *Linnea's Windowsill Garden* and *Linnea's Almanac* are about the same girl. Brooke's classic *Johnny Crow's Garden* has been reissued.

Picture books on a wide variety of subjects can be introduced to students by their settings. Griffith's *Georgia Music* is a heartwarming story of a Baltimore girl who spends the summers in Georgia with her grandfather who plays a mouth organ. When Grandpa becomes ill and has to live with them, Janetta brings back their good times in Georgia by playing some of his music on the mouth organ. Janetta first goes to her grandfather's home in the book *Grandaddy's Place*, which also appears in Pearson's third grade SB/Ginn basal reader, *Castles in the Sand*, on pages 56–69. Check page 70 of *Castles in the Sand* for Child's poem "Over the River and Through the Wood." Tom Burt and his cousins spend time *On Grandaddy's Farm* in Appalachia in the 1930s in a book by Allen. A girl describes life in the Colorado Rockies at her grandfather's house *High in the Mountains* in a book by Radin. Ben wants a place of his own to get away from the new toddler in the house in Titherington's *A Place for Ben*. In Spencer's *The Magic Room*, Phoebe is forbidden from the room where her parents practice their magic. However, when her parents accidentally make themselves smaller, Phoebe helps them to grow an inch with each laugh. *There's an Alligator Under My Bed* by Mayer is about the same boy from *There's a Nightmare in My Closet*. Elizabeth is afraid to go down into the cellar to get a jar of peaches in Josse's *Spiders in the Fruit Cellar*. A girl calls before going to Mary Bloom's so that the baby and all the pets will be ready for her to spend the night in Aliki's *Overnight At Mary Bloom's*, which is the sequel to *At Mary Bloom's*. *General Store* is the title of two picture books of Field's poem illustrated by Parker and by Laroche. Field's poem also appears on pages 24–25 of Pearson's third grade SB/Ginn basal reader series, *Castles in the Sand*. In Botter's *Zoo Story*, the lion, hippo, and bear antagonize each other instead of working in harmony. Joey draws scenes from a movie about a pirate on the sidewalks in Isadora's *The Pirates of Bedford Street*. Schotter's *Captain Snap and the Children of Vinegar Street* is about children who live down the road from a hermit. Pryor's *The House on Maple Street* shares 300 years of the history of one place. Annie visits with each neighbor and complains that there is nothing to do in *Once Around the Block* by Henkes. Christelow's *Robbery at the Diamond Dog Diner* is available in paperback/cassette format. Lola and Harry Dog's diamonds are saved by the chicken, Glenda Feathers, using her plan to hide the diamonds in eggs and in chocolate. Chorao's *Cathedral Mouse* is about a mouse who runs away from a pet shop to a cathedral. *School* by McCully is a wordless picture book about the littlest mouse who is left home when the eight others go to school. Corbett's *Song of Pentecost* is about the mice of Pentecost Farm who are forced to move, and face danger from snakes, owls, and foxes. In *Meanwhile Back at the Ranch* by Noble, Rancher Hicks drives 84 miles into Sleepy Gulch for some excitement, but only finds people watching a turtle cross the road. Meanwhile, back at the ranch his wife wins a refrigerator, gets a legacy, a winning lottery ticket, strikes oil, builds various buildings to house the new arrivals, goes on a diet, makes a movie, and becomes a diplomat at the request of the president while the cat has kittens, the dog has puppies, and the pig has piglets. *Meanwhile Back at the Ranch* is a featured book on the television program *Reading Rainbow*. In Martin and Archambault's *Barn Dance!*, a boy becomes involved in a magical square dance out in a barn. Hendershot's *In Coal Country* is about life in a company town in the 1930s. In Rockwell's *Come to Town*, children learn about various places in the community when the bear family visits. French's *Snow White in New York* is a version of Snow White set in the 1920s. *It Happened in Pinsk* by Yorinks is about Irv Irving, a show salesman, who is not content. Read aloud on March 19. In *Aurora Means Dawn* by Saunders, a family moves to Ohio in the 1800s only to find that the town Aurora is not what they expected. Sadler's

Alistair in Outer Space is a picture book featured on the television series *Reading Rainbow.*

Some books which include the place in the title are nonfiction. Hausherr's *The One-room School at Squabble Hollow* is based on a real school in Vermont that closed in 1986. The school had 18 students from first to sixth grades. *The Tower of London* by Fisher tells of the historic English fortress where princes and queens were imprisoned and often put to death. Kuskin's *Jerusalem, Shining Still* covers 4,000 years of history of a city that is home to three major religions. Laird's *The Road to Bethlehem: An Ethiopian Nativity* is a version of the Christmas story illustrated with Ethiopian manuscripts. Lessac's *My Little Island* is about a boy named Lucca, who returns to the Caribbean island of his birth, and is as much a documentary as it is a story of life on the island. *Anno's U.S.A.* shows the whole country in a wordless trip across time and distance. Two girls learn about biomes (environmental surroundings) in three books by Jean George: *One Day in the Desert*; *One Day in the Prairie*; and *One Day in the Woods*. *Beaver at Long Pond* by Lindsay and William George presents information about the lives of beavers. *The Hidden Life of the Pond* and *The Hidden Life of the Meadow* by Schwartz combine photographs and information. Color photos enhance Ekey's *Fire! in Yellowstone: A True Adventure* which tells about the fire of 1988.

For more titles, consult a section in Chapter 5 called BOOKS ABOUT BUILDINGS AND CITIES.

INTRODUCING BOOKS BY TITLES: HUMAN CHARACTERS [CU 24–29]. Many books can be introduced simply by describing the character in the title or telling one event that happens to that person. Share these books in a booktalk or informally with students.

Several books for intermediate students which have human characters named in the title take place in the past. Carrie in *Who Is Carrie?* by the Colliers is a kitchen slave at Samuel Fraunces Tavern. In the Colliers' *War Comes to Willy Freeman*, Willy is a 13-year-old free African-American girl who poses as a boy during the American Revolution and is involved in the trial of her uncle, whom she sues for freedom. Willy also works at Samuel Fraunces Tavern. Two books take place before the Civil War. Hurmence's *A Girl Called Boy* is about a modern African-American girl who goes back in time and is chased by slavers. Turner's *Nettie's Trip South* is about a girl who goes from Albany to Richmond with her brother, a newspaper reporter, in 1859. In Nettie's letter to her friend, she shares her opinion of slave quarters and slave auctions. In Beatty's *Turn Homeward, Hanalee*, 12-year-old Hanalee Reed is one of 2,000 textile workers taken from their mill in Georgia to make cloth for the Yankees at a mill in Indiana. The title is her mother's admonition: to turn her heart homeward no matter where she is taken. Because Hanalee's mother gives her a persimmon seed button as a charm to help her return home, Persephone's story from mythology could be briefly recounted when introducing the book. The sequel is *Be Ever Hopeful, Hanalee*. Beatty's *Charley Skedaddle* is a 12-year-old city boy who lives in New York's Bowery and is a member of a rough and tough gang. Charley joins the Union Army as a drummer to avenge the death of his older brother who was killed at Gettysburg. During his first battle at the Wilderness in Virginia, Charley "skedaddles" or runs away to the Blue Ridge Mountains. Descriptions of the mountain woman, Granny Jerusha Bent, with whom he stays, appear on pages 106 and 109. Although *Susanna of the Alamo* by Jakes appears in a picture book format, the book can be used with any history unit up through middle school that covers the Mexican War and the Alamo. The book is based on historical information that Susanna and her child were survivors of the Alamo. Eleven-year-old Bethany Brandt in Beatty's *Behave Yourself, Bethany Brandt* tells about her life after her mother dies. The setting in this book is Texas in 1898.

Trouble for Lucy by Stevens and Lawlor's *Addie Across the Prairie* are both fiction books about frontier and pioneer life. Another is Hudson's *Sweetgrass*, based on records of the Blackfoot Indians during the winter of 1837–38, won the Canadian Library Association Book of the Year for Children and the Canada Council Children's Literature Prize. During the summer of her fifteenth year, Sweetgrass's only concern is that Eagle-Sun will be able to collect enough horses for her father to accept them in return for her becoming Eagle-Sun's wife. During that winter, Sweetgrass's concern is that some of her family will be able to survive the smallpox epidemic. References to the prairie sweetgrass appear on pages 12, 25, 75, 116, and 155. Have students compare the marriage customs of the Blackfoot Indians with those found in the Cholistan Desert culture in Pakistan in the Newbery Honor Book, *Shabanu: Daughter of the Wind*. Marriage plans are made for 11-year-old Shabanu and her sister, Phulan.

Hannah's Fancy Notions by Ross is a story based on a woman from New Hampshire who made band-boxes at the turn of the century in Massachusetts.

Stolz's *Ivy Larkin* is a 14-year-old Depression era girl who lives in Manhattan. Burch's *Ida Early Comes Over the Mountain* is also set in Depression times and takes place on the Georgia side of the Blue Ridge Mountains. Ida just appears at the door to the Sutton house and offers to cook for them. The Sutton family is glad to have Ida stay because they have lost their mother and don't like their bossy aunt. Life is fun with unpredictable Ida who tells tall tales, wears unusual clothes, and has wild hair, but the Suttons don't really appreciate Ida until they lose her. The sequel is *Christmas with Ida Early*. Peck's Blossom Culp is a very unusual 14-year-old who lives in the early 1900s and whose second sight gets her into lots of trouble. Books about Blossom are: *Ghosts I Have Been*; *The Ghost Belonged to Me*; *The Dreadful Future of Blossom Culp*; and *Blossom Culp and the Sleep of Death*. A description of the books appears in Chapter 1 in a section called TIME TRAVEL: A BOOK-TALK.

Millie Cooper: 3B by Herman is about a third grader in New York City in 1946. Millie's problems include a strict teacher, fountain pens that blob ink, and her new expensive Reynolds Rocket ball point pen that is guaranteed for 15 years but only works a few days. References to radio programs and comic books of the time are included. In the sequel, *Millie Cooper: Take a Chance,* Millie forces herself to read a poem in front of her class. Schotter's *Rhoda, Straight and True* is set in Brooklyn, 1953. *The Girl on the Outside* by Walter is about Eve, an African-American girl who integrates a high school. It is based on the integration of Little Rock High School in Arkansas in 1957.

In Doherty's *Granny Was a Buffer Girl,* winner of the Carnegie Medal, a modern family shares memories at a gathering which occurs because Jess is going to France for a year abroad at university. It is Chapter 3, "The Buffer Girl," pages 29–41 in which Jess's grandmother Dorothy tells about what it meant to be a buffer girl, how she attracted the attention of the factory owner's son at a dance, and how her husband proposed to her. Check pages 37 and 38 for the meaning of "buffer."

Many books with names of girls in the title are about modern girls. Eleven-year-old Lucy and Rosie, friends, set up Shrinks, Inc., "a psychiatric consultants'" office in the basement of Lucy's home. Because Lucy's father is a child psychiatrist, the two girls meet a 5-year-old girl who intends to consult with Lucy's father in Shreve's *Lucy Forever and Miss Rosetree, Shrinks.*

Lowry's *Anastasia Krupnik* is one of two books featured on the sound filmstrip *Character* from the set *Literature For Children, Series 9* and is also available as a three-filmstrip set. Anastasia is 10 years old, gains a baby brother, loses a grandmother, and has a crush on a boy, and records important events in a green notebook. In the sequel, *Anastasia, Again,* Anastasia moves from the city to the suburbs. Each family member wants something special in the new home. Anastasia wants a tower; her father, a professor of English and a published poet, wants bookcases; and her mother, an artist, wants light. An older lady next door, Gertrude Stein, bakes cookies and Anastasia tries to get her to meet other senior citizens. A new boy asks Anastasia to play tennis and Anastasia misses her friend Jenny. Anastasia is also writing a novel. In *Anastasia at Your Service,* Anastasia puts an ad in the newspaper offering her services as a companion. Mrs. Bellinghorn answers the ad, but expects Anastasia to polish the silver and serve at her granddaughter's birthday party. When Anastasia ruins a piece of silver in the garbage disposal, it takes all of her wages to pay for it. *Anastasia at Your Service* is a Cliffhanger paperback/cassette set. In *Anastasia Has the Answers,* 13-year-old Anastasia has a crush on her black female gym teacher, matchmakes between her widowed uncle and a friend's mother, deals with a baby brother, and persists in rope climbing. In *Anastasia, Ask Your Analyst,* Anastasia is given two gerbils called Romeo and Juliet which she uses for her science project. Both turn out to be females and have 11 babies between them. The gerbils escape and have to be caught before mother sees them. The creative way the family rids themselves of the gerbils is humorous. Anastasia also has parent problems so she buys herself a bust of Freud at a garage sale and talks to him because her parents say she doesn't need a psychiatrist. Anastasia and her father cope with a variety of problems that come up while Mother is on a 10-day business trip in *Anastasia on Her Own*. Anastasia's "Non-sexist Housekeeping Schedule" falls apart during Sam's chicken pox, a visit from Father's old girlfriend, and Anastasia's first date. In *Anastasia's Chosen Career*, the 13-year-old favorite book character goes to downtown Boston to interview a bookstore owner for her composition on "My Chosen Career." That is Anastasia's cover so she can take a modeling course for her "real" career. *All About Sam* is about Anastasia's younger brother, Sam.

Boyd's *Charlie Pippin*, an African-American girl whose real name is Chartreuse, also has a school project—to write about the Vietnam War, in which her father served and about which he is bitter. Greenwald's *Give Us a Great Big Smile, Rosy Cole* is about 10-year-old Rosy whose uncle is a photographer. Uncle Ralph has already made books of her older sisters engaging in various activities. However, Rosy feels she is too ordinary for her uncle to want to take pictures of her violin classes. *Valentine Rosy* is the sequel. Program #11 of the instructional television series for third and fourth graders, *Readit!*, is *Give Us a Great Big Smile, Rosy Cole*. In *Rosy Cole's Great American Guilt Club*, Rosy learns that the rich girls in her class like to give things away so they don't feel too guilty about having so much and she forms the Great American Guilt Club. Whether or not it succeeds is the basis for the story. After Rosie and her friend Hermione read a series of romance novels, they embark on "Project Romance" which will mold Rosy's older sisters and their boyfriends into characters from their books. In spite of their disastrous project, romance happens right under their noses in *Rosy's Romance*.

Fosburgh's 10-year-old *Bella Arabella* is Arabella Fitzgerald, a wealthy girl with a stepfather. When she overhears her stepfather say she should be sent to a boarding school, Arabella escapes by turning into a cat. Readers may have seen this book featured on Program #15 of the educational television series *Books from Cover to Cover*. Delton's *Back Yard Angel* is Program #11 of this same series. Angel O'Leary is responsible for taking care of her 4-year-old brother because her mother works and Father has long ago left the family. The book is filled with her scrapes and her desire to get rid of her brother, Rags, until the day Angel really does lose him in a shopping center. Other books about Angel are: *Angel in Charge*; *Angel's Mother's Boyfriend*; *Angel's Mother's Wedding*; and *Angel's Mother's Baby*. Another girl who is concerned with her mother's wedding is the 8-year-old heroine from *Mitzi and the Terrible Tyrannosaurus Rex* by Williams. Mitzi doesn't think a wedding in the back yard and her mother in a colored dress is a proper wedding at all. When her mother marries Walter, Mitzi will have stepbrothers who are 11 and 3 years old. The youngest, Charles Darwin, can read better than Mitzi, who has just been promoted to the red reading group. Most of the time Darwin thinks he is a Tyrannosaurus Rex except for a lapse when he thinks he is a motorcycle. *Poor Gertie* of Bograd's book is 10 years old and lives with her mother because her father deserted them. Gertie's vivid imagination compensates for other lacks. A fifth grader in Hurwitz's *DeDe Takes Charge* helps her mother adjust to a divorce. DeDe's friend is Aldo Sossi, from other books by Hurwitz. There are sad parts when readers share DeDe's first Thanksgiving without her father and humorous parts when she attempts to fix her shop teacher up with her mother. DeDe and the shop teacher arrive unannounced on the doorstep when Mother has a vegetable pack on her face. Pevsner's *Sister of the Quints* is 13-year-old Natalie Wentworth, a child of divorced parents. Her father and his new wife have quints and her mother is moving to Colorado. Natalie feels that she has no identity either inside or outside the family. Strangers become interested in her only because of the quints, and her father and stepmother want her to give up activities to be a babysitter. Lowry's *Rabble Starkey*, a sixth grader, comes from a single-parent family. Rabble and her mother, Sweet Hosanna, live above a garage, and her mother is the housekeeper for the Bigelow family in this first person narrative. Rabble is friends with Veronica Bigelow, who is her age, little Gunther Bigelow, an elderly neighbor, and a bratty neighbor boy. Kib in *Thatcher Payne-in-the-Neck* by Bates always thought that having Thatcher for a brother would be fun. They have known each other for years because of the proximity of their lake homes, but now that Kib's father has married Thatcher's mother, she finds that Thatcher can be a pain. In Wood's *The Secret Life of Hilary Thorne*, Hilary is a voracious reader who has book friends rather than real ones.

Eleven-year-old Cory lives with her father after a divorce, goes to a private school, and does not make friends easily. Her one friend is a girl in her apartment building who also goes to her school. Rachel is always concocting pranks in school like spreading the word that Cory has been called to the principal's office because she left a love note on the window of his car. In fact Cory was called to the office to pick up the lunch she had left at home. Fisher's title reflects Cory's response: *"Rachel Vellars, How Could You?"*

Fourth grader Cybil is the object of the affections of both Simon and Tony in *The Cybil War* by Byars. When 4-year-old Ella comes into 11-year-old Amy's life, she becomes less selfish in Cleaver's *Sugar Blue*.

Fifth grader Cam Jansen has a photographic memory so she is called "The Camera" or "Cam" for short, and is described on pages 3 and 4 of Adler's *Cam Jansen and the Mystery of the Dinosaur Bones*. During a field trip to a museum, Cam notices that several bones are missing from the Ceolophysis's tail and proceeds to solve the mystery. Other books about Cam are listed in Chapter 10 in a section called INTRODUCING MYSTERIES. How would you like to be a fifth grader and have your look-alike sister promoted to your class? That's what happened to Mills's *The One and Only Cynthia Jane Thornton*. *Isabelle the Itch* and *Isabelle Shows Her Stuff* by Greene are about a fifth grader who is exceptionally lively. In the first book Isabelle takes over her brother's paper route.

In Lowry's *The One Hundredth Thing About Caroline*, 11-year-old

Caroline and her 13-year-old brother J. P. think that the man who is dating their mother wants to kill them when they see the letter that says "Eliminate the kids." Caroline's best friend Stacy wants to be an investigative reporter and Caroline wants to be a paleontologist and has a famous museum friend. Mom says that the one hundredth thing about Caroline "is that sometimes you're completely incomprehensible." *Switcharound* is the sequel. Caroline and J. P. go to visit their father, stepmother and 6-month-old twins for the summer. Eleven-year-old Dorrie's parents have triplets, Dierdre, Randolph, and Raymond, in *Dorrie's Book* by Sachs.

MacLachlan's *The Facts and Fictions of Minna Pratt* is about 11-year-old Melinda (Minna), who has a psychologist for a father and a writer for a mother. During her cello lessons, Minna plays with a chamber group and becomes friends with Lucas Ellerby who plays the viola. Minna likes Lucas's parents because their house is clean and orderly. Lucas likes Minna's family because they are lively and real. Lucas says if he were an animal, he would like to be a frog; Minna would like to be a ferret; and Twig, the Ellerby's housekeeper, would like to be a penguin. Ask students to write in their journals what animal they would like to be or ask the question in a booktalk. Margaret, in Dragonwagon's *Margaret Ziegler is Horse-Crazy,* dreams of getting a horse but never imagines it to be old and fat.

Eleven-year-old Lily, her 13-year-old brother Paul, and their parents are on the Greek island of Thasos while Father is finishing a book on the Children's Crusade in Fox's *Lily and the Lost Boy.* Paul and Lily are unusually close until a reckless and scruffy boy named Jack takes up Paul's time. However, when Jack causes the death of a Greek boy, it is Lily who helps him.

Showell's *Cecelia and the Blue Mountain Boy* is about music and the mountains. In Branscum's *Johnny May,* an 11-year-old girl lives in the Arkansas hills with her grandparents. Johnny May has read *Bluebeard* and thinks Mr. Berry has killed his wife. Now no one would believe that she had seen well-liked Homer Ragland kill Tom Satterfield in Huckleberry Hollow. Did the murder really happen? If so, what is Johnny May going to do about it? Growing up is the theme of Branscum's *The Adventures of Johnny May.* Lenski's Newbery Medal winner, *Strawberry Girl,* about Birdie Boyer and her family in backwoods Florida, has been reissued.

Two sixth grade girls have trouble with new girls. Erica in Klein's *Hating Alison Ashley* is an A student and is resentful when Alison comes to her sixth grade. Ashley is not only just as smart as she is but pretty and exquisitely dressed as well. In Shura's *Don't Call Me Toad,* 11-year-old Janie Potter is nicknamed "Toad" by the new girl, Dinah Dobbins. Learn how Janie gets her nickname in Chapter 1.

Twelve-year-old *Tallahassee Higgins* by Hahn is left by her mother with an aunt and uncle whom she has never met while her mother goes to Hollywood to become a star. Liz promises to write and to send for Tallahassee but she worries that Liz won't. Tally has trouble with her unusual name, given because she was born in Tallahassee, Florida. Tally learns about her mother's youth and the person who might be her father from the daughter of her mother's childhood friend and from a photo album. In Clymer's *My Mother Is the Smartest Woman in the World*, 13-year-old Kathleen Rowan decides that her mother has better ideas than the current mayor so she helps her mother run for mayor. Thirteen-year-old Lillian (Beanpole) is five feet six inches tall and has three wishes: to have a bra, to dance with a boy, and to become a member of the Pom Squad in Park's *Beanpole*. Fourteen-year-old Enid Irene Crowley wishes she had another name, so when she is baby-sitting she calls herself Cynthia and understands why 4-year-old Joshua Warwick Cameron IV wants to be called Tom Terrific in Lowry's *Taking Care of Terrific*. Fifteen-year-old Izzy, in Voigt's *Izzy, Willy-Nilly*, loses a leg in an automobile accident in which the driver has been drinking. Geraldine, nicknamed *Jellybean* in a book by Duder, has a mother who plays the cello professionally, and Jellybean meets a man she thinks is her father. Sixteen-year-old Japanese American Kim is also known as Kimi Yogushi in Irwin's *Kim/Kimi*.

How would you feel if you woke up in the hospital and learned that your life had been saved by transferring your neuron memory to the brain of a female chimpanzee? That's what happened to the main character in Dickinson's *Eva*.

Several books with the names of girls in the title are about girls with handicaps or with someone in the family who is handicapped. Shyer's *Welcome Home, Jellybean* is about how Neil feels when his 13-year-old retarded sister returns home to live. *M.E. and Morton* by Cassedy is also about a brother and sister. M.E. is short for Mary Etta, whose younger brother Morton is retarded. M.E. is a year younger than the other girls in her class at a private school and has no friends in her neighborhood. When a new girl, Polly, moves in, M.E. pretends she doesn't know Morton and even makes fun of him. M.E. can't understand why Polly becomes friends with her brother as well as with her. Howard's *Edith Herself* takes place in rural America in the 1890s when medication for and understanding of epilepsy were not common. Edith's problems include adjusting to her mother's death; moving in with her sister and her family, which includes a grandmother; as well as dealing with the blackness that sometimes creeps into her head. Greenwald's 11-year-old heroine in *Will the Real Gertrude Hollings Please Stand Up?* has dyslexia. Eleven-year-old Jenna has to spend time in the hospital in therapy and under medication because of rheumatoid arthritis in *Angie and Me* by Jones. Jenna's roommate Angie dies in the story. In Gorman's *Chelsey and the Green-haired Kid*, 13-year-old Chelsey is a paraplegic and her friend Jack has green hair. When she witnesses a murder at a basketball game, Chelsey becomes involved in hunting down the killers.

Each chapter in Hall's *In Trouble Again, Zelda Hammersmith?* can be read on its own. In one of them, the fourth grader plans an elaborate hoax to divert attention from the F on her report card. The worst day in Joshua Bates's life is the first day of school, when he has to repeat third grade. It is the worst day in his teacher's life also because Mrs. Goodwin's husband has moved out of the house. When Joshua becomes the only person in his third grade class to turn 11, Mrs. Goodwin tutors him at her home, while allowing him to help others in math and social studies, in which he already knows the answers. By the end of Shreve's *The Flunking of Joshua Bates*, readers learn whether or not Joshua passes his test so he can move on to fourth grade during that school year.

Ten-year-old Toby from Talbert's *Toby* has parents who are illiterate and a mother who became brain damaged as a teenager. The question posed is: Can the Thurston family stay together even though a local minister and a neighbor want to put Toby in a foster home because of their perception that the Thurstons are unfit parents?

Two books are about abuse. In *Don't Hurt Laurie!* by Roberts, 11-year-old Laurie and her mother Annabelle move frequently because people become too suspicious of the broken bones, cuts, and burns Laurie gets. *Cracker Jackson* goes to great lengths to keep Alma, his ex baby-sitter, from being abused by her husband, in a book by Byars.

In Cole's *The Goats*, two unpopular children on the brink of puberty are stripped of their clothing and left on Goat Island as a prank. However, rather than have the campers return in the morning to laugh at them, Laura and Howie swim ashore and hide.

Kaye has written several novels in the "sisters series" about the girls in the Gray family that are popular with intermediate and middle school students. Eleven-year-old *Phoebe* returns from summer camp to find that much has changed while she was gone. Her mother is busy getting ready to go back to teaching high school English and her friends are talking about bras, periods, and boys. The one place where Phoebe feels comfortable is the public library, where she becomes a volunteer. Then one of the mothers wants to ban all the books written by Betsy Drake, a writer similar to Judy Blume. Although Phoebe personally is not interested in those subjects written about by Betsy Drake, she goes to the city council to defend the books with the help of her cause-oriented sister, Lydia. Twelve-year-old *Daphne*, a shy poetess, is about to enter junior high and her two older sisters give her advice. Cassie signs her up for the pep club and Lydia signs her up to run for vice president of the seventh grade class. All shy Daphne wants is to join the Creative Writing Club but she doesn't have time because of the other two activities. Finally, as in the Robert Frost poem they are reading in English, Daphne has to make her choices. Thirteen-year-old *Cassie* is only interested in designer labels and boys. Lydia, the sister who is into causes, tells her about conspicuous consumption, but Cassie doesn't understand what that means. A new girl, Dana, whose parents are always away on business trips, lives in a big house with servants and shoplifts to get attention. Cassie is unknowingly drawn into Dana's web. Fourteen-year-old *Lydia*, daughter of a small-town newspaper editor and champion of causes, starts an alternative newspaper at her junior high school. Some of the issues she tackles are cafeteria food and girls on the football team. Lydia, unlike Cassie, has no time for boys, but a hint at the end of the story suggests a possible change in the wind. In Kaye's *A Friend Like Phoebe*, Phoebe hopes to be chosen for a television interview but her best friend is chosen instead. Phoebe has to decide what friendship means when Jessica asks for her help.

Hurwitz has written several books about members of the Sossi family—Aldo, Karen, and Elaine. Karen has the misfortune to be the middle child between a pair of paragons. Karen is 13 in *Tough-Luck Karen* with Aldo in the fifth grade and Elaine in the ninth grade. Karen blames her problems on breaking three chain letters sent to her by former classmates, but by the end of the book she decides she is responsible for her own actions. Karen's main interests are baby-sitting and cooking, but her parents ban both until Karen finishes her science project. Eventually, Karen combines her love of making bread with the discovery of a role for yeast in the process of making an excellent science presentation. Another member of the family is the 15-year-old main character in *Hurricane Elaine*. Elaine has a crush on her French teacher, Monsieur DuBois, and is devastated when she finds out he is married and has a child. She even breaks her first date with Scott to baby-sit with Monsieur DuBois's niece. Elaine gets her ears pierced, and generally has typical ninth grade problems with parents, friends, and siblings. Learn about Elaine's nickname on page 4. Books about Aldo include: *Aldo Applesauce*; *Aldo Ice Cream*; and *Much Ado About Aldo*. In the first book Aldo meets DeDe from *DeDe Takes Charge* and she is responsible for spilling his lunch so he gets the nickname "Aldo Applesauce." Check pages 32–35 for details. Also learn why DeDe wears a moustache on pages 118–20. Nine-year-old Aldo spends his summer vacation in the second book. Check pages 26–27 for references to ice cream. In *Much Ado About Aldo*, 8-year-old Aldo becomes a vegetarian while studying the food chain because he learns that the crickets in school are eaten by chameleons.

Third grader Jonah has to prove he is responsible before he can have a pet of his own in Honeycutt's *The All New Jonah Twist*. Granville Jones, the bully, threatens to kill Jonah with his bare hands. Third grader Lucas Cott is smart but clowns around, so he is chosen to be the clown in the class play when he would rather be the ringmaster in Hurwitz's *Class Clown*. Hurwitz's *The Adventures of Ali Baba Bernstein* is about a third grader named David Bernstein who changes his name to Ali Baba when he learns that there are 17 people with the same name as his in the Manhattan phone book. What would happen if he invited them to his ninth birthday party? Students will have to read the book to find out. Romance enters third grade in Kline's *What's the Matter with Herbie Jones?* Herbie Jones's friend Ray is worried when Herbie begins to enjoy dancing in P.E. and working in the library with Annabelle. The romance begins when Herbie takes get well cards from his class to Annabelle, who has the chicken pox. She listens to him read a poem he wrote, but doesn't know who is reading it because she has her head covered with a sheet so no one can see her. Other books about Herbie are: *Herbie Jones*; *Herbie Jones and the Class*

Gift; Herbie Jones and the Monster Ball; and *Herbie Jones and the Hamburger Head*. In the second book Herbie and a friend manage to bungle giving their teacher a going away gift. In the third book, Herbie learns to talk to a ball and tell it his troubles, a technique he learns from his uncle. In the last book, Herbie foils a bank robbery.

What's the matter with Matthew in Gaeddert's *Your Former Friend, Matthew?* Gail and Matthew have been friends for years and the last day of school they plan their science fair project together. However, when they return to school, Matthew ignores Gail in favor of the new male friends he has made while summer camping. Gail is especially hurt when her younger brother Benji gets to go to a football game with her dad, Matthew, and Matthew's father. Finally, Gail makes friends with Joyce, whose science fair project is sure to interest students, and with Amanda, who lives in Gail's apartment and who has recently lost her mother. After making Matthew look bad in public, Gail lets him have part of her science fair project when his friends ditch him.

Gilson is also a popular writer. *Hobie Hanson, You're Weird* is the third book about that hero. Nine-year-old Hobie's best friend goes off to computer camp so he is stuck with bossy Molly, a contestant in a preteen pageant. Molly and Hobie are paired to conduct interviews for a time capsule prepared by the Junior Chamber of Commerce for Stockton's 200th birthday. A picture of Molly kissing Hobie on the cheek at the Fourth of July pie-eating contest appears in the paper and mortifies Hobie. Other books in which Hobie appears are: *Thirteen Ways to Sink a Sub*; *Four-B Goes Wild*; *Double Dog Dare*; and *Hobie Hanson: Greatest Hero of the Mall*. Program #2 of the educational television series *Books from Cover to Cover* is *4-B Goes Wild*. In Gilson's *Hello, My Name is Scrambled Eggs*, Harvey wants to Americanize a Vietnamese boy named Tuan, whose family is being sponsored by Harvey's church. Harvey tries to change 12-year-old Tuan Nguyen's name to Tom Win. For a pronunciation and information about the incident, check pages 36–38. The family teaches vocabulary by placing name tags on items in the kitchen like "Hello my name is Jelly," but they stifle the urge to place a name tag on the scrambled eggs. Harvey Trumble also appears as a sixth grader in *Harvey the Beer Can King*. Harvey enters the newspaper's "Superkid contest" and brags about himself. Check pages 94–102, Chapter 10 for "The Boy Who Would Be King," to describe the title of the book. Contestants have to write a one-page essay describing their hobby, so teachers could have the class write a similar essay. The newspaper picks finalists and the class votes on them. Have students predict the outcome of the election.

Sometimes titles of books do not mention the character by name but rather by description. Ten-year-old Howard knows what it is like to be *The Kid in the Red Jacket* when he moves to another state in Park's book. *The Kid in the Red Jacket* is Program #8 of the educational television series *Books from Cover to Cover*, which is designed to motivate third and fourth graders to read.

Germy Blew It and *Germy Blew It Again* by Jones are books about Jeremy

Bluett who gets his nickname because he is always "blowing it." In the first book Germy tries to organize a city wide gum-chewing contest so he can get himself on television. In the second book, Germy tries to make money by raising gerbils. Anyone who has had plans go awry can identify with this fifth grader.

In *Kevin Corbett Eats Flies* by Hermes, fifth grader Kevin Corbett moves so much that he has to attract attention and establish himself by activities like eating flies at five cents each. Kevin meets his match when the new girl challenges him to chew and eat a goldfish. Kevin and Bailey become friends and plan a meal so Pop can meet their teacher, Miss Holt, fall in love with her, and not want to move again. In Robinson's *My Brother Louis Measures Worms*, 11-year-old Mary Elizabeth tells about how her brother keeps worms in a coffee can and how Aunt Rhoda makes coffee for a family reunion. Rockwell's *How to Eat Fried Worms* is about a boy who has to eat worms to win a bet.

Steiner's *Oliver Dibbs and the Dinosaur Cause* is about a fifth grader who always has wonderful ideas. In January, when the class doesn't know what to study next, they vote on Ollie's idea to study dinosaurs. Eventually the project gets so big that Ollie's class spearheads a campaign to make the stegosaurus the state fossil of Colorado. Some readers may already know Ollie from his campaign to save the prairie dogs in *Oliver Dibbs to the Rescue!*

Conford's *Lenny Kandell, Smart Aleck* wants to be a comedian so he tries out jokes on his friend Artie. Pair Conford's book with Hurwitz's *Class Clown*, described earlier. Simon's *Einstein Anderson, Science Sleuth* is always telling jokes to his friends. The sixth grader's real name is Adam, but he was given his nickname by his kindergarten teacher, Ms. Moore, when he used cobalt chloride to test for humidity in the air. For a description of this science sleuth, check pages 3, 4, and 7. Other books in the series include: *Einstein Anderson Tells a Comet's Tale*; *Einstein Anderson Lights Up the Sky*; *Einstein Anderson Goes to Bat*; and *Einstein Anderson Sees Through the Invisible Man*. Each of the books about this hero has 10 chapters, each one a science puzzle with answers at the end of the chapter. Simon is also the author of *Chip Rogers, Computer Whiz*. Wouldn't it be fun if Einstein Anderson and Encyclopedia Brown [CU 134–36] could meet? Encyclopedia Brown gets his name because he can remember so much and can solve mysteries by his wits. For a list of books about Encyclopedia Brown, check the section of Chapter 10 called INTRODUCING MYSTERIES. Have students prepare dialogue for a telephone conversation between Einstein Anderson and Encyclopedia Brown.

Clifford's *Harvey's Marvelous Monkey Mystery* and *Harvey's Horrible Snake Disaster* are about Harvey Wilson and his cousins. The first book is about a monkey and the second about a hognose snake.

Twelve-year-old Pip and his 10-year-old sister Emma spend the summer with their grandmother in rural Vermont in Bacon's *Pip and Emma*. Pip becomes ill with meningitis.

In *The Burning Questions of Bingo Brown*, Byars tells of 12-year-old Bingo, who was named by the doctor who delivered him. Some questions that bother him are: What does their teacher, Mr. Markham, think about when he closes his eyes? What should he do about being in love with two girls at one time? Has there ever been a successful writer named Bingo? Has there ever been a successful writer with freckles? When will the class bully realize that his new home is next door to Bingo Brown's? Students may wish to create burning questions of their own.

Eleven-year-old TJ and his younger brother Billy (the Moondance Kid) have been adopted and hope that Mop, another orphan, will also be adopted in *Me, Mop, and the Moondance Kid* by Myers. Eleven-year-old James has to change his name to Jimmy Jo when his family's country music group becomes successful in Paterson's *Come Sing, Jimmy Jo*, Program #10 of the instructional television series, *More Books from Cover to Cover* for fifth graders. Besides having his name changed, James learns something that may change his whole identity. *Park's Quest* is another book by Paterson. Park's quest is to find out something about his father, Parkington Waddell Broughton IV. Park doesn't know anything about his father except that he was killed in the Vietnam War. Finally Park's mother allows him to visit his father's family, where he learns the unhappy circumstances behind his father's death. Naturally, to know what Park found out, you must read the book. Information about Smith's *Mostly Michael* comes from Michael's own diary during the year he was 11.

Eleven-year-old Mitchell Dartmouth's hobby is entering sweepstakes. He wins the Dazzle-Rama Sweepstakes for a detergent company and appears on the television show "Have a Good Day" in Sharmat's *Rich Mitch*. Then Mitch begins to get letters asking him for contributions, and gives money to Dementia Lansdorf who owns 18 Doberman pinschers. Mitch gets Dementia on the television show "Isn't It Fantastic." The show is a disaster but puts Dementia in contact with Jed Buchanan. *Rich Mitch* is program #1 of the educational television series *Books from Cover to Cover.* Twelve-year-old Alex Frankovich, who appears in *Skinnybones* and *Almost Starring Skinnybones* by Park, also wins a contest and stars in a cat food commercial. Because he has to pose as a boy half his age, it isn't exactly the kind of fame and recognition Alex wants.

Thirteen-year-old Timothy Martin is lost in the Adirondack wilderness for three weeks in Blackwood's *Wild Timothy*. Pudgy, introverted Timothy puts his knowledge of the wilderness, gleaned from his reading, to good use.

How would you like to know that you could get away with anything and never have to suffer the consequences? What if someone else was there to receive any spankings you might deserve? That is what happens in the life of Prince Brat in Fleischman's *The Whipping Boy*. Jemmy is the official person who receives all the punishments that should go to Prince Brat because it is against the law to spank, thrash, or whack the heir to the throne. A sound filmstrip of this Newbery winner is also available. *The Whipping Boy* is also Program #15 of the educational television series, *More Books from Cover to Cover.*

Peck's *Soup* reminds readers of *Tom Sawyer* (Twain) and Tom Dennis in

The Great Brain (Fitzgerald) [CU 27]. Wouldn't it be fun to have these characters converse with each other? Projects could include role playing with conversations among these characters or written comparisons of those boys. Books by Peck about Soup and Rob include: *Soup*; *Soup and Me*; *Soup for President*; *Soup's Drum*; *Soup on Wheels*; *Soup in the Saddle*; *Soup's Goat*; *Soup on Ice*; *Soup's Uncle*; and *Soup on Fire*. Soup is Luther Wesley Vinson and his pal is Rob Peck. Soup thinks up the wild schemes and Rob goes along with him, even though he often has to do most of the work or take the most risk. Trouble finds them easily. The boys live in rural Vermont during the Depression. In *Soup*, Rob ties up his Aunt Carrie using Janice Riker's methods but his aunt is not amused. In *Soup and Me*, the boys don't have enough money to buy their teacher a present, so they leave her a note that they will ring the courthouse bells at 5 PM for her because they know she likes bells. However, they get caught up in the deserted bell tower when the ladder falls down. Read pages 96–115, Chapter 7, "A Christmas Bell," aloud at Christmas time. In *Soup for President*, Rob has to decide between voting for his best pal, Soup, and the girl of his dreams, Norma Jean Bissell. Soup's party, representing the boys, is called the Apes and Norma Jean's party is the Amazons. The U.S. election that year is between FDR and Alf Landon and Republican Vermont supports Alf. The outcome of the class election is a surprise to Rob, even though the class is evenly split between boys and girls. Then Rob realizes what accounts for Soup's winning. In *Soup's Drum*, Miss Boland organizes a band because an Italian french horn player, Romeo Farina, is coming to town. In the band Rob carries the drum and Soup gets to play it. In *Soup on Wheels*, Miss Boland's scheme is to have a Vermont Mardi Gras in June with prizes for the most unusual costume. Everyone in town enters, and Soup and Rob plan to be Margaret the mule until they see the mule costume Miss Boland and Mr. Jubert have. The boys paint stripes on their costume to make it a zebra and then add roller skates because Rob has a sore ankle. See the picture on page 92 before disaster strikes. Also in *Soup on Wheels*, Rob's girlfriend Norma Jean likes the new boy in school, Beverly, who looks like a sissy but, when attacked, fights Eddy Tacker to become the second toughest kid in school—after Janice Riker. In *Soup in the Saddle*, there is going to be a celebration in honor of their teacher, Miss Kelley. but the day may be ruined because the speaker, Dr. Uppit, wants to do away with one-room schools. How would painting spots on themselves help their cause? How can Miss Boland, the county nurse, help? In *Soup's Goat*, Miss Boland plans a goat race in honor of Dr. Frank Sumatra, the world famous South Seas explorer. Five students are chosen to drive the goat carts and Soup, Rob, and Janice Riker are three of them. Soup's goat Orbit is mean, but his twin Nesbit is calm. Because Nesbit has a calming effect on Orbit, Soup plans a joint venture. The boys build their cart from a baby buggy and laundry cart. Soup enlists the help of his prissy cousin Sexton Dilly, who knows lots of swear words. Check page 4 for a description of Soup in a paragraph that ends ". . . so I usually allowed him to be the boss. There is no sense in becoming his enemy. Because being Soup's pal is trouble enough." Also check page 27, "Work, I had observed, was not Luther Wesley Vinson's favorite pastime. Not that Soup was afraid of a dose of work. If *I* was doing it, he'd watch for hours." In *Soup on Ice,* the regular Santa can't help out so the boys talk Stanley Dubinsky (better known as Slosh, the owner of Slosh's Hot-Time Pool Parlor) to play the part. How they fly through the air and short the Christmas lights is part of the excitement. In the first chapter of *Soup on Fire,* Soup talks Rob into climbing the shaky old water tower to get away from Janice Riker. When the boys swim nude in the tower water, Janice swipes their clothes and the sheriff demands that they come down. The fire of the title is in a smelly wagon full of hay with Rob and Soup on it that goes wild the same day the radio hero Fearless Ferguson and Bishop Zion Zeal and the Golden Prophets of Eternal Glory come to town. Anyone who enjoys reading about Soup and Rob would enjoy Fitzgerald's books about Tom Dennis, another boy from the past, in: *The Great Brain*; *More Adventures of the Great Brain*; *The Great Brain Reforms*; *The Great Brain at the Academy*; *The Return of the Great Brain*; and *The Great Brain Does It Again.*

Haseley's *The Scared One* is an Indian boy who is timid and often teased. When he goes off to find the family goat, he is caught in a thunderstorm and wakes up to see a large injured bird who can't fly. Scared One saves the bird from Old Wolf, who collects stuffed animal heads, and from the other boys and tells the story of his rite of passage.

Aiken's new book is part of a series that includes: *The Wolves of Willoughby Chase*; *Black Hearts in Battersea*; *Nightbirds on Nantucket*; *Cuckoo Tree*; and *Stolen Lake.* In *Dido and Pa,* Dido Twite's father is plotting to do away with King Richard. Dido's friend Simon is now the Duke of Battersea. The healing powers of music are a theme in this book. All fans of Aiken's gothic mysteries will love this one.

Several books with human names in the title are fantasy, science fiction, time travel, or a combination of all of them. Sargent's *Weird Henry Berg* doesn't know that his pet lizard, Millie, is a baby dragon. Several books discussed in a section of chapter 1 called TIME TRAVEL: A BOOKTALK are: Senn's *The Double Disappearance of Walter Fozbek*; Sleator's *The Green Futures of Tycho*; and Curry's *Me, Myself and I: A Tale of Time Travel*; Greer's *Max and Me and the Time Machine*; Cresswell's *The Secret World of Polly Flint*; and Wiseman's *Jeremy Visick.*

In *The Lives of Christopher Chant* by Jones, Christopher has nine lives and is destined to become the next Chrestomanci, watch over the world's magic, and prevent it from misuse. At Chrestomanci Castle, Christopher learns that his travels for his uncle have been for illegal purposes and that Uncle Ralph is part of the evil he has to combat.

Some books do not have the name of one human person in the title, but have several names or the name of a group. There are several books for intermediate or middle school readers that fit this pattern. *The Homeward Bounders* by Jones are a group of children who are trying to escape THEM and get home. Twelve-year-old Jamie is the main character. Jeremy from Adler's *The Magic of the Glits* is also 12, and his story is described earlier. The Glits are described on pages 24–25. Holman's *The Wild Children* are a gang of children who are trying to survive alone during the Bolshevik Revolution in Russia. The main character is a boy whose parents are arrested in the middle of the night, and he is afraid he will be put in an orphanage. There are several books about Baker Street Irregulars in a series by Newman. The Irregulars are children who do odd jobs for Sherlock Holmes and include Andrew Tillett, Sara Wiggins, and Peter Wyatt of Scotland Yard. The newest book in the series is *The Case of the Watching Boy*. Peter Wyatt is now Andrew's stepfather. In this book, Andrew, Sara, and Markham solve a case involving deception, kidnapping, and murder. Other books in this series are described in Chapter 10 in INTRODUCING MYSTERIES. Pinkwater's books about the Snarkout Boys include a detective who disguises himself as Sherlock Holmes. Books in the series include *The Snarkout Boys and the Avocado of Death* and *The Snarkout Boys and the Baconburg Horror*. Walter Galt, Winston Bongo, and Rat (a girl with green-tinted hair) are masters in the art of "snarking out." A teacher or librarian wouldn't give away what that means but the information can be found in the book. One question that can be asked to pique interest is, "Can an avocado save the Earth from alien invaders?" *The Scorpions* are a gang in Harlem in the Newbery Honor Book by Myers. Twelve-year-old Jamal Hicks takes the place of his brother, who is in prison, as leader of the Scorpions. Avi's *The S.O.R. Losers* are 11 seventh grade students who are not interested in sports but are placed on a soccer team at South Orange River Middle School.

The Not-Just-Anybody Family by Byars is one of several about the unusual Blossom family. Members include Mother, Vicki Blossom, a trick rider who performs with the Wrangler Riders between events at rodeos; her late husband, Cotton Blossom, a World's Champion Single Steer Roper, who was killed by a steer; Pap, Vicki's father-in-law, a 72-year-old retired rodeo clown; Maggie, who is practicing to join the Wranglers; Vern, who wants a friend and finds one; and Junior, who invents things. In the first book Junior tries to fly off the barn roof and goes to the hospital with broken legs from his fall and meets Ralphie who has only one leg. Maggie helps Vern break into jail to be with Pap, and Vicki reads about all of them in the newspaper while she is on the rodeo circuit. In *The Blossoms and the Green Phantom*, Pap and his dog, Mud, fall into a dumpster while looking for empty pop cans and rescue an abandoned puppy they call Dump. Junior's invention, the Green Phantom, is successful the second time around. Check page 39 for a "Blossom Promise." In *The Blossoms Meet the Vulture Lady*, Junior invents a coyote cage to trap a coyote for a $100 reward. When the trap door shuts on Junior, he is found by Mad Mary who takes him home to her cave. Descriptions of Mad Mary appear on pages 21–22, 49, and 68. Check chapter 27, called "Baby Vultures." In *A Blossom Promise*, Maggie has the best and worst day of her life when she performs for the first time as one of the Wranglers on the rodeo circuit and discovers that her mother has a boyfriend. Maggie makes a "Blossom Promise" to herself and to Ralphie on page 141. A good description of Dump, the dog who is bitten by a snake, appears on page 66. Vern and his friend, Michael, build a raft and take it out on the Snake River which is swollen by floods. Pap throws his lariat out to catch them and suffers a heart attack. Ask students to explain the understatement found on page 98 of *The Not-Just-Anybody Family* in the quote "'We Blossoms,' Maggie said proudly, 'have never been just anybody.'" *The Not-Just-Anybody Family* is program #11 of the educational television series *More Books from Cover to Cover*. These books provide excellent character descriptions for models in writing classes.

Adult men are part of the title in several books for intermediate and middle school students. Clifford's *The Man Who Sang in the Dark* is Gideon Brown, a blind man of whom 10-year-old Leah is frightened. In Howker's *Isaac Campion*, a 96-year-old man reminisces about the death of his brother Dan in late 19th-century England. Magorian's *Good Night, Mr. Tom* is about a reclusive widower from an English village who takes in a refugee during World War II. Eight-year-old William has been abused and gradually begins to trust Mr. Tom. Then his mother wants him back. Gardiner's *Stone Fox* is an Indian who has never lost a dog sled race. Willie, who needs the $500 prize to save his grandfather's farm, races against him. Who will win the race? *Stone Fox* is program #5 of the instructional television series *More Books from Cover to Cover*. In Kherdian's *A Song for Uncle Harry*, 12-year-old Pet's Uncle Harry is an Armenian immigrant who was disabled in World War I. Hartling's *Crutches* is about a one-legged ex-German soldier from World War II. Twelve-year-old Thomas meets *Crutches* in Vienna and the story is told from Thomas's point of view. *Crutches* won a Batchelder Award for excellence in a foreign translation. In Garrigue's *The Eternal Spring of Mr. Ito*, Sara lives with an aunt and uncle in Vancouver during World War II. Mr. Ito, the gardener, teaches Sara to grow a bonsai tree but when Canadians of Japanese descent begin to be taken away to camps, Mr. Ito disappears. Readers learn what happens when Sara accidentally discovers his hiding place. Morgan in Howe's *Morgan's Zoo* is the keeper at the Chelsea Park Zoo which is often called Morgan's Zoo. When fewer and fewer people come to the zoo, the director and the mayor decide that it must close. However, the 11-year-old twins, Allison and Andrew Potter, don't want it to close. An English boy, James, has recently moved and is bored until he meets an older neighbor, in Walsh's *Gaffer Samson's Luck*. Gaffer gives James his bike and sends him in search of the "luck" that he buried 70 years ago. Service's narrative poem "The Cremation of Sam McGee" is in picture book format. Set in the Yukon, it is about a Tennessee prospector during the Gold Rush.

Some books for primary students can be introduced by telling about the men in the title. *Old Henry* by Blos is about a man whose neighbors do not like his yard full of junk, but miss and appreciate him after he leaves. *Captain*

Snap and the Children of Vinegar Street by Schotter is about a hermit. Small's *Paper John* has always been appreciated by everyone in his neighborhood for his paper gifts. This unusual man lives in a paper house. Pearson's *The Storekeeper* is a picture book. Craven's *What the Mailman Brought* is about a duck mailman who brings presents to William while he is home from school for a week. In Thiele's *Farmer Schulz's Ducks*, the Australian farmer figures out how to get his ducks safely across a busy highway on their daily trip to the river. Music is included in Parkinson's *The Farmer in the Dell*. In Hawthorne's *King Midas and the Golden Touch*, the king is granted his wish but it brings him nothing but trouble in this newly illustrated picture book of the famous Greek myth. *Sir Cedric* by Gerrard rescues Matilda from evil Black Ned on Walter, his faithful steed. When 67-year-old *Mr. Bunion* puts on his old school cap, he changes into a small boy in a book by Ward. Berger's *Grandfather Twilight* lives among the trees and when day is done, closes his book, combs his beard, puts on his jacket, and places a pearl (the moon) in the sky. *Hey, Al* by Yorinks, with illustrations by Egielski, is a Caldecott Medal winner. Al is a janitor and he and his dog, Eddie, live in a little room. When Eddie and Al are invited to go to an island paradise inhabited by exotic birds, they find that paradise isn't what it seems. *The Song and Dance Man* by Ackerman is a Caldecott Medal winner, illustrated by Gammell. The ex-vaudeville dancer is the children's grandfather who shares his act with them in their attic. Schwartz's *Bea and Mr. Jones* is a featured book on the television program *Reading Rainbow. Mr. Murphy's Marvelous Invention* by Christelow is about a housekeeping machine Mr. Murphy makes for his wife's birthday. Unfortunately, everything gets mixed up: the soup smells like soap; the laundry is in the cooking pots; and dinner is hanging on the washline. *The Shadowmaker* by Hansen replaces old shadows with new ones or trade-ins. Mufaro has two daughters, a selfish one and a kind and generous one, in Steptoe's *Mufaro's Beautiful Daughters,* an African folk tale. *Like Jake and Me* by Jukes is a Newbery Honor Book and a film and video about a boy who gets to know his stepfather, Jake. Lucky Kidd watches her father ride a rodeo bull called White Dynamite in Martin and Archambault's *White Dynamite and Curley Kidd.*

Several easy books include the names of adult women in the title. Boyd's *The Not-so-Wicked Stepmother* is about Hessie, who has heard that stepmothers are mean, terrible people. She is apprehensive when she has to spend the summer with her father and stepmother, but she is pleasantly surprised. In Russo's *Why Do Grown-Ups Have All the Fun?*, Hannah thinks her parents do exciting things after she goes to bed. One night when she can't sleep, Hannah checks on them several times, only to find out that they are doing mundane things like folding laundry, reading, or working crossword puzzles. In *Oma and Bobo* by Schwartz, Alice finally gets a dog, and names him Bobo. However, her grandmother, Oma, is not sold on the idea of a dog. This is the story about how Bobo wins Oma over while Alice is busy. *My Grandma Leonie* by Le Tord is about the death of a live-in grandmother. Seven-year-old Susie and her family gather at Grandma's funeral in *Saying Goodbye to Grandma* by Thomas. At first Marianne remembers only her grandmother's death and funeral in Egger's *Marianne's Grandmother.* Then she recalls all their good experiences together and the healing process begins. *Aunt Lulu* by Pinkwater is a librarian who carries books on a dog sled to gold miners in Alaska. Then Aunt Lulu moves to New Jersey. Ask students to guess what kinds of uses Aunt Lulu will have for her 14 dogs and dog sled in New Jersey. In Howard's *The Train to Lulu's*, Aunt Lulu is the person Beppy and Babs are going to visit on their trip from Boston to Baltimore in the 1930s. *My Teacher Sleeps in School* by Weiss is about primary children who believe that their teacher lives at school. After a field trip to her home, the children learn otherwise. Allard's favorite teacher appears in *Miss Nelson Is Missing, Miss Nelson Is Back,* and *Miss Nelson Has a Field Day.* The most unpopular substitute teacher is Viola Swamp, who takes Miss Nelson's place. Bulla's *The Stubborn Old Woman* won't leave her farm although her house is fast crumbling into the river below. Finally the stubborn old woman meets her match in a stubborn little girl. *The Little Old Lady Who Was Not Afraid of Anything,* by Williams, is about a woman who is not afraid even when spooky objects follow her through the woods. How would you like to be *Friends of Emily Culpepper?* Coleridge's Emily is plump, has white hair in a bun, wears glasses, and looks harmless. However, Emily makes the milkman small enough to fit in a jam jar, the postman in a coffee jar, and the plumber in a pickle jar. Emily lets them out each day to eat, visit, and play. Do you still want to be friends with Emily Culpepper? In *Love from Aunt Betty* by Parker, Aunt Betty sends an unusual chocolate cake recipe to Charlie. Three books by Brandenberg are: *Aunt Nina and Her Nephews and Nieces*; *Aunt Nina's Visit*; and *Aunt Nina, Good Night.* Tina, a first grader, can't wait to show her basal reader to her mother but mom keeps making excuses not to look at it until they finally talk about the pictures in Stanek's *My Mom Can't Read.* Mom gets a tutor and the first note Tina ever writes is the first note her mom ever reads. "Dear Mom. I love you. Tina." Rosie Jones is a rancher in Gerrard's *Rosie and the Rustlers.*

Several books for primary students have titles which include the names of groups. *The Cut-Ups* and *The Cut-Ups Cut Loose* by Marshall are easy readers, and include Spud, Jo, and Mary Frances. Erlich's *Leo, Zack and Emmie* and *Leo, Zack and Emmie Together Again* are about second graders. There are several short stories in these easy reader books. Brandenberg's *Leo and Emily, Leo and Emily and the Dragon, Leo and Emily's Big Ideas,* and *Leo and Emily's Zoo* are also easy to read. *Commander Toad and the Space Pirates* is the newest easy reader by Yolen. Others are included in Chapter 6 of this book, "Sharing Easy Readers." Rylant's *The Relatives Came* is a picture book about carloads of relatives who come from Virginia for a visit. They eat, visit, and sleep everywhere imaginable, have a wonderful time, and then go home. Besides being a Caldecott Honor Book, the book has won several other accolades. Graham's *First There Was Frances* is about a family that has to move to the country when it expands to include over 16 others, including a cat, goats, and guinea pigs. Kuskin's *The Dallas Titans Get Ready for Bed* is a humorous picture book about what happens to a football team after the game is over. As the various team members undress at home and get ready for bed, readers realize many types of individuals make up a team and various types of gear are part of the game. In *The Philharmonic Gets Dressed*, also by Kuskin, 105 musicians prepare in different ways for a concert. Readers learn in Stanley's *The Conversation Club* that it takes listeners and talkers to make a conversation. There is always lots of excitement on Scotland's Isle of Struay when the boy cousins come to visit. The fourth book by Hedderwick is *Katie Morag and the Big Boy Cousins*. Others in the series are: *Katie Morag and the Tiresome Ted*; *Katie Morag and the Two Grandmothers*; and *Katie Morag Delivers the Mail*.

There are several picture books and easy readers about boys whose names appear in the title. One of the most famous is Sharmat's *Nate the Great*. One of the newest books in this series is *Nate the Great and the Boring Beach Bag*, in which the young detective in Sherlock Holmes clothing investigates the disappearance of Oliver's beach bag. Each book contains cases. Other easy readers in the series are included here in INTRODUCING MYSTERIES (Chapter 10).

In *Where's Julius?* by Burningham, Julius is too busy to join his parents for meals because he is pretending to have adventures, like crossing Russia in a sleigh. Daly's *Not So Fast, Songolo*, is about a South African boy, Malusi, and his grandmother, Gogo, who go off shopping for shoes. In Faulkner's *The Amazing Voyage of Jackie Grace*, Jackie steps into a Victorian-style bathtub which is seized by pirates. Jack stows away on a British warship during the Napoleonic Wars in Dupasquier's *Jack at Sea*. Gerstein's *Arnold and the Ducks* is about a boy who turns into a duck. What would happen if you turned into a person no larger than a mouse? That happens to George in Joyce's *George Shrinks*. Eight-year-old Earl swings with gorillas and plays jazz with an alley cat in Komaiko's *Earl's Too Cool for Me*. Burningham's *John Patrick Norman McHennessy—The Boy Who Was Always Late* has several unusual excuses for why he is late for school. Excuses include a lion, an alligator, and a tidal wave. Titch always has to wear hand-me-downs in *You'll Soon Grow into Them, Titch* by Hutchins. King's *Because of Bozo Brown* is a rhyming book about a giant boy who has a green tongue and rats living in his hair. Seven-year-old Hemi takes his 3-year-old sister, Rata, to school for the pet show because she meets the requirements of being alive as well as someone he looks after, in *Hemi's Pet* by De Hamel. Hemi wins a prize for having the most original pet. According to Oscar, an imaginary boy named Billy is really responsible for causing trouble in *Oscar Got the Blame* by Ross. Harry dangles a garter snake in a classmate's face and pins a boy to the ground and makes him say "I love girls" in Kline's *Horrible Harry in Room 2B*. In Sharmat's *Go to Sleep, Nicholas Joe*, little Nicholas does not want to go to sleep. Ira and Reggie are friends in *Ira Sleeps Over* and *Ira Says Goodbye*, by Waber. In the first book, Ira sleeps over at

Reggie's house for the first time and in the second book, Reggie is moving away. A Chinese boy faces discrimination during the Gold Rush in *Chang's Paper Pony* by Coerr, an easy reader. In Wood's *Elbert's Bad Word*, a bad word sneaks into Elbert's mouth from his pocket and causes an uproar.

Hurwitz's *Russell Sprouts* is the sequel to *Rip-Roaring Russell* and *Russell Rides Again*. In the first book, Russell is 5; in the sequel, 6. The books may be too long and difficult for children this age to read for themselves, but they are excellent books to read aloud. In "Bad Words," pages 9–18 of *Russell Sprouts*, the first grader learns that there are some words that a person just does not say, so he makes up a word to use for those occasions when strong language is called for. In "The Science Project," pages 55–68, Russell learns patience when his potato doesn't grow as fast as the beans and sweet potatoes that the other children have chosen to grow for their science projects. In *Russell and Elisa*, Russell is in second grade. Cameron's *The Stories Julian Tells* is about a father and two sons. Other books which contain short stories about Julian include *More Stories Julian Tells* and *Julian's Glorious Summer.* Smith's *The Kid Next Door and Other Headaches: Stories About Adam Joshua* contains several stories. Stories about Adam Joshua's dog, George, appear in *It's Not Easy Being George: Stories About Adam Joshua (and His Dog).* Another *Helping of Chips* is about the same children who appear in *Chips and Jessie,* also by Hughes. Five stories in cartoon style appear in *Chips and Jessie.* Chips is a boy and Jessie is a girl. In one of Hughes's stories, "Anybody Here Seen Chico?" the class hamster gets lost. British children will catch the double entendre in the title *Another Helping of Chips* by connecting Chips to French fries but others may not. Subjects in the four stories include camping, Christmas caroling, a dog, and a cat. These books by Hughes are for students in grades two to four.

There are easy and picture books for primary students that have the names of girls in the title. *Poor Esme* by Chess is about a little girl listeners can identify with because everyone is always too busy to play with her. *It's Just Me, Emily* by Hines is about a preschool child who makes a variety of noises for which her mother makes up fanciful causes. Then Emily pops up and says, "It's just me, Emily." Koci's *Sarah's Bear* is adopted by a little girl after it is swept overboard in a storm. *Lucy and Tom's A.B.C.* by Hughes is just one of several books about these two children. Others include: *Lucy and Tom's Christmas* and *Lucy and Tom's Day.* In *Imogene's Antlers* by Small, Imogene wakes up one Thursday to find that she has grown antlers. *Imogene's Antlers* is a featured book in the *Reading Rainbow* television series. *Janet's Thingamajigs* by Cleary is about twins. In this story, Jimmy wants to get into Janet's "thingamajigs." Although Katharine and Molly are best friends, they fight over the doll Charlotte in Winthrop's *Katharine's Doll.* In Havill's *Jamaica's Find*, Jamaica has to decide whether or not to keep the stuffed dog she finds in the park. Gauch's *Christina Katherina and the Time She Quit the Family* is about a little girl who changes her name to Agnes and quits her family to live under the dining room table. Naturally that becomes a bit boring, so she decides to rejoin the family. Lotta wants a bike for her fifth birthday in Lindgren's *Lotta's Bike*. Blegvad's *Anna Banana and Me* is about a city boy and girl. Anna Banana is brave and inspires her friend to overcome his fear. *Annie Bananie* has a pet porcupine in Komaiko's book which is told in rhyme. In *Bethany for Real* by Hines, Bethany and Timmy pretend. In Cohen's *Molly's Pilgrim*, a Jewish girl makes a Jewish Russian immigrant doll for her contribution to the model of a Pilgrim village for her school's Thanksgiving project because her family are pilgrims too. Learn why Donna is chased by cows in the humorous rhyming picture book *Donna O'Neeshuck Was Chased by Some Cows* by Grossman. When Ruthie goes to school she meets a real girl named Jessica to replace her imaginary friend in *Jessica* by Henkes. Four-year-old Sophie in King-Smith's *Sophie's Snail* loves all animals, especially snails. *Kirsty Knows Best* by McAfee is also told in rhyme. A film is based on Urdry's *What Mary Jo Wanted*.

The setting for Olson's *The Lighthouse Keeper's Daughter* is Maine in the 1850s. Although the book is fiction, it is based on a real incident. *Keep the Lights Burning, Abbie*, by the Roops, is another book about a similar incident which was featured on *Reading Rainbow*. Levinson's *Clara and the Bookwagon* is an easy reader about early bookmobiles at the beginning of this century.

Use the filmstrip of *Brave Irene* to introduce Steig's book. When Irene Bobbin's dressmaker mother becomes ill and can't deliver a ball gown to the duchess, Irene braves the winds and snow to deliver the dress. *Brave Irene* is also available in book/cassette combinations. Alderson's *Ida and the Wool Smugglers* is about a little girl from an island belonging to British Columbia, Canada, who saves sheep from wool smugglers. Rosie wonders about a stepsister she has never met in Dragonwagon's *Diana, Maybe*. In *Emmie and the Purple Paint* by Edwards, preschooler Emmie makes a mess with her finger paints. Five-year-old Nancy has trouble with her role as the middle child in Hoffman's *Nancy No-Size*. When Anna moves to a new town she is lonely until she receives gifts in the family mailbox from another little Asian girl in Tsutsui's *Anna's Secret Friend*. Another Anna is African-American in Carlstrom's *Wild Wild Sunflower Child Child*. *Nadia the Willful* by Alexander does not agree with her father, a Bedouin sheik, that no one should say her dead brother's name, so she alleviates her grief by remembering and talking about her brother. A magic bone helps the spoiled Pookins to improve her behavior in Lester's *Pookins Gets Her Way*. Jenny finds out what fairies do with baby teeth in Richardson and Dodd's *Jenny and the Tooth Fairy*. Abigail gets her nickname because she is the bossiest girl in Australia in *Bossyboots* by Cox. However, Abigail's bossiness saves the day when the bushranger Flash Fred holds up the stagecoach in which she is riding. In *Duncan and Dolores* by Samuels, Dolores chases and makes loud noises around Duncan the cat so that he prefers her sister Faye.

Literary characters in titles do not have to be humans. *Nata* by Griffith is a fairy. Lulu is a little witch in O'Connor's *Lulu Goes to Witch School*. *Heckedy*

Peg is a wicked witch who transforms seven children into food and makes the children's mother play a guessing game to break the spell in a book by Wood. Helen is a ghost in Hahn's *Wait Till Helen Comes,* a book for intermediate students. A brother and sister do not like their new 7-year-old stepsister Heather, but try to save her from a ghost that wants to drown her in a watery grave.

INTRODUCING BOOKS BY TITLES: ANIMAL CHARACTERS [CU 26].   Books for intermediate students that have animals named in the titles can be introduced to students by describing the animal or telling something about its activities in the book. This first group of books can be used in booktalks for intermediate and middle school students.

Wallace's *A Dog Called Kitty* has an intriguing title. Ricky is afraid of dogs because one attacked him when he was an infant and the resulting stitches and treatments for rabies were painful. When a stray dog arrives at his Oklahoma farm and eats with the kittens, Ricky calls the dog Kitty, so it won't seem like a dog. This book is excellent to use for a divided reading project. Take a paperback book apart by chapters and staple each chapter separately. In a few cases, the last page of a chapter has to be copied because it backs the first page of the next chapter. Give the chapters to different students and have them read their chapters silently before telling the rest of the class about it. Sometimes the teacher or school library/media specialist can paraphrase the first chapter to set the standard and share the last chapter so it can be telescoped or lengthened according to time availability. A remedial ninth grade group of students can finish this book in one 50-minute class period. Times will vary according to the students. The only reference to fifth grade appears on page 83 of the hardback and page 70 of the paperback. *A Dog Called Kitty* is an excellent book to read aloud as well as for use in a literature-based program.

A number of books have the names of dogs in the title. Readers who like the sadness of Wallace's book will enjoy Aronsky's *Gray Boy.* The part-Lab dog was given to Ian by his father shortly before the father's accidental death. The dog kills a neighbor's pet rabbit and runs away, but later, the dying Gray Boy saves Ian's life. *Stories About Rosie* by Voigt contains four, told from the point of view of a dog. *Duchess* by Aaron is a border collie pup on a sheep ranch in northern California where Marty, a 13-year-old underachiever, is sent because he has gotten into trouble with the law. Six-year-old Blair, in Snyder's *Blair's Nightmare,* wakes up every night to feed Nightmare, the dog that he has saved from abuse. Older children in the family eventually help him hide the dog. Naturally the parents are the last to find out. In *Foxy* by Griffith, Jeff is happy until he learns that someone else wants Foxy, another abused dog. *Rafa's Dog* is also by Griffiths. Rafa meets a mongrel dog, Moro, who helps him get over his lonesomeness for his home in Madrid and his dead mother. When Dan's dog dies, he doesn't want another until he finds Lady, a dog near death in *Comeback Dog* by Thomas. Sixth grader Kim Bowman's family doesn't want her to have a dog so she gets Misty from the pound and keeps her at Mrs. Mac's place until she can find the right time to tell her parents in Girion's *Misty and Me*. Meanwhile, several disasters occur before she can find the right time. *The Trouble with Tuck*, a 3-year-old golden Labrador named Friar Tuck, is that he is going blind. Helen's solution is to get a retired Seeing Eye dog for her dog. Be sure to mention in a booktalk that Friar Tuck was a friend of Robin Hood. *The Trouble with Tuck* is also Program #10 of the instructional television series *Books from Cover to Cover*. The trouble with Hazen's *Fang* is that he looks big and has a fierce name, but he is a cream puff who is afraid of the bulldog next door, as well as some neighborhood children. Guy's *Paris, Pee Wee and Big Dog* presents the adventures of 12-year-old Paris on Saturday when his mother works. In Kline's *Herbie Jones and the Hamburger Head*, a dog with a rash on his hairless pate is called Hamburger Head. Harold the dog narrates the story of Howe's *Bunnicula*, a rabbit with habits like Dracula. Other books about these animals are: *The Howliday Inn*; *The Celery Stalks at Midnight*; *Nighty-Nightmare*; *Scared Silly: A Halloween Treat*; and *The Fright Before Christmas*.

Beauty by Wallace is about 11-year-old Luke who moves to the Oklahoma farm of his crochety grandfather because of a divorce. Beauty, an elderly mare, becomes Luke's confidante, but Luke has to put Beauty out of her misery when she suffers an accident. A selection from Shub's *The White Stallion* appears on pages 72–81 of the third grade SB/Ginn basal reader, *Castles in the Sand*, edited by Pearson et al. Corcoran's *A Horse Named Sky* is about 13-year-old Georgina and her mother, who move to Montana to get away from an abusive father and husband. The horse dies in this story.

Ned receives a Daisy air rifle for a birthday present from his uncle. His dad forbids him to keep it so he hides it in the attic, but takes it out one night and shoots it. When a one-eyed cat appears, Ned wonders if he is responsible in *The One-Eyed Cat*, a Newbery Honor Book, by Fox. Grissi the cat gets out, is chased by dogs, and disappears. Dee Dee finds homes for other cats she comes across, but never does find Grissi. Shura's *The Search for Grissi* may have already been introduced to children by the television series *Books from Cover to Cover*, Program #14. Selden's favorite characters, Harry Kitten and Tucker Mouse, are back. A new book explains how Tucker got his name and how he and Harry met. *Harry Kitten and Tucker Mouse* takes place before Selden's classic *The Cricket in Times Square*. Other titles include: *Chester Cricket's New Home*; *Chester Cricket's Pigeon Ride*; *The Genie of Sutton Place*; *Harry Cat's Puppy*; and *Tucker's Countryside*. McHugh's *Wiggie Wins the West* is about a cat that travels west to Idaho with pioneers. *Blitzcat* by Westall is a cat that scours England for her master during World War II.

Stolz's *Quentin Corn* is a pig who learns that he is destined for the barbecue so he runs away. Quentin poses as a boy and only three precocious and very clever children—Emily, Andy, and the terrible Pete Benway—can see that he is a pig. Will they tell? Those who like Stolz's book will like King-Smith's

Pigs Might Fly. Daggie Dogfoot is a runt who escapes death, learns to swim, saves his home and family during a flood, and even flies. *Babe, the Gallant Pig* is another pig book by King-Smith in which a pig is trained by a dog to be a "sheep pig." King-Smith's *Magnus Powermouse* is a greedy mouse who doesn't appreciate his family until he is carried off by Jim the Rat Catcher. What good is a farm cat that keeps mice as pets instead of eating them? Readers learn what happens to Martin the cat in *Martin's Mice* by King-Smith. King-Smith is also the author of *Harry's Mad*, about an African gray parrot named Madison who can understand human language, talk on the telephone, and play the piano. Madison is left to Harry by his great-uncle. Aiken's *Mortimer Says Nothing* is about a talking raven who belongs to Arabel. The raven is always talking so when it becomes silent, everyone worries. Another book about the same character is *Mortimer's Cross.* Bawden's *Henry* is a baby squirrel that the narrator, her two brothers, and mother adopt while they are living on a farm in the English countryside to avoid the bombings of London during World War II. Dana's *Zucchini* is a zucchini-shaped animal, a ferret, who lives in a zoo but hears that there is a wonderful place called a prairie where other ferrets live. After his escape, Zucchini meets shy 10-year-old Billy, with whom he becomes friends. In Wallace's *Ferret in the Bedroom, Lizards in the Fridge*, 12-year-old Liz's home is lively because her father is a zoologist.

Nimmo's *The Snow Spider* is a fantasy about Gwydion Gwyn, who is sent off to find his missing sister. Gwyn is helped by Arianwen, a silver spider or the Snow Spider.

The Shadow Shark in Thiele's book is Scarface, a legendary shark of South Australia. *Alice and the Boa Constrictor* by Adams is about a girl who is studying snakes and decides she wants a boa constrictor for a pet, so she saves money to buy Sir Lancelot.

Carly and a friend watch condors flying and dancing on a California ranch in Snyder's *And Condors Danced. The Case of the Elevator Duck* by Berends is about 11-year-old Gilbert, who finds himself riding the elevator in his apartment building with a duck. Gilbert's detective work leads him to apartment 13B and readers will learn what he finds. Some children may already have been introduced to the book through the television series *Books from Cover to Cover,* Program #4. Another book which appears on Program #4 is Erickson's *Wharton and the Castaways.* Wharton and Morton are toad brothers who meet their tree toad cousins Hester and Cora when they escape from a raccoon.

Many books for primary children have names of animals in the title. *Jimmy's Boa Bounces Back* is a sequel to Noble's *The Day Jimmy's Boa Ate the Wash.* A misunderstanding between Max and Mrs. Goosebump is resolved in *Max, the Bad-Talking Parrot* by Demuth. Cole's *Norma Jean, Jumping Bean* is a beginning reader about a kangaroo who has to learn that there is a time and place for jumping. Use this book with Kent's *Joey* and *Joey Runs Away.* The second book is available as a sound filmstrip or hardcover/cassette package and tells about how Joey runs away because his mother complains about his messy room. The animal in Baker's *Benjamin's Portrait* is a hamster who decides to draw a self-portrait after he sees the paintings at the Animal Portrait Gallery. *Tyrone the Horrible* by Wilhelm is a dinosaur bully who makes life miserable for others. Hadithi's *Hot Hippo* explains why a hippo lives where he does. *Hot Hippo* is also available as a sound filmstrip. Hadithi's *Crafty Chameleon* is tired of being bothered by a leopard and a crocodile, so he outwits them by tying their tails together. *Monty* and *No Need for Monty* by Stevenson are about an alligator who gives three animal children a ride to school on his back until the parents decide they don't need Monty anymore. *Bill and Pete Go Down the Nile* by de Paola is about William Everett Crocodile and his friend Pete, his bird toothbrush, who go on a field trip down the Nile with Mrs. Ibis. A bad guy tries to steal the Sacred Eye of Isis. A lion protects various animals from a crocodile in Jorgensen's *Crocodile Beat*, which is written in rhyme. *Funny, Funny Lyle* is Waber's newest book about Lyle. Other books about Lyle include: *The House on East Eighty-eighth Street*; *Lovable Lyle*; *Lyle and the Birthday Party*; *Lyle Finds His Mother*; and *Lyle, Lyle, Crocodile* [CU 688]. A new video called *Lyle, Lyle Crocodile* is an adaptation of Waber's *House on East Eighty-eighth Street*. *The House on East Eighty-eighth Street* is one of the selections included on pages 164–77 of the third grade SB/Ginn basal reader *Castles in the Sand*, edited by Pearson, et al. Check page 160 of that basal for Carroll's poem "How Doth the Little Crocodile" and Galdone's retelling of an Indian folk tale, "The Monkey and the Crocodile," pages 150–59. Flannel board figures for "The Monkey and the Crocodile" appear on pages 196–202 of Sierra's *The Flannel Board Storytelling Book*. Other books about the crocodile are: Aruego and Dewey's *Rockabye Crocodile*; Guy's *Mother Crocodile*; and Lionni's *Cornelius*. Lionni's book is available in a cassette/hardback package. Some nonfiction titles include the Carricks' *Crocodiles Still Wait*, Behler's *Audubon Society Field Guide to North American Reptiles and Amphibians*, and Stone's *Alligators and Crocodiles*. Tworkov's *The Camel Who Took a Walk* is about an encounter between a sly tiger and a proud camel. It is also available as a video and film. Mahy's *Seventeen Kings and Forty-Two Elephants* is a nonsense jungle journey. Chorao's *George Told Kate* contains three stories about sibling elephants concerned with messy rooms, school, and a moving van. The left side of the page contains words and illustrations and the right side of the page contains nonverbal information. Wild raccoons visit a cornfield at night in Aronsky's *Raccoons and Ripe Corn*. *William the Backwards Skunk* by Jones has his stripe on the front instead of the back. *Gregory the Terrible Eater* by Sharmat is a goat whose story is a feature on the television program *Reading Rainbow*. Leaf's *Gordon the Goat* follows his leader into a tornado before he learns to think for himself. In Hadithi's *Greedy Zebra*, readers learn how the zebra got his stripes and how other animals got their colors. Fox's *Koala Lou* lives in the Australian bush and enters the Bush Olympics. Even though Lou does not win the race to the top of the gum tree, her mother loves her anyway. *Basil of Bywater Hollow* by Baker is a clumsy bear who does not have much self-confidence. However, he saves the day at the fair when he holds up the big top after it collapses in the storm. *Solomon: The Rusty Nail* by Steig is about a rabbit that can turn itself into a nail. *Do I Have to Take Violet?* is the lament of Elly bunny in Stevenson's book. Elly doesn't want to take her sister Violet with her. Sometimes it is good to be small. The other sheep laugh at *Friska, the Sheep That Was Too Small* by Lewis but wolf doesn't see her so she bites his tail to save the other sheep. Harald throws the king's hunters off the trail of the legendary Great Stag in Carrick's *Harald and the Great Stag.*

A number of books for primary students are about chickens, ducks, geese, and penguins. The Australian writer Mem Fox has written *Hattie and the Fox* which is also available as a big book. Hattie the Hen sees a sharp nose in the bushes and eventually all the parts that make up a fox. Macaulay's *Why the Chicken Crossed the Road* is a circular story that includes a herd of cows, a bridge, a train, a robber, the fire department, and some hydrangeas. *Maria Theresa* by Mathers is a chicken who escapes and travels around New York City. *Petook, an Easter Story* by Houselander is about a rooster who crows in honor of the Resurrection. In Kent's *Little Peep*, the chick tries to wake up the sun. *Wolf's Chicken Stew* by Kasza is about a hungry wolf who wants to eat a chicken but decides to fatten her up first with a variety of goodies. The ending is a delightful surprise. In the chapter book *Wolf Story* by McCleery, the vain Waldo matches wits with Rainbow the hen in a hilarious story-within-a-story. Marshall's *Wings: A Tale of Two Chickens* is about Harriet and Winnie and how Harriet's reading saves their lives. Lyon's *The Runaway Duck* is the feature book on a *Reading Rainbow* television segment. Other books on that segment include *Dabble Duck* by Ellis, *The Story About Ping* by Flack, and *Jamaica's Find* by Havill. George's *William and Boomer* is about the summer friendship between William and his pet goose. *Petunia the Silly Goose Stories* contains four books about Duvoisin's favorite goose in one volume. Lester's *Tacky the Penguin* is a misfit whose differences save the other penguins from hunters. Gay's *Bibi Takes Flight* is about a baby penguin who, unlike other penguins, can fly. *The Tiny Patient* by Pedersen is a picture book about a little girl and her grandmother who care for a sparrow with a broken wing.

Books about cows and horses for primary students can be introduced by titles. A Vermont farmer's Hereford cow is courted by a wild moose in this photo essay about a real situation in Wakefield's *A Moose for Jessica. Daisy* by Wildsmith is a cow who wants to see the world and does. Farmer Dakin is forced by finances to sell his cow, Blossom, in Herriot's *Blossom Comes Home.* When Blossom escapes from the market drover and comes home, Dakin decides to let her stay and nurse calves for her keep. Herriot's *Moses the Kitten* gets his name because he was found in the rushes. The famous Yorkshire veterinarian tells how a family of piglets adopts Moses. Herriot's *The Christmas Day Kitten* is about an independent cat who gives Mrs. Pickering a kitten for Christmas. Herriot's *Bonny's Big Day* is about an old, very large cart horse who is entered in the family pet class in the Darrowby Pet Show because she and another horse are retired and kept on as pets. *The Mare on the Hill* by Locker is a beautifully illustrated book about a year in the life of a white mare and two boys who try to tame her. Anyone who can ride Scott's *The Magic Horse* can travel anywhere they want in no time at all and the Persian prince has to outwit an evil magician to marry a princess. Cohen's *The Donkey's Story* is a picture book about the biblical prophet Balaam and the donkey, Sosi, who refuses to pass an angel on the road. The angel tells Balaam what to do when he meets the Moabite king.

Books about other animals that can be introduced by title appear in various chapters in this book. Check Volume 2 of this book for sections called ANIMAL STORIES IN VERSE, POEMS AND STORIES ABOUT DOGS, and POEMS AND STORIES ABOUT CATS. Numerous books about bears that can be introduced by title appear there in a section called BEARS, BEARS, EVERYWHERE. Check sections of Chapter 5 in this book titled MICE ARE NICE, FOXY BOOKS, PIG OUT ON PIG BOOKS, and INTRODUCING OWLS for books about those animals that can be introduced by titles.

Books with animals in the titles can be used to introduce other books about the same subject. *Koko's Story* and *Koko's Kitten* by Patterson can be used to introduce books about experiments with gorillas and chimps. When she was a graduate student at Stanford, the author became fascinated with the idea of teaching a gorilla to communicate. Beginning in 1972, Patterson taught Koko for 14 years and Koko learned 500 words in sign language. When she was 5 years old, Koko was mated with Michael to see if they would teach their baby. In *Koko's Kitten*, Patterson gives Koko a kitten. *Gorilla* is a video about Koko. NIM is a chimp who learns sign languages. In Michel's *The Story of NIM the Chimp Who Learned Languages*, a chimp learned 125 different signs. Between December 1975 and February 1977, a baby chimp raised by a family was taught American Sign Language just like a human child. The author was one of the volunteers. Eventually NIM was returned to his birthplace. Landsman's *Castaways on Chimp Island* is a fiction book about a chimp from a language lab who is returned to the wilds. Danny pretends that he has forgotten what he has learned in the language lab so he is sent with three other chimps, Roger, Tarzan, and Nibbles, to an island to return to nature. Dickinson's *Eva*, for middle school students, is about returning chimps to their natural habitat with Eva as their mentor. Eva is a 13-year-old girl whose brain has been implanted in the body of a chimp. Jane Goodall is a student of chimps. Goodall's books are *The Chimpanzees of Gombe* in which she celebrates 26 years of research and *My Life with the Chimpanzees* in which Chapter 6 is about Gombe National Park. This book also tells about ethology and how naturalists observe animals. Photographs enhance *Jane Goodall's Animal World of Chimps*. Fox's *Jane Goodall: Living Chimp Style* is an easy biography of a woman who studied animals by living among them. Two 16mm films or videos about Goodall and her studies are *Introduction to Chimpanzee Behavior* and *Miss Goodall and the Wild Chimpanzees*. Some nonfiction books to be used with these are:

Chivers's *Gorillas and Chimpanzees*; Green's *Gorilla*; Amon's *Reading, Writing, Chattering Chimps*; Powzyk's *Tracking Wild Chimpanzees in Kiriba National Park* (Africa); and Klingsheim's *Julius* (a chimpanzee in a Norwegian zoo). Students who are fascinated with the idea of animals that have a close relationship with people will also enjoy Leslie-Melville's *Daisy Rothchild: The Giraffe That Lives with Me*.

INTRODUCING BOOKS BY TITLES: INANIMATE OBJECTS OR NON-HUMAN CHARACTERS [CU 26]. Introduce books to students by describing a main character from the title that may not be a human character. A description of Taylor's *The Gold Cadillac*, a new 1950 Coupe de Ville with gold leather seats, gold carpeting, and gold dashboard, appears on page 12 of the book. Because they already have a year-old Mercury, Mother-Dear is angry that Father has spent money that should have been put toward a new house. Against the advice of friends, Father drives the family to Mississippi to visit relatives. They encounter hostile police and signs forbidding them to eat and drink where white people do. Clifton's *The Lucky Stone* contains four short stories about four generations of African-American women who own a lucky stone. The stone brings good fortune and has been passed down since slavery days. The stories, related in dialect, are told to Tee by her great-grandmother. Rylant's Newbery Honor Book, *A Fine White Dust*, refers to the pieces of a broken ceramic cross which Peter, the narrator, holds as he tells of his conversion by a revival preacher and how the preacher disappoints him. Garfield's *December Rose* is about an orphaned chimney sweep in Victorian England who overhears a spy plot and the words "December Rose." Barnacle, so named because he can cling to the sides of a chimney, learns that the *December Rose* is a ship that sails from Hamburg every month and is somehow involved in the mystery. Check page 75 of *December Rose* for more information. The *Frog* in Paulsen's *The Voyage of the Frog* is a sailboat given to 14-year-old David Alspeth by his Uncle Owen when he was dying of cancer. When David sails out to scatter Owen's ashes at sea, he is caught in a freak storm. Clymer's *Horse in the Attic* is a painting of a racehorse that 12-year-old Caroline finds in the house they have just bought. Who do you suppose painted it? Could they sell it for much-needed cash? Shura's *The Josie Gambit* is a chess move which is explained within the text on pages 11–13, 119, and at the end of the book on pages 151–60. Twelve-year-old Greg is unhappy because the wealthy Tory is using the queen's gambit not only in chess, but with the life of his friend Josie. Josie and her family are to be sacrificed so that Tory can get her way in a custody battle.

Several time travel books can be introduced by their titles. Mahy's *Aliens in the Family* is about a young alien named Bond who is on Earth to complete his coming of age quest. McDonald's *The Ghosts of Austwick Manor* is about 15-year-old Don who is given the family records and a model of the old family home. Most of the action of the book centers on the dolls in the model doll house. Winthrop's *Castle in the Attic* is a model of a medieval castle in which a silver knight comes alive. In Voigt's *Building Blocks* Brann, who builds a fort of the blocks, falls asleep, and wakes up during the Depression when his father is 10 years old. *The Indian in the Cupboard, The Return of the Indian,* and *The Secret of the Indian* are books by Banks in which a plastic toy cowboy and Indian are brought to life when placed in an old cupboard. Cresswell's *Moondial* is a sundial that Minty finds in a garden that helps to bring two children from the past into the present. *The Time Piper* and *The Humboldt Effect* by Huddy are about Tom Humboldt's experiments with a time machine. *Thimbles* by Wiseman is about a modern girl who is given a thimble which takes her back to a march on St. Peter's Fields in 1819 where she meets Kate and Sophie. The "Piggy" is a pawn in an intergalactic game in Sleator's *Interstellar Pig*. Park's *Playing Beatie Bow* is a game that takes Abigail into life in Sydney, Australia, during Victorian times.

Christina's Ghost by Wright is about a ghost boy Christina is involved with when she stays for part of a summer with an uncle in a Victorian house in the Wisconsin woods. Hoover's *Orvis* is a robot. Ten-year-old Toby West finds a 400-year-old robot, Orvis, built in the 21st century. Orvis is described on pages 9, 25, 59, 61, and 179 of Hoover's *Orvis*. Because Orvis is obsolete, the "multi-purpose unit, self-contained, self-repairing, and self-assured" robot is programmed to go to the dump. While trying to save Orvis, Toby and Thaddeus are left in an empty wilderness with the robot, and their survival depends on his memory and logical thinking. *My Robot Buddy* by Slote is Danny I, a robot designed by 10-year-old Jack Jameson to play with him. *That Game from Outer Space: The First Strange Thing That Happened to Oscar Noodleman* by Manes is about a video machine that is really a spaceship with occupants who want Oscar to help repair it so they can go home. Other books include *The Oscar J. Noodleman Television Network: The Strange Thing That Happened to Oscar Noodleman* and *Chicken Trek: A New Oscar J. Noodleman Story.* There are two books about Space Case, written by Marshall. Buddy McGee first meets his friend from outer space when he comes at Halloween time in *Space Case*. The second book, *Merry Christmas, Space Case* occurs during the Christmas holidays when Buddy and his family are at Grannie's.

Walsh's *The Green Book* is about a family that is allowed to take one or two personal items, a change of clothing, and a book on their voyage to Shine, a colony on a new planet. Father takes a technical dictionary but his youngest child takes a blank green book. Later, when Father wants to write up some important information, Father thinks of Pattie's blank book. However, Pattie has filled it with an account of their activities since leaving earth. *The Green Book* is Program #16 of the instructional television series *Books from Cover to Cover*. Hoover's *The Shepherd Moon* is about Mikel, who comes from an artificial moon, the shepherd moon, to dominate earth in the 48th century. In *The Blossoms and the Green Phantom* by Byars, the Green Phantom is the invention of 7-year-old Junior Blossom. Check pages 53–54 for a description of the Green Phantom. Use this book to introduce other books about the Blossom family to intermediate students.

Townsend's *The Persuading Stick* is about a strange silvery stick that serves as a magic wand for Beth. Beth is unable to get rid of the stick and after each incident in which she uses it, including getting free ice cream for her friends, Beth is drained. Beth's best use of the stick is when she persuades her brother not to commit suicide. York's *Miss Know It All and the Wishing Lamp* is about how the girls at the Good Day Orphanage make wishes on an old brass lamp. Stolz's *The Cuckoo Clock* is about 10-year-old Erich, a foundling, who becomes an assistant to old Ula, a clockmaker near Germany's Black Forest. Rather than make a clock for an overbearing baron, Ula says he is too busy making a special clock for himself. Ula and Erich dream the cuckoo bird to life. When Ula dies, the baron comes to claim the clock. Shub's *Cutlass in the Snow* is a short book about a sword Sam and his grandfather find in 1797 on Fire Island in Long Island Sound. A picture of the cutlass appears on page 34. They also find a chest with gold coins, a coin of which is passed on to the eldest Campbell son on his tenth birthday. There is a reissue of Bulla's *The Sword in the Tree* in which Shan, the youngest son of Lord Weldon, makes a journey to King Arthur's Camelot. Brooks's *The Sword of Shannara* is the only weapon that can combat Brona, the evil warlock lord. The only person who can use the sword is a descendant of Jerle Shannara who is Shea, the adopted son of Innkeeper Olmsford. Sequels include *Elfstones of Shannara* and *Wishsong of Shannara*. When 13-year-old Brian survives a plane crash, all he has to keep him alive is a hatchet given to him by his mother in *Hatchet*, a Newbery Honor Book by Paulsen.

Sutcliff's *Flame-Colored Taffeta* is about 12-year-old Damaris, who hides a wounded man whom she suspects is a smuggler, and helps him escape with the assistance of 13-year-old Peter. The setting is England in the middle of the 18th century. Eitzen's *The White Feather* takes place in early 19th-century Ohio during a Shawnee Indian uprising. The Quaker family does not move out as other settlers do and Father even gets rid of his gun. When the Shawnees arrive and find gifts of biscuits and molasses instead of a gun, they leave. However, the leader returns and puts a white feather from his headdress above the family's doorway as a sign of friendship. Minshull's *Cornhusk Doll* is another book about pioneers and Indians.

In Hanlon's *The Swing*, it is the swing that provokes the conflict between a stepbrother and sister. Eleven-year-old Beth is deaf and 14-year-old Danny resents her use of the swing at the summer house in this contemporary story. Bellairs's *The Lamp from the Warlock's Tomb* is an ordinary kerosene lamp that, if lighted under the wrong circumstances, summons Ashtaroth, the ancient Phoenician goddess of the moon.

The Bear's House by Sachs is about a fourth grader who wants to own the dollhouse her teacher keeps in the back of the classroom. The dollhouse, to be given away to the most deserving student at the end of the year, is important to Fran Ellen; the bear family that lives there provides the support that her own family does not. Fran Ellen and her 12-year-old brother care for their little sister and hide the fact that their father is gone and their mother is depressed and cannot help them. In the sequel, *Fran Ellen's House*, the three children are reunited after spending two years in different foster homes. Little Flora wants to return to her foster family and doesn't remember her sister Fran Ellen who took such good care of her in the first book. Fran Ellen gives her dollhouse to her sister who needs the emotional prop that she herself no longer needs. In Cassedy's *Lucy Babbidge's House*, the dollhouse in the basement of Norwood Hall, a school, provides Lucie a retreat from reality similar to the one experienced by Fran Ellen.

Paulsen's *Dogsong* is the quest that a 14-year-old Eskimo boy goes on to find himself and his "song." Paulsen's *The Crossing* refers to the Texas-Mexican border crossing made by an American soldier who meets a little Mexican street urchin.

In King-Smith's *The Queen's Nose*, 10-year-old Harmony Parker receives from her uncle a coin that can grant wishes. In Coven Tree in rural England where covens of witches gather, 14-year-old Ellen McCabe and Calvin Huckabee are caught between good and evil in Brittain's *Dr. Dredd's Wagon of Wonders*. The narrator is Stewart Meade (Stew Meat), owner of the Coven Tree General Store. Drought has stricken Coven Tree and Dr. Dredd promises to make rain. Check page 7. His conditions for making rain include a bargain like the one in *The Devil and Daniel Webster* by Benét, which might be discussed in a booktalk.

Several books are about trees. In Clapp's *The Tamarack Tree*, 17-year-old Rosemary Leigh becomes trapped in the Union's siege of Vicksburg during the Civil War. Check page 103 to find out why Rosemary and her brother Derek call their new home the Tamarack Tree. Mattingley's *The Miracle Tree* helps a family reunite after they are separated by the explosion of the atomic bomb. Ten-year-old Dexter Drake listens to stories about his town's heritage oak tree in Lisle's *The Great Dimpole Oak*. Greenfield's *Under the Sunday Tree* is brightly illustrated poetry from the Bahamas. Some primary books about trees include Martin and Rand's *The Ghost-Eye Tree*, Coats's *The Oak Tree*, Patent's *Christmas Trees*, and Parnall's *The Apple Tree*. A number of books about trees that would be suitable to introduce by their titles appear in Volume 2 of this book, in a section called EGG TREES, COOKIE TREES, BIRD TREES, AND MORE TREES.

There are also books for primary children that contain inanimate objects in the title. Allen's *Hidden Treasure* is an Australian picture book with the theme that money does not ensure happiness. Two brothers are fishing partners until they find a treasure. Herbert pushes Harry overboard, keeps the treasure, and spends all his life protecting it while Harry lives a happy life and has grandchildren. *Iktomi and the Boulder* by Goble is a Plains Indian trickster tale in which Iktomi boastfully attempts to outwit a boulder. Geringer's *Molly's*

Washing Machine is delivered by two rabbits even though Molly hasn't ordered it. Caple's *The Purse* is about Kate's purchase of her first real purse. *Daniel's Gift* by Helldorfer is a shepherd boy's gift of a wooden pipe to the Christ child. Winter's *Follow the Drinking Gourd* contains the song that blacks sang in Underground Railroad days. The Big Dipper, which points north, is the drinking gourd which leads to freedom. Leaf's *The Eyes of the Dragon* are one thing the painter says cannot be finished in the huge dragon he is painting on the wall of a Chinese village. Because the magistrate cannot follow directions, the dragon comes to life and flies away in a storm. Ginsburg's *The Chinese Mirror* is a picture book about a man who brings the first mirror home to his Korean village. Birch's *The King's Chessboard* is about a king who learns to distinguish between arithmetic and geometric progression. The king demands that a wise man accept a reward, so the man accepts a grain of rice for the first square of the king's chess board, two grains for the next, etc. *The Bridge Across* by Bollinger is a Swiss book about two families that live on either side of the river. Naturally, the family on the left bank wants to live on the right bank and vice versa. *The Sign in Mendel's Window* by Phillips is about a stranger who rents half of Mendel's butcher shop because he sees the sign in the window. The stranger listens to Mendel count his money and accuses Mendel of stealing from him. Mendel's wife proves that the money belongs to Mendel by throwing it in a pot of hot water. *The Incredible Painting of Felix Clousseau* by Agee is about a duck that comes alive and steps out of a painting. San Souci's *The Enchanted Tapestry* is stolen from a widow by the fairies of Sun Mountain and her three sons try to get it back. A rich fat man, Wing Fat, is given a magic axe in Demi's *Chen Ping and His Magic Axe*. The Chinese dragon in the story represents wealth, wisdom, and power. Pellowski's *Magic Broom* is easy to read and features Brenda, a rabbit girl. The story is also available on videocassette. *The Magic Leaf* by Morris is a Chinese tale about a man who thinks he is invisible. Herman's *Jenny's Magic Wand* is the stick she uses because she is blind. Whoever eats the honey from Bohdal's *The Magic Honey Jar* will never be cold or hungry. Hearn's *The Porcelain Cat* is brought to life by a sorcerer to get rid of mice. In Mauser's *Patti's Pet Gorilla*, Patti tells everyone during "show and tell" that she has a pet gorilla because she wants to be special. *The Velveteen Rabbit* is a toy in a book by Williams which has become a classic. In Fuchshuber's *Cuckoo-Clock Cuckoo*, the cuckoo in the Zeitler family's cuckoo clock flies off to play with a ghost and is gone for 24 hours.

Martin and Archambault's *Knots on a Counting Rope* are the knots Grandfather makes to help tell the story of the birth of his grandson "Boy-Strength-of-Blue Horses." *Grandpa's Slide Show* by Gould is about pictures Grandpa shares with his grandchildren. After his death, Grandmother shows the slides to help the grief by remembering. Anna gets a new coat even though times are difficult after World War II in Ziefert's *A New Coat for Anna*. Hest's *The Purple Coat* and other stories about clothing appear in a section of this book in Chapter 5 called CONSIDERING CLOTHING.

Coerr's *The Josefina Story Quilt* is an easy reader about Faith, her pet hen, and the quilt Faith made while journeying to California in a covered wagon. Check for more books about quilts in a section called QUILTS in volume 2 of this book.

Fleischman's *Rondo in C* is a picture book about a Beethoven piece that shows the music eliciting a different reaction from each listener. *Clementina's Cactus* by Keats is a wordless book about a cactus blooming in the desert. Fussenegger's *Noah's Ark* and Geisert's *The Ark* are both stories about the rains, the ark, and the rainbow. Kroll's *Biggest Pumpkin Ever* and Johnson's *The Vanishing Pumpkin* and *Witch's Hat* can be read at Halloween time. Other holiday books include Sharmat's *The Best Valentine in the World* about a purple valentine and a misunderstanding.

Share the title and ask children to guess what *Polar Express* is about. Van Allsburg's *Polar Express* is excellent for reading aloud before Christmas. Howard's *The Train to Lulu's* is about another train that takes two black girls on a visit to Aunt Lulu in the 1930s. Goble's *Death of the Iron Horse* is a story based on a real event from 1867 in which Cheyenne Indians attack a Union Pacific freight train. The story is told from the Indian point of view. Two books by Cole are about a magic schoolbus that takes Ms. Frizzle's class on field trips to places to investigate the water cycle and geology. Students become part of raindrops, reservoirs, pipes, the earth's inner core, and a volcano. *The Magic Schoolbus at the Waterworks* and *The Magic Schoolbus Inside the Earth* will be followed by similar titles and children will be eagerly waiting for them. Willard's *The Voyage of the Ludgate Hill* is about a voyage on a ship that Robert Lewis Stevenson took from London to America in 1887. The unusual cargo is described in the poem. What begins as a 400-mile race between two bullock teams who are carrying wool from the interior of Australia to the sea ends in a cooperative venture during the 19th century in Page's *The Great Bullocky Race*. Giblin's *Let There Be Light: A Book About Windows* links facts about windows with events in history.

In Tapp's *Moth-Kin Magic*, a human giant puts the humanoid Moth-Kin in a terrarium. The escape of the Moth-Kin is just one of the adventures of Ripple and other folk. The Moth-Kin, introduced in *The Moth-Kin*, are no bigger than an inch tall when full grown. Hansen's *The Shadowmaker* is an inept wizard whose job is selling new shadows, and 9-year-old Drizzle and her brother help by opening a shadow-mending shop. In Downer's fantasy *The Spellkey*, Caitlin and Badger search for the meaning of the Spellkey. Belden's *Frankie* is a griffin whose family is attacked by the the evil Morgan le Fay. Everyone in Frankie's family is magical except Mike.

Multimedia can help to introduce books with inanimate objects as characters. Mara Lori and her mother save money to buy a chair in *A Chair for My Mother* by Williams. The book is available as a sound filmstrip, video, and a book/cassette package. *A Chair for My Mother* is a featured book on the television series *Reading Rainbow*. Steig's *Sylvester and the Magic Pebble* is available as a cassette/book package. Show the 16mm film or video of Gramatky's horse-drawn fire engine, *Hercules*. Several books for intermediate students appear on television series which are designed to motivate reading. *The Whistling Teakettle* by Skolsky and *The Witch of Fourth Street* by Levoy appear on Program #15 of *Readit!* for third and fourth graders. *The Skates of Uncle Richard* by Fenner is Program #10 of *Book Bird* for fourth graders.

CHAPTER THREE

Introducing Books
by Authors

Books can be introduced by the author in booktalks or displays when students are familiar with the authors and want to read their other books, as in the case of such popular authors as Judy Blume, Betsy Byars, Jean Fritz, and Beverly Cleary. Teachers, librarians, and school library/media specialists who have heard authors speak at conferences can give students information based on what the author said or what the author did. Those who have not heard authors speak or visited with them briefly can rely on sets of biographies about authors or articles about authors in professional periodicals [CU 710].

Cleary's autobiography, *A Girl from Yamhill: A Memoir,* begins with Beverly's early life on the farm, Yamhill, in Oregon. It tells of her family's move to town, her uneasy relationship with her mother, relationships with teachers, an uncle who wants to become too friendly, a boyfriend who pleases her mother more than herself, and her father's loss of job during the Depression. Martin's biography is *Beverly Cleary: She Makes Reading Fun.* Check Volume 2 of this book, in a section called TOYS AND DOLLS, for information about Cleary's books. For annotations and awards about Cleary's books, check in Chapter 1, BOOKTALKING 118 AWARD-WINNING TITLES. Also check the section of Chapter 10 called INTRODUCING REALISTIC FICTION. Cleary is the 1975 winner of the Laura Ingalls Wilder Award given for "a substantial and lasting contribution to literature for children." "Lee Bennett Hopkins Interviews Beverly Cleary" appears on pages 72–77 of the SB/Ginn third grade basal reader, *On the Horizon,* edited by Pearson, et al. A selection from *Ramona and Her Father* appears on pages 78–95 of *On the Horizon.* An author profile and a selection from *Ramona Forever* appear on pages 164–86 of the fifth grade HBJ basal reader, *Skylines,* in the Laureate edition, collected by Cullinan, et al. A selection from *Dear Mr. Henshaw* appears on pages 14–27 of the fifth grade SB/Ginn basal reader, *Dream Chasers.* Cleary also appears in *Something About the Author,* volumes 2 and 43 and in *More Junior Authors.* A profile of Cleary appears on page 404 of Cullinan's *Literature and the Child. Meet the Newbery Author: Beverly Cleary* is a sound filmstrip.

Jean Fritz's novel *Homesick: My Own Story* is autobiographical and is a Newbery Honor Book and an American Book Award winner. Fritz also won the Regina Medal from the Catholic Library Association for "excellence in writing of literature for children" and the Laura Ingalls Wilder Award. "Is That a Fact, Jean Fritz?" appears on pages 40–43 of the August 1984 issue of *Instructor* magazine. *Homesick* is also available in a three-cassette set. Fritz's memories of a childhood in China, her amah, her friend Andrea, and thoughts about returning to the United States appear in *Homesick*. A selection from *Homesick* appears on pages 312–27 of the sixth grade HBJ basal reader, *Treasures*, from the Laureate edition collected by Cullinan, et al. A selection from *Homesick* appears on pages 478–90 of the SB/Ginn fifth grade basal reader, *Dream Chasers*, edited by Pearson, et al. A selection from Fritz's *China Homecoming* appears on pages 330–43 of *Treasures*. In *China Homecoming*, after about 50 years, Fritz returns to China which she left at the age of 13. *China Homecoming* is the winner of the Christopher book award because of its ability to "affirm the highest values of the human spirit." Information about Fritz's biographies appears in a section of Chapter 10 called INTRODUCING BIOGRAPHIES.

There are several places in this book where information about authors is given. In Volume 2, Chapter 1, check sections called ILLUSTRATORS AND AUTHOR/ILLUSTRATORS OF CHILDREN'S BOOKS for information about Margot Zemach, Trina Shart Hyman, Erik Blegvad, Ipcar Dahlov, Gail Haley, Charles Schultz, Mitsumasa Anno, Barbara Cooney. For information about Beatrix Potter, check the sections of Volume 2, Chapter 1 called TOYS AND DOLLS and NEEDLEWORK IN ART. Chapter 7 in this volume called EXPANDING BASAL READERS contains works by favorite authors. Check a section of Chapter 13 called BIRTHDAYS OF FAMOUS PEOPLE INCLUDING AUTHORS for ideas about celebrating the birthdays of authors.

Multimedia can be used in conjunction with units in which an author's book is being read. *Meet the Newbery Author: E. B. White* can be used effectively when a class or a teacher is reading *Charlotte's Web*, or it can be used to introduce *The Trumpet of the Swan* and *Stuart Little*. *Reading Together— A Wrinkle in Time, A Wind in the Door, A Swiftly Tilting Planet* is a cassette narrated by Madeleine L'Engle and her husband, the late Hugh Franklin, once a soap opera star from *All My Children*. Other books discussed on the tape include *A Ring of Endless Light, Love Letters*, and *Circle of Quiet*. L'Engle has had honors such as the Regina Medal from the Catholic Library Association and the Newbery Medal. The sound filmstrip *Jack London* can be shown when a class is reading *Call of the Wild* or *White Fang*. Three other sound filmstrips about classic authors are *Mark Twain, Jules Verne*, and *Robert Louis Stevenson*. Use the large print edition of Baum's classic with the filmstrip or video, *The Real, the True, The Gen-u-ine Wizard of Oz: L. Frank Baum*.

Use multimedia when reading Fleischman's *The Whipping Boy*. *The Whipping Boy* is a sound filmstrip or video about the 1987 Newbery winning book which is about a prince who is a spoiled brat and his "whipping boy," Jemmy. Questions and answers about *The Whipping Boy* appear on the sound filmstrip or video *Meet Sid Fleischman: The Newbery Author*. Viewers also learn that Fleischman became interested in magic in the fifth grade and published a magic book at 19. Excerpts from *Humbug Mountain* are included. *Humbug Mountain* is one of two books featured on the sound filmstrip, *Style*, from the set *Literature for Children, Series 9*. *The Whipping Boy* is also a program on the educational television series, *More Books from Cover to Cover.* Other books by Fleischman include *By the Great Horn Spoon!*, California Gold Rush; *Chancy and the Grand Rascal*, frontier and pioneer life; *Humbug Mountain*, the West; *Jingo Django*, orphan apprentice; *McBroom Tells the Truth*, *McBroom the Rainmaker*, *McBroom and the Big Wind*, *McBroom's Zoo*, *McBroom's Ear*, tall tales; *Me and the Man on the Moon-eyed Horse*, the West; *Mr. Mysterious and Company*, magic. *Mr. Mysterious* is introduced on the sound filmstrip *Sports and Hobbies* from the set *Nonfiction Too Good to Miss*, Series 5.

Some books by Sid Fleischman's Newbery-winning son Paul include: *Finzel the Farsighted*, fortunetelling; *Graven Images*, Newbery Honor Book of short stories with a supernatural twist; *Half-a-Moon Inn*, kidnapping and mutism; *Path of the Pale Horse*, yellow fever epidemic; *Phoebe Danger, Detective in the Case of the Two-minute Cough*, mystery. "The Binnacle Boy" and "The Man of Influence" are read on the cassette *Graven Images*.

Multimedia can be used in conjunction with books by and about authors. *Meet the Newbery Author: Katherine Paterson* can be used with books by this two-time Newbery winner who wrote *Jacob Have I Loved* (1981) and *Bridge to Terabithia* (1978). *The Great Gilly Hopkins* is a Newbery Honor Book (1979). *The Master Puppeteer* is a National Book Award winner, and *Sign of the Chrysanthemum* can be used with units of study about Japan. The first book is available as a sound filmstrip and the second is available as a recording. Check page 436 of Cullinan's *Literature and the Child* for a profile. *The Spying Heart: More Thoughts on Reading and Writing Books for Children* is the second volume of her speeches, book reviews, and essays. In *The Spying Heart*, Paterson tells about the experiences that led to the writing of *Jacob Have I Loved* and *Come Sing, Jimmy Jo.*

Betty Miles narrates the sound filmstrip, *Meet the Newbery Author: Betty Miles*, and tells of her early life in Baghdad where her parents were missionaries. She discusses the books *The Trouble with Thirteen*, *The Real Me*, and *Save the Earth.*

Use the filmstrip *Meet the Newbery Author: Laurence Yep* to introduce his books: *Child of the Owl*, learning about heritage; *Dragon of the Lost Sea*, dragon fantasy; *Dragonwings*, immigration; *Mark Twain Murders*, mystery; *Sea Glass*, San Francisco Chinatown; *Serpent's Children*, 19th-century China; and *Sweetwater*, science fiction. The Newbery Honor Book, *Dragonwings*, appears on the sound filmstrip *Meet the Newbery Author: Laurence Yep*. *Dragonwings* is also available as a sound recording. Check pages 422–27 of the sixth grade SB/Ginn basal reader, *Wind by the Sea*, edited by Pearson and others for "Lee Bennett Hopkins Interviews Laurence Yep."

Use the sound filmstrip *Maude Hart Lovelace, 1892–1980* to introduce the books: *Betsy-Tacy*; *Betsy-Tacy and Tib*; *Betsy and Tacy Go over the Big Hill*; and *Betsy and Tacy Go Down Town.*

Multimedia can be used to explain works by an author. The video *Tomi*

Ungerer: Storyteller tells of the Frenchman who came to the United States in 1956. Ungerer, who has been persecuted because of differences, tells of his heroes who are unpopular. Viewers learn how *Moon Man, The Three Robbers,* and *The Beast of Monsieur Racine* were written.

Multimedia can introduce a whole genre of literature to students. Use the video *A Visit with Scott O'Dell,* or the sound filmstrip *Meet the Newbery Author: Scott O'Dell* to introduce historical fiction. Because O'Dell has set such a high standard, there is a Scott O'Dell historical fiction award. Some favorites by him are: *Black Pearl,* pearl fishing; *Island of the Blue Dolphins* and *Zia,* Indians; *The King's Fifth,* old Southwest; *Sarah Bishop,* American Revolution; and *Sing Down the Moon,* Indians. Check pages 132–40 of the seventh grade SB/Ginn basal reader, *Star Walk,* edited by Pearson, et al. for "Lee Bennett Hopkins Interviews Scott O'Dell." *Star Walk* also contains a selection from *The Black Pearl* on pages 140–55.

The genre of mysteries or mysteries by Sobol in particular can be introduced by the sound filmstrip *The Case of the Model-A Ford and the Man in the Snorkel Under the Hand: Donald J. Sobol.* Sobol's books about Encyclopedia Brown are included in Chapter 10 in this book in a section called INTRODUCING MYSTERIES.

Use the video *A Visit with Lois Lowry* to introduce her books: *Anastasia Again!; Anastasia, Ask Your Analyst; Anastasia's Chosen Career; Anastasia At Your Service; Anastasia Has the Answers; Anastasia Krupnik; Anastasia on Her Own; All About Sam; The One Hundreth Thing About Caroline; Find a Stranger, Say Goodbye; Rabble Starkey; Summer to Die; Switcharound;* and *Taking Care of Terrific.*

A Visit with Elizabeth George Speare is another video in the Houghton Mifflin series. Other author/illustrators available from the same source are: *David Macaulay in His Studio, James Marshall in His Studio,* and *Bill Peet in His Studio. Bill Peet: An Autobiography* is a Caldecott Honor Book.

Introduce poetry with a pair of sound filmstrips: *Meet the Newbery Author: Nancy Willard* and *A Visit to William Blake's Inn: Poems for Innocent and Experienced Travelers,* also available in video format. Another way to introduce poetry to students is to share information about Baylor when viewing *The Byrd Baylor Video Series,* which includes *Hawk, I'm Your Brother, The Way to Start a Day,* and *The Other Way to Listen.*

A new biography of the 1978 Nobel Prize winner is Kresh's *Isaac Bashevis Singer: The Story of a Storyteller.* Use the book with the sound filmstrip *Meet the Newbery Author: Isaac Bashevis Singer,* which includes an excerpt from *Zlateh the Goat;* the documentary video, *Isaac in America;* and Singer's *Day of Pleasure: Stories of a Boy Growing Up in Warsaw,* which includes 18 stories from 1904–1918 and is a National Book Award winner. "Lee Bennett Hopkins Interviews Isaac Bashevis Singer" appears on pages 286–90 of the fifth grade SB/Ginn basal reader, *Dream Chasers,* edited by Pearson, et al.

Use the sound filmstrip *Who's Dr. Seuss?,* along with the biography *Dr.*

Seuss: We Love You. MacDonald's *Dr. Seuss* is from the Twayne series which provides in-depth studies of authors. These are most often used by high school students but are now beginning to include authors of books for younger children. *Dr. Seuss from Then to Now* contains 250 photos, sketches, and drawings from an exhibition originally shown at the San Diego Museum of Art, which is now on tour. The video *Dr. Seuss's Caldecotts* includes *McElligot's Pool, Bartholomew and the Oobleck,* and *If I Ran the Zoo.* Geisel is the winner of the Laura Ingalls Wilder Award, Regina Medal, and a Pulitzer Prize. In addition to his rhyming books for children, Seuss has written *The Butter Battle Book,* which is about the dangers of nuclear war, and *You're Only Old Once: A Book for Obsolete Children* which is an excellent book for a child to give to a grandparent or great-grandparent.

Those who have enjoyed the 16mm film *Maurice Sendak—1965* now will enjoy a new film and video called *Sendak.* Sendak discusses his childhood and how the Holocaust and Lindbergh kidnapping affected his life. Sendak also appears on the video *Where Artists Get Their Ideas: The Fantasists* in which he tells about *Where the Wild Things Are.* Trina Schart Hyman and Chris Van Allsburg also appear on that video. Sendak's *Caldecott & Co.: Notes on Books and Pictures* is a collection of Sendak's critical writing and includes essays and reviews. The book also includes autobiographical essays and interviews and the texts for the following acceptance speeches: 1964 Caldecott Medal, 1970 Hans Christian Andersen Medal, and the 1983 Laura Ingalls Wilder Award. Sound filmstrips and videos are available for the following Nutshell Library picture books: *Alligators All Around,* alphabet; *One Was Johnny,* counting; *Pierre,* behavior and apathy; and *Chicken Soup with Rice,* rhyming months. The film and video of *Really Rosie* which includes the Nutshell Kids, is still popular.

Bill Peet: An Autobiography is a Caldecott Honor Book. Titles by Peet that are available in hardback and paperback are: *Big Bad Bruce; Buford the Little Bighorn; The Caboose Who Got Loose; Capyboppy; Chester the Worldly Pig; Cowardly Clyde; Cyrus the Unsinkable Sea Serpent; Eli; Ella; Encore for Eleanor; Farewell to Shady Glade; Fly Homer Fly; The Gnats of Knotty Pine; How Droofus the Dragon Lost His Head; Hubert's Hair-Raising Adventure; Huge Harold; The Kweeks of Kookatumdee; The Luckiest One of All; Merle the High Flying Squirrel; No Such Things; Pamela Camel; The Pinkish, Purplish, Bluish Egg; Randy's Dandy Lions; Smokey; The Spooky Tail of Prewitt Peacock; The Whingdingdilly;* and *Wump World.*

Lotus Seeds includes 13 written essays on her life in children's literature by Marcia Brown, including three Caldecott acceptance speeches for *Cinderella,* 1955; *Once a Mouse,* 1962; and *Shadow,* 1983. The book also contains observations about her techniques and recollections of people she has known. *Randolph Caldecott: The Man Behind the Medal* is a sound filmstrip about the famous illustrator. *Wanda Gag 1893–1946* is a sound filmstrip about the artist and writer responsible for the classic picture book *Millions of Cats.* *Before the War: 1908–1939* is an autobiography in pictures that Goodall originally intended for his wife. Check Volume 2 of this book in the section called BOOKS WITH UNUSUAL FORMATS and in a section of Chapter 5 in this volume called PIG OUT ON PIG BOOKS for titles by Goodall. Green's *Hans Christian Andersen: Teller of Tales* and Quackenbush's *Once Upon a Time: A Story of the Brothers Grimm* can be used when comparing folk tales and literary folk tales.

Two picture books by James Stevenson are about his own childhood. *When I Was Nine* tells about a summer vacation to New Mexico in the 1930s. *Higher on the Door* is the sequel and tells about marking his height on the doorway, a train trip to New York, and his relationship with his brother. *When I Was Nine* appears on pages 14–23 of the third grade SB/Ginn basal reader, *Castles in the Sand*, edited by Pearson, et al. The two autobiographical books are similar in format to other favorite Stevenson books: *Are We Almost There?*; *Emma*; *Worse Than Willy*; *That Dreadful Day*; *We Can't Sleep*; *The Great Big Especially Beautiful Easter Egg*; *Could be Worse!*; *What's Under My Bed?*; *Will You Please Feed Our Cat?*; *That Terrible Halloween Night*; *There's Nothing to Do!*; and *No Friends*.

Endersbee's "In the Library with Roald Dahl" is Chapter 12 in Hancock and Hill's *Literature-Based Reading Programs at Work* and explains how an author can be the focus of a literature-based reading unit. Information about any of the authors included in this section can be used with literature-based reading programs. During the study of Dahl, read his autobiography *Boy: Tales of Childhood* which tells of his childhood in Norway and England and his experiences as a pilot during World War II. Books by Dahl to be introduced include: *Charlie and the Chocolate Factory*; *Charlie and the Great Glass Elevator: The Further Adventures of Charlie Bucket*; *Willy Wonka, the Chocolate Maker Extraordinaire*; *James and the Giant Peach*; *The Enormous Crocodile*; *George's Marvelous Medicine*; *The Twits*; and *Witches*. Two of his books made into plays are *Charlie and the Chocolate Factory: A Play* and *James and the Giant Peach: A Play*.

The Canadian author Jean Little's autobiography, *Little by Little: A Writer's Education* can introduce books she enjoyed in childhood, such as Burnett's *The Secret Garden*, Spyri's *Heidi*, and Montgomery's *Anne of Green Gables*. Because of her own sight problem, Little is able to write sensitively about problems of others in her books: *From Anna*, poor eyesight; *Look Through My Window* and *Kate*, friendship; *Mama's Going to Buy You a Mockingbird*, death; *Mine for Keeps*, cerebral palsy; *One to Grow On*, honesty; *Stand in the Wind*, siblings and disappointment; and *Take Wing*, mentally handicapped.

Meltzer's *Starting from Home: A Writer's Beginnings* can be used to introduce nonfiction to middle school students. Some nonfiction by Meltzer includes *Black Americans: A History of Their Own* and *Never to Forget: The Jews of the Holocaust*.

Erlanger's *Isaac Asimov: Scientist and Storyteller* can be used to reinforce the concepts of fiction and nonfiction. Gather as many of the almost 100 books Asimov has written as you can and have students divide them into fiction and nonfiction. Place a temporary tape over the call numbers, give two teams of students a list of Asimov titles and have them guess which titles are fiction and which are nonfiction. You might give a synopsis of Asimov books and ask students to divide them into the two categories. Use the Asimov biography with science fiction, as Asimov is a master of that genre. The film of Asimov's book *Fantastic Voyage* could be shown to introduce his science fiction. Five miniaturized scientists in a submarine enter the bloodstream and have a fantastic voyage. Isaac and Janet Asimov have written several science fiction books about Jeff Wells, a student at the Space Academy, and his tutor robot, Norby: *Norby the Mixed-Up Robot, Norby and the Invaders, Norby and the Lost Princess,* and *Norby and the Queen's Necklace.* There are four mysteries to be solved, Encyclopedia Brown–style, in Asimov's *Key Word and Other Mysteries.* Some of the newer nonfiction books by Asimov in the series *How Did We Find Out About* are *How Did We Find Out About Antarctica?; How Did We Find Out About Black Holes?; How Did We Find Out About Comets?; How Did We Find Out About Computers?; How Did We Find Out About Genes?; How Did We Find Out About Oil?; How Did We Find Out About Our Human Roots?; How Did We Find Out About the Atmosphere?; How Did We Find Out About the Beginning of Life?; How Did We Find Out About the Speed of Light?;* and *How Did We Find Out About the Universe?* A very different type of book by Asimov found in many libraries is *Words from the Myths.*

There are a number of books and multimedia about authors of classic children's books. Quackenbush's *Mark Twain? What Kind of Name Is That?* and Frevert's *Mark Twain: An American Voice* are biographies of Samuel Langhorne Clemens that can be used with the filmstrip *Mark Twain. The Real, the True, the Gen-u-ine Wizard of Oz: L. Frank Baum* is part of the *Meet the Author Series.* Information about the book and movie *The Wizard of Oz,* as well as Baum's life, are included. Kuznet's *Kenneth Grahame* is a biography in the Twayne series. Green's *Beyond the Wild Wood: The World of Kenneth Grahame, Author of The Wind in the Willows* is another biography of Grahame. Bassett's *Very Truly Yours, Charles L. Dodgson, Alias Lewis Carroll* is for adults who are reading *Alice in Wonderland* and *Through the Looking Glass* to students. *To the Point: A Story About E. B. White* by Collins is for intermediate students. *C. S. Lewis and His World* can be used with the fantasy books in the Narnia series which are, in sequence: *The Lion, the Witch and the Wardrobe; Prince Caspian: The Return to Narnia; Voyage of the Dawn Treader; The Silver Chair; The Horse and His Boy; The Magician's Newphew;* and *The Last Battle.* Interesting tidbits about Lewis can be gleaned from Dorsett and Mead's *C. S. Lewis, Letters to Children.* The book contains letters written between 1898 and 1963. On page 28 the pronunciation of Aslan is given, as well as the information that it is Turkish for lion and in *The Arabian Nights* meant the Lion of Judah. A sketch of Lewis's childhood appears on pages 8–16. Quackenbush's *Who Said There's No Man on the Moon? A Story of Jules*

Verne can be used in conjunction with the science fiction books of Verne. *A Woman of Passion: The Life of E. Nesbit, 1854–1924* by Briggs discusses Nesbit's books for children and how she uses other sources like H. G. Wells's *Time Machine* to write modern fantasy books on time travel. Use Hurwitz's *Astrid Lindgren: Storyteller to the World* when reading *Pippi Longstocking*. The filmstrip *Robert Louis Stevenson* can be used to introduce the poet and storyteller of *Treasure Island*. Information about poems by Stevenson can be found in the chapter in Volume 2, "Introducing Poetry." Critical essays on Baum, Carroll, Grahame, Lewis, Nesbit, Stevenson, Verne, and Wells appear in Bingham's *Writers for Children*. Turner's *William Shakespeare* can introduce the bard to children and be paired with the Lambs' *Tales from Shakespeare*. Burleigh's *A Man Named Thoreau* contains a bibliography and list of important dates in the life of a major American writer. Quotes from *Walden* appear throughout the book. Brown's *Dreamcatcher: The Life of John Neihardt* is about a writer of poetry and stories of the West and of Indians. Mitchell's *"Good Morning Mr. President": A Story About Carl Sandburg* is about the author and poet. In Avi's fiction book, *The Man Who Was Poe*, Edmund persuades Poe to solve the mystery of his aunt's disappearance. Gentry's *Paul Laurence Dunbar* is about the black poet.

There are many students who are interested in becoming authors and like to read about them. Many of the biographies and autobiographies already mentioned would be of interest. Have Goffstein's *A Writer* available for students in intermediate grades who are in young author groups. In that book a writer is compared to a gardener. In a poetic manner, Goffstein tells what it's like to be a writer. Broekel's *I Can Be an Author* is about writing careers in fiction, nonfiction, newspapers, and magazines. There is information about first drafts, revising, final drafts, word processing, and self-discipline. If the book has a flaw it is that too many men and not enough women are represented. *If You Were a Writer* by Nixon is a picture book in which Melia's mother is a writer and through their conversation children learn about the creative process of writing a book.

Horn Book Magazine is an excellent source of articles about authors. The articles can celebrate an author's life, as in the case of Bach's "Ellen Raskin: Some Clues About Her Life," from pages 162–67 of the March/April 1985 issue, which is a eulogy for the author and illustrator of such books as *The Westing Game* and *Figgs and Phantoms*. Silvey's article, "An Interview with Cynthia Rylant," pages 695–702 of the November/December 1987 issue of *Horn Book*, gives insight into Rylant's personal life, her writing habits, what she wants in illustrators for her books, and her relationship with her editor.

Check the "Profile" articles in issues of *Language Arts* for author profiles such as "Profile: Patricia MacLachlan" from pages 783–87 of the November 1985 issue; "Profile: Arnold Lobel" from pages 489–94 of the September 1988 issue; and "Profile: Arnold Adoff" from pages 584–91 of the October 1988 issue.

Numerous books contain information about authors that would be helpful to children and adults. One popular series from H. W. Wilson that has a cumulative index is the newest *Sixth Book of Junior Authors and Illustrators*, edited by Holtze. Previous titles include Haycraft's *Junior Book of Authors*; Fuller's *More Junior Authors*; DeMontreville and Hill's *Third Book of Junior Authors*; DeMontreville and Crawford's *Fourth Book of Junior Authors and Illustrators*; and *Fifth Book of Junior Authors and Illustrators*, edited by Holtze. Another series, *Something About the Author* from Gale, edited by Commire, reached Volume 57 in 1989 and continues to provide new information. Carpenter and Prichard's *Oxford Companion to Children's Literature* contains 2,000 entries, 900 of which are biographies. Kirkpatrick's *Twentieth Century Children's Writers*, 2nd edition contains 700 entries with biographical information, critical commentary, and a list of the author's publications. Bingham's *Writers for Children* includes 84 critical essays on writers for children from the 17th to the 20th centuries. *American Writers for Children Since 1960: Fiction* by Estes is part of Gale's *Dictionary of Literary Biography* series. Numerous awards are included in *Children's Books: Awards and Prizes* by the Children's Book Council. Senick's *Children's Literature Review* is a Gale publication that reached Volume 15 in 1988 and includes reviews of children's books. Public libraries and many high school libraries own the following sets of author books that may be used by adults: *Contemporary Authors, Authors in the News, Who's Who in America,* and *Who's Who of American Women.*

Kingman's *Newbery and Caldecott Medal Books 1976–1985* is Volume 5 in a series and includes speeches, biographies, and essays about Robin McKinley, Beverly Cleary, Cynthia Voigt, Nancy Willard, Katherine Paterson, Joan Blos, Ellen Raskin, Mildred Taylor, and Susan Cooper. Essays by Barbara Bader, Ethel Heins, and Zena Sutherland are also included in *Newbery and Caldecott Medal Books 1976–1985.* Previous books by Kingman include *Newbery and Caldecott Medal Books: 1956–65* and *Newbery and Caldecott Medal Books, 1966–75.* Miller and Field's book is *Newbery Medal Books, 1922–1955.*

An Author a Month, for Pennies, by the McElmeels, outlines a plan for activities and biographical information relating to Marcia Brown, Carol Carrick, Beatrice Schenk De Regniers, Dr. Seuss, Arnold Lobel, Eric Carle, Tomie de Paola, Steven Kellogg, Margot Zemach, Bill Peet, Chris Van Allsburg, and Bernard Waber. Asher's *Where Do You Get Your Ideas?* shares stories behind the stories for Lloyd Alexander, Lois Lowry, Jan Greenberg, Carol Kendall, Peter Cohen, Jamie Gilson, Lila Perl, Irene Bennett Brown, William Sleator, Dorothy Frances Patricium, Ruth Giff, Marjorie Sharmat, Bernice Rabe, C. S. Adler, Robert Burch, Robert Kimmell Smith, Mary Frances Shura, Ellen Conford, and others.

Readers As Writers is a packet of letters and photos about Nina Bawden, Betsy Byars, Jean Fritz, Marguerite Henry, M. E. Kerr, Evaline Ness, Ed Radlauer, Judith St. George, and Yoshiko Uchida. Profiles of the following authors appear in Cullinan's *Literature and the Child:* Jan Omerod, Gail Gibbons, Donald Crews, Arnold Lobel, Chris Van Allsburg, William Steig, Maurice Sendak, Tomie de Paola, Trina Schart Hyman, A. A. Milne, Natalie Babbitt, Isaac Asimov, Judy Blume, Beverly Cleary, Lois Lowry, Betsy Byars, Jean Little, Jean Craighead George, Katherine Paterson, Jean Fritz, Mildred Taylor, Milton Meltzer, Seymour Simon, Laurence Pringle, Yoshiko Uchida, Isaac Bashevis Singer, and Louisa May Alcott.

The Laureate edition of the HBJ basal readers edited by Cullinan, et al. contain author profiles, along with a story by each author. Byrd Baylor appears on pages 53–54 of the fourth grade book, *Crossroads*; Ann McGovern appears on pages 118–19 of the fifth grade *Skylines*; Elizabeth George Speare appears on pages 118–19 of the sixth grade *Treasures*; William Pené du Bois appears on pages 136–37 and Robert Silverberg appears on pages 286 of the seventh grade *Patterns*; and J.R.R. Tolkien appears on page 134 of the eighth grade *Panoramas*.

Norton's *Through the Eyes of a Child: An Introduction to Children's Literature* contains essays by authors throughout the book in sections called "Through the Eyes of an Author." Articles by the following authors are included: Jamake Highwater, Beverly Cleary, Patricia Clapp, Virginia Hamilton, Jack Denton Scott, Jean Fritz, Tomie de Paola, Madeleine L'Engle, and Jack Prelutsky.

Childhood experiences with books appear in *Once Upon a Time: Celebrating the Magic of Children's Books in Honor of the Twentieth Anniversary of Reading Is Fundamental*. Contributors include Natalie Babbitt, Stan and Jan Berenstain, Barbara Helen Berger, Judy Blume, Ashley Bryan, Beverly Cleary, Tomie de Paola, Leo and Diane Dillon, Jean Fritz, M. B. Goffstein, Edward Gorey, Virginia Hamilton, Jamake Highwater, Trina Schart Hyman, Steven Kellogg, Myra Cohn Livingston, Arnold Lobel, James Marshall, Katherine Paterson, Jack Prelutsky, Maurice Sendak, Dr. Seuss, Shel Silverstein, Margot Tomes, Jim Trelease, Tasha Tudor, and Ed Young.

Celebrating Children's Books: Essays on Children's Literature in Honor of Zena Sutherland, edited by Hearne and Kaye, is now available in paperback. Twenty-three prominent persons knowledgeable about children's literature contributed pieces: Lloyd Alexander, Susan Cooper, Paula Fox, Jill Paton Walsh, Robert Cormier, Virginia Hamilton, E. L. Konigsburg, Arnold Lobel, Jean Fritz, Milton Meltzer, David Macaulay, Laurence Pringle, Millicent Selsam, Myra Cohn Livingston, Ursula Nordstrom, Mimi Kayden, John Rowe Townsend, Betsy Hearne, Marilyn Kaye, Amy Kellman, John Donovan, Mary Orvig, and Sophie Silverberg.

Seventy-seven New Zealand and Australian authors and illustrators are included in Dunkle's *The Story Makers: A Collection of Interviews with Australian and New Zealand Authors and Illustrators for Young People*. Another Australian book is Ingram's *Making a Picture Book*. Interviews with Canadian writers and illustrators appear in *Canadian Children's Literature*, a quarterly publication. Articles about North American authors appear in the Canadian periodical for teacher/librarians, *The Emergency Librarian*.

CHAPTER FOUR

Using Sequels, Series, and Favorite Characters to Introduce Books

After a child has read and enjoyed a book, it is not easy to find "another book just like it." However, a sequel or other books in a series can help to solve that problem. My motto is "Never introduce just one book when you can introduce two, or three, or more." Sequels and series are the easiest way to accomplish this [CU 81–84, 726].

Sequels can be introduced in several ways. Read aloud a picture book that is about a special character in a series during holiday time and make the other books about that character available to listeners. Read the newest book in a series aloud or share it in a booktalk because it will be a welcome addition for those who loved the previous books and will stimulate others to read them. Introduce a character through a film, filmstrip, video, or sound recording and then share the many books in the series with students. Introduce the idea that authors write books and illustrators draw the pictures by providing information about these book creators. Books in series are especially helpful in literature-based reading programs or when extending basal readers, because they provide more books about a familiar character for students to read. Any of the books in this section that are available in paperback can be used in reading programs. Even if a whole classroom set is not available, a dozen copies of several titles by one author could be purchased so that half a class could be reading one title and half of the class could read another at the same time. Then one group could trade books with the other. In this way the money for one set could be stretched to two titles. A big book can be read aloud to students before they read individual paperbacks of the same story.

It is not too early to teach the word "sequel" to primary students. Read the humorous book or show the sound filmstrip of *The Day Jimmy's Boa Ate the Wash* and tell students that the sequels are Noble's *Jimmy's Boa Bounces Back* and *Jimmy's Boa and the Big Splash Birthday Bash*. Then make all books available to students. The first book is available in paperback so it could be used as a literature-based reading book by a whole class. Teach the word "series" to primary students when the complete book of Duvoisin's stories about Petunia is introduced. *Petunia the Silly Goose* includes five books about Petunia that were previously published separately. There are numerous favorite animal characters that appear in sequels or series.

Some authors have written several series. Learn more about Nancy Carlson and then introduce other books in series that she has written. Some books about Carlson's Louanne Pig are: *Louanne Pig in Making the Team*; *Louanne Pig in the Mysterious Valentine; Louanne Pig in the Perfect Family; Louanne Pig in the Talent Show*; and *Louanne Pig in the Witch Lady*. *Harriet's Recital* is available as a sound filmstrip. Carlson's Harriet the dog appears in five cassette/paperback packages: *Harriet and the Garden*; *Harriet's Halloween Candy*; *Harriet and Walt*; *Harriet's Recital*; and *Harriet and the Roller Coaster*. Harriet's cousin is Loudmouth George, who appears in the following cassette/paperback packages: *Loudmouth George and the Big Race*; *Loudmouth George and the Coronet*; *Loudmouth George and the Fishing Trip*; *Loudmouth George and the New Neighbors*; and *Loudmouth George and the Sixth Grade Bully*. Carlson and books by her can be introduced to first graders who read "Harriet and the Garden" on pages 88–99 of the HM basal reader, *Carousels*, by Durr et al. Series and sequels about the following pigs appear in Chapter 5 in a section called PIG OUT ON PIG BOOKS: Goodall's Paddy Pork; Gretz's Roger Pig; McPhail's Pig Pig; and Yolen's Piggins.

Waber's Lyle can be introduced through the newest book *Funny, Funny Lyle*; the new animated video *Lyle, Lyle, Crocodile*, which is based on *The House on East Eighty-eighth Street*; or *Lovable Lyle* from the Red Module in the television series, *Picture Book Park*. *Lyle, Lyle, Crocodile* and *The House on East Eighty-eighth Street* are both available in cassette/book packages. Other books about Lyle include *Lyle and the Birthday Party* and *Lyle Finds His Mother*.

Horse stories are always a favorite. Read aloud from the reprint of *Flip and the Cows* by Dennis in which Flip is afraid of the cows. Then provide 15 paperback copies each of *Flip* and *Flip and the Morning*. After half a class has read one book, exchange books and have them read the other one.

Introduce Brown's Arthur after a third grade spelling test by sharing the sound filmstrip *Arthur's Teacher Trouble* in which Arthur and Prunella, the Brain, are finalists in a spellathon. The teacher is Mr. Ratburn. A video is called *Arthur's Teacher Trouble/Arthur Goes to Camp*. After showing the videos or filmstrip, place all the other books in the reading/listening/viewing center in the classroom. Arthur and his sister D. W. are anteaters who also appear in the following books: *Arthur's April Fool*; *Arthur's Christmas*; *Arthur's Halloween*; *Arthur's Thanksgiving*; *Arthur's Valentine*; *Arthur's Baby*; *Arthur's Eyes*; *Arthur's Nose*; *Arthur's Tooth*; *The True Francine*; *D. W. All Wet*; and *D. W. Flips*. Hoban's Arthur is a monkey. Use the newest book, *Arthur's Loose Tooth* to introduce other books about Arthur: *Arthur's Christmas Cookies*; *Arthur's Funny Money*; *Arthur's Halloween Costume*; *Arthur's Honey Bear*; *Arthur's Pen Pal*; and *Arthur's Prize Reader*. All of the books except *Arthur's Halloween Costume* and *Arthur's Loose Tooth* are available in cassette/paperback packages.

The cassette *Angelina Ballerina and Other Stories* can be placed in the reading/listening/viewing center in the classroom or in a special multimedia corner of the school library/media center because it includes the following books: *Angelina Ballerina*; *Angelina and the Princess*; *Angelina at the Fair*; *Angelina's Christmas*; and *Angelina on Stage*. Two other books by Holabird are *Angelina and Alice* and *Angelina's Birthday Surprise*.

Prepare a display in the school library/media center called "Christmas Cats" to introduce *Rotten Ralph's Rotten Christmas* by Gantos; *Church Mice at Christmas* by Oakley; and *Marmalade's Christmas Present*. During the winter, read Wheeler's *Marmalade's Snowy Day* and make *Marmalade's Nap* and *Marmalade's Picnic* available too. When students are having show and tell, produce *Rotten Ralph's Show and Tell*, about another cat, to introduce other books by Gantos: *Rotten Ralph*; *Rotten Ralph's Trick or Treat*; and *Worse Than Rotten Ralph*. The newest book about Oakley's cat and mice, which can be read aloud in January, is *Diary of a Church Mouse* which can be used to introduce: *Church Mouse*; *Church Cat Abroad*; *Church Mice Adrift*; *Church Mice and the Moon*; *Church Mice in Action*; *Church Mice at Bay*; and *Church Mice Spread Their Wings*. For other series about cats check a section of Volume 2 of this book for POEMS AND STORIES ABOUT CATS. Some favorite cats in series include: Calhoun's Henry; Clymer's Horatio; Griffith's cat that's a friend of Alex; Pearson's Porkchop; Poulin's Josephine; Selden's Harry Kitten; and Wynne-Jones's Zoom. Two of Poulin's books are also available in French: *Peux-tu Attraper Joséphine?* and *Pourrais-Tu Arrêter Joséphine?*

The mice in Oakley's series can be introduced with Celestine mouse in Vincent's series beginning with *Ernest and Celestine*.

Show the sound filmstrip, *Ernest and Celestine*, to introduce the bear and mouse to students. Provide multiple copies of the paperback, *Ernest and Celestine's Picnic*, for a whole class to read, then provide students with other books about the bear and mouse for them to read on their own. Sound filmstrips, or cassette/paperback and cassette/hardback packages are available for *Ernest and Celestine* and *Ernest and Celestine's Picnic*. Other books include *Breakfast Time, Ernest and Celestine*; *Ernest and Celestine's Patchwork Quilt*; *Smile, Ernest and Celestine*; *Merry Christmas, Ernest and Celestine*; *Feel Better, Ernest!*; and *Where Are You, Ernest and Celestine?* After reading these books, have students locate other picture books about mice and bears in the subject card catalog. There are probably enough titles so that each member of a class can be assigned to look up and locate a book about either a bear or a mouse or one of each. The books can be taken back to the classroom and shared. Bears and mice can be used to study the adjectives big and little.

Use the live action film *Angus Lost* to introduce other books by Flack: *Angus Lost*; *Angus and the Ducks*; and *Angus and the Cat*. Three sound filmstrips are available for Dodd's books about the New Zealand dog, Hairy Maclary: *Hairy Maclary from Donaldson's Dairy*; *Hairy Maclary—Scattercat*; and *Hairy Maclary's Bones*. Sometimes a film or video gives new life to a series that has long been popular, as in the case of the multimedia versions of *Harry, the Dirty Dog*, which can motivate students to read other books by

Zion: *Harry and the Lady Next Door*; *Harry by the Sea*; *Harry, the Dirty Dog*; and *No Roses for Harry.* Series about the following dogs appear in Volume 2 of this book in a section called POEMS AND STORIES ABOUT DOGS: Adler's My Dog; Bridwell's Clifford; Carlson's Harriet; Griffith's Alex; Hill's Spot; Kellogg's Pinkerton; and Rylant's Mudge.

Use the new film or video of *Frog and Toad Together* which includes four stories to introduce other books by Lobel: *Days with Frog and Toad*; *Frog and Toad All Year*; *Frog and Toad Are Friends*; *Frog and Toad Pop-Up Book*; and *Frog and Toad Together.* Yolen's series about Commander Toad are also easy readers.

Television can introduce students to favorite characters. Use *Bedtime for Frances* from the Blue Module of *Picture Book Park* to introduce these books about Frances the badger by Hoban: *A Baby Sister for Frances*; *A Bargain for Frances*; *Bedtime for Frances*; *Best Friends for Frances*; *A Birthday for Frances*; and *Bread and Jam for Frances.*

There is a series about a moose named Morris. Wiseman's Morris appears in the following books: *Morris the Moose*; *Morris Goes to School*; *Morris the Moose Goes to School*; *Morris Has a Birthday Party*; *Morris Has a Cold*; *Morris and Boris at the Circus*; and *Morris Tells Boris Mother Goose Stories and Rhymes.* Two holiday books are *Halloween with Morris and Boris* and *Christmas with Morris and Boris.* Boris is a bear.

Mousekin's Thanksgiving is now available in paperback format. Other books by Miller that are available in paperback that could be used in literature-based reading programs are: *Mousekin Finds a Friend*; *Mousekin Takes a Trip*; *Mousekin's ABCs*; *Mousekin's Birth*; *Mousekin's Close Call*; *Mousekin's Thanksgiving*; *Mousekin's Christmas Eve*; *Mousekin's Easter Basket*; *Mousekin's Fables*; *Mousekin's Family*; *Mousekin's Mystery*; and *Mousekin's Woodland Sleepers.*

Early primary students can learn about authors and illustrators James Marshall (who is also Edward Marshall) and Harry Allard as a prelude to enjoying many books by these men. Marshall provides an opportunity to introduce the term "pseudonym." Edward Marshall's books about Fox, illustrated by James Marshall, include: *Fox and His Friends*; *Fox All Week*; *Fox at School*; *Fox in Love*; and *Fox on Wheels.* *Fox on the Job* is written and illustrated by James Marshall. Books in series by Edward Marshall include *Three by the Sea* and the sequel *Four on the Shore* about Lolly, Spider, and Sam. The books about Fox can be read by first and second graders.

Use James Marshall's recent book, *George and Martha Round and Round*, to introduce other books in the series: *George and Martha*; *George and Martha Tons of Fun*; *George and Martha Back in Town*; *George and Martha Encore*; *George and Martha One Fine Day*; *George and Martha Rise and Shine.* After reading *George and Martha* aloud to a class, make the cassette/paperback package available to students so they can read along with it and practice their reading skills. Have students take the other books about the humorous hippos home and read them with their parents or older brothers and sisters.

James Marshall also illustrated Allard's humorous books about Miss Nelson. Use all of the books either written by or illustrated by Marshall together after reading about the Caldecott Honor Book illustrator. First graders who are reading the easy books about the fox will enjoy having the books about Miss Nelson read aloud to them. In *Miss Nelson Is Missing*, which is also available in paperback/cassette, 16mm, and video formats, the rowdy students in Room 207 get a stern substitute while Miss Nelson is gone, so they appreciate her more. In the sequel, *Miss Nelson Is Back*, the teacher announces to her class that she is having her tonsils out and will be gone for a week. Students are afraid that Miss Viola Swamp will be their substitute. The students in Horace B. Smedley School are down in the dumps in *Miss Nelson Has a Field Day* because the football team has not won a game. Viola Swamp becomes the coach and whips them into shape. *Miss Nelson Is Back* is available in cassette/paperback format. *Miss Nelson Is Missing* is one story in the film *Fables of Harry Allard*.

There are a number of books about human characters in series that can be introduced to students so that they can be encouraged to read many books. Parish's favorite character is the maid Amelia Bedelia. Because the books are easy to read and are available in paperback editions, they would make great choices for literature-based reading in second grade. The following books are available on two cassettes in a set called *Amelia Bedelia*; *Come Back, Amelia Bedelia*; *Play Ball, Amelia Bedelia*; *Amelia Bedelia and the Surprise Shower*; and *Merry Christmas, Amelia Bedelia*. Four of the newer books are *Amelia Bedelia Goes Camping*; *Thank You, Amelia Bedelia*; *Amelia Bedelia and the Baby*; and *Amelia Bedelia's Family Album*. The 25th anniversary of Amelia Bedelia was in 1988.

A Chair for My Mother by Williams can be used to introduce the concept of the Caldecott Medal and Caldecott Honor Books to primary students as well as the terms *sequel* and *series*. The book, which is available in paperback, can be used in a literature-based reading program. A sound filmstrip and a paperback/cassette package are available. In the sequel, *Something Special for Me*, Rosa is allowed to buy something for her birthday with the money in the big jar. The previous major purchase made from money in the jar had been the chair. In *Music, Music for Everyone*, Rosa and her friends raise money through their music to help pay for Grandmother's illness. Students will enjoy *Cherries and Cherry Pits*, also by Williams.

A favorite series by Stevenson is about a grandfather. *That Dreadful Day* is about the first day of school; *No Friends* is about moving to a new neighborhood; *Will You Please Feed Our Cat?* is about feeding a vacationing neighbor's dog. Other books about Grandpa, Mary Ann, and Louie are: *Are We Almost There?*; *Could Be Worse!*; *Grandpa's Great City Tour*; *The Great Big Especially Beautiful Easter Egg*; *Grandpa's Too Good Garden*; *There's*

Nothing to Do!; *We Can't Sleep!*; *Worse Than Willy*; and *We Hate Rain*. Stevenson illustrated Griffith's *Georgia Music* and the sequel *Grandaddy's Place*, both of which are excellent to read aloud.

Madeline, by Bemelmans, is a children's literature classic that is available in big book format. Teachers and school library/media specialists can read to the whole class from the big book and then students can read the paperback for themselves. A video of *Madeline* is also available. A pop-up book, while not suitable for circulation, can be made available as a display to stimulate interest. Books about Madeline that are available as cassette/paperback packages include: *Madeline*; *Madeline and the Bad Hat*; *Madeline and the Gypsies*; *Madeline in London*; and *Madeline's Rescue*. Have the class read these books prior to Christmas so that the newest book, *Madeline's Christmas*, can be time for the holiday. *Madeline's House* includes *Madeline*; *Madeline's Rescue*; and *Madeline and the Bad Hat*.

Alfie and the baby sitter cope with a burst pipe in *An Evening at Alfie's* by Hughes. *Alfie's Feet* is available in paperback format. In *Alfie Gets in First*, Alfie, his mother, and sister Annie Rose come back from shopping and Alfie goes into the house first by mistake and locks the other two out. The catch is too high so Alfie goes to find a chair. Meanwhile, the neighbor, her daughter, the milkman, and the window cleaner try to help. Stop reading the book when Alfie discovers that the catch is too high for him to reach and have students suggest what should be done next. Other books about this character include *Alfie Gives a Hand* and *The Big Alfie and Annie Rose Storybook*. Preschool children will enjoy Lucy and Tom, created by Hughes in *Lucy and Tom's A.B.C*; *Lucy and Tom's 1–2–3*; *Lucy and Tom's Christmas*; and *Lucy and Tom's Day*.

Alfie is English and Jafta is African. Introduce Lewin's books to children: *Jafta*; *Jafta: The Journey*; *Jafta: The Town*; *Jafta's Father*; *Jafta's Mother*; and *Jafta and the Wedding*.

Basal reader selections often come from books in series. Giff's *Watch Out, Ronald Morgan!* appears on pp 160–67 of the second grade SB/Ginn basal reader series edited by Pearson, et al. Other books are *Happy Birthday, Ronald Morgan* and *Ronald Morgan Goes to Bat*. "A Day When Frogs Wear Shoes" from Cameron's *More Stories Julian Tells*, appears on pages 214–25 of the third grade SB/Ginn basal reader, *Castles in the Sand*. The book is the sequel to *Stories Julian Tells*.

A collection of five stories about Adam Joshua appear in Smith's *The Show-and-Tell War and Other Stories About Adam Joshua*. Other books include *The Kid Next Door and Other Headaches: More Stories About Adam Joshua*; *The Monster in the Third Dresser Drawer and Other Stories About Adam Joshua*; and *It's Not Easy Being George: Stories About Adam Joshua (and His Dog)*.

Primary students will enjoy the Polk Street Gang series by Giff which include: *The Beast in Mrs. Rooney's Room*; *Fish Face*; *The Candy Corn Contest*; *December Secrets*; *In the Dinosaur's Paw*; *The Valentine Star*; *Lazy Lions, Lucky Lambs*; *Snaggle Doodles*; *Purple Climbing Days*; *Say "Cheese"*;

Sunny Side Up; and *Pickle Puss*. Second grade teachers may wish to use Giff's *A Teacher's Guide to the Kids at the Polk Street School Books*. A recipe for latkes (potato pancakes) appears on page 12 to be used with *December Secrets*. A pamphlet called "Patricia Reilly Giff Visits the Kids of the Polk Street School" is an interview with the author when she visits Ms. Rooney's class at the Polk Street School. One of the girls from the Polk Street series, Dawn, appears in another series by Giff, the Polka Dot Private Eye series, which includes: *The Mystery of the Blue Ring*; *The Riddle of the Red Purse*; *The Secret at the Polk Street School*; and *The Powder Puff Puzzle*. Since all the books about the Polk Street School are available in paperback, three of each title could be purchased and kept in a special box which could be loaned from the school library/media center to second grade classrooms. The box could be sent from second grade classroom to second grade classroom after a one-or-two month visit. During that time, a classroom of second graders could each have a book to read at the same time. Faster readers might read all of the titles while others may read only one or two in the same time period.

Bright's *Georgie's Halloween* is a children's literature classic. Read the story aloud in October to introduce the other books about Georgie: *Georgie and the Buried Treasure*; *Georgie and the Little Dog*; *Georgie and the Magician*; *Georgie and the Robbers*; *Georgie and the Runaway Balloons*; *Georgie Goes West*; and *Georgie's Christmas Carol*.

Introduce Mariana's *Miss Flora McFlimsey and the Baby New Year* in January and discuss all the holidays that occur all year through *Miss Flora McFlimsey's Valentine*; *Miss Flora McFlimsey's Easter Bonnet*; *Miss Flora McFlimsey's May Day*; *Miss Flora McFlimsey's Halloween*; and *Miss Flora McFlimsey's Christmas Eve*. Have students place *Miss Flora McFlimsey's Birthday* into the correct sequence according to their own birth months and arrange the other books in chronological order.

Strega Nona, created by de Paola, is a witch. Use the sound filmstrip, video, or 16mm film to introduce this Italian character to students. Place the recording *Strega Nona's Magic Lessons and Other Stories* in the reading/ listening/viewing area in the classroom to introduce or reinforce other books by de Paola besides those about Strega Nona, because seven stories are included on the recording. Copies of *Strega Nona's Magic Lessons* in paperback could be used as a class set for literature-based reading programs. In this book, Strega Nona gives magic lessons to Bambolona, the baker's daughter. Big Anthony becomes jealous and disguises himself as a girl in order to take magic lessons too. Another book about Big Anthony and the witch is *Merry Christmas, Strega Nona*. Because de Paola has written and illustrated so many picture books, students could be introduced to several of them. The project could include recognizing and discussing de Paola's art style. Sharing the books helps to teach the meaning of author and illustrator.

Hoban's *The Laziest Robot in Zone One* is the sequel to *Ready, Set, Robot!* which is about Sol-1, a tubby little robot.

There are a number of books for students in grades four through eight that are sequels. Students who enjoyed Fitzgerald's books about *The Great Brain* will enjoy Peck's *Soup*, who also appears in *Soup and Me*; *Soup for President*; *Soup in the Saddle*; *Soup on Fire*; *Soup on Ice*; *Soup on Wheels*; *Soup's Drum*; *Soup's Goat*; and *Soup's Uncle*. *Soup for President* is available in video format. *The Great Brain* is available on five cassettes and *The Great Brain Does It Again* appears on four cassettes. Other books by Fitzgerald in this series include: *The Great Brain at the Academy*; *The Great Brain Reforms*; *Me and My Little Brain*; *More Adventures of the Great Brain*; and *The Return of the Great Brain*.

Some other books in series about boys that appear in a section of Chapter 2 in this book called: INTRODUCING BOOKS BY TITLES: HUMAN CHARACTERS are: Klein's *Herbie Jones*; Gilson's *Hobie Hanson*; Jones's *Germy*; Clifford's *Harvey*; Steiner's *Oliver*; and Hurwitz's *Aldo*.

Check this same chapter for sequels and series for intermediate students that are about girls and women including: Branscum's *Johnny May*; Burch's *Ida Early*; Delton's *Angel*; Green's *Isabel*; Greenwald's *Rosey*; Peck's *Blossom Culp*; the Gray family by Kaye; *DeDe, Karen*, and *Elaine* by Hurwitz; and *Anastasia Krupnik* by Lowry.

Twelve-year-old Alex wins a contest in Park's *Skinnybones* and the prize is a chance to be in a TV commercial in the sequel *Almost Starring Skinnybones*. Lowry's *Switcharound* is the sequel to *The One Hundredth Thing About Caroline*. Giff's *The Fourth-Grade Celebrity* is the sequel to *The Girl Who Knew It All*. Blume's *Superfudge* is the sequel to *Tales of a Fourth Grade Nothing*. Twelve-year-old Harvey Trumble appears in Gilson's *Harvey the Beer Can King* and in *Hello, My Name Is Scrambled Eggs*. *Only My Mouth Is Smiling* is the sequel to Riley's *Crazy Quilt*, both of which are for junior high students.

The Stanley children meet a new stepsister, Amanda, in Snyder's Newbery Honor Book and winner of the Christopher Award, *The Headless Cupid*. Amanda is preoccupied with the occult. In the sequel, *The Famous Stanley Kidnapping Case*, Amanda is kidnapped but all five of the Stanley children are together. The third book in the series is *Blair's Nightmare* in which all of the Stanleys help keep David's secret. In the fourth book, *Janie's Private Eyes*, 8-year-old Janie founds a detective agency to find out who is dognapping pets in the neighborhood.

Middle school students will enjoy books by Voigt. In *Homecoming*, 13-year-old Dicey Tillerman takes care of her younger brothers and sister when they are deserted by their mother. Dicey's goal is to take 10-year-old James, 9-year-old Maybeth, and 6-year-old Sammy to their great-aunt Cilla's house in Maryland. The sequel is *Dicey's Song*, winner of the 1983 Newbery Medal. In *Sons from Afar* by Voigt, James is 15 and Sammy is 12. James is interested in learning more about the father who abandoned them. Voigt's *The Runner* is a prequel to the other two books and features Samuel "Bullet" Tillerman. In another spinoff, Jefferson Greene, who was a minor character in another book, is the main character of *Solitary Blue*, a Newbery Honor Book. Minna Smith from *Dicey's Song* is the main character in *Come a Stranger*. These last two books are for high school readers.

Another series of books which contains a spinoff is for intermediate readers. Taylor's *Let the Circle Be Unbroken* is a sequel to the Newbery winner, *Roll of Thunder, Hear My Cry*, which is a sequel to *Song of the Trees*. Taylor's novella, *The Friendship*, is narrated by Cassie Logan from the other books. This book is about a black-white relationship during the Depression.

Riko, a Japanese-American girl living in California during the Depression, is the main character in Uchida's *The Best Bad Thing* and the sequel, *The Happiest Ending*.

Use Greene's recent book, *Just Plain Al*, to introduce other books about Al: *A Girl Called Al*; *I Know You, Al*; and *Your Old Pal, Al*. Al develops a social conscience in *Just Plain Al* and helps street people and nursing home patients. Use Robertson's newest book about Henry Reed, *Henry Reed's Think Tank*, to introduce *Henry Reed, Inc.*; *Henry Reed's Journey*; *Henry Reed's Big Show*; and *Henry Reed's Baby-Sitting Service*. The *Not-Just-Anybody Family* by Byars is an unusual rodeo family consisting of a mother, grandfather, a sister, and two brothers. Other books in the series include: *The Blossoms Meet the Vulture Lady*; *The Blossoms and the Green Phantom*; and *A Blossom Promise*. Byars is the winner of the 1986 Regina Medal given by the Catholic Library Association for excellence in the field of literature for children.

Fifth graders using Pearson's SB/Ginn basal reader, *Dream Chasers*, will read "A Paying Job" from Stolz's *Explorer of Barkham Street*. That book about the bully, Martin, follows *The Dog on Barkham Street* and *The Bully of Barkham Street*. The first two books tell similar stories. The first is from Edward's point of view and the second is from Martin's point of view. Martin tries to reform in the third book.

Pinkwater's *The Snarkout Boys and the Avocado of Death* is the sequel to *The Snarkout Boys and the Baconburg Horror*. Use *Dido and Pa* to introduce Aiken's series which includes: *Wolves of Willoughby Chase*; *Black Hearts in Battersea*; *Nightbirds on Nantucket*; *Cuckoo Tree*; and *Stolen Lake*.

Hamilton's *Mystery of Drear House* is the sequel to *The House of Dies Drear*. Beatty's *Be Ever Hopeful, Hannalee* is the sequel to *Turn Homeward, Hannalee*. Aiken's *Bridle the Wind* is the sequel to *Go Saddle the Sea*. Siegal's *Upon the Head of a Goat: A Childhood in Hungary, 1939–1944* is a Newbery Honor Book about a family that lives through the Holocaust. The sequel is *Grace in the Wilderness: After the Liberation, 1945–1948*. Holocaust books for middle students include Sender's *The Cage* and the sequel, *To Life*. Garrigue's *The Eternal Spring of Mr. Ito* is the sequel to *All the Children Were Sent Away*, in which World War II comes to Japanese-Canadians.

Wrightson's *The Ice Is Coming* is followed by *The Dark Bright Water* and *Journey Behind the Wind*. These stories about Wirgun, a young aborigine, are a blend of realism and fantasy. The conflict between good and evil involves the terrible Wulgaru who steals men's spirits. Numerous fantasies that appear in sequels and series appear in a section of Chapter 10 in this book called IN-TRODUCING FANTASY. Lindbergh's *The People in Pineapple Place* and the sequel, *The Prisoners of Pineapple Place*, are space and time fantasies that can introduce other time travel books found in Chapter 1 of this book under TIME TRAVEL: A BOOKTALK. At the end of the first book, the unusual family trapped in time is about to move. In the sequel, something happens and the family moves to Athens, Connecticut, instead of Athens, Greece, as expected. Students can use an atlas to find out and locate many places in the world that are named after Athens, Greece. Hunter's *The Three-Day Enchantment* is a sequel to *Knight of the Golden Plain* which is a space and time book about the Middle Ages and knights. Quite often, successful books with a sequel turn into a series. Banks's *The Return of the Indian* and *The Secret of the Indian* follow *The Indian in the Cupboard.*

Howe's Bunnicula series includes *Bunnicula; The Celery Stalks at Midnight; Howliday Inn;* and *Nighty-Nightmare.* These books are for intermediate students, but two picture books about these characters are called *The Fright Before Christmas* and *Scared Silly: A Halloween Treat.* An abridged version of *The Celery Stalks at Midnight* is available on cassette.

Two fantasies that have prequels are by McKinley and by Jacques. The Newbery Honor Book *The Blue Sword* is the prequel to the Newbery Winner *Hero and the Crown* by McKinley. *Mossflower* is the prequel to *Redwall* by Jacques. Students can learn more about an author who has written one or more series. Fantasy and science fiction series that are popular include the Time Quartet series by L'Engle, the Chronicles of Narnia by Lewis, the Dragon series by McAffrey. Christopher has written several successful series. The White Mountain series includes *The White Mountains; Pool of Fire; City of Gold and Lead;* and the prequel *When the Tripods Came.* The Fireball series includes: *Fireball; New Found Land;* and *Dragon Dance.* The titles in Christopher's Sword of the Spirits trilogy are: *The Burning Lands; The Prince Is Waiting;* and *The Sword of the Spirits.* Harrison's *Doom of the Gods* is a sequel to *The Curse of the Ring*, which retells the Norse myths of the Volsung saga. *Devil on My Back* by Hughes, a Canadian writer, is the sequel to *The Dream Catcher,* in which 14-year-old Ruth lives in Ark Three, a city established after the earth's oil supplies dry up.

For books about Cam Jansen by Adler, Encyclopedia Brown by Sobol, and Einstein Anderson by Simon, check the section of Chapter 10 in this book called INTRODUCING MYSTERIES. A selection from *Einstein Anderson Makes Up for Lost Time* appears in the fourth grade HBJ basal reader in the Laureate edition compiled by Cullinan, et al. beginning on page 174 of *Crossroads.* Some series and sequels that are mysteries, that are included in a section of this chapter called INTRODUCING MYSTERIES include books about: My Dog by Adler; Incognito Mosquito by Hass; the Ghost Squad series by Hildick;

Sebastian by Jones; Pinkerton by Kellogg; Something Queer series by Levy; Mr. Sniff by Lewis; the Baker Street series by Newman; Miss Mallard by Quackenbush; and Nate the Great by Sharmat.

Favorite characters from series that appear in this book in Chapter 7, EXPANDING BASAL READERS, are: de Brunoff's Babar; Minarik's Little Bear; Sharmat's Nate the Great; McGregor and Pantell's Miss Pickerell; Robertson's Henry Reed; Lowry's Anastasia; Lewis's Narnia characters; Farley's Black Stallion; Henry's Misty; Lobel's Frog and Toad; and Yolen's Commander Toad.

Cresswell's *Bagthorpes Liberated: Being the Seventh Part of the Bagthorpe Saga* takes place after the family return from a vacation in Wales and finds that a tramp is in their home. Use Cresswell's seventh book in the Bagthorpe saga to remind students of the other six titles: *Ordinary Jack: Being the First Part of the Bagthorpe Saga*; *Absolute Zero: Being the Second Part of the Bagthorpe Saga*; *Bagthorpes Unlimited: Being the Third Part of the Bagthorpe Saga*; *The Bagthorpes vs the World: Being the Fourth Part of the Bagthorpe Saga*; *The Bagthorpes Abroad: Being the Fifth Part of the Bagthorpe Saga*; *Bagthorpes Haunted: Being the Sixth Part of the Bagthorpe Saga*.

CHAPTER FIVE

Multimedia Introduce Books by Subject

WHALES, DOLPHINS, SHARKS [CU 52–53; 99–104; 730]. One of the *Reading Rainbow* television episodes features *Humphrey the Lost Whale: A True Story*. Review books for the *Reading Rainbow* segment are: Patent's *All About Whales*; Behrens's *Whalewatch!*; and Hogan's *The Life Cycle of the Whale*. Humphrey, a real humpback whale, is famous because of his swim 64 miles up the Sacramento River where he was stuck for 25 days. Two books about Humphrey are Takuda and Hall's *Humphrey the Lost Whale: A True Story* and Goldner's *Humphrey the Wrong-Way Whale*. Patent's *Humpback Whales* makes a good companion to the books about Humphrey. *Whale Rescue*, for an older audience, is a NOVA TV production available also as a video or 16mm film. *Whale Rescue* is about pilot whales beached along the Cape Cod coast of Massachusetts where 27 of them die. Whittell's *The Story of Three Whales* is about real whales who were trapped in the icy waters of Barrow, Alaska in 1988. *Whales* is the joint effort of WETA TV and the National Audubon Society, and it is available as a video. A teacher's guide is available with this history of the North American right whale. A National Geographic video, *The Great Whales*, includes the birth of a killer whale and discusses whale conservation. Basic information about whales is included in the National Geographic sound filmstrip, *Whales,* and the video, *Whales*. A video produced by the Sierra Club is *Sierra Club: Whales.*

Sattler's *Whales: The Nomads of the Sea* is one of the best books about whales for intermediate students. The whales are categorized by families and excellent drawings explain physical characteristics, habits, and their natural environment. "A Glossary of Whales" appears on page 51 and Chapter 5 is devoted to the language of whales and Chapter 6 is about babies. Twenty species of whales appear in Berger's *Whales. Whalewatch!* by Behrens is easy to read and includes color photos on every page. A two-page chart gives a scale for whales that compares them to a schoolbus. Moby Dick and Orca are mentioned by Behrens. The artwork in Milton's easy-to-read book, *Whales: The Gentle Giants*, is especially noteworthy. Several general overviews of whales include Patent's *All About Whales*; Hoyt's *Whale Watcher's Handbook*; and Bunting's *The Sea World Book of Whales*. Use the *Audubon Society Field Guide to North American Fishes, Whales and Dolphins* to identify whales. McClung's *Thor, Last of the Sperm Whales* has been reissued. The whale is one of five animals in McGrath's *Saving Our Animal Friends*. Color photos enhance Martin's *Whales*, which is part of the series *Wildlife in Danger* for primary students and Simon's *Whales* which appeals to all ages. Whales are among the giants in *Giants of Land, Sea, and Air: Past and Present* by Peters. MacQuilty's *Side by Side* discusses symbiosis and includes whale barnacles. Information about the sound of the beluga whale appears in McGrath's *How Animals Talk*. The Harrars' *Signs of the Apes, Songs of the Whales: Adventures in Human-Animal Communication* also addresses whale communication.

Johnson's *Whale Song* contains beautiful illustrations by Young, and advances the idea that whale songs are counting. Baker's *Who's a Friend of the Water-Spurting Whale?* is a picture book illustrated by de Paola. Smyth's *Crystal: The Story of a Real Baby Whale* is a fictionalized account of Crystal's birth in the West Indies to sojourns along the coast of New England and includes much factual information about the humpback whales. *Davy's Dream: A Young Boy's Adventure with Wild Orca Whales* is about a boy who paints his sailboat to look like the killer whales who help him. A wordless segment appears in Lewis's story. Thrush's *The Gray Whales Are Missing* is for intermediate students. Ten-year-old Pence and a friend investigate the disappearance of the gray whales during their migration off the coast of California.

Students may wish to investigate the history of whaling. One of the best sources is the April 1988 issue of *Cobblestone* magazine which contains 13 articles about whales and whaling. Articles include "Sailor-Made Songs" by Calkins; "Women at Sea" by Germer; "The Last Whaler" by Morgan and Blohm; "Honolulu: Nineteenth-Century Yankee Seaport" by Plude; and "The Sail Maker: A Sailor's Best Mate" by Greco. Hall's "Make Your Own Scrimshaw," pages 16–17, tells about the art of scratching designs into the teeth and bones of whales using ink or soot. Information is given for engraving on ivory or plastic piano keys or other plastic. Bunting's *The Sea World Book of Whales* has an excellent chapter on the history of whaling whereas the Shapiros' whole book, *The Story of Yankee Whaling*, is devoted to the topic. The building of a wooden whaling ship in the 1870s is the topic of *The Wooden Ship* by Adkins. *Arctic Adventure* by Dekkers is about two Dutch brothers who keep a pirate whaling boat from harpooning a Greenland whale. In George's *Water Sky*, Lincoln, a young man from an old New England whaling family, goes to Alaska to find his uncle and gets involved in whaling the Eskimo way. The materials about whales in this section can be used in a literature-based unit using *Water Sky* as the main book. Students may also wish to branch out to study dolphins and sharks.

Some poems about whales include "Constant Whales," pages 22–23 of Holman's *The Song in My Head* (gray whales); "If You Ever Met a Whale," page 39 of *More Surprises* collected by Hopkins (humorous); "Whale," page 16 of Bodecker's *Snowman Sniffles and Other Verse* (humorous); and Dearover's "Whale," page 354 of *The Book of a Thousand Poems*. Drawing a whale from the letter "W" appears in MacDonald's alphabet picture book, *Alphabatics*. *Draw Along*, a primary art program produced by AIT and the Oklahoma Educational Television Authority, contains a program which shows how to draw a diver, shark, whales, and an octopus in Program #30, *Underwater Animals*.

An interview by Cooper, "Sylvia Earle, Swimming with Humpback Whales" appears in the seventh grade HM basal reader, *Pageants*, edited by Durr, et al. "The Voice of the Whale" is a personal narrative by Mowat on pages 434–48 of the eighth grade HM basal reader, *Triumphs*, edited by Durr, et al. *Draw 50 Sharks, Whales, and Other Sea Creatures* by Ames shows how to draw a dozen kinds of sharks and whales.

Differences among varieties of whales and dolphins are pointed out in Strachan's *Whales and Dolphins*. The following books include information about dolphins as well as whales: Bender's *Whales and Dolphins*; Sattler's *Whales: The Nomads of the Sea*; Berger's *Whales*; and Behrens's *Whales of the World*.

Check Rinard's *Dolphins: Our Friends in the Sea, Dolphins and Other Toothed Whales* for legends about the dolphin from world mythology, as well as information about killer whales. A list of aquariums and parks of the world that contain dolphins and whales is included. Color photos enhance Leatherwood's *Sea World Book of Dolphins* for intermediate students. *The Sea World Book of Dolphins* gives information about evolution, feeding and raising of dolphins as well as conservation. *Dolphins* is a 16mm film and video. *The Dolphin Adventure* is a video about a crew of researchers who are communicating with wild dolphins near the Bahamas. Experiments with dolphin communication appear in L'Engle's fiction book, *A Ring of Endless Light*, also available in a two-filmstrip set. Clarke's science fiction book, *Dolphin Island*, also includes dolphin communication. L'Engle's book would make an excellent literature-based selection for middle school students. *A Ring of Endless Light* is the fourth book in the Austin series that begins with *Meet the Austins* and includes *Moon by Night* and the spinoff, *Arm of the Starfish*.

Primary students can enjoy color photographs as well as information about dolphins in *Dolphins!* by Behrens. Patent's *Dolphins and Porpoises* gives information about the habits of these mammals, sonar, birth of a dolphin, raising and feeding the young. Smith's *A Dolphin Goes to School: The Story of Squirt, a Trained Dolphin* shows the step-by-step process for training a bottle-nosed dolphin for a marine show. Squirt comes from the Gulf of Mexico near Florida and is trained in North Carolina. Students K–6 will enjoy the film or video *Dolphins* which includes the birth of a baby dolphin. Dolphins appear in Goodall's picture book, *Paddy Under Water*. In *Demo and the Dolphin* by Benchley, Demosthenes wants to help his fisherman father who is afraid of the sea because his own father drowned. The father fishes along the coast but does not catch much. The dolphin Simo is a character in this book, which takes place in Piraeus (the port of Athens), in Delphi, and Mt. Parnassus (above the Gulf of Corinth).

Lauber's nonfiction article "The Friendly Dolphins," and the Greek folk tale "Arion" appear on pages 70–82 of the third grade Ginn basal reader, *Mystery Sneaker*, edited by Clymer and Venezky. Extend basal reader stories by providing other materials on dolphins. Siderell's *Whale in the Sky* is a folk tale of the Northwestern Indians that includes Raven and Thunderbird. Bierhorst's

The Sacred Path: Spells, Prayers, and Power Songs of the American Indian includes a prayer to the whale on page 131.

Some companion books are Anton's *Sharks, Sharks, Sharks*; Cole's *Hungry, Hungry Sharks*; Freedman's *Sharks*; Reed's *Sevengill. The Shark and Me*; and Sattler's *Sharks, the Super Fish*. Sharks appear in *Giants of Land, Sea and Air: Past and Present* by Peters. *The Sharks* is a National Geographic video. *Sharks* is a sound filmstrip in the *Animal Kingdom* series. McGovern's "Eugenie Clark: Shark Lady" appears on pages 343–52 of the fourth grade HM basal reader *Flights*, edited by Durr, et al. Ciardi's poem "The Shark" appears on page 353 of *Flights*.

DISCOVERING DINOSAURS [CU 53–54; 714].   The study of fossils is a natural precursor to studying dinosaurs. Read Lilian Moore's poem, "Fossils," from *Dinosaurs* by Hopkins before examining the many books about fossils. One of the best books about fossils for intermediate students is Lauber's *Dinosaurs Walked Here: And Other Stories Fossils Tell.* Drawings and photographs help explain theories and how discovery of the same fossils in different parts of the world supports these theories. Arnold's *Trapped in Tar: Fossils from the Ice Age* concentrates on fossils from the La Brea Tar Pits. Many of these fossils are from creatures which came after the time of the dinosaurs. The La Brea Tar Pits contain fossils from 135 different species of birds, 300 kinds of animals and over 100,000 plants. Other finds include a woman's skull, mastadons, and mammoths. Chapter 7 of Gallant's *Fossils* is devoted to Dinosaur National Monument and early discoveries by Douglas. Some of the items covered are: what fossils are and what they tell us; how to collect fossils; and the ages of the earth. Lambert's *A Field Guide to Prehistoric Life: A True Field Guide to Fossil Life from One-Celled Plants to Homo Sapiens* includes information on all types of fossils and hundreds of drawings, diagrams, and maps. Smith's *Living Fossils* tells about the oldest living animal fossils. A chart giving samples of plant and animal life from the Precambrian to the present day is included in *Fossils* by Curtis, which also tells how fossils are formed and how they tell us information. Baylor's *If You Are a Hunter of Fossils*, in lyrical prose, shares the record of the earth through fossils. *Fossils Tell of Long Ago* by Aliki is easy reading and makes a good companion book to the other books written and illustrated by Aliki that are part of the Let's-Read-and-Find-Out series: *Evolution* by Cole; *Digging Up Dinosaurs*; and *Dinosaur Bones. Evolution* describes how fossils tell us about our origins. *Digging Up Dinosaurs* and *Dinosaur Bones* explain how scientists gather, label, organize, and make deductions from dinosaur bones. Cobb's *The Monsters Who Died: A Mystery About Dinosaurs* tells about fossil reconstruction. The five basic processes of fossilization appear in the film or video *Fossils! Fossils!*

Information about dinosaurs is available in various multimedia formats. Students can create their own dinosaur fossil skeletons by mixing and matching bones from several dinosaurs in a section of the computer program *Designa-*

saurus called "Build-a-Dinosaur." Other sections of the program include "Print-a-Dinosaur," which prints out a dozen dinosaurs, and "Walk-a-Dinosaur" which takes several dinosaurs through four ecosystems. *First Dinosaur Reader* is a computer program that contains four large-print stories which share information about dinosaurs in an interactive manner for students in grades one to four. *Digging Up Dinosaurs* by Aliki is available as a read-along. The video of *Digging Up Dinosaurs* which appears as Program #6 of the television series *Reading Rainbow*, is available for purchase. *Dinosaurs: Puzzles from the Past* is a National Geographic film or video in which viewers visit Dinosaur Provincial Park in Canada and see excavations of dinosaur fossils. Reconstructions of dinosaurs and details of how they are assembled in an Ottawa museum are shown. Photographs of reconstructions showing terrain, vegetation, habitat, and weather conditions for dinosaurs are included in Dixon and Burton's *The Age of Dinosaurs: A Photographic Record*. Books in the New Dinosaur Library series by Dixon are: *The First Dinosaurs: Hunting the Dinosaurs and Other Prehistoric Animals*; *The Jurassic Dinosaurs*; and *The Last Dinosaurs*. A four-filmstrip set, *The Magnificent Dinosaurs*, tells about new discoveries as well as information about the fossils from Dinosaur National Monument in Colorado and Utah. The same filmstrip series adapted for younger students is called *All About Dinosaurs*, and a video version is also available. The video for intermediate students, *Where Did They Go?: A Dinosaur Update*, shares museum exhibits and a fossil dig. *Where Are They Now?: A Dinosaur Update* explains new theories. *More Dinosaurs* is a video showing dinosaurs in humorous cartoons, as well as footage from various movies, to examine the myths and truths of dinosaurs. A sound filmstrip based on the book *Dinosaurs* by Gibbons covers 14 dinosaurs. The cassette and 30 paperbacks, *Dinosaurs: Giant Reptiles*, is for primary students. A film or video, *Stanley and the Dinosaurs* is based on Hoff's easy reader, *Stanley*. A program from Season VI of the instructional television series *3–2–1 Contact* for 8 to 12-year-olds, called *Detectives*, has a section called *Dinosaur Detectives*, #609. Gary Owens has hosted two videos which are appropriate for all ages: *Dinosaurs* and *Son of Dinosaurs*. The following posters are available: a poster called "Awakening of Hunger" from *Dinosaurs Past and Present* by Czerkas and Olson, a set of 16 color posters from the *Dinosaur Poster Book*, and a poster with cassette called *Dinosaurs*.

Any adult preparing to rediscover dinosaurs with youngsters should read Wilford's *The Riddle of the Dinosaur*, a book of information based on new evidence about dinosaurs, including: not all dinosaurs were coldblooded, as previously thought; some cared for their young; and their extinction wasn't based on maladaptation but was probably due to a catastrophe such as global floods or colliding asteroids. Another helpful book is Roop's *Dinosaurs: Opposing Viewpoints*, which includes various theories. Bakker's *The Dinosaur Heresies* contains controversial theories. Current theories also appear in Lampton's *New Theories on the Dinosaurs* and two books by Lauber: *New Facts About Dinosaurs* and *The News About Dinosaurs*.

Cohen's *Dinosaurs* is approached from the standpoint of how we know about dinosaurs rather than by type of dinosaur. Information includes fossils, time periods, eggs, and family life. The newest theories on how they became extinct, climate change or a catastrophe from space, such as a meteorite or asteroid, are included. Some types mentioned are: armored, duckbilled, horned, winged, and feathered. Norman's *The Illustrated Encyclopedia of Dinosaurs* is an excellent all-around book containing dinosaur information for all ages. Sattler's *Dinosaurs of North America* is an oversize book that describes the three periods of the Mesozoic era as well as 80 types of dinosaur, with information about them. Pages 147–48 include the North American dinosaur discoveries by location. It is interesting to note that 35 have been found in Alberta, Canada; 25 in Wyoming; 23 in Montana; 15 in Utah; and 14 in western Canada. Students might like to locate them on a map or check to see if any discoveries have been made in their own state or province. Sattler's *Illustrated Dinosaur Dictionary* is an excellent alphabetical listing of over 300 dinosaurs from all over the world. Lambert's *A Field Guide to Dinosaurs* discusses dinosaur definitions, fossilization, discoveries dating, identification, restoring, and displaying. Chapter 5 lists the names of scientists involved in discoveries and research, so students could be challenged to look up more information on each. The double-page spread of the six main groups of dinosaurs is especially good and would be an excellent addition to a bulletin board. Elting's *Macmillan Book of Dinosaurs and Other Prehistoric Creatures* is an oversize book divided according to time periods. Benton's *The Dinosaur Encyclopedia* is an alphabetical illustrated book. Pictures with names, pronunciations, and descriptions are a useful feature of Parker's *Dinosaurs and Their World*. Cobb's *The Monsters Who Died: A Mystery About Dinosaurs* explains how deductions about fossils are made, and shares some of the theories about the extinction of the dinosaurs. Although Lambert's *The Age of Dinosaurs* is a revised edition in the All-About series, none of the new theories about extinction are included. However, the paperback includes a large poster. Branley's *Dinosaurs, Asteroids, and Superstars*; Branley's *What Happened to the Dinosaurs?*; Cohen's *Dinosaurs*; Murphy's *Last Dinosaur*; and Milburn's *Let's Look at Dinosaurs* contain extinction theories. Murphy's *The Last Dinosaur* is fiction based on fact and speculates how and why the triceratops might have been the last dinosaur left.

Dinosaurs can be studied by specific type and several books deal with only one type or highlight several. *The Illustrated Dinosaur Dictionary*, winner of the 1984 Golden Kite Award, would be helpful if this approach is used. Jacobs's *Supersaurus* is an easy-to-read book about the supersaurus and Dr. James Jensen, a field paleontologist, and what he does. Selsam's *Tyrannosaurus Rex* deals with the discovery made in Mahoshika State Park in Montana. Cauley's *The Trouble with Tyrannosaurus Rex* is a large picture book in which TR wants to gobble up other dinosaurs. Share Carroll's *How Big Is a Brachiosaurus?* Benton's *How Dinosaurs Lived* is about a day with a diplodocus, the dinosaur with the helmet-like head and armor spikes. Brontosaurus, brachiosaurus, stegosaurus, and the triceratops are featured in Cobb's *The Monsters Who Died.* *Dodosaurus: The Dinosaurs That Didn't Make It* is by Meyerowitz. Knight's *Dinosaurs That Swam and Flew* includes the thecodonts, dimetrodon, mixosaurus, placodont and early echthyosaurus. Sattler's *Peterosaurs: The Flying Reptiles* describes various species of flying reptiles. Simon's *The Largest Dinosaurs* includes the brachiosaurus, diplodocus, apatosaurus, camarasaurus, supersaurus and ultrasaurus. Captioned drawings appear in Norman and Milner's *Dinosaur.* Only creatures from the Mesozoic period appear in Sattler's *Tyrannosaurus Rex and Its Kin: The Mesozoic Monsters.*

Several books that have been written about baby dinosaurs can be shared with younger children. Sattler's *Baby Dinosaurs* tells about comparative size, physical features, habitat, eating habits and parental care of young dinosaurs, and has good color paintings. Because of the repetition of categories, the book lends itself to chartmaking for intermediate students. Some interesting facts are: the camarasaurus hatched from eggs just a little larger than basketballs or the size of a large rabbit; the protoceratops had 18 potato-shaped eggs the size of baby pigs; the oval eggs of the maiasaura babies were the size of a squirrel. Silverman's *Dinosaur Babies* is a similar book that includes a few more dinosaurs but does not have the time chart. Horner's *Maia: A Dinosaur Grows Up* is fiction but is based on new information about the baby duckbill dinosaur and follows it from birth to maturity. Fossil evidence indicates that the maiasauras were good parents, contrary to previous speculation. Freedman's *Dinosaurs and Their Young* is based on a find in Montana in 1978 that also shows that dinosaurs reared their young. Photographs of the duckbilled dinosaur appear in Lauber's *Dinosaurs Walked Here: And Other Stories Fossils Tell.*

Nancy Renfro Puppets sells the following dinosaur puppets: brontosaurus, dimetrodon, pteradactyl, stegosaurus, and tyrannosaurus. Spizzirri Company has 9 dinosaur mask puppets: tyrannosaurus, pachycephalosaurus, stegosaurus, ceratosaurus, triceratops, apatosaurus, parasaurolophus, euoplocephalus, and deinonychus. The Troll catalog *Dinosaurs Plus . . .* contains the following stuffed animals: pentaceratops, brontosaurus, tyrannosaurus, triceratops, stegosaurus, and dimetrodon.

What would happen if dinosaurs returned? Check Most's *If the Dinosaurs Came Back*; *Whatever Happened to the Dinosaurs?*; and *Dinosaur's Cousins.* Have children speculate what would happen.

Students may wish to branch out into prehistoric animals of other time periods from those in which dinosaurs lived. "The Boy Who Loved Mammoths" is told by Rolf Martin on his cassette *The Boy Who Loved Mammoths and Other Tales.* Aliki's *Wild and Woolly Mammoths* and *Giants from the Past: The Age of Mammals* center on other prehistoric beasts. Cole's *Saber-toothed Tiger and Other Ice Age Mammals* includes 12 ice-age mammals from the La Brea Tar Pits. Miller's *Prehistoric Mammals* tells about 36 early mammals and possible reasons for their extinction. *Prehistoric Animals* by Gibbons tells about early animals but has a confusing time table.

Several nonfiction books about dinosaurs are geared for early readers. Parish's *Dinosaur Time* has long been a favorite in which children can learn to read the names of 11 dinosaurs by themselves. *Dinosaurs* by Gibbons continues in her tradition of nonfiction for beginning readers. Pictures and footprints of dinosaurs are included with a discussion of fossils and paleontologists. Read-along cassettes for *Dinosaurs* by Gibbons and *My Visit to the Dinosaurs* by Aliki are available. Children will enjoy seeing the dinosaurs in the museum and learning characteristics of each one. Aliki's other book, *Dinosaurs Are Different*, helps children learn how to tell the jawbone of a lizard-hipped saurischian from the beak of a bird-hipped ornithischian. Teachers can look at page 32 and divide the class into two groups, saurischia and ornithischia. Then students can go off looking for information to place in each category. Kingdon's *The ABC Dinosaur Book*, a picture book, includes phonetic pronunciations for dinosaurs from Ankylosaurus to Zancladon. Even the youngest children can learn about dinosaurs through Barton's *Dinosaurs, Dinosaurs* and Blumenthal's *Count-a-Saurus,* a counting book.

One of the funniest picture books about dinosaurs is Kellogg's *Prehistoric Pinkerton.* Pinkerton, everyone's favorite Great Dane, is dressed up in a stegosaurus costume and taken on a field trip to the museum. Pinkerton's owner didn't want to leave him at home because he is teething and has already eaten 13 pencils, a broom, and a bedpost. As can be expected, Pinkerton is far from harmless around all those dinosaur bones. *What Happened to Patrick's Dinosaurs?* by Carrick is available as a read-along cassette with paperback. When Patrick goes to the zoo with his brother Hank, he is amazed at the size of the elephant. Hank then explains dinosaurs in terms of elephants: a brontosaurus is heavier than 10 elephants. Patrick imagines that he sees a dinosaur everywhere, including one that follows them home. When Hank says that dinosaurs have been extinct for over 60 million years, the dinosaur disappears. *What Happened to Patrick's Dinosaurs?* by Carrick is excellent for reading aloud. When Patrick asks Hank what happened to the dinosaurs, his brother gives the reasons that are found in the newer books: it was too hot or too cold for them, or an asteroid covered the earth with dust when it hit. Then Patrick makes up a story about how dinosaurs do all the work for people, but when people only want recess and lunch, the dinosaurs get on a spaceship and go away. However, the dinosaurs miss people and check on them every day. A cassette/paperback package is available. In Klein's *Thing,* Emily has a pet rock because her landlord does not allow live pets. However, the rock is really a little stegosaurus which Emily calls "Thing." When the landlady finds out, she says they have to leave, but when Emily comes home from school, the landlady is feeding Thing a large meal because he has just foiled burglars. This Australian picture book is excellent for reading aloud. Talbott's *We're Back! A Dinosaur's Story* is about a tyrannosaurus who is lured into a spaceship where he swallows Brain Grain that enables him to learn language and comprehend advanced studies. On a trip to 20th-century New York, the dinosaurs are rescued by Dr. Bleb of the Museum of Natural History. Bradman's *Dilly the Dinosaur* includes four stories about a dinosaur who refuses to take a bath, throws a tantrum on his sister's birthday, paints his room, and waits for it to rain cats and dogs after his father uses the expression. Both the Talbott and Bradman books have cartoon-type illustrations. *In Granny's Garden* by Harrison, a boy sees a brontosaurus in his grandmother's garden. Berenstain's *The Day of the Dinosaur* gives information about dinosaurs in rhyme, as does Harrison's book. Joyce's *Dinosaur Bob and His Adventures with the Family Lizardo* is about a family that finds a green dinosaur while they are on vacation in Africa. The dinosaur causes nothing but trouble after they get home, until they interest him in playing on the Pimlico Pirates baseball team. *Dinosaur Bob* is a feature on Program #60 of the television series *Reading Rainbow.* In *Dinosaur's Halloween* by Donnelly, a boy and his dog go trick or treating and meet a dinosaur who turns out to be real when they are attacked. Wilhelm's *Tyrone the Horrible* is a bully. Kellogg's *The Mysterious Tadpole* is available as a hardback/cassette, paperback/cassette, sound filmstrip, 16mm film, and video. The tadpole Louis receives from Uncle McAllister for his birthday turns out to be a dinosaur. Richter's *Jacob Two-Two and the Dinosaur* is about 8-year-old Jacob, who receives a tiny green lizard, the last surviving diplodocus. A cassette is available. Professor Potts puts together dinosaur bones in an unusual way in Carrick's *Big Old Bones: A Dinosaur Tale.*

Show the film or video *Dinosaur* to intermediate students before introducing fiction books about dinosaurs. Philip's report on dinosaurs is boring until the prehistoric animals came to life. In Steiner's *Oliver Dibbs and the Dinosaur Cause,* Oliver chooses the study of dinosaurs for his class project and eventually lobbies the Colorado State Legislature to vote the stegosaurus as the official state fossil. In Adrian's *Mystery of the Dinosaur Graveyard,* Chris, her twin Tom, and her cousins are camping in Utah with a map for a dinosaur graveyard when they become lost. *Cam Jansen and the Mystery of the Dinosaur Bones* by Adler is available as a read-along. Butterworth's classic *The Enormous Egg* hatches into a triceratops. Use the read-along Cliffhanger series which contains a word-for-word narration of the first third of the story and then leaves the reader with the desire to finish the book. In Senn's *The Double Disappearance of Walter Fozbek,* a boy changes into a dinosaur through a time lock or black hole. Senn's book is part of the CBS-TV program "CBS Storybreak." Logan's *Dinosaur Adventure* is a choose-your-own-ending book with eleven possible endings. Through Uncle Max's time machine, readers go back to dinosaur days with Max the dinosaur, who runs away with a time bearer. In Seidler's *The Tar Pit,* whenever Edward has troubles, he talks to an imaginary friend, a 20-foot dinosaur Alexander the Allousaurus, who lives in a tar pit. In addition to Edward's friend, a tar pit excavation reveals a real dinosaur fossil. In *Mitzi and the Terrible Tyrannosaurus Rex* by Williams, Mitzi's mother remarries and she gets two new stepbrothers. The creative 3-year-old, Darwin, thinks he is a dinosaur.

Teachers, librarians, and school library/media specialists will appreciate the 10 activities for teachers by Schatz in *Dinosaurs: A Journey Through Time*. Anyone planning preschool programs should consult Idea #17 in MacDonald's *Booksharing* for programs about dinosaurs. A set of punch-out models is part of Dimond's *Dinosaurs*. Moseley's *Dinosaurs: A Lost World* contains pop-up pictures which can be used in displays. The 1989 *A Dinosaur Year Calendar* by Peters shows 19 dinosaurs and gives a list of permanent dinosaur exhibits in the United States and Canada. Songs include: "The Dinosaur Song" from the recording *Rainbows, Stones and Dinosaur Bones*; "Dinosaurs" from the recording *When the Rain Comes Down*; and "Doing the Dinosaur Rock," from the recording of the same title.

Enjoy poetry about dinosaurs. *Dinosaurs* is a collection of 18 illustrated poems about dinosaurs edited by Hopkins. Prelutsky's *Tyrannosaurus Was a Beast* includes 14 humorous dinosaur poems, one for each of the following types: tyrannosaurus, brachiosaurus, leptopterygius, stegosaurus, deinonychus, ankylosaurus, diplodocus, coelophysis, triceratops, corythosaurus, allosaurus, iguanodon, quetzalcoatlus, and seismosaurus. Armor's poem "Pachycephalosaurus" appears on page 79 of *Sing a Song of Popcorn* by De Regniers. Use the poem "The Museum Door" by Hopkins from page 12 of *Sing a Song of Popcorn* and from pages 12–13 of *Dinosaurs* to introduce Thomson's *Auks, Rocks and the Odd Dinosaurs: Inside Stories from the Smithsonian's Museum of Natural History*, winner of one of the 1986 *Boston Globe–Horn Book* Awards.

Add a zesty bulletin board to a classroom, a library, or a school library/media center by placing Lillian Fisher's poem "Brontosaurus—A Gentle Giant Dinosaur" found on page 36 of *Dinosaurs* by Hopkins on a large colored sheet of paper shaped like a brontosaurus. Use a primary typewriter or computer enlarging program, or the enlarging feature on a copy machine for greater visibility. The poems "Tyrannosaurus," pages 4–5 and "Seismosaurus," pages 30–31 of Prelutsky's *Tyrannosaurus Was a Beast*, are also suitable poems for placing on appropriate dinosaur shapes. When making a display of dinosaur books, be sure to include *Dinosaurs Divorce* and *Dinosaurs Beware! A Safety Guide* both by Laurene and Marc Brown, to give them exposure. The first book helps children to understand divorce and the second contains 60 safety tips. Both books rely on the illustrations for nonverbal clues. A sound filmstrip is available for *Dinosaurs Beware!*

Lighten up the study of dinosaurs with some riddles. "What do you do with a blue dinosaur and a green dinosaur?" You cheer one of them up and wait until the other ripens, according to two riddles in Keller's *Colossal Fossils, Dinosaur Riddles*. If you can stand to read more dinosaur riddles, consult Sterne's *Tyrannosaurus Wrecks: A Book of Dinosaur Riddles*; Heck's *Dinosaur Riddles*; Rosenbloom's *The Funniest Dinosaur Book Ever*; the Waltons'

Fossil Follies! Jokes About Dinosaurs; and Adler's *The Dinosaur Princess and Other Prehistoric Riddles*. Osband's *The Dinosaur Fun Book* contains games, crafts, jokes, and facts.

There are many ways to make a dinosaur unit even more exciting. Troll's Fall/Winter, 1987 *Dinosaur Plus* catalog includes: stuffed toys; dino heads and costumes to wear for plays and skits; models; book bags and backpacks; puzzles; templates and stencils; T-shirts and sweat shirts; and skeleton model kits for dinosaurs. Two other catalogs of dinosaur supplies are *Dinosaur Catalog* and *The Nature Catalog*. Dinosaur puppets can be found in here as well as from Nancy Renfro Studios. Directions for making a dinosaur sock puppet and a mobile appear on pages 26–27 and 29 of Glovach's *The Little Witch's Dinosaur Book*.

Coordinate the study of dinosaurs with the art teachers. Caket's *Model a Monster: Making Dinosaurs from Everyday Materials* contains 61 projects for making dinosaurs of clay, sand, papier maché, plasticine, pipe cleaners, corrugated cardboard, and coathangers. Directions for kites, costumes, and desserts are also given in Caket's book. Dean's *Make a Prehistoric Monster* includes instructions for making 12 different projects arranged in order of prehistoric evolution beginning with a mobile from the Carboniferous era of dragonflies. The tyrannosaurus is one of the dinosaurs represented. Masks, costumes, and dioramas are included in Dean's book. The video *Dinosaurs* uses clay animation to tell about a boy and his science project. West's *Dinosaur Discoveries: How to Create Your Own Prehistoric World* tells how to create nine 3-D dinosaurs within a setting of sand, gravel, and grass. More projects appear in *The Better Homes and Gardens Dandy Dinosaurs*. Check page 48 of *Finger Frolics* by Cromwell et al. for a fingerplay called "Dinosaurs." Program #21, *Dinosaurs*, of the instructional television series *The Draw Man* includes instructions for drawing dinosaurs for intermediate and junior high school students. Program #27 of the instructional television series *Draw Along* for primary students, *Animals of the Past (Dinos)*, shows how to draw a tyrannosaurus rex. *Draw Fifty Dinosaurs and Other Prehistoric Animals* by Ames; *How Do You Draw Dinosaurs?* by DuBosque; and *Dinosaurs: A Drawing Book* and *More Dinosaurs and Other Prehistoric Beasts*, both by Michael Emberley, are helpful. Have children draw authentic pictures only after they have matched his pictures of specific types of dinosaurs with those found in other books with recent copyright dates. For example, Emberley's stegosaurus is shown with two rows of plates down the back and recent information says there is only one row. Also, the brontosaurus in Emberley's *Dinosaurs* is called an apatosaurus on pages 13–15 of Simon's *The Largest Dinosaurs*. The old concept of its mouth is seen on page 12 in Emberley's book instead of the real skull which was found in 1979.

Have students find books about dragons, such as *A Book of Dragons* by the Baskins, and compare dragons and dinosaurs.

MICE ARE NICE [CU 64–68; 721].   Mice are favorite book characters. Use "Mice Are Nice" as a bulletin board caption for a circulating display of books about mice. The books could include fiction, easy books, or nonfiction. The title of the bulletin board comes from Fyleman's poem "Mice" that begins "I think mice are rather nice." and can be found on page 56 of Cole's *The Read-Aloud Treasury*, page 71 of De Regniers's *Sing a Song of Popcorn*, and on card #77 of *Bill Martin Junior's Treasure Chest*. The poem called "Cats and Dogs" on page 7 of Bodecker's *Snowman Sniffles and Other Verse* is about mice and the fourth line in the first stanza is "—but I myself like mice." For a preschool story program called "Mice Are Nice," consult Idea #75 of MacDonald's *Booksharing*.

A number of books about mice appear in series. *Angelina Ballerina and Other Stories* is recorded by Sally Struthers with readings of the following picture books: *Angelina Ballerina; Angelina at the Fair; Angelina's Christmas; Angelina on Stage;* and *Angelina and the Princess. The Diary of a Church Mouse* is the newest of Oakley's books in his series. In this book Humphrey, a schoolmouse, decides to write a year's worth of his life adventures with the cat-friend Sampson. Other books in the series are: *Church Cat Abroad; Church Mice Adrift; Church Mice and the Moon; Church Mice at Christmas; Church Mice in Action; Church Mice Spread Their Wings;* and *Church Mouse.* Taylor has written about a dormouse named Dudley: *Dudley and the Strawberry Shake; Dudley Bakes a Cake; Dudley Goes Flying;* and *Dudley in a Jam. Mousekin's Thanksgiving* is the newest book about Miller's mouse which also appears in: *Mousekin's Golden House; Mousekin Finds a Friend; Mousekin Takes a Trip; Mousekin's ABC; Mousekin's Christmas Eve; Mousekin's Close Call; Mousekin's Fables; Mousekin's Family; Mousekin's Mystery; Mousekin's Woodland Birthday;* and *Mousekin's Woodland Sleepers.*

Several authors have written and illustrated more than one mouse book. Favorite stories by Beatrix Potter that contain mice are: *Tailor of Gloucester; Tale of Two Bad Mice; Tale of Mrs. Tittlemouse; Tale of Johnny Town Mouse;* and *Sly Old Cat. Two Bad Mice* is in pop-up format. *The Tale of Two Bad Mice* is told on the cassette *Peter Rabbit and Friends from the Picture Book Parade.* Lionni's *Nicholas, Where Have You Been?* is about a field mouse who is abducted by a bird, dropped in a nest, and accepted by birds he had been told were his enemies. Lionni's *Frederick* is included on pages 284–93 of the second grade SB/Ginn basal reader, *Garden Gates*, edited by Pearson, et al. *Alexander and the Wind-Up Mouse* is available in paperback. Lionni's *Tillie and the Wall* is about a curious mouse who wants to see what is on the other side of the wall.

Doctor De Soto by Steig is a picture book winner of the National Book Award. A mouse dentist named Dr. De Soto does not take as patients large animals who are enemies of mice. Then a fox comes begging Dr. De Soto to take him on as a patient. *Doctor De Soto* appears on pages 234–41 of the third grade SB/Ginn basal reader, *On the Horizon,* edited by Pearson, et al. Steig's *Doctor De Soto* is available in video as well as audio cassette format. Caldecott winner *Sylvester and the Magic Pebble* has been reissued. A young donkey finds a red stone that grants wishes. Sylvester accidentally changes himself into a rock, to escape a lion. A video of Steig's *Abel's Island* is available. Two books by Kraus are about mice: *Come Out and Play, Little Mouse* and *Where Are You Going, Little Mouse?* A *Friend for Oscar Mouse* by Majewski is the sequel to *Oscar Mouse Finds a Home.*

All of the characters in the following wordless books by McCully include the same mice: *Picnic*; *School*; *New Baby*; *First Snow*; and *Christmas Gift.* Goodall's *Naughty Nancy Goes to School* and *Little Red Riding Hood* are also wordless books about girl mice. Books discussed in Volume 2, Chapter 1 of this book, in a section called WORDLESS MICE BOOKS, include Henstra's *Mighty Mizzling Mice* and the sequel, *Mizzling Mouse and the Red Cabbage House.* Aronsky's two books are wordless: *Mouse Numbers and Letters* and *Mouse Writing.* In Vincent's *Breakfast Time, Ernest and Celestine,* Celestine is a mouse and Ernest is a bear. For the titles of six other books about Celestine and Ernest, check USING SEQUELS, SERIES, AND FAVORITE CHARACTERS TO INTRODUCE BOOKS in this volume, Chapter 4.

Mice are frequent characters in picture books. *Sheila Rae, the Brave* by Henkes is about a mouse who tries to prove that she is brave by not only taking a new route home from school but by doing it backwards. In Jeschke's *Lucky's Choice,* a cat is lonely until he finds a mouse for a companion. *Henri's Mouse* by Mendoza is about an artist. Oechsli's *Mice at Bat* is an easy reader about Kevin and his mice friends who play baseball at night in an empty stadium. Allen's *Where Is Freddy?* and Hoff's *Mrs. Brice's Mice* are also easy readers. Tweedy and Rollo solve the mystery of Mrs. Twombly's grandson Freddy, who has disappeared. Lily mouse terrorizes bullies who are picking on Chester and Wilson in *Chester's Way* by Henkes. Chorao's *Cathedral Mouse* runs away from a pet shop and is helped by a stonecarver working in the cathedral. *Shy Charles* by Wells is a mouse who does not talk but when he finally does, he performs a heroic deed. Bunting's *Mother's Day Mice* is a good holiday book for reading aloud. Numeroff's *If You Give a Mouse a Cookie* is a circular story that is available in big book format. Ivimey's *The Complete Story of the Three Blind Mice* is a picture book of the famous song. Use the cassette of Hurd's *Pea Patch Jig* to provide the music for the story of how a baby mouse saves his family from a fox. A priceless possession is lost in Martin's *Bizzy Bones and the Lost Quilt.* Dan Mouse tells the cat that they are really porcupines in Pryor's *Porcupine Mouse.* A video of Low's Caldecott Honor Book, *Mice Twice,* is available. *Thomas in Trouble* by DaRif has a mouse who sails down the river in a raft, falls in, and is saved by Badger. In *Uncle Foster's Hat Tree* by Cushman, a mouse hears four stories about hats from his uncle. Two mice play with shapes in Gundersheimer's *Shapes to Show.* In Stanley's *The Conversa-*

tion Club, Peter Fieldmouse learns that conversation requires interaction between people or animals. Johnny Mouse and his friends, Percy Pig and Charlie Rooster, ride bicycles together in Heine's *Friends.* While Nathan the elephant falls asleep, a mouse named Nicholas Alexander moves into his toy chest in Delacre's *Nathan and Nicholas Alexander,* the theme of which is sharing and friendship. A mouse and a cricket become friends in Johnston's easy-to-read book, *Little Mouse Nibbling.* Baby Mouse teases the pigs, cows, and chickens in Hurd's *Blackberry Ramble.* Four toy mice come to life in Ginsburg's story in rhyme, *Four Brave Sailors.* Freschet's *Bernard of Scotland Yard* is a detective mouse. Some other mice do not want to ride in a rattletrap bus so they build their own in Peppe's *The Mice and the Clockwork Bus.*

Two nonfiction books about caring for mice as pets are Broekel's *Gerbil Pets and Other Small Rodents* and Pope's *Taking Care of Your Rats and Mice.* Stein's *Mouse* is about eight baby mice from birth until maturity. Silverstein's *Mice: All About Them* gives a history of rodents and includes mouse heroes and heroines on pages 29–33: "A Frog Went A-Courtin'"; Mickey Mouse; Mighty Mouse; Tom and Jerry; Lawson's *Ben and Me*; and White's *Stuart Little.* Morimoto's *Mouse's Marriage* is a new picture book of a favorite Japanese folk tale in which a mouse girl's parents check out the sun, clouds, wind, and a stone wall to find a husband for her. Gackenbach tells a similar story in *The Perfect Mouse.* Two books of an Aesop fable have the same title—*The Town Mouse and the Country Mouse.* One picture book is by Stevens and the other is by Cauley. Cauley's book is available as a sound filmstrip. Another picture book, *Country Mouse and the City Mouse,* is illustrated by Lydecker.

The following fiction books are about mice. Moore's *I'll Meet You at Cucumbers* is about country mice who visit the city. Corbett's *The Song of Pentecost* is about a city mouse who leads the harvest mice to new quarters and helps a snake obtain his inheritance. Another title is *Pentecost and the Chosen One.* Matthias, the hero in *Redwall* and *Mossflower* by Jacques, is a mouse. Conly's *Rasco and the Rats of NIMH* is the sequel to O'Brien's *Mrs. Frisby and the Rats of NIMH,* both of which are about a mouse family befriended by rats. *Runaway Ralph,* based on a book by Cleary, is now available in 16mm film and video formats. Other books about him are *The Mouse and the Motorcycle* and *Ralph S. Mouse.* Ralph goes to school with Ryan Bramble, son of the housekeeper at Mountain View Inn, where he lives. Brad the bully fights Ryan and the motorcycle is destroyed. King-Smith's *Power Mouse* is larger than usual and *Martin's Mice* are pets a barn cat keeps instead of eating. Read both books aloud. All of the Selden books beginning with *The Cricket in Times Square* include Tucker Mouse. One of the newer picture books, *Harry Kitten and Tucker Mouse,* tells how the two animals met. Readers who are interested in ancient Egypt will enjoy Kirby's *Secret of Thut-Mouse III or Basil Beaudesert's Revenge* which features a museum cat and two mice. Van Leeuwen's *The Great Christmas Kidnapping Caper* is about how Santa is kidnapped from Macy's department store in New York City. Santa is a friend of Marvin the

Magnificent and his mice friends. *The Great Cheese Conspiracy* comes before it and *The Great Rescue Operation* is the sequel. When Fats is accidentally sold from the toy department, Raymond and Marvin face the dangerous city of New York to rescue him. When they finally find him living on Fifth Avenue with a poor little rich girl, Fats does not want to be rescued.

FOXY BOOKS [CU 69–71; 716].   Here are more books to add to a display called "Foxy Books" or to a unit on foxes. Such a unit could be a spinoff from reading any of the fables of Aesop. A unit might begin with the showing of the film *Three Fox Fables*. Then have students investigate various collections of fables by Aesop to find more fox fables. For example, Hague's *Aesop's Fables* contains three fox fables: "The Fox and the Goat," pages 6–7; "The Fox and the Grapes," pages 20–21; and "The Fox and the Crow," pages 24–25. In the first fable, a fox falls in a well and calls the goat to come down, then jumps on his back to get out and leaves the goat in the well. "Look before you leap" is the admonition of that fable. The second is well known as the origin of the phrase "sour grapes." In the third fable, the fox flatters the crow so that the cheese she is holding in her mouth falls out and the fox snatches it. *Foxy Fables* by Ross contains six fables by Aesop: "The Fox and the Crow"; "The Cat and the Fox"; "The Fox and the Goat"; "The Fox and the Stork"; "The Stag and His Mirrors"; and "The Hare and the Tortoise." *Anno's Aesop* contains 21 fables from a book that Freddy Fox finds in the forest. Freddy asks his father to read the book to him and the second story on the page is Father Fox's version of the fable. Fables about foxes include: "The Fox and the Grapes," pages 4–5; "The Fox and the Goat," pages 15–17; "The Fox and the Crow," page 25; and "The Fox and the Stork," pages 30–31. "The Fox and the Raven" is one of several fables found in Bollinger's *Tales of a Long Afternoon*. Lavine's *Wonders of Foxes* is an excellent companion book. Chapters on the origins, folklore, and superstitions of foxes are included. Check the chapter of Volume 2, "Enjoying Poetry," for a section called AESOP IN AND OUT OF RHYME for more fox fables. Check pages 36–43 of Crouch's *The Whole World Storybook* for "Prince of Nettles," a Hungarian version of "Puss in Boots" that has a fox instead of a cat as a main character. Compare this story to other versions of "Puss in Boots." Galdone's *What's in Fox's Sack?* is a favorite tale that is available in a paperback edition. Compare that fox with the famous one in Galdone's *Henny Penny*. Conover's *Mother Goose and the Sly Fox* is a version of the Grimm folk tale, "The Wolf and the Seven Kids." King-Smith's fantasy *The Fox Busters* tells how the chickens at Foxearth Farm outsmart the foxes. Read aloud!

If the emphasis of the unit is on real foxes, the following books will be helpful. McDearman's *Foxes* is about four species of North American foxes: red; gray; kit; and Arctic. Schnieper's *On the Trail of the Fox* contains colored photos by a zoologist, and explains the life cycle of the red fox. Lane's *Fox* is also about the red fox in the United States. A large two-page spread with photos of a red fox appears in Schwartz's *The Hidden Life of the Forest*. Leighner's *Reynard:*

The Story of a Fox contains black and white photos which help tell how a red fox is found by a volunteer from Wildcare, which cares for injured or abandoned wild animals and releases them back into the wild after rehabilitation. Korschunow's *The Foundling Fox* is an orphan fox whose mother has been killed by hunters. The baby fox is taken in reluctantly by a vixen who has three kits of her own, but eventually she can't tell the difference between her own and the foundling. Aronsky's *Watching Foxes* shares sketches in lead and colored pencils and watercolor wash of four fox pups who play while mother is hunting. Because the book has large print, read it aloud as you would a big book, and then lay it aside for children to read to themselves later. Plants and animals that live in Northeastern dunes are featured in Roach's *Dune Fox*. Include MacQuilty's *Discovering Foxes* with these nonfiction books about foxes.

Japanese woodcuts enhance Tejima's view of a fox on a winter night in *Fox's Dream*. The poetic language makes it excellent for reading aloud.

Multimedia can be incorporated into the study of foxes. A cassette of Roald Dahl reading his book *The Fantastic Mr. Fox*, the cassettes of Steig's picture book *Doctor De Soto*, or Byars's *Midnight Fox* could be placed in the reading/viewing/listening area of the classroom for students to listen to at their leisure. Some questions or projects could accompany the tapes. *Midnight Fox* is one of the titles featured on the sound filmstrip *Setting*, from the set *Literature for Children, Series 9*.

The film, video, or filmstrip of Steig's *Doctor De Soto* can be used to introduce other picture books about foxes. The book is also excellent for reading aloud. Use it to introduce Miller's *Frederick Ferdinand Fox* who is appointed to carry secret messages and, as a reward, is made postmaster general. Shannon's *Dance Away* is about a fox outwitted by rabbits he has trapped. Oakley's *Hetty and Harriet* are chickens who go off to find the perfect place to live. A fox den is one of the unsuitable places they investigate. McKissack's *Flossie and the Fox* is a delightful story about a Southern girl who goes through the woods with a basket of eggs. The fox tries to get the eggs but the girl outfoxes the fox. Despite the dialect, this book is too much fun not to read aloud. In Aoki's *Santa's Favorite Story*, Santa tells the story of the Nativity to a fox. In Stehr's *Quack-Quack*, a mother duck leads a fox away from her nest to protect her eggs, and later finds her lost duckling with the fox in pursuit. Christelow's *Henry and the Red Stripes* is a rabbit who paints himself with red stripes and attracts a fox. How Henry escapes makes for an interesting story. Freddie Fox hurts himself while skiing in Watson's *Tales for a Winter's Eve*. While he recuperates, Grammer, Bert Blue Jay, and Nellie Mouse tell him stories. Read Kellogg's *Tallyho, Pinkerton!* aloud. Pinkerton becomes involved in the craziest fox hunt involving a hot air balloon. In *Fox in a Trap* by Thomas, Daniel is not able to accept the fact that his Uncle Fred traps foxes.

One of Marshall's series of easy readers is about foxes. *Fox on the Job* is the sixth book. Other titles include: *Fox All Week*; *Fox and His Friends*; *Fox At School*; *Fox in Love*; and *Fox on Wheels*. There are four stories in *Fox and*

His Friends, which is available in a paperback/cassette package. In "Fox in Trouble," Fox baby-sits his little sister who climbs a telephone pole; in "Fox All Wet," Louise gets into more trouble while fox is supposed to have his eye on her. In "Fox on Duty," Fox shirks his duty on traffic patrol to go swimming at the beach with friends. *Fox in Love* has three more good stories: in "Fox in Luck," Fox does not want to take Louise to the park until he meets a girl fox there; in "Fox and the Girls," Fox goes with different girls each day; and in "Fox Trot," fox enters a dance contest. There are three stories in *Fox on Wheels*: Fox watches TV instead of watching Louise in "Doctor Fox"; Millie taunts Fox into climbing a tree and then she is too scared to climb down in "Fox and the Grapes"; and Fox has to help on Saturday instead of racing his bike in "Fox on Wheels."

Use the film, filmstrip, or video of Spier's picture book *The Fox Went Out on a Chilly Night* to inspire students to find other variants of the old folksong. "A Ballad of a Fox" is card #98 of *Bill Martin Junior's Treasure Chest* while "Fox Went Out on a Chilly Night," can be found on page 118 of *Time to Read*, vol. 2 of *Childcraft*. For further sources check Volume 2 of this book for the section called ANIMAL SONGS.

INTRODUCING OWLS [CU 71–74; 723]. One of the most famous picture books about owls is now available as a sound filmstrip and can be used to introduce a unit. Yolen's *Owl Moon,* illustrated by Schoenherr, is the 1988 Caldecott Medal winner. A father and child walk out in the woods on a cold moonlit night hoping to catch a glimpse of a great horned owl. "Owling" is a shared family event that will never be forgotten. For ideas for a preschool program called "Owls in the Night," consult MacDonald's *Booksharing,* Idea #32.

There are several poems that include owls. Children can illustrate Lear's poem "The Owl and the Pussy-cat" as sung by Carfra on her cassette *Songs for Sleepyheads and Out-of-Beds!* Check pages 49–51 of Fleischman's *I Am Phoenix: Poems for Two Voices* for "Owls." The selection is to be read in two-part voices by two people or two groups. Read Shaw's poem "Owls Aren't so Smart" on page 27 of *Potato Chips and a Slice of Moon* by Hopkins and Arenstein. "Owl" appears on pages 80–81 of *Tail Feathers from Mother Goose* by the Opies.

Owls provide interesting subjects for art projects. Illustrate Tomlinson's *The Owl Who Was Afraid of the Dark* which is available as a sound recording. The letter *O* changes into an owl's eye in MacDonald's Caldecott Honor Book, *Alphabatics.* Beautiful owl patterns appear in Heller's coloring book, *Designs for Coloring: Owls.* Check pages 38–39 of Haddad's *Potato Printing* for directions on making an owl. Directions for making "Ollie the Owl" from a cardboard box are given on pages 50–53 of *Make and Do,* vol. 11 of *Childcraft.* On the lighter side, check page 19 of Corbett's *Jokes to Read in the Dark* for a joke about "The Poor Old Owl" which could also be illustrated.

Students can compare the way various artists view the owl. Piatti's picture book, *The Happy Owls*, is available as a video or 16mm film. Pomerantz's *One Duck, Another Duck* is illustrated by Aruego and Dewey. Danny the owl and his grandmother practice counting up to 10 while watching ducks at the pond. The same illustrators are responsible for Kraus's *Owliver*, the little owl who wants to be an actor even though his parents give him doctor and lawyer toys. Thaler's *Owly* is a 2-year-old owl who asks his mother questions like "How high is the sky?" or "How deep is the ocean?" "Owly" appears in the first grade HBJ basal reader, *Sand Castles*, in the Laureate edition, compiled by Cullinan, et al. The story "Two Hoots and the King" by Cresswell and the poem "How Wise Is an Owl?" by Orleans appear on pages 90–98 of *Ribbons*, the primer in the same series. Enhance the basal story with any of these owl books. When school library/media specialists know that the story is soon to be read in the basal, they can arrange a display of books about owls or read an owl story during story time.

Bunting's *The Man Who Could Call Down Owls* is excellent for reading aloud. Children can learn about screech owls, barn owls and elf owls from the Owl Man. The owls go to him when they need help. Then a stranger comes in the man's place and wears his clothes to get the owls in his power. However, the owls dive at the stranger and frighten him away. "The Sad Story of Owl" is a song based on a story from Wolkstein's book *The Magic Orange Tree and Other Haitian Folktales,* and is performed by Heather Forest on her cassette *Songspinner: Folktales and Fables Sung and Told.* Mowat tells of two owls from his boyhood in *Owls in the Family.* One of the 13 Chinese fables in Demi's *Fables* is about owls.

The previous stories could enhance a unit on owls that is part of a study module on birds. The following nonfiction books are essential: Selsam and Hunt's *A First Look at Bird Nests* and *A First Look at Owls, Eagles, and Other Hunters of the Sky*; Catchpole's *Owls*; and Zim's *Owls.* Two life cycle books about snowy owls are important: Hunt's *Snowy Owls* and Hopf's *Biography of a Snowy Owl.* Mitchell's *A Field Guide to Your Own Back Yard* contains information about the great horned owl and screech owls. Hurd's *Mother Owl* is about a screech owl. There are 18 types of owls in Sadoway's *Owls, Hunters of the Night.* In Dewey's *Clem: The Story of a Raven,* a wildlife artist tells of the death of her husband's burrowing owl, Clyde. When someone brings them a screech owl to rehabilitate, they do not name it because they don't want to become attached to it before they help it and then let it go.

PIG OUT ON PIG BOOKS [CU 42–43; 724].   Teachers and librarians don't have to wait until the next Year of the Pig (1995) to have a pig celebration. A bulletin board could contain the caption "Pig Out on Pig Books." Or take a tree branch hanging with pigs and surround it with books about pigs, including Lobel's *A Treeful of Pigs* and *Book of Pigericks*, pig limericks. Nursery rhymes about pigs appear in Lubin's *The Little Pig: A Mother Goose Favorite.* Latta's

This Little Pig Had a Riddle includes such gems as "What do pigs write with?" and "Who was a famous pig painter?" The answers, of course, are "pigpens" and "Pigasso." "How do pigs keep from getting a suntan?" appears in Adler's *The Carsick Zebra and Other Animal Riddles.* Have students look for riddles about pigs in other riddle books. Directions for making items out of circles, including a pig, appear in Dondiego's *Year-Round Crafts for Kids*, pages 118–19. For a preschool story program called "Portly Pigs" consult MacDonald's *Booksharing.*

Pigs are featured in several series of books. Use the sound filmstrip of *Mr. and Mrs. Pig's Evening Out* by Rayner to introduce that pig family in other titles too: *Mrs. Pig's Bulk Buy*; *Garth Pig and the Ice Cream Lady*; and *Mrs. Pig Gets Cross and Other Stories.* The piglets want to put catsup on everything in *Mrs. Pig's Bulk Buy* and The Ice Cream Lady is really a wolf who is interested in kidnapping little pigs in *Garth Pig and the Ice Cream Lady.* In the title story from *Mrs. Pig Gets Cross and Other Stories*, the 10 piglets are so messy that a wolf slips on their toys and loses what he has stolen. The moral of the story is not to be messy but "Be careful not to make your mother and father so cross that they forget to bolt the doors." In "The Potato Patch," pages 27–32, Garth plants bananas, squash, and a felt-tip pen in the garden.

McPhail has four books about Pig Pig. Something unusual happens to Pig Pig, who practices saying "cheese" while looking at a photo album, in *Pig Pig and the Magic Photo Album.* In *Pig Pig Rides*, the pig tells Mother of all the wild activities he has planned for the day, but all she says is to be home before dark. In *Pig Pig Goes to Camp*, Pig Pig goes to Camp Wildhog for the first time and attracts a group of frogs. Pig Pig saves a baby from harm in *Pig Pig Grows Up* which is available as a hardback/cassette paperback/cassette or group of paperbacks and cassettes.

Two female pigs are familiar to first and second graders who devour easy readers: Amanda Pig and Louanne Pig. The six books in Van Leeuwen's series are *Tales of Oliver Pig*; *More Tales of Oliver Pig*; *Tales of Amanda Pig*; *Amanda Pig and Her Big Brother Oliver*; *More Tales of Amanda Pig*; *Oliver and Amanda's Christmas*; and *Oliver, Amanda, and Grandmother Pig.* Grandmother Pig appears in *Tales of Oliver Pig* which has a chapter about baking oatmeal cookies. Grandmother is slowing down in *Oliver, Amanda, and Grandmother Pig.* In *Tales of Amanda Pig*, Oliver and Amanda fight while playing monsters. The problem in *Amanda Pig and Her Big Brother Oliver* is that Amanda wants to do everything her big brother Oliver does. Check pages 16–22 for "The Secret," which can be used with the book or sound filmstrip *The Surprise Party* by Hutchins. Paperback/cassettes of *Amanda Pig and Her Big Brother Oliver*, *Tales of Oliver Pig*, and *More Tales of Oliver Pig* are available. In *Oliver and Amanda's Christmas*, the siblings bake cookies and pick out a tree.

Louanne Pig in the Mysterious Valentine is a sound filmstrip or a book by Carlson in which Louanne tries to find out the identity of the person who has sent her a huge valentine. Hardback/cassette or paperback/cassettes are available for: *Louanne Pig in the Talent Show*; *Louanne Pig in the Perfect Family*; *Louanne Pig in the Witch Lady*; and *Louanne Pig in Making the Team*. Louanne helps out when the M.C. for the school talent show develops laryngitis. Louanne envies the rabbits who have a large family until she spends two days with them. Louanne tries out for cheerleader and Arnie tries out for the football team but they find out that they are better suited for each other's activity. While playing near the feared witch lady's house, Louanne twists her ankle and finds out that the witch lady is an interesting lady who likes birds and makes cookies and tea in *Louanne Pig in the Witch Lady*. A girl pig learns self-esteem in Carlson's *I Like Me*, which is available as a book, a sound filmstrip, and a hardcover/cassette.

Goodall's wordless books with half pages about Paddy Pork are fun and include *The Adventures of Paddy Pork*; *Paddy Goes Traveling*; *Paddy Under Water*; *Paddy to the Rescue*; and *The Ballooning Adventures of Paddy Pork*. Two other books about pigs and balloons are Cox's *Louella and the Yellow Balloon* and Geisert's *Pa's Balloon and Other Pig Tales*.

Roger Pig's neighbor is in charge of his baby brother, Nelson, while their mother is away in *Roger Takes Charge!* Roger doesn't want to set the table in Gretz's *It's Your Turn, Roger!* Pig William appears in Dubanevich's *Pig William*, *Pigs at Christmas*, and *Pigs in Hiding*. Yolen has three books about a pig who is a very proper Edwardian butler: *Piggins*, *Picnic with Piggins*, and *Piggins and the Royal Wedding*. In the first book, Mr. and Mrs. Reynard are having a party to show off Mrs. Reynard's new diamond necklace which disappears during the party. Piggins comes to the rescue. In the second book, Piggins follows three clues which lead him to his own surprise birthday picnic. In the third book, Rexy Reynard is to be ring bearer at a royal wedding but the ring disappears and Rexy is blamed. It is Piggins who uncovers the thief.

Leonard's *Little Pig's Birthday* is a choose-your-own adventure book for primary students. Kasza's *The Pig's Picnic* is about a pig who is on his way to a picnic and gets advice and gifts from a fox who gives him a tail, a lion who gives him hair, and a zebra who gives him stripes. However, when the pig stops to pick up a friend, she is frightened and won't go on the picnic with him. Have students add other unusual features to the pig. The outline of a pig standing up could be on a transparency and students could add the features from the story as well as make up their own features. The story could also be retold using the transparency. This story is suitable for playing out and is similar to Waber's *You Look Ridiculous Said the Rhinoceros to the Hippopotamus*. Kaza's book can also be compared to Freeman's book or filmstrip, *Dandelion*.

Show Heine's *The Pigs' Wedding* to a group of children. Porker and Curlytail decide to hose down their smelly guests and then paint on wedding clothes. Jeschke's *Perfect the Pig* is a featured book on the television program *Reading Rainbow*. Because the pig can fly, he is exploited by a not-so-nice man before he is returned to his owner. Two noodlehead pig stories can be read aloud. In Gackenbach's *Harvey the Foolish Pig*, Harvey wants to be rich so he asks the king for advice. The advice Harvey gets sends him back to a surprise ending. Hewitt's *The Three Sillies* has pigs for the main characters but follows the traditional lines of the familiar folktale. Galdone's *The Amazing Pig* is an old Hungarian tale in which a king promises his daughter in marriage to anyone who tells him something that he can *not* believe. The peasant tells the king many things about the amazing pig his family owns until the king finds something in the story that he cannot believe—that his own father is the swineherd for the pig. Have students make up more attributes for this amazing pig. A farmer gives golden sovereigns to his three sons and the choice of any animal that they wish. The oldest chooses a black stallion, the middle son chooses a fierce hound, and the third son chooses a pig in *Crispin and the Dancing Piglet* by Jennings. Emil is a French pig who can sniff out truffles, a delicacy, but faces the danger of being fattened up to eat in Ernst's *The Prize Pig Surprise.* Two elderly boars are neighbors in Aruego and Dewey's *Rockabye Crocodile.* Mrs. Piggott, a human, gets tired of picking up after her messy husband and son and leaves home in Browne's *Piggybook.* Simon and Patrick Piggott realize that they really are "pigs" and clean up their act. In Schwartz's *Spiffen: A Tale of a Tidy Pig*, soapy water is used to put out a dragon's fire. Tyler's *The Sick-in-Bed Birthday* is about a pig child who has chicken pox on his birthday and has to stay in bed. In Winthrop's *Sloppy Kisses*, Emmy Lou Pig's family kisses a lot until her friend Rosemary says that kissing is yucky and is for babies. When Emmy Lou changes her ways, she learns the value of a good-night kiss. Geraldine can't wait until it snows so she can go out and play in Keller's *Geraldine's Big Snow.* In *Tommy at the Grocery Store* by Grossman, a small pig is left at a grocery store by his mother and is accidentally sold to some other pigs. Geisert's *Pigs from A–Z* is a hidden picture book. On the pages for each letter, readers have to find not only the seven pigs, but also items which begin with that letter and at least one item from the previous letter and one from the next letter.

Herriot's *Moses the Kitten* is a tale the famous veterinarian gleaned from his long practice in Yorkshire. The kitten, named Moses because he is found in the rushes, is adopted by a family of piglets. Read this one aloud and share the pictures.

Theodora is warned in Tusa's book with the same title, to *Stay Away from the Junkyard!* However, Theodora doesn't and meets Clarissa the pig and Old Man Crampton there. Tusa's story is Program #57 of the television series *Reading Rainbow.*

Marshall's "The Pig and the Pencil" is a story in the HM preprimer *Trumpets,* edited by Durr, et al. A turtle, pig, frog, and fox are part of that story. McPhail's *Boo Bear Takes a Rest,* which also appears in *Trumpets,* has a fox, pig, and frog in the story. Use books about these animals with the basal readers. "If Pigs Could Fly," a poem by Reeves, appears on page 141 of Saltman's *Riverside Anthology of Children's Literature* and on page 116 of *Skylines,* the fifth grade HBJ basal reader in the Laureate edition, collected by Cullinan, et al. Use the poem in connection with King-Smith's *Pigs Might Fly* in which Mrs. Barlycorn's runt, with front feet like a dog's paws, becomes a hero. Another by King-Smith is *Babe, The Gallant Pig*. A selection from this fantasy appears on pages 106–15 of *Skylines*. In that story, Babe is taught to be a sheep dog (pig) by a sheep dog named Fly. *Babe, the Gallant Pig* is the winner of the Guardian Award (England) and the California Young Reader's Medal. Other fantasies about pigs can be introduced to intermediate students.

Stolz's *Quentin Corn* is a pig who runs away when he learns that he is about to be eaten. Quentin heads for the city where he lives in a boardinghouse. Only three precocious children are able to see that Quentin is a pig. In Rodda's *The Pigs Are Flying!* Rachel is sick in bed and dreams of flying off on a unicorn with pink pigs flying around. The pigs are part of a storm warning system, UEF (Unlikely Events Factor). Add pig features to long pink balloons and float them on the ceiling when introducing this book. Don't forget the most famous fantasy pig of all, Wilbur, in White's *Charlotte's Web*. Another famous pig from fantasy is Piglet from Milne's *Winnie-the-Pooh*.

Scott's *The Book of the Pig* includes characteristics, habits, history, and relatives of the pig. Unusual information includes: eyes of the pig are more like those of humans than those of any other animal; the snout can seek out truffles; and the digestive system is being studied by scientists. Lavine's *Wonders of Pigs* utilizes black and white photos to share information about wild and domestic pigs, uses of pigs, raising pigs, and pork cuts. Photographs enhance Nicholson's *Wild Boars* about the Eurasian wild boar which was originally brought to North America for hunting.

BULLIES IN CHILDREN'S LITERATURE [CU 711].   Books about bullies can be part of a booktalk that includes realistic fiction, a display that includes many types of problems in fiction, or as an essential component of the study of characterization. Reading these books can also stimulate writing projects. Even though each student reads a different book, the writing assignment can be the same: ask students how they would have reacted to the bully in the story. In this way, books about bullies can be incorporated into literature-based reading programs or the whole language approach to the language arts.

The most famous bully in children's literature is Martin from Stolz's *The Bully of Barkham Street* and *The Dog on Barkham Street*. In the newest book, *The Explorer of Barkham Street*, Martin is determined to live down his bad reputation. He is trying to improve his disposition and act more responsibly, especially in his baby-sitting job; make friends; lose weight; and understand his father. Can a bully reform? Martin is really trying and readers hope he makes it.

Dexter and Howlie plan to trick the bully, Bulldog Calhoun, when he appears at *The Great Dimpole Oak* by Lisle. However, Bulldog does not show up. In Talbert's *Toby*, a minister is trying to take Toby away from his illiterate parents while the minister's son, a bully, makes life miserable for him.

When bullies pick on 8-year-old Guy Gibbs and a dog with no identification, Guy does what he thinks Isabelle would do—he fights them until they knock him out—in Greene's *Isabelle Shows Her Stuff*. Bullies plague Ernest in Lawlor's *How to Survive Third Grade*. Herman's *Millie Cooper: 3B* is about a third grader in New York City in 1946. When Millie becomes monitor and has to turn in the class bully, she uses psychology on him so he won't beat her up. Fourth grader Jason's talking rabbit, Robot, insults the school bully in *Stop the Presses!*, a book in the Bad News Bunny series by Saunders. Nat, a fourth grader with diabetes, is plagued by a bully in *Tough Beans* by Bates. Lenny, the bully, calls Barney a wimp and plays tricks on him in Carrick's *What a Wimp*. In Mauser's *A Bundle of Sticks*, a fifth grader learns martial arts to combat a bully. Mouse is afraid of Marv Hamerman in *The Eighteenth Emergency* by Byars. When Billy makes friends with Juan, a Hispanic, bullies torment him also in Bograd's *The Fourth Grade Dinosaur Club*.

In Snyder's *And Condors Danced*, 11-year-old Carly challenges a 1907 school bully. Henry Quigley Babcock has bribed students to vote for him so he can ride the float in the Fourth of July parade. When the teacher chooses Carly because she has answered more questions in social studies, Henry spooks the horses into running away. Eleven-year-old Lucy is bullied by Melanie Prosser in *Present Takers* by Chambers. Soup and Rob are bullied by Janice Riker in Peck's *Soup* and all the books that follow. Chapter 9, "Eddy Tacker Was a Bully," on pages 77–83 of *Soup*, is devoted to Eddy.

Eleven-year-old Peter in Shura's *The Search for Grissi* has to walk his younger sister home from school, and the two encounter a bully together. The bully in Steiner's *Oliver Dibbs and the Dinosaur Cause* is Lester, who ruins a birthday party and disrupts Oliver's presentation to the state legislature. *The Scared One* by Haseley is about an Indian boy who is teased because he is afraid, but when bullies want to take an injured bird from him, he becomes strong. Alan bets Billy $50 he can't eat 15 worms in Rockwell's *How to Eat Fried Worms*. Russell is tired of being bullied by Eddie and wants to scare Eddie at Halloween time in Coville's *The Monster's Ring*. Russell buys a ring which turns him into a monster, who scares Eddie and tells him not to pick on Russell anymore. Later, Russell needs Eddie's help to turn back to his own self. In Smith's *Jelly Belly*, the nickname is bestowed by a bully on 11-year-old Nathaniel Robbins until Nathaniel goes to Camp Lean-Too and loses 15 pounds. In Pascal's *The Hand-Me-Down Kid*, 11-year-old Ari Jacobs gets in trouble because the school bully "borrows" a bike for a race and it gets stolen. Ari's new friend Jane teaches her to stand up for herself. Twelve-year-old Janie's business enterprise in the book *Kid Power* by Pfeffer slumps when school starts, so Janie decides to go into the snow shoveling business to revive Kid Power. A bully, Johnny Richards, causes problems in *Kid Power Strikes Back*.

Pat, a seventh grader, has problems with the bully, Chuck McGrew, in Adler's *Once in a While Hero*. Despite problems with Albert Hamilton, the bully in Avi's *Romeo and Juliet—Together (and Alive!) at Last,* the eighth grade play and the romance come off . . . sort of.

Bullies also appear in books for younger children. In Browne's picture book, *Willy the Wimp* is a chimpanzee who is able to stand up to the bullying gorilla gang after he takes a bodybuilding course. Peet's *Big Bad Bruce* is available as a hardback or a paperback/cassette package. Big Bad Bruce is a bear who is the biggest bully in the forest until a witch shrinks him to the size of a chimpunk. In Porte's *Ruthann and Her Pig,* her cousin Frank decides that Ruthann's pet pig, Henry Brown, can protect him on the school bus from bullies. *Ruthann and Her Pig* is a first chapter book. On the first day of school, a bully takes George's lunch, so Harriet helps him keep it from happening again in *Loudmouth George and the Sixth Grade Bully* by Carlson. Harriet puts garlic in his tunafish, vinegar in his vegetable soup, hot pepper in his fruit cocktail, and lard in his cream-filled cookies. Ask students if the bully will ever eat George's lunch again. It is possible to include these books in the selections for intermediate students, making them optional reading "just for fun." Remember, it is not a sin to read a picture book after third grade.

THE 1980s: THE DECADE OF THE GRANDPARENTS. Grandparents are characters in many books for children published in the 1980s. Some are minor characters and some are very important to the story. Some are stereotypes and others are as varied as real people are. Some of them are very much alive and some are old or dying. In many stories the grandparents pass on the heritage to their grandchildren through stories about family history. These books help students to write down family stories and traditions. Check a section of Chapter 12 called IMMIGRANT AND FAMILY STORIES INSPIRE WRITING PROJECTS. Thirteen titles about grandparents and 26 questions appear in Greenson and Taha's *Name That Book! Questions and Answers on Outstanding Children's Books.* Check the index on page 229 for grandparents and on page 239 for a companion topic, old age, which has nine titles and 18 questions. One good time to highlight books about grandparents in a booktalk for intermediate students or to prepare a display of books would be the week including September 11, Grandparents' Day.

● *Famous Grandparents.* If a vote were taken to produce the most famous grandfather, Stevenson's Grandpa would win by an overwhelming majority. Preschoolers and primary students can be introduced to Grandpa through the wordless alphabet book *Grandpa's Great City Tour.* The other books are wonderful read-alouds or can be introduced to students through filmstrips and cassettes. Use the award-winning filmstrip, *We Can't Sleep,* to introduce Mary Ann, Louie, and their Grandpa. The ALA Notable filmstrip is also a *Learning Magazine* award winner. When Mary Ann and Louie tell Grandpa that they can't sleep, he tells them he had the same problem many years ago when he was their age. The beginnings of Stevenson's books about Grandpa follow the same pattern, but then they erupt into the most wonderfully imaginative tales. In *We Can't Sleep*, the wild tale involves sharks, icebergs, polar bears, walruses, dragons, zebras, and crocodiles. *We Can't Sleep* is a Christopher Medal winner for "affirming the highest values of the human spirit." *What's Under My Bed?* can be used with the ALA Notable cassette. After Grandpa tells a scary story, Mary Ann and Louie are afraid to go to bed. The two run down and tell Grandpa that something is under their beds and he replies "Why, the very same thing happened to me once . . ." and he launches into his story. When the two children complain that their new brother is no fun, Grandpa tells them about his brother in *Worse Than Willie*. Children will enjoy hearing how Wainey saves Grandpa's life and will be tickled when Wainey comes for a visit. When Mary Ann and Louie complain that they are bored, Grandpa tells them what he and his brother Wainey did when they were bored in *There's Nothing to Do!* The adventure includes baby-sitting, disaster on the farm, and a twister. When Uncle Wainey comes in time for ice cream and Grandpa asks him, "What's new?" the children listening to the story will know the answer. When Mary Ann and Louie complain that they have no friends because they have just moved, Grandpa has another humorous story to tell about his own experiences in *No Friends*.

Chapter 3 in Van Leeuwen's easy reader, *Tales of Oliver Pig*, is about Grandmother's visit. In *Oliver, Amanda and Grandmother Pig*, the grandmother comforts the children during a loud thunderstorm.

One of the most famous grandmothers is the one Little Red Riding Hood visits. In the Grimms' *Little Red Cap*, the woodcutter rescues Grandmother by cutting open the belly of the sleeping wolf, removing Grandmother and replacing her with stones. Peter and Andrew in McPhail's *Grandfather's Cake* are asked by their grandmother to take some chocolate cake to Grandpa, who is in the hills tending his sheep. The boys keep the cake away from a fox, bear, robber, and even from themselves. When they arrive, they are rewarded because Grandmother has packed pieces of cake for all three of them. Compare these two books with various versions of "Little Red Riding Hood." Nokomis is the grandmother of Nanabozho, a Canadian/American Indian sometimes called Manabozho. In Toye's *The Fire Stealer*, Nanabozho changes himself into a tree and a rabbit to obtain fire for his grandmother. "The Theft of Fire" is also found on pages 11–19 of Leekley's *The World of Manabozho: Tales of the Chippewa Indians*. Nokomis is also given as the grandmother of Hiawatha in Longfellow's poem. Two picture books of that story are *Hiawatha*, illustrated by Jeffers, and *Hiawatha's Childhood*, illustrated by Le Cain. "Hiawatha" is read by Hal Holbrook on the recording *Best Loved Poems of Longfellow*.

● *Grandmothers in Children's Literature.* Sometimes grandmothers are characters in children's books without any fanfare or didacticism about generation gaps. Preschool and primary students will enjoy the helpfulness of two grandmothers in stories that contain ducks. In Lloyd's *Duck*, Tim calls all animals "duck" and all vehicles "truck" until his grandmother teaches him the right names. In Pomerantz's *One Duck, Another Duck*, Danny Owl counts ducks at the pond by saying "one duck, another duck," until his grandmother teaches him the numbers up to 10. After these two stories are read aloud in the library, the children go to tables where books are placed in front of each seat. Some of the books could contain other pictures of ducks. Whenever a child identifies one of the ducks, the teacher, librarian, or library/media specialist can hold up the picture for all to share. Because some of the children are faster "readers" than others, have extra books in the middle of the table so that anyone who is finished looking at a book can exchange it for another. Not all the books need a duck in them because there would not be enough time to share all of them anyway. Some books with ducks could include: Flack's *Angus and the Ducks*; Flack's *The Story About Ping*; Gerstein's *Arnold and the Ducks*; Hurd's *Last One Home Is a Green Pig*; McCloskey's *Make Way for Ducklings*; Potter's *The Tale of Jemima Puddleduck*; Stevenson's *Howard*; Tafuri's *Have You Seen My Duckling?*; and Thiele's *Farmer Schulz's Ducks*.

One grandmother, important in the resolution of the plot in a book containing numbers, saves the day in *The Doorbell Rang* by Hutchins. Ma makes cookies and Sam and Victoria take six cookies each. However, each time the doorbell rings, their share becomes less. Listeners will hold their breath when each child is down to one cookie as the doorbell rings again. Fortunately, it is Grandmother with a tray of cookies. Seven-year-old Raven Hannah in Purdy's *Least of All* teaches herself to read from the family Bible while churning and boasts of her accomplishment. After her wise grandmother tells her that "People can be strong in differing ways," Raven Hannah teaches the whole family to read during the long-ago Vermont winter. A boy sees a brontosaurus in his grandmother's garden in Harrison's *In Granny's Garden*. In *Brother to the Wind*, by Walter, Emeke's job is to herd the family goats. The African boy sees Good Snake, whom his grandmother says can make any wish come true. Emeke's secret wish is to fly, and Good Snake tells him to make a kite and wait for the right wind. In order to protect Hush in Fox's *Possum Magic*, Grandma Poss makes her invisible. One day Hush wants to be visible so she can see herself, but Grandma doesn't remember how to reverse the spell. When they finally discover the secret, Hush eats the three foods that make her visible once a year on her birthday so she can be visible for that day. Because the book comes from Australia, Hush eats various foods special to parts of that country. Read the book aloud, especially to classes that are studying Australia. In *Oma and Bobo* by Schwartz, Alice gets a dog she calls Bobo from the animal shelter for her birthday. Grandmother doesn't want the dog, but Oma is won over while she teaches him how to pass the obedience school tests. In Komaiko's *I Like the Music*, a grandmother and granddaughter have different tastes in music but respect each other's choices.

Books in which grandmothers tell family heritage stories include: Clifford's

The Remembering Box; Miller's *My Grandmother's Cookie Jar*; Greenfield's *Childtime: A Three Generation Memoir*; Clifton's *The Lucky Stone*; Rogers's *From Me to You*. A grandmother and grandson walk through empty rooms of the house where Grandma and Grandpa lived for many years before she moves to a new place in Shecter's *Grandma Remembers*. Parent's cassette *Sundays at Grandma's* includes original stories and traditional French songs that evoke childhood memories of two cultures. "Grandmother's Pictures" is a story that appears in *The Big Alfie and Annie Rose Storybook* by Hughes. Grandmother tells Alfie stories about her childhood and about her brother Will.

Some grandmothers appear in books for intermediate students. Fourth grader Molly Bosco's grandmother comes to school and goes on the class campout in Gilson's *Thirteen Ways to Sink a Sub*. Compare Molly's grandmother with Grandpa Day in Cleary's *Ramona Forever*. In Wright's *The Secret Window*, Meg is bothered with pre-cognition, shared by her grandma, who seems to handle it better than Meg.

• **Grandfathers in Children's Literature.** Grandfathers appear in books for students in intermediate grades. The grandpa in Cleary's *Ramona Forever* is retired and living in a sunshine state. When Ramona's aunt gets married, Grandpa comes to give the bride away, stays in a motel to be away from the fuss, and hires a limo to transport his daughter to the church. Check pages 129–35 and 141–45 of *Ramona Forever* to learn more about Grandpa. Twelve-year-old Carl tries to heal the breach between his father and grandfather in *The Golden Pasture* by Thomas, a story horse lovers in intermediate grades will enjoy.

The grandfathers are a vital part of the following picture book stories. When a boy's smaller cousin comes to visit, he doesn't want to share his teddy bear, then relents. When the cousin wrecks the bear, Grandy fixes it by taking out the stuffing, washing, drying, restuffing, and sewing the bear back together again. When the cousin comes for a return visit, the boy, his bear, and Grandy go off for a walk in *As Good As New* by Douglas. Gina and her grandfather check out all the shortcuts in town so they can reach the hot air balloon first on their bikes and win a free balloon ride in *The Great Town and Country Bicycle Balloon Chase* by Douglass. In *Jesse and Abe* by Isadora, Abe goes with his grandfather to work backstage at Brown's Variety Theater. One night when Grandfather is late, Abe learns how important his grandfather is to the cast. Tamika, a black child, sees her grandfather rehearsing for a play and is frightened in Greenfield's *Grandpa's Face*. A little girl and her grandfather count from one to 10 while going on a walk in *When We Went to the Park* by Hughes. Another little girl goes on a biweekly walk in Hest's *The Crack-of-Dawn Walkers*. Sadie enjoys this time alone with her grandfather and resents the intrusion of her younger brother. Louis Rabbit hides his grandfather's shoes so he is late to work in Gazet's *Big Shoe, Little Shoe*. There is a grandmother in the background of the story. *Talk to Me* by Bellanger is a book and cassette about a small boy who can relate to his grandfather and tell him his troubles. *Talk to Me* is available in big book and small book formats. A grandfather and grandson tame a mare in upper New York State in Locker's *The Mare on the Hill*. Cole's *The Trouble with Granddad* is a humorous book in which Granddad grows vegetables so big that he is arrested for having a dangerous vegetable. Barrett's *Cloudy with a Chance of Meatballs* is a bedtime story that Grandpa tells. Gauch's "My Grandpa and Me" appears on pages 176–87 of the third grade SF basal reader, *Golden Secrets*, edited by Aaron and Carter. In Graham's *Grandad's Magic*, Alison has learned juggling tricks from her granddad. Compare Alison's granddad with the one in Ackerman's *Song and Dance Man*.

Poems about grandfathers include "The Grandfather I Never Knew" and "Grandfather" from Livingston's *Worlds I Know and Other Poems*. "Zuni Grandfather" appears on page 5 of Streich's *Grandparents' Houses*, a book of 15 poems about grandparents.

Some books in which grandfathers impart stories of their heritage are Hughes's *Blaine's Way*; Highwater's *Legend Days*; Hirsh's *I Love Hanukkah*; Martin and Archambault's *Knots on a Counting Rope*; and Ackerman's *The Song and Dance Man*.

● *Nontraditional Grandparents.* We might expect grandmothers to make quilts as they do in Flournoy's *The Patchwork Quilt*, Roth's *Patchwork Tales*, and Willard's *The Mountains of Quilt*. However, not all grandparents in children's literature are so predictable. In Olson's *Hurry Home, Grandma!*, Grandma is an explorer who is busy having wild adventures in the jungle, while Timothy and Melinda are preparing for a traditional Christmas. Grandma flies her own plane to make it on time to celebrate with them. In McCully's easy reader, *The Grandma Mix-Up*, Grandma Nan is neat and orderly and has white hair and glasses, while Grandma Sal is laid back and mod looking. In Hedderwick's *Katie Morag and the Two Grandmothers*, Katie has an island grandmother who is a farmer and Gramma on the mainland, who wears frills and cosmetics and dislikes large animals. In Hoffman's *My Grandma Has Black Hair*, the grandmother is unlike traditional grannies and wants to be called Sylvia. One of the stories Sylvia tells is about when she was a kid in the circus where her parents were trapeze artists. Compare this story with Ackerman's *Song and Dance Man*. In the ALA Notable Book *Tales of a Gambling Grandma* by Khalsa, originally published in Canada, Granny is a card shark. After her grandchildren leave, Elzibah Swan decides that life is dull and she learns to swim on her 75th birthday in *Sea Swan* by Lasky. Grandma is an alien in Cole's *The Trouble with Gran*. Her activities include winning the Glamorous Grandma contest by making herself over to fit a bikini, taking the field trip to her home planet, and opening an extraterrestrial travel agency. Other books by Cole are *The Trouble with Mom*, who is a witch, and *The Trouble with Dad*, who invents robots. The grandparents in Skoofield's *Snow Country* are nontraditional role models because the woman works in the barn and the man does the dishes. Justin's Grandpa is also an excellent role model, winning a biscuit-baking contest, and teaching Justin how to make beds, clean, and cook in Walter's *Justin and the Best Biscuits in the World.*

• **Visiting Grandparents.** One of the most touching stories about a girl who visits a grandparent is Griffith's *Granddaddy's Place*, illustrated by Stevenson. Janetta rides on the train to see her granddaddy for the first time and is disappointed in the farm home where her mother grew up. There is a mean old cat, a mule, a small house, and a bare, red dirt yard. Janetta doesn't want to stay, but after getting to know her grandfather they establish a rapport. In *Georgia Music*, a sequel, Grandfather comes to live with Janetta's family. Both stories are excellent read-alouds. Bo is another child who spends the summer with Grandpa. The two play ball, work in the garden, grill outside, carve soap, and make willow baskets. Bo learns the names of many wild things from Grandpa, and they also establish a marvelous rapport. When it is time to leave they both wish on a star. Similar out-of-door experiences, such as looking at constellations and sailboating, are told about in the first person in Lasky's *My Island Grandma.* Barney spends the day with his grandparents in Cazet's picture book, *Sunday.*

Large clear photographs illustrate Krementz's *Jamie Goes on an Airplane,* a board book. Preschoolers learn all about an airplane trip that begins with packing and ends with seeing grandparents at the end of the flight. Preschoolers and kindergarteners will also enjoy McPhail's *First Flight,* in which a small boy and his teddy bear visit Grandma. A bear also appears in Oechsli's *Fly Away!*, which is about a first plane ride to visit Gram and Grampa. Carlstrom's *The Moon Came Too* is about a small child packing everything but the moon for a trip to Grandmother's house. Some of the things a little girl shares with her grandparents every week are a new song, playing, and trying on jewelry in Oxenbury's *Grandma and Grandpa.* Burningham's *Grandpa* is considered by the *New York Times* one of the best illustrated books. After hearing Hooker's *At Grandma and Grandpa's House,* children can list all the special things that they do at Grandma and Grandpa's house. In that story, Grandma tells stories and has a cookie jar shaped like a rabbit.

Children may be familiar with MacLachlan's *Through Grandpa's Eyes* from seeing it on the television series *Reading Rainbow.* John learns from his blind grandfather to appreciate the world through his senses while visiting his grandparents. *I Go with My Family to Grandma's* by Levinson is about five girl cousins and their families who come from Manhattan, Brooklyn, Queens, the Bronx, and Staten Island by bike, trolley, wagon, train, and ferry to visit Grandma. The book is helpful for learning the geography of New York City. Children will enjoy the family feeling as well as the humor of the family photo. Gomi's *Coco Can't Wait* is also humorous. Coco and her grandma each go to visit the other but keep bypassing each other. They finally meet in the middle. The following two stories are more serious. In Caseley's *Apple Pie and Onions*

Rebecca visits her grandmother's apartment and goes with her to the market so they can make an apple pie. On the marketing trip, Rebecca is embarrassed by her grandmother's ethnicity. "My Grandma" by Letty Cottin Pogrebin, on pages 52–56 of Thomas's *Free to be . . . a Family*, is a first-person story about another girl who is ashamed of her grandmother who lives in a basement, comes from the old country, and speaks Yiddish. Five young cousins stay overnight together at Grandma's in *Grandma Gets Grumpy* by Hines. The children have fun making a mess and noise until they break a lamp and Grandma yells at them for the first time ever. This contemporary grandma wears a T-shirt and sandals. The grandmother in Roe's *Staying with Grandma* is also modern looking.

Vigna's *Grandma without Me* has a different theme from most other picture books. A boy is upset because he won't be spending Thanksgiving with his grandmother because of his parents' divorce. In this first-person narrative, the boy tells how he and his grandmother write to each other and how he puts the letters in a scrapbook she has given him. At the end of the story, the boy's mother takes a large sheet of paper and makes an outline of the boy to send to his grandmother. "Grandma without Me" appears on pages 202–8 of the second grade HBJ basal reader, *Weather Vanes*, in the Laureate edition, collected by Cullinan, et al.

Several books about grandparents are birthday books. In Wolf's *The Best Present Is Me*, a little girl loses the present she was going to give Oma, but the girl's mother traces the granddaughter on a large sheet of paper and they make a birthday card. Naturally, Oma loves the gift. Martha gives her blind grandfather a birthday card made out of construction paper, a paper doily, a shiny heart, and stick-on letters that say "Grampie, I love you." Everything on the card has a different texture that Grampie can feel. Pair this book with MacLachlan's *Through Grandpa's Eyes*. That story appears on a cassette, *Mama One, Mama Two and Other Stories*. Tom and Lucy have much to do and count before going to Grandma's 60th birthday party in Hughes's *Lucy and Tom's 1, 2, 3*. In Cazet's *December 24th* Emily and Louie Rabbit bring a present to Grandfather and make him guess what holiday the present represents. Finally after exhausting all the other holidays, Grandfather guesses that it is a birthday present for him. Marshall's *Fox All Week* is an easy reader about Grannie's birthday. Oldham's "Grandma's Birthday Surprise" appears on pages 112–19 of the HBJ primer, *Ribbons*, in the Laureate edition, collected by Cullinan and others.

Two books where children go on trips with a grandparent are Locker's *Where the River Begins* and Daly's *Not So Fast, Songolo*. Josh, Aaron, a collie dog, and Grandfather go on a camping trip to find the source of a river. A small black South African boy, Malusi, takes a trip to the city with his grandmother, Gogo, to help her shop. At the end of the story, Gogo buys Malusi new tackies (shoes).

Sometimes it is the grandparents who are the visitors. In *Anna, Grandpa, and the Big Storm* by Stevens, Anna and her grandpa experience what becomes known as the "Great Blizzard of 1888" in New York City.

• *Living with Grandparents.* The following stories are about children who live with grandparents or grandparents who live with their children and grandchildren. Use the filmstrip *When I Was Young in the Mountains*, winner of a *Learning Magazine* award, to introduce the Caldecott Honor Book by Rylant. A young girl tells how her grandfather and grandmother were part of her young life in the mountains of long ago. Greenfield's *Grandma's Joy* is a Coretta Scott King Honorable Mention Book. Rhody, whose parents have been killed in an accident, lives with her grandmother and begs grandmother to tell her again how she came to do so. *When Grandpa Came to Stay* by Caseley is about how Grandpa comes to live with the Golds after Grandma dies. Benny and Grandpa sing Yiddish songs and do things together, but sometimes Grandpa is sad, so the two plant tulips together on Grandma's grave. In Langner's *Freddy My Grandfather*, the little girl shares her thoughts about things that are irritating and the things that are good about her grandfather, who lives with her and her parents. In Kibbey's *My Grammy*, Amy's grandmother, who has Alzheimer's disease, comes to live with them.

Thirteen-year-old Katie McNeill lives with her grandparents in a little town in Oregon where her granddad owns a drug store in Morrison's *Whisper Goodbye*. When her grandparents decide to relocate close to Portland, Katie has to leave her horse Whisper behind. Boarding the horse in Portland is too expensive, and she can't get a job in exchange for board so Katie decides to live with her friend Allison so she can keep her horse. A dramatic experience during a storm shows Allison that her family is more important to her than her horse. In Smith's *The War with Grandpa*, fifth grader Peter Stokes tells how he had to give up his room when grandfather came to live with them and how he shows his resentment. In the end, Grandfather's carpentry skills help him to create his own basement apartment. The love of grandfather and grandson are put to the test in this book that has won several awards, chosen by children in Kansas, Nebraska, South Carolina, Vermont, and the Pacific Northwest. In *My Old Granddad* by Harranth, Granddad comes to to the city to live with his family after Granny dies, but goes back to the country because he is lonesome for it. While his parents are building a new home, a boy and his younger brother stay on their grandma's farm for a year in Nilsson's *If You Didn't Have Me*, a Batchelder Award winner from Sweden. In a sequel to *Only My Mouth Is Smiling*, 14-year-old Merle and her brother and sister come to live with their grandmother in Riley's *Crazy Quilt* because their mother is mentally ill. Thirteen-year-old Wren and 16-year-old Kevin live with their grandparents while their mother is busy with her career and father is in a mental hospital in *Notes for Another Life* by Bridgers. *Johnny May Grows Up* by Branscum is the sequel to *Johnny May*. Johnny May's grandparents don't have enough money to send her to high school with her best friend from Huckleberry Hollow, Aron McCoy, and 13-year-old Johnny May worries that Aron will find new friends. After a disastrous party where her clothes are all wrong, Johnny May really feels left out of Aron's life. So when city boy Mike Conway comes for the summer, Johnny May pretends he is her boyfriend, to make Aron jealous. Twelve-year-old Greg lives with his grandmother for six months while his mother is in Europe on business. Greg gets involved in the chess club and his neighbor, Josie Nolan, in Shura's *The Josie Gambit*. Twelve-year-old Maggie lives with her grandmother in Houston because her actress mother is dead and her father, a famous movie producer, is out of the country making a movie in Nixon's *And Maggie Makes Three*. Casey goes to live with her grandmother Paw-Paw in San Francisco's Chinatown in the 1960s and learns about her heritage in Yep's *Child of the Owl*. Paw-Paw tells Casey the legend of the owl spirit in a book for students in intermediate grades and above.

• **Grandparents Who Are Ill.** *Grandma Drives a Motor Bed* by Hamm is for primary students. When Josh visits his grandmother at her home, he is fascinated by the motorized bed. Life in a sickroom is experienced realistically as Josh watches some of the routines, like Grandma getting her exercise. Because his grandma wears disposable diapers, the room sometimes has a bathroom smell. The big chair, in the book *A Chair for My Mother* by Williams, is empty because Grandmother is sick. The granddaughter and her friends play music on the accordian for this same grandmother in *Music, Music for Everyone*. Three books contain role reversals of grandparent or older person and child. In Wittman's *A Special Trade*, Bartholomew, a neighbor, pushes Nelly in her baby carriage and now that she is older, Nelly pushes Bartholomew in his wheelchair. In Aliki's *The Two of Them*, a girl sings to her grandfather and tells him stories just as he did when she was a baby. In de Paola's *Now One Foot, Now the Other*, it was Bobby's Grandfather Bob who taught him to walk. After Bob's stroke, Bobby teaches his grandfather to walk. De Paola's story appears on pages 206–14 of the HBJ third grade reader, *Celebrations*, from the Laureate edition compiled by Cullinan, et al. In *Georgia Music* by Griffith, Grandaddy leaves Georgia for Maryland to live with his daughter but he pines for his cabin.

Fifteen-year-old Emma always looks forward to spending the summer with her grandmother on her farm in Vermont, but this year there is a shadow: Emma knows her grandmother is dying of cancer in Bacon's *Shadow and Light*.

• **Old Age.** In Delton and Tucker's book, *My Grandma's in a Nursing Home*, Grandma has Alzheimer's disease and is in a nursing home called Meadowbrook. Everyone in the family has a different idea about the place: Mom says it sounds like a cemetery, Dad says it sounds like a golf club, but all grandmother says is that she wants to go home. Intermediate and middle school students will want to look at Landau's *Alzheimer's Disease* for more information about care of persons with that disease. Landau explains symptoms, mental changes, and problems of caring for a patient in an anecdotal manner. Fox's

Wilfrid Gordon McDonald Partridge is a picture book about a boy who goes next door to an old folks' home and meets Miss Nancy Alison Delacourt Cooper who has four names like he does. Having learned that memories can be warm, come from long ago, make you cry or laugh, and are as precious as gold, Wilfrid shares his memories with Miss Cooper who has lost hers. When Wilfrid shows his shells from long ago, his puppet that makes people laugh, the medal his grandfather gave him that made him sad, and the football that is as precious as gold, Miss Cooper holds the objects and remembers stories of her own to tell. *Wilfrid Gordon McDonald Partridge* is also available as a sound filmstrip and could begin or end a unit about older people. Even though her grandmother doesn't remember her, a little girl remembers the good times they shared in the past in Nelson's *Always Gramma*. Sally, in Zolotow's *I Know a Lady*, learns to appreciate the old lady on her block who grows flowers and gives treats. Sally wonders what the lady was like when she was a girl, and if she had an older person to give her Halloween treats, Christmas cookies, and flowers. Grandpa retires as a barber, and a party is given for him in Knox-Wagner's *Grandpa Retired Today*. A circus dog retires in Hoff's easy reader *Barkley* because he thinks he is no longer useful but becomes a teacher to younger dogs. Farber's *How Does It Feel to Be Old?* contains information about hospices, senior centers, money matters, legal questions about retirement, medical alternatives, contributions of older people to society, and case studies. In the case studies, one person likens aging to a long poem, someone suggests that they no longer have to listen to parents' advice, and another says that there is so much to be done and so little time in which to do it. Henderson's poem "Growing Old" appears on Card #24 of *Bill Martin Junior's Treasure Chest*. Howker's *Badger on the Barge*, an International Reading Association winner, contains five stories, each of which describes interaction between young and older people. Le Shan's *Grandparents: A Special Kind of Love* tells about this unique relationship and discusses its joys as well as problems.

DEATH IN FICTION AND NONFICTION. Some of the vocabulary in bolder type that is defined in Arnold's *What We Do When Someone Dies* are: death certificate, postmortem, embalming, mortician, undertaker, casket, coffin, burial plot, epitaph, mausoleum, vault, pyre, life insurance policies, sympathy cards, obituary, eulogy, pallbearers, hearse, mourning, will, estate, executor, intestate and soul. In *The Kids' Book About Death and Dying*, Rofes uses a different approach—case histories and student writing. Krementz's *How It Feels When a Parent Dies* shares taped interviews with 18 children between the ages of 7 and 16. Teachers may find "Helping Your Students Deal with a Death," pages 86–89 of the April 1986 issue of *Learning Magazine*, to be helpful.

• **Death of a Grandparent.** A primary age child narrates Le Tord's *My Grandma Leonie* and remembers little things done with grandmother that are a comfort after her death. One of the things Grandma liked to do was listen to the radio, so the narrator turned on the radio and "thought how much she loved me." When grandfather dies in Aliki's *The Two of Them,* his granddaughter sits in the orchard he loved and thinks of how the blossoms will come year after year. Townsend and Stern's *Pop's Secret* is told by Mark, whose 85-year-old grandfather whom he calls "Pop" comes to live with them, goes into the hospital, and then dies. Mark tells how he feels about Pop's death by putting together a pictorial story of his life. The three parts to *Saying Goodbye to Grandma* by Thomas are the family gathering, the funeral, and after the funeral, as seen through the eyes of a child. Holden's *Gran-Gran's Best Trick* is an account of a girl whose grandfather dies of cancer. *Grandpa's Slide Show* by Gould is guaranteed to bring tears to the eyes of readers. Whenever Sam and his younger brother Douglas stay over at their grandparents' house, they watch Grandpa's slide show. Then Grandpa dies. The boys are finally able to say goodbye to Grandpa when Grandma shows the slides and they remember him on the screen and celebrate his life. Nine-year-old Austin is reluctant to visit his grandmother's farm the summer after his grandfather's death, because all the traditions he had built up with his grandfather would now be gone. *Blackberries in the Dark* by Jukes tells how Austin and his grandmother deal with their loss and discover each other. Austin doesn't want to fish with neighbors because his grandfather had been going to teach him to fly-fish. Grandmother gives Austin his grandfather's fishing knife and a promise to teach him to use the old Farmall Cub tractor so he can cut the long grass. When Austin goes off to pick blackberries, his grandmother comes to Rock Creek in Grandfather's green rubber boots and fishing vest and they learn to fly-fish while eating blackberries. They throw back their first catch of the season, as Grandfather always did.

Annie and the Old One, by Miles, and *The Happy Funeral,* by Bunting, are multicultural books. Miles's book, a Newbery Honor Book, is available as a recording. *Annie and the Old One* is one of two books used to introduce the concept of theme in the sound filmstrip *Theme in Literature for Children, Series 9.* Annie's grandmother tells her how to accept her impending death in this classic story. In Bunting's book, about a Chinese-American family, Grandfather's funeral will be a happy one, his daughter tells May-May, because Grandfather has led a long and happy life. The poem "Zuni Grandma" appears on page 19 of Streich's *Grandparents' Houses.*

Hall's *The Rose Behind the Wall* is about a middle school student, Rachel Lincoln, and her grandmother's last days. Rachel is the one who finds Grandmother Potter on her bathroom floor. After a hospital visit, Grandmother is released to their care and is visited by a young hospice nurse. All the stages of death are included here, as well as the hospice concept. Rachel's brother Dan denies his grandmother's impending death and won't come near her, because he had been close to his grandfather and knew how painful that loss had been to him. There is realism here as readers see how Rachel's mother's constant vigil wears her out; how Rachel's father wants to go out to eat and get away from the house just for a while. Chemotherapy, loss of hair, and depression are realistically portrayed. The chemotherapy ends because the cancer is growing anyway, and gradually Grandmother slips away. The close relationship between Grandmother and Rachel is evident throughout the book, as they visit together, look at old photo albums, and discuss death. Grandmother's comforting poem appears at the end of the book. Rachel is also the name of the main character in Mazer's *After the Rain*. Fifteen-year-old Rachel Cooper doesn't really know her grandfather, even though she and her parents visit him every weekend. Then Rachel becomes her grandfather's baby-sitter and learns he is dying. The crotchety old man and his granddaughter establish a relationship that is touching. Toward the end Rachel doesn't even want to go to school. *After the Rain* is a Newbery Honor Book. In Wallace-Broder's *Steps in Time*, 16-year-old Evangeline (Evan) spends the summer with Gram on Whaleback Island off the coast of Maine because her parents are touring Russia on an exchange program for newspaper editors, her brother Andrew has a job, and her sister Tory is at gymnastics camp. This is the first summer Evan has spent on the island since Grandy died. Evan had been Grandy's favorite. Although Evan thinks Gram likes her siblings best, they come to an understanding.

● *Death of a Parent.* Clifton's *Everett Anderson's Goodbye*, a Coretta Scott King Award winner, is a story in verse that shares with primary students a boy's coming to terms with his father's death.

The death of a parent appears in several books for intermediate students. Jeremy, his mother, and his sister face the death of a husband and father in Little's *Mama's Going to Buy You a Mockingbird*. The books by Byars, beginning with *The Not-Just-Anybody Family* about the Blossom family, all mention the death of Cotton, the father who was gored by a bull in a rodeo accident. In MacLachlan's *Sarah, Plain and Tall*, the children have lost their mother. A young girl on the prairie loses first the new neighbor's child, and then the new neighbor in Conrad's *Prairie Songs*. Ten-year-old Ashley and 7-year-old Kristi in Hahn's *The Doll in the Garden* have the deaths of Ashley's father and Kristi's grandfather as a common bond.

● *Death of a Young Person.* Sometimes it is more difficult to explain the death of a child or teen than it is someone who has lived a long and productive life. Paterson's *Bridge to Terabithia* has become a classic for intermediate and middle school students. Ten-year-old Jess experiences the death of his new friend, Leslie. In *Cave Beyond Time* by Bosse, Ben's father and brother are killed in an accident, so he spends the summer with his archaeologist uncle. It is not until Ben falls into another time period that he learns to deal with death and his new situation. In *The Baby Project* by Ellis, 11-year-old Jessica's baby sister dies of crib death. Joel has the added burden of feeling responsible for the death of his best friend by drowning in Bauer's Newbery Honor Book, *On My Honor.*

There are several new books about death for primary students. Cohn's *I Had a Friend Named Peter: Talking to Children About the Death of a Friend* contains an introduction about death and children which answers questions like "When do children understand the concept of death?" In the story, Peter has been hit by a car and his friend Betsy asks the question "Can I die, too, like Peter?" The teacher talks about what they remember best about Peter. The idea that sleep is very different from death is covered. Some children might respond easier to the more natural book, Clardy's *Dusty Was My Friend: Coming to Terms with Loss.* Eight-year old Benjamin tells the story about Dusty, who was the same age as his 2-years-older brother Peter but was still friendly to him. Dusty dies in an accident on the way home from visiting his grandparents for Christmas and is buried far away. Thinking about Dusty's death scares Ben, but remembering good things about Dusty, such as his knock-knock jokes and their violin lessons, helps him. Ben comes to terms with not being able to say goodbye by writing a letter to Dusty and putting it in a drawer. At the end of the book Ben says, "Dusty was my friend and I am glad that he was."

• *Death of an Animal.*   Some books make it seem less painful to talk about death by talking about the death of an animal. In the picture book *Badger's Parting Gifts* by Varley, all the animals remember something special about Badger: he helped fox tie his first knot in a tie; he helped frog to ice skate; and he gave Mrs. Rabbit his recipe for gingerbread rabbits. "He had given them each something to treasure: a parting gift that would become all the more special each time it was passed on to others." It is clear in the story that Badger was old and knew he would die soon.

Primary students who have ever lost a pet will identify with the narrator in Wilhelm's *I'll Always Love You.* Elfie was "the best dog in the world" and was a member of the family. The narrator tells how other family members forgot to tell Elfie they loved her. As Elfie got older, she had to be carried upstairs, until finally she died in the night. The narrator doesn't want another dog right away but will probably want one some day. Other books for primary students that contain the death of a dog are Cohen's *Jim's Dog Muffin* and Keller's *Goodbye Max.*

The most famous of all stories about death is the classic *Charlotte's Web,* by White. Children can learn about life cycles when everyone's favorite spider dies. The death of the dogs in *Where the Red Fern Grows* by Rawls also provides tear-jerking moments. Both books can be read independently by intermediate or junior high students or read aloud to younger children. Books for intermediate students that contain the death of a dog include Aronsky's *Gray Boy,* Thomas's *Comeback Dog,* and Wallace's *A Dog Called Kitty.* In *Hurricane Elaine* by Hurwitz, Elaine's younger brother Aldo loses one of his cats when it is run over by a neighbor. Aldo doesn't want another cat but everyone, including himself, thinks he needs a dog, so he gets four dogs for his birthday, all from different sources.

ENJOYING CAMPING. A display of books about camping can be featured in school library/media centers right before school is out for the summer or in public libraries any time during the summer. Although Tafuri's *Do Not Disturb!* is a children's picture book, the humor can be enjoyed by readers of all ages. A family with three children, a dog, and two parents go on a camping trip and make lots of noise while unpacking their camping gear. The family disrupts the lives of large and small animals in the area. In retaliation, the animals disturb the family with regular nighttime animal sounds. The Carricks' picture book, *Sleep Out,* is available as a cassette. Carlson's *Arnie Goes to Camp* is about a reluctant camper who wins the "Best New Camper Award." Arnie is Harriet's cousin from the books *Harriet and the Garden, Harriet and the Roller Coaster, Harriet and Walt, Harriet's Halloween Candy,* and *Harriet's Recital.* In Roche's picture book, *Webster and Arnold Go Camping,* a mouse and his big brother Arnold go on a first campout in the back yard accompanied by Pandy Bear and Larry Dog. The mice brothers tell scary stories. In Levy's *Dracula Is a Pain in the Neck,* Robert and Sam frighten themselves after an evening of Dracula stories at camp. Three favorite picture book characters go to camp: Brown's *Arthur Goes to Camp;* McPhail's *Pig Pig Goes to Camp;* and Parish's *Amelia Bedelia Goes Camping.* Ask primary students to predict who the camp director will be in Marshall's *The Cut-Ups at Camp Custer* after they have read *The Cut-Ups* and *The Cut-Ups Cut Loose. The Ghost in Tent 19,* by the O'Connors, is an easy-to-read book that takes place at Camp Tall Pines. Two boys, their grandfather, and a collie dog go camping in Locker's *Where the River Begins.*

Any display of camping books should include Bernstein and Cohen's *Riddles to Take on Vacation,* which includes a section called "Camp Jokes." Another nonfiction book about camping is Arnold and Loeb's *Lights Out! Kids Talk About Summer Camp.*

Several books for intermediate students can be part of the display of camp books or can be booktalked. Erica Yurken, nicknamed Yuk, learns more about the new girl during camp in Klein's *Hating Alison Ashley.* The first three chapters, which end on page 29 of McDonnell's *Just for the Summer,* are about three girls who go to day camp and dislike it very much. The "Three Sillies," Lydia, Emily, and Ivy, are reunited when Lydia visits her aunts while her father is in the hospital. The three girls previously appeared in *Lucky Charms and Birthday Wishes.* Sheila attends day camp in Blume's *Otherwise Known as Sheila the Great.* Blue's *The Secret Papers of Camp Get Around* is a paperback original about Marcy's adventures with a newspaper at summer camp. Ten-year-old Abby plans to go to camp with her best friend, but Merle breaks her ankle and can't go. Abby's adjustment is revealed in letters which are signed with the title of O'Connor's book, *Yours Till Niagara Falls, Abby.* O'Connor's book is a winner of Nebraska's Golden Sower Award, chosen by children. Conford's *Hail, Hail Camp Timberwood* is the winner of two awards chosen by children—The Young Readers' Choice Award, given by six states and Canadian provinces in the Pacific Northwest, and the California Young Reader's Medal for junior high school. In this book Melanie learns to sing the Camp Timberwood song to the tune of the Notre Dame fight song, gets to know little Dougie when she is swimming with the 6-year-olds because she can't swim, and meets his older brother Steve, her first boyfriend. Melanie stands up to Ricky and wins the most improved rider award. Danziger's *There's a Bat in Bunk Five* is for the same age group. Use *4-B Goes Wild*, program #2 of the television series *Books from Cover to Cover*, to introduce this sequel to Gilson's *Thirteen Ways to Sink a Sub*. Miss Ivanovitch, the substitute teacher, is one of the chaperones when Hobie Hanson, his friends, and the entire fourth grade class go off to Camp Trotter in Wisconsin. Hobie is homesick and calls home but no one answers and he is afraid his parents are getting a divorce, when in fact his father is having a gallstone operation. Encounters with scary stories around the campfire and a skunk make the story interesting. At the end of the book the students learn that Miss Ivanovitch has been hired to teach 5B. A 12-year-old stepchild learns to belong during a summer at camp in Martin's *Bummer Summer*. Twelve-year-old Tiffin and her brother go to camp for the summer in Parker's *Camp Off-the-Wall*. The last chapter, pages 137–46, of *Sixth Grade Can Really Kill You* by De Clements finds Helen in trouble at the school camp during "outdoor education." Cole's *The Goats* is about two shy campers, a boy and a girl, who are stripped naked and left on an island to fend for themselves as a prank by fellow campers. Howe's *Bunnicula: A Rabbit-Tale of Mystery* is the winner of seven book awards chosen by children. Sequels are *The Celery Stalks at Midnight, Howliday Inn*, and *Nighty-Nightmare*. In the last book, the Monroe family goes camping and the animals become lost during a dark and rainy night in the woods by Boggy Lake. Chester the cat's imagination runs wild. As usual, Harold the dog is the narrator.

FINDING MANNERS IN CHILDREN'S BOOKS [CU 481–82; 720]. The 1959 Caldecott Honor Book, *What Do You Say, Dear?* by Joslin and Sendak is still a winner, especially since the paperback and sound filmstrip are available. What to say when you bump into a crocodile and other bits of humorous advice are given. The filmstrip could be an introduction to a unit on manners. The companion book, *What Do You Do, Dear?* is available in a cassette/paperback combination.

Several books are available for preschool through grade one. In the Hawkins' *Max and the Magic Word,* Max the dog learns the word "please" in a humorous book that is excellent for reading aloud. The audience will be only too glad to answer the question Max poses at the end of the book: "What IS the magic word?" *Shy Charles* by Wells doesn't say please or thank you. McLeod's *The Bear's Bicycle* and McPhail's *First Flight,* both illustrated by McPhail, are similar to each other. In the first title the boy observes proper bicycle safety and etiquette, but his bear does not. In the second, a boy and teddy bear visit Grandmother for the first time, but the bear pushes and slurps food in an unacceptable manner. Four-year-old Dolores plays too hard with the cat who prefers Faye in *Duncan and Dolores* by Samuels. Use this book to discuss manners in dealing with pets. In Oxenbury's *The Birthday Party*, a girl wants to keep the markers she has chosen to give as a birthday gift, as John, the birthday boy, ungraciously asks her "What did you bring me?" Bernard isn't very good at a birthday party in *Alfie Gives a Hand* by Hughes. In Gackenbach's *Binky Gets a Car*, Binky McNab gets a small riding car for his birthday, but does not ride it properly.

Good Manners is a set of two sound filmstrips on manners. Berry's *Every Kid's Guide to Good Manners* discusses manners in meeting people, using other people's things, and manners as we talk, eat, play, work, and visit. Cartoons help define manners in Berry's book. On page 3 of *Manners Can Be Fun*, Leaf says "Having good manners is really just getting along well with other people." This idea is reinforced in *Four-and-Twenty Watchbirds* by Leaf, a new compilation of several older books that portray such manner-less creatures as the Bully and the Bathroom-wrecker. Television manners appear on page 44 of Leaf's book. Ringalina, the Telephone Fairy, shares manners in *Telephone Time: A First Book of Telephone Do's and Don'ts* by Weiss. Table manners are just one type of behavior that appears in Anastasio's *Pass the Peas, Please: A Book of Manners*, which uses humor and rhyme to introduce concepts.

Gedye's picture book *Dinner's Ready! A Pig's Book of Table Manners* contains a matter-of-fact sentence about manners on each page. However, it is the illustrations that make the book hilarious by depicting the pigs' unacceptable behavior. When using this book in a unit on manners, be sure to discuss the concept of nonverbal communication. Giblin's *From Hand to Mouth: Or How We Invented Knives, Forks, Spoons, and Chopsticks and the Table Manners to Go with Them* shares information about utensils and manners. Differences in eating customs appear in the picture book *How My Parents Learned to Eat*, by Friedman. Use that book with Giblin's book. Manners during mealtimes appear on pages 10–11 of Brown and Krensky's *Dinosaurs Beware!* which combines manners with safety by admonishing children to chew before swallowing, not to lean back in their chairs, and to pay attention when using sharp knives. Safety also appears in cartoon form in a 16mm film or video, *Every Dog's Guide to Complete Home Safety*.

Being messy is bad manners and so is leaving others to do all the work. In Browne's *Piggybook*, Mrs. Piggott's two sons and her husband watch TV and make demands on her while she slaves away. When Mrs. Piggott has had enough, she leaves home after writing a note "You are pigs." This very funny book puts its point across with pictures and words. Schwartz's *Spiffen: A Tale of a Tidy Pig* lives in Slobbyville but is different from all the other pigs because he is tidy and on time. The other pigs tease him but Spiffen saves the town from a dragon by his cleanness, and wins approval. Three short stories about manners which feature a good and a bad pig appear in Richard Scarry's *Pig Will and Pig Won't*.

Two poems about manners appear in Merriam's *Jamboree*: "Manners," page 68 and "Company Manners" page 70. The poem "Elephant" from page 17 of Bodecker's *Snowman Sniffles and Other Verse* adds humor to a lesson on manners because it is "gross—eating with your nose." The well-known rhyme about eating peas with honey appears in Bayley's *As I Was Going Up and Down and Other Nonsense Rhymes*. Check page 42 of Viorst's *If I Were in Charge of the World and Other Worries: Poems for Children and Their Parents* and page 80 of Low's *Family Read-Aloud Christmas Treasury*, for the poem "Thank You Note." Sandburg's "We Must Be Polite" is a humorous poem about what to say to a gorilla or elephant. Milne's "Politeness" and Sandburg's poem appear on page 97 of *Sing a Song of Popcorn* by De Regniers. "Table Manners" by Burgess features a goop in Prelutsky's *Read-Aloud Rhymes for the Very Young*, Cole's *Poem Stew*, and *Childcraft's* Volume 2, *Time to Read*, and ends, "So that's why I am glad that I am not a Goop. Are you?" Pat Carfra sings "The Goops" on her cassette *Songs for Sleepyheads and Out-of-Beds!*

Use the story "The Simple Prince" from the second grade HBJ basal reader, *Weather Vanes*, edited by Cullinan and others, to introduce books about manners to children.

CONSIDERING CLOTHING. *Carousels*, the first grade HM basal reader, edited by Durr, et al., contains the story "The Man and His Caps" on pages 228–40. This story would be a good springboard for a unit on clothing. Stories about hats appear in Volume 2 of this book in a section called MAKING OUT-RAGEOUS HATS. Any of the books about hats found in that section could be the basis for a literature-based reading program on hats that could be expanded to include other items of clothing.

The film and video *Charlie Needs a Cloak*, from a book by de Paola, is an excellent addition to a primary unit about clothing. Although it has no table of contents or index, Weil's *New Clothes: What People Wore—From Cavemen to Astronauts* provides useful information for primary students pursuing this topic. The 16mm film or video, *Clothing Around the World*, tells why people wear many different kinds of clothing and is suitable for grades two to four. Cobb and Hafner's *Getting Dressed* contains cartoon-style drawings to show the historical background of various inventions like zippers and buttons.

Several books are good for reading aloud. Watson's *The Walking Coat* is about Scott, whose uncle gives him a brown coat with green splotches. When Scott wears the coat on a cold day, it seems to be walking by itself. When a neighbor takes the walking coat to a bakery, the coat eats doughnuts and captures a thief. In Smath's *Up Goes Mr. Downs,* Mr. Downs floats up and away when his coat inflates. In Neitzel's *The Jacket I Wear in the Snow* tells of a little girl who is trapped in layers of winter clothes when her zipper sticks.

Spohn's *Clementina's Winter Wardrobe* is about a kitten that thinks about longjohns, shirts, sweaters, boots and other warm clothing. *Thomas' Snowsuit* by Munsch ends up on everyone but Thomas.

The poem "I look pretty" from Greenfield's *Honey, I Love and Other Poems* is about an African-American child who plays dress-up in in her mama's purple coat. Read that before reading Hest's *The Purple Coat.* Although her mother insists that her new coat be navy blue, her grandfather, a tailor, finds a way to get Gabrielle the purple coat she wants in Hest's book, which is a featured book on the television program *Reading Rainbow.* Ziefert's *A New Coat for Anna* is an ALA Notable Book, as well as a National Social Studies Notable. Read the story aloud or show the filmstrip to the class. The story takes place in Europe after World War II and Anna is due for a new coat. Anna's mother barters possessions with a sheep farmer, a spinner, weaver and a tailor. After a year, Anna has a new coat and all the people are invited to celebrate. The poem "As Soon As It's Fall" appears on Card #33 of *Bill Martin Junior's Treasure Chest.* In the poem children learn that animals don't need to buy coats.

Carlstrom's *Jessie Bear, What Will You Wear?* is a nonsense rhyme that includes shirt and pants and some unconventional clothing. Gackenbach's *Poppy the Panda* is a toy panda who wants proper clothing. In Rockwell's *First Comes Spring,* Bear's clothes change with the seasons. In spring he wears a flannel shirt and a windbreaker, and in fall he wears corduroy pants, a sweater, and a book bag. Patrick dresses himself in Yektai's *Crazy Clothes,* but his pants appear on his head and his sweater goes on like pants.

Katie keeps her money in a Band-aid box but when she buys a purse she has no money to put in it. Readers add up with Katie as she earns money for various chores in Caple's *Purse.* Two other books about purses are *The Lady with the Alligator Purse* by Westcott and Giff's *The Riddle of the Red Purse.*

Several board books introduce clothing vocabulary to children. A double-page spread on clothing vocabulary appears in Hill's *Spot's Big Book of Words.* Preschoolers will like *One Wet Jacket* and *Two New Sneakers* by Tafuri and Zimmerman-Hope's *Find Your Coat, Ned.* Hoban's *Red, Blue, Yellow Shoe* introduces 10 colors through photos. Have first graders read these to younger children at home or to parents and grandparents. There are several books about shoes. *Shoes in Twos* is a big book that contains the repeated refrain "But all shoes come in twos." *Two Shoes, New Shoes* by Hughes is about many types of clothing. Carlstrom's *Shoes, Shoes, Shoes* and Morris's *Hats, Hats, Hats* are companions. Roy's *Whose Shoes Are These?* contains 38 photos and children have to guess who would wear the shoes. Two books about shoes are part of the *Reading Rainbow* television series: *Alligator Shoes* by Dorros and *Shoes* by Winthrop. *Shoes* is also available in a paperback/cassette combination. In Riddell's *Bird's New Shoes,* the problem begins when Bird wears new shoes. Then Rat, Warthog, Buffalo, Goat, Anteater, and Rabbit all have to wear the newest fashions. While they are arguing and sulking, Bird walks by without any shoes. When asked where they are, Bird answers, "Oh, I like to be different." Balian's *Socksnatchers* must be read aloud. These creatures steal socks from the Perkins family. Anyone who has lost socks will consider the possibility of socksnatchers living in their own home.

Marzollo's *The Three Little Kittens* is about Daisy, a white cat; Brownie, a brown cat; and Smokey, a silvery gray cat, who forget their brand new mittens in the snow. The poem "The Three Little Kittens" appears at the end of the book. Use this picture book with *The Three Little Kittens*, which has illustrations by Galdone. Allen's poem "The Mitten Song" is card #63 in *Bill Martin Junior's Treasure Chest* and appears in Cole's *The Read-Aloud Treasury.* "Mittens" appears on page 25 of Esbensen's *Cold Stars and Fireflies: Poems of the Four Seasons.* Arnold's *The Winter Mittens* is about a silver box containing a worn pair of mittens that have the ability to bring snow. To develop thinking skills, have children list other magical powers that the mittens might have. In *The Runaway Mittens* by Rogers, an Eskimo boy named Pica finds his lost mittens in a box behind the stove, where the sled dog has just had puppies. Two picture book versions of the Ukrainian folktale *The Mitten* are retold by Tresselt and Brett.

In de Paola's *Pajamas for Kit,* Kit sleeps over at Grandma and Grandpa's house, but forgets to take along his pj's. Clothing without any people in them appears in Lynn's *Clothes.* Items include shirt, overalls, socks, shoes, sweater, coat, mittens, and hat. Max hates what he is supposed to wear to a party so he dresses himself and goes to the party with mixed-up clothing in *Max's New Suit* by Wells.

BOOKS ABOUT BUILDINGS AND CITIES. During the last 10 years, many children's books have been devoted to city life, as well as to the metamorphosis from country to town to city. Muller's *The Changing City* shows changes in a European city as a neighborhood turns into an area of high rises between 1953–1976. In his *The Changing Countryside,* Muller tells of how open country changes into a town. Both books use fold-outs, eight in the first book and seven in the second. My favorite book on this subject is a gem I encountered in Australia. *My Place* by Wheatley and Rowlins takes an area in Australia from 1988 back by decades to the days when only aborigines lived there. Each era includes a map of the area, the date, name and nationality of the child who lived there during those years. Three decades of Greek immigrants lived in the area: Mike, 1978; Sofia, 1968; and Michaelis/Mick, 1958. The Irish lived there from 1848 to 1928, preceded by the British, back to 1888. The years 1878 and 1868 saw Germans Heinrich and Minna living there. An American boy born in San Francisco lived there in 1858 and 1848, the days of the gold boom. The year 1838 saw bushrangers and then two decades of early immigrants back to Sarah and her mother, who came on a convict ship in 1808. Finally, when 1788 is reached, we have Barangaroo, an aborigine. The contrast between the natural times in 1788 and the derelict neighborhood of 1988 is sharp. The ages of the children range from 7–11 in this picture story, which not only shows changes in neighborhoods but some of the history of Australia. Roennfeldt's *A Day on the Avenue* is a wordless picture book about a day on a street in Australia. Two girls find a tiny china cup and an arrowhead at their home in contemporary America in Pryor's picture book *The House on Maple Street*. Readers learn who lived at 107 Maple Street during the last 300 years. Loeper's *The House on Spruce Street* shares the history of a house in Philadelphia from when Thomas Morton built it in 1772 to when it was restored in the 1980s.

Seventy-seven years of change to a fictional town square from 1910 to 1987 are shown in *New Providence: A Changing Cityscape* by Von Tscharner and Fleming and the Townscape Institute. Not only are the physical changes shown, but one can see the economic, political, and architectural changes which have taken place in countless American towns during that period. The disintegration and restoration of the downtown area is especially significant. The Provensens show changes in an area of countryside in *Shaker Lane*. The area begins to be developed when two sisters sell their farm and it is subdivided into plots for poor and middle income people. These residents learn that a reservoir is planned which will flood much of their area. Despite protests by the neighbors, many of whom have a casual lifestyle with yards full of "stuff," the land is purchased for the reservoir and bulldozers come. The water level rises and new middle class homes replace the unzoned look of the area, and old man Van Sloop builds a houseboat. The area depicted is Foster County, Pennsylvania. Changes in a marsh from the American Revolution to the present are depicted in Turner's *Heron Street*.

Hoff's *Barney's House* is an easy reader about how a community changes. Children will enjoy seeing the old-time street peddler and elevated train. Changes caused by urbanization are colorfully depicted in Burton's Caldecott Medal Winner, *The Little House*, which is available as a sound filmstrip, paperback/cassette and hardback/cassette. Contrast between urban and rural areas is shown by the Provensens in *Town and Country*. Objections to the book are that while the city, New York City, is shown as multiethnic, the country, populated only by whites, is not, and the city is portrayed as being modern while the country is old-fashioned. Rylant's *Night in the Country* features night sounds, owls, frogs, dogs, or an apple falling from a tree. *From Path to Highway: The Story of the Boston Post Road* by Gibbons shows what happens along an Indian path as it changes to a major East Coast highway. Share *New Road* by Gibbons with students studying highways.

Goodall is a master of wordless picture books. In this section are those of his books about changes to places. In his usual style, Goodall uses watercolor paintings on full and half pages. Roennfeldt's Australian *A Day on the Avenue* can be compared with Goodall's *The Story of a Main Street*, in which one street in an English town is shown from the Middle Ages to the present. Some of the periods covered are Elizabethan, Restoration, Georgian, Regency, Vic-

Victorian, and Edwardian. *The Story of an English Village* depicts changes from a medieval village to a modern town between 1170 and 1970. *The Story of a Castle* traces the alterations to a castle up through modern times. The actual building of a castle appears in Macaulay's *Castle*, which appears in book, sound filmstrip, or video formats. Davison's *Looking at a Castle* shows children visiting a castle with a moat, keep, and dungeons. Other books about castles include Sancha's *Castle Story*, Smith's *Castles*, and Unstead's *See Inside a Castle*. Goodall's *Victorians Abroad* shows the cities visited during a "Grand Tour" of the last half of the 19th century: Venice, Florence, Paris, Versailles, Bombay, and Calcutta.

Individual cities have been the subject of books which show changes down through the ages. Kuskin's *Jerusalem, Shining Still* covers 4,000 years of invaders and conquerors. This poetic recounting of all the groups to have conquered Jerusalem is told mainly from a Jewish perspective, and shares the periods of David, Nebuchadnezzar and the Babylonian Empire, Greeks, Maccabees, Romans, Jesus, Christians, Constantine and the Holy Roman Empire, Persians, Moslems, Mohammed, Fatimid and Egyptians, Seljuk Turks, the Crusades, Saladin, Mameluke Egyptians, Ottoman Turks, Suleiman the Magnificent, British, Jews, and Arabs. Unstead's *How They Lived in Cities Long Ago* gives information about cities in Egypt, Babylonia, China, Greece, Rome, and Mexico in a straightforward manner. Dunrea's *Skara Brae: The Story of a Prehistoric Village* traces a stone village in the Orkney Islands from 3500 B.C., when it was first inhabited by neolithic families, through various inhabitants until it was abandoned in 2400. Information about unearthing the ruins from 1850–1972 are given. What was the Roman/Italian town of Pompeii like before a volcano eruption destroyed it in 79 A.D.? The black and white photos and text by the Goors (which make use of primary sources from Pliny the Younger and Tacitus, a historian) help tell that story. Information is also given about its archaeological discovery. Macaulay's *City* shows the design, construction and population of a Roman community. Ventura's *Venice: Birth of a City* is a history of Venice with emphasis on the 15th and 16th centuries when it was at its height as a trading city.

There are many books about modern cities of the world. Aska's lyrical poetry in *Who Goes to the Park?* shares Toronto's High Park with children through the seasons. Other books about Canadian cities are: *Ah! Belle Cité!/ A Beautiful City ABC*, a bilingual alphabet book by Poulin about Montreal, and Moak's *A Big City ABC* an alphabet book about Toronto. *In Love with Paris* is a video that can be used with Green's *In the City of Paris*. Explanations for what readers are seeing in Munro's *The Inside-Outside Book of London* appears at the end of the book. Krementz's photo essay, *A Visit to Washington, D.C.*, shows the city from the tourist viewpoint of a 6-year-old boy and his family. *The Inside-Outside Book of Washington, D.C.* by Munro shows the interiors and exteriors of a dozen landmarks in our capital city. A favorite picture could be the beautiful main reading room of the Library of Congress. Munro used the same oversized format for *The Inside-Outside Book of New York City,* which was chosen by the *New York Times* as a best illustrated book. Descriptions of the buildings at the end of the book are helpful, and the angles at which they are shown is the most unusual feature of these books. We hope more will follow. Another Munro book, *Christmastime in New York City* shares the special glow of the city, from the Macy's Thanksgiving Day Parade until the ball is dropped at Times Square on New Year's Eve. Stevenson's wordless picture book *Grandpa's Great City Tour: An Alphabet Book* shows New York City from an airplane. St. George's *The Brooklyn Bridge: They Said It Couldn't Be Built* crosses New York's East River, and can be used with books about that city. The Maestros' *Taxi: A Book of City Words* is important for building vocabulary. *The Best Town in the World* by Baylor is a prose poem depicting a town in the American Southwest, where the narrator's father grew up. A selection appears in the fourth grade HBJ basal reader in the Laureate edition, *Crossroads,* compiled by Cullinan, et al. A contrasting town would be the African *Village of Round and Square Houses* by Grifalconi, which changed after a volcanic eruption. Use either the book or the filmstrip in a unit about places where people live. A child's view of life in an Ohio coalmining town in the 1930s is given in Hendershot's *In Coal Country.*

The following books by Davis and Hawke provide information about specific cities: *Chicago; London; Los Angeles; Mexico City; Moscow; New York City; Washington, D.C.* Other books about specific places are: *Chicago, Illinois* by Turck; *Denver, Colorado* by Deegan; *Los Angeles, California* by Lee; *New York, New York* and *Nashville, Tennessee* by Deegan; *Orlando, Florida* by Stephenson; and *Washington, D.C.* by Turck.

A selection from Walt Whitman's "Song of the Broad-Axe" entitled "The Place Where a Great City Stands" appears on pages 38–40 of Sullivan's *Imaginary Gardens: American Poetry and Art for Young People.* Sandburg's "Skyscraper" appears on pages 40–41 with a photograph entitled "New York City: Showing the Construction of the Esso Building As Iron Workers Raise Steel and the 32nd Floor, 1954."

A number of picture books depict cities but do not name them. The hazy handtinted photographs in *City/Country A Car Trip* by Robbins show a car leaving the high-rise apartment and traveling through the city over bridges, through tunnels, past factories, the airport, malls, and finally on back roads to the mountains or the sea. The book is written from a child's perspective. A very different book to compare with that one is *Round Trip* by Jonas, which takes readers through a city and then at the end, has them turn the book upside down and read back through it. Rockwell's *Come to Town* takes a bear family on a visit to a school, supermarket, office and the library. Florian's *The City* is a wordless picture book. Rice's *City Night* follows a family to a street fair at night and shows what the city and skyline looked like between twilight and midnight. Black and white photographs show various letters of the alphabet in

Isadora's *City Seen from A to Z. My City* by Adams shows a map with places of interest and a city around the year.

Skyscrapers are an important part of a city's landscape. *The Story of the Empire State Building* is told by Clinton. Make sure that when readers see the dismantling of the Empire State Building used as an example of how a skyscraper can be taken down in Macaulay's *Unbuilding* that they don't think that the famous skyscraper has actually been removed. Another Macaulay book explains the complex support systems for buildings which are *Underground. Up Goes the Skyscraper!* by Gibbons tells about forms, piles, anchor bolts, screed, H-beams, girders, decking, and core. A whole range of people involved in the building of a skyscraper, and their specific jobs, are identified. Cobb and Strejan's *Skyscraper Going Up!* is a pop-up book which shows the inside and outside of the Equitable Center in New York. Ostler's *Skyscraper* is about the construction and functions of a skyscraper. Program #1 of the instructional television program *Explorers Unlimited*, for primary and intermediate students, is called *Skyscraper* and explores the inside of a building in Cleveland. *Department Store* by Gibbons tells about a building for a specific purpose. *Let There Be Light: A Book About Windows* by Giblin recounts the history of blown glass in the Roman empire to glass walls of skyscrapers today.

Building an ordinary house is also depicted in picture books. In Maynard's *New House*, Andy watched the progress of a new house being built next to his in the country. Andy ate with the workers at noon and used scraps to build a treehouse. Eventually, a boy his age came to live there. Photographs share the process of *Building a House* in a book by Robbins. Another picture book, Barton's *Building a House*, stresses the tools and people who use them in the building of a house, from the bulldozer operator to the painters. Weil's *The Houses We Build* takes a different approach, showing houses and the customs of the people who live there. Some of the places shown are: caves, hotels, hospitals, huts, pyramids and churches. Isaacson's *Round Buildings, Square Buildings, and Buildings That Wiggle Like a Fish* gives a list of 93 structures at the end and includes cathedrals, the Parthenon, mills, museums, bridges, and churches. Shefelman's picture book, *Victoria House*, is about moving and renovating an old house. *Our House on the Hill* is a wordless book by Dupasquier that shows a family through the seasons in a two-story rural house. Hindley and Reys's *Once There Was a House and You Can Make It* tells how to make a box into a house with shutters, flowerbox, roof, antenna, etc. The instructional television series *Images and Things* for students in intermediate grades and above, contains five programs about buildings in the green module: 201-*Spaces to Live In*, 202-*All Kinds of Houses*, 203-*Buildings for Work and Play*, 204-*Plazas, Malls and Squares*, and 205-*Here to There*.

Check the category, "In the City" of Kennedy's *The Forgetful Wishing Well* for poems about the city. Another poem which would be helpful for this unit is "This Is the Key to the Kingdom" on pages 62–63 of *The Random House*

Book of Mother Goose. "Buildings" appears on page 34 of Holman's *The Song in My Head.* Livingston's "Buildings" is Card #12 of *Bill Martin Junior's Treasure Chest* and Hughes's "City" is on Card #50. "Cityscape" appears on page 28 and "Development" appears on pages 22–26 of Bodecker's *Pigeon Cubes and Other Verses.* The second poem shows 10 steps for taking a choice piece of nature and changing it into landscape architecture. Hoberman's "A House Is a House for Me" appears in Cole's *The Read-Aloud Treasury. Roomrimes* by Cassedy contains 26 poems about different types of rooms arranged in alphabetical order. Blegvad's *The Parrot in the Garret and Other Rhymes About Dwellings* is another poetry book. Yoeman's *Our Village* contains 21 nostalgic poems about a village. Lenski's *Sing a Song of People* is a collage-illustrated poem in picture book format, which shows contemporary Boston while a boy walks his dog through town. "Houses" by Fisher is a poem that appears on page 102 of Pearson's SB/Ginn second grade basal reader, *Garden Gates.* "Pueblos of the Southwest" by Westcott, a selection from Clark's picture book in poetry, *In My Mother's House,* called "My Pueblo Home," and "The House That Nobody Wanted" by Moore appear on pages 114–49 of *Garden Gates.*

There are also books about types of buildings and specific buildings around the world, and three of them are written by Fisher: *The Tower of London* which has been a fortress, prison, museum, residence, and zoo since 1078; *The Alamo,* a mission and a fort important to the history of Mexico and Texas; *The White House* which includes anecdotes about the presidents and the families who lived there. Macaulay's *Mill, Cathedral, Castle, Underground,* and *Pyramid* all include step-by-step processes of planning and constructing the various architectural designs. *A Williamsburg Household* by Anderson tells of life in colonial Williamsburg. Yue's *The Igloo* is about the homes and lifestyle of the Inuit in Alaska. Eleven different kinds of homes from igloos, tepees, adobe, and log homes appear in *Shelters from Tepee to Igloo* by Weiss. Climo's *Chester's Barn* is on Prince Edward Island, Canada. Parnall's *Winter Barn* is in the eastern United States. *Animal Homes* is a video which compares animal and human shelters. *Plants and Animals in the City,* a National Geographic filmstrip set, could be part of this unit. A very different kind of city is shown in *Ant Cities* by Dorros, which is a *Reading Rainbow* TV program.

READING ABOUT TRUCKS, TRAINS, AND OTHER FORMS OF TRANSPORTATION. Many primary teachers introduce units about transportation to students. It is not too early to present the concept of nonfiction to primary and even preschool students whenever nonfiction books are shared with children, by using the terms nonfiction and information books and showing students the call number on the spine. When stories about the same subject are introduced, they should be identified as such and the *E* on the spine should be shown. The books in this section can also be used to introduce particular authors because several of the books are by Barton, Crews, Gibbons, the Maestros, Marston, and Rockwell.

Cole's *Cars and How They Go*, illustrated by Gibbons, shows what makes an automobile function through illustrations and straightforward text. *Fill It Up! All About Service Stations* by Gibbons shows people at work; the attendant and owner are female. Readers learn how hydraulic lifts, cylinders, and pistons work, where gas is stored, and how it is pumped. Preschool and primary students will enjoy Rockwell's *Cars*. Pop-ups and pull-tabs help students to understand the operation of automobiles in Marshall's *The Car: Watch It Work by Operating the Moving Diagrams*. *In the Driver's Seat*, by the Goors, describes how to drive a car. Fans of detective Encyclopedia Brown will enjoy information about cars found in Sobol's *Encyclopedia Brown's Book of Wacky Cars*. Fletcher's *Cars and Trucks* is for intermediate students. Toy cars and trucks explain scientific principles to primary students in Wyler's *Science Fun with Toy Cars and Trucks*. Introduce the concept of magazines to students by providing *Car and Driver* or *Motor Trend*. Students can use pictures from these magazines to make bulletin boards or collages.

Have students listen to the cassette or view the 16mm film or video of Fleischmann's story, *Alexander and the Car with a Missing Headlight*. *Sam's Car* is by Lindgren. *Traffic: A Book of Opposites*, by the Maestros, has vehicles going over and under bridges, making left and right turns, and going through dark and light tunnels. Related information appears in *Tunnels* and *New Road* by Gibbons.

The youngest children can find out about trucks from Barton's *Trucks*. Another book illustrated by Barton is Siebert's *Truck Song*, which shares the travels of a transcontinental truck in rhyme. The book is available in cassette/paperback format from one source and in 16mm or video from another. *Truck*, by Crews, is a wordless book which uses traffic signs to show the progression of a truck to its destination, where it delivers the load of bicycles. The Caldecott Honor Book is also available in a sound filmstrip format. The picture book *Truck* is shown in the background of another picture book, *Holes and Peeks* by Jonas. Magee's *Trucks You Can Count On* describes the elements of a powerful 18-wheeler. Children learn how an 18-wheeler is handled in *In the Driver's Seat* by the Goors. Many types of trucks are shown in the following books for primary students: *Trucks* by Gibbons; *Trucks, Trucks, Trucks* by Lippman; *Trucks* by Rockwell; *Trucks* by Seiden; and *Truck Book* by Wolfe. *Trucks of Every Sort* by Robbins is more difficult to read. Zim and Skelly's *Trucks* has long been used in transportation units. *City Trucks* by Quackenbush shows the Macy's Thanksgiving Day parade. A dump truck spreading gravel is shown in Haddock's *Truck and Loader*. Rich's *Diesel Trucks* explains trucks which have diesel engines and use diesel fuel. Trucks from 1900–1940 appear in Dorin's *Yesterday's Trucks*. *Snoopy's Facts and Fun Book About Trucks* is shared by Schultz in cartoons. Fire trucks appear in Gibbons's *Fire! Fire!*; Johnson's *Firefighters*

A to Z; Marston's *Fire Trucks*; Rockwell's *Trucks*; Seiden's *Trucks*; and *Ed Emberley's Big Red Drawing Book*. Horowitz's *Night Markets: Bringing Food to a City* shows how meat, fruit, and vegetables arrive by truck, train, and plane. A personified red truck takes a seven-hour trip to bring strawberries to market in the middle of the night in Lyon's *The Biggest Truck*.

How Many Trucks Can a Tow Truck Tow? by Pomerantz shares a rhyme about another personified truck. In *Dad's Car Wash* by Sutherland, a little boy who has gotten dirty playing with his cars and trucks gets an evening bath which is described in automotive terms. William lines up all his cars and trucks in *William the Vehicle King* by Newton. Tim calls all animals "duck" and all vehicles "truck" until his grandmother helps him distinguish between them in Lloyd's picture book *Duck*. A green truck appears in Adoff's poetry book *Greens*.

Marston's *Snowplows* describes removal equipment including snow throwers, sanders, plows, ice breakers, and plows on trains. Burton's *Katy and the Big Snow* is a classic picture book. *School Bus* by Crews is a wordless book about the travels of a yellow school bus.

The Bulldozer Cleared the Way and *Wheels at Work* by Zubrowski can be used to introduce large machines with students. Small books are also available. "The Bulldozer" by Francis appears on page 30 of Janeczko's *Pocket Poems*. An informative article by Mullett called "The Bulldozer" appears on pages 12–15 of the HBJ primer, *Ribbons*, from the Laureate edition compiled by Cullinan, et al. Bulldozers and cranes are just two of the large machines that appear in Olney's *Construction Giants*. Color photos enhance Bushey's *Monster Trucks and Other Giant Machines on Wheels*. Many vehicles appear in Rockwell's *Big Wheels*. Photos of 16 *Monster Movers* appear in Ancona's book of the same title. Marston's *Load Lifters: Derricks, Cranes, and Helicopters* is for intermediate students. Photos enhance Rich's *Earth Movers*.

Use Bennett's poem "The Steam Shovel" from page 80 of *Sing a Song of Popcorn* by De Regniers to introduce that favorite story by Burton, *Mike Mulligan and His Steam Shovel*. It is available in paperback/cassette format as well as 16mm and video format. A real steam shovel appears in Seiden's *Trucks*.

A variety of machines appear on farms. *Farm Combine* by Olney traces the harvester from the McCormick reaper to date. Use that book with Patent's *Wheat: The Golden Harvest*. *In the Driver's Seat* by the Goors tells what the driver of a combine does. Other books include Marston's *Machines on the Farm*, Sheffer's *Tractors*, and Bowman's *Agriculture*. A milk tanker and a livestock truck appear in Seiden's *Trucks*. Climo's *Clyde* is a Canadian story of a Clydesdale horse that is replaced by a new tractor.

Numerous books about boats are available. *Harbor* by Crews is a beginning book about boats and shows wharves, docks, piers, warehouses, tankers, tugboats, and barges. Ship shapes are shown at the end. *The Boat Book* by Gibbons shares the following water craft with a few words: kayaks, rowboats, canoes, sailboats, cruise ships, fireboats, police boats, aircraft carriers, submarines, tugboats, freighters, and tankers. Photos enhance Ancona's *Freighters: Cargo Ships and the People Who Work Them.*

Black and white photos of tugboats, ship loaders, and floating cranes appear in Ancona's *Monster Movers.* Maestro and Del Vecchio's *Big City Port* uses vivid colors to describe activities at a busy port. *Big City Port* is featured on the television program *Reading Rainbow. Fire! Fire!* by Gibbons tells how to fight fires on the waterfront, among other places. Cargo ships and tugboats are in *Ed Emberley's Big Red Drawing Book.* A father and two children cross on a ferry in *Ferryboat* by the Maestros. This book contains a historical note about the Chester-Hadlyme Ferry in Connecticut which began in 1769 and is the oldest ferry service in continuous use in the United States. *Sailing Ships* by McGowan and Van Der Meer recounts the history of sailing vessels. *The Story of Mississippi Steamboats* is a brief factual history of steamboats by Stein.

Picture books for preschool and primary students include Hurd's *Mystery on the Docks*, Gay's *Little Boat*, and the sound filmstrip or Gramatky's classic book, *Little Toot.*

Trains are fascinating modes of transportation. The freight train, electric train, passenger train, caboose, and steam engine are all introduced to preschool and primary children in Barton's *Trains.* Those same children will enjoy learning colors through the book or sound filmstrip, *Freight Train* by Crews, a Caldecott Honor Book. Rockwell uses foxes to introduce toy trains, freight trains, passenger trains, as well as subways and monorails in *Trains. Trains* by Gibbons shares historic and modern trains and shows steam, diesel, and electric engines as well as boxcars, piggyback, tank, hopper, and refrigerator cars. Pop-ups and pull-tabs help children understand the operation of steam, diesel, and electric locomotives, as well as railroad signals, in Marshall's *The Train: Watch It Work by Operating the Moving Diagrams! In the Driver's Seat* by the Goors allows readers to be a train engineer. Retan's *Big Book of Real Trains* is for primary and early elementary students. Scarry's *Aboard a Steam Locomotive* shows models and diagrams of locomotives throughout their history. Roop's informational article, "Steam-Engine Trains" appears on pages 50–57 of the third grade HBJ basal reader, *Fanfares*, in the Laureate edition compiled by Cullinan, et al. Frost's poem "Trains at Night" appears on page 58 of *Fanfares.* Sattler's *Train Whistles* shares the language of train whistles. More railroad terminology appears in Yepsen's *Train Talk: An Illustrated Guide to Lights, Hand Signals, Whistles, and Other Language of Railroading.* Goble's *Death of the Iron Horse* is about Cheyenne braves who attack a freight train because an Indian prophet said the Indians would starve and Mother Earth would be bound in iron bands. Miller's *The Transcontinental Railroad* is for intermediate and middle school students.

Preschool and primary students can listen to a cassette/paperback which is an adaptation by Retan of Piper's *The Little Engine That Could,* called *The*

Easy-to-Read Little Engine That Could. For a preschool story program called "Here Comes the Train," consult Idea #69 of MacDonald's *Booksharing.*

The letter P leans forward to become a plane in MacDonald's *Alphabatics.* Rosenblum's *Airplane ABC* is another alphabet book. Barton's *Airport* is for preschool and primary students and shows cars, buses, taxis, the waiting room, cargoes, fuel, pilots, and the control tower. Unfortunately the outdated word "stewardess" rather than "flight attendant," is used. *Flying,* by Crews, is for the same children and tells of boarding, taxiing, and flying in a prop plane over the city, suburbs, and countryside. All types of flying machines—seaplanes, pontoons, helicopters, and hang gliders—appear in Rockwell's *Planes. Flying,* by Gibbons, is a basic introduction to modern air travel and the history of flight from the Wright brothers to blimps, hang gliders, propeller planes, and jumbo jets. *In the Driver's Seat* by the Goors helps readers learn how a Concorde is piloted. Zisfein's *Flight: A Panorama of Aviation* recounts the story of Lindbergh's solo flight and the first American in space. Rutland's *See Inside an Airport* is for intermediate students. The Provensens' Caldecott winning book, *The Glorious Flight,* available in cassette/paperback, sound filmstrip, and video, tells of Bleriot's flight across the English Channel on July 25, 1909. Helicopters appear in Marston's *Load Lifters: Derricks, Cranes, and Helicopters,* Rockwell's *Planes,* and Berliner's *Helicopters.*

Picture books help take the trauma out of first experiences on airplanes. McPhail's *First Flight* is about a little boy and his teddy bear who are going alone to visit Grandmother. Krementz's *Jamie Goes on an Airplane* is a photographic board book about Jamie's trip to visit his grandparents. Photos enhance *Going on an Airplane* by Mr. Rogers.

If these books are introduced to students via a display, be sure to include Rockwell's *Bikes. Les Bikes* is a film or video that tells of a children's bicycle race in France.

The instructional television series *Draw Along,* for primary students, includes lessons on drawing transportation vehicles: Program #21 is *Cars and Trucks,* Program #22 is *Aircraft,* and Program #29 is *Boats and Water.* Drawing books about transportation by Ames include: *Draw Fifty Airplanes, Aircraft, and Spacecraft; Draw Fifty Boats, Ships, Trucks, and Trains;* and *Draw Fifty Vehicles.*

The following story programs about vehicles appear in *Storytimes for Two-Year-Olds* by Nichols: boats, pages 33–35; trains, pages 108–10; and vehicles, pages 111–13.

CHAPTER SIX

Sharing Easy Readers

First graders can be introduced to the idea that authors write books. They can become acquainted with authors such as Aliki, Brandenberg, Brown, Carlson, de Brunhoff, Ehrlich, Hoban, the Lobels, E. Marshall, J. Marshall, Parish, Rylant, Wheeler, Wiseman, and Van Leeuwen. Since these authors have written several easy books, information about them could be shared with students as the books are shown to them [CU 715]. The idea that students often like books by a certain author or about a certain character should be introduced in first grade.

Jane Yolen's Commander Toad books are probably the most exciting easy readers to come along in some time. In *Commander Toad and the Big Black Hole*, the Commander and his ship *Star Warts* are swallowed into a black hole and only the secret weapon can get them out. Space travelers eat pills for food and ETT is Extra Terrestrial Toad. *Commander Toad in Space* is the 1983 Garden State Award winner, a children's choice book award in New Jersey. *Commander Toad and the Planet of the Grapes* is full of puns and word play; i.e., "Have a grape day." Jake Skyjumper is one of the heroes in this easy science fiction book. *Commander Toad and the Intergalactic Spy* has a Toad Code, a spy convention, and makes readers wonder which monster is telling the truth. *Commander Toad and the Dis-Asteroid* is also in the Break-of-Day easy reader series and is full of references to food. All of the Commander Toad books could be used to introduce the genre of science fiction to primary students as early as first grade. Because the books are so much fun, they can be used as remedial reading for older students.

Louanne Pig and Oliver and Amanda Pig appear in two series of easy readers. When first graders are getting into the swing of reading in February, show the sound filmstrip *Louanne Pig in the Mysterious Valentine*. Use this book to introduce other books by Carlson about Louanne. In *Louanne Pig in Witch Lady*, Louanne learns that the woman they think is a witch is an inter-esting bird lady who gives her tea and cookies. Van Leeuwen's *Tales of Oliver Pig* is the first in a series of books about Oliver and his sister Amanda. Each contains five chapters and can be used to introduce the concept of chapters to first graders. The chapters include such topics as baking, bad days, sharing, Grandmother's visit, the snow season, and hiding. In *Amanda Pig and Her Big Brother Oliver*, little Amanda Pig wants to do everything Oliver does. In *Tales of Amanda Pig*, the pigs play airplane, monsters, fight with each other, and avoid bedtime. *More Tales of Amanda Pig* can be used to introduce the term *sequel* to first graders. All five stories in *Oliver, Amanda, and Grand-mother Pig* are about Grandmother's visit. Read-alongs are available for *Tales of Oliver Pig, More Tales of Oliver Pig* and *Amanda Pig and Her Big Brother Oliver.* In a first grade classroom, the books about Louanne, Oliver, and Amanda can form the nucleus of a group of easy readers about pigs. Anita Lobel's easy readers *The Pancake*, a Danish version of the runaway pancake story, and *A Treeful of Pigs*, would be a natural part of this collection of easy readers about pigs. After reading *A Treeful of Pigs* to students, place a pink pig with the name of each student in class on your "tree" (a large branch stuck in a pot of dirt). As each child reads one of the books, add the title of the book to that child's pig. Besides encouraging students to read, the concept of book titles and underlining written book titles can be introduced. Supplement these easy readers about pigs by sharing books from the section PIG OUT ON PIG BOOKS in Chapter 5.

There are easy readers available about dogs and cats. Mudge is a dog in an easy reader series by Rylant that contains: *Henry and Mudge*; *Henry and Mudge and the Forever Sea*; *Henry and Mudge in Puddle Trouble*; *Henry and Mudge Get the Cold Shivers*; *Henry and Mudge in the Green Time*; *Henry and Mudge Under the Yellow Moon*; and *Henry and Mudge in the Sparkle Days.* The last three titles are available in filmstrip or video. *Mr. Sniff and the Motel Mystery* and *Call for Mr. Sniff* by Lewis are about a dog detective. Cohen's *Three Yellow Dogs* contains only five words. In Porte's *Harry's Dog*, readers learn how Harry acquires a dog before asking permission of his parents, because he knows that his father is allergic to them. Aunt Rose comes to the rescue when she takes the dog, and Harry buys his father a goldfish instead of the dog his father has always wanted. Other titles include *Harry's Mom*; *Harry's Visit*; and *Harry in Trouble.* A dog appears in Griffith's *More Alex and the Cat.* Three stories are found in *Alex and the Cat.* Easy-to-read books by Wheeler about Marmalade the cat include: *Marmalade's Nap*; *Marmalade's Picnic*; *Marmalade's Yellow Leaf*; *Marmalade's Snowy Day*; and *Marmalade's Christmas Present.* *Pat the Cat* by Hawkins features words that contain "at." Parish's *Scruffy* is about the kitten that Todd chooses for his birthday present at the animal shelter.

Also read aloud from poems and books about dogs and cats described in Volume 2 of this book in sections called POEMS AND BOOKS ABOUT DOGS and POEMS AND BOOKS ABOUT CATS. After reading aloud, share easy books about dogs and cats that children can read by themselves. A temporary classroom collection of easy books on the subjects should accompany the poems or stories. If the list is to be expanded to all easy books about animals, the media specialist can read an animal story and then give each student a slip of paper containing the title of an easy book about an animal. Children can read the title, locate the book in the card catalog, and then locate the book on the shelf. It is always a good idea to check the shelves beforehand to make sure the books are in. First grade is not too early to teach children about book titles and locations of books in the library. Matching the E for easy and the author letter with the shelves that contain that letter provides students with a treasure hunt.

Media specialists may wish to enlist students in grades three and above as "buddies" for the first graders. These older students would provide help in locating the card in the card catalog and on the shelf. This provides review as well as self-satisfaction for the older students.

There are many easy readers about animals that appear in series. Marshall's books about a fox include: *Fox and His Friends*; *Fox in Love*; *Fox at School*; *Fox on Wheels*; and *Fox All Week*. All of these titles except the last one appear on a two cassette set called *Fox*. Hoban's Arthur is a chimpanzee who appears in: *Arthur's Christmas Cookies*; *Arthur's Funny Money*; *Arthur's Honey Bear*; *Arthur's Loose Tooth*; *Arthur's Pen Pal*; *Arthur's Prize Reader*; and *Arthur's Halloween Costume*. Another Arthur is an anteater. Use Brown's easy reader *Arthur's Halloween* to introduce other books about this Arthur: *Arthur Goes to Camp*; *Arthur's April Fool*; *Arthur's Baby*; *Arthur's Christmas*; *Arthur's Eyes*; *Arthur's Nose*; *Arthur's Teacher Trouble*; *Arthur's Thanksgiving*; *Arthur's Tooth*; and *Arthur's Valentine*. Three books about Arthur's sister and friends include Brown's: *D. W. All Wet*; *D. W. Flips*; and *The True Francine*. Books about Babar the elephant by de Brunhoff that are easy readers are *Babar and the Ghost* and *Babar's Little Circus*. *Hocus and Pocus at the Circus* by Manushkin is another easy book about the circus. Wiseman's *Morris and Boris at the Circus* can be used to introduce other easy readers in this series about a moose and a bear: *Morris the Moose*; *Morris the Moose Goes to School*; *Christmas with Morris and Boris*; *Morris Has a Birthday Party*; and *Morris Tells Boris Mother Goose Stories and Rhymes*. In *Hello, Goodbye* by Lloyd, a bear says hello to bees and animals, but says goodbye to them when it rains. The tree says hello to the rain and welcomes it. Komori's *Animal Mothers* begins with a mother cat carrying her kittens in her mouth and then shows how other animal mothers move their babies from place to place. Harry the hare and Shellburt the tortoise appear in Van Woerkom's easy reader, *Harry and Shellburt*. A turtle and raccoons appear in Hoban's *The Case of the Two Masked Robbers*. Introduce Ryder's *Fireflies*, the Hawkins's *Zug the Bug*, and Hall and Eisenberg's *Buggy Riddles*. Tripp's *Baby Koala Finds a Home* and *Norma Jean, Jumping Bean* can be used to introduce easy readers to animals found in Australia. Show a map of that country when introducing the books or point out Australia on a globe and show it in relationship to the United States and Canada. Pair Aliki's dinosaur books from the Let's-read-and-find-out series: *Dinosaurs Are Different* and *My Visit to the Dinosaurs*.

Human characters also appear in easy reading books. Brandenberg's *Leo and Emily* contains three stories. In "Early in the Morning," pages 6–15, Leo and Emily dress themselves in the dark before anyone else is up but find they have their clothing on inside out. In "The Swap," pages 26–39, Emily swaps her grandmother's wig for Leo's rabbit. Emily and Leo have a magic show in "Magic," pages 40–55. In the two stories in *Leo and Emily and the Dragon*, the friends go on a dragon hunt and make Harold, the baby sitter, earn his money by recreating a camping trip in "The Hunt" and "The Baby Sitter."

Other books by Brandenberg include *Leo and Emily's Big Ideas*, and *Leo and Emily's Zoo*. Spud and Joe meet their match in practical jokers when they meet Mary Frances Hooley in *The Cut-Ups*. Other easy-to-read books by Marshall include *Three up a Tree* and *Three by the Sea*. In one of the four stories in Ehrlich's *Leo, Zack, and Emmie*, they sing a song to the tune of "Jawbones." One of the four chapters in *Leo, Zack, and Emmie Together Again* is called "Chicken Pox," pages 27–40. Krasilovsky's *The Man Who Entered a Contest* is about a man who bakes a cake every Saturday and enters a baking contest. In *Harry's Mom*, Harry learns more about his dead mother, a writer who traveled all over the world. Although she sky dived, rode elephants, and rode horses bareback, she was afraid of bees. In Porte's other book, *Harry's Visit*, Harry is not excited about visiting Betty, Charlie, their three children, and their turtle; but after his visit, he can't wait to go back. There are five chapters to Krensky's *Lionel at Large*. In "Vegetables," pages 7–16, Lionel doesn't want to eat green beans. In "The Baby," pages 35–43, Lionel makes a sandbox. In "Sleepover," Lionel thinks he is too old to kiss his mother goodbye on his way to a sleepover but has trouble sleeping so Mother gives him a kiss over the phone.

Surprises and *More Surprises* contain poems collected by Hopkins which are easy to read. Check section 2 of *More Surprises* for poems about body parts like "On Wearing Ears" by Harris, page 15; "My Nose" by Aldis, pages 16–17; "Whistling" by Prelutsky, pages 18–19; and "This Tooth" by Hopkins, pages 20–21.

Little's *David and the Giant* is an easy reader depicting the Bible story of David and Goliath in cartoon-style watercolors. Bang's *Tye May and the Magic Brush* is about a Chinese orphan who is given a magic brush that makes everything she draws become real. Tye May uses her gift to help people, but her wicked landlord and then the emperor want to take her gift away from her. Several easy books make history interesting. One is Coerr's *Chang's Paper Pony*, set in American gold rush days which tells how Chang is mistreated by the miners. In Levinson's *Clara and the Bookwagon*, readers learn how roving librarians brought books to people early in the 20th century. Brenner's *Wagon Wheels* is about an African-American pioneer family that moves to Kansas after the Civil War.

There are a number of easy reading books that can be shared at special or holiday times. Levinson's *Clara and the Bookwagon* can be introduced in November during Children's Book Week or in April during National Library Week. Children can learn to fold and cut a red sheet of paper to make a valentine in Lexau's *Don't Be My Valentine*. Silly Tilly Mole smells jelly beans in Hoban's *Silly Tilly and the Easter Bunny*. Scott's *Memorial Day* tells how and why we celebrate that holiday. Three easy readers about Thanksgiving include Adler's *The Purple Turkey and Other Thanksgiving Riddles*, Cohen's *Don't Eat Too Much Turkey*, and Nixon's *The Thanksgiving Mystery*. Among easy books suitable for Halloween are: Brown's *Arthur's Halloween*; Cole's

Baba Yaga; Hoban's *Arthur's Halloween Costume*; Kessel's *Halloween*; Segal's *The Scariest Witch*; and Schwartz's *In a Dark, Dark Room and Other Scary Stories*. Some books for winter include: Florian's *A Winter Day*; Goffstein's *Our Snowman*; and Quackenbush's *Mr. Snow Bunting's Secret*. Easy Christmas books include: Bonsall's *Twelve Bells for Santa*; Davidson's *Teddy's First Christmas*; and Parish's *Merry Christmas, Amelia Bedelia*.

Easy readers can help students to understand concepts. *ABC Games* by Lopshire and *Busy ABC* by the Hawkinses are both easy alphabet books. Eleven color words are introduced in Burningham's *John Burningham's Colors*. A boy and his father share the concept of size in Barrett's *I'm Too Small, You're Too Big*. *Floating and Sinking* by Jennings contains experiments. Children can learn about a community from Hoff's *Barney's House*. In Levinson's *Touch! Touch!*, a preschooler says "Touch Cat" and a chain reaction begins when the cat upsets a bowl of cake mix that runs down the counter so the dog eats it and makes footprints on the older sister's clothing.

Students who need help with reading can read along with a cassette. Some easy readers that are available in cassette/paperback format are: Hoban's *Arthur's Funny Money*; Kessler's *Here Comes the Strikeout*; Lewis's *Hill of Fire*; and Lobel's *Owl at Home*. Use the video of Pellowski's *Magic Broom* to introduce the book.

A picture book with easy vocabulary is Tafuri's *The Ball Bounced*. Two books by Weiss contain four words per double spread, the last of which rhymes with the last word in the next double spread. There are only 57 words in *Sun Sand Sea Sail*, but together with the pictures, they form a story. *Dog Boy Cap Skate* is another book by Weiss that uses the same format. The next double spread is "Snow Scarf Leash Gate." Florian's *Nature Walk* contains only 26 words. The pattern for the book is set by the first two pages "On the trail, Cottontail."

A list of 200 outstanding first readers as well as profiles of 1,600 books appear in Barstow and Riggle's *Beyond Picture Books: A Guide to First Readers*. *Books for Children to Read Alone: A Guide for Parents and Librarians* by Wilson and Moss includes 350 fiction and nonfiction books for beginning readers.

CHAPTER SEVEN

Expanding Basal Readers

Although many teachers have incorporated literature-based reading into their reading programs, basal readers are still used by a majority of school systems in the United States. Two of the new basal readers, the Laureate edition of Harcourt Brace Jovanovich (HBJ), edited by Cullinan, et al, and the Silver Burdett/Ginn (SB/Ginn) series edited by Pearson, et al, contain many selections from several types of children's literature. Selections from favorite pieces of literature and popular topics in the basals are also covered in *Creative Uses of Children's Literature* [49–58; 710] and in both volumes of this book. Because basal reader selections should be enhanced by other books and multimedia whenever possible, selections from several basal reader series are woven into the text of this book whenever the appropriate books or topics are discussed.

In order for children to want to read, they need to be introduced to as many complete books as possible. School library/media specialists should be familiar with the basal readers being used in their schools. There are several ways basals can be expanded. One is to provide bibliographies of related books and multimedia by checking the lists in teacher's editions against the collection and ordering books on those topics or other good books that didn't get into the teacher's manual. Another is for school library/media specialists to base picture book reading and storytelling on themes or topics from basal selections. These related books should be made available to classes through floating classroom collections or brought to the attention of students through displays in the school library. Also, library instruction can be related to basal reading through providing booktalks on books in the genre of the story that is being read, by reinforcing retrieval skills, or by having students look up topics found in basal reader articles or stories. A search of the card catalog will reveal books, vertical files, and a variety of multimedia on those subjects. In addition, basal reader topics can be looked up in the following magazine indexes: *The National Geographic Index, 1888–1988*; *The Abridged Readers' Guide to Periodical Literature*; and *The Children's Magazine Index*. Also teach students to use the following poetry indexes to find poems on topics in basal readers: *Index to Children's Poetry* and its first and second supplements *Index to Poetry for Children and Young People, 1964–1969* by the Brewtons and *Index to Poetry for Children and Young People, 1970–1975*; *Index to Poetry for Children and Young People, 1976–1981*; and *Index to Poetry for Children and Young People, 1982–1987* by Blackburn.

Teach students to use reference sources such as the index to Commire's *Something About the Author* and the index in Holtze's *The Sixth Book of Junior Authors and Illustrators* to locate information about a famous author whose selection is included in the basal. For sources of author information, consult Chapter 3 of this book called "Introducing Books by Authors." Also make sure that a hardback copy and several paperback copies of the complete book are available for students whenever an excerpt from a longer book is included in a basal. Multimedia on various subjects introduced in basals can become the nucleus of the classroom reading/listening/viewing center. Books with accompanying projects, multimedia and individual equipment with earphones or listening centers can be part of these areas. Materials should flow in and out of these centers constantly from the school library/media center. Basals can also be used to introduce various literary genres, art projects, whole picture books, or whole fiction books for intermediate students.

Begin as early as first grade to spin off from the basal readers. A selection from *Eddie Couldn't Find the Elephants* by Battles from pages 58–65 of the Laureate edition of the HBJ primer, *Ribbons*, edited by Cullinan, et al., can be expanded with stories and poems about elephants. Two elephant poems appear in Prelutsky's *Read-Aloud Rhymes for the Very Young*: the anonymous "An Elephant Carries a Great Big Trunk," page 10 and "Holding Hands," page 11. The old chant that begins "I asked my mother for 50 cents" appears on card #190 of *Bill Martin Jr.'s Treasure Chest*. The humorous poem "Elephants," from page 17 of Bodecker's *Snowman Sniffles and Other Verse*, can be used to introduce elephant riddles. "Elephonty" by Richards appears on page 17 of *Poems for Young Children* by Royds. "All I Want for Christmas is an Elephant!" from pages 18–19 of Muncy's *Springboard to Creative Thinking* is a thinking exercise about elephants. Information on how female elephants talk is included in McGrath's *How Animals Talk*. Yoshida's *Elephant Crossing* shows typical activities of an African elephant herd. Books about zoos, like *Zoo* by Gibbons, can help children to understand the concept of nonfiction. Hadithi and Kennaway's *Tricky Tortoise* could be read aloud. When the big-headed elephant steps on tortoise and doesn't worry about it because he is the most important animal in the forest, Tortoise and his brother, who looks exactly like him, trick Elephant. Some books which contain elephants are: Bos's *Ollie the Elephant*; Caple's *Biggest Nose*; Chorao's *George Told Kate* and *Kate's Snowman*; de Brunhoff's *Babar's Anniversary Album*; Jenkin-Pearce's *Bad Boris and the New Kitten*; Lobel's *Uncle Elephant*; Peek's *The Balancing Act*; Sadler's *Alistair's Elephant*; and the Seuss classic *Horton Hatches the Egg*. Edge's big book and small books are available for *One Elephant Went Out to Play*, which also appears on the cassette *Music Is Magic*. Black line masters for that story are available so each child can have a book to color, reread, take home and read to parents, and use as a nucleus for a home library. Listen to songs on the cassette, *A Sunny Song*, in which Little Sara Sunshine, a circus elephant, sings. For multimedia about the circus, check Volume 2 of this book, for sections called ANIMAL SONGS and POEMS AND STORIES ABOUT THE CIRCUS. "How a Clown Makes Up" appears on pages 188–189 of the fourth grade Macmillan basal *Rhymes and Reasons*, edited by Smith and Arnold.

Parades, the first grade HM basal reader, edited by Durr, contains many subjects that are included in this book and can be located in the index. There is a selection, "A Good Place to Play," pages 12–22, by James Marshall, who has written many picture books that can be introduced. Have children go with the school library/media specialist to the author card catalog where the titles can be located on the cards and the shelves. Books about the color red can be introduced with the selection "The Little Red Hen," pages 40–41, "Pam and Lee Bake Bread," an information article, pages 53–57, can be supplemented with displays and storytelling about food. A section called POEMS AND STORIES ABOUT FOOD appears in Volume 2 of this book. Pape's "Doghouse for Sale," pages 78–89 and Chute's poem, "Dogs" on page 90 can be supplemented with books and poems about dogs from *A Dog's Life: Poems Selected by Lee Bennett Hopkins*. For more books about dogs, also check Volume 2 for a section called POEMS AND STORIES ABOUT DOGS. Leverich's *The Hungry Fox* who wants to eat ducks, can be expanded with books from this chapter called FOXY BOOKS or books about ducks which can be located through the index of this book. Check Volume 2 of this book for a section on BEARS, BEARS, EVERYWHERE to expand the informational story, "Who Helps Bear Cubs?"; the nonsense play "The Five Silly Bears"; Waber's book, *Ira Sleeps Over*; and Chute's poem, *My Teddy Bear*.

Selections about bears also appear in the first grade HBJ basal, *Sand Castles*, edited by Cullinan, et al. Minarik's *Little Bear Goes to the Moon*, pages 158–73 of the Ginn primer *Birds Fly, Bears Don't*, edited by Clymer and Venezky, and a selection from *Little Bear's Friend* appears on pages 10–19 of the SB/Ginn primer, *A New Day*, edited by Pearson. The basal reader stories can be used to introduce other books about bears or other books by Minarik about this bear such as: *Father Bear Comes Home*; *A Kiss for Little Bear*; *Little Bear*; *Little Bear's Friend*; and *Little Bear's Visit*. Sound filmstrips, cassette/paperbacks, and cassette/hardbacks are available for *A Kiss for Little Bear* and *Little Bear's Visit*. Paperback/cassette sets are available for *Little Bear, Little Bear's Friend,* and *Little Bear's Visit*. Two HM preprimers contain stories that can introduce books about several animals. Sections of this book called PIG OUT ON PIG BOOKS and FOXY BOOKS provide titles about those two animals. McPhail's "Come In, Boo Bear" and "Boo Bear and the Kite" can be used with picture books about bears, pigs, or foxes. The second can be used with books about kites. The stories could also be used in conjunction with other books by McPhail. "Lee Bennett Hopkins Interviews David McPhail" appears on pages 154–59 of the SB/Ginn primer, *Make a Wish*, edited by Pearson, et al. McPhail's story "The Bear's Toothache" appears on pages 160–69 of *Make a Wish*.

Basal readers can be used to introduce books about favorite characters in literature. Sharmat's favorite detective is introduced by *Nate the Great and the Lost List* from pages 186–96 of the second grade Ginn basal reader *Give Me a Clue*, edited by Clymer and Venezky. *Nate the Great* also appears on pages 71–96 of the first grade HM basal reader, *Carousels*, edited by Durr, et al. Other easy reading books about that detective include: *Nate the Great and the Boring Beach Bag*; *Nate the Great and the Fishy Prize*; *Nate the Great and the Lost List*; *Nate the Great and the Missing Key*; *Nate the Great and the Phony Clue*; *Nate the Great and the Snowy Trail*; *Nate the Great and the Sticky Case*; *Nate the Great Goes Undercover*; and *Nate the Great Stalks Stupidweed*. Books about Nate the Great can also be used to introduce the type of fiction called mysteries. For more mystery titles, consult the section of this book called INTRODUCING MYSTERIES.

Introduce the term *characterization*, the genre of historical fiction, and the meaning of Caldecott Honor Books through "Thy Friend, Obadiah" by Turkle found in the third grade SB/Ginn basal reader edited by Pearson, et al., *Castles in the Sand*. Other books by Turkle about Obadiah include: *The Adventures of Obadiah*; *Obadiah the Bold*; and *Rachel and Obadiah*. Several books are available as sound filmstrips.

Miss Pickerell and Paddington Bear are two characters that are introduced by the third grade Macmillan basal reader, *Orbits*, by Smith and Arnold. A chapter from MacGregor's *Miss Pickerell Goes to Mars* appears on pages 218–29. Check the author and the title indexes to *Creative Uses of Children's Literature* for out-of-print titles of MacGregor's books that may be found in libraries. Newer books about Miss Pickerell are written by MacGregor and Pantell. Titles currently in print include: *Miss Pickerell and the Blue Whales*; *Miss Pickerell and the Supertanker*; *Miss Pickerell Meets H.U.M.*; and *Miss Pickerell on the Trail*. A selection from *Paddington Abroad* by Bond appears on pages 232–42 of *Orbits*. A list of books and multimedia about Paddington appear in Volume 2 of this book in a section called TOYS AND DOLLS.

Books by Robertson that can be introduced with the sixth grade HM story "Henry Reed's Engineering Problem," pages 12–28 of Durr's *Celebrations* are: *Henry Reed's Think Tank*; *Henry Reed, Inc.*; *Henry Reed's Baby-sitting Service*; *Henry Reed's Big Show*; and *Henry Reed's Journey*.

A selection from Lowry's *Anastasia Again!* which appears on pages 346–58 of the sixth grade HBJ basal, *Treasures*, edited by Cullinan and others, can be used either to introduce realistic fiction books or to discuss characterization. *Anastasia Krupnik* is one of the books discussed on the sound filmstrip *Character in Literature for Children, Series 9*. Take this opportunity to introduce the following books about Anastasia: *Anastasia Krupnik*; *Anastasia Again!*; *Anastasia's Chosen Career*; *Anastasia, Ask Your Analyst*; *Anastasia at Your Service*; *Anastasia Has the Answers*; and *Anastasia on Her Own*. The story can also introduce other favorite books by Lowry: *The One Hundredth Thing About Caroline*; *Rabble Starkey*; *A Summer to Die*; and *Taking Care of Terrific*.

Books contained in basal readers can be used to introduce a favorite author. Authors in the following paragraphs who have articles written about them in Commire's *Something About the Author* include: James Howe, volume 29; Lois

Lowry, volume 23; William Steig, volume 18; Bernard Waber, volumes 40, 47; and Betty Wren Wright, volume 48. Authors who appear in the Wilson Junior Author Series include: Howe, 6; Lowry, 5; Steig, 3; Waber, 3; and Wright, 6.

Third grade students who are reading *Amos and Boris* in the SF basal reader, *Golden Secrets*, edited by Aaron and Carter, will enjoy other books by Steig. Teach students to use the author card catalog to locate: *Abel's Island*; *The Amazing Bone*; *Brave Irene*; *Caleb and Kate*; *Doctor De Soto*; *Dominic*; *Farmer Palmer's Wagon Ride*; *Sylvester and the Magic Pebble*; and *Yellow and Pink*. The *Long Ago and Far Away* television series from WGBH in Boston shares the Steig book *Abel's Island*. The mouse is stranded in Robinson Crusoe fashion on an island far away from everyone he loves. Baron's article "Who Is Beatrix Potter?" appears on pages 128–35 of the first grade Ginn basal reader, *Across the Fence*, edited by Clymer and Venezky. Levy's "Beatrix Potter" appears on pages 222–33 of the second grade Macmillan basal reader, *Magic Times*, edited by Smith and Arnold. Books by Potter appear in Volume 2 of this book in sections called NEEDLEWORK and TOYS AND DOLLS. Two books by Waber appear in the third grade SF basals, *Hidden Wonders* and *Golden Secrets*, edited by Aaron, et al. The books are *You Look Ridiculous Said the Rhinoceros to the Hippopotamus* and *An Anteater Named Arthur*. Have students check the card catalog for other books by Waber, especially those in the series *Lyle, Lyle Crocodile*. The first book about Lyle is available in a paperback/cassette package. Two books by Waber about Ira include *Ira Sleeps Over* and *Ira Says Goodbye*. The first title is available as a sound filmstrip as well as in a paperback/cassette package.

Introduce Eth Clifford and Betsy Byars to fourth grade students from selections beginning on pages 6 and 48 of the HBJ basal reader, *Crossroads* collected by Cullinan, et al. The selections come from *Help! I'm a Prisoner in the Library* and *The Midnight Fox*. Have students locate other books by those authors.

Beverly Cleary writes realistic fiction as well as fantasy and selections from her books appear in basals. A profile of Cleary and a selection from *Ramona Forever* appears in the fifth grade HBJ basal *Skylines*, edited by Cullinan, et al. on pages 164–87. "Letters to Mr. Henshaw" appear on pages 14–27 of the fifth grade SB/Ginn basal, *Dream Chasers*, edited by Pearson, et al. A selection from *Ramona and Her Father* appears on pages 78–95 of the third grade SB/Ginn basal, *On the Horizon*, edited by Pearson, et al. Introduce *The Mouse and the Motorcycle*, *Runaway Ralph*, and *Ralph S. Mouse* through the selection "Adventures in the Night" from pages 232–43 of Smith and Arnold's third grade Macmillan basal, *On the Track*. For more information about Cleary, consult a section of this book called INTRODUCING BOOKS BY AUTHORS.

Basal readers can be used to introduce specific types of literature. Such a fable as Aesop's "The Hare and the Tortoise" is introduced on pages 78–84 of the SB/Ginn primer, *Make a Wish*, edited by Pearson. Another fable by Aesop appears in the second grade SB/Ginn basal, *Going Places:* "The Bundle of

Sticks," pages 38–45. "The Vain Bird and the Peacock Feathers" appears on pages 129–33 of the second grade Ginn basal reader, *Give Me a Clue*, edited by Clymer and Venezky. The second grade Macmillan basal, *Mirrors and Images* edited by Smith and Arnold, contains two fables on pages 228–31: "The Dog and the Bone" and "The Lion and the Mouse." Check page 231 for a picture of paper bag puppets of lion and mouse and mitten puppets of dog and bone. "The Fox and the Stork," appears on pages 186–87 of the third grade Ginn basal reader, *Mystery Sneaker*, edited by Clymer and Venezky. "The Boy Who Cried Wolf" appears on pages 312–23 of the first third grade SB/Ginn basal reader *Castles in the Sand*, edited by Pearson, et al. and "The Wind and the Sun" appears on pages 260–67 of the second third grade SB/Ginn basal reader, *On the Horizon*. "The Crow and the Pitcher" appears on pages 165–66 of the fifth grade HM basal, *Explorations*, edited by Durr, et al. "The Town Mouse and the Country Mouse" appears on page 263 of the sixth grade HM basal, *Celebrations*, edited by Durr, et al. Three Chinese fables appear in the fifth grade Macmillan basal, *Echoes of Time*, edited by Smith and Arnold, on pages 82–84 and include "The Fox and Grapes," "The Dog in the Manger," and "Phrases from Fables." Check Volume 2 of this book in a section called AESOP IN AND OUT OF RHYME for titles of books which include fables, or a section of this volume called FOXY BOOKS.

Mythology appears in basal readers. Young's retelling of "Daedalus and Icarus" appears on pages 44–51 of the third grade Macmillan basal, *Orbits*, edited by Smith and Arnold. A retelling of "King Midas and the Golden Touch" appears on pages 130–37 of the third grade SB/Ginn basal reader, *On the Horizon*, edited by Pearson, et al. A radio play, "King Midas and the Golden Touch" appears on pages 245–63 of the fifth grade Macmillan basal, *Echoes of Time*, edited by Smith and Arnold. Two modern books about a 20th-century boy named John Midas appear in Catling's *The Chocolate Touch* and *John Midas in the Dreamtime*. "Arachne," the myth retold by Coolidge, appears in the seventh grade HM basal, *Pageants*, edited by Durr, et al. and "Arachne" from *The Warrior Goddess: Athena* by Gates appears on pages 496–501 of the sixth grade SB/Ginn basal, *Wind by the Sea*, edited by Pearson, et al. The informational article "Spider Silk" from Naylor's *Spider World* also appears in *Wind by the Sea*. "Athene's City," retold by Coolidge, appears on pages 205–09 of the HM eighth grade basal, *Triumphs*. "Odysseus and the Sea Kings" by Reeves appears on pages 327–28 of Pearson's *Dream Chasers*, the fifth grade basal in the SB/Ginn series. "Pegasus and Bellerophon" from Price's *A Child's Book of Myths and Enchantment Tales*, appears in the eighth grade SB/Ginn basal reader, *Worlds Beyond*. For more mythology titles, check Volume 2 of *More Creative Uses of Children's Literature*.

Second graders love riddles. Use Fleischman's *Kate's Secret Riddle Book*, in which Kate collects riddles from many people and makes a book for Wally, who is sick, to introduce a whole riddle spree. The story appears on pages 197–203 of the second grade Ginn basal reader, *Give Me a Clue*, edited by Clymer and Venezky. Check Volume 2 of this book for a section called RIDDLES, which includes titles and ideas for introducing them. Also check "Puns Anyone" which begins on page 227 of Smith and Arnold's sixth grade Macmillan basal, *Catch the Wind*. Volume 2 also includes a section on folktales, so use Malcolmson and McCormick's "Stormalong Goes to Sea" which appears on pages 192–203 of the fifth grade HM basal, *Explorations*, to introduce a unit on folklore.

Allow selections that represent a particular genre to provide the opening to introduce other books in that genre. A selection from Ullman's novel, *Banner in the Sky*, pages 71–98 of the eighth grade HM basal reader *Triumphs*, edited by Durr, et al., can be used in conjunction with the multimedia in a section of Chapter 1 called SURVIVAL BOOKS: A LITERATURE-BASED UNIT OF BOOKTALK TOPIC. A selection from Verne's *Journey to the Center of the Earth*, pages 506–524 of *Triumphs*, can be used to introduce multimedia in a section of Chapter 10 called INTRODUCING SCIENCE FICTION. A selection from the sixth grade HBJ basal reader, *Treasures*, collected by Cullinan, et al. comes from *Prince Caspian: The Return to Narnia* by Lewis and can be used to introduce books in a section of Chapter 10 called INTRODUCING FANTASY and in TIME TRAVEL: A BOOKTALK in Chapter 1. "Letters to Children" from Dorsett and Mead's *C. S. Lewis, Letters to Children* appears on pages 376–85 of *Treasures*, a HBJ basal edited by Cullinan, et al. The play, "The Diary of Anne Frank," by Goodrich and Hackett, appears on pages 74–99 and "A Diary Worth Saving" appears on pages 100–01 of the seventh grade SB/Ginn basal reader, *Star Walk*, edited by Pearson, et al. A selection from *The Upstairs Room* by Reiss, pages 60–71, can be used to introduce multimedia found in a section of Chapter 1 called THE HOLOCAUST: A BOOKTALK, as well as to introduce the genre of historical fiction. Several pioneer selections appear in basal readers and could be used with the books that appear in Chapter 10 in a section called If you like the *Little House* Books. Heiderstadt's biographical sketch "Ezra Meeker: Marker of the Oregon Trail," appears on pages 160–64 of the sixth grade Macmillan basal, *Catch the Wind*, edited by Smith and Arnold. An essay by Rounds, "The Prairie Schooner," appears on pages 500–11 of the fifth grade Macmillan basal, *Echoes of Time*, edited by Smith and Arnold. Also appearing in *Echoes of Time* are "Westward Ho!," page 512; the first two chapters of Wilder's *Little House on the Prairie*, pages 525–36; and the song "Sweet Betsy from Pike," pages 538–39. "Taming the West" appears on pages 212–19 of the sixth grade HM basal reader, *Celebrations*, edited by Durr, et al. The selection from *Trouble River* by Byars which begins on page 66 of the fourth grade HBJ basal, *Crossroads*, edited by Cullinan, can also be used with pioneer units. Holocaust and pioneer books are both subthemes in the genre of historical fiction.

Introduce poetry and other nonfiction at holiday time. "Life in Pilgrim Times" by Dunn and "Over the River and Through the Wood" by Child from pages 38–45 and page 70 of the third grade reader, *Castles in the Sand*, in the

SB/Ginn series edited by Pearson, et al. can be used to introduce Thanksgiving books and poems found in Volume 2 of this book, in a section called THANKS-GIVING IN STORY AND VERSE. "Arthur's Thanksgiving Emergency" begins on page 59 of Pearson's fourth grade SB/Ginn basal, *Silver Secrets*, and comes from Pinkwater's *The Hoboken Chicken Emergency*.

Basal reader stories can introduce specific subjects to students. A boy practices ballet with a sister to limber himself up for athletics in Isadora's *Max*. *Max* appears on pages 36–41 of the second grade SB/Ginn reader, *Garden Gates* edited by Pearson, as well as on pages 100–05 of the third grade Macmillan basal, *Secrets and Surprises* edited by Smith and Arnold. "Ballet for Everyone" by Harper appears on pages 294–99 of the fourth grade HBJ basal, *Crossroads*, edited by Cullinan, et al. "Maria Tallchief: Dancer with a Dream," pages 32–45 of the sixth grade HM basal reader, *Celebrations*, edited by Durr, et al, can be used to introduce books found in the BALLET section of Volume 2 of this book. The fictionalized biography can also be used with ethnic studies or in units about Native Americans.

Young's "If I Rode a Dinosaur," pages 93–102 of Aaron's third grade SF basal, *Golden Secrets*, can be used with books in a section of this volume called DISCOVERING DINOSAURS or from the ART MUSEUMS section of Volume 2. Prelutsky's poem, "The Museum" appears on page 206 of the second grade SB/Ginn basal, *Garden Gates*, edited by Pearson, et al. "The Mexican Museum" appears on pages 290–93 of the third grade Macmillan basal, *Secrets and Surprises*, edited by Smith and Arnold. Adults will be interested in *Developing Library/Museum Partnerships to Serve Young People* by the Jays. A selection from Hurwitz's *Baseball Fever* on pages 252–63 of the fifth grade SB/Ginn basal reader, *Dream Chasers*, edited by Pearson, et al. can be used to introduce the books in the SHARING BASEBALL section of Volume 2 of this book. "The Story of the Statue of Liberty" by the Maestros appears on pages 276–85 of the second grade SB/Ginn basal, *Going Places*, edited by Pearson, et al. and an interview with Betsy and Giulio Maestro appears on pages 272–86 of the same basal. A biographical sketch of Emma Lazarus is found on pages 18–22 of the fifth grade Macmillan basal, *Echoes of Time*, edited by Smith and Arnold. The poem "The New Colossus" by Lazarus, carved on the base of the Statue of Liberty, appears on page 23 of *Echoes of Time*. Expand these two basal reader articles with books from a section of this book called VISITING THE STATUE OF LIBERTY.

Books about horses can be shared when students are reading selections in basal readers about horses. A selection from Shub's *The White Stallion* appears on pages 26–37 of the third grade HM basal reader, *Caravans*, edited by Durr, et al. A selection from *The Black Stallion* is on pages 102–14 of the fourth grade HBJ basal, *Crossroads*, edited by Cullinan, et al. There is a selection from Farley's *The Black Stallion* on pages 336–60 of the seventh grade HM basal reader, *Pageants*, by Durr, et al and on pages 282–97 of the seventh grade SB/Ginn basal reader, *Star Walk*, by Pearson, et al. The following books by

Farley make up the Black Stallion series: *The Black Stallion*; *The Black Stallion: An Easy-to-Read Adaptation*; *The Black Stallion and Flame*; *The Black Stallion and Satan*; *The Black Stallion and the Girl*; *The Black Stallion Challenged*; *Black Stallion: A Comic Book Album*; *The Black Stallion Legend*; *The Black Stallion Mystery*; *The Black Stallion Picture Book*; *The Black Stallion Returns*; *The Black Stallion Returns: Movie Storybooks*; *The Black Stallion Returns: A Comic Book Album*; *The Black Stallion Revolts*; *The Black Stallion's Courage*; *The Black Stallion's Filly*; *The Black Stallion's Ghost*; *The Black Stallion's Sulky Colt*; *The Island Stallion*; *The Island Stallion Races*; *The Island Stallion's Fury*; *Man O' War*; and *Son of the Black Stallion*. A recent addition is *The Young Black Stallion* by Walter Farley and Steven Farley, a prequel which tells how the horse came from an Arab sheik to Alex Ramsey.

Make the following fiction titles about horses available to students who are reading about either the black or white stallion in their basal readers: Bagnold's *National Velvet*; Brown's *Last Hurdle*; Campbell's *A Horse of Her Own*; Climo's *Clyde*; Diggs's *Everyday Friends*; Dragonwagon's *Margaret Ziegler Is Horse-Crazy*; Gates's *Filly for Melinda*; Hoppe's *Pretty Penny Farm*; Morrison's *Somebody's Horse*, *Whisper Again*, and *Whisper Goodbye*; Pollack's *Stall Buddies*; Savitt's *Horse to Remember*; Sewell's *Black Beauty*; Thomas's *Golden Pasture*; Waddell's *Harriet and the Haunted School*; Wallace's *Beauty*. Horse books by Doty include: *Dark Horse*; *Can I Get There by Candlelight?*; *Summer Pony*; *Winter Pony*; and *Yesterday's Horses*. Horse books by Hall include: *Danza*; *Dragon Defiant*; *Megan's Mare*; *Mrs. Portee's Pony*; *Mystery of the Plum Park Pony*; *Mystery of Pony Hollow*; *Mystery of Pony Park Panda*; *Ride a Dark Horse*; and *The Something Special Horse*. Three paperback originals by Bryant for intermediate students include *Horse Crazy*; *Horse Sense*; and *Horse Sky*. Sewell's *Black Beauty* has been adapted by McKinley and illustrated by Jeffers. Horse books by Henry appear in Chapter 3 of this volume, "Introducing Books by Authors." Chapter 2 of Green and Sanford's *The Wild Horses* is about horses at Assateague Island in the National Wildlife Refuge. Bullaty's *The Little Wild Ponies* is about the Chincoteague and Assateague Island ponies. Use these two books with Henry's *Misty of Chincoteague*, *Sea Star: Orphan of Chincoteague*, and *Stormy, Misty's Foal*. A selection from Henry's *Justin Morgan Had a Horse* appears on pages 458–71 of the fifth grade HBJ basal reader *Skylines*, collected by Cullinan, et al. Four nonfiction books about breeds of horses include Patent's *Appaloosa Horses*; *Arabian Horses*; *Quarter Horses*; and *Draft Horses*. Featherly's *Mustangs: Wild Horses of the American West* contains color photographs and dwells on the social order of the herd. Information about wild horses in the American west from the time of the Spanish settlers to the present appears in Patent's *Where the Wild Horses Roam*. Other nonfiction books about horses include: Jurmain's *Once Upon a Horse: A History of Horses and How They Shaped Our History*; Ludell's *Harold Roth's Big Book of Horses*; Patent's *A Horse of a Different Color*; Quicke's *Let's Look at Horses*, and Saville's *Horses in the Circus Ring*. Nine stories from folklore are included in *If You Had a Horse* by Hodges. Poems appear in a collection by Hopkins, *My Mane Catches the Wind: Poems About Horses.* Isenbart's *Birth of a Foal* includes photos of birth and the first few hours of life. There are horses in Rahn's *Animals That Changed History.* Philp's *Rodeo Horses* can be used with books about the Blossom family that begin in *The Not-Just-Anybody Family* by Byars.

Brown's "Shackleton's Epic Voyage" appears on pages 170–82 and the photo essay, "Antarctica" appears on pages 184–90 of the HM fifth grade basal, *Explorations,* edited by Durr, et al. "Arctic Fire," a story by Houston, and a personal narrative by Davis as told to Tripp, "Living at the Bottom of the World: My Year in Antarctica" appear on pages 270–88 and 346–57 of the sixth grade HM basal, *Celebrations.* The latter tells of a husband and wife science team that studies penguins for a year. Books about penguins appear in Chapter 9 of this volume in a section called STUDYING NONFICTION CLUSTERS. Introduce Stolz's *The Explorer of Barkham Street* in which Martin has been reading books of this type. More books about the Arctic and Antarctic appear in Volume 2 in a section called GIFT BOOKS.

Basal reader stories help students to understand about handicaps and can encourage them to read other stories about handicapped children. A selection from Peterson's *I Have a Sister—My Sister Is Deaf,* appears on pages 79–88 of *Golden Secrets,* the third grade basal reader from Scott Foresman, edited by Ira Aaron et al. Litchfield's *Making Room for Uncle Joe,* about a retarded uncle who comes to live with a grown sibling and her family, appears on pages 22–36 of the fourth grade HBJ basal reader, *Crossroads,* edited by Cullinan, et al. Books about several handicaps appear in Chapter 8 of this volume in a section called LITERATURE-BASED READING: *THE TROUBLE WITH TUCK.*

The text of whole picture books or chapters from books appear in basal readers and can encourage students to read the original book or the entire book. Friedman's *How My Parents Learned to Eat* appears on pages 256–67 of the second grade basal SB/Ginn reader *Going Places* and Cooney's *Miss Rumphius* appears on pages 22–32 of the third grade *On the Horizon* in the same series edited by Pearson, et al. Stories can include favorites such as Payne's *Katy-No-Pocket* from pages 258–74 of the second grade HM basal, *Adventures,* edited by Durr, et al. or a selection from Knight's *Lassie, Come Home* as found in the sixth grade HM basal, *Celebrations.* Selections from two classics appear in the SB/Ginn series edited by Pearson, et al.: "In Which Piglet Meets a Heffalump," pages 324–41 of the third grade reader, *Castles in the Sand,* and "Escape from Charlotte's Web" by White on pages 242–53 of the fifth grade reader, *Silver Secrets.* Be sure to make complete copies of White's *Charlotte's Web* and Milne's *Winnie-the-Pooh* available to students. "Toad of Toad Hall," a play by Milne based on Grahame's *The Wind in the Willows* appears on pages 132–40 of the second grade SB/Ginn basal reader, *Going Places,* by Pearson, et al. and a selection from *The Adventures of Ali Baba Bernstein* appears on pages 42–55 of the third grade reader, *On the Horizon*, from the same series. A selection from Miles's *Annie and the Old One* appears on pages 476–88 of the fourth grade Macmillan basal, *Rhymes and Reasons*, edited by Smith and Arnold. A selection from Bulla's *Shoeshine Girl* appears on pages 130–45 of the fifth grade SB/Ginn basal *Dream Chasers*, edited by Pearson, et al. Selections from Salten's *Bambi*, pages 278–81; George's *Gull Number 737*, pages 380–90; George's *My Side of the Mountain*, pages 480–91; as well as De Jong's *A Horse Came Running*, pages 502–622, appear in the Macmillan sixth grade basal, *Catch the Wind*, edited by Smith and Arnold. A selection from O'Brien's *Mrs. Frisby and the Rats of NIMH*, Wier's *The Loner*, and Heyerdahl's *Kon-Tiki* appear in the sixth grade HM basal, *Celebrations*, edited by Durr, et al. A selection from Burnford's *The Incredible Journey* appears in the seventh grade SB/Ginn basal, *Star Walk*, edited by Pearson, et al.

Basal reader selections can be used to introduce music. Wadsworth's version of *Over in the Meadow* appears on pages 178–81 of Smith and Arnold's third grade Macmillan basal reader, *Full Circle*. More editions of this song appear in Volume 2 of this book in a section called ANIMAL SONGS. Check a section called INDIVIDUAL PICTURE BOOKS CONTAINING SONGS for other stories set to music.

Basal readers can stimulate art projects. The collage illustrations in "Arion," pages 70–76 of the third grade Ginn basal reader, *Mystery Sneaker*, edited by Clymer and Venezky, can be followed by a study of picture books illustrated with collage as listed in a section called COLLAGE IN PICTURE BOOKS in Volume 2 of this book. Even kindergartners reading *Kites* and *Rainbows* from the HBJ Laureate edition edited by Cullinan, et al., can appreciate the illustrations on the covers and realize that they are collages which include relief figures. Stories which include colors can be springboards for the many picture books which feature colors. Smith and Arnold's first grade basal, *Rainbow World*, contains O'Neill's poem "Red" as well as Anastasio's story "Rico and the Red Pony" and Lionni's *Little Blue and Little Yellow*. For more books about color check COLOR IN PICTURE BOOKS in Volume 2 of this book. Charlip and Supree's *Harlequin and the Gift of Many Colors* appears on pages 86–104 of the third grade Macmillan basal, *Full Circle*, edited by Smith and Arnold. Directions for making an origami drinking cup appear on pages 322–26 of the same book.

Basal reader articles can stimulate bulletin boards and displays created by adults or students. Check Volume 2 of this book for a section called DISPLAYS ABOUT BALLOONS. Basal reader stories about balloons include *The Bicycle Balloon Chase* by Douglass from pages 28–34 of the third grade HBJ basal reader, *Celebrations*, collected by Cullinan, et al. Lindop's "The First Balloon Flight in North America" appears on pages 122–29 of Clymer and Venezky's third grade Ginn basal reader, *Mystery Sneaker*. A selection from *Twenty-One Balloons* by du Bois appears on pages 138–57 of the seventh grade HBJ basal, *Patterns*, edited by Cullinan, et al. Dean's article, "Ballooning Today," appears on pages 118–21 of the eighth grade basal reader, *Triumphs*, edited by Durr, et al.

Books about frogs and toads for primary students can be introduced through Lobel's favorite characters in stories found in basal readers. Lobel's "Alone," from pages 24–35 of *Days with Frog and Toad* appears in the SB/Ginn primer, *A New Day*, edited by Pearson, et al. Check pages 14–21 of the second grade SB/Ginn reader, *Garden Gates* for "Frog and Toad," a selection from *Frog and Toad Together*. Lobel's "The Surprise" from *Frog and Toad All Year* appears on pages 110–19 of the first grade Ginn basal reader, *Across the Fence*, edited by Clymer and Venezky. "The Kite" from *Days with Frog and Toad* appears on pages 186–97 of the first grade HBJ basal, *Sand Castles*, collected by Cullinan and others. "The Garden" from *Frog and Toad Together* by Lobel appears on pages 66–76 of the second grade HM basal reader, *Adventures*, edited by Durr, et al. *Frog and Toad* appears on pages 44–53 of *Time to Read*, volume 2 of *Childcraft*. *The Arnold Lobel Video Showcase* contains selections from *Frog and Toad Are Friends, Frog and Toad Together, Fables, Mouse Soup*, and the revised edition of the film, *Meet the Newbery Author: Arnold Lobel*. Nine frog and toad stories are part of films using puppet animation: *Frog and Toad are Friends, Frog and Toad Together*, and *Frog and Toad: Behind the Scenes*, which are part of the PBS television series *Long Ago and Far Away*. Teachers, librarians, and school library/media specialists will appreciate Polette's *The Frog and Toad Thinking Book* which contains activities based on Lobel's books: *Frog and Toad All Year, Days with Frog and Toad, Frog and Toad Together, Frog and Toad Are Friends, The Frog and Toad Coloring Book*. Thinking skills included in Polette's book are fluency, flexibility, originality, elaboration, planning, forecasting, decision-making, and problem solving. In her book *Presenting Reader's Theater*, Bauer includes a play for eight or more characters, "Dragons and Giants" from Lobel's *Frog and Toad Together*. Wolkstein reads stories from *Frog and Toad Are Friends* on her recording *Romping*.

Another series of easy readers about toads are Yolen's books about Commander Toad: *Commander Toad and the Big Black Hole; Commander Toad and the Dis-Asteroid; Commander Toad and the Intergalactic Spy; Commander Toad and the Planet of the Grapes; Commander Toad and the Space Pirates*; and *Commander Toad in Space*. Yolen's *Commander Toad in Space* and Erickson's *A Toad for Tuesday* are available as paperback/cassette packages.

Some fiction books about frogs include: Anderson's *Time for Bed, the Babysitter Said*; Blake's *Story of the Dancing Frog*; Lionni's *It's Mine*; Maris's *Better Move on, Frog*; Noll's *Off and Counting*; and Yeoman's *The Bear's Water Picnic*. Potter's *The Tale of Mr. Jeremy Fisher* appears on the cassette *Peter Rabbit and Friends from the Picture Book Parade*. Edge's *I've Got a Frog* is available in big book and small book format as well as on her cassette *Music Is Magic*. A black line master is included with Edge's book, so small books can be made for students each to have a personal copy. "The Frog Prince" appears on pages 57–60 of Wainwright's *A Magical Menagerie: Tales from Perrault, Andersen, La Fontaine, and Grimm*. *The Frog Prince* by the Grimms has been retold by Tarcov and illustrated by Marshall. *The Princess and the Frog* is a picture book by Vesey. For more titles about princes, princesses, and frogs, consult COMPARING FOLKTALES from Volume 2 of this.

Some nonfiction books about frogs include Cole's *A Frog's Body*; Dallinger's *Frogs and Toads*; Florian's *Discovering Frogs*; Johnson's *Tree Frogs*; Lane's *Frog*; Linley's *Discovering Frogs and Toads*; Petty's *Frogs and Toads*; Selsam and Hunt's *A First Look at Frogs, Toads, and Salamanders*; and Webster's *Frog and Toad Watching*. A video from National Geographic, called *Tadpoles and Frogs*, shows the stages of metamorphosis in two species.

A commercial package is available which correlates basals and trade books. Lynch has created "Text Extenders," which are basal-correlated paperback libraries by Scholastic. A dozen basal reader series have been analyzed and the basal selection is correlated with books of the same content, books about the same character, books of the same genre, the complete book, books with the same theme, and extra books. These "Text Extenders" are available for grades one to six.

CHAPTER EIGHT

Whole Language, Literature-Based Reading, and Language Experience

The integration of all language arts is the key to the whole language approach. The combination of reading, writing, listening, speaking, researching, and thinking are manifestations of the whole language approach.

Goodman's *What's Whole in Whole Language?* shares information about whole language teaching. Check page 8 for a list of 12 items that make language very easy to learn and 12 factors that make language very hard to learn. Check pages 31–33 for information on what makes a whole language classroom. Check page 34 for six teaching practices that are rejected by the whole language approach. Check pages 38–40 for principles of whole language in reading and writing and teaching and learning. "What's Whole about Whole Language" appears on pages 40–42. Goodman's "Whole Language Research: Foundations and Development" appears on pages 207–21 of the November 1989 issue of *The Elementary School Journal.* That issue contains nine articles about whole language, some of which are Yetta Goodman's "Roots of the Whole-Language Movement," pages 113–27; Watson's "Defining and Describing Whole Language," pages 129–41; McCaslin's "Whole Language: Theory, Instruction, and Future Implementations," pages 223–29; Pearson's "Treading the Whole-Language Movement," pages 321–41; and Harste's "The Future of Whole Language," pages 243–49.

Also check Ken and Yetta Goodman's *Linguistics, Psycholinguistics, and the Teaching of Reading* and Hood and the Goodmans' *The Whole Language Evaluation Book.* Bird and the Goodmans have compiled *The Whole Language Catalog* which contains 1500 contributions from 500 educators, researchers, parents, and students from ten countries. The seven sections covered are: learning; language; literature; teaching; curriculum; community; and understanding whole language. Of special interest are features called "Network," which includes excerpts from teacher-support newsletters in the U.S., Canada, and Australia, and "Book Notes," which gives information about professional books. Information about the dangers of "basalizing literature" is given.

A number of books provide excellent background reading: *Whole Language: Beliefs and Practices* by the Mannings; *Whole Language: What's the Difference?* by Edelsky, Atwerger, and Flores; *Portraits of Whole Language Classrooms* by Mills and Clyde; *The Whole Language Kindergarten* by Raines; and *Whole Language: Theory in Use* by Newman. For more titles, check the

211

card catalog under English Language—Study and Teaching (Elementary); Language Acquisition; Language Arts; Language Experience Approach in Education; and Reading (Elementary) Language Experience Approach.

Two booklets about whole language by Butler are useful. *Whole Language: A Framework for Thinking* includes Butler's philosophy of literacy learning, page 3; pages 4–8 share the six conditions of learning: immersion, demonstration, expectation, responsibility, employment, and approximation, and discuss the integration of the four language modes: reading, writing, listening, and talking. Butler's *The Elements of the Whole Language Program* includes eight conditions for achieving literacy, page 4. The remainder of the booklet is devoted to explaining the 10 elements of a whole language program: reading to children; shared book experiences; sustained silent reading; guided reading; individualized reading; language experience; children's writing; modeled writing; opportunities for sharing; and content area reading and writing. Hardt edited *Oregon English Theme: Whole Language*, a whole issue of *Oregon English* which is devoted to the teaching of reading, writing, literature, and oral language and which can be obtained from the National Council of Teachers of English. Chapter 9 of Trelease's *The New Read-Aloud Handbook* is "SSR: Read Aloud's Natural Partner." A 16mm film, *Reading Aloud*, brings that world-famous lecturer to teacher in-service or parent programs. A cassette, *Turning On the Turned-Off Reader*, is a preview of the film and is accompanied by a companion tape, *Read-Aloud: Questions and Answers*. Use Kimmel and Segel's *For Reading Out Loud!* with Trelease's *The New Read-Aloud Handbook*. For techniques on reading out loud as well as more books which contain read-aloud lists, consult Volume 2 of this book.

Ten statements from Anderson's *Becoming a Nation of Readers*, with which psycholinguistics and whole language advocates agree, appear on pages 167–68 of Weaver's *Reading Process and Practices, from Socio-Psycholinguistics to Whole Language*. Components and implementation of the whole language program appear in Chapter 8 of Weaver's book. Incorporating Bloom's *Taxonomy of Educational Objectives* into the whole language approach is an important ingredient because questions given to students need to include all six aspects of the higher levels of thinking: knowledge, comprehension, application, analysis, synthesis, and evaluation. Often questions tend to be on the lowest level, knowledge, which asks students to repeat facts learned from a text as a means of assessing their comprehension. Using just such fact questions is dangerous because it makes learning superficial and boring to students. Consult Volume 2 of this book for ideas about applying Bloom's thinking skills to literature. There is a section on each thinking skill under the headings beginning BLOOM'S TAXONOMY: LEVEL 1—KNOWLEDGE; LEVEL 2—COMPREHENSION; LEVEL 3—APPLICATION; LEVEL 4—ANALYSIS; LEVEL 5—SYNTHESIS; LEVEL 6—EVALUATION.

Literature-based reading is based on the premise that children can learn to read and to enjoy it by actually reading children's literature rather than slugging through basal readers containing articles, stories, and edited versions of children's literature. The philosophy of literature-based reading is similar to that of Jeannette Veatch's theory of individualized reading, popular during the 1960s. Individualized reading emphasizes student selection of materials, self-pacing, and learning through doing. Evaluation of such reading takes place through individual conferences with students and writing projects. Literature-based reading is also linked with the whole language approach which has long been popular in Australia, New Zealand, and Canada.

Some of the 90 items in the bibliography of my research for an Ed.S. from Western Michigan University in 1971, *A Study of the Materials Used in the Teaching of Reading by Teachers With and Without a Library-Media Center with a Full-Time Media Specialist*, are classic articles and books about basal readers and individualized reading. Some especially helpful citations include: Chall's *Learning to Read: The Great Debate*; Duker's *Individualized Reading: An Annotated Bibliography*; Duker's "Master's Studies of Individualized Reading," *Elementary English*, Vol. 40, March 1963, pages 280–82; Larrick's "The Reading Teacher and the School Library," *Reading Teacher*, Vol. 17, December 1963, pages 149–51; and Veatch's *Individualizing Your Reading Program*. A more recent Veatch book is *How to Teach Reading With Children's Books*. An article by Veatch is "Individualized Reading; A Personal Memoir" on pages 586–93 of the October 1986 issue of *Language Arts*. Check pages 177–81 of the 1987 Yearbook of the Claremont Reading Conference, *Return to Reason: Individualized Reading*. Bader, Veatch, and Eldridge's "Trade Books or Basal Readers?" appears on pages 62–67 of the Spring, 1987 issue of *Reading Improvement* and shares five experiments in which trade or library book programs were compared with basal programs. The study found that of the 20 statistically significant differences, 14 of them were in favor of the literature program supplemented with special decoding, and two were in favor of the traditional basal supplemented with special decoding strategies.

Finding articles on literature-based reading has not been easy because that topic is not used in *Library Literature* or *Education Index*. Aiex's "Literature-Based Reading Instruction," *Reading Teacher*, Vol. 41, January 1988 contains a bibliography of 13 articles as well as hints about searching monthly issues of *Resources in Education*, and *Current Index to Journals in Education* under the headings "Reading Instruction," "Reading Programs," "Children's Literature," "Literature Appreciation," and "Reading Materials Selection." Check various combinations of these topics in a Boolean Logic search of the ERIC database which is available at many teaching universities on CD-ROM (Compact Disk, Read Only Memory). Topics to consult in *Education Index* include: Reading—Motivation; Reading—Teaching; Reading—Teaching Methods; Literature—Correlation with Other Subjects; Literature—Teaching Methods; and Children's Literature—Reading Aloud. Articles to be found include Bergenski's "The Missing Link in Narrative Story Mapping," from pages 333–35 of the December 1987 issue of *Reading Teacher*, published by the International

Reading Association. Topics to consult in the card catalog are: Children—Books and Reading; Children's Literature—Study and Teaching—Aids and Devices; Children's Literature—Study and Teaching (Primary); Libraries, Children's—Activity Programs; Literature—Study and Teaching (Elemenary); and School Libraries—Activity Programs. If your computer card catalog has the capability of using Boolean Logic to combine any of the terms used in various indexes, be sure to do so.

The techniques used in *Creative Uses of Children's Literature* and in both volumes of this book, *More Creative Uses of Children's Literature*, can be incorporated into the literature-based reading program. Introducing books through music, art, poetry, puppetry, creative dramatics, storytelling, booktalks, television, 16mm film, filmstrips, videos, and sound recordings can stimulate enjoyment of children's literature in creative ways. My sunburst technique of finding one piece of literature and then radiating out to many other points of interest is similar in concept to Jean Roos's method in *Patterns of Reading*, or Charlotte Huck's "webbing" technique for which samples appears on page 652 of *Children's Literature in the Elementary School* by Huck et al., or in the magazine *Charlotte's Web*, edited by Huck and Hickman. Check pages 657–61 of *Children's Literature in the Elementary School* for a "Web of Possibilities" for Speare's *Sign of the Beaver*. On page 657 there are nine questions for an in-depth study of *The Sign of the Beaver* using sequential hierarchies (cognitive levels of questions and reading comprehension) and nonsequential hierarchies (literary appreciation and type). Consult Bromley's *Webbing with Literature: Creating Story Maps with Children's Books*. *Webbing Your Idea* is program #3 of the educational television program, *Fins, Feathers, and Fur.* A mapping of "Survival on Islands," featuring O'Dell's *Island of the Blue Dolphins*, appears on pages 414–18 of Norton's *Through the Eyes of a Child: An Introduction to Children's Literature*. *Mapping Mysteries* is a filmstrip from the set *Literature to Enjoy and Write About*, which uses two books to teach story maps: *The House with a Clock on Its Walls* by Bellairs, and *Bunnicula* by Howes. "Mapping Story Structure for Storytelling" appears on pages 38–39 of *Storytelling: Process and Practice* by Livo and Reitz.

Background reading for implementing literature-based reading programs is available. Rudman's *Children's Literature: Resources for the Classroom* deals with every challenge raised when teaching children's literature in the classroom. Articles deal with authors, genres, evaluation and criticism, censorship, and school and family partnerships. Contributors include Nancy Larrick, Anita Silvey, Donna Norton, Jane Yolen, and others. Stewig and Sebesta's *Using Literature in the Elementary Classroom* contains six essays with background as well as practical information for using children's literature in the classroom, and includes the nature of language, strategies for approaching literature, book illustration, reading leading to writing and comprehension, and creative dramatics. Hickman, a colleague of Charlotte Huck, edited *Children's Literature in the Classroom: Weaving Charlotte's Web* which contains contributions by former students of Huck about literature-based reading programs. Benefits of a literature-based reading program and information about setting up a program are included.

The eighth edition of Sutherland and Arbuthnot's classic, *Children and Books*, contains a section edited by Peggy Sullivan called "Arenas and Issues" which focuses on literature-centered classroom activities. Two books by Vandergrift are essential reading: *Child and Story: The Literary Connection* and *Children's Literature: Theory, Research, and Teaching*. Two other books of interest are McConaughy's *Children Learning Through Literature: A Teacher Researcher Study* and Hart-Lewins's *Real Books for Reading: Learning to Read with Children's Books*.

Seven functions of literature in the curriculum appear on page 54 of Lamme's *Learning to Love Literature: Preschool Through Grade 3*. Hancock and Hill's *Literature-Based Reading Programs at Work* provides information on making a change from a basal reading program to a literature-based one. The first five articles tell about setting up a literature-based reading program and the last seven tell how various types of literature such as poetry, fairy tales, biography, and science fiction are shared in reading and writing programs. The teachers mentioned in Hancock and Hill's book are from Australia and New Zealand. Thomas and Perry's *Into Books: 101 Literature Activities in the Classroom* was published first in Australia and New Zealand and contains frameworks for three levels of literature programs: ages 5–7; ages 8–9; and ages 10–12. Projects and specific titles for each level are included. Some themes include: color; mice; bears; giants; circuses; pirates; cats; dogs; magical and mythical beasts; dragons; and heroes. *Literacy Through Literature* by Johnson and Louis is another Australian title which includes information about developing a literature-based language arts curriculum, integrating the language arts, and developing literacy. Some projects include literary report cards, posters, letters, journals, awards, sociograms, news reports, plot profiles, interviews, and dramatization.

There are other books about using literature in the classroom. Bennett's *Learning to Read with Picture Books* is now in the third edition and gives information about incorporating real books into the reading program. The books listed in the bibliographic entries are especially useful for United Kingdom and Commonwealth countries. Four elements of literary activity for children mentioned by Bennett include: hearing good stories told or read aloud; seeing their own stories written out; seeing older children reading and enjoying books; and reading and discussing stories with a teacher. Organizing and selecting the books is discussed by Bennett. Moss's *Focus Units in Literature: A Handbook for Elementary School Teachers* provides 13 units on different topics. Somers and Worthington's *Response Guides for Teaching Children's Books* contains 27 guides for 10 picture books, 4 transitional novels, and 13 longer novels according to the whole language approach. The books have literary merit and child appeal. Polkingharn and Toohey's *Creative Encounters: Activities to*

Expand Children's Responses to Literature contains books, activities, materials and directions for introducing 50 picture books. Tway's *Writing Is Reading: 26 Ways to Connect* contains reading and writing activities for elementary through junior high school students. Watson edited *Ideas and Insights: Language Arts in the Elementary School*, which includes language activities.

In *Developing Learning Skills Through Children's Literature*, Laughlin and Watt divide children's literature into groups by grade: kindergarten/first grade; first grade/second grade; second grade/third grade; third grade/fourth grade; fourth grade/fifth grade; and fifth grade and up. The books within these sections are organized by favorite authors which include Tana Hoban, Pat Hutchins, Marie Hall Ets, Jose Aruego and Ariane Dewey, Rosemary Wells, Steven Kellogg, Mercer Mayer, Charlotte Zolotow, Leo Lionni, Millicent Selsam, Anita and Arnold Lobel, Beatrice Schenk de Regniers, Brian Wildsmith, Eric Carle, Robert McCloskey, Ezra Jack Keats, Maurice Sendak, Judith Viorst, Roger Duvoisin, James Stevenson, James and Edward Marshall, Karla Kuskin, Bill Peet, Carol and Donald Carrick, Bernard Waber, Byrd Baylor, James Flora, Marcia Brown, Clyde Bulla, Hans Christian Andersen, Aileen Fisher, Glen Rounds, Beverly Cleary, Sid Fleischman, Jack Prelutsky, Jean Fritz, Gerald McDermott, A. A. Milne, Jack Denton Scott, Jean George, Laura Ingalls Wilder, Marilyn Burns, Robert Burch, Mary Shura, Myra Livingston, and Betsy Byars. Laughlin and Watt list student objectives, recommended reading, biographical sources, group introductory activities and follow-up activities for teachers and students to share.

Landes and Flender have created "Book Wise Literature Guides" for a number of books which include the following information: what the book is about; how to read the book; how to review the book; how to connect the book to experience; and how to connect the book to others. Discussion questions, writing topics, and activities are included. Guides are available for Babbitt's *Tuck Everlasting*; Holman's *Slake's Limbo*; George's *Julie of the Wolves*; Lewis's *The Magician's Nephew*; MacLachlan's *Sarah, Plain and Tall*; Gardiner's *Stone Fox*; Potter's *The Tale of Peter Rabbit*; Leaf's *The Story of Ferdinand*; de Paola's *Charlie Needs a Cloak*; Taylor's *Roll of Thunder, Hear My Cry*; Paterson's *Bridge to Terabithia*; and White's *Charlotte's Web*. A guide to Juster's *The Phantom Tollbooth* has been written by Landes and Moross. The guide *Picture Books by Gerald McDermott* was prepared by Francis and Stott. The guide *Picture Books by William Steig* was prepared by Baxter. Avi's *The Fighting Ground*; the Colliers' *Who Is Carrie?*; O'Dell's *Streams to the River, River to the Sea*; and McLachlan's *Sarah, Plain and Tall* are only several of the fifteen books included in the McGowans' *Telling America's Story: Teaching American History Through Children's Literature*.

Although annual handbooks by DeBruyne and Sherman were created for use by teachers and school library/media specialists working with students reading the nominees for the Young Readers' Choice Award sponsored by the Pacific Northwest Library Association, they can be assets to any literature-based reading program. The 1988 book is called *The Handbook for the 1988 Young Readers' Choice Award Nominees.* Look for the newest one. Fifteen nominees for 1988, which appeal to fourth through eighth graders, were selected in eight genre categories: animal stories; contemporary realistic fiction; fantasy; historical fiction; humor; multicultural; mystery; and science fiction. The following information is given for each book: genre(s); theme(s); readability; interest level; reviews; awards; author information; plot summary; reading aloud; booktalk 1; booktalk 2; curriculum implementation (language arts, class discussion); other books like it; other books by this author. Books in the 1988 edition include *Cracker Jackson* by Byars; *Sixth Grade Can Really Kill You* by DeClements; *Deep Wizardry* by Duane; *The Eternal Spring of Mr. Ito* by Garrigue; *Devil on My Back* by Hughes; *The Everlasting Hills* by Hunt; *Babe, the Gallant Pig* by King-Smith; *Anastasia on Her Own* by Lowry; *Switcharound* by Lowry; *Come Sing, Jimmy Jo* by Paterson; *Babysitting Is a Dangerous Job* by Roberts; *Julie* by Taylor; *The Castle in the Attic* by Winthrop; and *Christina's Ghost* by Wright. Books in the *Handbook for the 1990 Young Readers' Choice Award Nominees* include: *Dr. Dredd's Wagon of Wonders* by Brittain; *The Blossoms and the Green Phantom* by Byars; *The Riddle of the Rune* by Chetwin *Angel's Mother's Wedding* by Delton; *Wise Child* by Furlong; *Tallahassee Higgins* by Hahn; *Edith Herself* by Howard; *Redwall* by Jacques; *Harry's Mad* by King-Smith; *Different Dragons* by Little; *Beetles, Lightly Toasted* by Naylor; *The Kid in the Red Jacket* by Park; *Hatchet* by Paulsen; *There's a Boy in the Girls' Bathroom* by Sachar; and *Too Much Magic* by the Stermans.

The theme for the December 1990 issue of *Language Arts*, published by the National Council of Teachers of English, is "Literature in Language Arts Learning and Teaching."

The method used by many high school English teachers is similar to that used in literature-based reading. A piece of literature is investigated through character, plot, setting, style, and theme. Spelling vocabulary, writing projects, listening to literature, listening to reports of others, and journal writing are all incorporated into the project. Reading related materials and conducting research are part of the process. Five filmstrips, *Character, Plot, Setting, Style,* and *Theme,* in *Literature for Children, Series 9* teach these concepts by introducing books which are popular with students in grades four through six. For more ideas on introducing these components of literature, check INTRODUCING FICTION BY THEME, PLOT, SETTING, STYLE AND CHARACTERS in Chapter 10.

Highlights from Kulleseid and Strickland's *Literature, Literacy, and Learning: Classroom Teachers, Library Media Specialists, and the Literature-Based Curriculum* appear on the video, *Literature, Literacy, and Learning.* The book summarizes theory and research and their effects on the curriculum as well as giving processes for implementing the program.

Until the publication of *Creative Uses of Children's Literature* in 1982, few books integrated children's literature with the curriculum. Now there are numerous books which do so: Blass and Jurenka's *Responding to Literature: Activities for Grades 6, 7, and 8*; Bosma's *Fairy Tales, Fables, Legends, and Myths: Using Folk Literature in Your Classroom*; the Butzows' *Science Through Children's Literature*; Fiday's *Authors and Illustrators Through the Year: Ready-to-Use Literature Activities for Grades K–3*; Freeman's *Books Kids Will Sit Still for*, 2nd ed.; Hall's *Using Picture Storybooks to Teach Literary Devices*; Irving's *Fanfares: Programs for Classrooms and Libraries*; Kruise's *Learning Through Literature: Activities to Enhance Reading, Writing, and Thinking Skills*; Laughlin and Kardaleff's *Literature-Based Social Studies: Children's Books and Activities to Enrich the K–5 Curriculum*; Laughlin and Street's *Literature-Based Art and Music: Children's Books and Activities to Enrich the K–5 Curriculum*; Laughlin and Swishner's *Literature-Based Reading: Children's Books and Activities to Enrich the K–5 Curriculum*; Laughlin and Watt's *Developing Learning Skills Through Children's Literature: An Idea Book for K–5 Classrooms and Libraries*; McCracken's *Stories, Songs, and Poetry to Teach Reading and Writing*; Mohr, Nixon, and Vickers's *Thinking Activities for Books Children Love*; Olsen's *Creative Connections: Literature and the Reading Program, Grades 1–3*; Polkingharn and Toohey's *Creative Encounters: Activities to Expand Children's Responses to Literature* and *More Creative Encounters: Activities to Expand Children's Responses to Literature*; Raines and Canady's *Story S-t-r-e-t-c-h-e-r-s: Activities to Expand Children's Favorite Books*; Stull's *Children's Book Activities Kit: Easy-to-Use Projects for the Primary Grades*; and Sullivan's *Starting with Books: An Activities Approach to Children's Literature*.

THE LIBRARY AND WHOLE LANGUAGE AND LITERATURE-BASED PROGRAMS. School library media specialists and public librarians can be valuable partners to teachers engaged in literature-based reading and whole language programs. Librarians can assist teachers in locating materials to be used in instruction as well as help teachers to create a framework for ways of teaching students to locate, interpret, and use materials that they have found on any given topic. Certain skills learned by librarians in their professional training are helpful to the process used in literature-based reading programs: sources and criteria for selecting children's books; the techniques for locating types of materials through special indexes for poetry, short story, quotations, storytelling, multimedia, and magazines; the breadth of knowledge of children's books which allows them to link similar themes in literature or types of literature together; skills in locating and selecting various types of literature (novels, short stories, poetry, plays, essays, biography, folktales, periodical articles); creating bibliographies; compiling materials for units; sharing fiction and nonfiction; incorporating science and math concepts and materials; integrating storytelling, fingerplays, puppetry, and creative dramatics into lessons; sharing picture books which contain various art techniques; books in poetry and song; booktalking; and incorporating multimedia and mass media (filmstrips, 16mm films, audio cassettes, video cassettes, study prints, vertical files, microforms, compact disks, and computer programs) into units. Increasingly, librarians have greater access to a network of other libraries through interlibrary loans which can supply them materials owned by others. Librarians have skills for purchasing materials at the lowest price possible as well as cataloging, organizing, advertising, and circulating those materials once they arrive. In addition to their library training, school library/media specialists have taken the same education courses as other teachers so they can help to integrate the use of materials into the curriculum. Some courses offered in programs training school library/media specialists also teach them to undertake instructional design. *Designing Instruction for Diverse Abilities and the Library Media Teacher's Role* by the Jays is a practical guide for helping teachers and school library/media specialists to prepare units of study using a variety of materials. Sample units which can be changed to fit differing ability levels of students are on the solar system; animal research; dinosaurs; Ancient Greece; Native Americans; producers and consumers; geography; nutrition; and visual literacy.

Check the November 1990 issue of *Language Arts* for articles on the theme, "Libraries and the Language Arts." On his cassette *Turning On the Turned-Off Reader,* Trelease says "Dollar for dollar the greatest bargain in the world today is the American free public library system and less than 10% of us use it regularly." On page xiv of *The New Read-Aloud Handbook*, Trelease says "Public library cards are free and therefore the most expensive and beautiful children's books in the world are yours, free for a lifetime." Also consult his Chapter 6, "Home and Public Libraries." Two books to consult about literature programs in public libraries are Carlson's *Early Childhood Literature-Sharing Programs in Libraries* and Colburn and Feeny's *First Steps to Literacy: Library Programs for Parents, Teachers, and Caregivers.* Also read *Library Programs for Children* by Jones and Wilkins's *Supporting K–5 Reading Instruction in the School Library Media Center. Pubic Library Services for Children* by Rollock is a classic. For information about preschool story hours and storytelling, consult *More Creative Uses of Children's Literature, Volume 2.*

School library/media specialists and public librarians can provide teachers with books from the lists in the following section.

WHERE TO FIND BOOKS FOR LITERATURE-BASED READING PROGRAMS. Because several thousand children's books are published each year, it is impossible for teachers to read them all. All of the books available at any one time are listed in Bowker's annual compilation, *Children's Books in Print*, which provides a staggering 60,000 titles, 8,000 which are new in any given year. Two excellent sources of selected books include: the 15th edition of the H. W. Wilson's *Children's Catalog* which includes 5,715 titles in the newest main volume, is revised about every five years but is kept up-to-date with annual supplements; and *Elementary School Library Collection*, published by

Brodart, now in its 17th edition. The latter includes an annual list of 8,271 books, 116 periodicals, and 2,082 multimedia.

There are other key selection sources for books for literature-based reading programs and whole language programs. There are 800 titles in *Let's Read Together: Books for Family Enjoyment* by ALSC. Every three years ALSC publishes a list of about 60 titles in "The USA Through Children's Books" which are representative of "the cultural diversity and pluralistic nature of the lifestyles and peoples of the U.S." Two titles published by the National Council of Teachers of English are Manson's *Adventuring with Books: A Booklist for Pre K–Grade 6* with 1,700 titles and the Davises' *Your Reading: A Booklist for Junior High and Middle School Students* with 3,000 titles. Wilson and Moss's *Books for Children to Read Alone* contains 379 titles pre-K through grade 3. Two especially good sources include Gillespie and Gilbert's *Best Books for Children: Pre-School Through the Middle Grades* and Sutherland's *The Best in Children's Books: The University of Chicago Guide to Children's Literature, 1979–1984*. Kobrin's *Eyeopeners! How to Choose and Use Children's Books About Real People, Places, and Things* contains 500 nonfiction titles. Horning and Kruse's booklet *Multicultural Children's and Young Adult Literature* is an annotated list. The Black Experience in Children's Books Committee of the New York Public Library has published *The Black Experience in Children's Books*. The New York Public Library (NYPL) also has a book called *Children's Books: 1911–1986, Favorite Children's Books from the Branch Collections of the New York Public Library*. The NYPL also publishes an annual best book list arranged by subject, *Children's Books 1989: One Hundred Titles for Reading and Sharing*. *Horn Book Magazine* publishes a pamphlet called *Children's Classics: A Book List for Parents*. The Child Study Children's Book Committee of the Bank Street College of Education has an annotated list of 600 titles for children preschool to age 14, *Children's Books of the Year*. Two favorite read-aloud titles are Kimmel and Segel's *For Reading Out Loud!* with 140 titles, and Trelease's *The New Read-Aloud Handbook*, with over 400 titles. Books especially helpful to parents are Larrick's *A Parent's Guide to Children's Reading*, Hearne's *Choosing Books for Children*, and Lipson's *New York Times Parents Guide to the Best Books for Children*.

Seek the guidance of committees of professional educators to help in determining which books to select. Many professional organizations have committees which select outstanding books, and annual lists can be found in their journals. The Association for Library Service to Children (ALSC) of the American Library Association (ALA) has committees which choose an annual list of about 50 books called the "ALA Notable Children's Books." The March 15th issue of *Booklist* reports on these books as well as the multimedia chosen for a list called "Notable Children's Films and Videos, Filmstrips and Recordings." The ALSC books and multimedia are for children through 14 years old. *School Library Journal* also includes an annual list of outstanding books reviewed for the year in its December issue. The ALA/ALSC and *SLJ* lists are combined in the *Bowker Annual*, under the heading "Best Children's Books of 19—." "Fanfare" is a feature in the March/April issue of *Horn Book Magazine*, highlighting the books the editors have chosen as outstanding for the year.

A committee of the National Council of Teachers of English has prepared between 1981 and 1986, an annual list called "Teachers' Choices," which appears in *Language Arts* in the April issue. After that time the issue varies. The focus of the list is not popularity, but rather books that children and adolescents might not select on their own, but would enjoy if they were introduced. The list is divided into primary, intermediate, and advanced. Since 1987, the International Reading Association has a list called "Teachers' Choices" of books that are exceptional in curriculum use. A list called "Notable Children's Trade Books for the Language Arts" for 1985 and 1986 appears in the March and November 1987 issues of *Language Arts*. The International Reading Association has an annual list called "Children's Choices" found in the October issue of *Reading Teacher*. An annual list of science trade books appears in the March issue of *Science and Children*, a publication of the National Science Teachers Association and is called "Outstanding Science Trade Books for Children in 19—." The annual list of social studies trade books appears in the April/May issue of *Social Education*, published by the National Council for the Social Studies and is called "Notable 19— Children's Trade Books in the Field of Social Studies."

There are also other sources of annual lists. The Library of Congress publishes an annual list prepared by Coughlan, an authority in children's literature at the Library of Congress, called "Books for Children. The Cooperative Children's Book Center at the University of Wisconsin publishes an annual list called "CCBC Choices," chosen by Horning and Kruse. A prominent library educator at Rutgers University, Dr. Kay Vandergrift, compiles an annual list called "A Gift: A Selected List of Children's Books for Holiday Giving, 19—."

For an annual list of winners of individual state contests of books chosen by children, check under the heading "Literary Prizes, 19—" in the *Bowker Annual*. Lists of Children's Book Award winners appear in *Children's Books in Print*. The Children's Book Council's *Children's Books: Awards and Prizes* lists those states where children choose the best book and gives titles of the winning books. *Children's Literature: Awards and Winners* by Jones also lists book awards chosen by children. A section of the "Hunt Breakfast" in each issue of *Horn Book Magazine* is devoted to awards and many child-chosen state awards are reported there. Recent state award winners chosen by children are also reported in *The Journal of Youth Services* (JOYS), a quarterly publication of the Association for Library Service to Children and the Young Adult Library Services Association, formerly the Young Adult Services Division of the American Library Association. An annual publication begun in 1990 that will feature awards is Criscoe's *Award-Winning Books for Children and Young Adults: An Annual Guide*.

Check the public library for lists of books similar to these distributed by the Detroit Public Library Children's Services: *Books for Pre-School Children*, a 15-page pamphlet of book titles and *Children's Books to Own*, a 16-page annotated list. Educators interested in the core list used by the State of California for its literature-based program should obtain a copy of *Recommended Readings in Literature, Kindergarten Through Grade Eight*, published by the California State Dept. of Education. Those interested in the California Reading Initiative, begun in 1986, may wish to read Alexander's Chapter 13, "The California Reading Initiative" from Cullinan's *Children's Literature in the Reading Program*. The book, edited by Cullinan, contains 14 articles written by experts under five categories.

The film *What's a Good Book? Selecting Books for Children* interviews authors, teachers, and librarians about book selection.

LITERATURE-BASED READING: *THE TROUBLE WITH TUCK*. Third or fourth grade students would enjoy reading Theodore Taylor's *The Trouble with Tuck*. In his acknowledgment, Taylor thanks the Orser family for sharing the story of the exploits of their blind Lab, Bonanza. This acknowledgment answers the question students often ask authors: "Where did you get the idea for this book?" For information about Taylor, consult Commire's *Something About the Author*, Volume 5, and de Montreville and Crawford's *The Fourth Book of Junior Authors*.

A first activity is to view Program #10 of the WETA-TV series, *Books from Cover to Cover*, which tells enough about the book to entice third and fourth grade students to read it. The teacher's guide accompanying the series gives a synopsis, pre- and post-viewing activities, information about the author, and related fiction and nonfiction reading. All on-air passages are listed by page number. A full-length film of *The Trouble with Tuck* has been shown on prime time television from another source. Use that version as a culminating activity.

In the story, 9-year-old Helen Ogden is given a yellow Labrador puppy by her father, to help her to overcome her shyness. Helen names the pup Friar Tuck Golden Boy because his mother is Maid Marian Golden Girl and his father is Golden Mack. Naturally the name is shortened to Tuck. Several editions of *Robin Hood* could be placed in the reading/listening/viewing corner of the classroom for students who are interested in finding out more about Robin Hood, Maid Marian, and Friar Tuck. On page 17 readers learn that the dog does not resemble Friar Tuck from the *Robin Hood* stories, because the dog is neither old nor fat. Students could locate information and stories about Friar Tuck to make further comparisons. Crestwick's *Robin Hood* is a reissue with the Wyeth illustrations. Anthony Quayle reads from the Crestwick edition on the recording *The Adventures of Robin Hood*. The four parts of the recording include: "How Robin Hood Became an Outlaw"; "The Outlaw Band of Sherwood Forest"; "Robin's Adventures with Little John"; and "Robin and His Merry Men." There are 22 stories in Pyle's *The Merry Adventures of Robin Hood of Great Renown in Nottinghamshire. Robin Hood, His Life and Legend* by Miles is illustrated by Victor Ambrus. McKinley's *The Outlaws of Sherwood* is another interpretation of the famous Robin Hood. *Robin Hood* is a recent retelling by Hayes. Robin Hood is one of the legends that appears in the film-strip *Epics and Legends* from the set *Literature for Children, Series 6*. Check the *Children's Magazine Guide* for articles about Robin Hood like Wilson's "The Real Robin Hood" from pages 5–9 of the January 1987 issue of *Child Life* magazine.

A natural writing assignment to come out of the study of *The Trouble with Tuck* would be to write descriptions. Helen's description of herself appears on page 11. Have students write a description of themselves. Descriptions of Tuck appear on many pages. Check pages 17, 20, 21, 23–24. On page 93, Helen calls Tuck "bullheaded." Have students write a description of an animal. This could be a family pet, an animal in a park or zoo, an animal from a classroom, or one belonging to a neighbor. Have students compare the German shepherd Lady Daisy with Friar Tuck. Students could look in newspapers for incidences of a dog saving the life of a person. Tuck saves Helen twice, once from drowning and again from a man in the park.

The Trouble with Tuck is a very emotional book. Have students compare the reactions of the family to Tuck's blindness and to Helen's training of Daisy and Tuck. The Ogden family consists of Mr. and Mrs. Ogden; Stan, who is two years older than Helen; and Luke, who is four years older.

On page 106 Helen hears the music from the movie *The Bridge on the River Kwai*, based on a book by Boulle. Teachers and librarians can provide that music from the movie soundtrack or from the video of the movie.

It is an unusual twist for a dog to be a guide dog for another dog. Helen's critical thinking powers are what led her to come up with that solution. Students may wish to read more about guide dogs. A well-known author, Beverly Butler, has had several Seeing Eye dogs since becoming blind at age 16. When her first dog, Una, dies of cancer, Beverly has to investigate places around the country that train guide dogs to find the right dog for her. Butler's experiences appear in the book *Maggie by My Side*. Butler shares with readers what it was like to go to the Pilot Dogs, Inc. of Columbus, Ohio, and meet with Maggie, a German shepherd. Butler explains how the two train together and what is necessary to be a guide dog trainer or to raise a 4-H dog that will eventually be a Seeing Eye dog. Butler also discusses correct etiquette of other people toward Seeing Eye dogs and reminds readers not to feed or bother them while they are working. She stresses understanding of why they are allowed by law to use public transportation. Students may wish to make their own list of eti-quette toward blind people and their guide dogs through further reading or interviews with blind people.

Have students investigate the Yellow Pages of their telephone book for organizations like California Companion Dogs for the Blind, Inc., and have someone find out if the local 4-H clubs have a guide dog program. Community resources may have speakers from similar organizations. In Kuklin's *Mine for a Year,* Evelyn Henderson and her foster children raise dogs for the 4-H program "Puppy Power." In that program, 8- to 12-week-old puppies are placed with families for a year, and are trained to be guide dogs. In the book, 12-year-old George helps to train a black Lab named Doug. Students could make a list of dogs most used for Seeing Eye dogs. Have them list characteristics of those breeds which make them the most useful. Wolf's *Connie's New Eyes* is a photographic essay about a 15-year-old 4-H member who raises a dog for a 22-year-old blind teacher. McPhee's *Tom and Bear: The Training of a Guide Dog Team* is about a diabetic who goes to the Guiding Eyes Association in Yorktown Heights, New York, to learn with his new dog, Bear. Readers have a chance to find out about commands, corrections, street crossings, matched and solo pairs, traffic checks, night walks, rides on buses, escalators and subways, and exit interviews. Background information is given about the story by Dorothy Eustis (which appeared in *The Saturday Evening Post* in 1927 and brought the attention of the world to the term "Seeing Eye"), as well as the school in New Jersey which began in 1932, and the 4-H families which began to prepare guide dogs in 1942. Readers also share the joy of "Puppy Raisers' Day," pages 6–28, when the families who raise the dogs come to see their dogs with new partners. The addresses of eight schools which train guide dogs are included. Readers see Tom's journal in McPhee's *Tom and Bear* and learn about the Annual Walk-A-Thon in October which raises money for training programs. Students learn about people who work at schools for the blind—apprentices, instructors and trainees. Smith's *A Guide Dog Goes to School: The Story of a Dog Trained to Lead the Blind* relates the steps through which Cinderella, a golden retriever born in the kennel of a guide-dog training school, becomes a Seeing Eye dog. Cindy has to go through tests at 6 weeks of age; 12-year-old Benjamin and 9-year-old Amy are the 4-H volunteer puppy raisers. The picture on page 21 of the dog leaving the 4-H family shows the forlorn look on the dog's face. Cindy goes to training school for three months before meeting her blind master, an 18-year-old high school senior girl, Belveria. The dog's graduation is attended by the 4-H puppy raisers. A special message is given in the book to people who see a dog working. *Greff: The Story of a Guide Dog* by Curtis is also about a Labrador from birth to guide-dog graduation. Check pages 34–50 of *Animal Partners: Training Animals to Help People* and pages 34–42 of Fichter's *Working Dogs* for chapters about Seeing Eye dogs. "Dogs at Work" by Hoffman is an article about Seeing Eye and Hearing Ear dogs from the second grade HBJ basal reader, *Weather Vanes,* edited by Cullinan, et al. The previous books and articles are all nonfiction. However, Garfield's *Follow My Leader* is a classic Seeing Eye story that is found in most libraries and which is now available in video or 16mm format. "Merry's Winter Walk" by Burns is a magazine story from pages 47–50 of the December 1988 issue of *Cricket.* Merry and her golden retriever, Boone, go outside for the first time with snow on the ground and Boone helps Merry to avoid disaster. Have this magazine article available in the reading/listening/viewing area of the classroom.

After investigating guide dogs, students may wish to read more books about working dogs or just about dogs in general. Books about sled dogs for primary students are: Pinkwater's *Aunt Lulu*; Quackenbush's *Dogsled to Dread: A Miss Mallard Mystery*; and Standiford's *The Bravest Dog Ever: The True Story of Balto*.

Books for students in intermediate grades and above are: Calvert's *Hour of the Wolf*; Casey's *Sled Dogs*; Gardiner's *Stone Fox*; London's *Call of the Wild*; Morey's *Kavik the Wolf Dog* and *Scrub Dog of Alaska*; O'Dell's *Black Star, Bright Dawn*; Paulsen's *Dogsong*; Reit's *Race Against Death*; Riddles's *Race Across Alaska: First Woman to Win the Iditarod Tells Her Story*; and Ungerman's *The Race to Nome: The Story of the Heroic Alaskan Dog Teams That Rushed Diphtheria Serum to Stricken Nome in 1925*. Multimedia include: *Race Against Death*, Program #12 of the television series *Book Bird*, and the cassette *Women of Courage: Libby Riddles*. More literature about all types of dogs appears in POEMS AND STORIES ABOUT DOGS in Volume 2 of this book.

Helen takes Tuck to a veterinarian in *The Trouble with Tuck*. Students may wish to read books about veterinarians from the career education point of view, or just to learn more about the occupation. Some newer books about veterinarians include: Kuklin's *Taking My Dog to the Vet* and *Taking My Cat to the Vet*; Imersheim's *Animal Doctor*; and even Paige's *A Day in the Life of a Zoo Veterinarian*.

Blindness by Weiss is about how Sarah, blind since birth, copes with everyday life. Photos accompany Frevert's book, *Patrick, Yes You Can*, which is about an African-American child, born with glaucoma and poor eyesight, until an injury at age 8 blinds him. Blindness is one of six handicaps discussed on pages 5–23 of Kamin's *What If You Couldn't? A Book About Special Needs*. Check pages 19–30 of *Like It Is: Facts and Feelings About Handicaps from Kids Who Know* by Adams for information about being visually impaired. Parker's *Living with Blindness* explains which parts of the body are diseased, treatments, and ways that patients cope. Information about physical conditions is appended in Bergman's photo essay *Seeing in Special Ways: Children Living with Blindness*.

Students may wish to read about famous blind people. Graff's *Helen Keller: Toward the Light* and Peare's *The Helen Keller Story* are easy enough for third and fourth graders. Wepman's *Helen Keller* is for students in middle school and above. Because Helen Keller's autobiography may be too difficult for many third and fourth graders to read, the three cassettes of *The Story of My Life* could be made available to them in the reading/listening/viewing corner of the classroom. Two biographies about Braille are Davidson's *Louis Braille: The Boy Who Invented Books for the Blind* and Keeler's *Louis Braille*. Braille is also one of those included in Fradin's *Remarkable Children: Twenty Who Made History*. Fort's *Redbird* is a picture book that is fascinating for children as well as adults. The story about an airplane introduces each new object in Braille and the art is reproduced in raised bas-relief that is molded so readers can feel and identify the images by touch and sight. Two books by Jensen also provide readers a chance to compare Braille with the standard alphabet. Jensen's *Catching: A Book for Blind and Sighted Children with Pictures to Feel as Well as to See* is about two shapes, Little Rough and Little Shaggy, who play tag. Children can feel the shape of the answers in Braille or read them in Jensen's *Red Thread Riddles*.

Two authors who are blind can be investigated. Find information about Midwesterner Beverly Butler in *Something About the Author*, Volume 7, and about Canadian Jean Little in Commire's *Something About the Author*, Volume 5 and De Montreville's *The Fourth Book of Junior Authors*. Butler became blind at 16 and *Light a Single Candle* is fiction about a girl who becomes blind at the same age. The same girl goes to college in the sequel, *Gift of Gold*. Have students make a list of other books by Butler and make a circulating display of those books owned by the school and public library. One title by Butler is *Ghost Cat*, which is a mystery about 14-year-old Annabel, a crying cat, an old feud and an abandoned house. The nonfiction book, *Maggie by My Side* has already been mentioned. Some books by Jean Little are: *From Anna*, about a refugee girl who is having trouble with her eyes, and the sequel *Listen for the Singing*; *Look Through My Window* and its sequel, *Kate*, which are about an old house and friendship between Emily and Kate; *Mama's Going to Buy You a Mockingbird*, about the death of a father; *Mine for Keeps*, about a girl with cerebral palsy and the sequel *Spring Begins in March*; *One to Grow On*, about a girl who exaggerates; *Stand in the Wind*, about camping; and *Take Wing*, about a girl with a mentally retarded brother. A selection from *From Anna* appears on pages 120–41 of the fourth grade HBJ reader *Crossroads*, edited by Cullinan, et al. A profile of Jean Little appears on pages 118–19. *Mama's Going to Buy You a Mockingbird* is Program #6 on *More Books from Cover to Cover*, a television series to motivate reading in fifth and sixth graders. If the video of the TV program were made available to advanced students, they could be motivated to stretch themselves and read *Mama's Going to Buy You a Mockingbird* and other books by Little.

Students may also wish to read other books by Taylor. *Tuck Triumphant* is the sequel to *The Trouble with Tuck*. In *The Cay*, Philip is evacuated by a ship sunk during World War II and stranded on an island in the Caribbean. Philip, who is blinded while he is on the island, has a black man as his companion. *Teetoncey* is the first in the Hatteras Banks trilogy and is followed by *The Odyssey of Ben O'Neal* and *Teetoncey and Ben O'Neal*.

Animal lovers who empathize with Tuck may also enjoy reading two books about blind horses by Rounds. *Blind Colt* is about 10-year-old Whitey, who adopts a blind colt. *Blind Outlaw* is about a boy who can save a wild mustang if he can tame him. Irvine's *The True Story of Corky the Blind Seal* tells how 7-year-old Corky, a blind performing seal in the San Diego Zoo, overcomes his handicap. Although the book is mainly for primary students, it could be included in a classroom collection of books in third or fourth grades where the class is reading Taylor's *The Trouble with Tuck*. Students of all ages enjoy reading easier books occasionally. Students could be asked to compare Corky and Tuck and how their handicaps affect them. There are several other picture books that have blind characters. Cohen's *See You Tomorrow, Charles* is about first graders in Cohen's series who meet a new boy who happens to be blind. A blind girl named Maria has a secret friend in Brighton's *My Hands, My World*. A blind Indian boy, Boy-Strength-of-Blue Horses, hears the story of his birth once again from his grandfather in Martin and Archambault's *Knots on a Counting Rope*. John visits his Grandpa in MacLachlan's *Through Grandpa's Eyes* and learns to use and appreciate his senses. Students can brush up on time-telling skills when they learn that Grandpa learns to eat his food on his plate because it is placed in order like a clock. *Through Grandpa's Eyes* is also available in 16mm and video format and also appears on pages 44–58 of the third grade HM basal reader, *Caravans*, edited by Durr, et al. Martha makes a special raised birthday card for her blind grandfather in Pearson's *Happy Birthday, Grampie*. *Sound of Sunshine, Sound of Rain* was nominated for an Oscar in the Animated Short Film category. The story is based on a book of the same name by Heide and is about a 7-year-old African-American boy whose sister leaves him in the park. He encounters experiences which help viewers to understand what it means to be physically handicapped, as well as a member of a minority group. Hermann's *Jenny's Magic Wand* is a photo essay about a blind girl who is mainstreamed, and her cane (wand). The woodcarver in Yolen's *The Seeing Stick* gives the blind Chinese princess a cane carved with stories. Compare the purpose of the canes in the stories. Winthrop's *Journey to the Bright Kingdom* is a Japanese folktale. A blind woman is taken by her daughter to the legendary kingdom of Kakure-Sato where no one is blind. There the woman's sight is restored for a day. "Why the Raccoon Has Rings on His Tail" is a Chippewa Indian legend about Manabozho that appears on pages 91–94 of Walker's *Legends of Green Sky Hill*. The markings we see today on the raccoon's tail remind us that he stole from two blind brothers. Check pages 22–25 of Arico's *A Season of Joy: Favorite Stories and Poems for Christmas* for the story by Powers called "The Little Blind Shepherd." Another handicapped child who appears in a Christmas story is the lame Amahl from Menotti's *Amahl and the Night Visitors*.

Apt. 3 by Keats is a picture book that transcends age levels. The blind man knows that Sam and Betsy like each other. Secrets come out in the blind man's music, including the happy music of friendship. Ten-year-old Leah was once afraid of Gideon Brown, a blind man who lived on another floor of her apartment building in Clifford's *The Man Who Sang in the Dark*. Gideon Brown plays the guitar and sings.

Although few children have personal experience with blindness, many of them are concerned with wearing glasses. One of the TV programs in WGBH's new series, *Long Ago and Far Away*, is about a boy who gets glasses for the first time. The Danish film, *As Long As He Can Count the Cows*, is about a boy whose family raises cows in a mountain village in Bhutan, and a teacher who finally persuades them to get glasses for him. Cromwell is a nearsighted rabbit who hates his glasses in Keller's *Cromwell's Glasses*. Although his family picks on Cromwell about his glasses they don't allow others to do so. Arthur is reluctant to wear glasses, and a video segment of the television program *Reading Rainbow*, narrated by Bill Cosby, features Brown's *Arthur's Eyes*. Iris in Raskin's *Spectacles* is nearsighted. Libby, in Tusa's *Libby's New Glasses*, runs away so no one will see her new glasses, and meets an ostrich who buries his head in the sand to hide his glasses. The two learn from each other. La Fleur's poem "The Cat Who Wore Glasses" appears on pages 40–44 of the November 1987 issue of *Humpty Dumpty*. *Lenses, Spectacles, Eyeglasses and Contacts: The Story of Vision Aids* by Kelley shares the history of vision aids from the Middle Ages to the present. Some magazine articles about contacts include: Samz's "Caring for Your Contacts" from page 4 of the October 2, 1987 issue of *Science World*; "Throwaway Contact Lenses Developed," page 8 of the November 20, 1987 issue of *Current Science*; and Steinkamp's "How Safe are Contact Lenses?," on pages 6–7 of the March 13, 1987 issue of *Current Science*.

Students can find information about the eye in the card catalog, magazine indexes, and reference books. The structure and function of the eye are discussed in Rahn's *Eyes and Seeing* and Ward's *The Eye and Seeing*. A large model of the eye would be fascinating for students to examine. Subjects in *The Abridged Readers' Guide to Periodical Literature* and *The Children's Magazine Guide* are under headings such as eye, sensory receptors, contact lenses, vision, blindness, and so on. Have students look for magazine articles about the eye such as: "The Human Camera: The Eye" on pages 3–9 of the March 1988 issue of *Current Health*; "Your Eyes: Picture Windows" by Fine and Josephson on pages 36–39 of the April/May 1988 issue of *Humpty Dumpty*; "The Eyes Have It" by Hicks on pages 46–47 of the February/March 1987 issue of *Jack and Jill*; or "The Eye" by Schwartz on pages 18–21 of the September 1986 issue of *3-2-1 Contact*. Have students check volume 18, the index, to the reference set *Science and Technology Illustrated* under blindness, contact lenses, eye banks, eyeglasses, senses, and vision. There are over 11 different references under the heading "Eye."

Two stories about older girls who are blind can be included in the collection. *The Absolute, Ultimate End* by First is about Maggie, an eighth grader, who tutors a blind girl, Doreen. When the school proposes cutbacks in the program, Maggie stages a demonstration to prevent the budget cut even though her own father is running for election to the school board and is interested in cutting the budget. Eyerly's *The Seeing Summer* is about Carey, who is dismayed when she learns that her new neighbor is blind. However, Jenny Anne Lee dispels Carey's misconceptions and they become friends.

Students may wish to branch out and read about other handicaps. Curtis also wrote *Cindy, A Hearing Ear Dog,* about a stray dog named Cindy who becomes a helper for a deaf junior high school girl named Jennifer. Golder and Memling's *Buffy's Orange Leash* is about how Buffy receives his training at Red Acre Farms Hearing Dog Center so he can help a husband and wife, both of whom are deaf. Yeatman's *Button: The Dog Who Was More Than a Friend* is also a hearing ear dog. Students may also wish to read about Thomas Hopkins Gallaudet, founder of the first school for the deaf in the United States, in Neimark's *A Deaf Child Listened: Thomas Gallaudet, Pioneer in American Education.* A selection from Neimark's book appears on pages 236–49 of the eighth grade HBJ basal reader, *Panoramas,* edited by Cullinan, et al. Helen Keller was both deaf and blind. Peterson's *I Have a Sister—My Sister Is Deaf* is about two real sisters. The sister telling the story says "her ears don't hurt, but her feelings do when people do not understand." *I Have a Sister—My Sister Is Deaf* was introduced in the television series, *Reading Rainbow.* Wolf's *Ann's Silent World* is about a girl who was born deaf. Compare these two girls with Walker's *Amy: The Story of a Deaf Child* and Levine's *Lisa and Her Soundless World.* Leardi's "Ludwig van Beethoven: Master of a Silent World" appears on pages 216–23 of the third grade SB/Ginn basal reader, *On the Horizon,* edited by Pearson, et al. Use Greenberg's *What Is the Sign for Friend?* to introduce the following books about sign language: Baker's *My First Book of Sign* (150 words); Bourke's *Handmade ABC: A Manual Alphabet*; Charlip and Ancona's *Handtalk: An ABC of Finger Spelling and Sign Language*; and Butterworth's *Perigree Visual Dictionary of Signing: An A to Z Guide to Over 1,200 Signs of American Sign Language.* Sign language is just one of the ways Michael communicates with his deaf parents in Litchfield's story, *Words in Our Hands.* A selection from Litchfield's book appears on pages 152–61 of the third grade textbooks basal reader, *Celebrations,* edited by Cullinan, et al. and on pages 78–91 of the third grade HM basal, *Journeys,* edited by Durr, et al. An interview appears on pages 164–71 of *Celebrations* and is called "Listen with Your Eyes." A photo essay, "The National Theatre of the Deaf," appears on pages 92–93 of *Journeys.* Photographs and sign language help tell the story of a woman who is surprised on her birthday in *Handtalk Birthday: A Number and Story Book in Sign Language,* by Charlip, Miller, and Ancona. Sakri's "Hand Talk" is a magazine article that appears on page 43 of the May 1988 issue of *Highlights.* More books about sign language appear in a section called SIGN LANGUAGE FOR THE DEAF in Volume 2 of this book. Have students check the index in volume 28 of *Science and Technology Illustrated* for the terms *ear, hearing, and hearing aids.*

Students may wish to investigate books about other handicaps. Brown's *Someone Special, Just Like You* is a photo essay of exceptional children engaged in all types of school activities. *Like It Is: Facts and Feelings about Handicaps from Kids Who Know* by Adams contains first-person stories of hearing, speech, and sight impairments, and mental and physical handicaps. The six handicaps in Kamin's *What If You Couldn't? A Book about Special Needs* are blindness, deafness, mental retardation, dyslexia, emotional problems, and impaired mobility. The five handicaps in Sullivan's *Feeling Free* are blindness, deafness, learning disabilities, cerebral palsy, and dwarfism. Rosenberg and Ancona's *Finding a Way: Living with Exceptional Brothers and Sisters* is a photo essay that tells about 6-year-old Danielle's brother who is a diabetic; 11-year-old Rachel's brother who has spina bifida; and 10-year-old Danny's two sisters, who have asthma. Black and white photos share the daily life of Angie, a brain-damaged child, in Prall's *My Sister's Special.* Drimmer's *Born Different: Amazing Stories of Some Very Special People* contains stories of seven people, like the Elephant Man and Tom Thumb, who were different. Kuklan's *Thinking Big: The Story of a Young Dwarf* is a photo essay about an 8-year-old dwarf. Matthew sees a boy with cerebral palsy and a man who has a hook for an arm in Stein's *About Handicaps: An Open Family Book for Parents and Children Together.* In Rosenberg's *My Friend Leslie: The Story of a Handicapped Child,* Leslie is blind, has a cleft palate, muscular problems, ptosis of the eyelids, and a hearing disability. *Cushla and Her Books* by D. Butler is about a girl born with several birth defects that affect her speech and motor skills. *The Quiet Revolution: The Struggle for the Rights of Disabled Americans* by Haskins helps students to understand the civil rights of handicapped people. A visit from a handicapped person in the community can personalize the topic, and make it more relevant.

Roy's *Move Over, Wheelchairs Coming Through!* shares the lives of seven children, ages 9–19, who use wheelchairs. White's *Janet at School* is about a girl who is in a wheelchair because she has spina bifida. Read Greenfield's *Alesia* to find out about Alesia Revis, who became crippled at the age of nine. Paul Jockimo was born without a right hand and foot in Wolf's *Don't Feel Sorry for Paul.* In Kaufman's *Rajesh,* a kindergarten boy, born with a hand and both legs missing, learns to use prostheses and enters school. The boy whose leg is amputated in Martin's biography *Ted Kennedy, Jr.: A Lifetime of Challenges* is the nephew of President John F. Kennedy. Smith's *A Service Dog Goes to School: The Story of a Dog Trained to Help the Disabled* is about Licorice, a black Labrador who is born at Canine Companions for Independence School, lives with a family, and returns to school to learn to be a helper. Licorice becomes the dog of Scott, a 12-year-old boy who is paralyzed from the waist down.

Although the main characters in Gorman's *Chelsey and the Green-haired Kid* are a 13-year-old girl named Chelsey who is a paraplegic and her friend Jack who has green hair, the story centers on the mystery that takes place at a basketball game. Eleven-year-old Beth from Hanlon's *The Swing* is deaf. *Edith Herself* in Howard's book, which takes place in the late 19th century, is an orphan who has epileptic seizures. An understanding teacher insists that she attend school, even though her sister does not think she should. Sherburne's *Why Have the Birds Stopped Singing?* is a time travel book in which a modern girl sees a portrait of a girl from the past who looks just like her. The modern girl, Katie, has an epileptic seizure and is transported to the time of her great-great-great-grandmother Kathryn, who also suffered from epilepsy. Based on these last two books, students can compare the perception of epilepsy then and now. A modern 11-year-old girl, Jenna, learns to live with rheumatoid arthritis in *Angie and Me* by Jones. Grollman's *Shira: A Legacy of Courage* is the journal of a girl suffering from a rare incurable form of diabetes.

It is easier to read and talk about physical handicaps than it is to discuss people who have mental handicaps such as those in the following stories. Carrick's *Stay Away from Simon!* is about Simon the miller's son, whom the children think is a big dumb ox and whom they call "Simple Simon." The setting is Martha's Vineyard in the 1830s and the children attend a one-room schoolhouse. One day, Lucy and Josiah are let go early from school because of an impending storm, and they cut through the woods because Lucy thinks Simon is chasing her. The story ends with Simon saving the lives of the children and Lucy learning compassion and gratefulness. Read this book aloud. It is no easy feat to conclude the story without didacticism. The reaction of several boys to a retarded adult/child also provides another great listening experience. It is worth eleven minutes of the time of sixth graders to listen to Donald Davis tell the story "LS/MFT" on the cassette *Live and Learn*. Neil tells about how his 13-year-old retarded sister returns home to live in Shyer's *Welcome Home, Jellybean*. Eleven-year-old Mary Ella of Cassedy's *M. E. and Morton* never had a best friend before, so when a new girl comes to live with her grandmother in Mary Ella's neighborhood, she and Polly become friends. M.E. is a scholarship student at a private school and none of those students lives in her neighborhood or is a friend of hers at school. To impress Polly, M.E. pretends that her retarded brother Morton is no relation of hers and even teases him cruelly. Then, much to M.E.'s chagrin, Polly becomes friends with both of them, but in a different way. The book can stimulate discussion of several questions. How did you feel when you found out that Morton and M.E. were brother and sister? What did you think of the jokes played on Morton, especially the one about leaving the *t* out of his name? How did you feel about the fact that Morton had to be hurt before his family appreciated him? List the good and bad qualities of M.E. Eleven-year-old Gertrude Hollings, in Greenwald's *Will the Real Gertrude Hollings Please Stand Up?*, has dyslexia and has been labeled learning disabled. Amy has a retarded sister in Wright's *The Dollhouse Murders*, and often wishes that she didn't always tag along. Mrs. Bigelow, the mother of Veronica and Gunther in Lowry's *Rabble Starkey*, is unbalanced. Rabe's *Where's Chimpy?* is a photographic picture book about a little girl with Down's Syndrome who has lost her toy monkey. The father and child finally find Chimpy. The book provides awareness of special children to primary children. Litchfield's book *Making Room for Uncle Joe* is about an adult with Down's Syndrome who leaves the institution and moves in with his sister and his 10-year-old nephew. Bergman's *We Laugh, We Love, We Cry: Children Living with Mental Retardation* is enhanced with photos.

Teachers who wish to find other legends, biographies, and stories about blindness and deafness should check under blindness, Braille, deafness, mental retardation, and sign language in the subject index of *Creative Uses of Children's Literature* for entries on those subjects. Also be sure to check in the index of this book under those subjects. Teachers and librarians should help students locate the materials mentioned in this chapter by using the card catalog. More information under the various subjects could be located in encyclopedia indexes. Some books for teachers and librarians which include bibliographies about handicaps include *Notes from a Different Drummer: A Guide to Juvenile Fiction Portraying the Handicapped* and *More Notes from a Different Drummer: A Guide to Juvenile Fiction Portraying the Disabled* by Baskin and Harris and *Accept Me As I Am: Best Books of Juvenile Nonfiction on Impairments and Disabilities* by Friedberg, et al. *Your Reading* by the Davises and the Committee on the Junior High and Middle School Booklist for the National Council of Teachers of English includes a section called "Physical Disabilities" on pages 180–84 which contains 21 annotated books. Older titles about disabilities appear in three volumes of Dreyer's *The Bookfinder* under the following subjects: amputee; asthma; birth defects; blindness; braces on body/limbs; brain injury; cardiac conditions; cleft lip/palate; deafness; deformities; education: special; hemophilia; handicaps; limbs, abnormal or missing; multiple sclerosis; muteness; paraplegia; prejudice: toward handicapped persons; speech problems; visual impairment; and wheelchair, dependence on. Check to see if volume 4 of the *Bookfinder* has been published, for newer titles. Some subjects to pursue in *The Children's Magazine Guide* include: blindness; contact lenses; deaf; disabled children; disabled persons; eyeglasses; hearing impaired; sign language; and vision. There are 18 books and 36 questions about handicaps listed in the index on pages 229–30 of Greenson and Taka's *Name That Book!*

Opportunities abound for writing in journals. Students can write about the following topics: how they would feel if they suddenly lost their sight; how people can be more understanding of people with handicaps; a day in the life of a blind person who has a new guide dog; any incident in *The Trouble with Tuck* told from the point of view of any family member or either dog; taking chapters from the book and giving titles to them with reasons for the choices; reviewing a related book or magazine article; writing up an interview with a handicapped person; sharing how they would feel if their dog became blind, as Tuck did; comparing a golden retriever and a German shepherd; comparing either Tuck or Daisy to their own dog; and comparing Tuck with his namesake, Friar Tuck.

SPIDERS IN LITERATURE-BASED OR BASAL PROGRAMS [CU 709; 727]. Climo's *Someone Saw a Spider: Spider Facts and Folktales* is an essential book in the study of spiders. The book provides myths, folklore, and superstition about spiders. Some folktales are the Japanese "The Cloud Spinner," pages 17–24; the American Indian "The Spider Brothers Make a Rainbow," pages 29–38; the Moslem "The Prophet and the Spider," pages 55–62; the Portuguese "The Spellbound Spider," pages 91–100; and the American Ozark Mountain "Sally-Maude, Zachary Dee and the Dream Spinner." The poem "King Bruce and the Spider" and "The Spider King" are about Robert the Bruce of Scotland. Another poem is Howitt's "The Spider and the Fly," pages 87–88. A Japanese legend, "The Goblin Spider," appears on pages 160–65 of San Souci's *Short and Shivery.* The Japanese emperor sends Tsuna and Raiko out to get rid of a goblin spider near Kyoto. The description of the spider is wonderfully terrible in this scintillatingly creepy story. Superstitions about spiders appear in two books by Sarnoff and Ruffins: on page 25 of *If You Were Really Superstitious,* and on page 127 of *Take Warning: A Book of Superstitions.*

There are two Christmas stories about spiders. Climo's picture book, *Cobweb Christmas,* tells about the German Tante, or Auntie, who lives in a cottage and has animals in her barn. Tante cleans, cuts a tree, and bakes cookies. Although Tante puts something on her tree for every animal except the spiders, whom she brushes away, the spiders turn the webs on her tree to silver and gold. A selection from Climo's story appears on pages 122–31 of Low's *The Family Read-Aloud Christmas Treasury.* "The De Angelis' Christmas Spider" from pages 96–97 of Miller's *Ten Tales of Christmas* is about a gray spider who spins a web in a stable where a baby is born and gives the web as a cover to keep him warm. Even today, spiders are good omens and we cover Christmas trees with angel's hair in memory of the gray spider's gift.

The most famous spider in folktales is Anansi [CU 709]. "How Spider Got His Waistline" is a Liberian folktale found on pages 43–52 of Climo's book. "Anansi and his Visitor, Turtle," appears on pages 201–03 of Cole and Calmenson's *The Laugh Book* and on pages 618–19 of Cole's *Best-Loved Folktales of the World.* "Anansi and Nothing Go Hunting for Wives" and "Anansi's Fishing Expedition" appear on pages 95–102 and 47–58 of Courlander's *The Cow-Tail Switch and Other West African Stories.* Courlander's famous story, "Anansi's Hat-shaking Dance," appears on pages 615–17 of Cole's *Best-Loved Folktales of the World* and on pages 313–14 of Sutherland and Livingston's *Scott, Foresman Anthology of Children's Literature.* "How Spider Obtained the Sky-God's Stories" appears on pages 620–23 of Cole's *Best-Loved Folktales of the World,* pages 24–26 of Yolen's *Favorite Folktales from Around the World,* and the Caldecott-winning picture book *A Story, A Story* by Haley. Check pages 102–111 for Haley's story in the third grade SB/Ginn basal reader, *On the Horizon,* edited by Pearson, et al. *A Story, A Story* is also available as a sound filmstrip, cassette/hardback, cassette/paperback, 16mm film, and video. Painter suggests using Miriam Makeba's music with Haley's *A Story, A Story.* For further information check page 108 of Painter's *Musical Story Hours.* A creative improvisation appears on the instructional television series for primary students, *The Folk Book,* on Program #2 *Stories of Stories,* "How Anansi the Spider Stole the Sky God's Stories." Courlander's "All Stories Are Anansi's" appears on pages

436–42 of the fourth grade Macmillan basal reader, *Rhymes and Reasons*, edited by Smith and Arnold. "Anansi" appears on pages 100–11 of Cole's *The Read-Aloud Treasury*. Check pages 627–31 of Cole's *Best-Loved Folktales of the World* for "The Rubber Man," a Hausa tale similar to "The Wonderful Tar-Baby Story" of Uncle Remus from pages 666–67 of the same anthology. Two Jamaican stories about Anansi outsmarting Tiger and being outsmarted by Guinea Fowl are "Anansi Play with Fire, Anansi Get Burned," pages 741–44 of Cole's anthology, and "Being Greedy Chokes Anansi," pages 131–32 of Yolen's *Favorite Folktales from Around the World*. Another Jamaican story, "Anansi and Mrs. Dove," appears on pages 145–50 of *Tales from the Enchanted World* by Williams-Ellis. Shedlock's "The Plantains" appears on pages 108–12 of Volume 3 of the set, *Childcraft: The How and Why Library*, in the book *Stories and Poems*. Aardema's retelling of "Anansi Finds a Fool" appears on pages 86–94 of the second grade Ginn basal reader, *Give Me a Clue*, edited by Clymer and Venezky. "Spider Anansi Finds Something" is from Togo, West Africa, and appears on pages 53–57 of Hamilton's Newbery Honor Book, *In the Beginning: Creation Stories from Around the World*. Another story, "Nyambi the Creator" appears on pages 65–67 of *In the Beginning*. *Why Spiders Hide in Dark Corners* is Program #10 of the television series *Magic Carpet*. The song "Anansi" appears on pages 8–9 of *Raffi's Singable Songbook* and on the recording *The Corner Grocery Store*. "The First Night of Sleep," a participation story, appears on pages 60–63 of McCauslin's *Creative Drama in the Primary Grades*.

A is for Anancy is the first letter of Agard's *Calypso Alphabet*. Several dozen Anansi stories appear in *West Indian Folk-Tales* and *Anansi the Spiderman*, both by Sherlock. Twenty stories from the West Indies appear in Berry's *Spiderman Anansy*. A dozen spider stories from Liberia and Ghana appear in anthologies by Arkhurst: *The Adventures of Spider* and *More Adventures of Spider*.

There are several picture books, besides Haley's *A Story, A Story*, which are based on an Anansi story. Aardema's *Oh, Kojo! How Could You!* is available as a book and a sound filmstrip. Kojo buys a dog, cat, and a dove from Anansi. Bryan's *The Dancing Granny* is about how lazy brother Anansi gets Granny Anika dancing so he can raid her garden. The source for this story is Antigua, British Antilles. Bryan reads this story on the recording *The Dancing Granny and Other African Stories*. Makhanlall's *Br'er Anansi and the Boat Race* comes from West Africa via the West Indies. After three days of rain, Br'er Rabbit and Br'er Bear go live on Br'er Rabbit's boat where they challenge Br'er Anansi to a boat race. Br'er Anansi suggests that the others lighten their load and then he steals their possessions when they aren't looking. *Brother Anansi and the Cattle Ranch/El Hermano Anansi y el Rancho de Granado* is a bilingual picture book in Spanish by De Sauza. Benitez's *How Spider Tricked Snake* is easy to read and comes from Jamaica. McDermott's picture book, *Anansi the Spider*, is available as a sound filmstrip and cassette/hardback package. Mc-

Dermott's book also appears on the filmstrip *Folktales From Afar,* from the set *Literature for Children, Series 8.* Check pages 69–72 of Lamme's *Learning to Love Literature, Preschool Through Grade 3* for "Sharing Anansi the Spider." Ideas are presented for sharing Anansi with children K–1 and 2–3. A picture of a glove puppet for animating McDermott's book is included.

Although Anansi stories appear all over the world where black Africans have been taken as slaves, they originated in Africa and the Ashanti word for spider is Anansi. Have students locate information about the Ashanti in sets of geography reference books. A search of the card catalog might reveal Bleeker's *The Ashanti of Ghana* and Musgrove's *Ashanti to Zulu,* a Caldecott Medal winner. *Ashanti to Zulu* is available as a sound filmstrip and as a cassette/hardback package. Have students make a list of other places where the stories are told, learn about them, and make a map showing the disbursement of the stories. Studying stories about Anansi can also be part of the social studies curriculum.

There are numerous nonfiction books about spiders. Goldin's *Spider's Silk* is from the Let's Read and Find Out science series. The best feature of Dallinger's *Spiders* is the color photos. Information is given about scientific classification and about trap door, crab, and wolf spiders in this book. Photos also enhance Schnieper's *Amazing Spiders.* Excellent color photos also appear in Penny's *Discovering Spiders,* which tells where they live and hunt and all about survival, reproduction, parts of the body, and how a web is made. McGrath's *How Animals Talk* discusses the communication of a male spider when he steps on the female spider's web. Patent's *Spider Magic* includes crab, jumping, wolf, cellar, black widow, tarantula, trapdoor, Fisher, and water spiders. Students could be divided into pairs and assigned to research a particular type of spider.

Directions for making a spider web and a Miss Muffet button spider appear on pages 22–23 and pages 20–21 of True's *Nursery Rhyme Crafts.* Directions for making fingerprint spiders, Sweet-Gum spiders, and Walk-Along spiders appear on pages 154–55, 161–63, and 86–87 of Dondiego's *Year-Round Crafts for Kids.* "Spider on the Floor" as well as on the leg, stomach, neck, face, and head is a song from page 84 of *Raffi's Singable Songbook* and the recording *Singable Songs for the Very Young.* Have older students plan one of these activities for first graders and then read Carle's *The Very Busy Spider* to them, or read Kraus's *The Trouble with Spider* with them. The pairing of an older student with a younger child can be accomplished though a "buddy" system between classrooms, or students could read to a relative, neighbor, or someone they baby-sit for, if they get a signed paper from an adult saying they have done so.

If all of the books containing spiders are part of a book display, include the fantasy *The Snow Spider* by Nimmo with the display. Ten-year-old Gwyn has inherited magical powers from his ancestors in Nimmo's book. White's classic, *Charlotte's Web,* could be part of the display also. A box office film of *Charlotte's Web* is now available in video format. All these other books on spiders enhance any classroom reading about Charlotte. The materials in this section would be invaluable to any teacher who is using *Charlotte's Web* in a literature-based reading program.

All of these books, stories, and poems about spiders can be used to enhance the seventh grade HBJ basal reader, *Patterns*, edited by Cullinan and others, which contains four selections about spiders. An informational article from *Animals Magazine*, Sleeper and Boyden's "What's a Spider Without a Web?," appears on pages 418–25. The Japanese legend, "The Cloud Spinner," from Climo's *Someone Saw a Spider: Spider Facts and Folktales* appears on pages 428–33. Climo's "The Spider Brothers Make a Rainbow," from Fisher's *Stories California Indians Told*, appears on pages 434–42 of *Patterns*. Carryl's poem, a parody of a famous nursery rhyme, "The Embarrassing Episode of Little Miss Muffet," appears on pages 444–45 of *Patterns*. An article by Adams, "Spiders and Webs," appears on pages 96–101 of the SF primer, *Hang on to Your Hats*, edited by Aaron, et al. *Pageants*, the seventh grade HM basal reader edited by Durr, et al. contains the myth of Arachne, retold by Coolidge on pages 160–66, and Coffin's poem, "The Spider," on page 167. Other versions include: "Arachne's Gift," pages 5–12 of Climo's *Someone Saw a Spider*; "Arachne," pages 45–48 of Low's *Macmillan Book of Greek Gods and Heroes*; and "The Spinning Contest," pages 64–67 of Russell's *Classical Myths to Read Aloud*. In that myth, the jealous Athena turns Arachne into a spider.

Use Anansi as an introduction to other tricksters in folk literature. Books about the following tricksters appear in Volume 2 of this book in TRICKSTER TALES: Br'er Rabbit (Southern black American); Coyote (American Plains Indians); Fox (French Reynard and Greek Aesop); Hodja (Turkish wise man); Kantjil (Indonesian deer mouse); Loki (Norse mythology); Raven (American Northwestern Indians).

CHAPTER NINE

Learning About Nonfiction

Chapter 11 of Huck's *Children's Literature in the Elementary School,* "Informational Books" on pages 588–618, contains information and titles in the following categories: accuracy and authenticity; content and perspective; style; illustrations and formats; types of informational books; and choosing and using informational books in the classroom. Of special interest are the "Guides for Evaluating Informational Books," page 604. "Nonfiction" is the title of Chapter 10, pages 525–71 of Cullinan's *Literature and the Child.* Criteria for evaluating nonfiction (integrity, tone, content) appear on pages 528–31. Learning to read critically (verifying, comparing sources, comparing with experience) appears on pages 531–35. Chapter 12 of Stewig's *Children and Literature* is "Information Books: The Desire to Know," pages 570–621. Information about evaluating information books (author qualifications, use of language, accuracy, illustrations, organizational and reference aids, and self-sufficiency) is included on pages 570–78. Nine categories of information books are shared: arts, animals, science, mathematics, social studies, sex and physical development, cycle of life, created objects, and language. Chapter 12, pages 544–609 of Norton's *Through the Eyes of a Child: An Introduction to Children's Literature,* contains information about evaluating informational books on pages 551–54: all facts should be accurate, stereotypes should be eliminated; illustrations should clarify the text; analytical thinking should be encouraged; organization should aid understanding; and style should stimulate interest. Twelve questions to consider when evaluating informational literature appear on pages 553–54. Chapter 10, beginning on page 151 of England and Fasick's *Childview: Evaluating and Reviewing Materials for Children* includes a checklist for informational materials on pages 163–64 with specific references to science and sex books.

Kobrin's *Eyeopeners! How to Choose and Use Children's Books About Real People, Places, and Things* contains 500 titles. Kobrin is an excellent speaker for encouraging the reading of nonfiction.

Early elementary students can be introduced to the concept of nonfiction through the following books of Gail Gibbons: *Boat Book; Check It Out!* (libraries); *Deadline: From News to Newspapers* (reporting and publishing); *Department Store* (retailing); *Fill It Up!* (gas stations); *Fire! Fire!* (firefighting and prevention); *From Path to Highway: The Story of the Boston Post Road* (highways); *Lights! Camera! Action!* (writing and producing films); *Playgrounds; The Post Office Book* (mail and how it moves); *The Pottery Place; Trucks; Tunnels; Weather Forecasting;* and *Zoo. Zoo* is also available as a sound filmstrip.

The concept of nonfiction can be introduced to primary students via the educational television program *Books That Answer Questions* from the series *Word Shop*. The following television programs are valuable for stimulating the reading of nonfiction: *3-2-1-Contact*; *Square One*; *Zoo Zoo Zoo*; *Naturescene*; *Nature*; *Smithsonian World*; *NOVA*; *Planet Earth*; *Conrad*; *Well, Well, Well with Slim Goodbody*; and specials by the National Audubon Society and the National Geographic Society.

For science nonfiction consult O'Connell's *Best Science Books and AV Materials for Children*, Wolff's *Best Science Books for Children*, and Wolff's *Best Science Films, Filmstrips, and Video Cassettes for Children*. Many of the books and multimedia have been recommended in the periodical *Science Books and Films*, from the American Association for the Advancement of Science. Because many science materials quickly become outdated, it is important to subscribe to periodicals which review the most recent science books.

Use the set of four sound filmstrips in the series *Literature for Children, Series 5* to introduce nonfiction to intermediate students. The filmstrips include *Sport and Hobby Books: Nonfiction Too Good to Miss*; *Art and Music Books: Nonfiction Too Good to Miss*; *Science Books: Nonfiction Too Good to Miss*; and *History Books: Nonfiction Too Good to Miss*.

The filmstrip *Sport and Hobby Books: Nonfiction Too Good to Miss* introduces Fleischman's *Mr. Mysterious's Secrets of Magic*, for those interested in making magic tricks, as well as his *Mr. Mysterious and Company*, a fiction book. The Radlauers' books are introduced through a discussion of gymnastics and their book, *Gymnastics School*. Viewers are shown how to look up sports figures in almanacs, record books, sports encyclopedias, and encyclopedia indexes. A biography of magician Houdini and two of soccer hero Pelé are mentioned. Lewis and Oppenheimer's *Folding Paper Puppets* is shown. A variety of hobbies are mentioned: model jets, pets, kites, stamps, origami, cooking, gardening, and riddles. Show this book in January, which is hobby month, or when introducing or reinforcing the value of reference books to students. *The World Almanac*, *The Guinness Book of World Records*; *The Lincoln Library of Sports Champions*; and an encyclopedia are shown. A list of recommended books in the guide is arranged under the topics "Sport" and "Hobby."

The filmstrip *Art and Music Books: Nonfiction Too Good to Miss* mentions Stevie Wonder, Beethoven, van Gogh, and Louis Armstrong. Jazz is especially highlighted and *The First Book of Jazz* by Hughes is mentioned. Individual picture books of songs include *Steven Kellogg's Yankee Doodle* by Bangs, and *I Know an Old Lady* by Mills. Garson and Herbert's *Laura Ingalls Wilder Songbook* is shown. All of the art books of Glubok can be introduced through her *Art of the North American Indian* and all of the art books of Raboff can be introduced through his book, *Paul Klee*. Two bibliographies accompany the filmstrip, one on art and the other on music. Activities are included so the filmstrip can be used individually.

The filmstrip *Science Books: Nonfiction Too Good to Miss* features *Octopus*, by the Carricks, as well as Asimov's *How Did We Find Out About Outer*

Space?, Selsam's *Questions and Answers About Ants*, and Harris's *Volcanoes*. Viewers are encouraged to find other books by Selsam and Asimov. Use the filmstrip when studying dolphins because that topic is used in conjunction with the following concepts: title page; importance of the copyright date; table of contents; glossary; and index. Forty-eight science starter questions are arranged in four categories in the guide: matter and energy; earth; universe; and living things. A bibliography is included. Activities are suggested.

The filmstrip *History Books: Nonfiction Too Good to Miss* features Macaulay's *Pyramid* and mentions his *Castle*, *Cathedral*, and *City*. Separate filmstrips sets, each containing two filmstrips, are available for two books by Macaulay: *Pyramid* and *Castle*. Videocassettes of Macaulay's Caldecott Honor Books *Castle* and *Cathedral* can also be shown to introduce his books or a study of the Middle Ages. *Shaw's Fortune* by Tunis and *This Is Historic Britain*, *This Is Hong Kong*, and *This Is Paris* by Miroslav Sasek are also introduced. Coerr's *Sadako and the Thousand Paper Cranes* and Milton's *Who Do You Think You Are? Digging for Your Family Roots* are also mentioned. The concepts of biographies and their place in history, and the Dewey Decimal System, are presented. The study of Egypt is used as a topic for exploration and viewers are lead through a search for materials. A sheet in the guide called "History—What Interests You Most?" lists about 60 subjects under three headings: people, events, and times and places. Activities are also suggested. History is compared to a time machine and students can write space and time books after researching an area of history and reading books from a section of Chapter 1 called TIME TRAVEL: A BOOKTALK.

A wealth of nonfiction articles appears in children's magazines and can be found by looking up individual subjects *The Children's Magazine Guide*, in *The Abridged Readers' Guide to Periodical Literature* and *The National Geographic Index: 1888–1988*. Stoll edited *Magazines for Children*, an annotated list that includes audience, contents, price, and addresses.

STUDYING NONFICTION CLUSTERS. Whenever a work of fiction is read aloud to students or when they read one by themselves, there are always nonfiction books that can add information to the topic, expand interest, and satisfy the natural curiosity of students. There are also numerous subjects that have built-in motivational power because the subjects are interesting to students.

Introduce the following books about robotics to intermediate and middle school students: Asimov's *Robots: Machines in Man's Image*; Pack and Baldwin's *Robots and Robotics*; Chester's *Robots: Facts Behind the Fiction*; Evans's *How to Draw Robots and Spaceships*; Hawkes's *Robots and Computers*; Irvine's *Satellites and Computers*; Knight's *Robotics: Past, Present, and Future*; Krasnoff's *Robots: Reel to Real*; Lauber's *Get Ready for Robots!*; Litterick's *Robots and Intelligent Machines*; McKie's *Robots*; Marsh's *Robots*; and the Silversteins' *The Robots Are Here. Robots and Artificial Intelligence* is the title of a sound filmstrip. *Robots and Computers* is Program #16 of the instructional television series for intermediate students, *Challenge.*

Orvis in Hoover's fiction book *Orvis* is an obsolete robot. Read *Orvis* aloud during a study of robots and to elicit examples about the difference between fiction and nonfiction. Slote's *My Robot Buddy* is a fiction book about how 10-year-old Jack gets his robot, Danny I, and how he protects him from robotnappers. The five P's of robots, as included in the book are: production, programming, physiognomy, personality, and power. *My Robot Buddy* is Program #2 of the instructional television series, *Readit!* A selection from Slote's *My Robot Buddy* appears on pages 252–69 of the fourth grade HBJ basal reader, *Crossroads*, edited by Cullinan, et al. Yount's informational article, "Ready, Set, Robots" appears on pages 242–49 of *Crossroads.*

It is never too early to teach children the difference between fiction and nonfiction. *Trumpets* is pre-primer #3 of the HM basal reader series edited by Durr, et al. "What Is a Robot?" from pages 52–54 is an informational article and Brown's "Mr. Robot" is a story, pages 55–63. These robot items can be displayed for everyone but pointed out to younger children. Students can learn to distinguish the *E* on the spine of the book as an easy fiction book and the number on the spine of the books as nonfiction.

If the above books are used in a display of books about robots, add the following easy fiction books: Waddell's *Harriet and the Robot*; Hoban's *The Laziest Robot in Zone One* and the sequel *Ready, Set, Robot!*; and *Mr. Murphy's Marvelous Invention* by Christelow.

On April 14, 1912 an unsinkable luxury oceanliner struck an iceberg and sank during her maiden voyage. It was not until September 1, 1985 that Dr. Robert Ballard and his crew found and explored the *Titanic.* A number of books have been written about the *Titanic* and icebergs. Ballard's *Exploring the Titanic* is the marine geologist and undersea explorer's own book for young people, and is the best book about the *Titanic.* Excellent color photos and diagrams, such as the cross section of the ship's different layers, enhance the book. Information on the sinking, as well as exploration and discovery, are included in Ballard's book. Three articles written by Ballard appear in the *National Geographic* magazine and even students who can't read the words can enjoy the pictures. The articles include: "How We Found the *Titanic*," December 1985, pages 696–719; "A Last Look at *Titanic*," December 1986, pages 698–727; and "Epilogue for *Titanic*," October 1987, pages 454–63. An article about Ballard appears on pages 17–31 of the 1986 *Current Biography.* Another book by Ballard for adults is *The Discovery of the Titanic.* An adult account of the tragedy is Lord's *A Night to Remember.* A new Lord title for adults is *The Night Lives On: New Ideas on the Titanic Disaster.* British journalist Davie's *Titanic: The Death and Life of a Legend* is also for adults, and includes black and white photo inserts of the rediscovery. Bonsall's *Titanic* contains many black and white illustrations about the design of the *Titanic* and other floating palaces, the maiden voyage, aftermath, and discovery of the wreck. Although written for adults, the pictures are valuable to younger students. Marshello's *Titanic Trivia* provides another source of information. Sloan's *Titanic*, from the First Book series, is for young people and includes Titanic trivia, a glossary, bibliography, and index. The introduction contains a poem by Thomas Hardy, "The Convergence of the Twain." Donnelly's *The Titanic Lost and Found* is an easy-to-read book accompanied by a cassette. *Secrets of the Titanic* is a video. Have students look in the card catalog under "Disasters" to find such books as Cohen's *Great Mistakes*. Searching out information about the *Titanic* can serve as an interesting way to teach reference skills. Use of the card catalog, magazine indexes, book and encyclopedia indexes, tables of contents, and brainstorming various subject headings and related topics are all related skills that can be taught. All of the topics surrounding the study of the *Titanic* can be placed on a sunburst map with rays extended for various side topics, for a literature-based reading program on nonfiction.

Persons interested in the *Titanic* can become interested in related subjects. The following two books about icebergs would also be of interest to readers: Simon's *Icebergs and Glaciers* and Gans's *Danger—Icebergs!* Students may also be interested in learning more about diving. Hackwell's *Diving to the Past: Recovering Ancient Wrecks* tells of the difficulties and dangers of exploring underwater wrecks and the types of historical information that have been found. Sullivan's *Treasure Hunt: The Sixteen-Year Search for the Lost Treasure Ship Atocha* is about a Spanish galleon that sank off the coast of Florida in a hurricane in 1622. On July 20, 1985, two divers discovered in it the biggest cache of sunken treasure ever found. Information is given about treasure hunter Mel Fisher, and the research that traced the last voyage of the *Atocha*. Lang's *Footsteps in the Ocean: Careers in Diving* is about salvage divers and underwater photographers. *Dive to the Coral Reefs* by Tayntor is a beautiful book about divers and photographers from the New England Aquarium in search of coral reefs of the Caribbean.

Multimedia can introduce nonfiction topics. The film or video *Portrait of a Coal Miner* is about how miners in West Virginia mine coal. Instructional television program #5, *Arch of Coal*, from the series *Explorers Unlimited*, shows how coal is loaded at the Penn Central docks in Ashtabula, Ohio. Nonfiction can be supported by fiction. Hendershot's *In Coal Country* depicts a mining town in the 1930s in Ohio, and tells what life was like in a company town. Rappaport's *Trouble at the Mines* is a fiction book for intermediate students about a coal strike in 1888–1900 in Pennsylvania seen through the eyes of Rosie, a miner's daughter. The strike was led by Mother Jones. *Goodbye and Keep Cold* by Davis is about Edda Combs and her childhood experiences in a Kentucky mining town.

George's fiction title, *The Talking Earth*, can be supported with nonfiction books about the Everglades including: Lauber's *Everglades Country: A Question of Life or Death*; Radlauer's *Everglades National Park*; and Stone's *Marshes and Swamps*. Wood's *Barometer of the Everglades* is a video about

the effect of draining the swamps. *Story of the Everglades* is two sound filmstrips about the geography, vegetation, and wildlife in the Everglades. The
video *Everglades National Parks: Everglades, Big Cypress, Biscayne, and Ft.
Jefferson* provides information about Florida swamps.

Dana's fiction book *Zucchini*, about Billy and a ferret, can be enhanced
by reading nonfiction about ferrets. *Time for Ferrets* by Hess is about the care
of a ferret at an animal rescue shelter, and information about ferrets as pets is
included. Casey's *Black-footed Ferret* tells of the characteristics, habits, life
cycle, and history of black-footed ferrets. Casey's *The Friendly Prairie Dog* is
about the life of the black-tailed prairie dog. Other animals that appear in this
book are eagles, snakes, and coyotes. Read Lerner's *Seasons of the Tallgrass
Prairie* or George's *One Day in the Prairie* in connection with Zucchini's desire
is to get out of the zoo and go to the prairie. Two videos to show include *The
Mysterious Black-Footed Ferret* and *Protecting Endangered Animals*. The
second is available as a film or video.

Locating and reading nonfiction books about penguins can be an offshoot
of reading fiction such as *Mr. Popper's Penguins* by Atwater, or *The Explorer
of Barkham Street*, by Stolz. Penguins are endearing animals and books about
them can appear in display cases with stuffed penguins or pictures of penguins.
Somme's *Penguin Family Book* features the chinstrap and Marconi penguins
on Antarctica's Bouvet Island. Strange's *Penguin World* is about the rockhopper
penguins on the Falkland Islands. *Penguin Year* by the Bonners is about the
Adelie penguins of the Antarctic. Crow's *Penguins and Polar Bears: Animals
of the Ice and Snow* contains more pictures than text and includes the following
types of penguins: Adelie, Marconi, chinstrap, Gentoo, and emperor. The bush-
tailed, emperor, and Adelie penguins and their role at Sea World appear in
Todd's *Sea World Book of Penguins*. Eighteen different species of penguins
appear in Coldry's *Penguins*. The sound filmstrips *Antarctica* tell how scientists
work in an outdoor lab. The first filmstrip is *The Environment and Research*,
and the second, *The Animals*, includes penguins. *The Hunters of Chubut* is
one of Lorne Green's wilderness video series and includes sea lions, penguins,
and killer whales. Two picture books about penguins are Lester's *Tacky the
Penguin* and Gay's *Bibi Takes Flight*.

USING SNAKES TO TEACH NONFICTION. *That Snake in the Grass*
by Hess contains such fascinating topics as snakes as pets; idioms concerning
snakes; how pythons coil and kill; milking venom; eggs hatching; and snake
catching equipment. Huge color photos enhance Leetz's *Book of Snakes*, which
tells of the care, feeding, breeding, ailments, and cures for snakes. An interesting question answered by the book is "Why keep snakes?" Lauber's *Snakes
Are Hunters*, from the Let's-Read-and-Find-Out science series, dwells on how
snakes are alike. Johnson's *Snakes*, of Japanese origin, describes general physical characteristics common to all snakes and gives information about their life
cycles. One chapter of Mattison's *Snakes of the World* tells about differences

and similarities between snakes and their relatives. Other information covered is reproduction, food, defense, ecology, camouflage, size, and modes of loco-motion. Hoffman's *Snake* contains information about habitat. Elting's *Snakes and Other Reptiles* includes snakes, chameleons, and relatives. *Discovering Snakes and Lizards* by Curtis can broaden the topic. Selsam and Hunt's *A First Look at Poisonous Snakes* categorizes and identifies poisonous snakes including cobras, coral snakes, vipers, rattlesnakes, cottonmouths, and copper-heads. Three hundred out of 2,500 kinds of snakes are poisonous. The book includes maps, how to avoid being bitten, and eight things to look for in snakes. Simon's *Poisonous Snakes* is complimentary to snakes. Black and white photos enhance Freedman's *Rattlesnakes. Museums* by Gibbons includes a section called "How a New Rattlesnake Exhibit Is Made." Drawings enhance Bender's *Pythons and Boas. Clem: The Story of a Raven* is a memoir written by a wildlife artist and her husband, who rehabilitate wild animals. In this book, Dewey tells how the harmless snake they are rehabilitating slithers into their bed one night.

Reptiles and How They Grow is a cassette with 30 paperbacks, a booklet, teacher's guide, and six activity sheets for primary students. *Snakes* is a sound filmstrip in a series called *Animal Kingdom. Snakes* is a 15-minute instructional television program for primary and intermediate students produced by New Hampshire Public Television and the Corporation for Public Broadcasting. Pro-gram #7 of *Up Close and Natural* is about two helpful snakes: a garter snake and a seven-foot indigo snake.

Don't forget to include folktales and riddles. The cassette *Tales of the Southwest* by Hayes contains the story "Softchild," a how-and-why story about why the snake contains poison. *Snakes Alive!* by Burns contains jokes and riddles about snakes.

Sneak a little poetry into the lives of children when studying snakes. The poems "The Python" by Gardner and "Boa Constrictor" by Silverstein appear on page 177 of Bauer's *Celebrations.*

Magazines can provide further sources about snakes. Teach students to use *The National Geographic Index: 1888–1988, Children's Magazine Guide,* or *The Abridged Readers' Guide to Periodical Literature* to locate articles about snakes. Interesting articles from these sources include Brown's "Hidden Life of the Timber Rattlesnake" from pages 128–38 of the July 1987 issue of *National Geographic;* McDonald's "Mousetrap" from pages 16–21 of the October 1988 issue of *National Wildlife;* Phillips's "A Talk With Two Sea Snakes" on pages 24–26 of the October 1986 issue of *Ranger Rick,* Swanson's "Pythons: The Big Squeezers" on pages 24–33 of the August 1988 issue of *Ranger Rick;* Elinick's "The Boa's Lost Legs" on page 20 of the September 4, 1987 issue of *Science World;* and Laycock's "Snakes with Poison" on pages 32–35 of the June 1988 issue of *Boy's Life.*

Easy books and fiction for intermediate students can be used with nonfic-tion to teach students the difference between fiction and nonfiction. Use the poems with Noble's humorous picture books *The Day Jimmy's Boa Ate the Wash, Jimmy's Boa Bounces Back,* and *Jimmy's Boa and the Big Splash Birthday Bash*; Ungerer's *Crictor*; and Adams's *Alice and the Boa Constrictor.* Alice, who attends a private girls' school in Manhattan, is studying snakes and wants a boa for a pet, so she makes money to buy Sir Lancelot. Intermediate students will be interested in Clifford's *Harvey's Horrible Snake Disaster* which features a hognose snake. When making a bulletin board to introduce snake books, use an S-shaped snake to help spell out the words "Sneak" and "Snake" in the caption, "Sneak into a Snake Book."

EXPLORING SPACE FLIGHT THROUGH NONFICTION. Branley explains the functions of rockets, satellites, and space shuttles for primary students in *Rockets and Satellites.* Although *Spaceborne,* an ALA Notable film and video, was copyrighted in 1977, it still makes an excellent introduction to space flight. There are appropriate sound effects, but no narration. NASA archives provide the sources for the video. Smith's *One Giant Leap for Mankind* begins with Goddard and von Braun and then on to John Glenn's orbit, Ed White's Gemini space walk, the Apollo flights, *Skylab* and space stations. The names of the seven astronauts who died in the *Challenger* are listed. Branley's *From Sputnik to Space Shuttles: Into the New Space Age* gives past, present and future use of space technology for various purposes. The history of space flight from 1957 to 1984 is included in *Space* by Furniss. *Where Are We Going in Space?* by Darling begins at *Sputnik* and ends with the *Challenger* disaster. The video *John Glenn and the Lunar Astronauts* ends with the moon landing in 1969. The *Kennedy Space Center* is the title and focus of Gaffney's book about the history of NASA, moon landings, and shuttles.

Smith's *Daring the Unknown: A History of NASA* is a history of the space program from *Sputnik* through the *Challenger.* Vogt's *Twenty-Fifth Anniversary Album of NASA* takes the program through the space shuttles of the early 1980s. A brief history of NASA appears in *Women in Space* by Briggs. NASA Teacher Resource Centers have videos, 16mm films, slides, publications, cassettes, computer software, laser discs, teacher's guides, student activities. Centers are located in Huntsville, AL; Moffett Field, CA; Pasadena, CA; Colorado Springs, CO; Kennedy Space Center, FL; Chicago, IL; Evansville, IN; Greenbelt, MD; Marquette, MI; Rochester, MN; National Space Technology Laboratories, MS; Cleveland, OH; Mankato, MN; St. Cloud, MN; New York City; Pittsburgh, PA; Johnson Space Center, Houston, TX; Hampton, VA; Milwaukee, WI; and LaCrosse, WI.

Begin with Barton's *I Want to Be an Astronaut* for primary students, and then introduce other books about astronauts and space personnel to students. Barton's book has few words and is intended for preschool and early primary students but could be included in a classroom reading/listening/viewing center for those who are poor readers. Jobs in space are listed and information about shuttles is included. Moche's *If You Were an Astronaut* includes male and female, as well as African-American, astronauts. *Space Challenger: The Story of Guion Bluford* by Haskins and Benson is about the first black astronaut. Lampton's *Space Sciences* tells about astronauts, astronomers, and other scientists who work in the space program.

Books about female astronauts provide good role models. Fox's *Women Astronauts: Aboard the Shuttle* is an overview of six women astronauts including Sally Ride as well as teacher Christa McAuliffe. Information about training programs, shuttles, and experiences are included. *Women in Space: Reaching the Last Frontier* by Briggs includes Valentina Tereshkova, Svetlana Savitskaya, and the eight female American astronauts. Sally Ride, the first American female astronaut, tells about her experiences in a space shuttle and discusses weightlessness, walking in space, and special fears, in *To Space and Back*. Use the ALA Notable Recording, *Women of Courage: Sally Ride*, for a "You Were There" type broadcast to introduce Ride's book. Ride is also included in Fox's collective biography, *Women Astronauts: Aboard the Shuttle*. Selection and training of astronauts appears in O'Connor's *Sally Ride and the New Astronauts: Scientist in Space*. Blacknall's *Sally Ride: America's First Woman in Space* is easy reading. Billing's biography of the first teacher in space was rewritten after January 28, 1986. *Christa McAuliffe: Pioneer Space Teacher* tells about her personal life, space training, and the lessons and experiments she was planning for her trip. Another biography is *Christa McAuliffe: Reaching for the Stars* by Martin. Two related biographies of early female pilots written by Chadwick are *Anne Morrow Lindbergh: Pilot and Poet*, and *Amelia Earhart: Aviation Pioneer.*

Dickinson's poem "Because I Could Not Stop for Death" is accompanied by a photograph of Christa McAuliffe on pages 104–05 of Sullivan's *Imaginary Gardens: American Poetry and Art for Young People*. Magee's poem "High Flight" appears on pages 52–53 of Sullivan's anthology along with the photographs "Astronaut Edward H. White (Gemini IV), the First American to 'Float in Space,' June 3, 1965" and "Africa and Other Areas of the Earth, Seen from Apollo 17 Spacecraft." "High Flight" ends: "And, while with silent, lifting mind I've trod / The high untrespassed sanctity of space / Put out my hand and touched the face of God."

Use the three filmstrips in the series *Today and Tomorrow in Space: The Space Shuttle and Beyond* to introduce books about space shuttles. The titles of the three individual filmstrips are: *The Space Shuttle*; *Satellites and How They Help Us*; and *Living and Working in Space*. Dwiggins's *Flying the Space Shuttles* contains information about 100 trips. A glossary and index are helpful. Students can answer questions about eating, sleeping, sponge baths, as well as the *Columbia, Challenger, Discovery,* and *Atlantis* missions. Students learn about how astronauts conduct private experiments for corporations or individuals who pay a fee. Cooper's *Before Lift-Off: The Making of a Space Shuttle Crew* tells about the year of preparation for the October, 1984 launch, which was Sally Ride's second journey. Joels and Kennedy's *Space Shuttle Operator's*

Manual details mechanical aspects of the spacecraft. Lord's *A Day in Space* provides photos of activities in a space shuttle for primary students. *Space Shuttle Disaster* by McCarter tells about arrangements aboard the *Challenger* as well as the disaster. The history of the shuttles and living in space appear in Begarnie's *The Space Shuttle Story*. For student projects that have been aboard the space shuttle contact the Space Shuttle, Student Involvement Project, National Science Teachers Association, 1742 Connecticut Ave. N.W., Washington, D.C. 20009.

McPhee and McPhee's *Your Future in Space: The U.S. Space Camp Training Program* tells about a camp in Huntsville, Alabama where there are programs available for grades five, six, and seven in Level I and for grades eight, nine, and ten in Level II. Addresses for obtaining more information on space and space-related careers are appended. Colored photographs are included and readers learn about shuttles, gravity, and living in space. The book is dedicated to the *Challenger* crew. Program #11 of the instructional television science series for intermediate students, *Challenge*, is called *Space Camp* and shows students at the camp and activities leading up to a simulated flight.

Chapter 7 of Branley's *From Sputnik to Space Shuttles: Into the New Space Age* is about space stations. Billings's *Space Stations: Bold New Step Beyond Earth* is illustrated with drawings and photographs. What it would be like to live in space as well as types of jobs available, is included. Apfel's *Space Station* is even more helpful. Also use Kerod's *See Inside a Space Station*. Langley's *Spacecraft* includes a variety of vehicles. Vogt's *Space Walking* includes information on Russian and American walks in space.

Four big book titles that are available include: *Moon Buggy, Space Shuttle, First on the Moon*, and *Skylab*. Individual small sized books are also available for each title.

Use the informational article "A Giant Step into Space" by Steele on pages 200–07 of the HBJ fourth grade basal reader, *Crossroads*, in the Laureate edition edited by Cullinan and others to introduce further study of space exploration.

Although it isn't a joking matter, Roop's *Space Out! Jokes About Outer Space* can add fun to any assignment about space. Sample riddles are "What's a space creature's favorite food?" and "What goes up when you count down?" The answers, of course, are human beans and a rocket.

Teach the use of magazine indexes through the study of space. *The National Geographic Index: 1888–1988* includes such topics as: space flight; space colonies; space medicine; space shuttles; space stations; space walk; spacecraft; spacelab; and Soyuz-Apollo Mission, as well as sun; moon; Mars; Uranus; Saturn; and Neptune. *The Abridged Readers' Guide to Periodical Literature* contains such subjects as: space biology; space centers; space flight; space museums; space flight to Mars; space flight to Neptune; space flight to Saturn; space flight to the sun; space flight to Uranus; moon; sun; and names of individual planets. Some subjects found in the *Children's Magazine Guide* include

Alpha Centauri; astronomy; black holes; comets; constellations; eclipses; galaxies; meteors; Milky Way; moon; moon—legends; names of planets; outer space—exploration; planets; solar system; space flight to the moon; Star of Bethlehem; stars; sun; supernovas; astronauts; camps; NASA; space colonies; space flights; space stations; space sciences; and space suits. One magazine which is especially useful is *Odyssey,* a full color magazine about astronomy and outer space.

Take advantage of the natural interest in space flight to teach the use of index volumes to general and special encyclopedias. Teach the use of the index volume #25, of *Space and Technology Illustrated: The World Around Us* to locate many topics. Also teach the use and importance of indexes in individual books. *The Macmillan Book of Astronomy* by Gallant is available in hardcover and paperback and includes much material.

Books about space flight can be related to books about outer space. Because knowledge of our universe has expanded with what we have learned from space travel, it is only logical to include some of the new books. Seymour Simon's books are especially good and include: *Earth, Jupiter, Mars, Moon, Saturn, Stars, Sun,* and *Uranus.* The photographs are outstanding. Several books by Branley are important additions to a display or classroom collection: *Star Guide, What the Moon Is Like,* and *Journey into a Black Hole.* Check pages 116–17 of Jespersen and Fitz-Randolph's *From Quarks to Quasars: A Tour of the Universe* for information about black holes. A filmstrip, *Black Holes in Space,* is available. Other new books to include are Rutland's *Planets* and Kandoian's *Under the Sun.* Books about comets include Anderson's *Halley's Comet;* Branley's *Comets;* Krupp's *The Comet and You;* Petty's *Comets;* Simon's *Long Journey from Space;* and the filmstrip *Halley's Comet.*

Another related area is aviation books. Zisfein's *Flight: A Panorama of Aviation* is a history of flying. Gunston's *Aircraft* contains photographs and diagrams to help readers understand principles of flight, aircraft construction and safety. A chart of important dates is included, as well as a glossary and index. Boyne's *The Smithsonian Book of Flight for Young People* contains photos and drawings from the Wright brothers and Lindbergh to Chuck Yeager. Rosenblum's *The Golden Age of Aviation* includes pioneers such as Lindbergh, Byrd, and Earhart and ends at the beginning of World War II. Two biographies about Earhart include Chadwick's *Amelia Earhart: Aviation Pioneer* and Randolph's *Amelia Earhart.* More information about her disappearance is included in the Chadwick book. Chadwick also wrote *Anne Morrow Lindbergh: Pilot and Poet* for intermediate students. Other aviation books are listed in Chapter 5 in the section READING ABOUT TRUCKS, TRAINS, AND OTHER FORMS OF TRANSPORTATION.

Because information goes quickly out of date in books about space, teach students the importance of the copyright date in determining which books are of historical interest and which ones include the latest information. Teachers, librarians, and school library/media specialists who wish to find the latest titles should consult the periodical published by the American Association for the Advancement of Science called *Science Books and Films*. AAAS also publishes books of science books such as O'Connell's *Best Science Books and AV Materials for Children*.

Be sure to include some creative projects in the space unit. Khoury's *The Space Shuttle Mystery* is a kit with a cassette and 10 paperbacks, in which readers must locate a missing space shuttle in the year 3020 A.D. Read aloud from Livingston's *Space Songs*, 13 poems about asteroids, comets, satellites, the sun, moon, and Milky Way. The Model Rocketry Safety Code is a feature of Olney's *Out to Launch; Model Rockets*. The Blocksmas' *Space-Crafting: Invent Your Own Flying Spaceships* shows how to turn household items such as plastic straws, cardboard cartons, can lids, margarine tubs, thread, spools, and pipe cleaners into flying objects. An earlier book by the Blocksmas is *Easy-to-Make Spaceships That Really Fly*. Three drawing books include: *Drawing Spaceships and Other Spacecraft* by Bolognese; *How to Draw Robots and Spaceships* by Evans; and *How to Draw Star Wars Heroes, Creatures, Spaceships, and Other Fantastic Things* by Ames. Program #23 of the instructional television series, *Draw Along*, is *Outer Space* which helps primary students to draw an imaginary scene on an unknown planet. Use the last two to show how information about science provides us with background to enter the realm of science fiction.

UNCOVERING THE SECRETS OF ANCIENT EGYPT. Mummies and pyramids have always fascinated children and can be part of any social studies unit in which Egypt is studied. Lauber's *Tales Mummies Tell* contains information about Egyptian mummies but also mummies of the Peruvians, Scythians, and even woolly mammoths and gerbils. The illustrations in Aliki's *Mummies Made in Egypt* are based on Egyptian paintings. Detailed information on the mummification process, beginning with removing the inner organs is included. Also consult Milton's *Secrets of the Mummies. Egyptian Mummies* by Andrews contains exceptional photos which make this adult book suitable for middle school students. A selection from Pace's *Wrapped for Eternity* appears on pages 144–46 of Saltman's *Riverside Anthology of Children's Literature*. Perl's *Mummies, Tombs and Treasure: Secrets of Ancient Egypt* concentrates on Egypt. Information about the mummification process, building the pyramids as tombs, tomb robbers, the afterlife, archaeological sites, art and artifacts are included, with black and white photographs and drawings from various museums. A chart of the dynasties and a floor plan of Tut's tomb are included. Bendick's *Egyptian Tombs* contains information about looted tombs, curses, and funeral practices. The filmstrips about *Treasure of the Boy King Tut* could be used in conjunction with Ventura and Ceserani's *In Search of Tutankhamun* which discusses entering and recording information about the archaeological find. Donnelly's *Tut's Mummy: Lost and Found* is an easy-to-read account of finding Tut's tomb. Glubok's *The Art of Egypt Under the*

Pharaohs shows photographs of tombs, temples, reliefs, statues, and jewelry. Two new books cover all aspects of ancient Egypt: Oliphant's *The Egyptian World* and Hart's *Ancient Egypt. An Egyptian Craftsman* by Caselli tells about everyday lives of Egyptians during the reign of Pharoah Ramses II.

Although the text of Davies's *Egyptian Hieroglyphs* is aimed at adults, the many drawings make the book suitable for middle school students. Titles of other books about hieroglyphics appear in Volume 2 of this book in a section called THE RIDDLE OF COMMUNICATION. Information about papyris appears in Limousin's *The Story of Paper.* Robinson's *Ancient Egypt* includes information about the Rosetta Stone and the Pyramids. Other books include Pace's *Pyramids: Tombs for Eternity* and David's *Ancient Egypt.* Macaulay's book *Pyramid* is featured on the sound filmstrip *History Books: Nonfiction Too Good to Miss*, on a separate two filmstrip set or a video called *Pyramid.* Macaulay's *Pyramid* answers many questions about how and why the Pyramids were built. Students may also branch out and read about pyramids in the Americas in Fisher's *Pyramid of the Sun, Pyramid of the Moon.*

Teachers and librarians might find tales to tell to classes studying Egypt from El-Shamy's *Folktales of Egypt* which is arranged by genre. Twenty-eight stories appear in *Gods and Pharaohs* by Harris. Climo's *The Egyptian Cinderella* is about Rhodopis, a Greek slave girl, whose dancing slipper is stolen by a falcon. Read this book aloud during studies of ancient Egypt.

Two fiction books that could be part of a display or unit on Egypt are Carter's *His Majesty, Queen Hatshepsut* and Stolz's *Zekmet, the Stone Carver: A Tale of Ancient Egypt.* Carter's book is a historical novel beginning when Hatshepsut was 13 years old. Much detail is given about this historical person, who was married at 14 and ruled for 20 years. Historical notes and a bibliography are appended. Stolz's book tells how the Sphinx might have come into existence as a monument to the Pharaoh Khafre, who also had a pyramid built as a tomb. Several time travel books that include Egypt are: Alexander's *Time Cat*; Stolz's *Cat in the Mirror*; Peck's *Blossom Culp and the Sleep of Death*; and Wandelmaier's *Secret of the Old Museum.*

Use the study of Egypt as a vehicle for introducing magazine indexes to students. A wide variety of articles is available from many kinds of magazines. Some representative articles include: Blauer's "Finding the Source of the Nile," *Junior Scholastic*, April 22, 1988, pages 8–9; Miller's "Egypt" and "Nile File" pages 20–31 of the November 1987 *Ranger Rick*; El-Baz's "Finding a Pharaoh's Funeral Bark" and Miller's "Riddle of the Pyramid Boats" from pages 512–50 of the April 1988 *National Geographic*; Bianchi's "Pharaoh's Felines: The Cat in Ancient Egypt," *Faces*, May 1988, pages 4–9; Muller's "Ancient Egyptian Dances," *Cricket*, January 1988, pages 48–50; and "Ancient Secret Revealed" *Current Events*, December 11, 1987, page 3. Although the articles in *National Geographic* magazine may be too difficult for primary and some intermediate students to read, the pictures are worth their weight in gold. The magazines can also be used to stretch the reading vocabularies of gifted elementary students. Teach students to use the *National Geographic Index: 1888–1988*. The index yields 39 articles on Egypt under the following subjects: Egypt, ancient; pyramids, Egypt (as well as references under pyramids, the Americas); Tutankhamen; Abu Simbel; Cairo; and the Suez Canal. Students can learn about *see also* references by using magazine indexes. *Children's Magazine Guide: A Subject Index to Children's Magazines* includes volume 40 in 1988. Some topics are: Egypt—ancient; mummies; Nile River; pyramids; and Gods, Egyptian. Some elementary and most middle schools will subscribe to the *Abridged Readers' Guide to Periodical Literature* so that source can also be consulted.

De Paola's picture book, *Bill and Pete Go Down the Nile*, could be added to the previously mentioned books if a display in the library were being created. Bill the crocodile and his friend go on a class trip down the Nile to see the pyramids. Less able readers could be assigned to read this book aloud to a small group of primary children as a project during the study of Egypt. The project would be important to the self-esteem of the student by providing public recognition, as well as an opportunity for sharing a positive reading experience.

Teachers will find Boyd's *Ancient Egyptians Activity Book* helpful for the 13 games, word searches, maze crosswords, and other activities. Conway's *Ancient Egypt Independent Learning Unit: Treasures, Tombs, and Tutankhamen* covers 45 topics with one- or two-page descriptions. Two books could be used in displays in classrooms or the school library/media center. Six scenes in Wild's *The Egyptians Pop-Up* include the Great Pyramid, Sphinx, treasures of Tutankhamen, and Cleopatra and the Romans. There are five scenes in Ventura's *Journey to Egypt: A UNICEF Pop-Up Book*.

INTRODUCING FICTION AND NONFICTION THROUGH THE MIDDLE AGES. Books about knights, castles, and dragons are favorites for students to read on their own or as part of history projects about the Middle Ages.

Study of the Middle Ages is a good vehicle for teaching students to look under a variety of subjects. Some card catalog and index subjects include: Arthurian romances; castles; chivalry; civilization, medieval; crusades; dragons, knights and knighthood; and Middle Ages. Several articles about the Middle Ages appear in children's magazines. Check the *Children's Magazine Guide*, for articles such as: Lasker's "A Tournament of Knights," which appears on pages 27–33 of the November 1988 issue of *Cricket*; Glass's "Behind the Castle Walls, Parts 1 and 2," which appear on pages 44–47 in the November 1988 and pages 55–60 in the December 1988 issues of *Cricket*; Oakeshott's "A Knight and His Horse" which appears on pages 14–16 of the April 1987 issue of *Faces*; and Muller's "No Forks, No Spoons" which is an article in *Highlights for Children*, November 1987, on pages 12–13.

There are a number of recent books about life in the Middle Ages which also include information about knights and castles. Morgan's *Life in a Medieval Village* is about Freeman John's life in a 13th-century English village. Sancha's *The Luttrell Village: Country Life in the Middle Ages* shares life in an English village in 1328. Goodall's *The Story of an English Village* contains half pages to show how an English village evolved from medieval times to a modern village of today. Town and country life are just two of the topics covered in *The Middle Ages* by Oakes. In Aliki's *A Medieval Feast*, the Lord and Lady of Camdenton Manor prepare a feast for the king and his entourage. Information about the feast and the castle are included. Birds baked in a pie fly out at the feast to remind readers of the famous nursery rhyme which includes 4 and 20 black-birds. Lasker's *Merry Ever After* is a book, as well as a sound filmstrip, which shows two medieval wedding celebrations, one of a noble couple and one of a peasant couple. Goodall's *Above and Below the Stairs* is a wordless book uti-lizing half pages to show the contrasts between how the upper and lower classes have lived in England from the Middle Ages to the present.

Use the sound filmstrips or the video of Macaulay's *Castle* to show how a medieval castle was built. Other books include Sancha's *Castle Story*, Smith's *Castles*, Unstead's *See Inside a Castle*, and Goodall's *The Story of a Castle*. Directions for making a castle appear on pages 96–107 of Bottomley's *Paper Projects for Creative Kids of All Ages*.

Exploring the Past: The Middle Ages by Oakes contains information on all phases of life. Of special interest is a month by month account of peasants at work and information about making a book and creating illuminations for it. Hunt's *Illuminations* is an alphabet book of the Middle Ages. Schnurnberger's *Kings, Queens, Knights, and Jesters: Making Medieval Costumes* includes photos and illustrations. *The Middle Ages* is the title of one of the five filmstrips in the series *Music: Medieval to Modern*. Play Nelson and Haack's cassette, *The Way-Out Cassette for Children*, for information about the Middle Ages. *Anno's Medieval World* shares what people in the Middle Ages felt about changes in scientific thought. Scarry's *Looking into the Middle Ages: A Pop-Up Book* shares everyday life in the Middle Ages, and includes a castle and moving drawbridge, a festival, a village, and a cathedral. Use the video of Macaulay's Caldecott Honor Book, *Cathedral*, to show the construction of a fictional medieval French cathedral. Caselli's *Medieval Monk* is about a boy's first months in a 12th-century Benedictine monastery.

Lasker's *A Tournament of Knights* shows a young knight preparing for his first tournament. The life and duties of a knight appear in Gibson's *Knights*. Life in a village and the castle appear in Miquel's *Days of Knights and Castles*. The role of a knight as a soldier appears in Windrow's *Medieval Knight*. In Hindley's *Once There Was a Knight and You Can Be One, Too!*, a boy reads about knights and makes a garbage can lid shield and a broom lance with the help of a girl. Other information includes how to make a castle, dragon, armor and mail, a scepter, flags and banners, and how to hold a tournament. Gerrard's *Sir Cedric* is a picture book which contains a narrative poem in which Sir Cederic defeats Black Ned.

There are a number of books about Arthurian times. Sutcliff's trilogy about King Arthur begins with *Light Beyond the Forest*, in which King Arthur's knights, Sir Launcelot, Sir Galahad, Sir Bors, and Sir Percival search for the Holy Grail, the cup Jesus used for the Last Supper. In the second book, *Sword and the Circle*, readers learn about the sword in the stone, the round table, Sir Launcelot, Sir Gawain and the Green Knight, Launcelot and Elaine, Tristan and Iseult, Geraint and Enid, Percival, and Gawain and the Loathly Lady. In the third book, *The Road to Camlann: The Death of King Arthur*, Mordred, Arthur's illegitimate son, enters the story. Readers learn about Launcelot and Guenever, the last battle, and Avalon of the Apple Trees. Philips's *The Tale of Sir Gawain* uses Malory's *Le Morte D'Arthur* as a main source and includes the story "The Marriage of Sir Gawain," pages 39–46, which is also told in the picture books *Sir Gawain and the Loathly Lady* by Hastings and *Sir Gawain and the Loathly Damsel* by Troughton. As payment for having his life saved, King Arthur promises the ugly hag one of his knights to be her husband. The Loathly Lady has a nose like a pig's snout, a misshapen mouth, yellow horse's teeth, sores, a naked scalp, and gnarled fingers. The knight who marries her is Sir Gawain and he finds that she is under a spell which makes her ugly by day and beautiful by night. In another version Sir Gawain marries the damsel in order to solve a riddle that will save King Arthur's life. Philips's *The Tale of Sir Gawain* also includes stories about "The Sword in the Stone," pages 6–14; "The Quest for the Holy Grail," pages 65–77; and "Lancelot and Guinevere," pages 78–88. Two recordings which are appropriate for this unit of study include *Tales of King Arthur and His Knights: Excalibur* and *Tales of King Arthur and His Knights: Story of Sir Galahad*. Galahad, Lancelot's son, searches for the Holy Grail. The first recording tells how Arthur obtains the sword Excalibur.

Service's fiction book, *Tomorrow's Magic*, a sequel to *The Winter of Magic's Return*, is about how Heather, Willy, and Earl help King Arthur, who has returned from a long sleep. The land has been destroyed by a nuclear holocaust and is now in a nuclear winter. Morgan le Fay is planning to take over the world. Heather has magic skills and Earl is the ancient Merlin in adolescent form. There are other fiction books for intermediate students. Hunter's *Knight of the Golden Plain* is about Sir Dauntless, who tries to get a golden bird from an evil magician. Pierce's *Alanna: The First Adventure* is about a girl who wants to be a knight, and trades places with her twin brother Alan. In the sequel, *In the Hand of the Goddess*, which is for high school students, Alanna trains for knighthood.

These books can be used to expand the study of any book about knights in a literature-based reading program; to enhance basal readers; or in the social studies curriculum. Check pages 174–241 of the Macmillan third grade basal reader, *Secrets and Surprises*, edited by Smith and Arnold, for an article called "Monsters of the Middle Ages" which includes the manicore, mermaids, unicorns, and dragons. For stories about unicorns, check *The Unicorn Treasury* by Coville, *Dragons and Unicorns* by the Johnsgards, and the picture book *The Unicorn and the Lake* by Mayer and Hague.

The study of the Middle Ages can include books and multimedia about dragons. The picture book *Saint George and the Dragon*, retold by Hodges and illustrated by Hyman, is a Caldecott-winning book that can be used by students of all ages interested in knights and dragons. The source Hodges uses is part of Spenser's *Faerie Queene*. A sound filmstrip, a video, and a poster of this book are available. In the story George, the Red Cross Knight, slays the fearsome dragon that has been ruining the kingdom of Princess Una. Yolen's story "Great Grandfather Dragon's Tale," from her anthology *Dragons and Dreams*, tells the story of St. George and the dragon from the dragon's point of view. Prelutsky's poem about a dragon appears in *Once Upon a Time*, which celebrates the 20th anniversary of RIF, Reading Is Fundamental. Some picture books which include dragons are: Aitken's *Ruby the Red Knight*; Leaf's *The Eyes of the Dragon*; de Paola's *The Knight and the Dragon*; Krahn's *The Secret in the Dungeon*; Leedy's *Dragon ABC Hunt, Dragon Halloween Party,* and *A Number of Dragons*; Murphy's *Valentine for a Dragon*; Peet's *How Droofus the Dragon Lost His Head*; Stock's *Emma's Dragon Hunt*; Williams's *Everyone Knows What a Dragon Looks Like*; and Wilson's *Beware the Dragons!*

Nonfiction about dragons includes *Draw Fifty Monsters, Creeps, Super-heroes, Demons, and Dragons* by Ames, and *A Book of Dragons* by the Baskins. In Branley's *Eclipse, Darkness and Daytime*, the eclipse is described as a dragon that gobbles up the sun.

Some fiction about dragons for intermediate and middle school students includes: Grahame's *The Reluctant Dragon* (illustrated by Shepard or by Hague); Keller's *A Small Elderly Dragon*; Krensky's *The Dragon Circle* and sequel *The Witching Hour*; Lindgren's *Brothers Lionheart*; Nesbit's *Last of the Dragons*; Sargent's *Weird Henry Berg*; Tolkien's *Farmer Giles of Ham*; and Yep's *Dragon of the Lost Sea* with its sequel *Dragon Steel*. Older readers will enjoy Menolly and the dragons of Pern in McCaffrey's *Dragonsong, Dragonsinger,* and *Dragondrums,* and Yolen's *Dragon's Blood, Heart's Blood,* and *A Sending of Dragons*. Other fiction about dragons includes: Murphy's *Ivory Lyre* and *Nightpool*; Salsitz's *Where Dragons Lie*; and Yolen's *Dragons and Dreams: A Collection of New Fantasy and Science Fiction Stories*.

Dragons appear in basal readers. "Dragon, Dragon" by Gardner is a folk-tale that appears on pages 360–73 of *Patterns*, the seventh grade HBJ basal reader in the Laureate edition compiled by Cullinan, et al. The tale comes from Gardner's *Dragon, Dragon and Other Tales*. A selection from Mahy's fantasy, *The Dragon of an Ordinary Family*, appears on pages 62–71 of *Celebrations*, the third grade HBJ basal reader in the Laureate edition, edited by Cullinan, et al.

CHAPTER TEN

Introducing Books
by Genre

INTRODUCING BIOGRAPHIES [CU 105–07; 710]. Criteria for juvenile biography—choice of subjects, accuracy and authenticity, style, characterization, and theme—appear on pages 566–82 and 586–87 of *Children's Literature in the Elementary School* by Huck, et al.; guides for evaluating biographies appear on page 573. Also included in Huck's book are types of presentation and coverage, including picture books, simplified, partial, complete, collective, autobiography, and memoirs. Criteria for selecting historical books and biographies appear on pages 461–62. Criteria for a good biography are also found on page 725 of Sutherland and Livingston's *Scott, Foresman Anthology of Children's Literature*. "Biography: Bringing Personalities to Life" is Chapter 9 of Stewig's *Children and Literature*. Check pages 413–16 for ideas for evaluating biography. Other topics in Stewig's book on pages 385–430 include: a changing style in biography; types of biography; variety in subject; and sharing biography with children. Check "Historical Fiction and Biography," Chapter 9 of Cullinan's *Literature and the Child*, pages 458–524. Information about biographies and historical fiction are categorized here by time periods. There is discussion of Fritz's landmark biography, *And Then What Happened, Paul Revere?* on page 463 and a profile of Fritz appears on page 489 of Cullinan's book. Chapter 12 of Norton's *Through the Eyes of a Child: An Introduction to Children's Literature* is "Nonfiction: Informational Books and Biographies," pages 544–609. Check page 571 for an article by Jean Fritz called "On Writing Biography." Criteria listed by Norton for evaluating biographies for children are: accuracy and origin of facts; a worthy subject; a believable human; and a balance of fact and story line. Biographical subjects include explorers; political heroes and heroines of the past and present; achievers in science, arts, literature and sports; and people who have persevered. When giving a booktalk of biographies, be sure to present books from all categories. Chapter 9, "Biography and History" of England and Fasick's *Childview: Evaluating and Reviewing Materials for Children* contains information about biographies on pages 132–40, including: types and functions of biography; structure (style, theme, point of view); balance; collective biographies; and fictionalized and false biography. Check the Lindskoogs's *How to Grow a Young Reader* for a list of "10 Good Collective Biographies," page 110, and "20 Good Individual Biographies," pages 110–12. Breen's helpful *Index to Collective Biographies for Young Readers*, fourth edition, indexes 1,129 collective biographies which profile 10,000 people.

A sound filmstrip for intermediate and middle school students that is useful for introducing biographies is *Interviewing Biographies* from the series *Literature to Enjoy and Write About, Series 1*. The three biographies that are introduced are Fritz's *The Double Life of Pocahontas*, Freedman's *Lincoln: A Photobiography*, and McKissack's *Martin Luther King, Jr.* Through the filmstrip, students learn to write interview questions so they can interview a biographical subject. A list of 30 recommended books is part of a guide for teachers using *Interviewing Biographies*. Use the filmstrip in January to highlight King or in February to highlight Lincoln or use it for social studies classes. Freedman's biography of Lincoln, a Newbery winner, is a photodocumentary which combines over 80 photographs with a well-researched and interesting biography. Special features include quotes from Lincoln in a section called "A Lincoln Sampler" and lists of memorials in a section called "In Lincoln's Footsteps." The bibliography is also very useful. The book made history when, as a photobiography, it won the Newbery Medal in 1988.

Use the filmstrip *Interviewing Biographies* to talk about Pocahontas. Fritz's biography treats Pocahontas differently from other biographies by showing that her life was spent in two very different cultures. Another excellent biography of the Indian princess is Bulla's *Pocahontas and the Strangers*. Discuss the difference between biography and historical fiction by sharing O'Dell's *The Serpent Never Sleeps: A Novel of Jamestown and Pocahontas* in which Serena Lynn, who comes from Plymouth, England, in 1609 on the *Sea Venture* to Jamestown, meets Pocahontas. Sacajawea is one of 20 boys and girls who made an impact during their early lives and are included in Fradin's *Remarkable Children: Twenty Who Made History*. Use this book and LeVert's *Doubleday Book of Famous Americans* when defining the term "collective biographies."

Make sure that Pocahontas and Sacajawea are part of any study of Native Americans. *Quanah Parker*, by Hilts, is a biography of the Comanche chief, the last major holdout in the fight to keep the Comanches from being placed on a reservation. Parker also appears in Freedman's *Indian Chiefs*, which shares the lives of five other western American Indians. Freedman is the author of one of the other books on the filmstrip. Some nonfiction about Indians of the Americas includes: Hirschfelder's *Happily May I Walk: American Indians and Alaska Natives Today*; Harlan's *American Indians Today; Issues and Conflicts*; Marrin's *Aztecs and Spaniards: Cortes and the Conquest of Mexico*; and Ashabranner's *Children of the Maya*.

Two other biographies of ethnic Americans include *Señor Alcade: A Biography of Henry Cisneros*, by Cillies, and *West Coast Chinese Boy* by Lim. One is about the former mayor of San Antonio and the other is about life in Vancouver's Chinatown in the early 1920s. Biographies of African-Americans appear in Volume 2 of this book in a section called PLAYS AND BOOKS TO ENRICH AFRICAN-AMERICAN STUDIES. Not enough quality biographies have been written about people from other lands and cultures. Huynh Quang Nhuong's *The Land I Lost: Adventures of a Boy in Vietnam* is an example of a nonfiction book about how one boy lives in the central highlands of Vietnam. Students learn about the six months of rainy season, children who work at the age of six, memories of a grandmother, a college-educated father who taught at night and was a farmer and hunter. The war disrupts this boy's dreams. Read the introduction on pages ix–xi and use the information to introduce the book. Sometimes this book is not shelved with biography and appears with other nonfiction materials about Vietnam.

Biographies have long been written about explorers, pioneers, and military leaders. Gerrard's biography of Drake, a picture book in rhyme, is different from the norm. In *Sir Francis Drake, His Daring Deeds*, Drake first sets sail at the age of 10, and the book can be used to introduce the term *biography* to children at an early age. It is never too soon to introduce the vocabulary of literature to children. When vocabulary is introduced properly and at the appropriate times it can be assimilated in a natural way. Quotations from Columbus's journal are included in Soule's *Christopher Columbus: On the Green Sea of Darkness*, and from his log in *The Log of Christopher Columbus*, edited by Herzog. A more fictionalized account is Monchieri's *Christopher Columbus*. Fritz's *Where Do You Think You're Going, Christopher Columbus?* is a biography which combines facts and humor. A sound filmstrip, *Christopher Columbus*, is based on a picture book by the d'Aulaires. Another sound filmstrip, *Christopher Columbus*, is from the National Geographic series *People Behind Our Holidays*. All information about Columbus is suitable for use in October or during history units. Fritz's *Make Way for Sam Houston* brings alive the colorful first president of the Republic of Texas, U.S. senator, and later governor, as a very human character who has energy, vision, patriotism, arrogance, and ambition but also has a temper and drinks too much. Commodore Matthew Perry and four steampowered ships entered Edo (now Tokyo) Bay on July 8, 1853. After exchanges of gifts, a treaty was signed on March 31, 1854 to open trade between the United States and Japan. Blumberg's *Commodore Perry in the Land of the Shogun* is a winner of the Golden Kite Award, Boston Globe/Horn Book Award, and is an ALA Notable Book. Kent's *The Story of Admiral Peary at the North Pole* can introduce books about the Arctic.

Biographies of world leaders abound. Stanley's *Peter the Great* is an exceptional biography. Peter was the czar who brought Russia into the modern world of the late 17th and early 18th centuries. Not only did Peter work with the common people but he traveled to England to broaden his knowledge. He was a qualified surgeon, an accomplished carpenter, and city planner of St. Petersburg. A child who always asks "What does it do?" or "How does it work?" should be pointed in the direction of *Peter the Great*. As a villain of humanity we have "Der Führer." Marrin's *Hitler* shares the life of Hitler through the horrors of the Holocaust, and tells much of the history of Europe in the process. Aliki's *The King's Day* is a picture book about Louis XIV and daily life at the court of Versailles, it can be used with French classes in middle and high schools.

Biographies of persons involved in American history are popular for their curriculum connections. Jefferson is part of a set called *Harriet Tubman/ Thomas Jefferson* in the Famous American Read-Along series. A cassette and eight paperbacks are available for each person. Adler's *Thomas Jefferson: Father of Our Democracy* begins with Jefferson's childhood and includes his authorship of the Declaration of Independence. Hilton's *The World of Young George Washington* is for intermediate students and focuses on the first 20 years of Washington's life. Siegel's *George and Martha Washington at Home in New York* is about 16 months in the term in office of our first president. Fleming's *First in Their Hearts* is for intermediate and middle school students. Meltzer's *George Washington and the Birth of Our Nation* is well documented and contains photographs and makes Washington, the general and the man, come alive. Washington, Lincoln, Columbus, and Franklin are all subjects of picture book biographies by the d'Aulaires which are available again in paperback. Those who enjoy the d'Aulaires' book of Franklin will be able to read the Dell Yearling original paperback by Davidson, *The Story of Benjamin Franklin, Amazing American!* Meltzer's *Benjamin Franklin: The New American* is for the intermediate and middle school readers. Greene's *Benjamin Franklin: A Man with Many Jobs* can be read by second and third grade students. Fritz's *What's the Big Idea, Ben Franklin?* is still a favorite. Other biographies by Fritz include: *Where Do You Think You're Going, Christopher Columbus?*; *And Then What Happened, Paul Revere?*; *Brendan the Navigator*; *Can't You Make Them Behave, King George?*; *George Washington's Breakfast*; *The Great Little Madison*; *Stonewall*; *Traitor: The Case of Benedict Arnold*; *Where Was Patrick Henry on the 29th of May?*; *Why Don't You Get a Horse, Sam Adams?*; *Will You Sign Here, John Hancock?* and *Bully for You, Teddy Roosevelt*. Cassettes are available for the books about Revere, King George, Franklin, Columbus, Henry, Adams, Hancock and *Who's That Stepping on Plymouth Rock?*

Reische's *Patrick Henry* includes sources and can be used in conjunction with Fritz's book. A filmstrip is available for Carmer's book, *The Pirate Hero of New Orleans*, in which Jean Lafitte's life is told in verse. Hilton's *The World of Young Herbert Hoover* is about a Quaker boy from Iowa who became our 31st president. *Robert E. Lee, Brave Leader* by Baines is an easy biography that is available as a hardcover/cassette read-along. The Civil War is covered only briefly and focus is on Lee's early years. Lawlor's *Daniel Boone* will be popular for writing reports. Le Sueur's *Little Brother of the Wilderness: The Story of Johnny Appleseed* is a biography of a man and a myth.

Scientists, inventors, and artists have contributed to the history of the world. Da Vinci was probably the most talented person in all three fields of all time. The Provensens' *Leonardo da Vinci: The Artist, Inventor, Scientist in Three-Dimensional Movable Pictures* is an oversize book that shows his inventions in pop-up fashion. The *Mona Lisa* and anatomical drawings are only two of the things shared. Ventura's *Michelangelo's World* is told from the viewpoint of the great artist. Cobb's *Truth on Trial: The Story of Galileo Galilei* includes Galileo's support of the Copernican theory in the face of the danger from the Inquisition. Invented dialogue is part of this biography and the focus is on his accomplishments, not his personality. The fact that Lavoisier was also persecuted and beheaded during the French Revolution explains the title of Grey's book, *The Chemist Who Lost His Head*. Grey tells of Lavoisier's discoveries, devotion to science, and enjoyment of the good life. Kumin's *The Microscope* is a biography in rhyme of Antoni van Leeuwenhoek. The discoverer of microorganisms was a contemporary of Rembrandt and Vermeer. Share this book when microscopes are introduced, or place it in a display with a microscope. *Secret in a Sealed Bottle: Lazzaro Spallanzani's Work with Microbes* is by the Epsteins. The 18th-century scientist studied natural history but had to support himself as a professor of Latin, Greek, and mathematics. Introduce collective biographies of scientists with students by sharing Aaseng's *The Disease Fighters: The Nobel Prize in Medicine*. *Dr. Beaumont and the Man with a Hole in His Stomach* by the Epsteins is about Dr. William Beaumont, who observed digestion by looking through a hole in the stomach of a patient who was shot on Mackinac Island, Michigan. Two sound filmstrips, now videos, which are appropriate for primary students are *Meet Tom Edison: The Boy Who Lit Up the World*, and *Wilbur and Orville: The First to Fly*. Lampton's *Werner von Braun* left Nazi Germany to become a U.S. citizen and helped to develop the American space program. Mitchell's *Click! A Story about George Eastman*, who invented the Kodak camera, is easy to read. Ben Franklin was both a statesman and an inventor, and new biographies include Greene's *Benjamin Franklin: A Man with Many Jobs* for primary students, and Meltzer's *Benjamin Franklin* and Sandak's *Benjamin Franklin* for intermediate students. *Carl Sagan: Superstar-Scientist* by Cohen is not only a well-known living scientist but an educator, writer, and activist. This biography should be mentioned whenever stars are studied. *Isaac Asimov: Scientist and Storyteller* by Erlanger is about an amazing man who is a scientist, nonfiction author and fiction writer. Point any student who has an interest in robotics in the direction of Erlanger's book. Fisher's *Walt Disney* could be of interest to anyone who knows Mickey Mouse or has been to Disneyland, Disney World, or EPCOT Center. Brenner's *On the Frontier with Mr. Audubon* comes from the journal of Audubon's apprentice when they studied birds along the Mississippi River for 18 months. Teachers can introduce the book when students are writing journals. Reading biographies can stimulate students to read other related nonfiction books. For example, students who read Girard's *Earth, Sea, and Sky: The Work of Edmond Halley* may also wish to read Branley's *Comets*, Krupp's *The Comet and You*, Petty's *Comets*, and Simon's *The Long Journey from Space*, to learn about comets in general and Halley's Comet in particular. A sound filmstrip, *Halley's Comet*, is also available.

Most of the biographies about women are about those who have been written about frequently, such as Pocahontas and Sacajawea (or Sacagawea).

Bull's *Florence Nightingale* is an excellent example. In it readers learn about the nurse's struggle with medical authorities. Steelsmith's *Elizabeth Blackwell: The Story of the First Woman Doctor*, is written as though it is an autobiography and Blackwell is telling her own story. Two books are available about Margaret Mead, anthropologist and author. Ludel's *Margaret Mead* focuses on her influence on the study of heredity and environment; Rice's *Margaret Mead: A Portrait* focuses more on her personal life.

Chadwick's *Anne Morrow Lindbergh: Pilot and Poet* is about a female pilot who broke records with her even more famous husband, Charles Lindbergh. The tragic kidnapping of their infant son is included. This book could also be used with a unit on authors and poets. Lindbergh wrote books for adults but one of her daughters, also named Anne, has written several children's books: *The People of Pineapple Place*, *The Prisoner of Pineapple Place*, and *The Worry Week*. Amelia Earhart was the world's most famous woman pilot, married a member of the Putnam publishing family, and is told about in Chadwick's *Amelia Earhart: Aviation Pioneer*. The books on Lindbergh and Earhart can both be used in conjunction with American history studies of the 1930s. Emerson's *Making Headlines: A Biography of Nellie Bly* is about Elizabeth Cochrane, a journalist and reformer, who flew around the world in an attempt to beat Phineas Fogg's fictional record found in Verne's *Around the World in 80 Days*. *To Space and Back* by Sally Ride is a photographic essay that deals with what the astronauts do in the space shuttle from blastoff to touchdown. Ride, the first female astronaut, is an excellent role model for girls. This book is located with other nonfiction books about space flight but can also be placed in the biography section. For more biographies of women in space, consult a section of this book called EXPLORING SPACE FLIGHT THROUGH NONFICTION.

Women have made important and documented political and historical contributions. Adler's *Our Golda: The Story of Golda Meir* is about the American woman of Russian descent who became the prime minister of Israel. The book focuses on her life before becoming prime minister. Faber's *Margaret Thatcher: Britain's "Iron Lady"* is from the same series, "Women of Our Time." Most of those books are also available in paperback editions for late primary and intermediate grade readers. Two biographies of Indira Gandhi are available for middle school students: Fishlock's *Indira Gandhi* and Currimbhoy's *Indira Gandhi*. Leigh's *Mother Teresa* is another biography of a woman of modern India. Faber's *Eleanor Roosevelt: First Lady of the World* emphasizes her early years of political activities. There are two new biographies of Juliette Gordon Low, founder of the Girl Scouts: *Juliet Low: Founder of the Girl Scouts in America* by Behrens; and *Juliet Gordon Low: America's First Girl Scout* by Kudlinski. Brower's *Baden-Powell: Founder of the Boy Scouts* is a companion book. Two new biographies of Helen Keller are available: Hunter's *Helen Keller* and Wepman's *Helen Keller*. Wepman's biography is for middle and high school students. Keller is just one among other women in Fradin's *Remarkable Children: Twenty Who Made History*. After hearing traditionally about Crockett, Bowie, and Travis at the Alamo, we now have a heroine of the Alamo: a Texas woman and her child Angelina were survivors and the story appears in *Susanna of the Alamo* by Jakes. Susanna was responsible for telling Sam Houston what Santa Anna had done. Brown's *Belva Lockwood Wins Her Case* is about a 19th-century lawyer, activist, and presidential candidate who worked for equal rights for women. Levinson's *I Lift My Lamp: Emma Lazarus and the Statue of Liberty* shares the poet's concern for immigrants. Turner's biography *Mary Queen of Scots* can be paired with Uttley's *Traveler in Time*, a time travel fantasy that involves Mary Queen of Scots. Two women appear in Levine's *Secret Missions: Four True Life Stories*: "Lydia Darragh: Revolutionary Quaker Housewife and Spy," pages 1–24, and "Leesha Bos: Nazi Fighter," pages 89–116. For biographies about Anne Frank, consult the section of this book called THE HOLOCAUST: A BOOKTALK.

Some recent biographies of women who have made a contribution to the arts are Dorothea Lange, Grandma Moses, and Lena Horne. Meltzer's *Dorothea Lange: Life Through the Camera* is about a famous photographer. O'Neill's *Grandma Moses: Painter of Rural America* is about Anna Mary Moses who gained fame in her older years. *Lena Horne*, by Haskins, is for middle school students and above. Horne's political as well as musical activities are included. *Shirley Temple Black* by Haskins is available in a paperback edition.

Two books about the 11-year-old girl who corresponded with Andropov and then visited the USSR are Galicich's *Samantha Smith: A Journey for Peace* and *Journey to the Soviet Union*, an autobiography. Gish's *An Actor's Life for Me!* is told from the child's point of view to a writer named Lanes. Gish tells of her life in vaudeville and silent films.

Some of the biographical material on women is available as multimedia. *Harriet Tubman/Thomas Jefferson* is a cassette/paperback set that contains a cassette and eight paperbacks per person. Two tapes are worthy of mention: *Women of Courage: Libby Riddles* and *Women of Courage: Ida Lewis*. Riddles is the first woman to win the Iditarod Trail Sled Dog Race from Anchorage to Nome, Alaska. Lewis is famous for saving 18 people, including four whom she saved when she was 14, during her 50 years as a lighthouse keeper at Lime Rock Lighthouse. Two easy books share a similar story: Olson's *Lighthouse Keeper's Daughter* and the Roops's *Keep the Lights Burning, Abbie*. The second title is available as a paperback/cassette package.

Biographies of Washington, Lincoln, Teddy Roosevelt, and Thomas Jefferson appear in Volume 2 of this book in a section called SCULPTURE IN STONE AND CLAY. Biographies of Lincoln, Washington, and Martin Luther King appear there too, in a section called POEMS INTRODUCE BIOGRAPHIES. On the lighter side, there is Adler's *Remember Betsy Floss and Other Constitutional Colonial Riddles*. That collection includes riddles about Paul Revere, George Washington, Ben Franklin, Thomas Jefferson, and Betsy Ross.

Biographies of musicians appear in Volume 2 of *More Creative Uses of*

Children's Literature in a section called BIOGRAPHIES IN THE WORLD OF MUSIC. Biographies of artists appear there too, in sections called ART MASTERS and ILLUSTRATORS AND AUTHOR/ILLUSTRATORS OF CHILDREN'S BOOKS. Biographies of authors also appear in Chapter 3 of this volume, INTRODUCING BOOKS BY AUTHORS. Biographies of Louisa May Alcott and Laura Ingalls Wilder appear in a section of this book called INTRODUCING JO, CADDIE, AND LAURA.

INTRODUCING FICTION BY THEME, PLOT, SETTING, STYLE, AND CHARACTERS. Check pages 31–33 of Pilla's *Resources for Middle-Grade Reluctant Readers* for definitions of style, content, sentence structure, characterization, and format. *The Word Shop* is an instructional television series for primary students' use in the language arts. Helpful programs include: *Characters in Stories*; *Setting in Stories*; *Action in Stories*; *Structure in Stories*; and *Character Playing*. Check the section "Guidelines for Fiction" in England and Fasick's *Childview: Evaluating and Reviewing Materials for Children* for information about plot, pages 106–07; character, 107–09; and style, 109–12.

Several filmstrips are available which help explain the five components of fiction. The filmstrips can be viewed individually and students can complete the projects listed at the end or on the worksheets. Teachers using the whole language approach or a literature-based reading program will find the filmstrips helpful to show to a whole class. Be sure to have all the books mentioned in the filmstrips available to students; they will be motivated to read them after viewing the filmstrips. Use all five filmstrips in the set *Literature for Children, Series 9* (*Plot, Theme, Style, Setting,* and *Character*), as well as the filmstrip *Folktale Characters* from the set *Literature for Children, Series 8*, to introduce these concepts. A list of recommended books is included with each filmstrip that tells whether or not the book is available in paperback format. The list is useful also for identifying books about the four other components of fiction.

The two books featured in the filmstrip *Theme* are *Annie and the Old One* by Miles and *The Pushcart War* by Merrill. Theme is explained as the central idea about a universal concept or feeling. Books introduced in *Theme* are: Armstrong's *Sounder*; Paterson's *The Great Gilly Hopkins*; and Wojciechowska's *Shadow of a Bull*. Students learn to identify the central idea of the story, tell about the author's statement of that theme, and share their views of whether or not they think the theme is important and why.

The two books featured in the filmstrip *Plot* are *Get Out of Here, Philip Hall* by Greene and *How to Eat Fried Worms* by Rockwell. Babbitt's *Kneeknock Rise*, George's *Who Really Killed Cock Robin?*, and O'Brien's *Mrs. Frisby and the Rats of NIMH* are mentioned. Be sure to mention Greene's *Philip Hall Likes Me, I Reckon Maybe*. At the beginning of the filmstrip, Baum's *The Wizard of Oz* is dissected to illustrate the four elements of plot: the problem to solve; the rising action (complications); the climax (peak of interest and turning point); and ending (resolution).

The two books featured in the filmstrip *Setting* are *The Children of Green Knowe* by Boston and *The Midnight Fox* by Byars. Setting includes the time and place where the plot occurs. Other books introduced by the filmstrip include: Fritz's *Homesick*; George's *Julie of the Wolves*; and Neville's *It's Like This, Cat*. Fritz's book is the only one that is nonfiction because Fritz relates her own experiences in China as a girl. Setting can be introduced to primary students via the sound filmstrip *Exploring New Places* from the series *Literature for Children, Series 7B*. Books featured in the filmstrip include Taylor's *Henry Explores the Mountains* and Bemelmans's *Madeline*.

The description in the filmstrip *Style* shows style as the ways we express ourselves in everyday language and the way authors express themselves through their particular ways of using words and phrases. The two books featured in the filmstrip are *Humbug Mountain* by Fleischman and *White Archer* by Houston. Fleischman's style is shown as playful and Houston's style is affected by years spent with the Eskimos. Other books in which style (use of words and phrases) is identified include: Greene's *Beat the Turtle Drum*, conversational; O'Dell's *Sing Down the Moon*, simple and rhythmic; and Snyder's *Witches of Worm*, eerie and scary. A list of helpful words and projects is included in the guide. The filmstrip shows how style is related to other components of fiction—character, plot, setting, and theme.

The two books featured in the filmstrip *Character* are *Anastasia Krupnik* by Lowry and *Jennifer, Hecate, Macbeth, William McKinley, and Me, Elizabeth* by Konigsburg. Characterization is identified as the things you do, the way you look, ways you feel, places you go, things you say, and how you say them. Qualities that make up character are the sum of what we admire and don't admire in people, fictional or real, including their strong feelings and interesting actions. Descriptions of three other books are included in the filmstrip: Fitzgerald's *The Great Brain*; Paterson's *Bridge to Terabithia*; and Wier's *The Loner*.

Characters in folktales are less complicated and are often one dimensional in their representation of good or evil. The two books featured in the filmstrip *Folktale Characters* are *Jorinda and Joringel* by Grimm and *The Donkey Prince* by Craig. Check page 61 of Hancock and Hill's *Literature-Based Reading Programs at Work* for a checklist of 20 adjectives used to describe a character with spaces to check five various degrees of those descriptions which fit the characters. Huck et al. in *Children's Literature in the Elementary School* uses Paterson's *The Great Gilly Hopkins* as an example of an in-depth study of characterization on pages 663–64. Check page 90 of Galda's article "Teaching Higher Order Reading Skills with Literature: Intermediate Grades" from *Children's Literature in the Reading Program*, edited by Cullinan, for a chart of Gilly's character. The chart is based on an idea from Butler and Turbill's *Towards a Reading-Writing Classroom*. "Inferring Character Traits" and "Getting to Know a Character in a Book" appear on pages 89 and 101–03 of Galda's article using characters in Paterson's *The Great Gilly Hopkins* and Mac-

Lachlan's *Sarah, Plain and Tall*. Use the sound filmstrip *Scary Stories* from the series *Literature for Children, Series 7C* to share character and plot. Books discussed include Mayer's *Terrible Troll* and Galdone's *King of the Cats*.

Students can learn about characters from what the author says about them, how the characters look, how the characters behave and think, what the characters say, and how other characters feel and talk about them. The best books require readers to think and deduce things about the characters from the information they are given. Readers learn that an orchestra is made up of individuals whose work is to play a variety of instruments together in Kuskin's *The Philharmonic Gets Dressed*. Readers learn that the 105 members of the orchestra are individuals from their actions—from the various ways they shower, bathe, shave, and put on their underwear. Orchestra members carry their instruments in cases of different shapes and sizes and arrive at the hall by several different modes of transportation. Orchestra members wear different types of outdoor garments but readers learn that in the end, all are dressed in black and white for their performance together. In Drescher's picture book, *My Mother's Getting Married*, Katy tells readers how she feels about living alone with her mother and the prospect of having Ben live with them. In Christelow's picture book, *The Robbery at the Diamond Dog Diner*, readers learn about Glenda Feathers from her words and her actions. Glenda rushes to the diner to tell her friends Lola and Harry that diamond robbers are on the loose, and suggests that they hide the diamonds in the eggs in the refrigerator. However, Glenda boasts that the robbers will not find out where in the refrigerator the diamonds are, so the robbers, who are listening, take Glenda and the refrigerator. Readers have to deduce that Glenda is helpful, thoughtful of her friends, law abiding, enterprising in her scheme to hide the diamonds, and a boastful blabbermouth. Readers learn from Harry that hiding the diamonds in the eggs is not Glenda's first featherbrained idea. The robbers think Glenda is dumb, but Glenda thinks of a plan to trick them into returning to the diner while alerting her friends so the robbers can be captured. *The Robbery at the Diamond Dog Diner* is also available as a cassette/paperback package. In *Mitzi and the Terrible Tyrannosaurus Rex* by Williams, intermediate readers get differing views of Mitzi's little stepbrother Darwin who acts like a dinosaur. Mitzi thinks Darwin is spoiled, adults think Darwin is adorable and bright, and Darwin's 11-year-old brother, Frederick, thinks Darwin is as adorable as a rattlesnake. Intermediate readers can infer that the ferret Zucchini is curious, adventuresome, kind, from his escape and his interactions with Billy in Dana's *Zucchini*. Readers learn about 11-year-old Minna Pratt, her friend Lucas Ellerby, as well as their family and friends through dialogue and action in MacLachlan's *The Facts and Fictions of Minna Pratt*. Check the second to the last page of Lowry's *The One Hundredth Thing About Caroline* for her mother's reactions to Caroline. In Alexander's *Nadia the Willful*, readers can predict Nadia's character from the title. Readers learn about Nadia from what she says about her Bedouin brother who is lost to the desert. Although forbidden by her father, Sheik Tarik, to talk about Hamed's death, Nadia finds that talking about him helps her to remember him, keeps him with them, and helps the healing process. Intermediate-age readers can predict from the title of *The Not-Just-Anybody Family* by Byars that the Blossom family will be unusual. Byars shares perceptions of the Blossoms through how the characters behave, what they say, and how they look.

Readers of *The Blossoms Meet the Vulture Lady* by Byars learn about the characters in a variety of ways. Readers learn about Junior through his inventions. Readers learn about Mad Mary, the Vulture Lady, from her dialogue and actions on pages 7–9. Vern and Maggie watch Mad Mary on pages 20–21 and Pap tells about the Mary he has known since grade school on pages 21–23. Mary's actions are shown on pages 31–33 when she finds Junior caught in the coyote trap and takes him to her cave on pages 49–51, 59–61, 64–65. Later Junior learns about Mary by investigating her possessions in the cave, pages 81–83, and Junior and Mad Mary get to know each other through conversation, pages 97–101, 110–11, 114–15. The dog's reaction to Mary appears on pages 116–18 but the kids are scared of her long stick, pages 20–21, and many think she is a witch, page 23. A physical description of Mary appears on pages 24 and 31. Mary's eating habits, cooking, and attitude toward critters are given on page 22.

Simon learns about the father who has left home from his father's letters. On page 25 of *The Cybil War* by Byars, Simon says these letters were Robinson Crusoe descriptions of what he was eating and how he gathered wood and built fires and mended his clothes.

In Cleary's *Ramona Quimby, Age 8*, readers learn that Daddy is returning to college and Ramona is happy because he is happy. Ramona's attitude toward Willa Jean and Howie Kemp reflect their behavior as well as Ramona's feelings. Ramona believes her teacher thinks she is a nuisance and a showoff from something she mistakenly overhears. The behavior of Danny, the new boy on the bus, shows him to be a bully.

Garrigue's *The Eternal Spring of Mr. Ito* shares much information about Sara and Japanese-Canadian Mr. Ito, the gardener. Readers learn about Mr. Ito's old felt hat and his combination of Japanese and English on pages 3 and 4, his reverence for nature and family as he tells Sara how the pine tree was a gift from his father and will be a gift to his son; his service in World War I. Prejudice against the "Japs" after Pearl Harbor begins on pages 22–23 and continues through the people throwing rocks at their house on page 49, and the camps where the Itos and other Japanese are sent, pages 73, 123–25, and 147–58. The industriousness of the Ito family appears on pages 22–23, 57–58. After the family learns that David has been killed, Aunt Jean screams at Mr. Ito, calls him a "Jap" and asks him to leave. Later on page 63, Uncle Duncan destroys the bonsai trees. Sara's interaction with Mr. Ito in his cave appears on pages 112–20. The story of Mr. Ito's death is shared on page 153.

Books which have human characters in their titles appear in Chapter 2 of this volume in the section, INTRODUCING BOOKS BY TITLES: HUMAN CHARACTERS. Books which have animal characters in their titles are shared here in INTRODUCING BOOKS BY TITLES: ANIMAL CHARACTERS.

The Midnight Fox by Byars is seen through the eyes of the main character, a boy who watches the black fox catch a mouse. Check pages 62–65 for adjectives like "sharp pointed," used to describe the ears, and "graceful," used to describe the fox's movement. Verbs used to describe the foxlike movements include "stretches," "pauses," "watches," and "pounces."

Another set of filmstrips, English Composition for Children, Series 5, also explains the components of stories. The three stories which help to explain character in the filmstrip Developing a Character are: Stevenson's Treasure Island; Alcott's Little Women; and Shotwell's Roosevelt Grady. Vocabulary includes: character, individual, unique, and personality. Ideas for writing character sketches are included.

Other filmstrips in the series English Composition for Children, Series 5 further explain the components of a story. The filmstrip Elements of a Story defines and shows story elements (protagonist, antagonist, setting, conflict, climax, plot, and resolution) for Baum's The Wizard of Oz and a story about Robin Hood called "Shooting Match at Nottingham." A "Dial a Story" sheet is included so students can mix story elements at random. The filmstrip Creating a Beginning uses excerpts from Thurber's The Secret Life of Walter Mitty, Andersen's The Ugly Duckling, and the Grimm fairy tale, Little Red Riding Hood. This filmstrip stresses sensory description, creating a mood, and action as a "grabber" to catch the attention of the audience. Brown's picture book of the classic tale Dick Whittington and His Cat is the example used in the filmstrip Building a Conflict. The terms conflict, climax, and resolution are explained in the filmstrip and different kinds of endings are investigated.

INTRODUCING REALISTIC FICTION [CU 103–05]. Background information on realistic fiction, criteria for selecting it and Alcott's Little Women as a landmark in realistic fiction appears on pages 390–94 of Cullinan's Literature and the Child. A discussion of books in this category appears on pages 394–449 of Cullinan's book, broken down into the following types: growing up; peer relations; families (mothers, siblings); personal integrity; physical disabilities; laughter; courage; survival; aging; death; caring; mental and emotional disabilities (mental retardation and emotional disturbance); and learning disabilities. The types of realistic fiction listed on pages 89–108 of the Lindskoogs' How to Grow a Young Reader are: animal stories; historical fiction; contemporary life; adventure; mystery; and personal and social problems. Realistic fiction is defined on page 574 of Sutherland and Livingston's The Scott Foresman Anthology of Children's Literature. Selections from "Realistic Fiction: Life in the United States" begin on page 575 and "Realistic Fiction: Life in Other Lands" on pages 658–87. Chapter 9 of Children's Literature in the Elementary School by Huck et al. is "Contemporary Realistic Fiction" on pages 463–530. Values and issues relating to realistic fiction are discussed. Issues include: what is real?; how real may a child's book be?; sex-role stereotyping; the background of the author; and categorizing literature. The first section, "Becoming One's Own Person," is subdivided into living in a family, living with others, and growing toward maturity. Books in the living-in-a-family category include family relationships, extended families, families in transition, and foster children. Living with others includes finding peer acceptance and making friends. Growing toward maturity includes developing sexuality, finding one's self, and survival stories. The second section, "Coping with Problems of the Human Condition," includes physical disabilities, developmental disabilities, mental illness, aging, and death. The third section, "Living in a Pluralistic Society," discusses appreciating racial and ethnic diversity and includes guidelines for evaluating minority literature, African-American experiences in books for children, and books about other minorities which respect religious backgrounds, regional differences, and world cultures. The fourth section includes four types of realistic fiction: humorous stories, animal stories, sports stories, and mysteries. Chapter 9, pages 368–430 of Norton's *Through the Eyes of a Child: An Introduction to Children's Literature* is "Contemporary Realistic Fiction." Norton shares the following information about it: definition, how it has changed, criteria for evaluating, values, types of controversial issues surrounding it, and guidelines for selecting controversial fiction for children. Norton lists as types of realistic fiction for children: family life; family disturbances; interpersonal relationships; handicaps; aging; death; physical changes; emotional maturity; children as individuals; surviving unusual circumstances; animal stories; mysteries; sports stories; and humorous modern fiction. Check pages 99–100 of England and Fasick's *Childview: Evaluating and Reviewing Materials for Children* for information about realistic fiction. "Discussing Realistic Fiction," from page 65 of Chapter 6 of Cullinan's *Children's Literature in the Reading Program*, appears in Bishop's article "Extending Multicultural Understanding Through Children's Books."

Chapter 2, "Realistic Fiction with a Social Conscience," is just one of the chapters in *Shadow and Substance: Afro-American Experiences in Contemporary Children's Fiction* by Sims. Titles in this book provide an excellent guide for books about the African-American experience in America.

Use the filmstrip *Realistic Fiction* from the set *Literature for Children, Series 6* to introduce realistic fiction to students. Books introduced by the filmstrip include Burch's *Queenie Peavy*, Byars's *The TV Kid*, and Fitzhugh's *Harriet the Spy*. Viewers learn that settings and dialogue are similar to real life and that characters are a mixture of good and bad.

Three realistic fiction books which appear in *Literature to Enjoy and Write About, Series 1* on the sound filmstrip, *Diary-Journal, Realistic Fiction* are: *Dear Mr. Henshaw* by Cleary; *Where the Red Fern Grows* by Rawls; and *In the Year of the Boar and Jackie Robinson* by Lord.

Probably the most famous and most prolific of the writers of realistic fiction for children is Beverly Cleary. For a list of Cleary's books chosen for awards by children, check in Chapter 1 for BOOKTALKING: 118 AWARD-WINNING TITLES. Sixteen realistic fiction and four fantasy books by Cleary have been chosen by children to receive state awards. Two books by Cleary are Newbery Honor Books: *Ramona Quimby, Age 8* and *Ramona and Her Father. Dear Mr. Henshaw* is a Newbery Award winner. A list of books about Ramona appears in Volume 2 in a section called TOYS AND DOLLS. For biographical information about Cleary, check Chapter 3, INTRODUCING BOOKS BY AUTHORS. According to Cleary's biography, *A Girl From Yamhill: A Memoir,* one of the few realistic fiction books that was available to her when she was growing up was Rankin's *Dandelion Cottage*, set in Marquette, Michigan.

Judy Blume needs no introduction to students who want to read about contemporary realism. Six Blume books were chosen 19 times by children for awards and appear in Chapter 1, the section BOOKTALKING: 118 AWARD-WINNING TITLES. *Superfudge* was chosen by children about a dozen times and *Tales of a Fourth Grade Nothing* was chosen three times. Other Blume favorites include *Are You There God? It's Me, Margaret; Blubber; Deenie; Freckle Juice; It's Not the End of the World;* and *Starring Sally J. Freedman As Herself.* Information about Blume appears in *Something About the Author,* volumes 2 and 43, and in Fuller's *More Junior Authors.* A profile appears on page 401 of Cullinan's *Literature and the Child.* Lee's biography is *Judy Blume's Story.*

Jamie Gilson has written numerous books in the contemporary realism category. Children in four states picked *Thirteen Ways to Sink a Sub* as the winner of their state awards. *Thirteen Ways to Sink a Sub* is followed by *4-B Goes Wild.* A third book about Hobie is *Hobie Hanson, You're Weird.* Information about Gilson appears in Commire's *Something About the Author,* volumes 34 and 37, and Holtze's *Sixth Book of Junior Authors and Illustrators.*

Johanna Hurwitz has written a number of realistic fiction books that are included in this book in various sections. *Hot and Cold Summer* and *Aldo Ice Cream* were each chosen by children as the outstanding book of the year and *Baseball Fever* was an honor book. Other books include: *The Adventures of Ali Baba Bernstein; Aldo Applesauce; Cold and Hot Winter; DeDe Takes Charge; Hurricane Elaine;* and *Tough-Luck Karen.* Information about Hurwitz appears in *Something About the Author,* volume 20, and Holtze's *Sixth Book of Junior Authors and Illustrators.* "Lee Bennett Hopkins Interviews Johanna Hurwitz" is on page 206 of *Castles in the Sand,* the third grade basal from the SB/Ginn series edited by Pearson, et al. A selection called "The Recital" by Hurwitz appears on pages 196–205 of *Castles in the Sand.*

Betsy Byars has written over 15 books in the contemporary realism category. Check page 409 of Cullinan's *Literature and the Child* for a profile of her. Biographies of Byars appear in De Montreville and Hill's *Third Book of Junior Authors,* and volumes 4 and 6 of *Something About the Author.* A sound filmstrip called *Meet the Newbery Author: Betsy Byars* is available. *The Cybil*

War was chosen as a winner and an honor book, *Cracker Jackson* was chosen as a winner and an honor book, *Night Swimmers* was chosen as a winner, and *Pinballs* was chosen by children in three states as a winner and one state as an honor book. *Summer of the Swans* is a Newbery Award winner.

Katherine Paterson won the Newbery Medal twice—for *Bridge to Terabithia* and *Jacob Have I Loved*. *The Great Gilly Hopkins* is a Newbery Honor Book. Two of her books were chosen by children as the outstanding book of the year: *Bridge to Terabithia* and *The Great Gilly Hopkins*. Information about Paterson appears in *Something About the Author*, volume 13 and in Holtze's *Fifth Book of Junior Authors and Illustrators*.

Information about Blume, Byars, Cleary, and Paterson appears in the newest edition of Kirkpatrick's *Twentieth Century Children's Writers*.

Instructional television can be used to introduce books of contemporary realism. Programs #3 and #4 of *More Books from Cover to Cover* introduce fifth graders to *Won't Know Till I Get There* by Myers and *The Agony of Alice* by Naylor. Fourteen-year-old Stephen Perry's family adopts 12-year-old Earl Goins, who has a police record that includes armed robbery, in the book by Myers. Eleven-year-old Alice McKinley moves and decides to adopt a mother because her own died when she was four. Alice is assigned to unattractive Mrs. Plotkin's class when she would rather be in Miss Cole's class. However, through the year, Alice gets to know her teacher better and on the last day, Mrs. Plotkin gives Alice a ring that belonged to her great-grandmother that she had planned to give to a daughter she never had. Getting her period and a bra are highlights of Alice's sixth grade year.

After reading a book aloud to the class, or after the class reads a book in the contemporary realism genre, the librarian or teacher can give a booktalk about some of these books. The booktalk will help students to make their choices based on the theme of the book. Many of these books can be explained by the title. For more information about introducing books by title, consult Chapter 2 of this book.

Some titles of contemporary realism that appear elsewhere in this book include: Aronsky's *Gray Boy*; Avi's *Romeo and Juliet—Together (and Alive!) at Last*; Bates's *Thatcher Payne-in-the Neck*; Bauer's *On My Honor*; Blume's *Are You There, God? It's Me, Margaret*; *Blubber*; *Deenie*; *Freckle Juice*; *Iggie's House*; *It's Not the End of the World*, *Otherwise Known as Sheila the Great*, *Starring Sally J. Freedman as Herself*, *Superfudge*, *Tales of a Fourth Grade Nothing*, *Then Again, Maybe I Won't*, and *Tiger Eyes*; Bograd's *Poor Gertie*; Boyd's *Charlie Pippin*; Branscum's *Johnny May*, *Johnny May Grows Up*, and *The Adventures of Johnny May*; Bridgers's *Notes for Another Life*; Bulla's *Shoeshine Girl*; Bunting's *Karen Kepplewhite is the World's Best Kisser* and *Sixth Grade Sleepover*; Burch's *Queenie Peavy*; Byars's *The Burning Questions of Bingo Brown*, *Cracker Jackson*, *The Computer Nut*, *The Cybil War*, *The Eighteenth Emergency*, *The Midnight Fox*, *Pinballs*, *Summer of the Swans*, *The TV Kid*, *The Not-Just-Anybody Family*, *A Blossom Promise*, *The Blossoms and the Green Phantom,* and *The Blossoms Meet the Vulture Lady;* Carris's *When the Boys Ran the House;* Cassedy's *M. E. and Morton;* Cleary's *Dear Mr. Henshaw, Henry and Beezus, Henry Huggins, Ramona Forever, Ramona and Her Father, Ramona and Her Mother, Ramona Quimby, Age 8, Ramona the Brave,* and *Ramona the Pest;* Cleaver's *Sugar Blue;* Clifford's *Harvey's Marvelous Monkey Mystery* and *Harvey's Horrible Snake Disaster;* Clymer's *My Mother Is the Smartest Woman in the World;* Cole's *The Goats;* Conford's *Hail, Hail Camp Timberwood, Lenny Kandell, Smart Aleck;* Cresswell's *Absolute Zero, Bagthorpes Abroad, Bagthorpes Haunted, Bagthorpes Unlimited, Bagthorpes vs. the World,* and *Ordinary Jack;* Danziger's *The Cat Ate My Gymsuit;* DeClements's *Nothing's Fair in Fifth Grade* and *Sixth Grade Can Really Kill You;* Delton's *Angel in Charge, Angel's Mother's Boyfriend,* and *Angel's Mother's Wedding;* Fitzhugh's *Harriet the Spy;* Fisher's *Rachel Vellars, How Could You?;* Fox's *The One-Eyed Cat* and *Lily and the Lost Boy;* George's *Julie of the Wolves, My Side of the Mountain, The Talking Earth, Water Sky,* and *Who Really Killed Cock Robin?;* Gilson's *Can't Catch Me, I'm the Gingerbread Man, Do Bananas Chew Gum?, 4-B Goes Wild, Harvey the Beer Can King, Hello, My Name is Scrambled Eggs, Hobie Hanson, Hobie Hanson, You're Weird,* and *Thirteen Ways to Sink a Sub;* Greene's *Al(exander) the Great, A Girl Called Al, I Know You, Al, Just Plain Al, Isabelle the Itch, Isabelle Shows Her Stuff, Get Out of Here, Philip Hall, Philip Hall Likes Me, I Reckon Maybe;* Greenwald's *Alvin Webster's Sure Fire Plan for Success (and How It Failed, Give Us a Great Big Smile, Rosy Cole, Rosy Cole's Great American Guilt Club, Valentine Rosy,* and *Will the Real Gertrude Hollings Please Stand Up?;* Hahn's *Daphne's Book* and *Tallahassee Higgins;* Hermes's *Kevin Corbett Eats Flies;* Hall's *In Trouble Again, Zelda Hammersmith?* and *The Rose Behind the Wall;* Haynes's *The Great Mom Swap;* Holland's *Prisoners at the Kitchen Table or Run for Your Life;* Hurwitz's *Aldo Applesauce, Aldo Ice Cream, Much Ado About Aldo, The Adventures of Ali Baba Bernstein, Baseball Fever, Class Clown, Cold and Hot Winter, DeDe Takes Charge, Hot and Cold Summer, Hurricane Elaine, Rip-Roaring Russell, Russell Rides Again, Russell Sprouts, Teacher's Pet,* and *Tough-Luck Karen;* Jones's *Angie and Me, Germy Blew It,* and *Germy Blew It Again;* Jukes's *Blackberries in the Dark;* Kaye's *Cassie, Daphne, Lydia,* and *Phoebe;* Klein's *Hating Alison Ashley;* S. Kline's *Herbie Jones, Herbie Jones and the Monster Ball, Herbie Jones and the Class Gift,* and *What's the Matter with Herbie Jones?;* Konigsburg's *Jennifer, Hecate, Macbeth, William McKinley, and Me, Elizabeth;* Little's *Mama's Going to Buy You a Mockingbird;* Lord's *In the Year of the Boar and Jackie Robinson;* Lowry's *Anastasia Again!, Anastasia's Chosen Career, Anastasia, Ask Your Analyst, Anastasia at Your Service, Anastasia Has the Answers, Anastasia Krupnik, Anastasia on Her Own, The One Hundreth Thing About Caroline, Rabble Starkey, Switcharound,* and *Taking Care of Terrific;* McDonnell's *Just for the Summer;* MacLachlan's *The Facts and Fictions of Minna Pratt;* Manes's *Be a Perfect Person in Just Three Days!*; Mauser's *A Bundle of Sticks*; Mazer's *After the Rain*; Miles's *The Secret Life of the Underwear Champ*; Mills's *The One and Only Cynthia Jane Thornton*; Morrison's *Whisper Goodbye*; Myers's *Me, Mop, and the Moondance Kid* and *The Scorpions*; Nathanson's *The Trouble with Wednesdays*; Neville's *It's Like This, Cat*; O'Dell's *Black Star, Bright Dawn*; Park's *Skinnybones* and *Almost Starring Skinnybones*; Pascal's *Hand-Me Down Kid*; Paterson's *Bridge to Terabithia, Come Sing, Jimmy Jo, The Great Gilly Hopkins, Jacob Have I Loved,* and *Park's Quest*; Rawls's *Where the Red Fern Grows*; Roberts's *Don't Hurt Laurie*; Riley's *Only My Mouth Is Smiling* and *Crazy Quilt*; Robertson's *Henry Reed's Think Tank*; Robinson's *The Best Christmas Pageant Ever*; Robinson's *My Brother Louis Measures Worms*; Rockwell's *How to Eat Fried Worms* and *How to Fight a Girl*; Ruckman's *Night of the Twisters*; Sachs's *The Bear's House* and *Fran Ellen's House*; Sachar's *Sixth Grade Secrets*; Shreve's *The Flunking of Joshua Bates* and *Lucy Forever and Miss Rosetree, Shrinks*; Shura's *Don't Call Me Toad, The Josie Gambit,* and *The Search for Grissi*; Shyer's *Welcome Home, Jellybean*; D. Smith's *A Taste of Blackberries*; R. Smith's *Jelly Belly, Mostly Michael,* and *The War with Grandpa*; Snyder's *And Condors Danced, The Egypt Game, Blair's Nightmare, The Famous Stanley Kidnapping Case,* and *The Headless Cupid*; Steiner's *Oliver Dibbs and the Dinosaur Cause* and *Oliver Dibbs to the Rescue!*; Stolz's *The Bully of Barkham Street, The Dog on Barkham Street,* and *The Explorer of Barkham Street*; Talbert's *Toby*; Taylor's *The Trouble with Tuck*; Thiele's *Shadow Shark* and *Storm Boy*; Thomas's *The Comeback Dog*; Ullman's *Banner in the Sky*; Voigt's *Dicey's Song, Homecoming, A Solitary Blue,* and *Izzy, Willy-Nilly*; Wallace's *A Dog Called Kitty*; Williams's *Mitzi and the Terrible Tyrannosaurus Rex*; Wojciechowska's *Shadow of a Bull*; and Yep's *Child of the Owl*.

● **Facing Problems in Everyday Life Through Fiction and Nonfiction.** Fiction, as well as nonfiction books, can help children to cope with problems in their daily lives. While nonfiction provides facts and possible solutions, fiction puts readers in touch with others who have faced the same problem. Through fiction, readers can learn that they are not alone and that others with the same problem have survived. Cuddigan and Hanson's *Growing Pains: Helping Children Deal with Everyday Problems Through Reading* provides titles on many subjects including moving, death of a pet, child abuse, loneliness, foster families, lying, divorce, and others. Bernstein's *Books to Help Children Cope with Separation and Loss* includes books about death, divorce, stepparents, and war. Check several editions of Dreyer's *Bookfinder* under: adoption, blame, boasting, bully, children's home, death, divorce, drugs, family, friendship, guilt, harassment, identity, jealousy, loss, moving, peer relationships, stepparent, stepbrother/stepsister, stealing, shoplifting, sports, suicide, teasing, and others.

A variety of problems that face children are addressed in children's books.

Vigna's *I Wish Daddy Didn't Drink So Much* is a story for primary children about alcohol abuse. Adler's *In Our House, Scott Is My Brother*, for intermediate students, is about Jodi's stepmother who drinks and her stepbrother who shoplifts. Rules about keys and not opening doors to strangers are woven unobtrusively into Stanek's *All Alone After School*. A young child runs away in Johnson's *Today I Thought I'd Run Away*. The reason why he wants to run away is overshadowed by his having to pull tricks out of a bag which help him escape the ogre, dragon, demon, and monster he encounters along the way. Cheating is addressed in Brown's *The True Francine*. Francine is upset when her friend Muffy lets her take the blame for cheating on a test. Francine misses softball practice for the big game between the third grades until Muffy confesses. Arnie the cat wants both candy and markers so he steals the markers in Carlson's *Arnie and the Stolen Markers*. In Brown's *Arthur's Christmas*, D.W. selfishly thinks of presents for herself while Arthur is concerned about giving a gift to Santa.

Areas of concern are very different for different children at different ages. Small children may be concerned about going to day care and middle students may be preoccupied with new braces. Bethancourt's *Smile! How to Cope with Braces* and the Silversteins's *So You're Getting Braces* help preteens and teens cope with braces. *Going to Day Care* by Mr. Rogers prepares children for the day care experience. Leiner's *Both My Parents Work* contains interviews with 10 children ranging from a 5-year-old girl to a 13-year-old boy about how their families operate because both parents work.

Child abuse appears in children's books for students in intermediate grades and above. One of the topics covered in Cuddigan and Hanson's *Growing Pains: Helping Children Deal with Everyday Problems Through Reading* is child abuse. Books about dealing with abuse are Haskins's *The Child Abuse Help Book*; Terkel's *Feeling Safe, Feeling Strong: How to Avoid Sexual Abuse and What to Do If It Happens to You*; Dolan's *Child Abuse*; and Hyde's *Sexual Abuse: Let's Talk About It*. Two books that deal with causes and results of child abuse are Hyde's *Cry Softly! The Story of Child Abuse*, and Landau's *Child Abuse, An American Epidemic*. Parents will be interested in Hart-Rossi's *Protect Your Child from Sexual Abuse: A Parent's Guide*. Child abuse appears as a theme in several books for intermediate students. In *Cracker Jackson* by Byars, Cracker's former baby sitter, Alma, is married to a mechanic who beats her. Alma finally realizes she must fight her husband when he abuses their child. In *Don't Hurt Laurie* by Roberts, Laurie is abused by her mother. A sixth grade girl is abused by her dentist in Nathanson's *The Trouble with Wednesdays*. Eleven-year-old Megan's riding instructor molests her and asks her not to tell in Polese's *Promise Not to Tell*. Four short stories about children who have been inappropriately touched appear in Wacher's *No More Secrets for Me*.

Nonfiction books for primary children about sexual abuse include Anderson's *Margaret's Story: Sexual Abuse and Going to Court*; Freeman's *It's My*

Body!; Girard's *My Body Is Private*; and Kehoe's *Something Happened and I'm Scared to Tell: A Book for Young Children*. Puppets are used to share feelings of children who are touched in private parts in the video *Some Secrets Should be Told*.

There are several nonfiction books about avoiding strangers and child abuse for primary children. Girard's *Who Is a Stranger and What Should I Do?* gives rules for dealing with people they do not know. *Robin's Story: Physical Abuse and Seeing the Doctor* and *Michael's Story: Emotional Abuse and Working with a Counselor* are both by Anderson and Finne.

One problem that faces a large percentage of American children is learning to cope with divorce. Nonfiction exists on the topic of divorce for primary students. Stein's *On Divorce: An Open Family Book for Parents and Children Together* has two texts on each page. One text is for children to read and the other information in the left margin is for adults. The consultant for the book is a psychologist. Emotions caused by divorce, including sadness, fear, anger, alienation, and confusion, are addressed in Sinberg's *Divorce Is a Grown Up Problem*. Two books which have been helpful for primary students for some time are Grollman's *Talking About Divorce and Separation* and Hazen's *Two Homes to Live In: A Child's Eye View of Divorce*. A cartoon animated video called *Divorce Can Happen to the Nicest People* is for children ages 5 to 10. Mayle's *Why Are We Getting a Divorce?* replaces *Divorce Can Happen to the Nicest People*. The best book for children from kindergarten through grades three and four is Brown's *Dinosaurs Divorce*. Professionals can comfortably recommend this book for parents to give to their children and the paperback edition makes it even more accessible. Advice from pediatricians, child and adult psychiatrists, clinical and social workers has gone into this book, which is in cartoon form and features a dinosaur family. Information includes why parents divorce, living with one and visiting another, learning to live in two homes, problems at holiday times, friends of parents, and stepparents and stepbrothers and sisters. Coming to terms with one's own feelings is the primary purpose of *Dinosaurs Divorce*, which is also available in sound filmstrip format. The poem "Daddy's Gone" is on page 13 of Livingston's *Poems for Father*.

Divorce is a theme in numerous picture books. The parents in Girard's *At Daddy's on Saturdays* are supportive and both love Katie. The story is told from Katie's point of view, beginning when her father moves out and ending several months later after they have made adjustments. In Baum's *One More Time*, Simon and his dad are on an outing Sunday afternoon and they sail a boat in the park. They take the train home and Simon is left with his mother but wishes to prolong the visitation. In Boyd's *The Not-So-Wicked Stepmother*, Hessie dreads spending the summer with her father and his new wife, but after she gets to know Molly, she cannot resist her friendly stepmother. Two books by Dragonwagon are *Always, Always* and *Diana, Maybe*. *Always, Always* is told in the first person about a little girl who lives with her mother in New York City in the fall, winter, and spring and with her father in Colorado in the summer. The contrasts in location and lifestyle are recognizable, although sub-tle. *Diana, Maybe* is about Rosie who imagines what her unknown older half sister Diana must be like and what fun they might have together if they ever meet. In Vigna's *Mommy and Me by Ourselves Again* a little girl misses her mother's ex-boyfriend. *Splitting Up* by Petty and Kopper is about Sam's friend, Maria, who is unhappy because her parents fight and then separate. Changes in holidays after a divorce cause mental anguish and are depicted in two picture books. In Pomerantz's *Who Will Lead Kiddush?*, Debbie remembers when her father led the family celebration. Vigna's *Grandma Without Me* is a first-person story about a little boy who is having a first Thanksgiving without his paternal grandmother.

There are a number of nonfiction books about divorce for intermediate students. Gardner's *The Boys and Girls Book About Divorce*, a pioneer in the field of nonfiction, is still available in hardback and paperback editions. Kre-mentz's photo essay *How It Feels When Parents Divorce* shows 19 boys and girls from age 7 to 16 who share their feelings about divorce and tell about various patterns of living, including joint custody. A few African-American, Jewish, and Puerto Rican children are included. The only drawback to this excellent and highly recommended book is that in most cases both parents want the child and this is not always the case. Chapter 1 of Nickman's *When Mom and Dad Divorce* is about 10-year-old Sam. Other chapters include fighting, talking it out, stepfamilies, what children and adults can do about the situation, and suicidal tendencies. A black father and child are shown. Le Shan offers advice to children in *What's Going to Happen to Me? When Parents Separate or Divorce*. Nonrepression of feelings is part of LeShan's advice. Books for middle school students include Friedrich's *Divorce*, which tells about laws and attitudes toward marriage and divorce and their impact on children. Boeck-man's *Surviving Your Parents' Divorce* includes a last chapter of names and addresses of organizations that help children involved with family problems caused by alcohol, abuse, and mental illness. *Do Children Also Divorce?* is a live-action video which shows the effects of divorce on three children with information about how parents can best handle divorce. *Dad's House, Mom's House* is a 16mm film or video which discusses joint custody. A 16mm film or video, *Tender Places*, is a drama in which a 10-year-old actor shares his emo-tions about divorce and remarriage. *The Way It Is: After the Divorce* is a 16mm film which shows how different family members cope with the trauma.

A number of fiction books for intermediate students are about children who know divorce or desertion: Bates's *Thatcher Payne-in-the-Neck*; Byars's *The Animal, the Vegetable, and John J. Jones*; Byars's *Cybil War*; Carrick's *What a Wimp*; Cleary's *Dear Mr. Henshaw*; Dana's *Zucchini*; Danziger's *Divorce Express* and sequel *It's an Aardvark-Eat-Turtle World*; Fine's *My War with Goggle-Eyes*; Fisher's *Radio Robert*; Fisher's *Rachel Vellars, How Could You?*; Giff's *Rat Teeth*; Howe's *Morgan's Zoo*; Hurwitz's *DeDe Takes Charge*; Lindbergh's *People of Pineapple Place*; Lowry's *Rabble Starkey*;

Lowry's *Switcharound*; Park's *Playing Beatie Bow*; Paulsen's *Hatchet*; Pevsner's *Sister of the Quints*; Voigt's *Solitary Blue*; and Wright's *Secret Window*. Blume's *It's Not the End of the World* is a program from the reading motivation instructional television series, *Storybound*. Eleven books and 22 questions about fiction books that include divorce appear in the index on page 223 of Greenson and Taha's *Name That Book! Questions and Answers on Outstanding Children's Books*.

Getting along with stepparents and stepbrothers and sisters appears in nonfiction. Books for primary students include: Berman's *What Am I Doing in a Step-Family?*; Helmering's *I Have Two Families*; and Sobol's *My Other-Mother, My Other-Father*.

Hyde's *My Friend Has Four Parents* is for students in intermediate grades and above. *Stepdancing: Portrait of a Remarried Family* is a 16mm film and video about 11-year-old Oliver who has two families. Oliver lives in Toronto with his mother, brother, and stepfather and in New Hampshire with his father, stepmother, and half brothers. *The Boys and Girls Book About Stepfamilies* is by Gardner. Getzoff and McClenahan's *Stepkids: A Survival Guide for Teenagers in Stepfamilies* is for older students. Books about various family patterns include: Drescher's *Your Family, My Family*; Gilbert's *How to Live with a Single Parent*; Simon's *All Kinds of Families*; Tax's *Families*; and Thomas's *Free to Be . . . a Family*. *The Kids' Book About Parents by Students at Fayerweather Street School* by Rofes is a companion book to *The Kids' Book of Divorce*, in which students describe relationships from their point of view. In Drescher's picture book, *My Mother's Getting Married*, Kathy is afraid her mother won't love her as much after she marries Ben. Vigna shows jealousy of a baby stepsister in *Daddy's New Baby*. Ten-year-old Alex's mother and stepfather are expecting a baby in *Like Jake and Me* by Jukes, also available in film and video formats. Alex and his stepfather, Jake, learn to understand each other. A variety of family patterns is shown in two filmstrips called *Families*, which is for preschoolers through first graders. Lisa describes the people in the neighborhood to a newcomer in the film and video *Families Are Different and Alike*. A variety of lifestyles, family compositions, and ethnic groups is represented.

Some fiction about stepfamilies for intermediate students include: Adler's *In Our House, Scott Is My Brother*; Delton's *Angel's Mother's Boyfriend*, *Angel's Mother's Wedding*, and *Angel's Mother's Baby*; Hahn's *Wait Till Helen Comes*; Mahy's *Aliens in the Family*; Oppenheimer's *Gardine vs. Hanover*; Roberts's *Don't Hurt Laurie*; and Williams's *Mitzi and the Terrible Tyrannosaurus Rex* . Six titles and a dozen questions about stepfamilies appear on page 245 in the index to Greenson and Taha's *Name That Book! Questions and Answers on Outstanding Children's Books*.

Some books for intermediate students about foster families include: Byars's *Pinballs*; Paterson's *The Great Gilly Hopkins*; Place's *The Boy Who Saw Bigfoot*; and Sachs's *Fran Ellen's House*.

There are a number of books about adoption. The common theme in Rosenberg's *Being Adopted* is that the children were given up through no fault of their own. Ancona's photos of Korean and Indian children enhance Rosenberg's book. Interviews with 14 adopted children appear in Rosenberg's *Growing Up Adopted*. Sobol's *We Don't Look Like Our Mom and Dad* is a photo essay about two adopted Korean children. Jim tells about the new Korean baby that is coming into his family in Fisher's *Katie-Bo: An Adoption Story*. Seven-year-old Sarah is concerned about her own adoption circumstances when she learns that her parents are adopting another baby in Greenberg's *Adopted*. In Girard's *Adoption Is for Always*, primary student Celia has a variety of questions and emotions about her adoption. *Sesame Street*'s Susan and Gordon adopt a baby in Freudberg and Geiss's *Susan and Gordon Adopt a Baby*. Kremetz's *How It Feels to Be Adopted* is a photo essay in which 19 children ranging in age from 8 to 16 each discuss feelings about being adopted. Angel and her brother are adopted by their stepfather in Delton's *Angel's Mother's Wedding*.

Moving is a traumatic experience that appears as a theme in children's books. *Moving*, by Mr. Rogers, can help to ease the stress of moving for preschool children. Color photographs show a 3-year-old boy helping to pack some of his things and explains why people move, why adults seem cranky, sad, and busy at moving time; and holds out the prospect of new friends. A companion book in the First Experiences series is *Making Friends*. In Asch's *Goodbye House*, baby bear says goodbye to all his favorite places before he moves. Rhody's grandma is sad because they must move in Greenfield's *Grandma's Joy*. Rhody is a black orphan who lives with her grandmother. Louie and Mary Ann have moved in Stevenson's *No Friends*, and they lament to Grandpa that their neighborhood is awful because they have not made any friends. Grandpa tells them his own miserable experience being a new boy long ago. When Peter moves away, Robert misses him and writes in Aliki's *We Are Best Friends*. Eventually Robert and Peter both meet new friends. Seven-year-old Simon projects his feelings about moving onto his younger sister Maggie in O'Donnell's *Maggie Doesn't Want to Move*. In Zolotow's *A Tiger Called Thomas*, Thomas is afraid his new neighbors won't like him, but when he goes trick or treating, people call him by name, even though he is wearing his tiger suit. Gus chronicles his move in a journal in Rabe's *A Smooth Move*. Anna is lonely in her new town until she starts to receive gifts from a secret friend in Tsutsui's *Anna's Secret Friend*. Right after she moves, Molly meets Miranda Marie next door, quarrels and makes up with her in Malone's *A Home*. Sharmat's *Gila Monsters Meet You at the Airport* is a featured book on the television series *Reading Rainbow* with a supporting book, also by Sharmat, *Mitchell Is Moving*. In Sharmat's first book, a New York City boy dreads moving to the West where he expects to see cactus, buffalo, and gila monsters. At the airport, he meets another boy who dreads moving to the East because he expects gangsters and snow. Ira's best friend Reggie is moving away in Waber's *Ira Says Goodbye,* a sequel to *Ira Sleeps Over.* Annie is going to move in Komaiko's *Annie Bananie* which is told in verse.

Intermediate students find solace in reading books about others who have moved: Adler's *Always and Forever* and Adler's *Eaton Stanley and the Mind Control Experiment;* Bacon's *Pip and Emma;* Blume's *Superfudge* and *Tiger Eyes;* Bulla's *The Chalk Box Kid;* DeClements's *Nothing's Fair in Fifth Grade;* Giff's *Sunny Side Up;* Greene's *Isabelle Shows Her Stuff;* Hahn's *Wait Till Helen Comes;* Hermes's *Kevin Corbett Eats Flies;* Hurwitz's *Tough-Luck Karen;* Johnson's *Bats on the Bedstead;* Lindbergh's *The People of Pineapple Place;* Little's *Lost and Found* and *Mama's Going to Buy You a Mockingbird;* Lowry's *Anastasia, Again!;* Nilsson's *If You Didn't Have Me;* O'Brien's *Mrs. Frisby and the Rats of NIMH;* O'Dell's *Zia;* Park's *The Kid in the Red Jacket;* Roberts's *Don't Hurt Laurie;* Shura's *The Josie Gambit* and *The Search for Grissi;* Slepian's *The Broccoli Tapes;* Slote's *Moving In;* Smith's *Return to Bitter Creek;* Ure's *You Two;* Wallace's *A Dog Called Kitty;* Walsh's *Gaffer Samson's Luck;* White's *Sweet Creek Holler;* and Wright's *Christina's Ghost.* Books about moving from place to place by wagon train appear in this Chapter in a section called "If You Like the *Little House* Books."

"Poem" by Hughes on page 94 of Janeczko's *Don't Forget to Fly* is about moving. "Since Hanna Moved Away" appears on page 54 of Viorst's *If I Were in Charge of the World and Other Worries: Poems for Children and Their Parents.*

INTRODUCING MYSTERIES [CU 132–39]. The following children's literature anthologies include information about mysteries: pages 136–37 of Cullinan's *Literature and the Child;* pages 403–05 of Norton's *Through the Eyes of a Child: An Introduction to Children's Literature;* and pages 640–43 of Stewig's *Children and Literature.* Introduce primary students to mysteries through two 15-minute instructional television programs called *Mystery Stories* and *Mystery Books,* from the series *The Word Shop.*

A sound filmstrip, *Mysteries,* from the set *Literature for Children, Series 6,* features two books, Snyder's *The Egypt Game* and Hamilton's *The House of Dies Drear,* and introduces Raskin's *The Westing Game,* Sobol's *Encyclopedia Brown,* and Bellairs's *The House with a Clock on Its Walls.* The elements of mystery that are discussed in the filmstrip include: spine-tingling words; danger; suspense; plots with puzzles; clues and false clues; eerie settings in dark places or haunted houses; suspicious characters; and mood. Use the bibliography at the end of the guide, as well as the books listed in the card catalog under "Mystery and Detective Stories," to provide the titles for a booktalk.

Mapping Mysteries, a sound filmstrip from the set *Literature to Enjoy and Write About, Series 1,* describes the concept of mapping a story. The models for story mapping are *The House with a Clock on Its Walls* by Bellairs and *Bunnicula* by Howe. A review of Raskin's *The Westing Game* is included in the filmstrip. *The Westing Game* is also available as a separate sound filmstrip.

Two mystery sleuths for middle graders have photographic memories. Encyclopedia Brown gets his nickname because he can remember encyclopedias full of knowledge, and Cam(era) Jansen gets her nickname because she remembers facts as if she has taken a picture of them. Adler's character Cam Jansen appears in numerous books: *Cam Jansen and the Mystery at the Monkey House*; *Cam Jansen and the Mystery of the Corn Popper*; *Cam Jansen and the Mystery of the Babe Ruth Baseball*; *Cam Jansen and the Mystery of the Carnival Prize*; *Cam Jansen and the Mystery of the Circus Clown*; *Cam Jansen and the Mystery of the Dinosaur Bones*; *Cam Jansen and the Mystery of Flight 54*; *Cam Jansen and the Mystery of the Gold Coins*; *Cam Jansen and the Mystery of the Monster Movie*; *Cam Jansen and the Mystery of the Stolen Diamonds*; *Cam Jansen and the Mystery of the Television Dog*; and *Cam Jansen and the Mystery of the U.F.O.* Most of the books are in paperback for easy handling.

Begin a study about Encyclopedia Brown [CU 135–36] by viewing the sound filmstrip about Sobol—*The Case of the Model-A Ford and the Man in the Snorkel Under the Hand: Donald J. Sobol.* Use these materials with third graders who use the HBJ basal reader *Celebrations*, in the Laureate series by Cullinan, et al., in which "The Case of the Cave Drawings" appears on pages 114–21. Sobol's "The Case of the Whistling Ghost" appears on pages 208–17 of the Macmillan third grade basal reader, *Full Circle*, edited by Smith and Arnold. "The Case of the Missing Roller Skates" appears on pages 14–23 of Sebesta's fourth grade HBJ Odyssey basal reader, *Across Wide Fields.* Check pages 170–85 of volume 2, *Time to Read*, in the *Childcraft* set, for "Encyclopedia Brown."

The 17th book about the 10-year-old detective, *Encyclopedia Brown and the Case of the Treasure Hunt*, follows the same format as earlier ones. The first story explains how Encyclopedia Brown got his nickname, and how his police chief father relies on him to solve difficult cases at the dinner table. Although Encyclopedia Brown is joined by Sally Kimball in this book, Sally plays a minor role. Three of the 10 mysteries include "The Case of the Round Pizza," pages 9–15; "The Case of the Leaking Tent," pages 58–64; and "The Case of Bugs's Zebra," pages 16–22. Other titles about the boy detective include: *Encyclopedia Brown*; *Encyclopedia Brown and the Case of the Dead Eagles*; *Encyclopedia Brown and the Case of the Exploding Plumbing and Other Mysteries*; *Encyclopedia Brown and the Case of the Mysterious Handprints*; *Encyclopedia Brown and the Case of the Midnight Visitor*; *Encyclopedia Brown and the Case of the Secret Pitch*; *Encyclopedia Brown and the Case of the Treasure Hunt*; *Encyclopedia Brown, Boy Detective*; *Encyclopedia Brown Carries On*; *Encyclopedia Brown Finds the Clues*; *Encyclopedia Brown Gets His Man*; *Encyclopedia Brown Keeps the Peace*; *Encyclopedia Brown Lends a Hand*; *Encyclopedia Brown Sets the Pace*; *Encyclopedia*

Brown Shows the Way; *Encyclopedia Brown Solves Them All*; *Encyclopedia Brown Takes the Case*; and *Encyclopedia Brown Tracks Them Down*. *Encyclopedia Brown Takes the Cake: A Cook and Case Book* is by Sobol and Andrews. A set of books and cassettes, *Encyclopedia Brown Solves Them All*, contains *The Case of the Missing Clues*, *The Case of the Muscle Maker*, *The Case of Sir Biscuit-Shooter*, and *The Case of the Super-Secret Hold*. Cassette/paperback sets are available for the following titles: *The Best of Encyclopedia Brown: The Case of Natty Nat*; *The Case of the Hungry Hitchhiker*; *The Case of the Scattered Cards*; *The Case of the Whistling Ghost*; *The Case of the Missing Clues*; *The Case of Sir Biscuit-Shooter*; *The Case of the Muscle Maker*; *The Case of the Super-Secret Hold*; *The Case of Bugs Meany's Revenge*; *The Case of the Hidden Penny*; *The Case of the Mysterious Tramp*; and *The Case of the World Traveler*. *Encyclopedia Brown: The Boy Detective in Five E. B. Mysteries* and *Encyclopedia Brown: The Boy Detective in the Case of the Missing Time Capsule* are videos.

There are several two-minute mysteries that Sobol fans will also enjoy: *Two-Minute Mysteries*; *More Two-Minute Mysteries*; and *Still More Two-Minute Mysteries*. Books in the Encyclopedia Brown Wacky-But-True Series, which are available in paperback, include: *Encyclopedia Brown's Book of Wacky Animals*; *Encyclopedia Brown's Book of Wacky Cars*; *Encyclopedia Brown's Book of Wacky Crimes*; *Encyclopedia Brown's Book of Wacky Spies*; *Encyclopedia Brown's Book of Wacky Sports*; *Encyclopedia Brown's Record Book of Weird and Wonderful Facts*; *Encyclopedia Brown's Second Record Book of Weird and Wonderful Facts*; and *Encyclopedia Brown's Third Record Book of Weird and Wonderful Facts*. The books include a mystery, anecdotes, and trivia on the topics. For example, *Encyclopedia Brown's Book of the Wacky Outdoors* contains a mystery called "The Case of the Invisible Ray Gun" as well as anecdotes, hunting and fishing stories, and other trivia about the out-of-doors.

There are other books for students who like to solve mysteries, which offer clues in the text and answers at the end. Ecke's *The Castle of the Red Gorillas* includes 19 mysteries to solve, following clues. Solutions appear at the end of the book. Read one example to introduce the book to students. Twelve solve-it-yourself mysteries appear in Vivelo's *Super Sleuth and the Rare Bones*. Readers can help Larry and his father solve four mysteries in Asimov's *Keyword and Other Mysteries*. Clues are also given in the following volumes of the Incognito Mosquito series by Hass: *Incognito Mosquito, Private Detective*; *Incognito Mosquito Flies Again!*; *Incognito Mosquito Takes to the Air*; and *Incognito Mosquito Makes History*. *Meg Mackintosh and the Case of the Missing Babe Ruth Baseball* is a solve-it-yourself mystery. Another book by Landon is *Meg Mackintosh and the Case of the Curious Whale Watch*.

There are a number of other mysteries written for students in intermediate grades that are also part of a series. Scott Corbett's mysteries are popular. *The Trouble With Diamonds* is a revised edition of a previous title in which Jeff

Adams catches a jewel thief. Other Corbett mysteries include: *Witch Hunt*; *Grave Doubts*; *The Disappearing Dog Trick*; *The Hairy Horror Trick*; *The Hangman's Ghost Trick*; and *The Lemonade Trick*. In Giff's *Tootsie Tanner, Why Don't You Talk?*, Abby tries to solve a mystery in the Defense Department. Another Abby and Potsie book, which is available as Program #3 of the television series *Readit!*, is Giff's *Have You Seen Hyacinth Macaw?* The Arrow Adventure series by Walter Dean Myers is about Chris and Ken and their anthropologist mother who travel around the world and have adventures in *Adventure in Granada, Hidden Shrine, Ambush in the Amazon*, and *Duel in the Desert*.

Gorman's *Chelsey and the Green-haired Kid* is about a 13-year-old paraplegic named Chelsey who, with the help of a new kid in school who has green hair, becomes involved with a murdering drug ring. Kastner's *Emil and the Detectives* is a classic mystery with a European setting, in which Emil has his money stolen and a professor and a whole slew of detectives help him catch the thief. Readers will find out about triskaidekaphobia when they read Naylor's *The Bodies in the Besseldorf Hotel*. An orphaned chimney sweep in Victorian London, named Barnacle, overhears a plot and the words "December Rose" while up in a chimney, and gets himself involved in a web of murder, intrigue, and deceit. A locket and a silver-crested spoon can be used as props to introduce Garfield's *December Rose* because they are clues to solving the mystery. The mystery in Clymer's *The Horse in the Attic* begins when 12-year-old Caroline finds a painting of a horse called Sprite in the attic of her new home. There is a mystery in Shura's *Don't Call Me Toad!* Kate and Bobby find out who is sabotaging the Utah ski lodge by switching signs in Elsenberg's *Mystery at Snowshoe Mountain Lodge*. Jeff, Nguyen, and a mystery writer named Mrs. Larken solve a murder on a cross-country train trip in Cross's *Terror Train*. Cross is also the author of *Mystery at Loon Lake*, in which 12-year-old Jeff and Nguyen spend a summer at the lake and along with Jenny Weber get involved in a dangerous tunnel. Mickey, who wants to be a detective, and Kate, who is interested in science, are twins who pool their knowledge to solve the mystery in Markham's *The Halloween Candy Mystery*. A quilt that holds the key to their grandfather's treasure is stolen in Erwin's *Jamie and the Mystery Quilt*. Brian and Gary try to find out about Gary's grandfather's death and are chased, kidnapped, left to starve, and almost drowned in Wallace's *Trapped in Death Cave*. *Roscoe's Leap* by Cross is an old mansion, where a student working on a thesis about an ancestor who built the house helps to solve a mystery involving the family who live there now. A working model of a guillotine is the catalyst which helps 12-year-old Stephen to remember.

Some mysteries are spooky. Hamilton's *The House of Dies Drear* is followed by *The Mystery of Drear House: The Conclusion of the Dies Drear Chronicle*. In this sequel, the treasure has been found but to whom does it belong? In Konigsburg's *Up from Jericho*, Jeanmarie and Malcolm are involved with the ghost of a dead actress named Tallulah. In Dunlop's occult mystery,

House on the Hill, 12-year-old Philip Gilmore stays in a Victorian house in Scotland with his great-aunt Jane and his cousin Sarah. In Lunn's *The Shadow in Hawthorn Bay*, 15-year-old Mary, who has second sight, leaves Scotland for Canada to look for her cousin. *The Curse of the Blue Figurine* by Bellairs is a ghost story in which Johnny Dixon finds an old black book and a tiny figurine. In *The Dark Secret of Weatherend*, also by Bellairs, 14-year-old Anthony explores the mansion with a 68-year-old librarian and they discover a diary. Wilson's *Vampires of Ottawa* is a mystery in which Liz Austen tries to unravel the message of the vampires. In Coville's *The Ghost in the Third Row*, a ghost haunts an old theater where a murder had been committed 50 years ago. Sara and Sam, twins, are involved in a mystery with gold nuggets and a Nevada ghost town in Moore's *Ghost Town Mystery*. Winston, Bongo, and Rat are up against a beatnik poet and a werewolf in Pinkwater's *The Snarkout Boys and the Baconburg Horror*. Because his mother is in the hospital, Tom goes to live with his American Indian grandfather. Tom learns about the Swalalahist or Indian devils which live on the mountain, in Olson's *The Secret of Spirit Mountain*. Sixteen-year-old John Proud is tormented by the ghost of an ancestor with the same name who looks like him, and who met his death by hanging in 1854 for being a demon. Tapp's *The Scorpio Ghosts and the Black Hole Gang* is called *The Ghostmobile* in paperback, and tells how Ryan is visited by a ghostmobile run by a ghostly librarian. Two collections of horror and mystery by Stamper include *Tales for the Midnight Hour* and *More Tales for the Midnight Hour*. In Duncan's *Locked in Time*, a mother speaks to her daughter from the grave and warns that she and her father are in danger from his new wife and children. A booktalk for *Locked in Time* appears on pages 125–28 of Gillespie and Naden's *Juniorplots 3*. Other adventure and mystery booktalks appear in that book on pages 118–56.

Betty Ren Wright, a favorite mystery author for intermediate and middle school students, weaves the supernatural with reality. Ten-year-old Christina spends the summer with grumpy Uncle Ralph in an isolated Victorian house by a lake in Wisconsin where a ghost helps Christina solve an old crime. *Christina's Ghost* has won several child-chosen awards. In *Ghosts Beneath Our Feet*, a ghost warns Katie that the house in which her family is living is going to collapse, but no one will believe her. In *A Ghost in the Window*, Meg has dreams that help her solve an old mystery concerning the woman her divorced father will probably marry. The book is a sequel to *The Secret Window*, in which Meg discovers that her frightening dreams are coming true. Her grandmother, who also has the "gift," helps her to come to terms with it. In *Getting Rid of Marjorie*, Emily tries to get rid of her grandfather's new wife by scaring her. Wright's *The Dollhouse Murders* has won several child-chosen awards. A box of dolls representing Grandma and Grandpa Treloar and Aunt Clare come alive and Amy and Louann uncover the secret of the dollhouse and discover the answer to a family murder. A dollhouse family tries to save a human family from burglars in O'Connell's *The Dollhouse Caper*.

Sisters get trapped in a library after it closes in Clifford's *Help! I'm a Prisoner in the Library.* The police think the girls are crank callers and pay no attention to them, a display featuring children in an old school bus comes to life, something is flying around the room, and strange noises come from above. Another unusual book by Clifford featuring the same girls is *Just Tell Me When We're Dead.*

There are several easy readers that are mysteries. Use Sharmat's newest detective book, *Nate the Great Goes Down in the Dumps,* to introduce the others: *Nate the Great; Nate the Great and the Boring Beach Bag; Nate the Great and the Fishy Prize; Nate the Great and the Lost List; Nate the Great and the Missing Key; Nate the Great and the Phony Clue; Nate the Great and the Snowy Trail; Nate the Great and the Sticky Case; Nate the Great Goes Undercover;* and *Nate the Great Stalks Stupidweed.* The *Case of the Two Masked Robbers* by Hoban has the Raccoon twins, Arabella and Albert, discovering who stole Mrs. Turtle's eggs. *Mr. Sniff and the Motel Mystery* and *Call for Mr. Sniff* by Lewis are about a dog detective. Mike and Susan see a ghost that turns out to be someone dressed as a turkey going to practice in a Thanksgiving play in Nixon's *The Thanksgiving Mystery.* Two books from the Polka Dot Private Eye series are available in book/cassette packages. Giff's *The Riddle of the Red Purse* has several people claiming to have lost the purse and *The Secret at the Polk Street School* has Dawn investigating a threatening note in her locker that is signed "The Wolf." There are four mystery chapters in Cushman's *Aunt Eater Loves a Mystery.* Aunt Eater, an anteater, has her bag stolen on a train, sees a mysterious person at a party, reads a mysterious note, and has a missing cat. Two easy readers are available as cassette/paperback sets: Lawrence's *Binky Brothers, Detectives,* and Bonsall's *The Case of the Hungry Stranger.* Otto and Uncle Tooth solve two mysteries in the Step-Into-Reading series: *The Mystery of the Pirate Ghost* and *The Secret of Foghorn Island* by Hayes. Reluctant readers will also enjoy *Foghorn Island,* in which Otto and his Uncle Tooth solve the mystery of the four shipwrecks that have taken place in a short time.

Picture books also contain mysteries. In *What the Mailman Brought* by Craven, William is bored because he is sick and has missed a week of school, so he puts a sign in his window, SICK OF THIS, and mysterious presents appear. In *Mousekin's Mystery* by Miller, Mousekin is trying to figure out what makes the animals glow in the dark. Jane is a human who locates missing dogs for 25 cents in Bunting's *Jane Martin, Dog Detective.*

Several books have animal detectives. Christian's Sebastian is a dog who helps his human detective, John Quincy Jones. In *Sebastian (Super Sleuth) and the Stars-in-His-Eyes Mystery,* Chummy the Wonder Dog is starring in a television movie in Hollywood that is plagued by accidents. Books about Sebastian and John Quincy Jones are: *Sebastian (Super Sleuth) and the Bone to Pick Mystery; Sebastian (Super Sleuth) and the Crummy Yummies Caper; Sebastian (Super Sleuth) and the Egyptian Connection; Sebastian (Super*

Sleuth) and the Hair of the Dog Mystery; Sebastian (Super Sleuth) and the Purloined Sirloin; Sebastian (Super Sleuth) and the Secrets of the Skewered Skier; Sebastian (Super Sleuth) and the Clumsy Cowboy; and *Sebastian (Super Sleuth) and the Santa Claus Caper.* Many second graders, as well as older students, will enjoy these stories.

Some animal stories are for primary students. Jenny and her dog called My Dog solve mysteries in Adler's *My Dog and the Green Sock Mystery* and *My Dog and the Knock Knock Mystery.* In *My Dog and the Birthday Mystery,* Jenny thinks she is trying to find a stolen bike, when in reality it is a ploy to get her to her surprise birthday party. The butler solves a mystery that leads him to his own birthday party in *Picnic with Piggins* by Yolen, which is a sequel to *Piggins. Basil of Baker Street,* about a mouse detective by Titus, has been reprinted in paperback. Quackenbush's *Sherlock Chick's First Case* is about Detective Sherlock Chick who is looking for missing corn. *Sherlock Chick and the Peekaboo Mystery* is the sequel. Use Quackenbush's newest Miss Mallard mystery, *Danger in Tibet,* to introduce the others: *Dig to Disaster; Express Train to Trouble; Gondola to Danger; Rickshaw to Horror; Stairway to Doom; Surfboard to Peril;* and *Taxi to Intrigue.* Two other books by Quackenbush include *Detective Mole* and *Detective Mole and the Haunted Castle Mystery.* There are several books about the Dalmation, Pinkerton, by Kellogg: *Pinkerton, Behave!; Prehistoric Pinkerton; A Rose for Pinkerton;* and *Tallyho, Pinkerton! Pinkerton, Behave!* is available as a book/cassette as well as a sound filmstrip. Incognito Mosquito is a private "insective" created by Hass and *Incognito Mosquito Makes History* contains five time travel adventures complete with puns. *Bernard of Scotland Yard* by Freschet is about a mouse detective and his cousin who are after the Mole Gang, jewel thieves.

Jill, her basset Fletcher, her friend Gwen, and two other friends enter a TV rock music contest in which Fletcher howls on cue. After winning the first round of the contest, Fletcher disappears in Levy's *Something Queer in Rock and Roll.* The music and lyrics are included on the endpapers. Other books in the series are: *Something Queer at the Ball Park; Something Queer at the Haunted School; Something Queer at the Lemonade Stand; Something Queer at the Library; Something Queer is Going On;* and *Something Queer on Vacation.* This series is for intermediate students. Clifford's *Harvey's Marvelous Monkey Mystery* can be included on handicapped booklists because when 11-year-old Harvey Wilson and his cousin Nora solve the mystery, he learns that the monkey, Aloha, is trained to help a quadraplegic. Intermediate readers will also enjoy *Harvey's Horrible Snake Disaster.* There is a vampire rabbit in Howe's *Bunnicula.* Other books in the series that includes dogs and a cat are *The Celery Stalks at Midnight, Howliday Inn,* and *Nighty-Nightmare. Flash Fry, Private Eye* by Schoch is a mystery about an 11-year-old boy and his dog.

Several mysteries are also available in multimedia formats. The mystery in Kellogg's *The Mysterious Tadpole* is that Louis's tadpole isn't a tadpole at all. Have children guess what he might be and then have them listen to the cassette or read the book. Another Kellogg book is *Mystery of the Stolen Blue Paint*. In *Maggie and the Pirate* by Keats, Maggie's pet cricket, Niki, is missing. Christelow's *The Robbery at the Diamond Dog Diner* is available in a cassette/book combination. Christelow's book is also a featured book on the television series, *Reading Rainbow*. Cushman's *Aunt Eater Loves a Mystery* is a review book on that same program. In *The Robbery at the Diamond Dog Diner*, Glenda Feathers, a chicken, tells Lola and Harry Dog at the Diamond Dog Diner to hide the diamonds in blown-out eggs because there are robbers in town, but the idea backfires. *The Secret of Kelly's Mill* by Carus is available on two cassettes. Several 10-year-old boys help the police capture counterfeiters wanted by Interpol in an English seaside village.

Allow television to introduce mysteries to children. *The Case of the Elevator Duck* by Berends is Program #4 and *Top Secret* by Gardiner is Program #9 of *Books from Cover to Cover*, for third and fourth graders. *The Ghost Squad Breaks Through* by Hildick is Program #7 of *More Books from Cover to Cover* for fifth and sixth graders. Other books about the Ghost Squad by Hildick that can be introduced by the video are: *The Ghost Squad and the Prowling Hermits*; *The Ghost Squad and the Halloween Conspiracy*; and *The Ghost Squad Flies the Concorde*. *Have You Seen Hyacinth Macaw?* by Giff is Program #3 of *Readit!*, a television series for third and fourth graders. Hurd's *Mystery on the Docks* is a featured book on the television series *Reading Rainbow* and the *Nate the Great* mystery series by Sharmat is advertised in a book review on the same program. *Read All About It!* is an instructional television series of 10 15-minute programs for grades four to six. The mystery series emphasizes immediate on-screen reading skills and revolves around three students who discover an intergalactic conspiracy. Two robots, Theta (a computerized videoscreen), and Otto (a space-age typewriter), are able to solve the mysteries.

Share mysteries with students after they have read a mystery in their basal reader. Teach students to locate mysteries in the card catalog under "Mystery and Detective Stories" or give a booktalk about mysteries and have each student select a book to read. For mysteries about Sharmat's *Nate the Great*, check Chapter 7, EXPANDING BASAL READERS. A selection from Witter's *Mystery of the Rolltop Desk* appears in the fourth grade reader *Crossroads*, edited by Cullinan, et al., from the Laureate edition. A selection from Fleischman's *The Bloodhound Gang in the Case of the Flying Clock* appears on pages 152–67 of the sixth grade HBJ basal reader in the Laureate edition, *Treasures*, compiled by Cullinan, et al. An article about mysteries appears on pages 168–69 of that book followed by a selection by Hitchcock called "The Mystery of the Seven Wrong Clocks," from *Alfred Hitchcock's Solve-Them-Yourself Mysteries*. Introduce the following other Hitchcock books to students using that series: *Alfred Hitchcock's Daring Detectives*; *Alfred Hitchcock's Ghostly Gallery*; and *Alfred Hitchcock's Supernatural Tales of Terror and Suspense*. Also in *Treasures* is D'Ignazio's "The Case of the Missing Report Cards" from *The*

Case of the Chocolate-Covered Bugs on pages 264–77. *Treasures* also includes an author profile of Sir Arthur Conan Doyle on pages 178–79 and his story, "The Adventure of the Blue Carbuncle," adapted by Sadler from Doyle's *The Adventures of Sherlock Holmes,* on pages 280–303.

Newman's books are excellent companions to any stories about Sherlock Holmes. In *The Case of the Baker Street Irregulars,* Screamer's brother is a Baker Street Irregular, one of the street children who sometimes work with Holmes. They help Andrew when his guardian, Mr. Dennison, is missing, and Andrew meets the Wiggins family. In *The Vanishing Corpse,* Constable Wyatt dislikes Inspector Finch. A corpse disappears before it can be examined, and a jewel thief is on the loose. In *Somerville Secret,* several days after Andrew and Inspector Peter Wyatt of Scotland Yard see Sgt. Major Polk argue in a pub with a scarfaced man, Polk is murdered. There is a chimney sweep in the story, so it can be paired with Garfield's *December Rose.* Sara Wiggins doesn't return from dancing school and Sara's friend Maria, daughter of the first secretary of the Serbian Embassy, also disappears in Newman's *Threatened King.* Sara is in a play with Andrew's mother in *Frightened Friend,* and the main question is why the grandfather of Andrew's friend Cortland has become paralyzed and unable to speak. In *Etruscan Treasure,* Verna Tillett is in New York to star in a play and Andrew and Sara are there also. But why is Inspector Peter Wyatt there? Two actresses have been murdered in a case similar to an unsolved murder 10 years earlier in *Murdered Players.* The story involves Inspector Wyatt of Scotland Yard, Sara Wiggins, a handicapped boy named Jack Collins, an antique dealer named Baron Bealey, and of course Andrew Tillett and his mother Verna who is a famous London actress. While Inspector Wyatt is off on a honeymoon with Andrew's mother in *Indian Curse,* Sara and Andrew solve a mystery surrounding the statue of the Indian goddess Kali, which produces light and sound. Baron Beasley, the antique dealer, is also in this story. *The Case of the Watching Boy* is the newest book in the series. Sara, Andrew and his schoolmate Markham inadvertently help in a kidnapping involving the succession to the throne of Rumania, when the three help a woman rescue her child from an estranged husband.

Murray's *Mystery Plays for Young Actors* contains 10 one-act mysteries. The plays cover such topics as predicting disaster, courtroom drama, jewel thieves, a secret mission, computer crime, and revenge. Greenson and Taha's *Name That Book! Questions and Answers on Outstanding Children's Books,* contains 34 titles and 68 questions about mysteries. Check page 236 of the index for titles.

INTRODUCING FANTASY [CU 107–09]. Check page 1089 of Saltman's *Riverside Anthology of Children's Literature* for recommendations about what part fantasy should play in children's lives. Chapter 7 of *Children's Literature in the Elementary School* by Huck, et al. is "Modern Fantasy," pages 335–91. Included are roots of fantasy and guides for evaluating modern fantasy, page

345. Types of fantasy are described: animal fantasy; the world of toys and dolls; lilliputian worlds; eccentric characters and preposterous situations; extraordinary worlds; magical powers; suspense and the supernatural; and tricks with time. High fantasy includes ancient powers, the struggle between good and evil, and quests and adventures. A definition of fantasy appears on page 31 of Cullinan's *Literature and the Child* and types of fantasy on pages 279–315: light fantasy; animal fantasy; fantasy as mystery; time slip fantasy; quest stories or high fantasy; and literary lore. Discussion of White's *Charlotte's Web* as a landmark fantasy is found on page 281 of Cullinan's book while a profile of Natalie Babbitt, author of *Tuck Everlasting*, appears on page 313. Chapter 11 of Stewig's *Children and Literature*, pages 506–69 is "Fantasy: But Could It Really Happen?" Types of fantasy include: simple fantasy for younger readers; literary folktales; stories about animals with special abilities; stories involving unearthly creatures; fantasies about people with special abilities; stories involving toys and dolls; stories in which magical objects play a major role; trips through time and space; changes in size; fantasies about other transformations; and conflicts with evil powers. Characteristics of well-done fantasy, pages 507–19, are: logic and consistency; language; characterization; setting; and endings. The purposes of fantasy and a bibliography are also included in Stewig's book. Chapter 7 of Norton's *Through the Eyes of a Child: An Introduction to Children's Literature*, pages 256–317 is called "Modern Fantasy." Evaluating modern fantasy, pages 259–61, covers: point of view (suspending disbelief); setting (creating a world); characterization; themes; and six questions to ask when evaluating modern fantasy. Types of fantasy include: fairy stories; allegory; good versus evil and quests; power and responsibility; articulate animals, dolls, toys, and inanimate objects; eccentric characters, preposterous situations, and exaggerations; strange and curious worlds; little people; friendly presences, ghosts and goblins; time warps; and science fiction. A list of fantasies for all ages appears in the index to Lipson's *Parent's Guide to the Best Books for Children*. The following information appears in the Lindskoogs's *How to Grow a Young Reader*: descriptions of the "Top Ten Contemporary Fantasies," pages 62–73; an alphabetical list of "Twenty-One More Authors of Contemporary Fantasies," pages 73–84; and an author, title, and date list of "Over 50 Other Recommended Fantasy Writers," pages 85–87.

The third edition of Lynn's *Fantasy Literature for Children and Young Adults* is an annotated bibliography that includes 3,300 fantasy novels and story collections, 1,000 of them new to this edition. The grade range is from third grade through twelfth grade. The 10 fantasy categories in Lynn's book are: animal fantasy; magic adventure fantasy; high fantasy (heroic or secondary world); fantasy collections; time travel fantasy; allegorical fantasy and literary fairy tales; ghost fantasy; witchcraft and sorcery fantasy; humorous fantasy; and toy fantasy. The book is especially helpful for finding sequels. Egoff's *Worlds Within: Children's Fantasy from the Middle Ages to Today* begins with the roots of fantasy, types, and value. The text is arranged chronologically, beginning with the Middle Ages. *Worlds Within* contains information about 375 fantasy novels. Field and Weiss's *Values in Selected Children's Books of Fiction and Fantasy* identifies and discusses 700 books of fiction and fantasy and the values propounded in them. Aquino's *Fantasy in Literature* includes such topics as fantasy as an activity of the mind; teaching fantasy literature; characteristics of fantasy literature; and suggested readings in myths, fairy tales, and pure fantasy. Pflieger's *A Reference Guide to Modern Fantasy* is an alphabetical list of settings, authors, characters, and objects from fantasy books. Story plots are included. Check Elleman's bibliography, "Popular Reading—Animal Fantasy: Update" on page 1441 of the April 15, 1988 issue of *Booklist* for an annotated list. Check pages 101–04 of England and Fasick's *Childview, Evaluating and Reviewing Materials for Children* for information about fantasy. Selections from modern fantasy appear on pages 480–537 of Sutherland and Livingston's *The Scott, Foresman Anthology of Children's Literature*. *Your Reading*, edited by Davis, Davis, and the National Council of Teachers of English, contains over 50 annotated fantasy titles for middle school and junior high students on pages 90–101 in a section called "Fantasy" and further titles in a section called "Space and Time" beginning on page 197. Greenson and Taha list 21 titles and 42 questions about fantasy books in *Name That Book! Questions and Answers on Outstanding Children's Books*. Check the index on page 225 for titles.

Booktalks for the following fantasies appear in Gillespie and Naden's *Juniorplots 3*: Alexander's *Westmark*; Jones's *Howl's Moving Castle*; McCaffrey's *Dragonsong*; McKinley's *The Hero and the Crown*; Park's *Playing Beatie Bow*; Pascal's *Hangin' Out with Cici*; and Yolen's *Dragon's Blood*. Guides for initiating literature-based studies of the following fantasy titles from *Response Guides for Teaching Children's Books* by Somers and Worthington are: Sendak's *Where the Wild Things Are*; Potter's *The Tale of Peter Rabbit*; Steig's *Sylvester and the Magic Pebble*; Burton's *Mike Mulligan and His Steam Shovel*; Lawson's *Rabbit Hill*; White's *Charlotte's Web*; Lewis's *The Lion, the Witch, and the Wardrobe*; Norton's *The Borrowers*; and L'Engle's *A Wrinkle in Time*.

Selections from certain fantasies for intermediate students are in Chapter 12 of Saltman's *Riverside Anthology of Children's Literature*: Lofting's *The Story of Doctor Dolittle*; Collodi's *Adventures of Pinocchio*; Carroll's *Alice's Adventures in Wonderland*; Travers's *Mary Poppins*; Langton's *The Fledgling*; Norton's *The Borrowers*; Boston's *The Children of Green Knowe*; Pearce's *Tom's Midnight Garden*; Lively's *The Ghost of Thomas Kempe*; Lewis's *Prince Caspian*; E. B. White's *Charlotte's Web*; T. H. White's *The Sword in the Stone*; Cooper's *The Grey King*; Le Guin's *The Wizard of Earthsea*; and Tolkien's *The Hobbit*.

Introduce the genre of fantasy to primary students through two programs from the instructional television series, *Word Shop: Fantasy Stories* and *Books About Fantasy*.

Coville's *The Unicorn Treasury: Stories, Poems and Unicorn Lore* can be introduced to students by reading his first section, "The Lore of the Unicorn," which introduces the history and lore of unicorns. Middle school teachers who set aside a few minutes a day to read aloud from a different book can spend a few minutes reading this introduction and then set the book aside in the classroom. Students will be motivated to read other stories and poems from the anthology. Intermediate teachers can choose to read various poems and stories aloud. There are eight poems and 11 other selections. Introduce L'Engle's "Time Quartet" by reading a selection from the third book, A Swiftly Tilting Planet, in a selection called "The Valley of the Unicorns," pages 41–60 of Coville's book. Introduce the seven books in C. S. Lewis's series that begins with The Lion, the Witch, and the Wardrobe and ends with The Last Battle. A selection from the last book, "What News the Eagle Brought," appears on pages 105–19 of Coville's anthology. Introductions to both selections are included so listeners will know what is happening. Introduce the reading of Lindholm's "The Unicorn in the Maze," pages 7–22 by showing a figurine of a unicorn. A display of carved and glass unicorns can be placed in a display case to introduce the entire anthology, The Unicorn Treasury. Yolen's "The Boy Who Drew Unicorns," pages 157–66 can be used to stimulate an art project. Mayer's picture book Unicorn Alphabet will be of interest to unicorn lovers of all ages. A three-stanza poem called "Unicorns" appears on page 104 of Finger Frolics by Cromwell, et al. Also check page 102 of Cromwell's book for a song, "Unicorns," to be sung to the tune of "Mary Had a Little Lamb." "Pegasus" appears on page 101.

Another book from which fantasy stories can be read aloud is Spaceships and Spells: A Collection of New Fantasy and Science Fiction Stories collected by Yolen, et al. Only a few of the 13 stories are science fiction; the majority are fantasy for middle school students. Another anthology by Yolen and friends is Dragons and Dreams: A Collection of New Fantasy and Science Fiction Stories. Mayer and Hague's picture book, The Unicorn and the Lake, can also be shared with students.

A number of fantasies can be introduced through sequels, prequels, and other books in the series. Mossflower is the prequel to Redwall by Jacques. The setting for Mossflower is Mossflower Woods during the time of Martin the Warrior. In Redwall, a bumbling mouse apprentice, Matthias, emerges as a leader, with the help of Martin the Warrior's sword, to save the animals and the abbey from the evil rat, Cluny the Scourge. In the prequel, Harry Kitten and Tucker Mouse, readers learn how Harry and Tucker meet to introduce Selden's series that begins with The Cricket in Times Square. In Chester Cricket's New Home, Chester looks for a new home to replace his tree stump. Chester Cricket's Pigeon Ride is a picture book which introduces younger readers to Chester. In Tucker's Countryside, Tucker Mouse and Harry Cat save the meadow from developers, and in The Old Meadow, they save old Abner Budd's home on the meadow from those who think it is an eyesore. Conly's Rasco and the Rats of NIMH is a sequel to O'Brien's (her father) Mrs. Frisby *and the Rats of NIMH*. A selection from *Mrs. Frisby and the Rats of NIMH* appears on pages 296–315 of the sixth grade SB/Ginn basal reader, *Wind by the Sea*, edited by Pearson, et al. In the sequel, Mrs. Frisby's mouse son, Timothy, saves the life of Rasco, son of the rebel rat Jenver. The two try to save the valley from being flooded to make a tourist lake. In the newest book in Norton's Borrower series, *The Borrowers Avenged*, the Platters, who have kidnapped the Borrower family, lose them and try to get them back. Other books about the Borrowers include: *The Borrowers*; *The Borrowers Afield*; *The Borrowers Aloft*; and *The Borrowers Afloat*. Omri has a toy cowboy and Indian that come to life in *The Indian in the Cupboard, The Return of the Indian*, and *The Secret of the Indian*. Chetwin's books about the wizard Gom Gobblechuck include: *Gom on Windy Mountain*; *The Riddle of the Rune*; *The Crystal Stair: From the Tales of Gom in the Legends of Ulm*; and *Starstone*. Alexander's Westmark trilogy includes *Westmark, The Kestrel*, and *The Beggar Queen*. Le Guin's *Wizard of Earthsea* is followed by *The Tombs of Atuun, The Farthest Shore*, and *Tehanu*. Kooiker's *Legacy of Magic* is a sequel to *The Magic Stone*. Chris, the main character in the first book, is apprenticed to a witch. In the second book, Alec visits his grandfather and meets Chris. *Tomorrow's Magic* by Service is the sequel to *Winter of Magic's Return*, a tale of King Arthur, Merlin, and Morgan Le Fay set in the future. *The Guardian of Isis* by Hughes is the sequel to *Keeper of the Isis Light*. In the sequel, Jody N'Komo from the planet Isis in the year 2136 meets the Guardian and the Keeper. Charlotte, who was a 12-year-old in *Best of Enemies*, is now an adolescent in Bond's *A Place to Come Back To*.

Adults will appreciate Tunnell's *The Prydain Companion: A Reference Guide to Lloyd Alexander's Prydain Chronicles*. Arranged alphabetically, the book gives insights to the following books by Alexander: *The Book of Three*, book 1; *The Black Cauldron*, book 2; *The Castle of Llyr*, book 3; *Taran Wanderer*, book 4; and *The High King*, book 5.

The Sword of Shannara by Brooks takes place 2,000 years in the future, 1,000 years after the last Great War when many small communities of humans, dwarfs, elves, gnomes, and trolls populate the earth. Shea and Flick Olmsford live in Shady Vale with their father who is an innkeeper. Shea is half human and half elf and doesn't know that he is adopted and is the descendent of Jerle Shannara, a great Elfen king who once overcame Brona, the evil warlock. Now Brona the warlock lord plans to destroy the world and the only weapon that can stop him is the sword which can only be successfully used by a descendent of Jerle Shannara. The journey of the brothers begins in *Sword of Shannara* and continues in *Elfstones of Shannara* and *Wishsong of Shannara*.

Fans of King Arthur and Merlin will enjoy Berry's *Magicians of Erianne* about a boy named Roman and the master magician Yorba.

Dragons appear in numerous fantasies for students in middle school and above. Many of these titles are in a series. In *Dragon's Blood* by Yolen, a 15-year-old slave boy named Jakkin gets his own dragon when a baby hatches but is not listed on the inventory at the dragon nursery where he works. The setting is the Planet Austar IV of the galaxy Eratto, where breeding dragons is a main occupation. The girl Akki helps Jakkin raise and train his dragon for fighting. The dragon is renamed Heart's Blood because of his victory. The sequels are *Heart's Blood* and *A Sending of Dragons*. The dragon dies saving Jakkin's life in *Heart's Blood*. Jakkin and Akki hide with five hatchling dragons with whom they can communicate telepathically in *A Sending of Dragons*. "Aerin's Dragon," a selection from McKinley's *The Hero and the Crown* is on pages 310–23 of the eighth grade SB/Ginn basal reader *Worlds Beyond* by Pearson, et al. Check page 24 for the article "Lee Bennett Hopkins Interviews Robin McKinley." McKinley calls her Newbery Medal Book, *The Hero and the Crown*, a forerunner or prequel to the Newbery Honor Book, *The Blue Sword*, even though *The Blue Sword* takes place in time several hundred years before *Hero and the Crown*. In *The Blue Sword*, Harry Crewe is kidnapped by Corlath, King of the Hillfolk. With the help of the magical blue sword named Gonturan, Harry wins a battle against the Northerners and wins Corlath's love. In *The Hero and the Crown*, Princess Aerin battles and slays the black dragon, Maur, to save the kingdom of Damar and reclaim her birthright. Aerin is given the Blue Sword by the wizard Luthe, and must reclaim the Hero's Crown, the secret strength of Damar. In Murphy's *The Ivory Lyre*, 16-year-old Tebriel and his singing dragon, Tirror, sing about the past before the Dark Raiders came into control. Prince Tebriel seaches for his sister with the help of a female court page and his dragons, who masquerade as horses. *Nightpool* is the sequel. Princess Sharlin and Aarondar look for a gold dragon in Salsitz's *Where Dragons Lie*. Yep's *Dragon Steel* is about an underwater clan of dragons that has a steel sword. A dragon princess and human companion, Thorn, combat the Dragon King's jealousy. Nesbit's *Last of the Dragons and Some Others* is about the last dragon in Cornwall. For picture books about dragons, check Chapter 9 for the section called INTRODUCING FICTION AND NONFICTION THROUGH THE MIDDLE AGES.

Use Program #16 of the instructional television series *More Books from Cover to Cover* to introduce Cooper's *The Dark is Rising*. When he turns 11, Will Stanton receives a black metal circle quartered by two crossed lines which begins his quest for the six great Signs of the Light. Similar circles are made of bronze and wood. Other signs are of stone, fire, and water. Other books in the series are *Greenwitch*, *Silver on the Tree*, and the Newbery Medal winner, *The Grey King*. Compare this book to Nimmo's *The Snow Spider*, in which a 10 year-old Welsh boy, Gwyn, is given five gifts from his grandmother and is told that he is a magician, someone who appears every seven years in their family. Gwyn is teased by his classmates and is avoided by his best friend when he speaks of spaceships he has seen. With the help of Arianwen, the silver spider or Snow Spider, Gwyn brings harmony to his unhappy family.

Fantasies can be introduced to students through multimedia. Other instructional television programs from *More Books from Cover to Cover* that can introduce fantasy are: Brittain's *The Wish Giver*, Program #1 and Farmer's *The Summer Birds*, Program #2. Eager's *Half Magic* and Cleary's *The Mouse and the Motorcycle* are Programs #14 and 7 of the educational television series, *Book Bird*. *The Mouse and the Motorcycle* and *Runaway Ralph* are both available in 16mm and video formats. The sound filmstrip, *Fantasy*, tells about attributes of fantasy books and focuses on Selden's *The Cricket in Times Square*. Books by C. S. Lewis, Hugh Lofting, Mary Norton, Astrid Lindgren, Eleanor Cameron, and W. P. du Bois are mentioned. Selden's *The Cricket in Times Square* is also Program #1 on the television series, *Book Bird*.

The filmstrip *Fantasy Literature*, for an older audience, is one of five filmstrips in the *Fantastic Series* which includes *The Folktale, The Fairy Tale, Horror/Ghost Stories*, and *Science Fiction*.

Students enjoy animal fantasies. Howe's *Bunnicula, The Celery Stalks at Midnight, Howliday Inn*, and *Nighty-Nightmare* are animal fantasies in which two dogs named Harold and Howie and a cat named Chester keep a vampire rabbit in line. *Harry's Mad* by King-Smith is about a parrot called Madison. In *Pigs Might Fly* by King-Smith, Daggie Dogfoot is a pig who learns to swim, dive, and saves the farm animals during a flood.

Fantasy books for intermediate students listed elsewhere in this book include Adams's *Watership Down*; Babbitt's *Tuck Everlasting*; Bellairs's *Dark Secret of Weatherend*; *The House with a Clock in Its Walls* and *The Lamp from the Warlock's Tomb*; Bond's *A Bear Called Paddington*; Carroll's *Alice's Adventures in Wonderland*; Cleary's *Runaway Ralph* and *The Mouse and the Motorcycle*; Dahl's *Charlie and the Chocolate Factory* and *James and the Giant Peach*; Grahame's *The Wind in the Willows*; Jones's *Howl's Moving Castle* and *The Lives of Christopher Chant*; King-Smith's *The Fox Busters* and *Pigs Might Fly*; Milne's *Winnie-the-Pooh*; Pearce's *Tom's Midnight Garden*; Smith's *Night of the Solstice*; Stolz's *Cuckoo Clock* and *Quentin Corn*; Tolkien's *The Hobbit*; Townsend's *Persuading Stick*; White's *Charlotte's Web*; York's *Miss Know It All and the Wishing Lamp*; *The Green Knowe* series by Boston; the Tripod Trilogy by Christopher; and the Time Quartet by L'Engle; all appear in the section of Chapter 1 called TIME TRAVEL: A BOOKTALK for books which includes numerous other fantasies about space and time.

INTRODUCING SCIENCE FICTION [CU 119–21]. Information about science fiction appear on pages 316–28 of Cullinan's *Literature and the Child*. Verne's landmark science fiction book is cited on page 316 and criteria for selection of science fiction appears on pages 319–20. The types of science fiction are mind control, tomorrow's world, and survival, and a definition of science fiction appears on page 32 of Cullinan's book. There is discussion of science fiction on pages 378–84 of Chapter 7, "Modern Fantasy," in *Children's Literature in the Elementary School* by Huck et al. Science fiction is a category of fantasy noted on pages 288–91 of Norton's *Through the Eyes of a Child: An Introduction to Children's Literature*. "In Search of Truth," an essay by Madeleine L'Engle, appears on page 289 of Norton's book. Science fiction is a section in Chapter 13, "Special Interests: Children's Choices" on pages 651–57 of Stewig's *Children and Literature*. A section of England and Fasick's *Childview: Evaluating and Reviewing Materials for Children* called "Science Fiction and Science Fantasy" on pages 104–05 includes a good definition. Check Saltman's *Riverside Anthology of Children's Literature* for material about science fiction. Selections from four books appear under the heading "Science Fiction" in Sutherland and Livingston's *Scott, Foresman Anthology of Children's Literature*: *Twenty-One Balloons* by du Bois; *Space Cat* by Todd; *The Fallen Spaceman* by Harding; and *A Wrinkle in Time* by L'Engle. Check page 241 of the index to Greenson and Taha's *Name That Book! Questions and Answers on Outstanding Children's Books*. Seventeen science fiction titles and 34 questions are included. Booktalks for Sargent's *Earthseed* and Sleator's *Interstellar Pig* appear in Gillespie and Naden's *Juniorplots 3*, and author information is given. Almost 40 annotated science fiction titles for middle school students are given in a section of *Your Reading* by Davis and the National Council of Teachers of English on pages 188–96 in a section called "Science Fiction and the Future."

Science fiction books are introduced on instructional television programs. Third and fourth graders can watch *Readit! #2* which introduces two books by Slote: *My Robot Buddy* and *My Trip to Alpha 1*, and Program #6 which introduces a science fiction choose-your-own-adventure by Packard: *The Third Planet from Altair*. *Book Bird*, the instructional television series for fourth graders includes Cameron's *The Wonderful Flight to the Mushroom Planet* as Program #9.

Use the sound filmstrip *Science Fiction*, from the set *Literature for Children, Series 6*, to introduce the concept of science fiction to students. The filmstrip discusses how science and fiction combine and how science fiction writers get their ideas by examining scientific developments and social problems and projecting them into the future. Books which are introduced in the filmstrip include Christopher's *City of Gold and Lead* and a glimpse of L'Engle's *A Wrinkle in Time*. Christopher's book is one of the "Tripod Trilogy" which has recently been expanded by the prequel, *When the Tripods Came* and includes *The White Mountains*, *Pool of Fire*, and *The City of Gold and Lead*. L'Engle's "Time Quartet" includes *A Wrinkle in Time*, *The Wind in the Door*, *A Swiftly Tilting Planet*, and *Many Waters*. Ideas for teaching *A Wrinkle in Time* appear in Somers and Worthington's *Response Guides for Teaching Children's Books*. Sometimes L'Engle's quartet is considered fantasy. Have students read various definitions of fantasy and science fiction and have a debate on which category the book should appear in. The sound filmstrip *Science Fiction* from the *Fantastic Series* is for middle school students and above, and contains information about Wells's *The War of the Worlds* and Herbert's *Dune*. It is especially helpful for gifted students, many of whom are interested in fantasy and science fiction.

Selections from science fiction books appear in basal readers and can introduce the genre, the author, and the book to students. Use Hamilton's *Willie Bea and the Time the Martians Landed* with two selections from the SB/Ginn basal reader, *Worlds Beyond*. Koch's informational article "The Night the Martians Landed, the Panic Broadcast: Portrait of an Event" is on pages 344–55 and Wells's radio play "Invasion from Mars" is on pages 356–75. Science fiction selections are found in the fourth and fifth grade SB/Ginn basal reader series edited by Pearson, et al. Check pages 24–33 of the fourth grade *Silver Secrets* for Bell's "Teeny, Tiny, Tinny Visitors" and pages 386–410 of *Dream Chasers* for Bunting's "Day of the Earthlings." Science fiction as a literature study appears in two basal readers from the HBJ Laureate edition, edited by Cullinan, et al., pages 482–83 of the sixth grade *Treasures*, and pages 178–79 of the seventh grade *Patterns*. The definitions call science fiction a type of fantasy. Selections from books are available to sixth graders: Bradbury's *The Fantastic Universe*; Serling's *Stories from the Twilight Zone*; Asimov's *The Fantastic Voyage*; and Clarke's "Saturn Rising." Selections from books available to seventh graders are: Gallo's *Sixteen Short Stories by Outstanding Writers for Young Adults*; Asimov's *Earth Is Room Enough*; Reynolds's *Optical Illusion*; Heinlein's *Expanded Universe*; Algozin's *Odyssey: The Young People's Magazine of Astronomy and Outer Space*; and Silverberg's *Voyages in Time: Twelve Stories of Science Fiction*. An informational article, "Isaac Asimov: Scientist and Storyteller" by Erlanger appears on pages 504–11 of the sixth grade *Treasures*. Clarke's "The Wind from the Sun" from *Worlds of Wonder: 16 Tales of Science Fiction* appears on pages 410–29 of the SB/Ginn seventh grade basal reader, *Star Walk*.

Use science fiction survival stories with booktalks about survival on earth. Cooper's *Earthchange* has Rose, her grandmother, and a baby survive a catastrophe which turns the earth into a wilderness. Christopher's Tripod Series can be introduced as survival books.

Science fiction books introduced in other sections of this volume include: *The Watcher of Space* and *The Crystal City* by Etchemendy; *Top Secret* by Gardiner; *Wordchanger* by Haynes; *Orvis, Shepherd Moon*, and *This Time of Darkness* by Hoover; *Guardian of Isis, Keeper of the Isis Light*, and *Isis Pedlar* by Hughes; *That Game from Outer Space* by Manes; *Ralph Fosbek and the Amazing Black Hole Patrol* by Senn; *Interstellar Pig* and *Singularity* by Sleator; and *The Green Book* by Walsh.

INTRODUCING HISTORICAL FICTION [CU 121–23; 718]. Discussion of historical fiction appears on page 688 of Sutherland and Livingston's *The Scott, Foresman Anthology of Children's Literature*. Interesting selections from historical fiction appear on pages 689–724. Check pages 532–66 of *Children's Literature in the Elementary School* by Huck for information that includes values of, types of, and criteria for judging historical fiction. There are guides for evaluation and recurring themes. Chapter 8, pages 330–84 of Stewig's *Children and Literature*, is "Historic Fiction: Trips Through Time." Stewig defines historic fiction, provides information for evaluation (authenticity of setting, characters, and action, and importance of balance), and shares ideas for using historical fiction to develop children's writing skills. Chapter 10 of Norton's book *Through the Eyes of a Child: An Introduction to Children's Literature* is "Historical Fiction," pages 434–84. Criteria for evaluating historical fiction on pages 435–38 include: setting, characterization, theme, and seven important questions to ask. There is an essay by Patricia Clapp, "Making the Past Come Alive," on page 447. Check pages 101–04 of England and Fasick's *Childview: Evaluating and Reviewing Materials for Children* for more information about historical fiction. Criteria for selecting historical books and biographies appear on pages 461–64 of Cullinan's *Literature and the Child* and information about historical fiction on pages 464–73 of Chapter 9, "Historical Fiction and Biography." Subject categories by time periods include outstanding and landmark titles. Martin's *Writing Historical Fiction* discusses the genre from the viewpoint of the writer. Program #6 of the instructional television series for intermediate students is *Picture This* which tells about researching facts for historical fiction and then filling in with imagination.

Historical fiction can be introduced in a number of situations. Booktalks which introduce it can be presented to classes studying American, world, or ancient history. Booktalks which introduce historical fiction titles can also be used, after reading a selection from a basal reader or a book in a literature-based reading program. It is helpful for the school library/media specialist to provide a booktalk so students can select books from a specific time period. Books for use with frontier and pioneer life units can be taken from a section in this chapter called "If You Like the *Little House* Books." Check the section called THE HOLOCAUST: A BOOKTALK for books on that subject to supplement reading a play about Anne Frank or to supplement a study of World War II. Booktalks can be planned just to introduce the range of historical fiction.

Information for booktalks that include historical fiction is found in a section of Chapter 2 called INTRODUCING BOOKS BY TITLES: HUMAN CHARACTERS. Books include: *Who Is Carrie?* and *War Comes to Willy Freeman* by the Colliers and *Girl on the Outside* by Walter.

Instructional television and multimedia can be used to introduce historical fiction. Program #11 of *Storybound* features *The Witch of Blackbird Pond*, a Newbery winner by Speare. *The Witch of Blackbird Pond*, also available as a recording, is about Kit Tyler, who is friendly with a woman in colonial Connecticut who is accused of being a witch. This book could introduce other books about colonial settlement of America or other books by Speare, a Laura Ingalls Wilder Award winner. Her *Calico Captive*, a novel of a girl who has been captured by the Indians during the French and Indian War, has long been on lists of books about life in early America. The Newbery Honor Book *The Sign of the Beaver*, also available as a sound filmstrip and a recording, is about a 12-year-old boy who is left in the Maine woods in their new cabin until his father returns with the family. Matt's friendship with an Indian boy makes an interesting story, and his ability to stay alive makes this a survival book as well. Speare's other Newbery winner, *The Bronze Bow*, available as a sound recording, is about Daniel and his sister who is interested in the message of the new teacher, Jesus.

Another master of historical fiction is Scott O'Dell, for whom the Scott O'Dell Award for Historical Fiction is named. Recent winners of the award include O'Dell himself, for *Streams to the River*, 1987; MacLachlan's *Sarah, Plain and Tall*, 1986; and Avi's *Fighting Ground*, 1985. Two excellent examples of recent historical fiction by O'Dell include *The Serpent Never Sleeps: A Novel of Jamestown and Pocahontas* and *Streams to the River, River to the Sea: A Novel of Sacagawea*. In his novel about Sacagawea, O'Dell uses information from Journals of Lewis and Clark edited by two different men. The book begins with the capture of Sacagawea and her cousin by the Minnetaries. Sacagawea comes into Toussaint Charbonneau's life when he wins her in a game of hands with Red Hawk, the chief's son who later marries her. Because of a technicality in dealing with her kidnapping from her new village, three men claim Sacagawea: La Brogne, a brutal chief of the Hidatsa whose name is used to scare little Indian children; Red Hawk; and Charbonneau, a trader who is half white and half Sioux. The Lewis and Clark expedition hire both Charbonneau and Sacagawea, who have a small child. The difference between historical fiction and nonfiction can easily be shown by comparing and contrasting O'Dell's book with Blumberg's *The Incredible Journey of Lewis and Clark*. This book tells of the information that the explorers brought back about plants, animals, and Indian life in their charting of the area between the Mississippi River and the Pacific Ocean. In an "Aftermath," readers learn of Lewis's suicide. Through Blumberg's book, students can again learn the importance of using sources in creating books. Another fiction book is *Bold Journey* by Bohner and another nonfiction book is *The Lewis and Clark Expedition* by McGrath. *Sacajawea*, a cassette, can be used to show students the similarities in historical fiction, biography, and other nonfiction books.

Historical fiction can be introduced through basal reader stories, which can also introduce authors to students. An author profile of Rosemary Sutcliff is found on pages 294–95 of the eighth grade HBJ basal reader, *Panoramas*, in the Laureate edition by Cullinan, et al. A Sutcliff historical fiction piece, "A Crown of Wild Olive" from *Heather, Oak, and Olive: Three Stories* appears in *Panoramas*, as well as on pages 192–204 of the eighth grade HM basal, *Triumphs*. Two very different boys, Amyntas and Leon, compete in the Olympic Games during the time of the Peloponnesian War, 431–404 B.C. In *Flame-Colored Taffeta*, 12-year-old Damaris Croche discovers a young man shot in the woods near her home in England. Other historical fiction by Sutcliff introduces *Brother Dusty-Feet* and traveling players in Elizabethan England, and *Light Beyond the Forest: The Quest for the Holy Grail*, about King Arthur. A selection from Speare's *Sign of the Beaver* appears in the sixth grade HBJ basal *Treasures* and on pages 16–29 of the seventh grade HM basal reader,

Pageants, edited by Durr, et al. A selection from O'Dell's *Sarah Bishop* appears on pages 180–98 of the HM basal, *Pageants*. Selections from Fritz's *The Cabin Faced West* and Henry's *Justin Morgan Had a Horse* are in the HBJ fifth grade basal reader, *Skylines* on pages 440–53 and 458–69. Check "Historical Fiction," pages 456–57 which tells about the genre and gives background information about both selections.

Historical fiction titles are included in the computer quiz game, *Bookbrain*, for fourth through sixth graders. Titles with annotated entries are: *Caddie Woodlawn* by Brink; *Eight Cousins* by Alcott; *A Gathering of Days* by Blos; *The Little House in the Big Woods* by Wilder; *Constance* by Clapp; *In the Year of the Boar and Jackie Robinson* by Lord; *Mara, Daughter of the Nile* by McGraw; *Moccasin Trail* by McGraw; *Sarah Bishop* by O'Dell; *Sarah, Plain and Tall* by MacLachlan; *Sign of the Beaver* by Speare; *The Whipping Boy* by Fleischman; and *The Witch of Blackbird Pond* by Speare. Titles in other entries are: *The Cabin Faced West* by Fritz; *Calico Captive* by Speare; all of the *Little House* books by Wilder; *Little Women* by Alcott; *Devil in Vienna* by Orgel; *Magical Melons* by Brink; and *Sign of the Chrysanthemum* by Katherine Paterson.

There are a number of books about the Civil War that could be introduced while studying American history, following up fiction or nonfiction selections in a basal reader. A selection of Hunt's Newbery Honor Book, *Across Five Aprils*, appears on pages 594–616 of the seventh grade HBJ basal reader, *Patterns*, in the Laureate edition by Cullinan, et al. The informational article "Civil War Spies" by Foster appears in *Patterns* on pages 564–72 and "Appomattox" by Davis appears on pages 580–87. Some nonfiction books to introduce are: Reit's *Behind Rebel Lines: The Incredible Story of Emma Edmonds, Civil War Spy*, Kent's *The Story of the Surrender at Appomattox Court House*, Kent's *The Story of Ford's Theater and the Death of Lincoln*, Patterson's *Rebels from West Point*, and Weidhorn's *Robert E. Lee.*

Historical fiction can be introduced in a booktalk. Thirteen-year-old Charlie leaves New York City to join the Union Army as a drummer and avenge the death of his older brother in Beatty's *Charlie Skedaddle*. During his first battle in Virginia, Charlie "skedaddles" or runs away to the Blue Mountains. Sixteen-year-old Willie Delamer leaves Texas to join the Confederate Army in Wisler's *Thunder on the Tennessee*. In the beginning, war is parades and singing "Dixie," "The Bonnie Blue Flag," and "The Yellow Rose of Texas." Then the realities come with the Battle of Shiloh after which the South and the Delamer family are never the same again. Students may be interested to know that Wisler is one of 2,300 Shiloh Veteran Hikers who have completed all 11 trails of the famous Civil War battlefield. In Reeder's *Shades of Gray*, 12-year-old Will Page's father is a Confederate soldier, but his uncle refuses to fight for either side. Will wonders who is right. *Shades of Gray* won the 1989 Scott O'Dell Award for historical fiction. In Clapp's *The Tamarack Tree*, 18-year-old Rosemary tells how she survives Vicksburg. In Climo's *A Month of Seven*

Days, 12-year-old Zoe Snyder's pregnant mother must face the Yankees while her father is off fighting. When the Yankee troops take over the family's Georgia home and use it for their headquarters, Zoe tries to frighten Captain Hetcher away by convincing him that the house is haunted. Beatty's *Turn Homeward, Hanalee* is about a 12-year-old who is forced to leave Georgia and relocate in Indiana with other millworkers. Hanalee promises her mother that she will return home as soon as she is able. *Be Ever Hopeful, Hanalee* is the sequel. Lunn's *Root Cellar* is about Rose, a modern Canadian girl, who crosses time to the American Civil War. Hurmence's *A Girl Called Boy* is another space and time book in which a modern black girl is captured by slavers in the 1850s. Hansen's *Which Way Freedom?* is a novel based on an actual event, the massacre at Fort Pillow, Tennessee, in 1864. Quotes throughout the book come from the *Fort Pillow Massacre Report #65*, Joint Committee on the Conduct of the War, 4–10–1864. The book focuses on the role of the black soldier in the American Civil War. Use with Lester's classic nonfiction book, *To Be a Slave*, which includes firsthand accounts of slavery, and Hamilton's *Anthony Burns: The Defeat and Triumph of a Fugitive Slave*, which is about the escape and trial of 22-year-old Anthony Burns in the 1850s. Hamilton's story of a modern family that lives in a house used in the Underground Railroad, *The House of Dies Drear*, has a sequel, *The Mystery of Drear House*. For background information, introduce students to Levine's nonfiction book, *If You Traveled on the Underground Railroad*. Nonfiction about two female slaves who were abolitionists are *Go Free or Die: A Story About Harriet Tubman* and *Walking the Road to Freedom: A Story About Sojourner Truth*, both by Ferris.

Five titles and 10 questions about the Civil War appear on page 230 in the index of Greenson and Taha's *Name That Book! Questions and Answers on Outstanding Children's Books*. Check the index on pages 217–18 under "Blacks" for 27 titles and on page 230 under "Slavery" for six titles.

Historical fiction can be introduced to children via a booktalk while a class is studying the period in social studies or after a class has read a historical fiction selection in a basal reader or in a literature-based reading situation. If students are asked to select and read a historical fiction book set in a certain time period or periods, it is helpful for the school library/media specialist to give a booktalk from which they can select a book. One such booktalk could include the books in the following two sections which could be used with frontier and pioneer units and with various basal and literature-based books mentioned in those two sections.

• *Introducing Jo, Caddie, and Laura* [CU 123–25]. New materials are available about Louisa May Alcott, Laura Ingalls Wilder, and Carol Ryrie Brink, whose heroines are some of the most interesting girls in children's literature—Jo March, Laura Ingalls, and Caddie Woodlawn. Despite an uninspiring format, Greene's *Louisa May Alcott: Author, Nurse, Suffragette* is an important addition to studying Alcott's life and gaining appreciation of her writings. Each chapter begins with a selection from her books, poems, and journals. "Louisa May Alcott's Advice to a Young Writer" appears on page 121. Check pages 16–18 to learn what ideas from Alcott's life appear in her *Little Men* and *Little Women*. A bibliography and list of events in Alcott's lifetime are useful. McGill's *The Story of Louisa May Alcott* is an easy-to-read book for intermediate students which stresses her unsettled childhood, family life, and love of writing. Burke's *Louisa May Alcott* occasionally draws from Alcott's writings and tells about her talent, her father's inability to hold a job, and her personal and family life. Students in middle school and above will appreciate Burke's biography. A selection from *Invincible Louisa*, the Newbery Award-winning biography by Meigs, appears on pages 77–94 of the seventh grade HM basal reader, *Pageants*, by Durr, et al. Check pages 1–6 and 389–95 of Bingham's *Writers for Children* for critical essays about Alcott and Meigs. There is a profile of Alcott on page 661 of Cullinan's *Literature and the Child*. Information about *Little Women* as a landmark book in realistic fiction is given on page 391 of Cullinan's book. A book and cassette of Santrey's *Louisa May Alcott, Young Writer* is available. Alcott's childhood, the basis of much that happens to the March family, is discussed in the sound filmstrip *Louisa May Alcott*. "Jo's Literary Efforts" from *Little Women* appears on pages 111–19 of *More Classics to Read Aloud to Your Children* by Russell.

The whole December 1988 issue of *Cobblestone* magazine is devoted to Alcott and includes such articles as Lawler's "Amos Bronson and Abba May Alcott, Louisa May Alcott's Parents"; Little's "Louisa May Alcott: A Chronology"; Barton's "The Fruitlands Experiment"; Baldwin's "Keeping a Journal"; Delmar's "Louisa May Alcott, Poet"; Richardson's "Blood and Thunder, Louisa May Alcott's Mysteries and Thrillers"; Simon-Katler's "Holidays with the Alcotts"; Calkins's "Louisa As an Army Nurse"; Delamar's "One of the 'Little Women'"; and Tutt's "Louisa's Golden Egg, a Play." Plays about *Little Women* appear in *Christmas Play Favorites for Young People* and *The Big Book of Christmas Plays*, both by Kamerman. Excerpts from Alcott's books accompany recipes in Anderson's *The Louisa May Alcott Cookbook*.

Caddie Woodlawn by Brink is about Caddie and her brothers, Tom and Warren, in pioneer Wisconsin. Humorous incidents like letting the sheep eat the buttons off prissy cousin Annabelle's pretty dress make the book enjoyable. The sequel is *Magical Melons*. Program #15 of the instructional television series *Book Bird*, for fourth graders, shares part of the book. A two-filmstrip set, a video, and a 16mm film of *Caddie Woodlawn*, a Newbery Medal winner, are also available. The sound filmstrip, *Meet the Newbery Author: Carol Ryrie Brink*, is available. Check pages 85–90 of Bingham's *Writers for Children* for a critical essay on Brink.

Teachers and librarians who wish to know more about Wilder as an author should read Spaeth's *Laura Ingalls Wilder*. Laura becomes alive to readers of the *Little House* books in a biography by Giff called *Laura Ingalls Wilder: Growing Up in the Little House*, which tells of Laura's early years, marriage, life as a farmer, and as a writer. One of the events included in the biography, but not the stories, is the death of Laura's baby brother. Older readers will enjoy Zachert's *Laura: The Life of Laura Ingalls Wilder, Author of the Little House on the Prairie*. Blair's *Laura Ingalls Wilder* is an easy-to-read biography. A selection from Blair's biography is on pages 726–27 of Sutherland and Livingston's *The Scott, Foresman Anthology of Children's Literature*. A selection called "Painting Pictures with Words" from Giff's biography is on pages 6–17 of the fifth grade HBJ basal reader, *Skylines*, in the Laureate edition collected by Cullinan, et al. An article by Warner called "Laura Ingalls Wilder, Storyteller" appears on pages 200–03 of the third grade basal reader, *Mystery Sneaker*, edited by Clymer and Venezky. Check pages 611–16 of Bingham's *Writers for Children* for a critical essay on Wilder. *A Little House Sampler*, edited by Anderson, contains essays, articles, columns, poems, fiction, drafts, unpublished manuscripts, notes, and musings of Laura Ingalls Wilder and her daughter Rose Wilder Lane. A selection from Lane's *Let the Hurricane Roar* appears on pages 176–89 of the SB/Ginn eighth grade basal reader, *Worlds Beyond*, edited by Pearson, et al. That same book contains a selection from Cather's *O Pioneers!*, pages 262–79; a poem by Benét, "Western Wagons," on page 174; and an essay by L'Amour, "The Eternal Frontier," pages 254–60.

The entire February 1986 issue of *Cobblestone* magazine is "Laura Ingalls Wilder: Growing Up on the Prairie." Some of the articles include Anderson's "A Laura Ingalls Wilder Chronology"; Anderson's "We Knew the Ingalls Family"; Stoffel's "Little House Crossword"; Lake's "Laura's Home Sites." Pages 6–13 tell of memorials and museums related to the Wilder family in Pepin, Wisconsin; Independence, Kansas; Walnut Grove, Minnesota; Burr Oak, Iowa; De Smet, South Dakota; and Mansfield, Missouri. "A Rose in Full Bloom, Laura's Daughter," pages 25–27, is about Rose Wilder Lane (scholar, journalist, novelist, and political observer) who encouraged her mother to write, offered suggestions on plot and characterization, dealt with agents and publishers, and edited the manuscripts. It is interesting to note that Lane's *Let the Hurricane Roar* was actually written before the *Little House* books. Greco's "Playing the Part of Laura Ingalls Wilder," pages 35–37 is an interview with Melissa Gilbert, who played Laura in all 200 episodes of the television series, *The Little House on the Prairie* between 1974 and 1984. A "Wilder Reprint" of an article that appeared in the *Horn Book Magazine* is still available. A video, *Laura Ingalls Wilder: Up Close and Real*, is performed by a children's librarian who shares memorabilia from the *Little House* books. Biographies of Wilder can be used in conjunction with the sound filmstrip *Meet the Newbery Author: Laura Ingalls Wilder*. Check pages 617–23 of Bingham's *Writers for Children* for a critical essay on Wilder.

Information about *The Little House in the Big Woods* as landmark historical fiction is given on page 460 of Cullinan's *Literature and the Child*. A guide for teaching *The Little House in the Big Woods* appears on pages 61–66 of Somers and Worthington's *Response Guides for Teaching Children's Books*.

Program #2 of the instructional television series *Book Bird* is *Little House in the Big Woods*. "Christmas in the Little House" appears on pages 276–90 of *Time to Read*, volume 2 of *Childcraft*. "The Christmas Horses" from *On the Banks of Plum Creek* is on pages 38–47 of Miller's *Ten Tales of Christmas*. A selection from *Little House in the Big Woods*, "Two Big Bears," appears on pages 368–87 of the fourth grade HM basal reader, *Flights*, edited by Durr and others. "Crossing the Creek" from *Little House on the Prairie* appears on pages 143–61 of the fourth grade HBJ basal reader *Odyssey*, edited by Sebesta. "The First Week at School" from *These Happy Golden Years* is on pages 544–59 of the fifth grade HBJ basal reader, *Skylines*, in the Laureate edition collected by Cullinan and others. There is an informational article by Stratton from *Pioneer Women*, "Voices from the Frontier," on pages 536–43 of *Skylines*. "Two Big Bears" from *Little House in the Big Woods* is also in the fifth grade Silver Burdette/Ginn basal series edited by Pearson, et al.

For activities about the *Little House* books, check pages 202–08 of Laughlin and Watt's *Developing Learning Skills Through Children's Literature* in a section called "Pioneer Life with Laura Ingalls Wilder." See a description on making paper logs for a cabin on pages 85–87 of Bottomley's *Paper Projects for Creative Kids of All Ages*. Information about log cabin construction appears on pages 28–35 of *Shelters from Tepee to Igloos* by Weiss. Directions for making a log cabin out of pretzels are found on page 336 of Bauer's *This Way to Books*.

A 7½" Laura and a 7" Mary doll are available to introduce the *Little House* books to children during booktalks or in displays.

In 1954 the first Laura Ingalls Wilder Award was given to an author or illustrator whose books, published in the United States, have made a substantial and lasting contribution to literature for children. The award is given by the Association for Library Service to Children, a division of the American Library Association. Winners of the Laura Ingalls Wilder Award have been: Laura Ingalls Wilder, 1954; Clara Ingram Judson, 1960; Ruth Sawyer, 1965; E. B. White, 1970; Beverly Cleary, 1975; Theodor S. Geisel (Dr. Seuss), 1980; Maurice Sendak, 1983; Jean Fritz, 1986; and Elizabeth Speare, 1989.

• *If You Like the* **Little House** *Books* [CU 125–32]. Reruns of the television series *The Little House on the Prairie* continue to stimulate the reading of books by Laura Ingalls Wilder. Also, units on frontier and pioneer life are part of many intermediate school curricula. All nine of the Wilder books are available in paperback: *The Little House in the Big Woods*; *The Little House on the Prairie*; *Farmer Boy*; *On the Banks of Plum Creek*; *By the Shores of Silver Lake*; *The Long Winter*; *The Little Town on the Prairie*; *These Happy Golden Years*; and *The First Four Years*. There are many new books about the prairie and about frontier and pioneer life which can be used in conjunction with Wilder's books.

Anyone wishing to know more about how pioneer children lived should read Freedman's *Children of the Wild West*, Kalman's *Early Settler Children*, and Alter's *Growing Up in the Old West*. Photographs of pioneer children and their families are provided in *Children of the Wild West*. Sections of special interest are those about frontier schools, pages 59–69, and games, parties and celebrations, pages 83–95. The index is helpful for answering questions posed on reports about pioneer life and such topics as boys, girls, houses, Indians, log cabins, Oregon Trail, responsibilities, schools, sod houses, teachers, and wagon trains. Information is given about treaties broken with the Indians, and schools to assimilate Indians into the white culture. Illustrations and photographs enhance Kalman's book, which compares the role of children in society then and now. Information is provided about extended families, jobs, punishments, dress for boys and girls, adultlike clothing, work, samplers, daily chores, stowaways, orphans, child labor, schools, death, proper pastimes, pets, games, and influence of the Bible. Alter's *Growing Up in the Old West* is enhanced by drawings and photos which include a cornhusk doll. The information on sod houses is particularly interesting. Alter's index is very helpful for locating items on work, fun, school, and danger. Fisher's *The Schools* tells about American schools from colonial days through the 19th century. An article by Freeman, "Frontier Schools," appears on pages 30–34 of the June 1988 issue of *Cricket* magazine.

The spinning craft of pioneer women and the weaving of baskets by Indian women provide the theme of Siegel's *The Basket Maker and the Spinner.* Three generations of a pioneer family appreciate a plum tree that changes with the seasons in Johnson's *Yonder*. The poetic richness of the language in this book make it essential as a read-aloud. Although the text may be too difficult for elementary students, the black and white photos of pioneer women in Reiter's *Women* can add to any study. Children can learn about pioneer crafts from visits to living history museums, such as the Connor Prairie Pioneer Settlement featured in *The Glorious Fourth at Prairietown* and *Christmas on the Prairie*, both by Anderson. Roop's "A Visit to Old Sturbridge Village" in Massachusetts appears on pages 238–45 of the HBJ basal reader, *Fanfares*, in the Laureate edition, collected by Cullinan, et al. Information on making maple syrup is given on pages 67–70 of Webster's *Winter Book*. Further information appears in Lasky's *Sugaring Time* and on Program #9, *Sugar Bush*, of the television series, *Explorers Unlimited*. Two filmstrips are available: *Maple Sugaring Story* and *Sugaring Time*.

Other nonfiction books of interest are *Cowboys of the Wild West* and *Indian Chiefs*, both by Freedman. The first book traces the life of the cowboy from the late 1860s to the present and the second shows a map of the West in the 1840s and tells about six Western chiefs: Red Cloud, Satanta, Quanah Parker, Washakie, Chief Joseph, and Sitting Bull. Black and white photos enhance both books. The takeover of the West by white settlers and the efforts of Indians to survive is the thrust of Marrin's *War Clouds in the West: Indians and Cavalrymen, 1860–1890*. Ehrlich's *Wounded Knee: An Indian History of the American West* is adapted from Brown's *Bury My Heart at Wounded Knee*. The video *Charles Russell: An American Artist* contains old photos of St. Louis in 1864. Russell portrays the Indian with respect and compassion on canvas and in bronze. His watercolors provided contemporary coverage of the West in magazines and newspapers. For more sources about Russell and Frederic Remington, consult Volume 2 of this book for a section called ART MASTERS and SCULPTURE IN STONE AND CLAY. Eitzen's fiction book, *The White Feather*, is about a Shawnee uprising in early 19th-century Ohio. The feather above a Quaker family's doorway is a symbol that the home belongs to friends of the Indians.

An excellent book to read aloud because of its rich language is Baker's *Where the Buffaloes Begin*. Gammell's illustrations made this a Caldecott Honor Book. Little Wolf, who lives on the prairie, is inspired by a legend about a sacred spot where the buffaloes began, so Little Wolf and his pony look for that place. The book is excellent for introducing Indian legends as well as to stimulate discussions about the displacement of prairie Indians by the white settlers. Students will be interested to learn more about the prairie as they read stories of pioneers' hardships there. Hamlin Garland's poems "Prairie Fires" and "A Dakota Wheat-Field" appear on pages 182–83 of Hall's *The Oxford Book of Children's Verse*. Lerner's *Seasons of the Tallgrass Prairie* tells of plant life on the American prairie by seasons. The danger of fire is also mentioned. George's *One Day in the Prairie* is about animals in a wildlife refuge during a tornado in southwest Oklahoma. Animals include buffalo, prairie dogs, jackrabbits, meadowlarks, elk, and coyote. Information about prairie grasses is included. Hirschi's *Who Lives on the Prairie?* and Stone's *Prairies* also contain information about the prairie.

Journals of pioneer women and historical records have provided much information. Play the selection from Elenore Plaisted's journal on the recording *Pioneer Women: Selections from Their Journals* to introduce Harvey's *My Prairie Year: Based on the Diary of Elenore Plaisted*. Nine-year-old Elenore and her family leave Maine in 1899 to homestead in the Dakota Territory. Her granddaughter based this book on a diary which provides rich details about tornadoes, blizzards, prairie fire, washday, heating rainwater, ironing and mending, gardening, cleaning, cooking, baking, getting supplies, planting, and threshing. Teachers who use the book when studying frontier and pioneer life will agree that it is indeed a "Notable Children's Trade Book in the Language Arts" as it was chosen by the NCTE. Besides writings from the diary of Elenore, the recording *Pioneer Women* includes information from the diaries of Martha Summerhayes, Elinore Pruitt, and Mary Richardson. Turner's *Dakota Dugout* tells of life on the Dakota prairie in a sod house, as related by a grandmother who describes her own experiences as a young bride. The dugout has a hide door, paper windows, and newspaper on the walls. Have students compare and contrast a dugout with their own homes. Turner's book appears on pages 430–35 of the SB/Ginn fifth grade basal reader, *Dream Chasers*, edited by Pearson, et al. After reading the reminiscences, have students read fiction about prairie life and settlement.

Use those books based on primary sources to introduce fiction about prairie life. In Wilder's *By the Shores of Silver Lake*, the Wilder family leaves Minnesota to go to the Dakota Territory which is the setting for *The Little Town on the Prairie*. Talbot's *Sodbuster Venture* and Conrad's *Prairie Songs* are fiction for intermediate and middle school students about the prairies of Kansas and Nebraska. Belle Warren comes to Kansas in 1870 and finds that her fiancé is dead. Thirteen-year-old Martha has held the homestead for her. Conrad's *Prairie Songs* is a winner of the IRA Children's Book Award and makes an excellent companion to Talbot's *Sodbuster Venture*. Louisa, in a sod house on the Nebraska prairie, lives with buffalo chips, snakes, and Indians. The new doctor's wife, Emmeline, impresses Louisa, who does laundry for her in return for lessons. The harshness of the frontier results in the death of the Berryman baby at birth and the madness of Emmeline Berryman. In Turner's *Grasshopper Summer*, 11-year-old Sam moves from Kentucky to the Dakota Territory to experience a plague of grasshoppers. Grasshoppers also plague Nebraska in Talbot's *An Orphan for Nebraska* and there is information about homesteading. Brenner's *Wagon Wheels* is an easy reader about a black family that moves to Kansas after the Civil War, settles land through the Homestead Act, and lives in a dugout. Introduce MacLachlan's *Sarah, Plain and Tall* and Lawlor's *Addie Across the Prairie* at this time. Nine-year-old Addie Mills travels 500 miles by wagon from Sabula, Iowa, to the Dakota Territory to homestead land there. The sequel is *Addie's Dakota Winter*. Addie misses her best friend from Sabula and meets a Norwegian girl at school but knows that she will not be a best friend like Eleanor, one with whom she will be able to share her doll Ruby Lillian. Addie survives a prairie fire in *Addie Across the Prairie* and gets lost in a snowstorm in *Addie's Dakota Winter*. The Kansas prairie is the setting for *In the Face of Danger*, Book 3 in Nixon's series, The Orphan Train.

Nixon bases this series on true stories of over 100,000 children who were sent from the slums of New York City to St. Joseph, Missouri between 1854 and 1880 by the Children's Aid Society founded by Charles Loring Brace. The books include *A Family Apart*, *Caught in the Act*, *In the Face of Danger*, and *A Place to Belong*. In *A Family Apart*, Mrs. Kelly, a widow with six children, gives them up so they can have better lives and sends them west on the Orphan Train to St. Joseph, Missouri. The children are given homes, and Frances Mary pretends to be a boy so she won't be separated from a younger brother. One of their activities is helping a slave family in the Underground Railroad. In *Caught in the Act*, Mr. Friedrich, a prosperous farmer, takes Michael Kelly into his family, but thinks that Michael is dishonest and can be straightened out with lots of hard work and discipline that includes beatings. Gunther Friedrich, the son, also causes trouble for Michael. In *In the Face of Danger*, 12-year-old Megan Kelly, the middle child, goes to live on the prairie of the Kansas Territory. Megan thinks that all the disasters—the blizzard, wolves, and an armed fugitive—are her fault because of something a gypsy fortune-teller tells her. In *A Place to Belong*, Danny and Peg are placed with Alfrid and Olga Swenson. When Olga dies suddenly, the family decides that they can stay together if Alfrid finds a new wife. Talbot's *Orphan for Nebraska* is about 11-year-old Kevin O'Rourke, who is sent west by the Children's Aid Society to Nebraska in 1872 to help a newspaper editor. Kevin's Uncle Michael had sent money to Ireland for Kevin and his mother to come to America, but Mother dies on the ship coming over and Kevin arrives in New York to learn that Uncle Michael is in jail. After surviving on the streets by selling newspapers, Kevin takes shelter in the Newsboys' Lodging House run by the Children's Aid Society. Compare Talbot's metaphors of the prairie with those found in MacLachlan's *Sarah, Plain and Tall*. In Magnuson's *Orphan Train*, for older readers, 27 children go west in 1853 with Emma, the spinster niece of a minister.

The most touching story of life on the prairie is MacLachlan's *Sarah, Plain and Tall*, winner of the Newbery Medal, Christopher Medal, Garden State Children's Book Award, the Scott O'Dell Award for historical fiction, and the Golden Kite Award. Sarah arrives from Maine as a mail-order bride for a prairie farmer and as mother to his two children, Anna and Caleb. A cassette, sound filmstrips, and video are available for the story. A selection from *Sarah, Plain and Tall* appears on pages 568–98 of the fifth grade HBJ basal reader, *Skylines* from the Laureate edition collected by Cullinan, et al. and on pages 522–35 of the SB/Ginn 5th grade basal reader, *Dream Chasers*, edited by Pearson, et al. *Sarah, Plain and Tall* makes an excellent book for the nucleus of a literature-based reading program. Landes and Flender have created a *Book Wise Literature Guide to MacLachlan's Sarah, Plain and Tall*. A web for *Sarah, Plain and Tall*, created by the Marquette-Alger Reading Council, is available to anyone who sends a stamped self-addressed envelope to MARC, PO Box 574, Marquette, MI 49855.

Two related books are Lampman's *Bargain Bride*, about a girl who is married off and widowed at the age of 15 in the Oregon Territory, and *A Place to Belong*, the fourth book in Nixon's Orphan Train Quartet. Supplement these stories with interviews with local people who can share stories that have passed down to them through their family history. A retired teacher, Betty Zesiger, taped a brief account about her grandfather Jacobson, the first Lutheran minister in Minnesota, and how he received his bride, sight unseen, from the old country—Norway. The Jacobsons were contemporaries of the Wilder family and once slept at their cabin during a blizzard. Encourage students to bring in similar information from family histories. Be sure to check with the public library or the parents of children in the class to see if they have any family reminiscences that will help students to better understand the past. More information about family history appears in Chapter 12 in a section called IMMIGRANT AND FAMILY STORIES INSPIRE WRITING PROJECTS and in Volume 2 of this book, in a section called USING DIARIES, JOURNALS, AND LETTERS TO INSPIRE WRITING.

Journals and diaries provide sources and the framework for other books. Anderson's *Joshua's Westward Journal* is a photo essay intended to show a family that leaves Pennsylvania and travels over the National Road into Illinois in 1836. Black and white photos showing the Carpenter family have been taken at Conner Prairie Pioneer Settlement in Noblesville, Indiana and the Living History Farm in Des Moines, Iowa. The journal ends on July 27th with a new home and a wedding. A selection from a fictional diary of a girl appears on pages 530–45 of the eighth grade HM basal reader from the Laureate edition, *Panoramas*, selected by Cullinan, et al. and pages 230–46 of the eighth grade HM basal reader, *Triumphs*, edited by Durr, et al. The selections come from the Newbery winner, *A Gathering of Days: A New England Girl's Journal, 1830–1832* by Blos. Henry's *Log Cabin in the Woods: A True Story of a Pioneer Boy* is about the life of an 11-year-old boy on the Indiana frontier of 1832. The book is based on Oliver Johnson's reminiscences retold by his grandson, Howard.

Several fiction books have been written about settling the Midwest. In Saunders's *Aurora Means Dawn*, a family with seven children moves by wagon from Connecticut to Ohio in the 1800s to a town that is nothing more than a small surveyor's post. Extensive notes accompany this story based on a true incident. Disappointment also faces 14-year-old Shem's family when they arrive in Millfield, Michigan in *Brothers of the Heart: A Story of the Old Northwest, 1837–1838* by Blos. Swedish immigrants in Sandin's *The Long Way to a New Land* and *The Long Way Westward* travel by train and by steamboat to Minnesota. In Shaw's *Happy Birthday, Kirsten: A Springtime Story*, a 9-year-old Swedish immigrant and her family move to Minnesota in 1854. Check pages 53–59 for information about life on the frontier. Dolls are available for the books in the American Girls Collection. Cassettes accompany *Meet Kirsten: An American Girl* and *Kirsten Learns a Lesson: A School Story*. Other books about her include *Kirsten's Surprise: A Christmas Story*; *Kirsten Saves the Day: A Summer Story*; and *Changes for Kristen: A Winter Story*.

In Scott's *The Covered Wagon and Other Adventures*, the author tells of her family's trip by wagons from St. Paul, Minnesota to Thermopolis, Wyoming in 1906 and a later trip to Oregon. Any of the pioneer journals could be used to encourage children to read books about wagon train journeys, life in pioneer times, biographies of pioneers, or to write their own journals based on those readings.

Bloch's *Overland to California in 1859: A Guide for Wagon Train Travelers* includes quotes from sources actually used by pioneers, especially Marcy's *The Prairie Traveler*. *The Prairie Traveler: A Hand-Book for Overland Expeditions* tells of routes, food, animal treatment, water, sanitation, fording rivers, descending mountains, saddles, rattlesnake bites, colic, tents, jerking meat, gun accidents, guides and hunters, tracking and pursuing Indians, and hunting for deer, buffalo, antelope, bear, and bighorn sheep. Any students wishing to recreate a diary or write a short story about wagon train travel could find background information here. Ware's *Emigrants' Guide to California* is a reproduction of a book originally printed in 1849. Schlissel's *Women's Diaries of the Westward Journey* contains the diaries of three women as well as reminiscences of others. A table lists the characteristics of women who traveled west between 1851 and 1859 and charts age, marital status, family, accidents, and deaths. The first diary tells of Lydia and Harry Rudd, a childless couple, who set out for Oregon in 1852; it is on pages 187–98 of Schlissel's book. Amelia Stewart Knight left Iowa for Oregon Territory with her husband and seven children in 1853 and her diary is on pages 199–216. Jane Gould Tourtillott, her husband, two small sons, father-in-law, brother and sister-in-law went to California in 1862 and her diary appears on pages 217–31. Rothenberg's "Westward Ho!" is a magazine article on pages 12–13 of the November 18, 1988 issue of *Junior Scholastic Magazine*. *The Westward Movement: A Unit of Study* is a set of five filmstrips about the 18th and 19th centuries. Individual titles include: *The First Frontier*; *Early Frontier Life*; *Moving Deep into the Interior*; *Settling Westward Lands*; and *Sodbusters, Cowboys, and Indians*. Computer programs of interest are *America Moves West*, *Oregon Trail*, and *Wagons West*.

A number of fiction books tell about traveling west by wagon train. Ten-year-old Libby travels by covered wagon with her family for two months and a thousand miles from Virginia to Michigan in 1837 in Whelan's *Next Spring an Oriole*. When the family befriends a Potawatomi Indian child with the measles, the Indians help them survive the winter with gifts of corn and smoked fish. Anderson's *The Glorious Fourth at Prairietown* and *Christmas on the Prairie* are about travel by wagon to Indiana. Donahue's *Straight Along a Crooked Road* is for older readers. Levitin's *The No-Return Trail* is fiction but contains a bibliography of primary and secondary sources. Levitin's book is based on the life of the first American woman to travel from Missouri to California. Nancy Kelsey was a 17-year-old mother of an infant when she and her husband Ben left their home to travel to California with a small wagon train. Some of the train split off to go to Oregon and a reduced group arrived in California without wagons or animals. Two other brothers and sisters-in-law went off to Oregon. The epilogue on pages 151–52 explains what became of the real people who were members of the Bidwell-Bartleson expedition of 1841.

In *Trouble for Lucy* by Stevens, Lucy Stewart, her parents, and her dog travel from Independence, Missouri to Oregon on the wagon train of 1843. Marcus Whitman delivers her baby sister on the way. Each chapter begins with a quote from an actual wagon train diary. Lucy makes friends with a Quaker girl. When her dog is left behind, Lucy goes back to get him and she is returned to the wagon train by Pawnee Indians. *Trouble for Lucy* is a 15-minute segment of the instructional television series *Readit*, program #9. Kate Purdy smuggles her cat on board the wagon train from Missouri to Oregon in *Pioneer Cat* by Hooks. Kate had been told that she could take anything that would fit in a certain box so she brings along Snuggs. All turns out well because Snuggs gives birth to four kittens that are worth a fortune in Oregon. Coerr's *The Josefina*

Story Quilt is an easy reader about Faith who in May of 1850 leaves in a covered wagon for California from Missouri. Faith brings her pet chicken, Josefina, even though it doesn't lay eggs and is too tough to eat. Faith keeps a record of her trip by sewing a patchwork quilt. The first patch is called wagon wheel. For books about quilts, consult a section of Volume 2 of this book called QUILTS. Waddell's *Going West* is 9-year-old Kate's diary of a trip across the United States in a covered wagon.

In Lasky's *Beyond the Divide*, 14-year-old Miribah Simon follows her father from Pennsylvania to California in 1849 after her father has been "shunned" by his Amish family for attending the funeral of a non-Amish man. Check the right hand corner at the beginning of each chapter for the date and place where Meribah is in her journey. Fourteen-year-old Abigail Parker travels by wagon train to the gold fields in 1850 in Murrow's *West Against the Wind*, a book for middle school students. Abby travels the Overland Trail from Missouri to the Yuba River with her mother and other relatives to join father in the gold fields. Lots of information on wagon train travel is included as well as the birth of Abby's cousin, her first menstrual period, and first stirrings of romance for Matthew Reed, a young man with a secret. The book makes a good companion book for Levitin's *No-Return Trail*. Harvey's *Cassie's Journey: Going West in the 1860's* is a first-person account of a girl who travels by covered wagon from Illinois to California. Cassie experiences buffalo, Indians, terrible weather, illnesses, snakebite, and death. The incidents for this picture book come from Schlissel's *Women's Diaries of the Westward Journey*. Waddell's *Going West* contains 9-year-old Kate's diary of a trip across the United States by covered wagon. *If You Traveled West in a Covered Wagon* by Levine is about life on the Oregon Trail. Beatty's *Eight Mules from Monterey* is about a librarian and her daughter who travel by mule train to establish libraries in California.

In *Texas Footprints*, Kerr writes about her great-grandparents who go to Texas in 1823. Scandinavian pioneers appear in Nixon's *A Place to Belong*. Hanna's *Lantern in the Valley—The Story of Christina and Peter Swenson* is about Norwegian-Swedish pioneers who go to Texas. Shefelman's *The Spirit of Iron* is about German immigrants who go to Texas in the 1840s. Information about a Texas woman, Susanna, and her child Angelina, are told in *Susanna of the Alamo* by Jakes. Susanna's own writings provide sources for this book. Readers who know all about Jim Bowie, Robert Travis, and Davy Crockett at the Alamo, now have a chance to learn about Susanna Dickinson, a survivor of the Alamo massacre in 1836.

Students may wish to go further back in American history to read about the lives of children in the 18th century. Speare's Newbery Honor Book *The Sign of the Beaver* is about 13-year-old Matt, who is left alone in his family's cabin in Maine while his father goes back to get the family. Matt survives with the help of the Indian boy, Attean. *Sign of the Beaver* is available as a video. Teachers and librarians concerned with thinking skills should check pages 137–

45 of Kruise's *Those Blooming Books: A Handbook for Extending Thinking Skills* for suggestions on teaching *The Sign of the Beaver.* For webbing techniques for Speare's story, check pages 652–61 of *Children's Literature in the Elementary School* by Huck, et al. In Dalgliesh's classic, *The Courage of Sara Noble*, 8-year-old Sarah moves to the Connecticut wilderness to cook for her father in 1707 while he is clearing land. In an incident similar to the one in *Sign of the Beaver*, Sara's father leaves her with the Indians while he goes back to get the rest of the family. Dalgliesh's Newbery Honor Book is also available as a recording, 16mm film, and video. Adults who want to learn ideas for teaching Dalgliesh's *The Courage of Sarah Noble* in a literature-based program should consult pages 44–47 of Somers and Worthington's *Response Guides for Teaching Children's Books.* Suggestions for teaching *The Matchlock Gun* by Edmonds appear on pages 48–51 of that book. *The Cornhusk Doll* by Minshull is for younger readers but has a situation similar to the one in *Sign of the Beaver.* When Yellow Feather is caught in Pa's bear trap, the Indian is resentful that he and his daughter must stay with the white family while he recuperates. Young Mary's gift of her most prized possession, her cornhusk doll, thaws the Indian. A display case containing a cornhusk doll and white feather could be used to highlight *The Cornhusk Doll* and *The White Feather* by Eitzen, which is about a Quaker family in Ohio during a Shawnee uprising. Children love to bring in artifacts and items that explain vocabulary in the story to make it more meaningful and also to bring the story to life. Fritz's classic, *The Cabin Faced West,* is about Anne Hamilton who lives in a log cabin and misses her former home in Gettysburg. Anne confesses her lonesomeness in her diary. George Washington comes for supper in the book. *The Cabin Faced West* is Program #3 in the instructional television program *Books from Cover to Cover.* A selection from Fritz's book appears in the fifth grade HBJ basal reader, *Skylines,* in the Laureate edition collected by Cullinan, et al. In *Daniel's Duck* by Bulla, an easy reader, Jeff and Daniel live in a log cabin in Tennessee. Daniel carves a wooden duck and mother makes a quilt. Check pages 282–99 of Durr's second grade HM basal reader, *Discoveries,* and pages 156–67 of Pearson's second grade SB/Ginn basal reader, *Garden Gates* for this story. Second grade teachers may wish to choose one of the pioneer stories in this section to read aloud to the class.

On the lighter side, students will enjoy reading or listening to Kellogg's retelling of *Pecos Bill.* Kellogg also illustrated Purdy's *Iva Dunnit and the Big Wind.* In this humorous tall tale, pioneer Iva Dunnit has six children. Once during "The Big Wind," Iva is blown about so she takes off her petticoats to save the chickens. Iva climbs up on the roof to hold down the roofing and ties the chickens to her corset strings until the wind blows over. Dewey's *Febold Feboldson* is an easy reader containing seven tall tales about a farmer in Nebraska in 1848. Readers learn about cyclones, blizzards, and grasshoppers. *Chuck Wagon Stew* by Bird contains nine tall tales from the Old West. Rosenbloom's *Wild West Riddles* contains jokes and riddles about the West. Tales and biographies about Johnny Appleseed can also be used in pioneer units. Aliki's *The Story of Johnny Appleseed* appears in Pearson's *Garden Gates* on pages 184–91, the second grade basal reader in the SB/Ginn series. For other books about Chapman and about apple trees, consult Volume 2 of this book for a section called EGG TREES, COOKIE TREES, BIRD TREES, AND MORE TREES.

Twenty-four titles and 48 questions about frontier and pioneer life are listed in Greenson and Taka's *Name That Book! Questions and Answers on Outstanding Children's Books.* Check page 230 in the index. Frontier and pioneer books are included in the books that contain annotated entries in the computer quiz game, *Bookbrain,* for fourth through sixth graders. For specific titles, check INTRODUCING HISTORICAL FICTION in this chapter.

CHAPTER ELEVEN

Reintroducing the Classics

Many times students cannot be tempted to read a "classic" children's book because the illustrations are dated or the physical appearance of the book is unappealing. [See also CU 713.] Perhaps it is time to purchase some new paperback copies of classics, because students prefer paperbacks anyway. Or purchase a new hardback edition of a classic. Sometimes the anniversary of the publication of a book generates a new edition. A new recording, filmstrip, or video of a classic can be used to stimulate reading. Often when a classic book becomes a television program or movie, a new edition of the book becomes available and students can be lured into it because of the media tie-in.

Anne of Green Gables and *Anne of Green Gables: The Sequel* appeared on the television program *Wonderworks*. The videos of these programs are available to buy. *Anne of Green Gables* and *Anne of Avonlea* appeared on the Disney channel. A shorter performance is available on a video called *Anne of Green Gables*. A cassette of the musical based on the book is also available. Flo Gibson reads the unabridged book on eight cassettes. Two adaptations of the book include McHugh's *Anne of Green Gables* and Kesseley's *A Child's Anne*. All of the paperbacks in the series can be shared after any of these multimedia presentations: *Anne of Avonlea*; *Anne of the Island*; *Anne of Windy Poplars*; *Anne's House of Dreams*; *Anne of Ingleside*; *Rainbow Valley*; *Rilla of Ingleside*; and *Chronicles of Avonlea*. Other Montgomery books include *Emily of the New Moon*; *Emily Climbs*; *Emily's Quest*; *Story Girl*; and *The Golden Road*. Macdonald's *Anne of Green Gables Cookbook* features recipes for food mentioned in the book.

Fifty recipes based on classic children's books and poems appear in Greene's *Once Upon a Recipe*.

Two cassette versions of Burnett's *The Secret Garden* are available. A Yorkshire dialect narrated by Fitzgerald is used, and music is added to the Spoken Arts version. In the cassettes published by Audio Book Contractors, Gibson uses voice changes to suit the characters. Both sets contain six cassettes. An older recording contains excerpts read by Claire Bloom, who also uses dialects to represent various characters. New hardcover editions of *The Secret Garden* have been illustrated by Hague and by Hughes. Paperbacks are available from Bantam, Dell, Puffin, Scholastic, Signet, and Trophy.

Hague has also been busy illustrating other classics: a new edition of Barrie's *Peter Pan*, Sandburg's *Rootabaga Stories: Part 1* and *Part 2*, and Tolkien's *The Hobbit*. Lofting's *The Voyages of Dr. Doolittle* has been edited recently to remove racially offensive material. Color photos enhance *The New Adventures of Pippi Longstocking: The Storybook Based on the Movie*. The film of

Lindgren's classic can be used to interest students in other books about that character: *The New Adventures of Pippi Longstocking; Pippi Goes on Board; Pippi in the South Seas; Pippi Longstocking;* and *Pippi on the Run.* Other books by Lindgren include: *The Children of Noisy Village; Springtime in Noisy Village; Dragon with Red Eyes; The Tomten;* and *The Tomten and the Fox.*

Several new editions of *The Adventures of Pinocchio* by Collodi are available and are illustrated by the following artists: Ambrus, Innocenti, and Wainwright. A word-for-word reading from Spinner's adaptation appears on a cassette. A large print edition of Baum's *The Wonderful Wizard of Oz* is available. Caldecott winner Ed Young has illustrated Wilde's *The Happy Prince.* San Souci's retelling of Irving's *The Legend of Sleepy Hollow* is available in picture book format.

Check pages 181–91 of Bingham's *Writers for Children* for critical essays about Dickens. The play "A Christmas Carol" appears on pages 277–97 of Kamerman's *Big Book of Christmas Plays. A Christmas Carol: A Ghost Story for Christmas* illustrated by Foreman contains darker illustrations than those by Hyman in *A Christmas Carol* by Dickens. Hyman also illustrated *A Child's Christmas in Wales* by Dylan Thomas.

New editions of Carroll's *Alice's Adventures in Wonderland* are available, illustrated by Browne, Prachaticka, Tenniel, Weevers, and Wiggins. Wiggins also illustrated another title, *Alice in Wonderland and Through the Looking Glass.* Todd's illustrations are found in *Through the Looking Glass and What Alice Found There.* Browne's surreal illustrations are found in *Alice's Adventures in Wonderland.* An edition arranged by Edens contains illustrations from various illustrators over 125 years. The Disney version of *Alice in Wonderland* can be found in video stores. Selections from that movie, featuring Greenwood and Holloway, are available on the recording *Alice in Wonderland.* Christopher Plummer reads on the recording *The Complete Alice in Wonderland.*

Sewell's *Black Beauty* has been adapted by McKinley and illustrated by Jeffers to make an old classic come alive again. The video of an older film version of the story is available in video stores. A video is also available for Henry's *Brighty of the Grand Canyon.* Use this video about a donkey to stimulate interest in the books by Henry about horses. Some books by Henry include: *Album of Horses; All About Horses; Black Gold; Born to Trot; Justin Morgan Had a Horse; Mustang, Wild Spirit of the West; San Domingo: The Medicine Hat Stallion;* and *White Stallion of Lipizza.* Books in the King of the Wind series include: *A Colt Is Born; Sultan's Gift; Sire of Champions;* and *An Innkeeper's Horse.* Books in the Misty series include: *Misty of Chincoteague; A Pictorial Life of Misty; Stormy, Misty's Foal; Sea Star, Orphan of Chincoteague; Going Home;* and *Whirlpool.* Petula Clark reads an adaptation of Spyri's *Heidi* on cassettes. Video stores carry the Shirley Temple version of the classic film, *Heidi.* Hardyment's book *Heidi's Alps* is a travelogue written for adults which features places in Europe found in children's books. Two cassettes contain Lumley's reading of Dodie Smith's classic, *101 Dalmatians.* A film of

Cleary's *The Mouse and the Motorcycle* and a sound filmstrip of Cleary's Newbery-winning *Dear Mr. Henshaw* are available. A film or video using claymation share St. Exupery's classic, *The Little Prince*. An inexpensive video of Dahl's *Willy Wonka and the Chocolate Factory*, based on his *Charlie and the Chocolate Factory*, is available. Lionel Jeffries reads an abridgment of Fleming's *Chitty Chitty Bang Bang* on two cassettes of the same title. A soundtrack of the PBS TV special of *The Velveteen Rabbit* by Williams is available. Julie Harris reads from Wiggin's *Rebecca of Sunnybrook Farm* on a cassette. Hinkle retold the version of *Rebecca of Sunnybrook Farm* that appears on two cassettes by Troll. Barrie's *Peter Pan*, in the same series, is read from the exact text.

Television can stimulate the reading of classics. Grahame's *The Wind in the Willows* is part of the recent "Long Ago and Far Away" series. Editions of the book are illustrated by Rackham, Shepard, and Burningham. Other books to introduce include *The Wind in the Willows: The River Bank*; *The Open Road*; *Wayfarers All: From The Wind in the Willows*. An animated Disney version of *Wind in the Willows* is available at video stores.

Bauer has shared three classics in play form in her book *Presenting Reader's Theater*. The selections come from *The Arabian Nights*; Milne's *Winnie-the-Pooh*; and Juster's *The Phantom Tollbooth*. Pat Carroll reads from an abridged *Phantom Tollbooth* on a recording. Selections from *Winnie-the-Pooh* are performed on the recording *Carol Channing Sings "The Pooh Song Book."* Check in video stores for *Winnie the Pooh and Tigger Too* and *Winnie the Pooh and the Honey Tree*. Some other Milne titles to introduce include: *The House at Pooh Corner*; *The Pooh Birthday Book*; *Pooh Goes Visiting*; *The Pooh Sticker Book*; *Pooh's Adventures with Eeyore and Tigger*; *Pooh's Adventures with Piglet*; *Pooh's Pot of Honey*; *Winnie-the-Pooh*; *Winnie-the-Pooh: A Pop Up Book*; *Winnie-the-Pooh's Calendar Book*; *The World of Christopher Robin*; and *The World of Pooh*. Poetry books include *Now We Are Six* and *When We Were Very Young*.

Bingham's *Writers for Children* includes information about the following classic authors: Barrie, pages 29–35; Burnett, pages 103–10; Carroll, pages 117–27; Collodi, pages 129–37; Grahame, pages 247–54; Lofting, pages 365–71; Milne, pages 397–405; Montgomery, pages 415–22; Sandburg, pages 503–10; Sewell, pages 525–28; Spyri, pages 529–53; and Wiggin, pages 605–09.

The cassette *Dragon Slayer: The Story of Beowulf* is based on Sutcliff's book *Beowulf*. Two new picture book editions of Chaucer's *Canterbury Tales* are available. The four tales that appear in Cohen's book, illustrated by Hyman, are: "The Prologue to the Nun's Priest's Tale"; "The Nun's Priest's Tale"; "The Pardoner's Tale (Wife of Bath)"; and "The Franklin's Tale." The seven tales that appear in the collection by Hastings called *The Canterbury Tales by Geoffrey Chaucer: A Selection* are: "The Knight's Tale"; "The Reeve's Tale"; "The Nun's Priest's Tale"; "The Pardoner's Tale"; "The Wife of Bath's Tale"; "The Franklin's Tale"; and "The Miller's Tale." The last tale is about cuckoldry and makes this collection a better version for high schools where Chaucer is studied rather than for elementary schools. Illustrations in the book by Hastings are by Cartwright. "The Nun's Priest's Tale" appears in Cooney's picture book *Chanticleer and the Fox*, a Caldecott winner. Use the cassette or sound filmstrip to introduce the two new illustrated collections of Chaucer's stories, first told by 30 people on a pilgrimage from London to Canterbury in 1386.

A new edition of *Tales from Shakespeare* by the Lambs is now available. Color illustrations of Shakespeare's poems appear in the book *Under the Greenwood Tree: Shakespeare for Young People*. Claire Bloom and Derek Jacobi perform the poems on a cassette with period music from the Folger Consort of the Folger Shakespeare Library. Favorite poems include the title poem as well as "When Icicles Hang by the Wall"; "Double, Double, Toil and Trouble"; "Shall I Compare Thee to a Summer's Day"; "What's in a Name"; "To Be or Not to Be, That is the Question"; "Tomorrow, and Tomorrow, and Tomorrow"; and "All the World's a Stage." A bibliography accompanies Turner's biography *William Shakespeare*. Use the biography with Avi's humorous fiction title, *Romeo and Juliet—Together (and Alive!) at Last*.

Descriptions of 30 classics appear in Chapter 5, "Tried and True, Old Books for Young People," pages 39–57 of the Lindskoogs' *How to Grow a Young Reader*. Towards the ends of the 1980s, many publishers have taken a good look at their backlists and have returned titles to print. While not all of these, certainly, are classics, many are well-loved and several are very good indeed.

CHAPTER TWELVE

The Making of America: Immigration and Liberty

VISITING THE STATUE OF LIBERTY. It was no surprise that a group of books about the Statue of Liberty appeared when she celebrated her hundredth birthday in 1986. *The Story of the Statue of Liberty* by Betsy and Giulio Maestro is an oversize easy-to-read book which tells the story of how the famous statue was created and sent to the United States from France. Highlights include Bartholdi's sketches, pictures of the skeleton, the World's Fair in Paris, a table of dates, dimensions, items of major restoration work, Emma Lazarus's poem from the pedestal, and interesting tidbits. *The Statue of Liberty: America's Proud Lady,* by Haskins, includes black and white photos and prints to help tell the story in a straightforward, easy manner. Information about the birth, model, facelift, and vital statistics, as well as what the statue means to us, is included. Shapiro's *How They Built the Statue of Liberty* includes a step-by-step description of building the statue; the meticulous sketches would be of special interest to art students. Sketches include the first models, shaping the copper plates, the skeleton, raising and unveiling the statue. Shapiro's book won the Garden State Children's Book Award in the Young Nonfiction category. Fisher's *The Statue of Liberty* is an ALA Notable Book which includes over 50 photographs, plus drawings, by the author. Many black and white photos of Bartholdi are included, as well as early drawings and models, and schematic drawings of staircases. Joe Pulitzer and his campaign to raise money for the pedestal is included. Emma Lazarus's poem "The New Colossus," located on the pedestal, appears on page 61.

The books by Mercer, Burchard, and Harris are longer. Mercer's book is an updated centennial edition and the first six chapters emphasize Bartholdi. One bit of trivia about Bartholdi is that he designed his own tombstone. Attention is given to problems faced by the Americans in raising money for the project. Lazarus's words from the pedestal appear on page 91. Burchard's *The Statue of Liberty: Birth to Rebirth* tells about the 121 years from the birth of the idea to the 100th birthday. Information is included about what it was like to visit the statue and information on the celebrations of the 50th anniversary and bicentennial are given. One chapter is devoted to immigration. Two chapters are devoted to the restoration. Two pages of statistics, a chronology, and bibliography are helpful. An interesting bit of trivia in this book is that Bartholdi's mother was the model for the statue's face. *A Statue for America: The First Hundred Years of the Statue of Liberty* by Harris contains many anecdotes about the statue. The index is excellent and students could be given the specific task of looking up information in the index of this book as well as some of the others. The entire Lazarus poem is included on page 88. Information about Eiffel and his design of the interior framework and anecdotes about the statue in the movie *Planet of the Apes* are examples of information included.

Coerr's *The Lady with a Torch* contains cartoon illustrations which give the book a lighter touch than some of the others. Important dates are included. For a close-up view inside and outside the crown on the head of the Statue of Liberty, see Munro's *The Inside-Outside Book of New York City.*

I Lift My Lamp: Emma Lazarus and the Statue of Liberty by Levinson is a biography of the poet who wrote "The New Colossus." The book begins with the statue and then goes back to Emma's life as a well-to-do Jewish girl and woman; her work as an aide to immigrants; her life as a writer and poet; and literary exchanges with Emerson. Levinson tells how her poem was lost and rediscovered and how Miss Liberty became the immigrant's symbol. There is lots of information on the sculptor Bartholdi also. Lefer's *Emma Lazarus* is for middle and high school readers and tells of her personal life of privilege, acclaim as a poet, and assistance to Russian Jewish immigrants.

ELLIS ISLAND AND AMERICAN IMMIGRATION. The anniversary of the Statue of Liberty and her facelift also gave rise to books about Ellis Island. This was a natural corollary because Ellis Island became an official part of the Statue of Liberty National Monument in 1965. Siegel's *Sam Ellis's Island* is a history of the island from the time Sam Ellis was a wholesale fish merchant and Tory in 1763. The history includes Dutch settlers, rebellion, revolution, Castle Garden, and the change from Fort Clinton to Fort Gibson. Information is given about changing immigration patterns from the first immigrant to set foot on Ellis Island in 1892 until the doors were closed in 1954. The emphasis in Fisher's *Ellis Island: Gateway to the New World* is on the people who passed through there. Photographs help understanding of the procedures in processing immigrants. This book is a companion for Fisher's *The Statue of Liberty.* The books by Siegel and Fisher complement each other. Both can be introduced with the question "Did anyone in your family come to the United States as an immigrant between 1892 and 1954?" If so, they would have passed through Ellis Island.

BOOKS ABOUT IMMIGRANTS. Following on the heels of the books about the Statue of Liberty and Ellis Island are books about immigrants. Some of the books stand alone, and some are part of a series. *Into a Strange Land: Unaccompanied Refugee Youth in America* by the Ashabranners is one example of the several good nonfiction books available. Specific cases of children who came here without their parents and why they did so are included. Another book by the same authors is *The New Americans: Changing Patterns in U.S. Immigration.* Case histories of refugee immigrants from Asia, Africa, Haiti, Cuba, and the Caribbean, as well as undocumented immigrants, are included. Rosenberg's *Making a New Home in America* is about five children, ages 7 to 9, who came from Japan, Cuba, India, Guyana, and Vietnam. Problems of adjustment are included. Blumenthal's *Coming to America: Immigrants from the British Isles* describes English, Irish, Welsh and Scottish immigrants and their reasons for coming to the United States. Excerpts from letters, journals and contemporary books are included. A chronological list of U.S. immigration laws is helpful. Some other books about immigrants are: *The Lebanese in America* by Harik; *The Vietnamese in America* by Rutledge; and *The Danes in America* by Petersen.

A number of immigrant books read like stories. Primary students will enjoy Sandin's *The Long Way to a New Land*, about Carl Erik, who left Sweden to come to the United States. Posell's *Homecoming* is about how the six Jewish Koshansky children survive the 1917 Revolution in Russia, and escape the Ukraine for the United States. A grandfather tells how the family came to America from Russia in Heller's *Castle on Hester Street*, which won the Parents' Choice Award of the Association of Jewish Libraries. In Harvey's *Immigrant Girl: Becky of Eldridge Street*, a Jewish girl leaves Russia to escape the pograms in 1910 and comes to live in New York City with relatives. In *Apple Pie and Onions* by Caseley, a granddaughter enjoys hearing her grandmother tell about life in America after coming from Russia. However, when her grandmother speaks Yiddish on the street to a friend, the girl is embarrassed. Vinebert's *Grandmother Came from Sworitz* is about emigration from Russia. A selection from Blaine's *Dvora's Journey* appears on pages 84–93 of the fourth grade HBJ basal reader, *Crossroads*, from the Laureate edition, collected by Cullinan, et al. In this excerpt, a Jewish family escapes from Russia to Poland and then to the United States in 1904. Information about Hoguet's *Solomon Grundy* appears at the end of this text; Grundy is the child of a baker who comes from England to the United States in 1830. Bunting's *How Many Days to America?* is a different kind of immigrant story in which a Caribbean family leaves on a small fishing boat to America. Have students describe "boat people" as the term is generally used.

IMMIGRANT AND FAMILY STORIES INSPIRE WRITING PROJECTS. Many books, even though they are fiction, are based on some event that is connected to the writer. Books that are based on family stories and tradition can be read to or by students for inspiration to write about a family incident of their own. Levinson's *Watch the Stars Come Out* is an ALA Notable Book and a notable book of the National Council for the Social Studies. Grandma tells how she and her brother came alone on a boat to America to join her father, mother, and sister. Naturally the boat came in near the Statue of Liberty. The beginning and end of the book show a grandmother and child looking at pictures in an album while the grandmother tells the story. In Cooney's *Miss Rumphius*, "The Lupine Lady" is the narrator's great-aunt, Alice, whose grandfather came to America on a large sailing ship. He told her stories of faraway places so she too goes traveling but comes home to live by the sea. Her grandfather told her to do something to make the world more beautiful, so she plants lupines to give people joy. Both Levinson and Cooney's books are excellent for reading aloud or to inspire children to find family stories of their own and write about them. Rylant's *The Relatives Came* evokes the same feeling of family, as relatives come from Virginia one summer to stay for a visit. Ziefert's *A New Coat for Anna* uses the raw material of a true story for the plot. A mother gets a new coat for her daughter through a complicated process after World War II. Noble's *Apple Tree Christmas* is based on the experiences of the author. After a three-day ice storm which destroys their ancient apple tree, the family remembers what pleasure it had given to each of them. Four generations of a family live on Tibbetts Island off the coast of New England in Cooney's *Island Boy*. In Howard's *The Train to Lulu's*, two sisters go from Boston to the home of a great-aunt in Baltimore by train in the 1930s. Another trip, Turner's *Nettie's Trip South*, was inspired by the author's great-grandmother's diary of 1859. A black American grandmother, a mother, and a daughter share memories in Greenfield's *Childtime: A Three Generation Memoir*. A selection from that book appears on pages 418–27 of the fourth grade HBJ basal reader, *Crossroads*, edited by Cullinan, et al.

Have students write down stories that have passed from generation to generation in their families. In Hiser's *The Adventures of Charlie and His Wheat-Straw Hat*, Charlie was the author's Grandpop, who told the story to her when she was a little girl. Seven-year-old Charlie lived in Appalachia during the Civil War and his grandmother made him a hat out of straw. When the Confederate soldiers came, Charlie hid the hat in a straw stack so they wouldn't get it. This book appears on many lists, including the National Council for the Social Studies notable list. Hartley's *Up North in Winter* is a story that a father tells about *his* father who missed his train in 1911 and had to walk home six miles over a frozen lake. The man found a fox and wrapped it around his neck to take home so he could sell the pelt. When he reached home, the fox ran off, but their mutual body heat saved both of their lives. Cohen's *Gooseberries to Oranges* begins "Listen darlings, and I'll tell you a story about what happened to me when I was a little girl." The story is about how a Jewish girl lives with an aunt in Europe, survives cholera, and comes on a boat and then through Ellis Island to join her father in America. America is the golden land where you could earn two nickels and buy two oranges. In Martin and Archambault's *Knots on a Counting Rope* a blind Indian boy begs his grandfather to tell him the story about the night when he was born weak and sickly, how the wind stopped howling, and how he received his name. Each time Grandfather tells the story, he ties a knot in a rope, and tells the boy that "When the rope is filled with knots, you will know the story by heart and you can tell it to yourself." In *Legend Days: Part One of the Ghost Horse Cycle* by Highwater, 11-year-old Amanda learns about the courage of a warrior and the prowess of a hunter from Grandfather Fox. In Mattingley's *The Angel with a Mouth-Organ*, Father finds the glass angel while playing a mouth organ in the ruins of a church and it keeps him company while he searches for his family. The glass angel becomes the family symbol of new beginnings. While they are putting the glass angel on the Christmas tree, Mother tells about when she was a refugee after World War II and they were able to find Father, because people remembered his mouth organ and the songs he sang at every camp. In Miller's *My Grandmother's Cookie Jar*, a grandmother shares cookies and legends from an Indianhead cookie jar. An 80-year-old Granny tells a grandchild about the lace on a christening robe that came from a wedding dress in *From Me to You* by Rogers. Nine-year-old Joshua visits his Grandma Goldina every Sabbath because she is old and needs company. Grandma pulls out items from her remembering box to remind her of times past in Clifford's *The Remembering Box*. The memories are recalled in a manner similar to that found in Fox's *Wilfrid Gordon Mc-Donald Partridge*. A child and an 85-year-old grandfather look at photo memories in Gelfand's *My Great-Grandpa Joe*. Parents discuss memories of the last five birthdays of a little girl in Rylant's *Birthday Presents*.

Have students write about the occupations of their parents or grandparents or even an elderly neighbor. Judith Hendershot's father and both grandfathers worked in a coal mine. Her book, *In Coal Country*, comes from her own memories. Papa goes to work every night with his lunch bucket and a light on his miner's hat, and every morning he washes off the dirt in a tub. The family lives in Company Row near the Black Diamond Mine. A train comes and takes the coal to power plants and steel mills on the Ohio River. Mama has a garden and does her wash in a copper boiler on a stove. On summer Saturdays, Dad treats the kids to Eskimo Pies at the company store. The rich details in this book can help students to make lists of the types of questions they want to ask their own relatives about "what it was like in the olden days." This is especially helpful if students live in a community with a special occupation they are investigating to write about. In Ackerman's *The Song and Dance Man*, illustrated by Caldecott winner Gammell, Grandfather tells stories about his days as a vaudeville entertainer to his grandchildren.

Have students write about a family tradition. In *The Keeping Quilt*, Polacco's family has a quilt that has served as a Sabbath tablecloth, wedding canopy, and baby blanket. The quilt that began with Great-Gramma Anna, an immigrant from Russia, passes through four generations and now resides with Polacco. The book is executed in charcoal drawings and the only color is in the babushka of Great-Gramma Anna, which becomes part of the beautifully colored quilt. Tanya finishes the quilt Grandmother begins before she gets sick in Flournoy's *The Patchwork Quilt*, which also appears on pages 440–52 of *Crossroads*, the fourth grade basal reader in the Laureate edition collected by Cullinan, et al. Each patch has a story in Tanya's quilt. Gram tells the stories behind the patches in *Patchwork Quilt*. In Goffstein's *My Noah's Ark*, a carved wooden ark is passed down in the family. Students may wish to write about a similar item. In Clifton's *The Lucky Stone*, the story told to a black girl by her great-grandmother when she gives her the stone includes stories of how the stone has been handed down in the family since slavery days and brings good luck to some of its owners. *The Lucky Stone* is Program #7 of the instructional television program, *Readit*, for third and fourth graders. The tradition in Josse's *Jam Day* is for the whole family to take part in berry picking and jam making. Ben and Mama go by train to a family reunion at Grandmam and Grandpap's home. They sing "White Coral Bells" on the trip there, and Grandpap and Ben make biscuits while the others make 22 jars of strawberry jam. The 19th-century farm family in Johnson's *Yonder* commemorates each birth by planting a "tree of life." Shub's *Cutlass in the Snow* is a story that passed from generation to generation in the Campbell family. To follow the tradition, the oldest Campbell boy always receives a gold coin on his 10th birthday and his father tells him the story his father told him of how they came to get the cutlass.

Have students write about their own town using Baylor's *The Best Town in the World* as a model. The country town way back in the Texas hills is the one where the narrator's father grew up. Childhood remembrances and oral history provide the description for this book, as they could for any book written by children. This town has the best cooks, the best blackberries, and the children know how to make the best toys in the world. Baylor's book is a Notable Social Studies book. Check pages 532–44 of the fourth grade HBJ basal reader, *Crossroads*, edited by Cullinan and others for *The Best Town in the World*. In Lewis's *Long Ago in Oregon*, 17 autobiographical poems describe life in a small Oregon town in 1917 and 1918. Mother does a "reading" of Maeterlinck's "The Blue Bird" on pages 40–43 and they go to the graveyard on Decoration Day. Little's *Children of Long Ago* is a book of memories describing the life of a rural black family in the early 1900s. Stevenson's two autobiographical books, *When I Was Nine* and *Higher on the Door*, are good patterns for writing about growing up in a small town long ago. The 19th-century New England of the author's own family is part of Hall's *The Ox-Cart Man*, for which illustrator Cooney won a Caldecott Medal. In Rylant's Caldecott Honor Book, *When I Was Young in the Mountains*, the recollections of an Appalachian childhood include a swimming hole, country store, and a porch swing. In *Blaine's Way* by Hughes, a grandfather remembers growing up in rural Ontario and joining the Canadian Air Force in this story of the 1930s and 40s.

Pursuing the Past: Oral History, Photographs, Family History by the Provenzos would be helpful to teachers and librarians working with projects concerning family history.

UNDERSTANDING THE U.S. CONSTITUTION. Because the bicentennial of the U.S. Constitution was in 1987, a whole group of fine books about that subject surfaced. *We the People: The Constitution of the United States of America* is a picture book illustrated by Peter Spier that is interesting for all ages. Old and new interpretations of it show a colonial representation on the left and a modern representation on the right. The picture depicting the establishment of justice shows old and new courthouses and juries, law books, and the figure of blind justice. Making an audio tape to describe the pictures would be an excellent project for understanding the Constitution and amendments. The complete text is included in the books by Spier and the Maestros. *A More Perfect Union: The Story of Our Constitution* by the Maestros describes the process that produced the Constitution and the Bill of Rights. *Shh! We're Writing the Constitution* is written in Jean Fritz's witty and accurate style and is available as a book, sound filmstrip, or separately as a word-for-word cassette. The book introduces the delegates at the 1787 convention in Philadelphia. The only problem is that sometimes George Washington, Thomas Jefferson, and especially minor characters look as though they have just stepped off the pages of *Strega Nona*. Although there is no index, the book contains such interesting tidbits about how the Constitution was written that children enjoy reading it for themselves, as well as having it read aloud to them. Did you know that Elbridge Gerry of Massachusetts was called Grumbletonian because he worried so much? Notes, a list of signers, and the total text of the Constitution are included. Although intended for the elementary level, the Spier, Maestros, and Fritz books would be welcome additions to middle school collections for history units. Hauptly's *A Convention of Delegates: The Creation of the Constitution* includes a list of delegates and discusses the people who attended the Constitutional Convention of 1787 and what transpired there. Hauptly's title is an ALA Notable Book. Anderson's *Seventeen Eighty-seven* sees the convention through the eyes of an aide to James Madison. *The Constitution* and *The Bill of Rights* are both books written by Colman in the New True series. The language, examples, and photographs given in both books make the Constitution easy enough for elementary students to understand. Levy's *If You Were There When They Signed the Constitution* is a paperback original that is similar to other Scholastic books beginning with that title. Sgroi's *This Constitution* is one of the First Book series, which sets the stage for the Constitution while telling of the failure of the Articles of Confederation. The book is packed with information and using the index may be the best way of getting the most from the book.

Collier's *Decision in Philadelphia: The Constitutional Convention of 1787* won the 1986 Christopher Award "for books that affirm the highest values of the human spirit." *We the People: The Story of the United States Constitution Since 1787* by the Fabers emphasizes how and why the Constitution is a living document. This book would be good when studying current events because not only are decisions like Marbury vs. Madison and McCulloch vs. Maryland included, but also cases about school prayer and the Miranda decision. The book is rich in history also, and tells about the Continental Congress, compromises, writing and ratifying, adding the amendments, and interpretation. The Collier and Faber books are excellent for middle and even senior high school collections.

Three of the books emphasize that the Constitution is a living document.

Sgroi's *The Living Constitution: Landmark Supreme Court Decisions* tells how the document weathered the following decisions: Marbury vs. Madison; the Dred Scott Decision; and the U.S. vs. Nixon. Mabie's *Constitution: Reflection of a Changing Nation* begins with the need for a constitution, the process of creating one, and the role of the judiciary in keeping it relevant. *The Supreme Court* by Weiss discusses the history and role of the judiciary through famous cases in our history.

CHAPTER THIRTEEN

Introducing Books
On and About Birthdays

Celebrate the birthday of a child by allowing the child to choose the book to be read aloud to the others. The choice could be wide open, or could be made from a selection of books not yet read, or from the books that have already been read that year. Another alternative would be to have the selection of books from which to choose in which a character has a birthday. Directions for what to include in "A Birthday Time Capsule" appear on pages 20–21 of Weitzman's *My Backyard History Book*. Check pages 138–40 of Shenk's *Why Not Celebrate!* for information about birthdays. Corwin's *Birthday Fun* includes information about birthdays, cards, games, directions for making a birthday book on pages 39–40, and a recipe for a birthday cake on pages 54–55. The poem "Birthdays" appears on page 29 of Prelutsky's *Read-Aloud Rhymes for the Very Young*. "Birthday Present" appears on page 14 of Fisher's *Out in the Dark and Daylight*. One of the festivities observed through poems by Livingston in *Celebrations* is the birthday. *Birthday Poems*, collected by Livingston, contains 24 poems about birthdays. For a preschool story program called "Happy Birthday to Me," consult idea #57 of MacDonald's *Booksharing*.

CELEBRATING BIRTHDAYS OF FAVORITE BOOK CHARACTERS [CU 74–76]. Allow the publishers of book characters to help you celebrate their anniversaries by providing special promotional materials. For example, Parish created Amelia Bedelia in 1963, and when Amelia Bedelia celebrated her 25th birthday, a flyer was available from Avon, Greenwillow, Harper & Row, or Listening Library. Check professional literature for notification of anniversaries of children's books and the promotional offers available free for a limited time, usually the anniversary year. Suggestions on this particular flyer are to have an Amelia Bedelia Hat Day or throw her a party and invent a birthday cake. Ask students to tell how the literal-minded Amelia would make a sponge cake, marble cake, or pineapple upside-down cake. Use Amelia's birthday to reintroduce the following books: *Amelia Bedelia*; *Amelia Bedelia and the Baby*; *Amelia Bedelia Goes Camping*; *Amelia Bedelia Helps Out*; *Good Work, Amelia Bedelia*; *Merry Christmas, Amelia Bedelia*; *Teach Us, Amelia Bedelia*; *Thank You, Amelia Bedelia*; *Amelia Bedelia and the Surprise Shower*; *Come Back, Amelia Bedelia*; and *Play Ball, Amelia Bedelia*. The last three titles are available in paperback/cassette sets. Mr. Rogers has a birthday in Parish's *Amelia Bedelia Goes Camping*, which is a winner of the Garden State Children's Book Award in the easy-to-read category. Mr. Rogers forgets about all the trouble Amelia Bedelia causes on the trip when she brings out his birthday cake.

Bridwell's *Clifford the Big Red Dog* also celebrated a 25th birthday in 1988. The birthday offering is a book/cassette, *Clifford the Small Red Puppy*. Use *Clifford's Birthday Party* or the video *Clifford's Birthday Surprise* to introduce all the other books about Clifford which appear in Volume 2 of this book in a section called TOYS AND DOLLS. Have children make a display, have a party, contact the local newspaper for publicity, and enjoy the books about the character. Clifford was the mascot for the 20th anniversary of RIF, Reading Is Fundamental, celebrated between October 1986 and October 1987.

New editions of popular works are often issued on the anniversary of a publication date. The 25th anniversary of *Where the Wild Things Are*, the Caldecott Medal Book first published in 1963, was marked by a reprinting of the book, with new engravings made from the original art. Celebrate the birthday by viewing the video of the opera, reason enough for a Sendak celebration. *Babar's Anniversary Album: Six Favorite Stories by Jean and Laurent de Brunhoff* is an example of a book published on a 50th anniversary. Bemelmans's *Madeline* was 50 years old in 1989. Langley's *The Wizard of Oz* was written to celebrate the 50th anniversary of the MGM movie, *The Wizard of Oz*. Although the book was written for adults, information can be shared with children. Atwater's *Mr. Popper's Penguins* is 50 years old. Linda Gramatky Smith tells how her father came to write *Little Toot* in "Little Toot Turns Fifty," pages 746–47 of the November/December 1989 issue of *The Horn Book Magazine*. The 75th anniversary edition of *The Wind in the Willows*, illustrated by Shepard, has an introduction by Hodges and a commentary by Shepard. The 50th anniversary edition of Lofting's *The Voyages of Dr. Doolittle* appeared in 1988. Thayer's poem, "Casey at the Bat" is 100 years old so the occasion has produced picture books, and there are versions with illustrations to compare by Tripp, Moser, Bachaus, and Polacco. *Cricket* magazine celebrated its 15th birthday in 1988. Parker's *The United Nations from A to Z* is part of the 40th anniversary celebration from 1945–1985.

Other celebrations within the last few years have included the 100th anniversary of the Statue of Liberty and the bicentennial of the U.S. Constitution. These events have caused a flurry of books published on the subjects. Check Chapter 12 for UNDERSTANDING THE U.S. CONSTITUTION and VISITING THE STATUE OF LIBERTY.

Books about favorite characters, in which a birthday occurs, can be used to introduce other books about that character to children. Lists of books about Spot appear in Volume 2 in sections called TOYS AND DOLLS and STRIPES, SPOTS, AND PLAIDS IN FOLKLORE AND IN PICTURE BOOKS. Use *Spot's Birthday Book* to introduce other books about Spot to preschool children. In this ALA Notable Book, Spot plays hide and seek and finds all the animals attending his party. Children can lift the flap to find out which animals are at the party. Another title on the same theme is *Spot's Birthday Party*. The children who like Spot will like the board books about Max by Wells. Use *Max's Birthday* to introduce other books about the little rabbit and his big sister Ruby: *Max's First Word*; *Max's New Suit*; *Max's Ride*; *Max's Toys*; *Max's Bath*; *Max's Bedtime*; and *Max's Breakfast*. Max's sister Ruby gives him a wind-up toy dragon that scares, yet fascinates, him. Preschoolers will enjoy *Alfie Gives a Hand* by Hughes. When Alfie is invited to Bernard's birthday party, he takes his blanket with him. Ask children to tell all the ways that Bernard misbehaves at his own party. Use this book about Alfie to introduce other books about him: *Alfie Gets in First*; *Alfie's Feet*; and *An Evening at Alfie's*. Daniel's birthday occurs in Poulin's *Could You Stop Josephine?* Use this book to introduce other books about this favorite Canadian cat: *Have You Seen Josephine?* and *Can You Catch Josephine?* Children who have already read *Duncan and Dolores* and *Faye and Dolores* will not be surprised when the cat Duncan becomes part of Dolores's birthday cake in *Happy Birthday, Dolores* by Samuels.

Chapter 7 of Bond's *Paddington Marches On* is about birthdays. Read this chapter aloud to children on a child's birthday or Bond's birthday to introduce other Paddington books. Books about Paddington Bear appear in Volume 2 of this book in a section called TOYS AND DOLLS. Readers who know the holiday books about this doll will enjoy *Miss Flora McFlimsey's Birthday*.

Use *Arthur's Birthday* by Brown to introduce other books about Arthur and D. W.: *Arthur Goes to Camp*; *Arthur's Baby*; *Arthur's Eyes*; *Arthur's Teacher Trouble*; *Arthur's Tooth*; *D. W. All Wet*; *D. W. Flips*; and holiday books about Valentine's Day, April Fool's Day, Halloween, Thanksgiving, and Christmas.

BIRTHDAYS—OTHER TIMES AND OTHER PLACES [CU 77]. Perl's *Candles, Cakes and Donkey Tails: Birthday Symbols and Celebrations* is a nonfiction book which discusses birthday celebrations from history, astrology, patron saints, name meanings, why we light birthday candles, and party games. Special birthdays like the Masai coming of age, sweet sixteen, bar and bat mitzvahs are included. Check "Birthday Symbols" on pages 14–15 of *Holidays and Birthdays*, volume 9 of *Childcraft*. National holidays also appear in this volume on pages 218–31 in the articles "Happy Birthday, Canada" and "Happy Birthday, America."

Tobias Has a Birthday by Hertz comes from Denmark and tells how a boy from Greenland celebrates his 12th birthday. Special customs include a party where everyone doesn't come at the same time because there wouldn't be room for everyone in the house, and the giving of small but meaningful gifts. In Fox's *Possum Magic*, Hush has to find three appropriate Australian foods and eat them on her birthday in order to become visible. *Night Noises* by Fox culminates when Lily Laceby's relatives gather to celebrate her 90th birthday. Children can listen to the recording of Kaye's *The Ordinary Princess*, or read the book about the princess who receives the gift of being ordinary from a fairy godmother at a birthday party. About the time of Gregory's ninth birthday, his father loses his job and they move to a rundown place. Gregory draws a garden on the wall of a burned-out chalk factory in Bulla's *The Chalk Box Kid.* Shub's *Cutlass in the Snow* is a story about why the eldest boy in the family always gets a gold coin on his birthday. Bauer's *Touch the Moon* is about a china horse that comes to life after a girl is disappointed that she doesn't get a real horse for her birthday. There is a birthday in Clifton's *My Friend Jacob,* which is about Sammy, an 8-year-old African-American child whose best friend and neighbor Jacob is 17 years old and retarded. The birthday child gets to wear a shell necklace in Decker's *Stripe and the Merbear.* One of three stories in *King Henry's Palace* by Hutchins is "King Henry's Birthday." What could be worse than a birthday while you have chicken pox? Tucky Pig leaves school on the afternoon of his birthday in Tyler's *The Sick-in-Bed Birthday.* There is a birthday in *Something Special for Me* by Williams. Paule's *A Birthday Surprise!/Una Sorpresa de Cumpleaños* is a bilingual Spanish/English book. Spanish words appear in the text and in a glossary in Brown's *Hello, Amigos!,* which celebrates the birthday of Frankie Valdez, from San Francisco.

BIRTHDAY PARTIES [CU 77–78].   Preschool children will love Oxenbury's *The Birthday Party.* A birthday party is not complete without a birthday cake. The candles wouldn't blow out in the story called "Birthday Cake," one of five short stories in *Flicks* by de Paola. One cake and six candles are part of Jabar's *A Birthday Counting Book.* Robart's *The Cake That Mack Ate* is a cumulative story about the ingredients that go into a cake that Mack, a dog, eats. Benny's dog Ralph eats the birthday cake in Rice's *Benny Bakes a Cake.* Toddler Benny helps his mother bake his birthday cake by keeping Ralph out of the way. While they are out for a walk, Ralph eats the cake. Luckily Papa brings a cake with him when he comes home. In Da Rif's *The Blueberry Cake That Little Fox Baked,* Little Fox bakes a cake because he thinks it is his mother's birthday. A birthday cake is one of the items in the inside/outside photos in Daugherty's *What's Inside?* Marge makes a chocolate birthday surprise for Mr. Reynolds in *Marge's Diner* by Gibbons. Two of the three wishes granted by the genie in the jug in Heide's *Treehorn's Wish* are cake and candles. The book is the sequel to *Treehorn's Treasure.* Three other books about wishes and birthdays are Schweninger's *Birthday Wishes,* McDonnell's *Lucky Charms and Birthday Wishes,* and Stevenson's *The Wish Card.*

Music is also part of birthday parties. Carfra sings "The Birthday Song" on her cassette, *Songs for Sleepyheads and Out-of-Beds!* The year can be changed to suit the age of the child. The birthday song appears on the *Wee TV* video with Don Cooper and his puppet, McCoon. "Happy Birthday!" appears on page 34 of Edge's *Music Is Magic for Your Child and You!* Sharon, Louis, and Bram have a cassette, *Happy Birthday,* a collection of poems and songs that can be used to celebrate. "Happy Birthday" is sung in Yolen's easy reader,

Commander Toad and the Planet of the Grapes. Kathy Bear's birthday party is the scene for Peek's picture book about the folk song *Mary Wore Her Red Dress and Henry Wore His Green Sneakers.* Children can sing "Happy Birthday" to Duck with the other animals in Bunting's *Happy Birthday, Dear Duck.* The concepts of colors and numbers are reinforced in *Going Up! A Color Counting Book,* by Sis.

Rockwell's *Happy Birthday to Me* is about a boy who helps his mother make the cake; blow up balloons; fill baskets with nuts, gumdrops and raisins; make place cards; and set the table for his party. At the party they play pin the tail on the donkey, have a peanut hunt, open presents, and sing. Daniel in Pomerantz's *The Half-Birthday Party,* gives his half-year-old sister, Katie, a half-birthday party and asks each person to bring half a present. Daniel is so busy with preparations that he forgets about his own present for her until he sees the half moon. Have children think up other half-birthday presents. Noble's *Jimmy's Boa and the Big Splash Birthday Bash* is perfect for reading aloud. Jimmy's party at Sea Land is as funny as the events in *The Day Jimmy's Boa Ate the Wash* and *Jimmy's Boa Bounces Back.* Half-pages are part of Leonard's *Little Pig's Birthday.* Friends do not forget Pig's birthday in this choose-your-own-adventure book. Hugo, a dog, watches his owner go from shop to shop, but does not realize his owner is buying items for Hugo's birthday, in Rockwell's *Hugo at the Window.* Adler's *My Dog and the Birthday Mystery* is about Jenny's friend Ken, who asks her to solve a mystery about his stolen bike. Clues lead Jenny to her surprise birthday party. Ronald's birthday comes after school is out, so he is surprised when his friends plan a surprise party for him in Giff's *Happy Birthday, Ronald Morgan.* Use the birthday book or the sound filmstrip to introduce two other books about Ronald: *Ronald Morgan Goes to Bat* and *Watch Out, Ronald Morgan!* Marvin and Milton make a mess trying to make ice cream and cake for a birthday party in Modell's *Ice Cream Soup.* Mice who live in the White House hitch a ride to Mt. Vernon for George Washington's birthday in Blair's *Hurrah for Arthur: A Mount Vernon Birthday Party.* *Mickey's Birthday Party* is a 16mm film or video that celebrates Micky Mouse's birthday. Directions for making seven different birthday hats are in Glovach's *Little Witch's Birthday Book.* In Hurwitz's *Ali Baba Bernstein*, a third grader wants to change his name because there are over a dozen David Bernsteins in the New York City phone book. David invites them to his ninth birthday party, and seven of them come. A mystery needs to be solved by Horace and his 11 friends at his 11th birthday party in Base's *The Eleventh Hour.*

Adults are featured in several books about birthdays. Charlip and Ancona's *Handtalk Birthday* is about a woman who wakes to a surprise party complete with cake and punch. The entire story is told in sign language and color photographs. Brandenberg's *Aunt Nina and Her Nephews and Nieces* is a different kind of birthday book. Aunt Nina, who has neither husband nor children, always invites her nephews and nieces to her place for her cat's birthday. Fluffy is missing from the celebration because she is delivering a litter of kittens. Children might want to sing "Happy Birthday" to Fluffy and to her kittens after hearing the story. Another book about Aunt Nina that could be read at the same time is *Aunt Nina's Visit*. Farmer Festus always makes pancake pie for his cat Mercury's birthday in *Pancake Pie* by Nordqvist.

BIRTHDAY PRESENTS [CU 78–80]. Oxenbury's *The Birthday Party* can stimulate discussion of the difficulty of giving up presents one likes to someone else. *Peabody* by Wells is a bear that is a gift for Annie's birthday. The two do everything together until Annie's next birthday when she receives Rita, the talking doll. Robert, Annie's younger brother, saves the day so that Annie takes back Peabody and gives Rita to Robert. Binky McNab, in Gackenbach's *Binky Gets a Car*, gets a small riding car for his birthday but he doesn't stay inside the yard and wrecks a window so the wheels are taken off his car. Sam's present in *Happy Birthday, Sam* by Hutchins is a chair given to him by his grandparents so he can climb up and reach items. Presents, a wishing candle, and a birthday pancake are part of the easy reader, *Scruffy*, by Parish. Todd gets a kitten named Scruffy from the animal shelter for his present. A treasure hunt leads to a dollhouse that looks like her own house in Merriam's *The Birthday Door*. In Foreman's *Ben's Baby*, Ben wants a baby for his birthday present. Bibi's gift from Dad, the King of the Penguins, is a toy boat in Gay's *Bibi's Birthday Surprise*, translated from the French. Alice gets a black and white mutt from the pound for her birthday in Schwartz's *Oma and Bobo*. Eddie gives his sister a glass dragon for her birthday in Adler's *Eddie's Blue-Winged Dragon*. In Kellogg's *The Mysterious Tadpole*, Uncle McAllister gives Louis a birthday gift that turns out to be a dinosaur. A truck-driving father returns home on his birthday and learns that his daughter has spent Wednesdays teaching her grandmother to read as a surprise birthday present for him in Bunting's *The Wednesday Surprise*. Read this book aloud—if you can handle the emotion. Angelina Mouse receives a bike for her birthday in Holabird's *Angelina's Birthday Surprise*. Have students add other possible uses for the moon if it were given to a child as a birthday present. Other books about Angelina appear in Chapter 4, USING SEQUELS, SERIES, AND FAVORITE CHARACTERS TO INTRODUCE BOOKS.

Show the 16mm film, video, or sound filmstrip of the story to celebrate a birthday. Show the sound filmstrip, 16mm film, or video of Asch's *Happy Birthday, Moon* to celebrate the birthday of a preschool or kindergarten child. The film is a CINE Golden Eagle Award winner and an ALA Notable Film. A paperback/cassette combination makes a nice gift to suggest for preschoolers. It is about a bear who decides to give his friend the moon a hat for a present. *Mooncake* is a companion story. Other books about gift giving can be introduced by *Happy Birthday, Moon*. In Shannon's *The Surprise*, Little Squirrel doesn't know what to give his mother for her birthday. Finally, he gives her a huge box with boxes nestled inside, and he jumps out of the last box. Compare this present to the present given by children in two classics, Flack's *Ask Mr. Bear,* and Zolotow's *Mr. Rabbit and the Lovely Present.* Wolf's *The Best Present Is Me* has a theme similar to the one in Shannon's book. A girl loses her present for her grandmother so her mother traces the child on a large sheet of paper and makes it into a birthday card. In *Happy Winter* by Gundersheimer, two sisters make a clay bird for their mother's birthday gift. Sawicki's *Something for Mom* is about Matilda's mom, who keeps calling her to come for breakfast while Matilda is upstairs wrapping a birthday present for Mom. Martha makes a card for her grandfather's 89th birthday that has various textures that he can appreciate with his fingers because he is blind in Pearson's *Happy Birthday, Grampie.* Gelfand's *My Great-Grandpa Joe* is 85 and lives in an apartment while his wife lives in a nursing home. Memories are shared from a photo album. In Cazet's *December 24th,* Emily and Louie Rabbit bring a present to their grandfather and make him guess that the present is for his birthday. Nine-year-old Belinda visits her Granny May every August. Belinda does odd jobs so she can purchase a shell necklace from a gift shop at the end of the summer in time for Granny's birthday. However, when Belinda goes to get the necklace, it has been sold. The shopowner won't tell her who makes the necklaces but before the end of the book, Belinda finds out and the story has a happy ending. Read this longer book aloud.

In Orbach's book, *Please Send a Panda,* Agatha wants a panda for her birthday and writes letters to her grandmother, an animal doctor, asking for one. Agatha also asks for other animals, including an elephant, but is given a cat named Fuzzy. *Papa's Panda* by Willard is the story Papa tells about a panda. The duck in Bunting's *Happy Birthday, Dear Duck* receives unusual birthday presents from his animal friends. The swimsuit, sunglasses, a beach ball, and a scuba mask finally make sense when the final gift, an inflatable swimming pool, arrives. Before the end of the story, have children guess what the big present might be. When Moe Dog wakes up on his birthday, he sees the big letter H and later other letters scattered around in Heller's *Happy Birthday, Moe Dog.* A similar spelling game could be created in a classroom by leaving red letters around to spell presents, green letters to spell party, blue letters to spell food, and letters in other colors to spell additional words associated with birthdays. Gifted children in the class, who need to be challenged, could prepare the spelling words and hide them. Grandma and Grandpa Bear bring a 4-year-old bear a photo album of pictures from when he was a baby in Watanabe's *It's My Birthday!* A kangaroo doesn't feel happy about not sharing birthday candy or the new bike in Harper's *What Feels Best?*

BIRTHDAYS OF FAMOUS PEOPLE INCLUDING AUTHORS [CU 80–81]. Divide the class into six groups of four or five students. After teaching them to write a friendly letter, have students write a letter to be enclosed in a birthday card to be sent to an author. Give students a list of living children's authors arranged by month of birthday, and allow them to pick an author each month of the school year. So that authors born during the summer are not slighted, letters could be written, addressed, and stamped during the school year, but mailed by the teacher during the summer. In this manner, all the letters could be written at one time and then mailed at the appropriate time. If the objective is to have students reinforce their letter-writing skills, each group could choose an "author of the month" and write one letter per month. It follows that they would want to read and share some of the books by that author, either while they are researching their author, or on the actual birthday.

CHAPTER FOURTEEN

Motivating Reading Through Television

It is important to observe copyright law when using television programs to promote reading. The copyright law says that programs may be taken off the air and used in educational settings for 45 days but must be erased after that time, unless arrangements have been made in advance with producers for additional retention. Student use is permitted only within the first 10 days; the other 35 days are for faculty member evaluation. Copying of programs directly from television for indefinite future use is a violation of the copyright law. Many of these shows are available for purchase in video format. Some regional and state educational media centers have obtained rights to make copies for a specific number of years.

There are many fine television programs that introduce quality children's literature. [See also CU 85-103.] Some programs directly introduce books to motivate children to read them. Others deal with subjects that can be followed up with library materials of all types. Adults working with children can alert them to programs of interest before they air, and can follow up the programs after they have been viewed. A special display in the library can announce programs and provide books to stimulate interest in knowing more about the subjects.

Check with your public broadcasting station for a *Book Tie-In List* composed of books to accompany television programs. The list includes adult and children's programs and is listed by the title of the series. Adults can check television viewing guides and then find books which complement the programs by looking in the subject catalog.

Most Americans are familiar with *Sesame Street* which has had 2,500 episodes since 1969. The program, produced by the Children's Television Workshop and shown on Public Broadcasting stations, reaches 11 million households per week. The target is children of low income families, 2–5 years old. Viewers include six million preschoolers, three million children 6–11 years old, and five million adults over 18. It is seen in 75 countries. *Sesame Street* has received 28 Emmys. The hour-long program has a magazine format and includes Muppet characters and live actors. Susan and Bob are original live characters, and Big Bird, Bert, Ernie, Cookie Monster, Grover, and Oscar the Grouch are original Muppet characters created by Jim Henson that are still on the program. Introduce Henson's biography by Woods that is easy to read and has numerous photos: *Jim Henson: From Puppets to Muppets*.

Sesame Street is divided into 20–30 segments, each of which has a specific goal. The 220 curricular goals include those related to reading readiness; writing skills; emotions; human diversity; cooperation; career awareness; safety practices; social groups; and the environment. Some concept areas investigated include: letters; numbers; social values; math; adoption; marriage; cognitive skills; social-emotional attitudes; Spanish language; sign language; and getting along with others. When an original live character, Mr. Hooper the storekeeper, died in 1983, death was explored. *I'll Miss You, Mr. Hooper* by Stiles is a book based on that program. A number of *Sesame Street* specials include *Christmas on Sesame Street*, 1978, which is repeated each December and appears in the book by Stone, *Christmas Eve on Sesame Street*. Other specials include: *Sesame Street in Puerto Rico*, 1979; *Big Bird in China*, 1982; *Big Bird in Japan*, 1988; and *Don't Eat the Pictures*, 1983, about the Metropolitan Museum of Art. *Sesame Street Magazine* has been published since 1970. Over 300 related book titles include *Sign Language ABC*; *Sign Language Fun*; and *Susan and Gordon Adopt a Baby*. Hayward's *Sesame Street Dictionary* is popular.

The television program *Mr. Rogers' Neighborhood* celebrated its 20th anniversary in 1987. Twenty episodes a year for preschoolers are produced by WQED, Pittsburgh. The overall theme is "You Are Special" but other themes include love, war, divorce, creativity, competition, and death. Puppets and actors in costume are part of the weekly shows. A number of books by Rogers are available: *Daniel Striped Tiger Gets Ready for Bed*; *First Experiences: Going to Day Care*; *First Experiences: Going to the Doctor*; *First Experiences: Going to the Hospital*; *First Experiences: Going to the Potty*; *First Experiences: Making Friends*; *First Experiences: Moving*; *First Experiences: The New Baby*; *First Experiences: When a Pet Dies*; *Many Ways to Say I Love You* (songbook); *Mister Rogers' Songbook*; *A Trolley Visit to Make-Believe*; *When Monsters Seem Real*; *Wishes Don't Make Things Come True*; and *You Can Never Go Down the Drain*. *If We Were All the Same* and *No One Can Ever Take Your Place* are by Rogers and Sustendal. *Mister Rogers: How Families Grow*; *Mister Rogers: Playbook*; and *Mister Rogers Talks with Parents* are by Rogers and Head. A biography of Rogers is *Mister Rogers: Good Neighbor to America's Children* by the DiFrancos. Highlights from several television shows appear on the video *Mr. Rogers' Neighborhood: Music and Feelings*. Have children who know how to print their names sign a birthday card for Mr. Rogers on January 20.

Captain Kangaroo for preschoolers is no longer in production but has been syndicated for reruns. Bill Cosby is now hosting a daily five-minute *Picture Pages* feature on the *Captain Kangaroo* series. *Picture Pages* is designed to involve preschoolers and their parents in the development of vocabulary, verbal skills, social awareness, and visual perception. Cosby is also the star of the award-winning television program on the CBS network, *The Cosby Show*. Biographies of Cosby from easiest to the most difficult include: *Bill Cosby: Making America Laugh and Learn* by the Woods; *Bill Cosby* by Etkin; *Bill Cosby,*

Family Funny Man by Kettlekamp; *Bill Cosby—For Real* by Latham; and *Cosby* by Smith. Cosby is one of 101 famous Americans in LeVert's *Doubleday Book of Famous Americans*.

Reading Rainbow began in 1983 over Public Broadcasting Service stations. The series is for 5- to 8-year-olds and enters 95 percent of American homes or eight million children a week. *Reading Rainbow* is coproduced by GPN and WNED-TV Buffalo, New York, in association with Lancit Media Productions of New York City. Underwriters include the Corporation for Public Broadcasting, Public Broadcasting Stations, and the National Science Foundation. Programs are captioned for the hearing impaired. Picture books which appear on the program carry special *Reading Rainbow* stickers in bookstores, to draw the attention of parents and children. The host is LeVar Burton, but celebrity narrators read the books while the illustrations are shown on-screen. Real-life-on-the-spot situations are tied to the book. One book is featured but three others are introduced by children. The 55, 30-minute television programs for primary students include: #1—*Tight Times* by Hazen; #2—*Miss Nelson Is Back* by Allard; #3—*Bea and Mr. Jones* by Schwartz; #4—*Bringing the Rain to Kapiti Plain* by Aardema; #5—*Louis the Fish* by Yorinks; #6—*Digging Up Dinosaurs* by Aliki; #7—*Liang and the Magic Paintbrush* by Demi; #8—*Gila Monsters Meet You at the Airport* by Sharmat; #9—*Three Days on a River in a Red Canoe* by Williams; #10—*The Gift of the Sacred Dog* by Goble; #11—*Gregory the Terrible Eater* by Sharmat; #12—*Three by the Sea* by Marshall; #13—*Arthur's Eyes* by Brown; #14—*The Day Jimmy's Boa Ate the Wash* by Noble; #15—*Ty's One-Man Band* by Walter; #16—*Hot-Air Henry* by Calhoun; #17—*Simon's Book* by Drescher; #18—*The Ox-Cart Man* by Hall; #19—*Mystery on the Docks* by Hurd; #20—*A Chair for My Mother* by Williams; #21—*Paul Bunyan* by Kellogg; #22—*The Patchwork Quilt* by Flournoy; #23—*Hill of Fire* by Lewis; #24—*The Tortoise and the Hare* by Stevens; #25—*Perfect the Pig* by Jeschke; #26—*Animal Cafe* by Stadler; #27—*Alistair in Outer Space* by Sadler; #28—*Feelings* by Aliki; #29—*Watch the Stars Come Out* by Levinson; #30—*Mama Don't Allow* by Hurd; #31—*Space Case* by Marshall; #32—*Milk Makers* by Gibbons; #33—*Imogene's Antlers* by Small; #34—*Germs Make Me Sick* by Berger; #35—*Abiyoyo* by Seeger; #36—*The Life Cycle of the Honey Bee* by Hogan; #37—*Keep the Lights Burning, Abbie* by the Roops; #38—*Chickens Aren't the Only Ones* by Heller; #39—*The Paper Crane* by Bang; #40—*The Runaway Duck* by Lyon; #41—*A Three Hat Day* by Geringer; #42—*Rumpelstiltskin* by Zelinsky; #43—*Best Friends* by Kellogg; #44 *Meanwhile Back at the Ranch,* by Noble; #45—*My Little Island* by Lessac; #46—*The Bionic Bunny Show* by the Browns; #47—*Bugs* by Parker and Wright; #48—*The Robbery at the Diamond Dog Diner* by Christelow; #49—*Brush* by Calders; #50—*The Purple Coat* by Hest, 51—*Barn Dance!* by Martin and Archambault, 52—*Duncan and Dolores* by Samuels; #53—*Knots on a Counting Rope* by Martin and Archambault; #54—*Mummies Made in Egypt* by Aliki; #55—*Mufaro's Beau-*

tiful Daughters by Steptoe; #56—*Humphrey the Lost Whale: A True Story* by Takuda and Hall; #57—*Stay Away from the Junkyard!* by Tusa; #58— *Little Nino's Pizzeria* by Barbour; #59—*Ludlow Laughs* by Agee; #60—*Dinosaur Bob and His Adventures with the Family Lizardo* by Joyce. The 30-minute programs are available in video format. More titles are expected.

There are related *Reading Rainbow* materials such as T-shirts, buttons, and stickers available. A recording, *Reading Rainbow Songs*, is available. A newspaper, *The Reading Rainbow Gazette*, a magazine for children, is filled with games, puzzles, background information, bibliographies, and activities related to the television series. *Reading Rainbow 1: A Guide for Teachers* is also available. The following picture books have been reprinted with a special behind-the-scenes section and an activity section with games, projects, and puzzles: Stadler's *Animal Cafe*; Wolkstein and Brown's *The Banza*; Stevenson's *Could Be Worse!*; Sharmat's *Gregory the Terrible Eater*; Stadler's *Hector the Accordion-Nosed Dog*; Small's *Imogene's Antlers*; Jeschke's *Perfect the Pig*; and Levinson and Goode's *Watch the Stars Come Out*. These books are available from the *Weekly Reader* book club.

Teletales includes 15, 15-minute literature programs for primary students produced by AIT, the Agency for Instructional Technology, and Positive Image Productions, which contain the following folk and fairy tales: #1—*The Charmed Ring* (India); #2—*The Willow Tree* (England/China); #3—*Stan Bolovan* (Rumania); #4—*Hansel and Gretel* (Germany); #5—*Soongoora and Simba* (Zanzibar); #6—*The Bargain* (Ireland); #7—*The Chenoo* (Micmac Indians); #8—*Molly O'Mally* (Wales/England); #9—*Long Nose* (Germany); #10—*Bianchinetta* (Italy); #11—*The Sorcerer's Boy* (Russia); #12—*Half Chick*; and *The Squire's Bride* (Spain and Norway); #13—*Caliph Stork* (Iraq); #14—*Fiddy Wow Wow* (Denmark); and #15—*Paka'a* (Hawaii).

The Folk Book includes 15, 20-minute literature programs for primary students, produced by NEWIST at the University of Wisconsin–Green Bay and by AIT, the Agency for Instructional Technology. Programs are divided into three segments. *Hodgepodge* contains games, riddles, jokes, puppets, and stories from the oral tradition. *Stories of Stories* includes origins of storytelling and includes the story "How Anansi the Spider Stole the Sky God's Stories." *In the Beginning: Creation Stories from Around the World* by Hamilton tells how the world began and includes poems, puppets, and dance.

Long Ago and Far Away is a television series produced by WGBH in Boston, in partnership with the International Reading Association and the Association for Library Service to Children, a division of the American Library Association. Funding for the series was provided by the National Endowment for the Humanities, the Arthur Vining Davis Foundation, the George Gund Foundation, and the WGBH Educational Foundation. The first year of *Long Ago and Far Away* coincided with the celebration of "The Year of the Young Reader." The series includes 16 half-hour programs for children K–3 hosted by James Earl Jones. Helper's *Long Ago and Far Away Discussion and Activity*

Guide gives before and after viewing, a bibliography, and information about each story for all books in the series. A 16-page student newspaper is available in classroom sets and some newspapers around the country offered them as part of "Newspaper in Education Week" packages. A list of related paperbacks is provided by Baker and Taylor.

The programs from *Long Ago and Far Away* include: *The Pied Piper of Hamelin* from a poem by Browning; *The Reluctant Dragon* from a book by Grahame; *Abel's Island* from a picture book by Steig; *The Happy Circus* from stories by Girerd, Terrier, and Bauza; *Hungarian Folk Tales* from the folk tales "The Hedgehog" and "Pinko"; *The Talking Parcel* (two parts), from a book by Durrell; *The Wind in the Willows* by Grahame (two hours); *Svatohor* based on a Russian folktale; *The Sleeping Princess* based on Grimm's *Sleeping Beauty*; *As Long as He Can Count the Cows*, based on a familiar story of Bhutan; *The Man Who Planted Trees* from an original story by Giono; *The Silver Coronet* from an original story by Innes; *Billy and Bunny* based on a book by Bergstroms; *Frog and Toad* (two parts), based on books by Lobel.

Picture Book Park is a series of 16, 15-minute television programs for primary students, produced by the Metropolitan Cleveland ETC and distributed by National Instructional Television/Agency for Instructional Technology. *Picture Book Park: A Guide for Teachers* is available. Book programs in the blue module include: *Sylvester and the Magic Pebble* by Steig; *That's Right, Edie* by Johnson; *Bedtime for Frances* by Hoban; and *What Mary Jo Shared* by Udry. Books in the green module include: *Mighty Hunters* by Hader; *Folk Tales* ("The Three Billy Goats Gruff" and "The Three Little Pigs" from *Chimney Corner Stories* by Hutchinson); *Mice Are Nice* (*Henry the Untouchable Mouse* by Simon and *Frederick* by Lionni); *From Japan* (*A Pair of Red Clogs* by Matsuno). Books in the red module include: *Lovable Lyle* by Waber; *Friends* (*I Need a Friend* by Kafka, *My Friend John* by Zolotow, and *Robbie's Friend George* by Estes); *Spotty* by Rey. The brown module includes the books: *Happy Birthday* (*Birthday Presents* by Rylant and *A Tree for Rent* by Shaw); *Zoo* (*May I Bring a Friend?* by De Regniers and *Zoo, Where Are You?* by Mc-Govern); *Benjie* by Lexau; and *Presents* (*Mr. Rabbit and the Lovely Present* by Zolotow and *Ask Mr. Bear* by Flack).

The 10 30-minute television programs of *Ramona* are based on three books by Cleary: *Ramona Quimby, Age 8*; *Ramona and Her Mother*; and *Ramona Forever*. The target age is from 6 to 12 but includes anyone who has ever loved any of Cleary's books. The programs are produced by Atlantis Films, Ltd., in collaboration with Lancit Media Productions and are presented by WGBH in Boston. Underwriters include public television stations and the Corporation for Public Broadcasting. Videocassettes are distributed by Lorimar Home Video and audiocassettes are available from Listening Library. Programs are closed-captioned for the hearing impaired. The 10 segments which began in 1988 include: *Squeakerfoot* (Ramona shows off her new shoes); *Mystery Meal* (Ramona and Beezus refuse to eat the mystery meat so she and Beezus must make the next meal); *Ramona the Patient* (Ramona recuperates after throwing up in front of everyone at school); *Rainy Sunday* (Ramona becomes bored one Sunday); *Goodbye, Hello* (The family cat, Picky-Picky, dies); *New Pajamas* (Ramona decides to run away when Beezus makes fun of her wearing her pajamas under her clothes to school); *Ramona's Bad Day* (everything goes wrong for Ramona); *The Great Hair Argument* (Beezus pays for a haircut and gets an apprentice and a ruined haircut); *The Perfect Day* (Aunt Bea marries Howie's Uncle Hobart); and *Siblingitis* (Ramona worries that the expected new baby will replace her). For a list of books about Ramona, consult a section of Volume 2 called TOYS AND DOLLS. For information about Cleary, check Chapter 3, "Introducing Books by Authors" and a section of Chapter 10, INTRODUCING REALISTIC FICTION.

Readit! is a series of 16, 15-minute programs for reading motivation for students in grades three and four. The host is John Robbins. *A Teacher's Guide to Readit!*, by Moskowitz, is available. Programs include the following books: #1—*Blue Moose* and *Return of the Moose* by Pinkwater; #2—*My Robot Buddy* and *My Trip to Alpha I* by Slote; #3—*Have You Seen Hyacinth Macaw?* by Giff; #4—*My Father's Dragon* by Gannett; #5—*The Boxcar Children* by Warner; #6—*Deadwood City* and *The Third Planet from Altair* by Packard; #7—*Who's in Charge of Lincoln?* by Fife and *The Lucky Stone* by Clifton; #8—*The Rise and Fall of Ben Gizzard*; *The Parrot and the Thief*; and *The Contests at Cowlick* by Kennedy; #9—*Trouble for Lucy* by Stevens; #10—*The Comeback Dog* by Thomas; #11—*Give Us a Great Big Smile, Rosy Cole* by Greenwald; #12—*Groundhog's Horse* by Rockwood; #13—*A Grandmother for the Orphelines* by Carlson; #14—*Twenty and Ten* by Bishop; #15—*The Whistling Teakettle* by Skolsky and *The Witch of Fourth Street* by Levoy; and #16—*Ben and Me* by Lawson.

Books from Cover to Cover is a series of 16, 15-minute television programs of reading motivation for students in grades three and four that was produced by WETA-TV in Washington, D.C. The host is John Robbins. *Books from Cover to Cover, Teacher's Guide* is available. Books in the programs include: #1—*Rich Mitch* by Sharmat; #2—*4-B Goes Wild* by Gilson; #3—*The Cabin Faced West* by Fritz; #4—*The Case of the Elevator Duck* by Berends and *Warton and the Castaways* by Erickson; #5—*The Little Riders* by Shemin; #6—*Different Dragons* by Little; #7—*If You Didn't Have Me* by Nilsson; #8—*The Kid in the Red Jacket* by Park; #9—*Top Secret* by Gardiner; #10—*The Trouble with Tuck* by Taylor; #11—*Back Yard Angel* by Delton;, #12—*Be a Perfect Person in Just Three Days!* by Manes; #13—*Going Home* by Mohr; #14—*The Search for Grissi* by Shura; #15—*Bella Arabella* by Fosburgh; and #16—*The Green Book* by Walsh. Copies of the books are available from Follett Library Book Company.

Book Bird is a reading motivation television series of 16, 15-minute programs for grade four. The host is John Robbins. *A Teacher's Guide to Book Bird* was researched by the Montgomery County Public Library Staff. Books in the programs include: #1—*The Cricket in Times Square* by Selden; #2—*The Little House in the Big Woods* by Wilder; #3—*A Bear Called Paddington* by Bond; #4—*The Toothpaste Millionaire* by Merrill; #5—*Frozen Fire* by Houston; #6—*Along Came a Dog* by DeJong; #7—*The Mouse and the Motorcycle* by Cleary; #8—*The TV Kid* by Byars; #9—*The Wonderful Flight to the Mushroom Planet* by Cameron; #10—*The Skates of Uncle Richard* by Fenner and *Song of the Trees* by Taylor; #11—*Striped Ice Cream* by Lexau; #12—*Race Against Death* by Reit; #13—*Misty of Chincoteague* by Henry; #14—*Half Magic* by Eager; #15—*Caddie Woodlawn* by Brink; and #16—*Lost in the Barrens* by Mowat.

More Books from Cover to Cover is a reading motivation television series for students in grade five that is produced by WETA-TV in Washington, D.C. The host is John Robbins and it follows the series *Books from Cover to Cover*. *More Books from Cover to Cover, Teacher's Guide* is available. Books in the programs include: #1—*The Wish Giver* by Brittain; #2—*The Summer Birds* by Farmer; #3—*Won't Know Till I Get There* by Myers; #4—*The Agony of Alice* by Naylor; #5—*Stone Fox* by Gardiner; #6—*Mama's Going to Buy You a Mockingbird* by Little; #7—*The Ghost Squad Breaks Through* by Hildick and *Who Kidnapped the Sheriff?* by Callen; #8—*The Castle in the Attic* by Winthrop; #9—*Baby-Sitting Is a Dangerous Job* by Roberts; #10—*Come Sing, Jimmy Jo* by Paterson; #11—*The Not-Just-Anybody Family* by Byars; #12—*Tom's Midnight Garden* by Pearce; #13—*Midnight Is a Place* by Aiken; #14—*The Root Cellar* by Lunn; #15—*The Whipping Boy* by Fleischman; and #16—*The Dark Is Rising* by Cooper.

Storybound is a reading motivation series of 16, 15-minute television programs for grades five and six and is a companion to the *Books from Cover to Cover* series produced by WETA-TV, Washington, D.C. *A Teacher's Guide to Storybound* by Moskowitz is available. The books in the programs include: #1—*Pilot Down, Presumed Dead* by Phleger; #2—*Bridge to Terabithia* by Paterson; #3—*Konrad* by Nostlinger; #4—*Ghosts I Have Been* by Peck; #5—*Call It Courage* by Sperry; #6—*It's Not the End of the World* by Blume; #7—*Lizard Music* by Pinkwater; #8—*Pinballs* by Byars; #9—*Sounder* by Armstrong; #10—*A Wrinkle in Time* by L'Engle; #11—*The Witch of Blackbird Pond* by Speare; #12—*Tuck Everlasting* by Babbitt; #13—*Island of the Blue Dolphins* by O'Dell; #14—*Pinch* by Callen; #15—*Mojo and the Russians* by Myers; and #16—*Escape from Warsaw* by Serraillier.

Wonderworks is a new television series provided by the Corporation for Public Broadcasting and public television stations, with additional funding from the National Endowment for the Arts. *Come Along with Us* is a newsletter sponsored by WQED/Pittsburgh, KCET/Los Angeles, KTCA/Minneapolis–St. Paul, the South Carolina ETV Network, and WETA/Washington, D.C. *Wonderworks* programs based on books include: *The Boy Who Loved Trolls* from the play "Ofoeti" by Wheater; *Who Has Seen the Wind* by Mitchell; *All Summer in a Day* based on a short story by Bradbury; *Be a Perfect Person in Just*

Three Days! by Manes; *Words by Heart* by Sebestyen; *Bridge to Terabithia* by Paterson; *The House of Dies Drear* by Hamilton; *Hide and Seek*, from *Adolescence of P-1* by Ryan; *Anne of Green Gables* by Montgomery; *Miracle at Mreaux*, from *Twenty and Ten* by Bishop; *Walking on Air*, based on a short story by Bradbury; *The Haunting of Barney Palmer*, from *The Haunting* by Mahy; *Taking Care of Terrific* by Lowry; *A Little Princess* by Burnett; *The Horse Without a Head*, from *A Hundred Million Francs* by Berna; *The Wild Pony*, from *Year of the Black Pony* by Morey; *Anne of Green Gables—The Sequel*, from *Anne of Avonlea, Anne of the Island,* and *Anne of Windy Poplars* by Montgomery; *Gryphon*, based on a short story by Baxter; *The Fig Tree*, based on a short story by Porter; *A Waltz Through the Hills* by Glaskin; *Chronicles of Narnia: The Lion, the Witch, and the Wardrobe* by Lewis; *Jacob Have I Loved* by Paterson; *Girl of the Limberlost* by Porter; *Slake's Limbo* by Holman; *Caddie Woodlawn* by Brink; *Home at Last* by Nixon; and *Good Ole Boy* by Morris.

Word Shop is a series of 30, 15-minute programs produced by WETA-TV in Washington, D.C. to help primary students develop their language skills. Programs include: *Story Telling; Characters in Stories; Setting in Stories; Action in Stories; Structure in Stories; Action in Stories; Fantasy Stories; Tall Tales; Mystery Stories; Story Maker; Poems As Rhythm; Poems As Sounds; Nonsense and Made-Up Words in Poetry; Poems As Descriptions; Poems As Stories; Poets; Character Playing; Scene Playing; Story Playing; Playwrights; News Stories; Signs; Comic Strips; Folk Tales; Books That Answer Questions; Books About People; Books About Places; Books About Animals; Books About Fantasy; Mystery Books;* and *Making a Book.*

3-2-1-Contact is a television program produced by the Children's Television Workshop with grants from the National Science Foundation and the U.S. Department of Education. The program is for third through sixth graders and introduces science concepts through field trips around the world. A *3-2-1-Contact Teacher's Guide* is available for the third and fourth seasons. Student activities are included. Promotional posters are often available. *3-2-1 Contact* is a science and technology magazine for children 8 to 14 and is available in bulk subscriptions. The *3-2-1-Contact Data Base* gives brief descriptions of all 225 programs with segment-by-segment program rundowns and timings. A science index and correlations with leading textbooks makes it invaluable. Unlimited duplication rights are granted. Programs for the fourth season include: *Tropics; Light; Farms;* and *Stuff.* Programs for the fifth season include: *Signals; Oceans; Motion;* and *Eating.* Programs for the sixth season include: *Antarctica; Your Body; Australia; Structures; Greece;* and *Island.* Programs for the seventh include: *Japan; Detectives; Architecture; Mammals; Modeling;* and *In the Air.*

Challenge includes 16, 15-minute instructional television programs in science for intermediate students produced by WDCN, Nashville. Program titles include: *Simple Machines; Power to Do Work; Renewable Energy; Matter and*

Its Properties; Electricity; Light; The Earth (earthquakes and volcanoes); *Rocks, Fossils, and Minerals; Rocks to Rings; Journey into Space; Space Camp; The Heart; Plants; Vertebrates; Food for Tomorrow;* and *Robots and Computers.*

Square One, a television program of 140, 30-minute programs for 8–12-year-olds. The program is produced by the Children's Television Workshop and underwritten by the National Science Foundation, Corporation for Public Broadcasting, Andrew Mellon Foundation, U.S. Dept. of Education, IBM, and Carnegie Corporation of New York. The Emmy-award-winning program premiered in January of 1987 and the main objective is to bring new insights into math concepts. Concepts include: problem solving, measurement, arithmetic, prealgebra, probability, statistics, geometry, and logic. The game shows within the program include "Triple Play," "Piece of the Pie," "Square One Squares," and "Close Call." "Mathnet" is a popular feature which has had a two-hour special of its own. The *Square One Television Teacher's Guide* includes daily program information as well as activity pages. *The Mathnet Guide* provides math projects for each program. These two programs can be videotaped off the air for in-school classroom use, provided the tape is erased within three years.

Zoo Zoo Zoo is an instructional television program produced by the Greater Cincinnati Television Educational Foundation, WCET and contains 16, 15-minute programs on ecology and life sciences for primary and intermediate students. *Zoo Zoo Zoo: A Teacher's Guide* is available. Programs include: #1—*All About Eyes;* #2—*All About Feet;* #3—*All About Ears;* #4—*All About Tails;* #5—*Animal Costumes;* #6—*Animal Defenses;* #7—*The Importance of Predators;* #8—*Do Animals Talk?;* #9—*How and What Animals Eat;* #10—*How Animals Move;* #11—*How Animals Help Each Other;* #12—*Zoo Babies;* #13—*Animal Homes;* #14—*Animal Groups;* #15—*Who Works at the Zoo?;* #16—*Where Animals Live.* A variety of books in the 599 section of the library, as well as animal encyclopedias, will be helpful to any research assignments that are followed up by these programs.

Naturescene is a television series of 52 programs in 30-minute episodes per year for the past 10 years produced by South Carolina Educational Television and grants from the Close Foundation, Corporation for Public Broadcasting, and the ETV Endowment of South Carolina. The family-oriented weekly nature walk visits national parks, nature reserves and examines plants, animals, and geological formations. Sample programs include: #301—*Shipwrecks and Lighthouses* (off the North Carolina coast); #306—*Everglades* (Florida); #312—*Nags Head Woods* (hardwood forest); #313—*New England Autumn* (deciduous forests); #508—*Padre Island* (seashells, wildflowers, wildlife on America's longest barrier island off the coast of Texas); and #509—*Autumn Field* (beetles, bees, and spiders).

Nature is a weekly television series in its sixth year, which probes the mysteries of the natural world. *Nature* is produced by WNET in New York, in association with the Nature Conservation, public broadcasting stations and a grant from the American Gas Company. George Page is the host. One program, *Battle of the Leaves*, is about how trees protect themselves from predators and the elements. Books on leaves and trees can be displayed when this program is shown.

National Audubon Specials premiered in 1986. Programs are produced by the National Audubon Society, Turner Broadcasting System, WETA, Washington, D.C., and are underwritten by the Stroh Brewery Company. *National Audubon Specials*, intended for family viewing, include: *Condor* (California bird); *Mysterious Black-footed Ferret* (almost extinct animal); *Grizzly and Man* (bear); *Whales*; *Sharks*; *Messages from the Birds* (Delaware Bay); *On the Edge of Extinction: Panthers and Cheetahs*; *Wood Stork, Barometer of the Everglades*; and *Ducks Under Siege* (wetlands). Programs are narrated by celebrities such as Robert Redford, Johnny Carson, and Loretta Swit.

National Geographic Specials are hour-long television documentaries produced by the National Geographic Society and WQED Pittsburgh, with a grant from Chevron. Programs are intended for family viewing. Some specials include *Among the Wild Chimpanzees*, *Flight of the Whooping Crane*, and *Land of the Tiger*.

Smithsonian World is a television series coproduced by WETA, Washington, D.C. and the Smithsonian Institution, with a grant from the James S. McDonnell Foundation, and is underwritten by Southwest Bell. The host is David McCullough. The fourth season was 1988/89. A variety of books and *Smithsonian* magazine can be introduced by such programs as *Speaking Without Words* about the language of animals (gorilla Koko); abstract art; universal meaning in mathematics; clues from human bones; and regional accents of birds. *The Living Smithsonian* is about the variety of topics shared by the museum: music, song, dance, art, science, race and ethnicity, zoology, and space. *The Way We Wear*, hosted by James Earl Jones, is about contemporary fashion set against the backdrop of history.

NOVA is a science program for junior and senior high school students and adults produced for public broadcasting stations by WGBH in Boston. Programs should be pointed out to gifted students and books on related topics should be provided. *NOVA* is 16 years old. Sample programs include #1516—*Can the Next President Win the Space Race?* (30 years after Sputnik); and #1204 *In the Land of Polar Bears* (Wrangle Island, a Soviet possession off Alaska and walruses, snow geese, and polar foxes).

Well, Well, Well with Slim Goodbody is an instructional television series of 15, 15-minute programs on health and wellness for children in kindergarten and the primary grades, produced for the Agency for Instructional Television by Positive Image Productions. Baraloto's *A Teacher's Guide to Well, Well, Well with Slim Goodbody* contains masters for reproducing certificates for developing healthy habits, membership cards, and emergency telephone lists. Food, cleanliness, exercise, relaxing, the senses, safety, emergencies and wellness are program topics. A video, *Slim Goodbody's Daily Desk Exercises*, contains five sessions for each day of the week and covers balance, strength, agility, flexibility, and aerobics. A teacher's guide is available. Check the library for the book, *Healthy Habits Handbook* by Goodbody. A set of four filmstrips entitled *Slim Goodbody's Health Series* includes *A Healthy Day*, which discusses nutrition, exercise, rest, and hygiene. Other titles include *A Visit to the Dentist*, *A Visit to the Doctor*, and *A Visit to the Hospital*.

All Fit with Slim Goodbody is an instructional television series of 15, 15-minute programs designed to help primary and intermediate students improve their overall level of physical fitness, and identify and develop components of physical fitness, and positive mental attitudes about lifetime fitness. *All Fit* was produced by the Slim Goodbody Corporation and is available through AIT, the Agency for Instructional Television. A video of the same title contains information on exercise, health, and fitness. *A Teacher's Guide to All Fit with Slim Goodbody* was prepared by Gabor and Burstein. A dozen reproducible master activity sheets include an *All Fit* pledge; muscle name game; *Fit Chart* for heart, endurance, strength, and flexibility; monthly warm-up chart for arm stretch, bear hug, bear walk, leg stretch; Flexy the Puppet; strength and endurance chart; the pulse activity chart; energy calories for activities chart; directions for making an arm and muscle model; posture guidelines; pipe cleaner puppet; and stress buster chart with relaxer exercises.

The Inside Story with Slim Goodbody is a series of eight 15-minute instructional television programs in health and science for grades three, four, and five. The series is produced at the University of Wisconsin–Green Bay Center for Television Production for the Wisconsin Educational Communications Board, operator of the Wisconsin ETV Network, and is available for distribution by AIT, the Agency for Instructional Television. Thompson's *The Inside Story with Slim Goodbody: A Guide for Teachers* is available. The guide contains line drawings of the heart, respiratory system, bones and muscles, eye, and endocrine system, that are excellent for transparencies or dittos. The programs include #1—*Lubba Dubba: The Inside Story of Your Heart and Blood*; #2— *The Breath of Life: The Inside Story of Respiration*; #3—*Down, Down, Down: The Inside Story of Your Bones and Muscles*; #4—*The Team That Hustles: The Inside Story of Your Bones and Muscles*; #5—*The Smart Parts: The Inside Story of Your Brain and Nervous System*; #6—*The Sensational Five: The Inside Story of Your Senses*; #7—*The Little Giants: The Inside Story of Your Glands*; #8—*The Body Symphony: The Inside Story of Your Whole Body*. Introduce nonfiction books about the body through this series. Books about the human body include: Elting's *Macmillan Book of the Human Body*; Miller's *Human Body*; Broekel's *Your Skeleton and Skin*; the Bruuns' *The Human Body*; and Fekete and Ward's *Your Body*. A tutorial microcomputer program for the Commodore is *Human Body: An Overview*, which tells about the following systems: muscular, skeletal, circulatory, digestive, respiratory, and nervous. Some books by Ward include *Food and Digestion*, *The Heart and Blood*, and *Lungs and Breathing*. Others are Asimov's *How Did We Find Out*

About Blood? and the Silversteins' *Heart Disease: America's #1 Killer; The Story of Your Foot;* and *The Story of Your Hand. You Can't Make a Move Without Your Muscles* by Showers can be used with the recording from *Muscle Hustle* from Burstein's *Slim Goodbody: The Inside Story.* Some books about the brain include: Berger's *Exploring the Mind and Brain;* Kettlekamp's *The Human Brain;* Sharp's *Brain Power! Secrets of a Winning Team;* the Silversteins' *World of the Brain;* and Stafford's *Your Two Brains.* Information about the senses is included in two books by Parramon, *Taste* and *Touch,* Broekel's *Your Five Senses,* Martin's *Messengers to the Brain: Our Fantastic Five Senses,* and the set of 4 sound filmstrips from the TV series *3-2-1-Contact: Five Senses* which includes *Smell and Taste, Vision, Hearing,* and *Touch.*

Take this opportunity to teach students to use indexes to nonfiction books and reference sets, as well as magazine indexes. Numerous diagrams and photos in color enhance the 28-volume reference set, *Science and Technology Illustrated: The World Around Us.* Check the index volume under bone, blood, brain, circulatory system, digestive system, gland, heart, human body, lung, nervous system, nose and sinuses, respiration process, senses, smell, touch, and vision. Check similar subjects in *The Abridged Readers' Guide to Periodical Literature* under bone, blood, brain, ear, eye, glands, heart, lungs, mouth, muscle, nervous system, nose, salivary glands, sense organs, sensory receptors, and respiratory organs.

Conrad is an instructional television series of 24, 15-minute programs on health, ecology, and life sciences for intermediate students. *Conrad* is produced by the Office of Instructional Television and Radio, South Carolina State Department of Education, and is available through AIT. A teacher's guide is available. Jason Conrad is a detective who looks for information about the body's systems with the help of his boss (Sorelli), a crime lab reporter (Mary), and a computer (Roger). Topics include dental health, personal hygiene, colds, air pollution and the respiratory system, the heart and circulatory system, diets, exercise, physical fitness, and poison prevention.

Shining Time Station is a new weekly children's television series coproduced by WNET, New York and Quality Family Entertainment, and broadcast over public broadcasting stations. Although intended for children ages 2 to 5, viewers include ages 3 to 7 and adults 18–49. The 20, 30-minute programs include live action and animation. Ringo Starr is the conductor and he is 18" high. Other people on the show include an engineer and his granddaughter, the station master and her nephew, and an arcade owner. A puppet band lives inside the jukebox but only the audience knows this. Some programs include *Does It Bite?* (overcoming fears of meeting new people); *And the Band Played Off* (learning from mistakes); *Show and Yell* (try many times for success); *Whistle While You Work* (importance of helping out); *Ring in the Old* (appreciating older people); and *Impractical Jokes* (jokes at the expense of other people).

Timmy and Lassie appears on PBS television and the following programs can be correlated to topics found in the index of this book. In #5802 *The Owl,*

Lassie protects Timmy from an outraged mother owl. In #5805 *The Storm,* they survive a cyclone. Henry is afraid of dogs in #5807, *Lassie's Decision.* Kite flying appears in #5818, *The Young Flyers.* Lassie is injured in #5823, *The Christmas Story.* An apple tree is in danger of being cut down for a new highway in #5824, *The Tree.* Complications arise during *The Campout,* #5839.

DeGrassi Jr. High is a television series produced by WGBH, Boston, and Taylor Productions. The series won an Emmy in 1987, and numerous awards like the Parents' Choice and ACT Awards. A discussion and activity guide is available. The program portrays real-life situations facing adolescents of middle school age and covers such subjects as peer pressure, alcohol and drug abuse, teen pregnancy, sexual abuse, social responsibility, and relationships. Some programs include: *Fight* (bullying, fighting, cowardice, and peer pressure); *Can't Live with 'Em* (grief, guilt, and death). Subscribers to DELPHI/Boston can gain access to WGBH online through a computer and modem.

A variety of specials appear on public broadcasting stations. Mikhail Baryshnikov's *The Nutcracker,* an American Ballet Theatre Production underwritten by IBM and PBS, has been a Christmas tradition since 1976. *Baby Panda* is a documentary produced by KCTS in Seattle about the first eight months of life for Chu-Lin, a baby panda from the San Diego Wild Animal Park and Zoo. *The Great Circus Parade* celebrates the big top and recreates an authentic street circus parade of bygone days. Restored circus wagons from the Circus World Museum in Baraboo, Wisconsin are included. Spanish language translation is available. The host is Bob Keeshan, Captain Kangaroo.

There are programs on cable TV that are of interest to students. A weekly glance at the magazine *TV Entertainment Monthly,* provided by the local cable company, can give hints of upcoming programs that could have tie-ins. One permanent display in the school library/media center or public library could be called "What's New on TV?" with a space for books that are available that tie into the programs. The display needs only a sign and a special shelf for the books. Some recent programs on the Disney Channel that could be linked to books are *Kavik the Wolf Dog* (Morey); *Grinch Grinches the Cat in the Hat* (Seuss); *Wind in the Willows* (Grahame); *Born Free* (Adamson); *Huckleberry Finn* (Twain); and *Welcome to Pooh Corner* (Milne). *Babar* (de Brunhoff) is not only a theater movie, but an HBO-TV series. HBO's Project Knowledge includes children's TV programs. *Lyle, Lyle Crocodile: The Musical* is an animated musical of the favorite crocodile, based on *The House on East 88th Street* which can be used to introduce the other five books by Waber about Lyle: *Lyle, Lyle, Crocodile; Funny, Funny, Lyle; Lovable Lyle; Lyle and the Birthday Party; Lyle Finds His Mother.* An animated musical *Madeline* can be used to introduce all the books by Bemelmans: *Madeline; Madeline and the Bad Hat; Madeline and the Gypsies; Madeline in London; Madeline's Christmas;* and *Madeline's Rescue. You Don't Have to Die: Jason's Story* is a television program based on a book *My Book for Kids with Cansur,* written by Janson Gaes, age 8. All three programs are also available as half-hour videos.

Showtime has carried *How the Rhinoceros Got Its Skin and How the Camel Got Its Hump*, (Kipling). Nickelodeon has the *The Little Prince* (Saint Exupéry); *Sharon, Lois, and Bram's Elephant Show*; and the *Lassie* (Knight) series. Superstation TBS carries reruns of *The Little House on the Prairie* (Wilder). Turner Network Television has had *The Phantom Tollbooth* (Juster); *National Velvet* (Bagnold); *Gentle Ben* (Morey); and *The Muppet Show* (Henson). The Discovery Channel has animal series like *Natural World, World Alone, Amateur Naturalist,* and *New Animal World.* A variety of interesting topics appear on The Learning Channel. *Smart Pics: The Learning Channel's Programming Quarterly* is the newsletter for the channel. *Planet Earth* is a series of seven programs about recent achievements in geoscience. College credit is available. Although the programs are intended for adults, gifted science students should be informed of the possibilities for learning with the TV program.

Television can be used to teach art and music. *Musical Instruments* includes 15, 20-minute programs for students of all ages to learn about musical instruments of today as well as the past. The series, produced by WNPB, Morgantown West Virginia includes: #1 and #2—*Classical Percussion, Parts 1 and 2*; #3 and #4—*Majestic Brass, Parts 1 and 2*; #5 and #6—*Vibrant Strings, Parts 1 and 2*; #7 and #8—*The Colorful Woodwinds, Parts 1 and 2*; #9 and #10—*Early Instruments, Parts 1 and 2*; #11 and #12—*South American Instruments, Parts 1 and 2*; #13—*West African Instruments*; and #14 and 15—*East African Instruments, Musical Encounter* includes 15, 30-minute programs produced in several PBS stations for students in grades three through six and includes the following programs: #1—*A Team Show*; #2—*The Bassoon-Piano Show*; #3—*A Record Show*; #4—*The Piano Show*; #5—*Musical Families*; #6—*The Orchestra*; #7—*The Clarinet-Flute Show*; and #8—*The Pop Show.* For television programs on art topics, consult a section called ART VIA INSTRUCTIONAL TELEVISION in Volume 2 of this book.

BOOKS WITH TELEVISION AND MOVIE TIE-INS. Fiction and non-fiction books about television and movies can stimulate interest in reading. Introduce stories about television by singing a parody of "On Top of Old Smokey" called "On Top of the Teevee" which appears in Merriam's *A Poem for a Pickle.*

There are several books for intermediate children in which television is part of the plot. Eleven-year-old Mitchell Dartmouth in Sharmat's *Rich Mitch* enters sweepstakes for a hobby. After winning the Dazzle-Rama Detergent Sweepstakes, Mitch appears on the television show "Have a Good Day," for which he gets a haircut and new clothes paid for by the sponsor. After announcing on the television program that he plans to give most of his winnings to charity, Mitch receives many letters offering to relieve him of his money. *Rich Mitch* is Program #1 of the TV series *Books from Cover to Cover.* In *The Secret Life of the Underwear Champ* by Miles, 10-year-old Larry is discovered by the Zigmund Model Agency and makes TV commercials for Champ Win

Knitting Mills. During the commercials, Larry is shown playing baseball in his blue warm-up suit which turns into his sponsor's blue underwear. Twelve-year-old Alex in Park's *Skinnybones* and *Almost Starring Skinnybones* also makes an embarrassing TV commercial. Alex poses as a 6-year-old in a commercial for cat food.

Confessions of a Prime Time Kid by Harris contains the memoirs of 13-year-old Margaret O'Brien Muldaur. Meg shares what it is like to be a famous television star. Readers also learn how 11-year-old James, a country singer, deals with his life and fame in Paterson's *Come Sing, Jimmy Jo*. *The TV Kid* by Byars is on a sound filmstrip, *Realistic Fiction*, from the set *Literature for Children, Series 6*. In that book, Lenny escapes into television until a snakebite changes his life. *The TV Kid* is Program #8 of the *Book Bird* TV series. *The Boy Who Turned into a TV Set* by Manes watches so much TV that when his set is broken, voices spouting commercials come from Ogden's mouth and the 6 P.M. news shows through his stomach. Three books by Adams are about a group of kids who own a TV station: *Can This Telethon Be Saved?*, *The Not-Quite-Ready-for-Prime-Time Bandits*, and *Rock Video Strikes Again*. Jill and her friends enter a TV rock and roll contest in Levy's *Something Queer in Rock and Roll*. In Christian's *Sebastian (Super Sleuth) and the Stars-in-His-Eyes Mystery*, Sebastian goes undercover to find out who is causing accidents to happen to Chummy the Wonder Dog, while Chummy is making a TV movie. Pevsner's *Sister of the Quints*, in which the media descend on the Wentworth quints for another story, can be used to discuss the need for news vs. the right to privacy. Allison and Andrew Potter, 11-year-old twins of divorced parents, have a mother who is a TV news announcer in Howe's *Morgan's Zoo*. In Delton's *Back Yard Angel*, 10-year-old Angel climbs up the neighbor's TV antenna and has to be rescued. The story is also Program #11 of the television series *Books From Cover to Cover*.

There are books for primary students that include television or movies in the plot. A cat in Heilbroner's picture book, *Tom the TV Cat*, tries to mimic the television with unusual results. Paddington Bear appears on TV in Bond's *Paddington on Screen*. Wildsmith's *Daisy*, a cow, leaves home and becomes a television and movie star but gets homesick for her old field. *The Boy with Square Eyes* by the Snapeses and *The Day the TV Blew Up* by West can both stimulate discussion of television watching with primary students. When Ralph Bean's TV set blows up, his friend Thelma suggests that he go to the library to get some free books. Rebecca's father is too busy watching TV when she tries to tell him that there is a moose in their garden in Alexander's *Even That Moose Won't Listen to Me*.

Several biographies of movie and TV personalities exist: Leather's *The Picture Life of Steven Spielberg*; Di Franco's *Walt Disney: When Dreams Come True*; Fisher's *Walt Disney Story*; and Montgomery's *Walt Disney, Master of Make Believe*; Erlander's *Jane Fonda: More Than a Movie Star*; Cohen's *Carl Sagan: Superstar-Scientist*; Mabery's *This Is Michael Jackson*; and Matthews's *Michael Jackson*; and numerous books about Bill Cosby which appear elsewhere in this book.

Often there are books that can be successfully introduced to children because of their prior knowledge of a television program. *Victory Garden Kid's Book* by Waters is a companion to the PBS series, *Crockett's Victory Garden*. Stone's *Christmas Eve on Sesame Street* is based on a TV special of the same name which features the Muppets. *No One Can Ever Take Your Place* by Fred Rogers is a story from *Mr. Rogers' Neighborhood*. Levy's *Bill Cosby's Fat Albert and the Cosby Kids: Take Two, They're Small* is based on the character Fat Albert from television. Peck's *Soup and Me* and *Soup for President* were shown on ABC's *Afterschool Specials*. Numerous examples of book and television companions appear in the previous section of this book.

"From Idea to Air: Making a Television Documentary" is an article by Mekuria from pages 314–28 of the sixth grade HM basal reader, *Celebrations*, edited by Durr, et al. Extend the basal reader with other books about television. Many students watch the annual Macy's Thanksgiving Day parade from New York City on television. Shachtman's *Parade* is a photo-essay about how the parade is put together. *On Camera: The Story of a Child Actor* by Hewett is a photo essay about 8-year-old Philip Waller, who plays in the TV special *Mouse and the Motorcycle* based on Cleary's book. Scott's *Ramona: Behind the Scenes of a Television Show* tells how the PBS series *Ramona* is produced, filmed, and edited. The program is based on *Ramona Forever, Ramona and Her Mother*, and *Ramona Quimby, Age 8*. *Lights! Camera! Action! How a Movie Is Made* by Gibbons tells about all the people who work on a movie and steps for making a story into a movie. *Walt Disney's Snow White and the Seven Dwarfs and the Making of the Classic Film*, by Holliss and Sibley, is a book to celebrate the 50th anniversary of the Disney film. Another title by the same authors, *Mickey Mouse: His Life and Times*, gives information about a favorite cartoon mouse. Weinberg's *Star Wars: The Making of the Movie* includes a brief summary of the story on pages 62–69 and tells about real and make-believe places seen in the movie. Two characters are especially mentioned: R2-D2 and C-3P0. Techniques involved in movie and TV stunts are explained in *Stunt Work and Stunt People* by Emens. In Wetzel and Huberman's *Onstage/Backstage*, a 10-year-old girl tells about her part in a play based on Kipling's *Just So Stories*. A rabbit shows illustrations of his life as the Bionic Bunny, a character on a television show in the Browns' *The Bionic Bunny Show*. Primary and intermediate students will enjoy this cartoon story.

Nonfiction about movies and television are available. Middle school students who are making their own videos will find Shachtman and Shelare's *Video Power: A Complete Guide to Writing, Planning, and Shooting Videos* helpful. Berry's *Every Kid's Guide to Watching TV Intelligently* is about why TV can be harmful or helpful, how to watch moderately and safely, how to choose programs, and how to respond to commercials. Check pages 178–80 of Muncy's *Springboard to Creative Thinking* for a project called "Let's Improve TV."

Educators may wish to subscribe to the *AIT Newsletter* from the Agency for Instructional Technology or the *GPN Newsletter* from the Great Plains National Instructional Television Library.

Take advantage of movies seen in theaters to advertise books. Children who enjoyed the movie *Honey, I Shrunk the Kids* will enjoy reading the book by Faucher, as well as books about little people. Place all books about little people on a bibliography attached to a display advertising the film *Honey, I Shrunk the Kids*.

A number of books for intermediate readers include little people. The most famous imaginary little people are Norton's Borrowers who appear in *The Borrowers, The Borrowers Afield, The Borrowers Afloat, The Borrowers Aloft*, and *The Borrowers Avenged*. A cassette recording of *The Borrowers* is available. The Minnipins are different from the other small inhabitants of the Land Between the Mountains in Kendall's Newbery Honor Book, *The Gammage Cup*. Alice shrinks in Carroll's classic, *Alice in Wonderland*. The 16mm film or video, *Gulliver's Travels*, includes the section of Swift's classic that tells about his visit with the little people of Lilliput. Tapp's *The Moth-Kin* and *Moth-Kin Magic* are about little people. In Woodruff's *Awfully Short for the Fourth Grade*, Noah plays with plastic "guys" that come to life and he shrinks to the size of his playthings. Tim is made small by a stone goblin but is rescued by snails in "A Leaf in the Shape of a Key," pages 31–42 of Aiken's *The Last Slice of Rainbow*. Asimov's *The Fantastic Voyage* is for adults, but the video may be enjoyed by middle school students. People are miniaturized and sent into the bloodstream of a human.

Information about the following little people appear in McHargue's *The Impossible People: A History of Natural and Unnatural Beings*: Agogwe, Akka, brownies, Domovoi, dwarfs, elves, fairies, Gahongas, Ghdowas, gnomes, goblins, gremlins, Hobs, Hulderfolk, Kalanoro, Knockers, Kobolds, Lar, leprechauns, Lutins, Maribundas, Muryans, Nittaewo, Ovinniks, Piziwa, Poleviks, Tootegas, trolls, and Yarthkins. Many of these same little creatures also appear in *Encyclopedia of Fairies, Hobgoblins, Brownies, Bogies, and Other Supernatural Creatures* by Briggs. Small Cornish elves called piskies, spriggans, and knackers appear in Climo's *Piskies, Spriggans, and Other Magical Beings*.

"Snow White and the Seven Dwarfs" appears on pages 53–61 of *The Best of Grimm's Fairy Tales* by Bell and Rogers. Check pages 104–09 of that book for a story called "Thumling." "Thumbelina" also appears on pages 194–205 of Ehrlich's *The Random House Book of Fairy Tales* and pages 67–82 of Andersen's *Michael Hague's Favorite Hans Christian Andersen Fairy Tales*. "Inchelina" appears on pages 29–37 of Andersen's *Complete Fairy Tales and Stories* and on pages 178–88 of *Hans Andersen: His Classic Fairy Tales*, both of which are translated by Haugaard. A picture book translated by Bell, called *Thumbelina*, is available. A Japanese folktale is available as a picture book called *Inch Boy* by Morimoto. The story is called "Little One Inch" on pages 66–70 of Sakade's *Japanese Children's Favorite Stories*. Stories of the folk character

Tom Thumb appear in "The History of Tom Thumb," pages 155–74 of Crossley-Holland's *British Folk Tales, New Versions*; pages 45–50 of Haviland's *Favorite Fairy Tales Told Around the World*; pages 140–47 of Jacobs's *English Fairy Tales*; and pages 63–70 of Reeves's *English Fables and Fairy Stories*. The Grimm story "Tom Thumb" appears on pages 310–14 of Thompson's *One Hundred Favorite Folktales*. Compare English, German and French versions. An illustrated picture book of Perrault's version is called *Tom Thumb*. Another picture book, *Tom Thumb*, is written and illustrated by Watson. Information about the human midget, Tom Thumb, appears in Drimmer's *Born Different: Amazing Stories of Some Very Special People*, on pages 14–47.

A modern picture book by Joyce, called *George Shrinks*, is about a little boy who has difficulties when he shrinks in size. *Chickpea and the Talking Cow* by Glass is about tiny Chickpea, who when swallowed by the family cow, Sweet Esmeralda, pretends to be a talking cow. The hoax is discovered when the cow loses her balance while bowing to the king, and Chickpea falls out. In *Penny* by De Regniers, a girl no bigger than a penny is adopted by a couple who look for a husband for her. Phoebe's parents accidentally make themselves smaller through magic in Spencer's *The Magic Room*. A witch shrinks a bear to the size of a chipmunk because he is a bully in Peet's *Big Bad Bruce*. The book is also available as a paperback/cassette package.

Bibliographical Indexes

Index to Books

All books are listed here by author last name. Many entries are followed by a number beginning with the letter "M." This indicates a related item or items that can be cross-referenced in the *Multimedia Index*.

Aardema, Verna. *Bringing the Rain to Kapiti Plain*. Illus. by Beatriz Vidal. New York: Dial, 1981. Pied Piper pb. M186.
———. *Oh, Kojo! How Could You!* Illus. by Marc Brown. New York: Dial, 1984. Pied Piper pb. M974, M975.
———. *Tales for the Third Ear, from Equatorial Africa*. Illus. by Ib Ohlsson. New York: Dutton, 1969.
Aaron, Chester. *Duchess*. New York: Lippincott, 1982.
———. *Gideon*. New York: Lippincott, 1982. Vagabond pb.
Aaron, Ira and Carter. *Golden Secrets*. Glenview, IL: Scott Foresman, 1983.
———. *Hidden Wonders*. Glenview, IL: Scott Foresman, 1983.
Aaseng, Nathan. *The Disease Fighters: The Nobel Prize in Medicine*. Illus. with photos. Minneapolis: Lerner, 1987.
Abells, Chana Byers. *The Children We Remember*. New York: Greenwillow, 1986.
The Abridged Readers' Guide to Periodical Literature. Bronx, NY: Wilson. Cumulative and annual.
Ackerman, Karen. *The Song and Dance Man*. Illus. by Stephen Gammell. New York: Knopf, 1988. M1223a
Adams, Barbara. *Can This Telethon Be Saved?* New York: Dell pb., 1987.
———. *Like It Is: Facts and Feelings About Handicaps from Kids Who Know*. Photos by James Stanfeld. New York: Walker, 1979.
———. *The Not-Quite-Ready-for-Prime-Time Bandits*. New York: Dell pb., 1986.
———. *Rock Video Strikes Again*. New York: Dell pb., 1986.
Adams, Laurie. *Alice and the Boa Constrictor*. Illus. by Emily McCully. Boston: Houghton, 1983.
Adams, Richard. *Watership Down*. New York: Macmillan, 1974. Avon pb. M1413.
Adamson, Joy. *Born Free: A Lioness of Two Worlds*. New York: Pantheon, 1960. pb.

Adkins, Jan. *A Storm Without Rain*. Boston: Little, 1983.
———. *The Wooden Ship*. Boston: Houghton, 1978.
Adler, Carole S. *Always and Forever*. New York: Clarion, 1988.
———. *Eddie's Blue-Winged Dragon*. New York: Putnam, 1988.
———. *In Our House, Scott Is My Brother*. New York: Macmillan, 1980.
———. *The Magic of the Glits*. New York: Macmillan, 1979. Avon Cameolot pb., Scholastic pb.
———. *The Once in a While Hero*. New York: Coward, 1982.
Adler, David. *Cam Jansen and the Mystery at the Monkey House*. Illus. by Susanna Natti. New York: Viking, 1985. Dell pb.
———. *Cam Jansen and the Mystery of Flight 54*. New York: Viking, 1989.
———. *Cam Jansen and the Mystery of the Babe Ruth Baseball*. Illus. by S. Natti. New York: Viking, 1982. Dell pb. M210.
———. *Cam Jansen and the Mystery of the Carnival Prize*. Illus by S. Natti. New York: Viking, 1984. Dell pb.
———. *Cam Jansen and the Mystery of the Circus Clown*. Illus by S. Natti. New York: Viking, 1983. Dell pb.
———. *Cam Jansen and the Mystery of the Corn Popper*. Illus. by S. Natti. New York: Viking, 1986.
———. *Cam Jansen and the Mystery of the Dinosaur Bones*. Illus by S. Natti. New York: Viking, 1981. Dell pb. M211a.
———. *Cam Jansen and the Mystery of the Gold Coins*. Illus. by S. Natti. New York: Viking, 1982. Dell pb.
———. *Cam Jansen and the Mystery of the Monster Movie*. Illus. by S. Natti. New York: Viking, 1984. Dell pb.
———. *Cam Jansen and the Mystery of the Stolen Diamonds*. Illus by S. Natti. New York: Viking, 1980. Dell pb.

———. *The Black Cauldron*. New York: Holt, 1965. Dell pb. M1317.

———. *The Book of Three*. New York: Holt, 1964. Dell pb.

———. *The Castle of Llyr*. New York: Holt, 1966. Dell pb.

———. *The Foundling: Other Tales of Prydain*. Illus. by Margot Zemach. New York: Holt, 1973. Dell pb.

———. *The High King*. New York: Holt, 1968. Dell pb.

———. *The Kestrel*. New York: Dutton, 1982. Dell pb.

———. *Taran Wanderer*. New York: Holt, 1967. Dell pb.

———. *Time Cat*. Illus. by Bill Sokol. New York: Holt, 1963. Magnolia, MA: Peter Smith, n.d. Dell pb. Avon Camelot pb.

———. *Westmark*. New York: Dutton, 1981. Dell pb.

Alexander, Martha. *Even That Moose Won't Listen to Me*. Illus. by the author. New York: Dial, 1988.

———. *Nobody Asked Me If I Wanted a Baby Sister*. Illus. by the author. New York: Dial, 1971. Pied Piper pb.

Aliki. *At Mary Bloom's*. Illus. by the author. New York: Greenwillow, 1983. Puffin pb.

———. *Digging Up Dinosaurs*. Illus. by the author. New York: Crowell, 1988. Trophy pb. M348, M349.

———. *Dinosaur Bones*. Illus. by the author. New York: Crowell, 1988.

———. *Dinosaurs Are Different*. Illus. by the author. New York: Crowell, 1985. Trophy pb.

———. *Feelings*. New York: Greenwillow, 1984. Mulberry pb. M438, M1098.

———. *Fossils Tell of Long Ago*. Illus. by the author. New York: Crowell, 1972. Trophy pb.

———. *Giants from the Past: the Age of Mammals*. New York: Harper, 1983. Trophy pb.

———. *The King's Day: Louis XIV of France*. Illus. by the author. New York: Crowell, 1989.

———. *A Medieval Feast*. Illus. by the author. New York: Crowell, 1983. Trophy pb. M827, M828.

———. *Mummies Made in Egypt*. Illus. by the author. New York: Crowell, 1979. Trophy pb. M915. M916

———. *My Visit to the Dinosaurs*. Illus. by the author. New York: Crowell, 1969, 1985. Trophy pb. M933.

———. *Overnight at Mary Bloom's*. Illus. by the author. New York: Greenwillow, 1987.

———. *The Story of Johnny Appleseed*. Illus. by the author. Englewood Cliffs, NJ: Prentice Hall, 1963, 1987.

———. *The Two of Them*. Illus. by the author. New York: Greenwillow, 1979. Mulberry pb.

———. *We Are Best Friends*. Illus. by the author. New York: Greenwillow, 1982.

———. *Wild and Woolly Mammoths*. Illus. by the author. New York: Crowell, 1977. Trophy pb.

Allard, Harry. *Miss Nelson Has a Field Day*. Illus. by James Marshall. Boston: Houghton, 1985. Scholastic pb., Sandpiper pb. M665, M866.

———. *Miss Nelson Is Back*. Illus. by J. Marshall. Boston: Houghton, 1982. Scholastic pb. Sandpiper pb. M665, M867, M868.

———. *Miss Nelson Is Missing*. Illus. by J. Marshall. Boston: Houghton, 1977. Scholastic pb. M423, M665, M869, M870, M871, M872.

Allen, Laura. *Where Is Freddy?* New York: Harper, 1986.

Allen, Pamela. *Hidden Treasure*. Illus. by the author. New York: Putnam, 1986.

Allen, Thomas B. *On Grandaddy's Farm*. New York: Knopf, 1989.

Alter, Judith. *Growing Up in the Old West*. New York: Watts, 1989.

———. *Women of the Old West*. New York: Watts, 1989.

Ames, Lee J. *Draw Fifty Airplanes, Aircraft, and Spacecraft*. New York: Doubleday, 1977. Zephyr pb.

———. *Draw Fifty Boats, Ships, Trucks, and Trains*. New York: Doubleday, 1976. Zephyr pb.

———. *Draw Fifty Cars, Trucks, and Motorcycles*. New York: Doubleday, 1986. Zephyr pb.

———. *Draw Fifty Dinosaurs and Other Prehistoric Animals*. New York: Doubleday, 1977. Zephyr pb.

———. *Draw Fifty Horses*. New York: Doubleday, 1984. Zephyr pb.

———. *Draw Fifty Monsters, Creeps, Superheroes, Demons, and Dragons*. New York: Doubleday, 1983. Zephyr pb.

———. *Draw Fifty Vehicles*. New York: Doubleday, 1978. Zephyr pb.

———. *How to Draw Star Wars Heroes, Creatures, Spaceships, and Other Fantastic Things*. New York: Random, 1984. pb.

Ames, Lee J. and Warren Budd. *Draw Fifty Sharks, Whales, and Other Sea Creatures*. New York: Doubleday, 1980.

Amon, Aline. *Reading, Writing, Chattering Chimps*. New York: Atheneum, 1975.

Anastasio, Dina. *Pass the Peas, Please: A Book of Manners*. Illus by Katy Keck Arnsteen. New York: Warner, 1988.

Barrett, Judi. *Cloudy with a Chance of Meatballs.* Illus. by Ron Barrett. New York: Atheneum, 1978. Aladdin pb. M281, M282.
———. *I'm Too Small, You're Too Big.* New York: Atheneum, 1981.
Barrie, James. *Peter Pan.* Illus. by Michael Hague. New York: Holt, 1987. M1003, M1004.
———. *Peter Pan.* Large Print edition. Santa Barbara: ABC-CLIO, 1988.
———. *Peter Pan and Wendy.* Illus. by Michael Foreman. New York: Potter, 1988.
Barstow, Barbara and Judith Riggle. *Beyond Picture Books: A Guide to First Readers.* New York: Bowker, 1989.
Barton, Byron. *Airplanes.* Illus. by the author. New York: Crowell, 1986.
———. *Airport.* Illus. by the author. New York: Crowell, 1982. Trophy pb.
———. *Building a House.* Illus. by the author. New York: Greenwillow, 1981. Puffin pb.
———. *Dinosaurs, Dinosaurs.* Illus. by the author. New York: Crowell, 1989.
———. *I Want to Be an Astronaut.* Illus. by the author. New York: Crowell, 1988.
———. *Machines at Work.* Illus. by the author. New York: Crowell, 1987.
———. *Trains.* Illus. by the author. New York: Crowell, 1986.
———. *Trucks.* Illus. by the author. New York: Crowell, 1986.
Base, Graeme. *The Eleventh Hour.* Illus. by the author. New York: Abrams, 1989.
Bash, Barbara. *Desert Giant: The World of the Saguaro Cactus.* Illus. by the author. Boston: Little and San Francisco: Sierra, 1989. Tree Tales pb. M341, M1098.
Baskin, Barbara and Karen H. Harris. *More Notes from a Different Drummer: A Guide to Juvenile Fiction Portraying the Disabled.* New York: Bowker, 1984.
———. *Notes from a Different Drummer: A Guide to Juvenile Fiction Portraying the Handicapped.* New York: Bowker, 1977.
Baskin, Hosie and Leonard Baskin. *A Book of Dragons.* New York: Knopf, 1985.
Bassett, Lisa. *Very Truly Yours, Charles L. Dodgson, Alias Lewis Carroll.* New York: Lothrop, 1987.
Bates, Betty. *Thatcher Payne-in-the-Neck.* Illus. by Linda S. Edwards. New York: Holiday, 1985. Dell pb.
———. *Tough Beans.* Illus. by Leslie Morrill. New York: Holiday, 1988.
Battles, Edith. *Eddie Couldn't Find the Elephants.* Illus. by Tom Funkil. Niles, IL: Whitman, 1974.

Bauer, Caroline Feller. *Celebrations.* Bronx, NY: Wilson, 1985.
———. *Presenting Reader's Theater.* Illus. by Lynn Bredeson. Bronx, NY: Wilson, 1987.
———. *This Way to Books.* Illus. by Lynn Gates. Bronx, NY: Wilson, 1983.
Bauer, Marion. *On My Honor.* New York: Clarion, 1986. Dell pb. M481.
———. *On My Honor.* Large Print edition. Boston: G K Hall, 1989. M481.
———. *Touch the Moon.* Illus. by Aliz Berenzy. New York: Clarion, 1987. Dell pb.
Baum, Frank. *The Wizard of Oz.* Illus. by Michael Hague. New York: Holt, 1982. M398, M659, M1104, M1475.
———. *The Wonderful Wizard of Oz.* Large Print edition. Illus. by W. W. Denslow. Santa Barbara: ABC-CLIO, 1987. M359, M659, M1104, M1475.
Baum, Louis. *One More Time.* New York: Morrow, 1986.
Bawden, Nina. *Henry.* Illus. by Joyce Powzyk. New York: Lothrop, 1988. Dell pb. M1093.
Bayley, Nicola. *As I Was Going Up and Down and Other Nonsense Rhymes.* New York: Macmillan, 1986.
Baylor, Byrd. *The Best Town in the World.* Illus. by Ronald Himler. New York: Scribner, 1983. M196.
———. *Hawk, I'm Your Brother.* Illus. by Peter Parnall. New York: Scribner, 1976.
———. *If You Are a Hunter of Fossils.* Illus. by Peter Parnall. New York: Scribner, 1980. Aladdin pb.
———. *The Other Way to Listen.* Illus. by Peter Parnall. New York: Scribner, 1978.
———. *The Way to Start a Day.* Illus. by P. Parnall. Scribner, 1978. Aladdin pb.
Beatty, Patricia. *Be Ever Hopeful, Hannalee.* New York: Morrow, 1988.
———. *Behave Yourself, Bethany Brandt.* New York: Morrow, 1986.
———. *Charley Skedaddle.* New York: Morrow, 1987. Troll pb. M1069.
———. *Eight Mules from Monterey.* New York: Morrow, 1982.
———. *Turn Homeward, Hannalee.* New York: Morrow, 1984.
Bedard, Michael. *A Darker Magic.* New York: Atheneum, 1987. Avon Flare pb.
Begarnie, Luke. *The Space Shuttle Story.* New York: Scholastic, n.d.
Behler, John L. and F. Wayne King. *The Audubon Society Field Guide to North American Reptiles and Amphibians.* New York: Knopf, 1979.
Behrens, June. *Dolphins!* Chicago: Childrens Press, 1989.

———. *Whales of the World.* Chicago: Childrens Press, 1987.

———. *Whalewatch!* Chicago: Childrens Press, 1978.

———. *Juliet Low: Founder of the Girl Scouts in America.* Chicago: Childrens Press, 1988. pb.

———. *Sharks.* Chicago: Childrens Press, 1990.

Belden, William S. *Frankie.* Illus. by Stewart Daniels. San Diego: Harcourt, 1987.

Bell, Anthea and Anne Rogers. *The Best of Grimm's Fairy Tales.* Illus. by Otto S. Svend. New York: Larousse, 1979.

Bellairs, John. *The Curse of the Blue Figurine.* New York: Dial, 1983. Bantam Skylark pb.

———. *The Dark Secret of Weatherend.* New York: Dial, 1984. Bantam Skylark pb.

———. *The Figure in the Shadows.* New York: Dial, 1975. Dell pb.

———. *The House With a Clock on Its Walls.* New York: Dial, 1973. Dell pb. M596, M815.

———. *The Lamp from the Warlock's Tomb.* New York: Dial, 1988.

———. *The Letter, the Witch and the Ring.* New York: Dial, 1976. Dell pb.

Bellanger, Claude. *Talk to Me.* Crystal Lake, IL: Rigby, n.d. M1308.

Belle, William. *Crabbe's Journey.* Boston: Little, 1986.

Bemelmans, Ludwig. *Madeline.* Illus. by the author. Puffin pb. M410, M784, M785, M786, M787, M792.

———. *Madeline.* Adapted pop-up by Judy Wheeler. Illus. by David A. Carter. New York: Viking, 1987. M410, M784, M785, M786, M787, M792.

———. *Madeline.* Illus. by the author. Big book edition. New York: Scholastic, n.d. M420, M784, M785, M786, M787, M792.

———. *Madeline and the Bad Hat.* Illus. by the author. New York: Viking, 1957. Puffin pb. M788.

———. *Madeline and the Gypsies.* Illus. by the author. New York: Viking, 1959. M789.

———. *Madeline in London.* Illus. by the author. New York: Viking, 1961. Puffin pb. M790.

———. *Madeline's Christmas.* Illus. by the author. New York: Viking, 1985.

———. *Madeline's House.* Illus. by the author. New York: Viking, 1989. pb.

———. *Madeline's Rescue.* Illus. by the author. New York: Viking, 1953. M420, M793, M794, M795.

Benchley, Nathaniel. *Bright Candles: A Novel of the Danish Resistance.* New York: Harper, 1974.

———. *Demo and the Dolphin.* Illus. by Stephen Gammell. New York: Harper, 1981.

Bender, Lionel. *Pythons and Boas.* New York: Gloucester/Watts, 1988.

———. *Whales and Dolphins.* New York: Gloucester/Watts, 1988.

Bendick, Jeanne. *Egyptian Tombs.* Illus. by the author. New York: Watts, 1989.

Benet, Stephen Vincent. *The Devil and Daniel Webster.* Illus. by Harold Denison. New York: Farrar, 1937. M345.

Benitez, Mirna. *How Spider Tricked Snake.* Illus. by Dorothea Sierra. Milwaukee: Raintree, 1989.

Bennett, Jill. *Learning to Read with Picture Books.* Stroud, England: Thimble, 1985.

Benton, Michael. *How Dinosaurs Lived.* Illus. by Jim Robins. New York: Warwick/Watts, 1985.

———. *Dinosaur Encyclopedia.* New York: Messner, 1984. Wanderer pb.

Beowulf. See Crossley-Holland, Kevin, and Sutcliff, Rosemary.

Berends, Polly. *The Case of the Elevator Duck.* Illus. by James K. Washburn. New York: Random, 1973. pb. M224, M225.

Berenstain, Stan and Janice Berenstain. *The Day of the Dinosaur.* New York: Random, 1987.

Berger, Barbara. *Grandfather Twilight.* Illus. by the author. New York: Philomel/Putnam, 1984. pb.

Berger, Gilda. *Whales.* Illus. by Lisa Bonforte. New York: Doubleday, 1987.

Berger, Melvin. *Exploring the Mind and Brain.* New York: Crowell, 1983.

———. *Germs Make Me Sick.* Illus. by Marilyn Hafner. New York: Crowell, 1985. Trophy pb. M489, M1098.

Bergman, Thomas. *Seeing in Special Ways: Children Living with Blindness.* Milwaukee: Gareth Stevens, 1989.

———. *We Laugh, We Love, We Cry: Children Living with Mental Retardation.* Milwaukee: Gareth Stevens, 1989.

Berliner, Don. *Helicopters.* Illus. with photos. Minneapolis: Lerner, 1983.

Berman, Claire G. *What Am I Doing in a Step-Family?* Secaucus, NJ: Lyle Stuart, 1982.

Berna, Paul. *A Hundred Million Francs.* Illus. by Richard Kennedy. Trans. by John Buchanan-Brown. London: Bodley Head, 1957. Puffin pb.

Bernbaum, Israel. *My Brother's Keeper: The Holocaust Through the Eyes of an Artist.* Illus. by the author. New York: Putnam, 1985. M925.

———. *Twelve Bells for Santa.* Illus. by the author. New York: Harper, 1977. Trophy pb.

Bonsall, Thomas. *Titanic.* New York: Gallery Books, 1987.

Book of a Thousand Poems. New York: Peter Bedrick, 1989. pb.

Books from Cover to Cover: Teacher's Guide. Washington, DC: WETA-TV, n.d. M166.

Books in Print. New York: Bowker, 1948–. Annual.

Bos, Burny. *Ollie the Elephant.* New York: North-South, 1989.

Bosma, Bette. *Fairy Tales, Fables, Legends and Myths: Using Folk Literature in Your Classroom.* New York: Teachers College Press, 1987.

Bosse, Malcolm. *Cave Beyond Time.* New York: Crowell, 1980.

Boston, Lucy. *The Children of Green Knowe.* Illus. by Peter Boston. San Diego: Harcourt, 1955. Voyager pb. M1170.

———. *The Children of Green Knowe.* Large print edition. Boston: G K Hall, 1987. M1170.

———. *An Enemy at Green Knowe.* New York: Harcourt, 1964. Voyager pb.

———. *The River at Green Knowe.* New York: Harcourt, 1959. Voyager pb. M179.

———. *Stranger at Green Knowe.* New York: Harcourt, 1961. Voyager pb. M1270.

———. *The Treasure of Green Knowe.* New York: Harcourt, 1958. Voyager pb.

Botter, Barbara. *Zoo Story.* Illus. by Lynn Munsinger. New York: Scholastic, 1987.

Bottomley, Jim. *Paper Projects for Creative Kids of All Ages.* Boston: Little, 1983. pb.

Boulle, Pierre. *Bridge Over the River Kwai.* New York: Vanguard, 1954. Bantam pb. M179.

———. *Planet of the Apes.* New York: Vanguard, 1963. Bantam pb. M1045.

Bourke, Linda. *Handmade ABC: A Manual Alphabet.* Reading, MA: Addison & Wessley, 1981.

Bove, Linda. *Sesame Street Sign Language ABC.* Illus. by Tom Cooke. Photos by Anita and Steve Shevett. New York: Random, 1985. M1168.

Bowker Staff, "The Best of Children's Books of 19–." *The Bowker Annual.* New York: Bowker, 1961–.

———. *The Bowker Annual.* New York: Bowker, 1961–. Annual.

———. "Literacy Prizes, 19—." *The Bowker Annual.* New York: Bowker, 1961–.

Bowman, Keith. *Agriculture.* Morristown, NJ: Silver Burdett, 1987.

Boyd, Anne. *Ancient Egyptians Activity Book.* Cambridge: Press Syndicate of the University of Cambridge, 1981.

Boyd, Candy Dawson. *Charlie Pippin.* New York: Macmillan, 1987. Puffin pb.

Boyd, Lizi. *The Not-So-Wicked Stepmother.* New York: Viking, 1987. Puffin pb.

Boyne, Walter J. *The Smithsonian Book of Flight for Young People.* New York: Atheneum, 1988.

Bradman, Tony. *Dilly the Dinosaur.* Illus. by Susan Hellard. New York: Viking, 1987. Puffin pb.

Brandenberg, Franz. *Aunt Nina and Her Nephews and Nieces.* Illus. by Aliki. New York: Greenwillow, 1983. M101, M102.

———. *Aunt Nina, Good Night.* Illus. by Aliki. New York: Greenwillow, 1989.

———. *Aunt Nina's Visit.* Illus. by Aliki. New York: Greenwillow, 1984.

———. *Leo and Emily.* Illus. by Aliki. New York: Greenwillow, 1981.

———. *Leo and Emily and the Dragon.* Illus. by Aliki. New York: Greenwillow, 1984. Dell pb.

———. *Leo and Emily's Big Ideas.* Illus. by Aliki. New York: Greenwillow, 1982. Dell pb.

———. *Leo and Emily's Zoo.* Illus. by Yossi Abolafie. New York: Greenwillow, 1988. Dell pb.

Branley, Franklin. *Comets.* Illustrated by Giulio Maestro. New York: Crowell, 1984. Trophy pb.

———. *Dinosaurs, Asteroids, and Superstars.* Illus. by Jean Zallinger. New York: Crowell, 1982.

———. *Eclipse, Darkness and Daytime.* Illus. by Donald Crews. New York: Crowell, 1973.

———. *From Sputnik to Space Shuttles: Into the New Space Age.* Illus. with photos. New York: Crowell, 1986.

———. *Journey Into a Black Hole.* Illus. by Marc Simont. New York: Crowell, 1986.

———. *Rockets and Satellites.* Illus. by Giulio Maestro. New York: Crowell, 1987.

———. *Star Guide.* Illus. by Ellen Eagle. New York: Crowell, 1987.

———. *What Happened to the Dinosaurs?* Illus. by Marc Simont. New York: Crowell, 1989.

———. *What the Moon Is Like.* Illus. by True Kelley. New York: Crowell, 1986. Trophy pb.

Branscum, Robbie. *The Adventures of Johnny May.* Illus. by Deborah Howland. New York: Harper, 1984.

———. *Johnny May.* Illus. by Charles Robinson. New York: Doubleday, 1975.

———. *Johnny May Grows Up.* Illus. by Bob Marstall. New York: Harper, 1987.

Breen, Karen. *Index to Collective Biographies for Young Readers.* New York: Bowker, 1988.

Brenner, Barbara. *On the Frontier with Mr. Audubon.* New York: Coward, 1977.

———. *Wagon Wheels.* Illus. by Don Bolognese. New York: Harper, 1978.

Brett, Jan. *The Mitten: A Ukranian Tale.* Retold and illus. by J. Brett. New York: Putnam, 1989. Trophy pb.

Brewton, John E. and Sara. *Index to Children's Poetry: A Title, Subject, Author, and First Line Index to Poetry in Collection for Children and Youth.* Bronx, NY: Wilson, 1942.

Brewton, John E., Sara Brewton, and G. Meredith Blackburn. *Index to Poetry for Children and Young People, 1964–1969.* Bronx, NY: Wilson, 1972.

Brewton, John E., G. Meredith Blackburn, and Lorraine Blackburn. *Index to Poetry for Children and Young People, 1970–1975.* Bronx, NY: Wilson, 1978.

————. *Index to Poetry for Children and Young People, 1976–1981.* Bronx, NY: Wilson, 1984.

Bridbill, David. *Bones on Black Spruce Mountain.* New York: Dial, 1978. Bantam pb.

————. *Snow Shoe Trek at Otter River.* Illus. by Lorence Bjorklund. New York: Dial, 1976.

Bridgers, Sue Ellen. *Notes for Another Life.* New York: Knopf, 1981. Bantam pb.

Bridwell, Norman. *Clifford the Big Red Dog.* Illus. by the author. New York: Four Winds, 1963. M176, M177, M178, M179, M1269b.

————. *Clifford the Small Red Puppy.* Illus. by the author. New York: Scholastic, 1985. pb. M227, M1269b.

————. *Clifford's Birthday Party.* Illus. by the author. New York: Scholastic, 1988. M1269b.

Briggs, Carole S. *Women in Space: Reaching the Last Frontier.* Minneapolis: Lerner, 1988. M1239.

Briggs, Julia. *A Woman of Passion: The Life of E. Nesbit, 1854–1924.* New York: New Amsterdam, 1987.

Briggs, Katherine M. *Encyclopedia of Fairies, Hobgoblins, Brownies, Bogies, and Other Supernatural Creatures.* New York: Pantheon, 1976. pb.

Bright, Robert. *Georgie.* Illus. by the author. New York: Doubleday, 1944. Scholastic pb.

————. *Georgie and the Buried Treasure.* Illus. by the author. New York: Doubleday, 1979.

————. *Georgie and the Little Dog.* Illus. by the author. New York: Doubleday, 1983.

————. *Georgie and the Magician.* Illus. by the author. New York: Doubleday, 1966.

————. *Georgie and the Robbers.* Illus. by the author. New York: Doubleday, 1963. Scholastic pb.

————. *Georgie Goes West.* Illus. by the author. Doubleday, 1973.

————. *Georgie and the Runaway Balloons.* Illus. by the author. New York: Doubleday, 1983.

————. *Georgie's Christmas Carol.* Illus. by the author. New York: Doubleday, 1975.

————. *Georgie's Halloween.* Illus. by the author. New York: Doubleday, 1958.

Brighton, Catherine. *Five Secrets in a Box.* New York: Dutton, 1987.

————. *My Hands, My World.* New York: Macmillan, 1984.

Brink, Carol. *Caddie Woodlawn.* New York: Macmillan, 1935. Aladdin pb. M200, M201, M202, M203, M840.

————. *Caddie Woodlawn.* Large print edition. Santa Barbara, CA: ABC-CLIO, 1988. M100, M201, M202, M203, M840.

————. *Magical Melons: More Stories about Caddie Woodlawn.* Illus. by Marguerite Davis. New York: Macmillan, 1939, 1966.

Brittain, Bill. *All the Money in the World.* New York: Harper, 1979.

————. *Dr. Dredd's Wagon of Wonders.* Illus. by Andrew Glass. New York: Harper, 1987. Trophy pb.

————. *The Wish Giver: Three Tales of Coven Tree.* Illus. by A. Glass. New York: Harper, 1983. Trophy pb. M1470, M1471.

Broekel, Ray. *Gerbil Pets and Other Small Rodents.* Chicago: Childrens Press, 1983.

————. *I Can Be an Author.* Chicago: Childrens Press, 1986. pb.

————. *Your Five Senses.* Chicago: Childrens Press, 1984. pb.

————. *Your Skeleton and Skin.* Chicago: Childrens Press, 1984. pb.

Bromley, Karen D. *Webbing with Literature: Creating Story Maps with Children's Books.* Boston: Allyn and Bacon, 1991.

Brooke, L. Leslie. *Johnny Crow's Garden.* Illus. by the author. New York: Warne, 1935. pb. M676.

————. *Johnny Crow's New Garden.* Illus. by the author. New York: Warne, 1986.

————. *Johnny Crow's Party.* Illus. by the author. New York: Warne, 1907. pb.

Brooks, Terry. *Elfstones of Shannara.* New York: Ballantine, 1982.

————. *Scions of Shannara.* New York: Ballantine, 1990.

————. *The Sword of Shannara.* New York: Random, 1977. Ballantine pb.

————. *Wishsong of Shannara.* New York: Ballantine, 1985.

Broomfield, Robert. *The Twelve Days of Christmas.* Illus. by R. Broomfield. New York: McGraw, 1965. M1373, M1374.

Brower, Pauline. *Baden-Powell: Founder of the Boy Scouts.* Chicago: Childrens Press, 1989.

Brown, Dee. *Bury My Heart at Wounded Knee: An Indian History of the American West.* New York: Holt, 1970. Bantam pb.

Brown, Drollene. *Belva Lockwood Wins Her Case.* Illus. by James Watling. Morton Grove, IL: Whitman, 1987.

Brown, F. K. *Last Hurdle.* Illus. by Peter Spier. Hamden, CT: Linnet, 1988.

Brown, Marc. *Arthur Goes to Camp.* Illus. by the author. Boston: Joy Street/Little, 1982. pb. M83, M93.

——. *Arthur's April Fool.* Illus. by the author. Boston: Joy Street/Little, 1983. pb. M82, M84.

——. *Arthur's Baby.* Illus. by the author. Boston: Joy Street/Little, 1987. M85.

——. *Arthur's Birthday.* Illus. by the author. Boston: Joy Street/Little, 1989.

——. *Arthur's Christmas.* Illus. by the author. Boston: Joy Street/Little, 1984. pb. M82, M86.

——. *Arthur's Eyes.* Illus. by the author. Boston: Joy Street/Little, 1979. pb. Avon pb. M87, M88.

——. *Arthur's Halloween.* Illus. by the author. Boston: Joy Street/Little, 1982. pb. M82.

——. *Arthur's Nose.* Illus. by the author. Boston: Joy Street/Little, 1976. pb. Avon pb.

——. *Arthur's Teacher Trouble.* Illus. by the author. Boston: Joy Street/Little, 1986. M92, M93.

——. *Arthur's Thanksgiving.* Illus. by the author. Boston: Joy Street/Little, 1984. pb. M82, M94.

——. *Arthur's Tooth.* Illus. by the author. Boston: Joy Street/Little, 1986. pb. M95.

——. *Arthur's Valentine.* Illus. by the author. Boston: Joy Street/Little, 1980. pb. Avon pb. M82.

——. *D. W. All Wet.* Illus. by the author. Boston: Joy Street/Little, 1988.

——. *D. W. Flips.* Illus. by the author. Boston: Joy Street/Little, 1987.

——. *The True Francine.* Illus. by the author. Boston: Joy Street/Little, 1981. pb. Avon pb.

Brown, Marc and Laurene Brown. *The Bionic Bunny Show.* Boston: Little, 1984.

——. *Dinosaurs Divorce: A Guide for Changing Families.* Boston: Joy Street/Little, 1986. M359.

Brown, Marc and Stephen Krensky. *Dinosaurs Beware! A Safety Guide.* Boston: Joy Street/Little, 1982. pb. M358.

——. *Perfect Pigs: An Introduction to Manners.* Boston: Joy Street/Little, 1983. pb.

Brown, Marcia. *Dick Whittington and His Cat.* Retold and illus. by M. Brown. New York: Scribner, 1950, 1988. M190.

——. *Lotus Seeds: Children, Pictures, and Books.* New York: Scribner, 1986.

——. *Once a Mouse.* Retold and illus. by M. Brown. New York: Scribners, 1961. Aladdin pb.

Brown, Marcia. *Shadow.* See Cendrars, Blaise.

Brown, Marcia and Charles Perrault. *Cinderella.* Retold and Illus. by M. Brown. New York: Scribner, 1954. Aladdin pb.

Brown, Marion M. and Jane K. Leech. *Dreamcatcher: The Life of John Neihardt.* Nashville: Abingdon, 1983.

Brown, Ruth. *A Dark Dark Tale.* Illus. by the author. New York: Dial, 1981. M328, M329, M330.

Brown, Tricia. *Chinese New Year.* Photos by Fran Ortiz. New York: Holt, 1987.

——. *Hello, Amigos!* Photos by F. Ortiz. New York: Holt, 1987.

——. *Someone Special, Just Like You.* Photos by F. Ortiz. New York: Holt, 1984.

Browne, Anthony. *Piggybook.* Illus. by the author. New York: Knopf, 1986. pb.

——. *Willy the Champ.* Illus. by the author. New York: Knopf, 1986.

——. *Willy the Wimp.* Illus. by the author. New York: Knopf, 1984.

Browning, Robert. *The Pied Piper of Hamelin.* Illus. by Anatoly Ivanov. New York: Lothrop, 1986. M1018.

——. *The Pied Piper of Hamelin.* San Diego: Gulliver/Harcourt, 1988. M1018.

Brunhoff, Jean de. *Babar the King.* Illus. by the author. New York: Random, 1986. M105, M107, M108, M709a, M1269b.

Brunhoff, Jean de and Laurent de Brunhoff. *Babar's Anniversary Album.* New York: Random, 1981. M106, M108, M709a, M1269b.

Brunhoff, Laurent de. *Babar and the Ghost: An Easy-to-Read Version.* Illus. by the author. New York: Random, 1986.

——. *Babar and the Ghost.* Illus. by the author. New York: Random, 1981 pb.

——. *Babar's Little Circus Star.* Illus. by the author. New York: Random, 1988 pb.

Bruun, Ruth D. and Bertel Bruun. *The Human Body.* Illus. by Patricia Wynne. New York: Random, 1982.

——. *Your Skeleton and Skin.* Illus. by P. Wynne. New York: Random, 1982.

Bryan, Ashley. *The Dancing Granny.* Retold and illus. by A. Bryan. New York: Atheneum, 1977. Aladdin pb. M324, M1094.

——. *The Lion and the Ostrich Chicks and Other African Folk Tales.* Retold and Illus. by A. Bryan. New York: Atheneum, 1986. M1094.

Bryant, Bonnie. *Horse Crazy.* New York: Bantam, 1988.
———. *Horse Sense.* Bantam, 1988.
———. *Horse Sky.* Bantam, 1988.
Buchan, Elizabeth. *Beatrix Potter.* Illus. by Beatrix Potter and Mike Dodd. London: Hamish Hamilton, 1987.
Buckley, Helen E. *Someday with My Father.* Illus. by Ellen Eagle. New York: Harper, 1985.
Bull, Angela. *Anne Frank.* Illus. by Stephen Gulbis. London: Hamish Hamilton, 1984. M60, M61, M62, M490, M712, M715.
———. *Florence Nightingale.* Illus. by Karen Heywood. London: Hamish Hamilton, 1985.
Bulla, Clyde. *The Chalk Box Kid.* Illus. by Thomas B. Allen. New York: Random, 1987. Stepping Stone pb. M248.
———. *Daniel's Duck.* Illus. by Joan Sandin. New York: Harper, 1979.
———. *Pocahontas and the Strangers.* New York: Scholastic, 1988. pb.
———. *Shoeshine Girl.* Illus. by Leigh Grant. New York: Crowell, 1975. Trophy pb. M1187.
———. *The Stubborn Old Woman.* Illus. by Anne Rockwell. New York: Crowell, 1980.
———. *The Sword in the Tree.* Illus. by Paul Galdone. New York: Crowell, 1956.
Bullaty, Sonja and Angelo Lorneo. *The Little Wild Ponies.* New York: Messner, 1987. Simon and Schuster pb.
Bullock, Alan. *Hitler: A Study in Tyranny.* New York: Harper, 1952. Trophy pb.
Bunting, Eve. *Ghost's Hour, Spook's Hour.* Illus. by Donald Carrick. New York: Clarion, 1987.
———. *Happy Birthday, Dear Duck.* Illus. by Jan Brett. New York: Clarion, 1988.
———. *The Happy Funeral.* Illus. by Vo-Dinh Mai. New York: Harper, 1982.
———. *How Many Days to America? A Thanksgiving Story.* Illus. by Beth Peck. New York: Clarion, 1988.
———. *Jane Martin, Dog Detective.* Illus. by Amy Schwartz. San Diego: Harcourt, 1984. Voyager pb.
———. *Karen Kepplewhite Is the World's Best Kisser.* New York: Clarion, 1983. Archway pb. Scholastic pb.
———. *The Man Who Could Call Down Owls.* Illus. by Charles Mikolaycak. New York: Macmillan, 1984.
———. *Mother's Day Mice.* Illus. by Jan Brett. New York: Clarion, 1986. M903.
———. *The Sea World Book of Whales.* Photos by Hubbs-Sea World Research Institute. San Diego: Harcourt, 1980.
———. *Sixth Grade Sleepover.* New York: Harcourt, 1986. Scholastic pb.

———. *The Wednesday Surprise.* Illus. by Donald Carrick. New York: Clarion, 1989.
Burch, Robert. *Christmas with Ida Early.* New York: Viking, 1983. Penguin pb.
———. *Ida Early Comes Over the Mountain.* New York: Viking, 1980. Avon Camelot pb.
———. *Queenie Peavy.* New York: Viking, 1966. Penguin pb. M1105.
Burchard, Sue. *The Statue of Liberty: Birth to Rebirth.* San Diego: Harcourt, 1985.
Burke, Kathleen. *Louisa May Alcott.* New York: Chelsea House, 1988. M772, M835.
Burleigh, Robert. *A Man Named Thoreau.* Illus. by Lloyd Bloom. New York: Atheneum, 1985.
Burnett, Frances Hodgson. *A Little Princess.* New York: Bantam pb., Dell pb., Puffin pb., Trophy pb.
———. *The Secret Garden.* Illus. by Michael Hague. New York: Holt, 1987. M1158, M1159, M1160, M1161, M1162, M1163.
———. *The Secret Garden.* Illus. by Graham Rust. Boston: Godine, 1986. M1158, M1159, M1160, M1161, M1162, M1163.
———. *The Secret Garden.* Illus. by Tasha Tudor. New York: Lippincott, 1963, 1987. M1158, M1159, M1160, M1161, M1162, M1163.
———. *The Secret Garden.* Apple pb., Bantam pb., Dell pb., Puffin pb., Signet pb., Trophy pb. M1158, M1159, M1160, M1161, M1162, M1163.
Burnford, Sheila E. *The Incredible Journey.* Illus. by Cal Burger. Boston: Joy Street/Little, 1961. Bantam pb. M57.
Burningham, John. *Grandpa.* Illus. by the author. New York: Crown, 1985.
———. *John Burningham's Colors.* Illus. by the author. New York: Crown, 1986.
———. *John Patrick Norman McHennessy— The Boy Who Was Always Late.* Illus. by the author. New York: Crown, 1988.
———. *Where's Julius?* Illus. by the author. New York: Crown, 1987.
Burns, D. "Merry's Winter Walk." *Cricket.* December 1988. Pages 47–50.
Burns, Diane L. *Snakes Alive! Jokes About Snakes.* Illus. by Joan Hanson. Minneapolis: Lerner, 1988.
Burstein, John. *Slim Goodbody: The Inside Story.* Photos by J. P. Kirouac. Illus. by C. Phillips. New York: McGraw, 1979. M1204, M1205, M1206.
Burton, Virginia Lee. *Katy and the Big Snow.* Illus. by the author. Boston: Houghton, 1943. Sandpiper pb. M686.
———. *The Little House.* Illus. by the author. Boston: Houghton, 1981. pb. M741, M743, M744.

———. *Mike Mulligan and His Steam Shovel.* Illus. by the author. Boston: Houghton, 1939. pb. M858, M859, M860, M861.

Bushey, Jerry. *Monster Trucks and Other Giant Machines on Wheels.* Minneapolis: Carolrhoda, 1985.

Butler, Andrea. *The Elements of the Whole Language Program.* Crystal Lake, IL: Rigby, n.d.

———. *Whole Language: A Framework for Thinking.* Crystal Lake, IL: Rigby, n.d.

Butler, Andrea and Jan Turbill. *Towards a Reading Writing Classroom.* Portsmouth, NH: Heineman, 1984.

Butler, Beverly. *Ghost Cat.* New York: Dodd, 1984. Apple pb.

———. *Gift of Gold.* New York: Dodd, 1973.

———. *Light a Single Candle.* New York: Dodd, 1962. Archway pb.

———. *Maggie By My Side.* Illus. with photos. New York: Putnam, 1987.

———. *My Sister's Keeper.* New York: Putnam, 1980.

Butler, Dorothy. *Cushla and Her Books.* Boston: Horn Book, 1980. pb.

Butterworth, Emma. *As the Waltz Was Ending.* New York: Four Winds/Macmillan, 1983. Scholastic pb.

Butterworth, Rod. *The Perigree Visual Dictionary of Signing: An A to Z Guide to Over 1,200 Signs of American Sign Language.* Illus. by Mickey Flodin. New York: Perigree/Putnam, 1983.

Butterworth, Oliver. *The Enormous Egg.* Boston: Little, 1956. Dell pb. M407.

Butzow, Carol M. and John W. Butzow. *Science Through Children's Literature: An Integrated Approach.* Englewood, CO: Teacher Ideas Press, 1989.

Byars, Betsy. *The Animal, the Vegetable, and John J. Jones.* Illus by Ruth Sanderson. New York: Delacorte, 1982. M1093.

———. *Bingo Brown and the Language of Love.* New York: Viking, 1989. M1093.

———. *A Blossom Promise.* Illus. by Jacqueline Rogers. New York: Delacorte, 1987. Dell pb. M837, M1093.

———. *The Blossoms and the Green Phantom.* Illus. by J. Rogers. New York: Delacorte, 1987. Dell pb. M837, M1093.

———. *The Blossoms Meet the Vulture Lady.* Illus. by J. Rogers. New York: Delacorte, 1986. Dell pb. M837, M1093.

———. *The Burning Questions of Bingo Brown.* New York: Viking, 1988. M837, M1093.

———. *The Computer Nut.* Graphics by Guy Byars. New York: Viking, 1984. Puffin pb. M837, M1093.

———. *Cracker Jackson.* New York: Viking, 1985. Puffin pb. M837, M1093.

———. *The Cybil War.* Illus. by Gail Owens. New York: Viking, 1981. Scholastic pb. M837, M1093.

———. *The Eighteenth Emergency.* Illus. by Robert Grossman. New York: Viking, 1973. Puffin pb. M394, M837, M1093.

———. *The Midnight Fox.* Illus. by Ann Grifalconi. New York: Viking, 1986. Puffin pb. M837, M856, M1093, M1170.

———. *Night Swimmers.* Illus. by Troy Howell. New York: Delacorte, 1980. M837, M1093.

———. *The Not-Just-Anybody Family.* Illus. by J. Rogers. New York: Delacorte, 1986. Dell pb. M837, M965, M966, M1093.

———. *Pinballs.* New York: Harper, 1977. Trophy pb. M2031, M1032, M1033, M1093.

———. *Summer of the Swans.* Illus. by Ted CoConis. New York: Viking, 1970. Puffin pb. Avon Camelot pb. M481, M490, M837, M1093, M1105, M1287, M1288.

———. *The TV Kid.* Illus. by Richard Cuffari. New York: Viking, 1976. Puffin pb. Scholastic pb. M837, M1093, M1319, M1320.

———. *Trouble River.* Illus. by Rocco Negri. New York: Viking, 1969. Puffin pb. M1093.

Caket, Colin. *Model a Monster: Making Dinosaurs from Everyday Materials.* New York: Blandford/Sterling, 1986.

Calders, Pierre. *Brush.* Illus. by Carme S. Vendrell. Trans. by Marguerite Feitlowitz. Brooklyn, NY: Kane Miller, 1986. M188, M1098.

Calhoun, Mary. *Hot-Air Henry.* Illus. by Erick Ingraham. New York: Morrow, 1981. Mulberry pb. M589, M1098.

———. *The Night the Monster Came.* Illus. by Leslie Morrill. New York: Morrow, 1982. M1094.

California State Department of Education. *Recommended Readings in Literature, Kindergarten through Grade Eight.* Sacramento: California State Dept. of Education, 1986.

Callahan, Steven. *Adrift: 76 Days Lost at Sea.* Illus. by the author. Boston: Houghton, 1986. Ballantine pb.

Callen, Larry. *Pinch.* Illus. by Marvin Friedman. Boston: Little, 1975. M1034.

———. *Who Kidnapped the Sheriff?* Boston: Little, 1985.

Calvert, Patricia. *The Hour of the Wolf.* New York: Scribner, 1988. Signet pb.

Cameron, Eleanor. *Beyond Silence.* New York: Dutton, 1980. Dell pb. M432.

———. *The Wonderful Flight to the Mushroom Planet*. Illus. by Robert Henneberger. Boston: Joy Street/Little, 1954. pb. M432, M1481.

Cameron, Ann. *Julian, Secret Agent*. Illus. by Diane Allison. New York: Random, 1988.

———. *Julian's Glorious Summer*. Illus. by Dora Leder. New York: Random, 1987. M681.

———. *Julia's Magic*. Illus. by Gail Owens. New York: Dutton, 1984. Puffin pb.

———. *More Stories Julian Tells*. Illus. by A. Strugnell. New York: Knopf, 1986.

———. *The Private Worlds of Julia Redfern*. New York: Dutton, 1988.

———. *The Stories Julian Tells*. Illus. by A. Strugnell. New York: Pantheon, 1981. Knopf pb.

———. *That Julia Redfern*. Illus. by G. Owens. New York: Dutton, 1982.

Campbell, Joanna. *A Horse of Her Own*. New York: Bantam Skylark pb.

Caple, Kathy. *The Biggest Nose*. Illus. by the author. Boston: Houghton, 1985.

———. *The Purse*. Illus. by the author. Boston: Houghton, 1986.

Cargas, Harold J. *The Holocaust: An Annotated Bibliography*. Chicago: American Library Association, 1986.

Carle, Eric. *The Very Busy Spider*. Illus. by the author. New York: Philomel, 1984.

Carlson, Ann D. *Early Childhood Literature-Sharing Programs in Libraries*. Hamden, CT: Library Professional Publications, 1985.

Carlson, Natalie Savage. *A Grandmother for the Orphelines*. Illus. by David White. New York: Harper, 1980. Dell pb. M507.

Carlson, Nancy. *Arnie and the Stolen Markers*. Illus. by the author. New York: Viking, 1987.

———. *Arnie Goes to Camp*. Illus. by the author. New York: Viking, 1988.

———. *Harriet and the Garden*. Illus. by the author. Minneapolis: Carolrhoda, 1982. Puffin pb. M543.

———. *Harriet and the Roller Coaster*. Illus. by the author. Minneapolis: Carolrhoda, 1982. Puffin pb. M544.

———. *Harriet and Walt*. Illus. by the author. Minneapolis: Carolrhoda, 1982. Puffin pb. M545.

———. *Harriet's Halloween Candy*. Illus. by the author. Minneapolis: Carolrhoda, 1982. Puffin pb. M547, M548.

———. *Harriet's Recital*. Illus. by the author. Minneapolis: Carolrhoda, 1982, Puffin pb. M549.

———. *I Like Me*. New York: Viking, 1988. M618, M619.

———. *Louanne Pig in Making the Team*. Illus. by the author. Minneapolis: Carolrhoda, 1985. Puffin pb. M760.

———. *Louanne Pig in the Mysterious Valentine*. Illus. by the author. Minneapolis: Carolrhoda, 1985. Puffin pb. M761, M762.

———. *Louanne Pig in the Perfect Family*. Illus. by the author. Minneapolis: Carolrhoda, 1985. Puffin pb. M763.

———. *Louanne Pig in the Talent Show*. Illus. by the author. Minneapolis: Carolrhoda, 1985. Puffin pb. M764.

———. *Louanne Pig in the Witch Lady*. Illus. by the author. Minneapolis: Carolrhoda, 1985. Puffin pb. M765.

———. *Loudmouth George and the Big Race*. Illus. by the author. Minneapolis: Carolrhoda, 1983. Puffin pb. M766.

———. *Loudmouth George and the Coronet*. New York: Puffin, 1985. pb.

———. *Loudmouth George and the Fishing Trip*. New York: Puffin, 1983. pb.

———. *Loudmouth George and the New Neighbors*. Minneapolis: Carolrhoda, 1983. Puffin pb.

———. *Loudmouth George and the Sixth Grade Bully*. Illus. by the author. Minneapolis: Carolrhoda, 1983. Puffin pb. M770.

Carlstrom, Nancy. *Jessie Bear, What Will You Wear?* Illus. by Bruce Degen. New York: Macmillan, 1986.

———. *The Moon Came Too*. Illus. by Stella Ormai. New York: Macmillan, 1987.

———. *Shoes, Shoes, Shoes*.

———. *Wild Wild Sunflower Child*. Illus. by Jerry Pinkney. New York: Macmillan, 1987.

Carmer, Carl. *The Pirate Hero of New Orleans*. Illus. by Marilyn Hirsh. New York: Harvey, 1975. M1043.

Carpenter, Allan. *Minnesota*. Chicago: Childrens Press, 1978.

Carpenter, Humphrey and Mari Prichard. *The Oxford Companion to Children's Literature*. New York: Oxford, 1984.

Carrick, Carol. *Big Old Bones: A Dinosaur Tale*. Illus. by Donald Carrick. New York: Clarion, 1989.

———. *Crocodiles Still Wait*. Illus. by D. Carrick. Boston: Clarion, 1980.

———. *Octopus*. Illus. by D. Carrick. Boston: Clarion, 1978.

———. *Patrick's Dinosaurs*. Illus. by D. Carrick. Boston: Clarion, 1983. pb. M999.

———. *Sleepout*. Illus. by D. Carrick. New York: Seabury, 1973.

———. *Stay Away From Simon!* Illus. by D. Carrick. New York: Clarion, 1985. pb.

Charlip, Remy and Burton Supree. *Harlequin and the Gift of Many Colors.* Illus. by R. Charlip. New York: Parents, 1973.

Chaucer, Geoffrey. *Chanticleer and the Fox.* Illus. by Barbara Cooney. New York: Crowell, 1958. M249.

Chaucer, Geoffrey. See Cohen, Barbara.

Chess, Victoria. *Poor Esme.* Illus. by the author. New York: Holiday, 1982.

Chester, Michael. *Robots: Facts Behind the Fiction.* New York: Macmillan, 1983.

Chetwin, Grace. *The Crystal Stair: From the Tales of Gom in the Legends of Ulm.* New York: Bradbury, 1988. Dell pb.

———. *Gom on Windy Mountain.* New York: Lothrop, 1986. Dell pb.

———. *The Riddle of the Rune.* New York: Bradbury, 1987. Dell pb.

———. *Starstone.* New York: Bradbury, 1989. Dell pb.

Chew, Ruth. *Do-It-Yourself Magic.* New York: Hastings/Kampmann, 1988. Scholastic pb.

———. *The Magic Coin.* New York: Scholastic, 1983.

———. *Summer Magic.* New York: Scholastic, 1977.

———. *Trapped in Time.* New York: Scholastic, 1986.

———. *The Trouble with Magic.* Magnolia, MA: Peter Smith, 1988. Scholastic pb.

Child Study Children's Book Committee of the Bank Street College of Education. *Children's Books of the Year.* New York: Child Study Children's Book Committee, 1989. Annual.

Child, Lydia Maria. *Over the River and Through the Wood.* Illus. by Brinton Turkle. New York: Coward, 1974. Scholastic pb.

———. "Over the River and Through the Wood" in Pearson, P. D. *Castles in the Sand.* Needham, MA: Silver Burdett/Ginn, 1989. Pages 38–45.

Childcraft. *Childcraft: The How and Why Library.* Chicago: Field Enterprises, 1986.

———. *Holidays and Birthdays, Childcraft Vol. 9.* Chicago: Field Enterprises, 1986.

———. *Make and Do, Childcraft Vol. 1.* Chicago: Field Enterprises, 1986.

———. *Time to Read, Childcraft Vol. 2.* Chicago: Field Enterprises, 1986.

Children's Book Council, eds. *Children's Books, Awards and Prizes.* New York: Children's Book Council, 1986.

Children's Books in Print. New York: Bowker, 1969–. Annual.

Children's Catalog. Bronx, NY: Wilson. Annual and cumulative.

Children's Magazine Guide: A Subject Index to Children's Magazines. Madison, WI: 1981–.

Monthly, bi monthly, and semi annual cumulation.

Children's Television Workshop. *Square 1 Curriculum Connections, Teacher's Guide.* New York: Children's Television Workshop, 1990. M1246.

———. *Square One Game Shows Teacher's Guide.* New York: Children's Television Workshop, 1989. M1246.

———. *Square One Mathnet Teacher's Guide.* New York: Children's Television Workshop, 1988. M818, M1246.

———. *Square One Television Teacher's Guide.* New York: Children's Television Workshop, 1987. M1246.

———. *3-2-1-Contact Teacher's Guide.* New York: Children's Television Workshop, 1988. M1246.

Chivers, David. *Gorillas and Chimpanzees.* New York: Watts/Gloucester, 1987.

Chorao, Kay. *Cathedral Mouse.* Illus. by the author. New York: Dutton, 1988.

———. *George Told Kate.* Illus. by the author. New York: Dutton, 1987.

———. *Kate's Snowman.* Illus. by the author. New York: Dutton, 1982.

Christelow, Eileen. *Henry and the Dragon.* Illus. by the author. New York: Clarion, 1984.

———. *Henry and the Red Stripes.* Illus. by the author. New York: Clarion, 1982.

———. *Mr. Murphy's Marvelous Invention.* Illus. by the author. New York: Clarion, 1983.

———. *Robbery at the Diamond Dog Diner.* Illus. by the author. New York: Clarion, 1986. pb. M1120, M1121.

Christian, Mary Blout. *Sebastian (Super Sleuth) and the Bone to Pick Mystery.* Illus. by Lisa McCue. New York: Macmillan, 1983. Bantam pb.

———. *Sebastian (Super Sleuth) and the Clumsy Cowboy.* Illus. by L. McCue. New York: Macmillan, 1985.

———. *Sebastian (Super Sleuth) and the Crummy Yummies Caper.* Illus. by L. McCue. New York: Macmillan, 1983. Bantam pb.

———. *Sebastian (Super Sleuth) and the Egyptian Connection.* Illus. by Lisa McCue. New York: Macmillan, 1988.

———. *Sebastian (Super Sleuth) and the Hair of the Dog Mystery.* Illus. by L. McCue. New York: Macmillan, 1982.

———. *Sebastian (Super Sleuth) and the Purloined Sirloin.* Illus by L. McCue. New York: Macmillan, 1986. Minstrel pb.

Conrad, Pam. *Prairie Songs*. Illus. by Darryl Zudeck. New York: Harper, 1985.

Conway, Lorraine. *Ancient Egypt: Treasures, Tombs, and Tutankhamen*. Illus. by Linda Atkins. Carthage, IL: Good Apple, 1987.

Cooney, Barbara. *Island Boy*. Illus. by the author. New York: Viking, 1988.

———. *Miss Rumphius*. Illus. by the author. New York: Viking, 1982. Puffin pb.

Cooper, Clare. *Earthchange*. Minneapolis: Lerner, 1986.

Cooper, S. F. *Before Lift-Off: The Making of a Space Shuttle Crew*. Baltimore: Johns Hopkins, 1987.

Cooper, Susan. *The Dark Is Rising*. New York: Macmillan, 1973. Collier pb. M331.

———. *Greenwitch*. New York: Macmillan, 1983. Collier pb.

———. *The Grey King*. New York: Macmillan, 1975. Collier pb.

———. *Silver on the Tree*. New York: Macmillan, 1977. Collier pb.

Cooperative Children's Book Center. *CCBC Choices*. Madison, WI: University of Wisconsin. Annual.

Corbett, Scott. *The Disappearing Dog Trick*. Illus. by Paul Galdone. Boston: Little, 1963. Scholastic pb.

———. *Grave Doubts*. Boston: Little, 1982.

———. *The Hairy Horror Trick*. Illus. by P. Galdone. Boston: Little, 1969. Scholastic pb.

———. *The Hangman's Ghost Trick*. Boston: Little, 1977. Scholastic pb.

———. *Hockey Trick*. Illus. by P. Galdone. Boston: Little, 1974.

———. *Jokes to Read in the Dark*. New York: Dutton, 1980.

———. *The Lemonade Trick*. Boston: Little, 1960. Scholastic pb.

———. *The Mailbox Trick*. Illus. by P. Galdone. Boston: Little, 1961. Scholastic pb.

———. *Pentecost and the Chosen One*. Illus. by Martin Ursell. New York: Delacorte, 1987.

———. *Song of Pentecost*. Illus. by M. Ursell. New York: Dutton, 1982. Dell pb.

———. *The Trouble With Diamonds*. Illus. by Bert Dodson. New York: Dutton, 1985.

———. *Witch Hunt*. Boston: Little, 1985.

Corcoran, Barbara. *A Horse Named Sky*. New York: Atheneum, 1986.

Cormier, Robert. *The Chocolate War*. New York: Pantheon, 1974. Dell pb.

Corwin, Judith. *Birthday Fun*. New York: Messner, 1986.

Coughlan, Margaret N. *Books for Children*. Washington, DC: Library of Congress. Annual.

Courlander, H. *The Cow-Tail Switch and Other West African Stories*. New York: Holt, 1987.

Cover, Arthur B. *American Revolutionary*. New York: Bantam, 1985.

———. *Blade of the Guillotine*. New York: Bantam, 1986.

———. *Rings of Saturn*. New York: Bantam, 1985.

Coville, Bruce. *The Ghost in the Third Row*. New York: Bantam Skylark pb., 1987.

———. *The Monster's Ring*. Illus. by Katherine Coville. New York: Pantheon, 1982. Minstrel pb.

———. *The Unicorn Treasury: Stories, Poems and Unicorn Lore*. Illus. by Tim Hildebrandt. New York: Doubleday, 1988. pb.

Cowan, Lore. *Children of the Resistance*. New York: Meredith, 1969.

Cox, David. *Bossyboots*. Illus. by the author. New York: Crown, 1987.

Coxe, Molly. *Louella and the Yellow Balloon*. Illus. by the author. New York: Harper, 1988.

Craig, M. Jean. *The Donkey Prince*. Illus. by Barbara Cooney. New York: Doubleday, 1977.

Crane, Stephen. *The Red Badge of Courage*. New York: Modern Library, 1925. pb.

———. *The Red Badge of Courage*. Avon pb., Puffin pb., Scholastic pb., Vintage pb.

Craven, Carolyn. *What the Mailman Brought*. Illus. by Tomie de Paola. New York: Putnam, 1987.

Cresswell, Helen. *A Game of Catch*. Illus. by Ati Forberg. New York: Macmillan, 1971.

———. *Absolute Zero: Being the Second Part of the Bagthorpe Saga*. New York: Macmillan, 1978. Avon Camelot pb. Puffin pb.

———. *Bagthorpes Abroad: Being the Fifth Part of the Bagthorpe Saga*. New York: Macmillan, 1984. Puffin pb.

———. *Bagthorpes Haunted: Being the Sixth Part of the Bagthorpe Saga*. New York: Macmillan, 1985. Puffin pb.

———. *Bagthorpes Liberated: Being the Seventh Part of the Bagthorpe Saga*. New York: Macmillan, 1989.

———. *Bagthorpes Unlimited: Being the Third Part of the Bagthorpe Saga*. New York: Macmillan, 1978. Avon Camelot pb., Puffin pb.

———. *The Bagthorpes vs the World: Being the Fourth Part of the Bagthorpe Saga*. New York: Macmillan, 1980. Avon Camelot pb., Puffin pb.

———. *Moondial*. New York: Macmillan, 1987.

———. *Ordinary Jack: Being the First Part of the Bagthorpe Saga*. New York: Macmillan, 1977. Avon Camelot pb., Puffin pb.

―――. *Charlie and the Great Glass Elevator: The Further Adventures of Charlie Bucket and Willy Wonka, Chocolate-Maker Extraordinary.* Illus. by Joseph Schindelman. New York: Knopf, 1972.

―――. *The Enormous Crocodile.* Illus. by Quentin Blake. New York: Knopf, 1978. Bantam Skylark pb.

―――. *The Fantastic Mr. Fox.* Illus. by Donald Chaffin. New York: Knopf, 1970. Bantam Skylark pb. M429.

―――. *George's Marvelous Medicine.* Illus. by Q. Blake. New York: Knopf, 1982. Bantam Skylark pb.

―――. *James and the Giant Peach.* Illus. by Nancy Ekholm Burkert. New York: Knopf, 1961. Puffin pb. Bantam Skylark pb.

―――. *James and the Giant Peach: A Play.* New York: Puffin, 1983. pb.

―――. *The Twits.* Illus. by Q. Blake. New York: Knopf, 1980. Bantam pb.

―――. *Witches.* Illus. by Q. Blake. New York: Farrar, 1983. Puffin pb.

Dalgliesh, Alice. *The Courage of Sara Noble.* New York: Scribner, 1954, 1987. Aladdin pb. M298, M299, M300.

Dallinger, Jane. *Spiders.* Photos by Satoshi Kuribayoshi. Minneapolis: Lerner, 1981. pb.

Dallinger, Jane and Sylvia A. Johnson. *Frogs and Toads.* Photos by Hiroshi Tanemura. Minneapolis: Lerner, 1982.

Daly, Niki. *Not So Fast, Songolo.* Illus. by the author. 1985. New York: Macmillan, 1986. Puffin pb.

Dana, Barbara. *Zucchini.* Illus. by Eileen Christelow. New York: Harper, 1982. Bantam pb.

Danziger, Paula. *The Cat Ate My Gymsuit.* New York: Delacorte, 1974. Dell pb.

―――. *The Divorce Express.* New York: Delacorte, 1981. Dell pb. M365, M366.

―――. *It's an Aardvark-Eat-Turtle World.* New York: Delacorte, 1985. Dell pb.

―――. *There's a Bat in Bunk Five.* New York: Delacorte, 1980. Dell pb. M1326, M1327.

Da Rif, Andrea. *The Blueberry Cake That Little Fox Baked.* Illus by the author. New York: Atheneum, 1984.

―――. *Thomas in Trouble.* Illus. by the author. New York: McElderry/Macmillan, 1987.

Darling, David J. *Where Are We Going in Space?* Illus. by Jeannette Swofford. Minneapolis: Dillon, 1984.

Daugherty, Duane. *What's Inside?* New York: Knopf, 1984.

d'Aulaire, Ingri and Edgar Parin d'Aulaire. *Abraham Lincoln.* Illus. by the authors. New York: Doubleday, 1957.

―――. *Benjamin Franklin.* Illus. by the authors. New York: Doubleday, 1950. M132, M133, M145.

―――. *Christopher Columbus.* Illus. by the authors. New York: Doubleday, 1955.

―――. *George Washington.* Illus. by the authors. New York: Doubleday, 1936.

David, Rosalie and Anthony David. *Ancient Egypt.* New York: Warwick, 1985.

Davidson, Amanda. *Teddy's First Christmas.* Illus. by the author. New York: Holt, 1982.

Davidson, Josephine. *Teaching and Dramatizing Greek Myths.* Illus. by Fiona Starr. Englewood, CO: Libraries Unlimited, 1989.

Davidson, Margaret. *Louis Braille: The Boy Who Invented Books for the Blind.* Illus. by Janet Compere. New York: Hastings, 1971. Scholastic pb.

―――. *The Story of Benjamin Franklin, Amazing American!* Illus. by John Speirs. New York: Dell Yearling pb., 1988.

Davie, Michael. *Titanic: The Death and Life of a Legend.* New York: Knopf, 1987. Holt pb.

Davies, Andrew. *Conrad's War.* New York: Crown, 1980. Dell pb.

Davies, W. V. *Egyptian Hieroglyphs.* Berkeley: University of CA, 1988.

Davis, James E., Hazel K. Davis and the Committee on the Junior High and Middle School Booklist of the National Council of Teachers of English. *Your Reading: A Booklist for Junior High and Middle School Students.* Urbana, IL: NCTE, 1988.

Davis, Daniel S. *Behind the Barbed Wire: The Imprisonment of Japanese Americans During World War II.* New York: Dutton, 1982.

Davis, Jenny. *Goodbye and Keep Cold.* New York: Orchard, 1987.

Davis, James and Sharryl D. Hawke. *Chicago.* Milwaukee: Raintree, 1989.

―――. *London.* Milwaukee: Raintree, 1989.

―――. *Los Angeles.* Milwaukee: Raintree, 1989.

―――. *Mexico City.* Milwaukee: Raintree, 1989.

―――. *Moscow.* Milwaukee: Raintree, 1989.

―――. *New York City.* Milwaukee: Raintree, 1989.

―――. *Tokyo.* Milwaukee: Raintree, 1989.

―――. *Washington, D.C.* Milwaukee: Raintree, 1989.

Davison, Brian. *Looking at a Castle.* Illus. by Peter Dennis. New York: Random, 1987.

Dean, Audry V. *Make a Prehistoric Monster.* New York: Taplinger, 1977.

de Brunhoff. *See* Brunhoff, de.

DeBruyne, Betty and Gale W. Sherman. *The Handbook for the 1988 Young Readers'*

De Regniers, Beatrice Schenk, ed. *Sing a Song of Popcorn: Every Child's Book of Poems.* New York: Scholastic, 1988.

De Sauza, James. *Brother Anansi and the Cattle Ranch/El Hermano Anansi y el Rancho de Granado.* Adapted by Harriet Rohmer. Illus. by Stephen von Mason. Spanish version by Rosalma Zubizaretta. San Francisco: Children's Book Press, 1989.

Detroit Public Library. *Books for Pre-School Children.* Detroit: Children's/Youth Services Department, Detroit Public Library, 1989.

———. *Children's Books to Own.* Detroit: Children's/Youth Services Department, Detroit Public Library, 1989. Annual.

Dewey, Ariane. *Febold Feboldson.* Illus. by the author. New York: Greenwillow, 1984.

Dewey, Jennifer O. *Clem: The Story of a Raven.* Illus. by the author. New York: Putnam, 1986.

Dickens, Charles. *A Christmas Carol.* Illus. by Trina Schart Hyman. New York: Holiday, 1983.

———. *A Christmas Carol.* Illus. by Lisbeth Zwerger. Saxonville, MA: Picture Book Studio, 1988.

———. *A Christmas Carol: A Ghost Story for Christmas.* Illus. by Michael Foreman. New York: Dial, 1983.

———. *A Christmas Carol: Being a Ghost Story of Christmas.* Abridged and illus. by Mercer Mayer. New York: Macmillan, 1986.

Dickey, James. *Deliverance.* Boston: Houghton, 1970. Dell pb.

Dickinson, Peter. *Eva.* New York: Delacorte, 1989.

Dictionary of Literary Biography. See Estes, Glenn.

Di Franco, Anthony and JoAnn Di Franco. *Mr. Rogers: Good Neighbor to America's Children.* Minneapolis: Dillon, 1983. MM886, M887.

Di Franco, Joann. *Walt Disney: When Dreams Come True.* Minneapolis: Dillon, 1985.

Diggs, Lucy. *Everyday Friends.* New York: Atheneum, 1986.

D'Ignazio, Fred. *Chip Mitchell: The Case of the Chocolate-Covered Bugs.* Illus. by Larry Pearson. New York: Dutton, 1985. Lodestar pb.

———. "The Case of the Missing Report Cards" in Cullinan, B. *Treasures.* San Diego: Harcourt, 1989. Pages 264–77.

Dimond, Jasper. *Dinosaurs.* Englewood Cliffs, NJ: Prentice Hall, 1985. pb.

Dixon, Dougal. *The First Dinosaurs: Hunting the Dinosaurs and Other Prehistoric Animals.* Illus. by Jane Burton and Steve Kirk.

Milwaukee, WI: Milwaukee: Gareth Stevens, 1987.

———. *The Jurassic Dinosaurs.* Illus. by J. Burton and S. Kirk. Milwaukee: Gareth Stevens, 1987.

———. *The Last Dinosuars.* Illus. by J. Burton and S. Kirk. Milwaukee: Gareth Stevens, 1987.

Dixon, Dougal and Jane Burton. *The Age of Dinosaurs: A Photographic Record.* New York: Beufort, 1986. pb.

Dixon, Paige. *The Summer of the White Goat.* New York: Atheneum, 1977.

Dodd, Lynley. *Hairy Maclary from Donaldson's Dairy.* Illus. by the author. Milwaukee: Gareth Stevens, 1988. M523.

———. *Hairy Maclary—Scattercat.* Illus. by the author. Milwaukee: Gareth Stevens, 1988. M524.

———. *Hairy Maclary's Bone.* Illus. by the author. Milwaukee: Gareth Stevens, 1985. M525.

———. *Hairy Maclary's Caterwaul Caper.* Illus. by the author. Milwaukee: Gareth Stevens, 1989.

———. *Hairy Maclary's Rumpus at the Vet.* Illus. by the author. Milwaukee: Gareth Stevens, 1989.

Dodd, Mike and Jean Richardson. *Jenny and the Tooth Fairy.* Illus. by M. Dodd. New York: Oxford, 1988.

Doherty, Berlie. *Granny Was a Buffer Girl.* New York: Orchard, 1986.

Dolan, Edward. *Child Abuse.* New York: Watts, 1980.

Domanska, Janina. *Busy Monday Morning.* Illus. by the author. New York: Greenwillow, 1985.

Donahue, Marilyn Cram. *Straight Along a Crooked Road.* New York: Walker, 1985.

Dondiego, Barbara L. *Year-Round Crafts for Kids.* New York: TAB, 1984. pb.

Donnelly, Judy. *The Titanic: Lost and Found.* Illus. by Keith Hohler. New York: Random, 1987. pb. M1348.

———. *Tut's Mummy: Lost and Found.* Illus. by James Watling. New York: Random, 1988. pb.

Donnelly, Liza. *Dinosaur's Halloween.* New York: Scholastic, 1987.

Doren, Marion Walker. *Borrowed Summer.* New York: Harper, 1986.

Dorin, Patrick C. *Yesterday's Trucks.* Minneapolis: Lerner, 1982.

Dorros, Arthur. *Alligator Shoes.* Illus. by the author. New York: Dutton, 1982. Unicorn pb.

———. *Let's Read and Find Out About Ant Cities*. Illus. by the author. New York: Crowell, 1987.

Dorsett, Lyle W. and Marjorie L. Mead. *C. S. Lewis, Letters to Children*. New York: Macmillan, 1985. M432.

Doty, Jean S. *Can I Get There by Candlelight?* Illus. by Ted Lewin. New York: Macmillan, 1980.

———. *Dark Horse*. Illus. by Dorothy Chuy. New York: Morrow, 1983.

———. *If Wishes Were Horses*. New York: Macmillan, 1984.

———. *Summer Pony*. Illus. by Sam Savitt. New York: Macmillan, 1973.

———. *Winter Pony*. Illus. by T. Lewin. New York: Macmillan, 1975.

———. *Yesterday's Horses*. New York: Macmillan, 1985.

Douglas, Barbara. *As Good As New*. Illus. by Patience Brewster. New York: Lothrop, 1982.

Douglass, Barbara. "The Bicycle Balloon Chase" in Cullinan, B. *Celebrations*. San Diego: Harcourt, 1989. Pages 28–35.

———. *The Great Town and Country Bicycle Balloon Chase*. Illus by Carol Newsom. New York: Lothrop, 1984.

Downer, Ann. *The Spellkey*. New York: Atheneum, 1987.

Doyle, Arthur Conan. *The Adventures of Sherlock Holmes*. Secaucus, NJ: Castle, 1989. Airmont pb., Avon Camelot pb., Ballantine pb., Bantam pb., Berkley pb., and Penguin pb.

Dragonwagon, Crescent. *Always, Always*. Illus. by Ariel Zeldich. New York: Macmillan, 1984.

———. *Diana, Maybe*. Illus. by Deborah Hogan Ray. New York: Macmillan, 1987.

———. *Margaret Ziegler is Horse-Crazy*. Illus. by Peter Elwell. New York: Macmillan, 1988.

Drescher, Henrick. *Simon's Book*. Illus. by the author. New York: Lothrop, 1983. Scholastic pb. M1196, M1197.

Drescher, Joan. *My Mother's Getting Married*. New York: Dial, 1986.

———. *Your Family, My Family*. New York: Walker, 1980.

Dreyer, Sharon S. *The Bookfinder, Vol. 3: A Guide to Children's Literature About the Needs and Problems of Youth*. Circle Pines, NM: American Guidance, 1985.

Drimmer, Fred. *Born Different: Amazing Stories of Some Very Special People*. New York: Atheneum, 1988.

Duane, Diane. *Deep Wizardry*. New York: Delacorte, 1985. Dell pb.

Dubanevich, Arlene. *Pig William*. Illus. by the author. New York: Bradbury, 1985.

———. *Pigs at Christmas*. Illus. by the author. New York: Bradbury, 1986.

———. *Pigs in Hiding*. Illus. by the author. New York: Four Winds/Macmillan, 1983.

du Bois, William Pène. *Twenty-One Balloons*. Illus. by the author. New York: Viking, 1947, 1966. Puffin pb. M432.

DuBosque, D. C. *How Do You Draw Dinosaurs?* Portland, OR: Peel Productions, 1989. pb.

Duder, Tessa. *Jellybean*. New York: Viking, 1986. Puffin pb.

Duker, Sam. *Individualized Reading: An Annotated Bibliography*. Metuchen, NJ: Scarecrow, 1968.

Dumbach, Annette and Jud Newborn. *Shattering the German Night: the Story of the White Rose*. Boston: Little, 1986.

Dumas, Alexandre. *The Man in the Iron Mask*. New York: Dodd, 1944. Airmont pb.

Duncan, Lois. *Birthday Moon*. Illus. by Susan Davis. New York: Viking, 1989. pb. M1094.

———. *Locked in Time*. Boston: Little, 1985. Dell pb. M1094, M1404.

———. *Stranger With My Face*. Boston: Little, 1981. Dell pb. M1094, M1271.

———. *Summer of Fear*. Boston: Little, 1976. Dell pb. M1094, M1286, M1404.

———. *The Third Eye*. Boston: Little, 1984. Dell pb. M1094, M1404.

Dunkle, Margaret. *The Story Makers: A Collection of Interviews with Australian and New Zealand Authors and Illustrators for Young People*. New York: Oxford, 1987.

Dunlop, Eileen. *Clementina*. New York: Holiday, 1987.

———. *House on the Hill*. New York: Holiday, 1987. Troll pb.

———. *The Valley of Deer*. New York: Holiday, 1989.

Dunrea, Oliver. *Skara Brae: The Story of a Prehistoric Village*. Illus. by the author. New York: Holiday, 1986.

Dupasquier, Philippe. *Jack at Sea*. Illus. by the author. Englewood Cliffs, NJ: Prentice Hall, 1986.

———. *Our House on the Hill*. Illus. by the author. New York: Viking, 1988.

Durr, William, et al. *Adventures*. Boston: Houghton, 1986.

———. *Caravans*. Boston: Houghton, 1986.

———. *Carousels*. Boston: Houghton, 1986.

———. *Discoveries*. Boston: Houghton, 1986.

———. *Drums*. Boston: Houghton, 1986.

———. *Celebrations*. Boston: Houghton, 1986.

———. *Explorations*. Boston: Houghton, 1986.

———. *Flights*. Boston: Houghton, 1986.

———. *Journeys*. Boston: Houghton, 1986.

————. *Pageants*. Boston: Houghton, 1986.

————. *Parades*. Boston: Houghton, 1986.

————. *Triumphs*. Boston: Houghton, 1986.

————. *Trumpets*. Boston: Houghton, 1986.

Durrell, Gerald. *The Talking Parcel*. Illus. by Pamela Johnson. Philadelphia: Lippincott, 1975. M1309.

Duvoisin, Roger. *Petunia*. Illus. by the author. New York: Knopf, 1962. Puffin pb. M1007.

————. *Petunia the Silly Goose Stories*. Illus. by the author. New York: Knopf, 1987. MM1007.

Dwiggins, Don. *Flying the Space Shuttles*. New York: Dodd, 1985.

Dygard, Thomas. *Wilderness Peril*. New York: Morrow, 1985.

Eager, Edgar. *Half Magic*. Illus. by M. Bodecker. San Diego: Harcourt, 1954. Magnolia, MA: Peter Smith, n.d. M527.

————. *The Time Garden*. Illus. by M. Bodecker. San Diego: Harcourt, 1985. Magnolia, MA: Peter Smith, n.d. Voyager pb.

Ecke, Wolfgang. *The Castle of the Red Gorillas*. Illus. by Rolfe Rettich. Englewood Cliffs, NJ: Prentice Hall, 1983. pb.

Edelsky, Carole, Bess Altwerger, and Barbara Flores. *Whole Language: What's the Difference?* Portsmouth, NH: Heinemann, 1991.

Edge, Nellie. *One Elephant Went Out to Play*. Illus. by Sylvia Ion. Salem, OR: Resources for Creative Teaching, 1988.

————. *I've Got a Frog*. Resources for Creative Teaching, n.d.

————. *Music Is Magic for Your Child and You!* Resources for Creative Teaching, 1988. M919.

Education Index. Bronx, NY: Wilson, Cumulative and annual.

Edwards, Dorothy. *Emmie and the Purple Paint*. Illus. by Priscilla Lamont. New York: Oxford, 1987.

Edmonds, Walter. *The Matchlock Gun*. Illus. by Paul Lantz. New York: Putnam, 1941, 1971.

Educational Resources Information Center. See ERIC.

Egger, Bettina. *Marianne's Grandmother*. Trans. by Christopher Franceschelli. Illus. by Sita Jucker. New York: Dutton, 1987.

Egoff, Sheila A. *Worlds Within: Children's Fantasy from the Middle Ages to Today*. Chicago: American Library Association, 1988.

Ehrlich, Amy. *The Random House Book of Fairy Tales*. Illus. by Diane Goode. New York: Random, 1985.

————. *Leo, Zack and Emmie*. Illus. by Steven Kellogg. New York: Dial, 1981.

————. *Leo, Zack and Emmie Together Again*. Illus. by S. Kellogg. New York: Dial, 1987.

————. *Wounded Knee: An Indian History of the American West*. New York: Holt, 1974.

Eisenberg, Lisa. *Mystery at Snowshoe Mountain Lodge*. New York: Dial, 1987. Troll pb.

Eitzen, Ruth. *The White Feather*. Illus. by Allan Eitzen. Scottsdale, PA: Herald, 1987.

Ekey, Robert. *Fire! in Yellowstone: A True Adventure*. Milwaukee: Gareth Stevens, 1989.

Ellis, Sara. *The Baby Project*. Vancouver: Douglas and McIntyre, 1986.

Ellis, Anne Leo. *Dabble Duck*. Illus. by Sue Truesdell. New York: Harper, 1984.

El-Shamey, Hasan. *Folktales of Egypt*. Chicago: University of Chicago, 1980. pb.

Elting, Mary. *The Macmillan Book of Dinosaurs*. Illus. by Joe Hamberger. New York: Macmillan, 1984.

————. *The Macmillan Book of the Human Body*. New York: Macmillan, 1986. Aladdin pb.

————. *Snakes and Other Reptiles*. Christopher Santoro. New York: Messner, 1987. Little Simon pb.

Emberley, Ed. *Ed Emberley's Big Red Drawing Book*. Illus. by the author. Boston: Little, 1987. pb.

Emberley, Michael. *Dinosaurs: A Drawing Book*. Illus. by the author. Little, 1980. pb.

————. *More Dinosaurs and Other Prehistoric Beasts: A Drawing Book*. Little, 1983. pb.

Emens, Carol. *Stunt Work and Stunt People*. New York: Watts, 1982.

Elwood, Ann and John Raht. *Walking Out: A Novel of Survival*. New York: Tempo, 1979.

Emerson, Kathy L. *Making Headlines: A Biography of Nellie Bly*. Minneapolis: Dillon, 1989.

England, Claire and Adele Fasick. *Childview: Evaluating and Reviewing Materials for Children*. Littleton, CO: Libraries Unlimited, 1987.

Epstein, Helen. *Children of the Holocaust: Conversations with the Sons and Daughters of Survivors*. New York: Putnam, 1979.

Epstein, Sam. *Dr. Beaumont and the Man with a Hole in His Stomach*. Illus. by Joseph Scrofani. New York: Coward, 1978.

Epstein, Sam and Beryl Epstein. *Secret in a Sealed Bottle: Lazzaro Spallanzani's Work with Microbes*. New York: Coward, 1979.

ERIC Staff and James Houston. *Thesaurus of Eric Descriptors*. 11th ed. Phoenix, Orynx, 1987. M393.

Erickson, Russell. *A Toad for Tuesday*. Illus. by Lawrence Di Fiori. New York: Lothrop, 1974. M1349.

——. *Women Astronauts: Aboard the Shuttle.* New York: Messner, 1987. pb.

Fox, Mem. *Hattie and the Fox.* Illus. by Patricia Mullins. New York: Bradbury, 1986.

——. *Koala Lou.* Illus. by Pamela Lofts. San Diego: Harcourt, 1988.

——. *Night Noises.* Illus. by Terry Denton. San Diego: Harcourt, 1989.

——. *Possum Magic.* Illus. by Julie Vivas. Nashville, TN: Abingdon, 1987.

——. *Wilfrid Gordon McDonald Partridge.* Illus. by J. Vivas. Brooklyn: Kane Miller, 1985. pb. M1463. M1464.

Fox, Paula. *Lily and the Lost Boy.* New York: Orchard, 1987. Dell pb.

——. *Lily and the Lost Boy.* Large print edition. Boston: G. K. Hall, 1989.

——. *The One-Eyed Cat.* New York: Bradbury, 1984. Dell pb. M481, M491.

——. *Village by the Sea.* New York: Orchard, 1988.

Fradin, Dennis Brindell. *Disaster! Blizzards and Winter Weather.* Chicago: Children's Press, 1983.

——. *Remarkable Children: Twenty Who Made History.* Boston: Little, 1987.

Frank, Anne. *Anne Frank's Tales from the Secret Annex.* Trans. by Ralph Manheim and Michel Mok. New York: Doubleday, 1983. Washington Square pb.

——. *The Diary of a Young Girl.* Trans. by B. M. Mooyaart. New York: Doubleday, 1952. M60, M61, M62, M490, M712, M715, M1263.

Frankel, Ellen and Robin Stevenson. *George Washington and the Constitution.* New York: Bantam pb., 1987.

Freedman, Russell. *Children of the Wild West.* Illus. with photos. New York: Clarion, 1983.

——. *Cowboys of the Wild West.* Illus. with photos. New York: Clarion, 1985.

——. *Dinosaurs and Their Young.* New York: Holiday, 1983.

——. "Frontier School." *Cricket.* June 1988. Pages 30–34.

——. *Indian Chiefs.* Illus. with photos. New York: Holiday, 1987.

——. *Killer Snakes.* Illus. with photos. New York: Holiday, 1982.

——. *Lincoln: A Photobiography.* Illus. with photos. New York: Clarion, 1987. M721.

——. *Rattlesnakes.* New York: Holiday, 1984.

——. *Sharks.* Illus. with photos. New York: Holiday, 1985.

Freeman, Don. *Dandelion.* Illus. by the author. New York: Viking, 1964. Puffin pb. M325.

Freeman, Judy. *Books Kids Will Sit Still For: A Guide to Using Children's Literature for Librarians, Teachers, and Parents.* Hagerston, MD: Alleyside Pr., 1984.

——. *Books Kids Will Sit Still For: The Complete Read-Aloud Guide.* 2nd ed. New York: Bowker, 1990.

Freeman, Lory. *It's My Body!* Seattle: Parenting Press, 1983.

French, Fiona. *Snow White in New York.* New York: Oxford, 1987. pb.

Freschet, Bernice. *Bernard of Scotland Yard.* Illus. by Gina Freschet. New York: Scribners, 1978.

Freudberg, Judy and Tony Geiss. *Susan and Gordon Adopt a Baby.* New York: Random, 1986. pb. M1168, M1169.

Frevert, Patricia. *Mark Twain: An American Voice.* Mankato, MN: Creative Education, 1981. M817, M835.

——. *Patrick Yes You Can.* Mankato, MN: Creative Education, 1983.

Friedberg, Joan, et al. *Accept Me As I Am: Best Books of Juvenile Nonfiction on Impairments and Disabilities.* New York: Bowker, 1985.

Friedman, Ina R. *Escape or Die: True Stories of Young People Who Survived the Holocaust.* Reading, MA: Addison-Wesley, 1982.

——. *How My Parents Learned to Eat.* Illus. by Allen Say. Boston: Houghton, 1984. pb.

Friedrich, Liz. *Divorce.* New York: Gloucester/Watts, 1988.

Fritz, Jean. *Brendan the Navigator: A Mystery About the Discovery of America.* Illus. by Enrico Arno. New York: Coward/Putnam, 1979. M1093.

——. *Bully for You, Teddy Roosevelt.* New York: Putnam, 1991.

——. *The Cabin Faced West.* Illus. by Feodor Rojankovsky. New York: Coward/Putnam, 1958. Puffin pb. M199a, M1093.

——. *Can't You Make Them Behave, King George?* Illus. by Tomie de Paola. New York: Coward/Putnam, 1977. pb. M216, M1093, M1403.

——. *China Homecoming.* Photos by Michael Fritz. New York: Putnam, 1985. M1093.

——. *China's Long March: 6,000 Miles of Danger.* Illus. by Yang Zhr Cheng. New York: Putnam, 1988. M1093.

——. *The Double Life of Pocahontas.* Illus. by Ed Young. New York: Putnam, 1983. Puffin pb. M640. M1093.

——. *George Washington's Breakfast.* Illus. by Paul Galdone. New York: Coward/Putnam, 1969. M1093.

——. *The Great Little Madison.* Illus. with photos. New York: Putnam, 1989. M1093.

Gans, Roma. *Danger—Icebergs!* Illus. by Richard Rosenblum. New York: Crowell, 1987. Trophy pb.

Gantos, Jack. *Rotten Ralph.* Illus. by Nicole Rubel. Boston: Houghton Mifflin, 1976. Sandpiper pb. M1132.

———. *Rotten Ralph's Rotten Christmas.* Illus. by N. Rubel. Boston: Houghton, 1984. pb.

———. *Rotten Ralph's Show and Tell.* Illus. by N. Rubel. Boston: Houghton, 1989.

———. *Rotten Ralph's Trick or Treat.* Illus. by N. Rubel. Boston: Houghton, 1986. Sandpiper pb.

———. *Worse Than Rotten Ralph.* Illus. by N. Rubel. Boston: Houghton, 1978. pb.

Gardiner, John. *Stone Fox.* Illus. by Marcia Sewall. New York: Crowell, 1980. Trophy pb. M1252, M1253.

———. *Top Secret.* Illus. by Marc Simont. New York: Little, 1984. M1355.

Gardner, Richard A. *The Boys and Girls Book About Divorce.* Illus. by Alfred Lowenheim. New York: Aronson, 1983. Bantam pb.

———. *The Boys and Girls Book About Stepfamilies.* Cresskill, NJ: Creative Theraputus pb., 1985.

———. *Dragon, Dragon and Other Timeless Tales.* New York: Knopf, 1975. pb.

Garfield, James. *Follow My Leader.* Illus. by Robert Greiner. New York: Viking, 1957. M458, M459.

Garfield, Leon. *December Rose.* New York: Viking, 1987. Penguin pb.

Garrigue, Sheila. *All the Children Were Sent Away.* New York: Bradbury, 1976.

———. *The Eternal Spring of Mr. Ito.* New York: Bradbury, 1985.

Garson, Eugenia. *Laura Ingalls Wilder Songbook.* Music by Herbert Haufrecht. Illus. by Garth Williams. New York: Harper, 1968.

Gaskin, Carol. *Caravan to China.* New York: Bantam, 1987.

———. *The Legend of Hiawatha.* New York: Bantam, 1986.

———. *The First Settlers.* New York: Bantam, n.d.

———. *The Secret of the Royal Treasure.* New York: Bantam, 1986.

Gasperini, Jim. *Mystery of Atlantis.* New York: Bantam, 1985.

———. *Sail with Pirates.* New York: Bantam, 1984.

———. *The Secret of the Knights.* New York: Bantam, 1984.

Gates, Doris. *Filly for Melinda.* New York: Viking, 1984.

Gates, *The Warrior Goddess: Athena.* Illus. by Don Bolognese. New York: Viking, 1972. Puffin pb.

Gauch, Patricia Lee. *Christina Katherina and the Time She Quit the Family.* Illus. by Elise Primavera. New York: Putnam, 1987.

———. *Grandpa and Me.* Illus. by Symeon Shimin. New York: Coward, 1972.

Gay, Michel. *Bibi Takes Flight.* Illus. by the author. New York: Morrow, 1988.

———. *Bibi's Birthday Surprise.* Illus. by the author. New York: Morrow, 1987.

———. *Little Boat.* Illus. by the author. New York: Macmillan, 1985.

———. *Little Plane.* Illus. by the author. New York: Macmillan, 1985.

———. *Little Truck.* Illus. by the author. New York: Macmillan, 1985.

Gazet, Denys. *Big Shoe, Little Shoe.* New York: Bradbury, 1984.

Gedye, Jane. *Dinner's Ready! A Pig's Book of Table Manners.* Illus. by the author. New York: Doubleday, 1988.

Gehrts, Barbara. *Don't Say a Word.* Trans. by Elizabeth D. Crawford. New York: McElderry/Macmillan, 1986.

Geisert, Arthur. *The Ark.* Illus. by the author. Boston: Houghton, 1988.

———. *Pa's Balloon and Other Pig Tales.* Illus. by the author. Boston: Houghton, 1984.

———. *Pigs from A-Z.* Illus. by the author. Boston: Houghton, 1986.

Gelfand, Marilyn. *My Great-Grandpa Joe.* Photos by Rosmarie Hautsherr. New York: Macmillan, 1986.

Gentry, Tony. *Paul Laurence Dunbar.* New York: Chelsea, 1989.

George, Jean. *Gull Number 737.* New York: Crowell, 1964.

———. *Julie of the Wolves.* Illus. by John Schoenherr. New York: Harper, 1972. Trophy pb. M682, M683, M957, M1170.

———. *My Side of the Mountain.* Illus. by the author. New York: Dutton, 1959. Dutton pb. M920.

———. *On the Far Side of the Mountain.* Illus. by the author. New York: Dutton, 1990.

———. *One Day in the Desert.* Illus. by Fred Brenner. New York: Crowell, 1983.

———. *One Day in the Prairie.* Illus. by Bob Marstall. New York: Crowell, 1986.

———. *One Day in the Woods.* Illus. by Gary Allen. New York: Crowell, 1988.

———. *The Talking Earth.* New York: Harper, 1983. Trophy pb.

———. *Water Sky.* New York: Harper, 1987. Trophy pb.

——. *Who Really Killed Cock Robin? An Ecological Mystery.* New York: Dutton, 1971. M1052.

George, Lindsay Barrett. *William and Boomer.* New York: Greenwillow, 1987.

George, William T. and Lindsay Barrett George. *Beaver at Long Pond.* Illus. by L. B. George. New York: Greenwillow, 1988.

Geringer, Laura. *Molly's Washing Machine.* Illus. by Petra Mathers. New York: Harper, 1986.

——. *The Three Hat Day.* Illus. by Arnold Lobel. New York: Harper, 1985. Trophy pb. M1098, M1335.

Gerrard, Roy. *Rosie and the Rustlers.* Illus. by the author. New York: Farrar, 1989.

——. *Sir Cedric.* Illus. by the author. New York: Farrar, 1984. Sunburst pb.

——. *Sir Cedric Rides Again.* Illus. by the author. New York: Farrar, 1986. Sunburst pb.

——. *Sir Francis Drake, His Daring Deeds.* Illus. by the author. New York: Farrar, 1988.

Gerstein, Mordicai. *Arnold and the Ducks.* Illus. by the author. New York: Harper, 1983. Trophy pb.

——. *The Mountains of Tibet.* Illus. by the author. New York: Harper, 1987.

Getzoff, Ann and Carolyn McClenahan. *Stepkids: A Survival Guide for Teenagers in Stepfamilies.* New York: Walker, 1984. pb.

Gibbons, Gail. *Boat Book.* Illus. by the author. New York: Holiday, 1983. pb.

——. *Check It Out! The Book About Libraries.* Illus. by the author. San Diego: Harcourt, 1985. Voyager pb.

——. *Deadline: From News to Newspapers.* Illus. by the author. New York: Crowell, 1987.

——. *Department Store.* Illus. by the author. New York: Crowell, 1984. Trophy pb.

——. *Dinosaurs.* Illus. by the author. New York: Holiday, 1987. pb.

——. *Dinosaurs, Dragonflies and Diamonds: All About Natural History Museums.* New York: Four Winds/Macmillan, 1988.

——. *Fill It Up! All About Service Stations.* Illus. by the author. New York: Crowell, 1985. Trophy pb.

——. *Fire! Fire!* Illus. by the author. New York: Crowell, 1984. Trophy pb.

——. *Flying.* Illus. by the author. New York: Holiday, 1986.

——. *From Path to Highway: The Story of the Boston Post Road.* Illus. by the author. New York: Crowell, 1986.

——. *Happy Birthday.* Illus. by the author. New York: Holiday, 1986.

——. *Lights! Camera! Action! How a Movie Is Made.* Illus. by the author. New York: Crowell, 1985.

——. *Marge's Diner.* Illus. by the author. New York: Crowell, 1989.

——. *Milk Makers.* Illus. by the author. New York: Macmillan, 1987. Aladdin pb. M862, M1098.

——. *New Road.* Illus. by the author. New York: Crowell, 1983. Trophy pb.

——. *Playgrounds.* Illus. by the author. New York: Holiday, 1985.

——. *The Post Office Book: Mail and How it Moves.* Illus. by the author. New York: Crowell, 1982. Trophy pb.

——. *The Pottery Place.* Illus. by the author. San Diego: Harcourt, 1987.

——. *Prehistoric Animals.* Illus. by the author. New York: Holiday, 1988.

——. *Sunken Treasure.* Illus. by the author. New York: Crowell, 1988.

——. *Trains.* Illus. by the author. New York: Holiday, 1988. pb.

——. *Trucks.* Illus. by the author. New York: Crowell, 1981. Trophy pb.

——. *Tunnels.* Illus. by the author. New York: Holiday, 1984. pb.

——. *Up Goes the Skyscraper!* Illus. by the author. New York: Four Winds/Macmillan, 1986.

——. *Weather Forecasting.* New York: Four Winds, 1987.

——. *Zoo.* Illus. by the author. New York: Crowell, 1987. M1491.

Giblin, James. *Chimney Sweeps.* New York: Crowell, 1982. Trophy pb.

——. *From Hand to Mouth: Or How We Invented Knives, Forks, Spoons, and Chopsticks and the Table Manners to Go With Them.* Illus. with photos, prints, and drawings. New York: Crowell, 1987.

——. *Let There Be Light: A Book About Windows.* New York: Crowell, 1988.

Gibson, Michael. *Knights.* New York: Arco, 1979.

Gies, Meip and Alison Leslie Gold. *Anne Frank Remembered: The Story of the Woman Who Helped to Hide the Frank Family.* New York: Simon and Schuster, 1987. Touchstone pb. M60, M61, M62, M490, M712, M715, M1263.

Giff, Patricia. *The Beast in Mrs. Rooney's Room.* Illus. by Blanche Sims. New York: Delacorte 1986. Yearling pb., 1984.

——. *The Candy Corn Contest.* Illus. by B. Sims. New York: Delacorte, 1986. Yearling pb.

———. *December Secrets*. Illus. by B. Sims. New York: Delacorte, 1986. Yearling pb.

———. *Fish Face*. Illus. by B. Sims. New York: Delacorte, 1986. Yearling pb.

———. *The Fourth Grade Celebrity*. Illus. by Leslie Morrill. New York: Delacorte, 1979. Dell pb. M463.

———. *The Girl Who Knew It All*. New York: Delacorte, 1979. Dell pb.

———. *Happy Birthday, Ronald Morgan*. Illus. by Susanna Natti. New York: Viking, 1986. Puffin pb. M537, M538.

———. *Have You Seen Hyacinth Macaw?* Illus. by Anthony Dramer. New York: Delacorte, 1981. Dell pb. M555.

———. *In the Dinosaur's Paw*. Illus. by B. Sims. New York: Delacorte, 1986. Yearling pb.

———. *Laura Ingalls Wilder: Growing Up in the Little House*. Illus. by Eileen McKeating. New York: Viking, 1987. Puffin pb. M844.

———. *Lazy Lions, Lucky Lambs*. Illus. by B. Sims. New York: Delacorte, 1986. Yearling pb.

———. *The Left-Handed Shortstop*. Illus. by L. Morrill. New York: Delacorte, 1980. Dell pb.

———. *Love from the Fifth Grade Celebrity*. Illus. by L. Morrill. New York: Delacorte, 1986. Dell pb.

———. *The Mystery of the Blue Ring*. Illus. by B. Sims. Dell pb., 1987. Magnolia, MA: Peter Smith, n.d.

———. *Pickle Puss*. Illus. by B. Sims. New York: Delacorte, 1986. Yearling pb.

———. *The Powder Puff Puzzle*. Illus. by B. Sims. New York: Dell, 1987.

———. *Purple Climbing Days*. Illus. by B. Sims. New York: Delacorte, 1986. Yearling pb.

———. *Rat Teeth*. Illus. by L. Morrill. New York: Delacorte, 1984. Dell pb.

———. *The Riddle of the Red Purse*. Illus. by B. Sims. New York: Dell, 1987. Magnolia, MA: Peter Smith, n.d.

———. *Ronald Morgan Goes to Bat*. Illus. by S. Natti. New York: Viking, 1988. Puffin pb.

———. *Say "Cheese."* Illus. by B. Sims. New York: Delacorte, 1986. Yearling pb.

———. *The Secret at the Polk Street School*. Illus. by B. Sims. New York: Dell, 1987.

———. *Snaggle Doodles*. Illus. by B. Sims. New York: Delacorte, 1986. Yearling pb.

———. *Sunny Side Up*. Illus. by B. Sims. New York: Delacorte, 1986. Yearling pb.

———. *A Teacher's Guide to the Kids of the Polk Street School Books*. Illus. by B. Sims. Dell pb., 1985.

———. *Today Was a Terrible Day*. Illus. by S. Natti. New York: Viking, 1984. Puffin pb. M1351.

———. *Tootsie Tanner, Why Don't You Talk?* New York: Delacorte, 1987. pb.

———. *Valentine Star*. Illus. by B. Sims. New York: Delacorte, 1986. Yearling pb.

———. *Watch Out, Ronald Morgan!* Illus. by S. Natti. New York: Viking, 1985. Puffin pb.

Gilbert, Sara. *How to Live With a Single Parent*. New York: Lothrop, 1982.

Gillespie, John T. *Best Books for Junior High Readers*. New York: Bowker, 1991.

———. *More Juniorplots: A Guide for Teachers and Librarians*. New York: Bowker, 1977.

Gillespie, John T. and Christine B. Gilbert. *Best Books for Children: Pre-School Through the Middle Grades*, 3rd ed. New York: Bowker, 1985.

Gillespie, John T. and Diana Lembo. *Introducing Books: A Guide for the Middle Grades*. New York: Bowker, 1970.

———. *Juniorplots: A Book Talk Manual for Teachers and Librarians*. New York: Bowker, 1967.

Gillespie, John T. and Corinne Naden. *Juniorplots 3: A Book Talk Guide for Use with Readers Ages 12–16*. New York: Bowker, 1987.

Gillies, John. *Senor Alcade: A Biography of Henry Cisneros*. Minneapolis: Dillon, 1988.

Gilson, Jamie. *Can't Catch Me, I'm the Gingerbread Man*. New York: Lothrop, 1981.

———. *Do Bananas Chew Gum?* New York: Lothrop, 1980. Archway pb. Minstrel pb.

———. *Double Dog Dare*. Illus. by Elise Primavera. New York: Lothrop, 1988. Minstrel pb.

———. *4-B Goes Wild*. Illus. by Linda S. Edwards. New York: Lothrop, 1983. Archway pb. Minstrel pb. M462.

———. *Harvey the Beer Can King*. New York: Lothrop, 1978. Pocket Books pb.

———. *Hello, My Name Is Scrambled Eggs*. Illus. by John Wallner. New York: Lothrop, 1985. Minstrel pb.

———. *Hobie Hanson: Greatest Hero of the Mall*. Illus. by Anita Riggis. New York: Lothrop, 1989.

———. *Hobie Hanson, You're Weird*. Illus. by E. Primavera. New York: Lothrop, 1987. Minstrel pb.

———. *Thirteen Ways to Sink a Sub*. Illus. by L. Edwards. New York: Lothrop, 1982. Archway pb. Minstrel pb. M1229, M1330.

Ginsburg, Mirra. *The Chinese Mirror*. Illus. by Margot Zemach. San Diego: Harcourt, 1988.

———. *The Story of a Castle.* Illus. by J. Goodall. New York: McElderry/Macmillan, 1986.

———. *The Story of a Farm.* Illus. by J. Goodall. New York: McElderry/Macmillan, 1989.

———. *The Story of a Main Street.* Illus. by J. Goodall. New York: McElderry/Macmillan, 1987.

———. *The Story of an English Village.* Illus. by J. Goodall. New York: McElderry/Macmillan, 1979.

———. *Victorians Abroad.* Illus. by J. Goodall. New York: McElderry/Macmillan, 1981.

Goodbody, Slim. *Healthy Habits Handbook.* New York: Putnam, 1983. pb. M381, M637.

Goodman, Yetta. "Roots of the Whole-Language Movement." *Elementary School Journal,* Vol. 90, #2. November 1989. Pages 113–129.

Goodman, Kenneth. *What's Whole in Whole Language?* Portsmouth, NH: Heinemann, 1986.

Goodman, Kenneth S. and Yetta M. Goodman. *Linguistics, Psycholinguistics, and the Teaching of Reading: An Annotated Bibliography,* 3rd. ed. Newark, DE: International Reading Association, 1980.

Goodman, Kenneth S., Yetta M. Goodman, and Lois Bridges Bird. *The Whole Language Catalog.* Santa Rosa, CA: American School Publishers/Macmillan/McGraw-Hill, n.d.

Goodman, Kenneth S., Yetta M. Goodman, and Wendy Hood. *The Whole Language Evaluation Book.* Portsmouth, N.H.: Heinemann, 1989.

Goodrich, Frances and Albert Hackett. *The Diary of Anne Frank.* New York: Random, 1956. M60, M61, M712, M1263.

Goor, Ron and Nancy Goor. *In the Driver's Seat.* Photos by the authors. New York: Crowell, 1982.

———. *Pompeii: Exploring a Roman Ghost Town.* New York: Crowell, 1986.

Gorman, Carol. *Chelsey and the Green-Haired Kid.* Boston: Houghton, 1987.

Gould, Deborah. *Grandpa's Slide Show.* Illus. by Cheryl Harness. New York: Lothrop, 1987.

Graff, Stewart and Polly Graff. *Helen Keller: Toward the Light.* Illus. by Paul Frame. Champaign, IL: Garrard, 1965.

Graham, Bob. *First There Was Frances.* New York: Bradbury, 1986.

———. *Grandad's Magic.* Boston: Little, 1989.

Grahame, Kenneth. *The Open Road.* New York: Scribner, 1979.

———. *The Reluctant Dragon.* Illus. by Michael Hague. New York: Holt, 1983. M1110.

———. *Wayfarers All: From The Wind in the Willows.* Illus. by Beverly Gooding. New York: Scribner, 1981. M1269b.

———. *The Wind in the Willows.* Illus. by John Burningham. New York: Viking, 1983. M1269b, M1468, M1469a.

———. *The Wind in the Willows.* Illus. by Michael Hague. New York: Holt, 1980. M1269b, M1468, M1469a.

———. *The Wind in the Willows.* Illus. by Ernest H. Shepard. New York: Scribner, 1981. M1269b, M1468, M1469a.

———. *The Wind in the Willows: The River Bank.* Illus. by Val Biro. New York: Wanderer, 1987. M1269b.

Gramatky, Hardie. *Hercules.* Illus. by the author. New York: Putnam, 1940.

———. *Little Toot.* Illus. by the author. New York: Putnam, 1939.

Gray, Ronald. *Hitler and the Germans.* Minneapolis: Lerner, 1983.

Greaves, Margo. *Cat's Magic.* New York: Harper, 1981.

Green, Carol and William Sanford. *Gorilla.* Mankato, MN: Crestwood, 1986.

———. *The Wild Horses.* Mankato, MN: Crestwood, 1986.

Green, Hannah. *In the City of Paris.* Illus. by Tony Chen. New York: Doubleday, 1985.

Green, Phyllis. *Eating Ice Cream with a Werewolf.* Illus. by P. Stren. New York: Harper, 1983. Dell pb.

Greenberg, Judith. *What Is the Sign for Friend?* Photos by Gayle Rothchild. New York: Watts, 1985.

Greenberg, Judith and Helen Carey. *Adopted.* Photos by Barbara Kirk. New York: Watts, 1987.

Greene, Bette. *Get Out of Here, Philip Hall.* New York: Dial, 1981. Dell pb. M1052.

———. *Philip Hall Likes Me, I Reckon Maybe.* Illus. by Charles Lilly. New York: Dial, 1974. Dell pb.

———. *Summer of My German Soldier.* New York: Dial, 1973. Bantam pb.

———. *Summer of My German Soldier.* Large print edition. San Diego: ABC-CLIO, 1989.

———. *Morning Is a Long Time Coming.* New York: Dial, 1978.

Greene, Carol. *Benjamin Franklin: A Man with Many Jobs.* Chicago: Childrens Press, 1988. pb.

———. *Hans Christian Andersen: Teller of Tales.* Chicago: Children's Press, 1986.

Grossman, Bil. *Donna O'Neeshuck Was Chased by Some Cows.* Illus. by Sue Truesdell. New York: Harper, 1988.

Grossman, Bill. *Tommy at the Grocery Store.* Illus. by Victoria Chess. New York: Harper, 1989.

Gundersheimer, Karen. *Happy Winter.* Illus. by the author. New York: Harper, 1982. Trophy pb.

———. *Shapes to Show.* Illus. by the author. New York: Harper, 1986.

Gunston, Bill. *Aircraft.* Illus. with photos. New York: Watts, 1986.

Guy, Rosa. *Mother Crocodile: An Uncle Amadon Tale from Senegal.* Illus. by John Steptoe. New York: Delacorte, 1981. pb.

———. *Paris, Pee Wee and Big Dog.* Illus. by Caroline Binch. New York: Delacorte, 1984. Dell pb.

Hackwell, W. John. *Diving to the Past: Recovering Ancient Wrecks.* New York: Scribner, 1988.

Haddad, Helen R. *Potato Printing.* New York: Crowell, 1981.

———. *Truck and Loader.* Illus. by Don Carrick. New York: Greenwillow, 1982.

Hader, Berta. *Mighty Hunter.* New York: Macmillan, 1943.

Hadithi, Mwenye. *Crafty Chameleon.* Illus. by A. Kennaway. Boston: Little, 1987.

———. *Greedy Zebra.* Illus. by Adrienne Kennaway. Boston: Little, 1984.

———. *Hot Hippo.* Illus. by A. Kennaway. Boston: Little, 1986. M560, M561.

———. *Tricky Tortoise.* Illus. by A. Kennaway. Boston: Little, 1988.

Hague, Michael. *Aesop's Fables.* Retold and illus. by M. Hague. New York: Holt, 1985.

———. *Michael Hague's World of Unicorns.* Illus. by the author. New York: Holt, 1986.

Hahn, Mary Downing. *Daphne's Book.* New York: Clarion, 1983. Bantam Skylark pb.

———. *December Stillness.* New York: Clarion, 1988.

———. *The Doll in the Garden: A Ghost Story.* New York: Clarion, 1989.

———. *Tallahassee Higgins.* New York: Clarion, 1987. Avon Camelot pb.

———. *Wait Till Helen Comes: A Ghost Story.* New York: Clarion, 1986. Avon Camelot pb.

Haley, Gail E. *A Story, A Story.* Retold and illus. by G. Haley. New York: Atheneum, 1970. M1258, M1259, M1260.

Hall, Donald. *The Ox-Cart Man.* Illus. by Barbara Cooney. New York: Viking, 1979. Penguin pb., Scholastic pb. M989, M990, M991.

Hall, Donald, ed. *The Oxford Book of Children's Verse.* New York: Oxford, 1985.

Hall, Kristi D. *The Rose Behind the Wall.* New York: Atheneum, 1985.

Hall, Lynn. *Danza.* New York: Scribner, 1981.

———. *Dragon Defiant.* Illus. by Joseph Cellini. Chicago: Follett, 1977.

———. *In Trouble Again, Zelda Hammersmith?* San Diego: Harcourt, 1987.

———. *Megan's Mare.* New York: Scribner, 1983.

———. *Mrs. Portee's Pony.* New York: Scribner, 1986.

———. *The Mystery of the Plum Park Pony.* Champaign, IL: Garrard, 1980.

———. *The Mystery of Pony Hollow.* Champaign, IL: Garrard, 1978.

———. *The Mystery of the Pony Park Panda.* Champaign, IL: Garrard, 1983.

———. *Ride a Dark Horse.* New York: Morrow, 1987. Avon pb.

———. *Shadows.* Illus. by Joseph Cellini. Chicago: Follett, 1977.

———. *The Something Special Horse.* Illus. by Sandy Rabinowitz. New York: Scribner, 1985.

Hall, Kathy and Lisa Eisenburg. *Buggy Riddles.* Illus. by Simms Taback. New York: Dial, 1986. pb.

Hall, Susan. *Using Picture Storybooks to Teach Literary Devices: Recommended Books for Children and Young Adults.* Phoenix, AZ: Oryx, 1990.

Hamilton, Virginia. *Anthony Burns: The Defeat and Triumph of a Fugitive Slave.* New York: Knopf, 1988.

———. *Dustland.* New York: Greenwillow, 1980. Avon pb.

———. *The Gathering.* New York: Greenwillow, 1980. Avon pb.

———. *The House of Dies Drear.* New York: Macmillan, 1968. M592, M593, M934.

———. *Justice and Her Brothers.* New York: Greenwillow, 1978. Avon pb.

———. *The Mystery of Drear House: The Conclusion of the Dies Drear Chronicle.* New York: Greenwillow, 1987. pb.

———. *People Could Fly.* Illus. by Leo and Diane Dillon. New York: Knopf, 1985.

———. *Willie Bea and the Time the Martians Landed.* New York: Greenwillow, 1983.

Hamilton, Virginia, ed. *In the Beginning: Creation Stories from Around the World.* Illus. by Barry Moser. San Diego: Harcourt, 1988.

Hamm, Diane Johnston. *Grandma Drives a Motor Bed.* Illus. by Charles Robinson. Niles, IL: Whitman, 1987.

———. *The Shrinking of Treehorn*. Illus. by
Edward Gorey. New York: Holiday, 1971. Dell
pb.
———. *Treehorn's Treasure*. Illus. by E.
Gorey. New York: Holiday, 1981.
———. *Treehorn's Wish*. Illus. by E. Gorey.
New York: Holiday, 1984.
Heilbroner, Joan. *Tom the TV Cat*. Illus. by Sal
Murdocca. New York: Random, 1984.
Heine, Helme. *Friends*. Illus. by the author.
New York: Macmillan, 1982.
———. *The Pigs' Wedding*. Illus. by the author.
New York: Macmillan, 1986. M1027, M1028.
Heinlein, Robert. *The Expanded Universe*. New
York: Ace pb., 1980.
Helldorfer, M. C. *Daniel's Gift*. Illus. by J.
Downing. New York: Bradbury, 1987.
Heller, Nicholas. *Happy Birthday, Moe Dog*. Il-
lus. by the author. New York: Greenwillow,
1988.
Heller, Ruth. *Chickens Aren't the Only Ones*.
Illus. by the author. New York: Putnam, 1981.
Scholastic pb. M265, M1098.
———. *Designs for Coloring: Owls*. New York:
Putnam, n.d.
Heller, Linda. *The Castle on Hester Street*.
Philadelphia: Jewish Publication Society, 1982.
Helmering, Doris W. *I Have Two Families*.
Nashville: Abingdon, 1982.
Hendershot, Judith. *In Coal Country*. Illus. by
Thomas B. Allen. New York: Knopf, 1987.
M631, M632.
Henkes, Kevin. *Chester's Way*. Illus. by the au-
thor. New York: Greenwillow, 1988. Puffin pb.
———. *Grandfather and Bo*. Illus. by the au-
thor. New York: Greenwillow, 1986.
———. *Jessica*. Illus. by the author. New York:
Greenwillow, 1989.
———. *Once Around the Block*. Illus. by Victo-
ria Chess. New York: Greenwillow, 1987.
———. *Sheila Rae, the Brave*. Illus. by the au-
thor. New York: Greenwillow, 1987. Puffin pb.
———. *Two Under Par*. Illus. by the author.
New York: Greenwillow, 1987.
———. *A Weekend with Wendell*. New York:
Greenwillow, 1986. Puffin pb.
Henry, Joanne Landers. *Log Cabin in the
Woods: A True Story of a Pioneer Boy*. Illus.
by Joyce A. Zarins. New York: Four Winds/
Macmillan, 1988.
Henry, Marguerite. *Album of Horses*. Illus. by
Wesley Dennis. Chicago: Rand McNally, 1951.
New York: Checkerboard/Macmillan pb.
M1093.
———. *All About Horses*. New York: Random,
1962. M1093.

———. *Black Gold*. Illus. by W. Dennis. Chi-
cago: Rand McNally, 1950. Checkerboard/
Macmillan pb. M1093.
———. *Born to Trot*. Illus. by W. Dennis. Chi-
cago: Rand McNally, 1950, 1969. M1093.
———. *Brighty of the Grand Canyon*. Illus. by
W. Dennis. Chicago: Rand McNally, 1969.
Checkerboard/Macmillan pb. M184, M185,
M1093.
———. *A Colt Is Born*. Adapted by Joan Ni-
chols. New York: Checkerboard/Macmillan,
1988. M1093.
———. *Going Home*. New York: Checkerboard/
Macmillan, 1987. M2093.
———. *An Innkeeper's Horse*. Adapted by
Catherine Nichols. Illus. by Cindy Spenser.
New York: Checkerboard/Macmillan, 1988.
M1093.
———. *Justin Morgan Had a Horse*. Illus. by
W. Dennis. Chicago: Follett, 1945. Checker-
board/Macmillan pb. M1093.
———. *King of the Wind*. Illus. by W. Dennis.
New York: Macmillan, 1948. Checkerboard
pb. M57, M1093.
———. *Misty of Chincoteague*. Illus. by W.
Dennis. Chicago: Rand McNally, 1947, 1966.
Scholastic pb., Checkerboard/Macmillan pb.
M1093.
———. *Mustang, Wild Spirit of the West*. Illus.
by Robert Longheed. Chicago: Rand McNally,
1966. Checkerboard/Macmillan pb. M1093.
———. *A Pictorial Story of Misty*. Illus. by W.
Dennis. New York: Macmillan, 1976.
———. *San Domingo: The Medicine Hat Stal-
lion*. Illus. by Robert Longheed. Chicago:
Rand McNally, 1972. Checkerboard/Macmillan
pb. M1093, M1261.
———. *Sea Star: Orphan of Chincoteague*. Il-
lus. by W. Dennis. New York: Macmillan,
1949. Aladdin pb., Scholastic pb. M21093.
———. *Sire of Champions*. Adapted by Cather-
ine Nichols. Illus. by Steven J. Petruccio. New
York: Checkerboard/Macmillan, 1988. M1093.
———. *Stormy, Misty's Foal*. Illus. by W. Den-
nis. Chicago: Rand McNally, 1963. Checker-
board/Macmillan pb. M1093.
———. *Sultan's Gift*. Adapted by Joan Nichols.
Illus. by S. Moore. New York: Checkerboard/
Macmillan, 1988. M1093.
———. *Whirlpool*. New York: Checkerboard/
Macmillan, 1987. M1093.
———. *White Stallion of Lipizza*. Illus. by W.
Dennis. Chicago: Rand McNally, 1964. Check-
erboard/Macmillan pb. M1093.
Henstra, Frisco. *Mighty Mizzling Mice*. New
York: Lippincott, 1983.
Henstra, Frisco. *Mizzling Mouse and the Red
Cabbage House*. Boston: Little, 1984. pb.

———. *Angelina Ballerina.* Illus. by H. Craig. New York: Potter/Crown, 1983. M47c.

———. *Angelina on Stage.* Illus. by H. Craig. New York: Potter/Crown, 1986. M47.

———. *Angelina's Birthday Surprise.* Illus. by H. Craig. New York: Potter/Crown, 1989.

———. *Angelina's Christmas.* Illus. by H. Craig. New York: Potter/Crown, 1985. M47.

Holden, Dwight. *Gran-Gran's Best Trick: A Story for Children Who Have Lost Someone They Love.* New York: Magination pb., 1989.

Holdridge, Barbara, ed. *Under the Greenwood Tree: Shakespeare for Young People.* Illus. by Robin and Pat DeWitt. Owings Mills, MD: Stemmer House, 1986. M1378.

Holl, Kristi. *The Rose Beyond the Wall.* New York: Atheneum, 1985.

Holland, Barbara. *Prisoners at the Kitchen Table or Run for Your Life.* Boston: Clarion/ Houghton, 1979.

Holliss, Richard and Brian Sibley. *Walt Disney's Mickey Mouse: His Life and Times.* New York: Harper, 1986.

———. *Walt Disney's Snow White and the Seven Dwarfs and the Making of the Classic Film.* New York: Simon and Schuster, 1987.

Holman, Felice. *The Song in My Head.* Illus. by Jim Spanfeller. New York: Scribner, 1985.

———. *The Wild Children.* New York: Scribner, 1983. Penguin pb.

———. *Slake's Limbo.* New York: Scribner, 1974. Aladdin pb.

Holtze, Sally H. *The Fifth Book of Junior Authors and Illustrators.* Bronx, NY: Wilson, 1983.

———. *The Sixth Book of Junior Authors and Illustrators.* Bronx, NY: Wilson, 1989.

Honeycutt, Natalie. *The All New Jonah Twist.* New York: Bradbury, 1986.

Hooker, Ruth. *At Grandma and Grandpa's House.* Niles, IL: Whitman, 1986.

Hooks, William J. *Pioneer Cat.* Illus. by Charles Robinson. New York: Random, 1988.

Hoover, H. M. *Orvis.* New York: Viking, 1987.

———. *This Time of Darkness.* New York: Viking, 1980. Puffin pb.

———. *The Shepherd Moon: A Novel of the Future.* New York: Viking, 1984.

Hopf, Alice. *Biography of a Snowy Owl.* Illus. by Fran Stiles. New York: Putnam, 1979.

Hopkins, Lee Bennett. "Lee Bennett Hopkins Interviews David McPhail" in Pearson, P. D., *Make a Wish.* Needham, MA: Silver Burdett/ Ginn, 1989. Pages 154–59.

———. "Lee Bennett Hopkins Interviews Isaac Bashevis Singer" in Pearson, P. D. *Dream Chasers.* Needham, MA: Silver Burdett/Ginn, 1989. Pages 286–90.

Hopkins, Lee Bennett, ed. *Dinosaurs.* Illus. by Murray Tinkleman. San Diego: Harcourt, 1987.

———. *A Dog's Life: Poems Selected by Lee Bennett Hopkins.* Illus. by Linda R. Richards. San Diego: Harcourt, 1983.

———. *More Surprises.* Illus. by Megan Lloyd. New York: Harper, 1987.

———. *I Am the Cat.* Illus. by Linda Richard. San Diego: Harcourt, 1981.

———. *My Mane Catches the Wind: Poems About Horses.* Illus. by Sam Savitt. San Diego: Harcourt, 1979.

———. *Surprises.* Illus. by M. Lloyd. New York: Harper, 1984.

Hopkins, Lee Bennett and Misha Arenstein. *Potato Chips and a Slice of Moon.* Illus. by Wayne Blickenstaff. New York: Scholastic pb., 1976.

Hoppe, Joanne. *Pretty Penny Farm.* New York: Morrow, 1987. Troll pb.

Horgan, Dorothy. *The Edge of War.* New York: Oxford, 1988.

Horn Book Magazine. *Children's Classics: A Book List for Parents.* Boston: Horn Book, 1982.

Horner, John R. and James Gorman. *Maia: A Dinosaur Grows Up.* Illus. by Doug Henderson. Philadelphia: Courage, 1987. pb.

Horning, Kathleen and Ginny Moore Kruse. *Multicultural Children's and Young Adult Literature.* Madison, WI: Cooperative Children's Book Center, n.d.

Horowitz, Joshua. *Night Markets: Bringing Food to a City.* New York: Crowell, 1984.

Houghton, Eric. *Steps Out of Time.* New York: Lothrop, 1980.

Houselander, Caryll. *Petook: An Easter Story.* Illus. by Tomie de Paola. New York: Holiday, 1988.

Houston, Gloria. *The Year of the Perfect Christmas Tree: An Appalachian Tale.* Illus. by Barbara Cooney. New York: Dial, 1988.

Houston, James. *Frozen Fire.* Illus. by the author. New York: Macmillan, 1977. M487.

———. *White Archer.* San Diego: Harcourt, 1967. M1281.

Houston, James A., ed. *Songs of the Dream People: Chants and Images from the Indians and Eskimos of North America.* Illus. by the author. New York: Atheneum, 1972.

Houston, Jeanne W. and James D. Houston. *Farewell to Manzanar: A True Story of Japanese American Experience During and After the World War II Internment.* Boston: Houghton, 1973.

Howard, Ellen. *Edith Herself.* Illus. by Ronald Himler. New York: Atheneum, 1987.

———. *The Pea Patch Jig.* Illus. by the author. New York: Crown, 1986.

Hurmence, Belinda. *A Girl Called Boy.* Boston: Clarion, 1982.

Hurwitz, Johanna. *The Adventures of Ali Baba Bernstein.* Illus. by Gail Owens. New York: Morrow, 1985. Scholastic pb.

———. *Aldo Applesauce.* Illus. by John Wallner. New York: Morrow, 1979. Apple pb.

———. *Aldo Ice Cream.* Illus. by J. Wallner. New York: Morrow, 1981. Archway pb.

———. *Anne Frank: A Short Life.* Philadelphia: Jewish Publication Society, 1988. M60, M61, M62, M490, M712, M715, M1263.

———. *Anne Frank: Life in Hiding.* Philadelphia: Jewish Publication Society, 1988. M60, M61, M62, M490, M712, M715, M1263.

———. *Astrid Lindgren: Storyteller to the World.* New York: Viking, 1989. Penguin pb.

———. *Baseball Fever.* Illus. by Ray Cruz. New York: Morrow, 1981. Dell pb.

———. *Class Clown.* Illus. by Sheila Hamanaka. New York: Morrow, 1987. Scholastic pb.

———. *Cold and Hot Winter.* Illus. by Carolyn Ewing. New York: Morrow, 1988.

———. *DeDe Takes Charge.* Illus. by Diane de Groat. New York: Morrow, 1984. Scholastic pb.

———. *Hot and Cold Summer.* Illus. by Gail Owens. New York: Morrow, 1984. Apple pb.

———. *Hurricane Elaine.* Illus. by D. de Groat. New York: Morrow, 1986. Apple pb.

———. *Much Ado About Aldo.* Illus. by J. Wallner. New York: Morrow, 1978.

———. *Rip-Roaring Russell.* Illus. by Lillian Hoban. New York: Morrow, 1983.

———. *Russell and Elisa.* Illus. by L. Hoban. New York: Morrow, 1989.

———. *Russell Rides Again.* Illus. by L. Hoban. New York: Morrow, 1985.

———. *Russell Sprouts.* Illus. by L. Hoban. New York: Morrow, 1987.

———. *Teacher's Pet.* Illus. by S. Hamanaka. New York: Morrow, 1988.

———. *Tough-Luck Karen.* Illus. by D. de Groat. New York: Morrow, 1982.

Hutchins, Pat. *The Doorbell Rang.* Illus. by the author. New York: Greenwillow, 1986. Scholastic pb., Scholastic big book.

———. *Happy Birthday, Sam.* Illus. by the author. New York: Greenwillow, 1978. Puffin pb.

———. *King Henry's Palace.* Illus. by the author. New York: Greenwillow, 1983.

———. *The Surprise Party.* Illus. by the author. New York: Macmillan, 1969. Collier pb. M1292.

———. *Where's the Baby?* Illus. by the author. New York: Greenwillow, 1988.

———. *The Very Worst Monster.* Illus. by the author. New York: Greenwillow, 1985. Mulberry pb.

———. *You'll Soon Grow Into Them, Titch.* Illus. by the author. New York: Greenwillow, 1983. Puffin pb.

Hutchinson, Veronica S. *Chimney Corner Stories.* Illus. by Lois Lenski. Hamden, CT: Linnet Books, 1992.

Huynh, Quang Nhuang. *The Land I Lost: Adventures of a Boy in Vietnam.* New York: Harper, 1982. Trophy pb.

Hyde, Dayton O. *Island of the Loons.* New York: Atheneum, 1984.

———. *The Major, the Poacher, and the Wonderful One-Trout River.* New York: Atheneum, 1985.

Hyde, Margaret O. *Cry Softly! The Story of Child Abuse.* Louisville, KY: Westminster, 1980.

———. *My Friend Has Four Parents.* New York: McGraw, 1981.

———. *Sexual Abuse: Let's Talk About It.* Louisville, KY: Westminster, 1987.

Hyett, Barbara H. *In Evidence: Poems of the Liberation of Nazi Concentration Camps.* Pittsburgh: University of Pittsburgh, 1986. pb.

Imersheim, Betsy. *Animal Doctor.* New York: Messner, 1988. pb.

Ingram, *Making a Picture Book.* Sydney, Australia: Methuen, 1987.

Ireson, Barbara, ed. *Tales Out of Time.* New York: Philomel, 1979.

Irvine, Mat. *Satellites and Computers.* New York: Watts, 1984.

Irving, Georgeanne. *The True Story of Corky the Blind Seal.* New York: Scholastic, 1987.

Irving, Jan. *Fanfares: Programs for Classrooms and Libraries.* Illus. by Karen Myers. Englewood, CO: Libraries Unlimited, 1990.

Irving, Washington. *The Legend of Sleepy Hollow.* Retold by Robert D. San Souci. Illus. by Daniel San Souci. New York: Doubleday, 1986.

Irwin, Hadley. *Kim/Kimi.* New York: Macmillan, 1987.

Isaacman, Clara and Joan Grossman. *Clara's Story.* Philadelphia: Jewish Publication Society, 1984.

Isaacson, Phillip. *Round Buildings, Square Buildings, and Buildings That Wiggle Like a Fish.* New York: Knopf, 1988.

Isaacson, Richard W. *The Junior High School Library Catalog.* 5th ed. Bronx, NY: Wilson, 1985.

———. *A Tale of Time City.* New York: Greenwillow, 1987.

Jones, Dolores Bly. *Children's Literature: Awards and Winners.* Detroit: Neal-Schuman, 1983, 1988.

Jones, Rebecca. *Angie and Me.* New York: Macmillan, 1981.

———. *Germy Blew It.* New York: Dutton, 1987.

———. *Germy Blew It Again.* New York: Holt, 1988.

Jones, Taffy. *Library Programs for Children.* Jefferson, NC: McFarland, 1989.

Joosse, Barbara M. *Jam Day.* Illus. by Emily McCully. New York: Harper, 1987.

———. *Spiders in the Fruit Cellar.* Illus. by Kay Chorao. New York: Knopf, 1983.

Jorgensen, Gail. *Crocodile Beat.* Illus. by Patricia Mullins. New York: Bradbury, 1989.

Joslin, Sesyle. *What Do You Do, Dear?* Illus. by Maurice Sendak. New York: Harper, 1958. Trophy pb. M1429, M1430.

———. *What Do You Say, Dear?* Illus. by M. Sendak. New York: Harper, 1985. Trophy pb. M1431, M1432.

Joyce, William. *Dinosaur Bob and His Adventures with the Family Lizardo.* Illus. by the author. New York: Harper, 1988. M351, M1098.

———. *George Shrinks.* Illus. by the author. New York: Harper, 1985.

Jukes, Mavis. *Blackberries in the Dark.* Illus. by Thomas Allen. New York: Knopf, 1985. Dell pb. M149.

———. *Like Jake and Me.* Illus. by Lloyd Bloom. New York: Knopf, 1984. Borzoi pb. M720.

———. *No One Is Going to Nashville.* Illus. by L. Bloom. New York: Knopf, 1983.

Jurmain, Suzanne. *Once Upon a Horse: A History of Horses—and How They Shaped Our History.* New York: Lothrop, 1989.

Juster, Norton. *The Phantom Tollbooth.* Illus. by Jules Feiffer. New York: Random, 1961. pb. M1008, M1009, M1010.

Kafka, Sherry. *If I Need a Friend.* Illus. by Eros Keith. New York: Putnam, 1971.

Kahl, Virginia. *The Duchess Bakes a Cake.* Illus. by the author. New York: Scribner, 1955. M607.

Kalb, Jonah. *The Goof That Won the Pennant.* Boston: Houghton, 1976.

Kalman, Bobbie. *Early Pleasures and Pastimes.* New York: Crabtree, 1983.

———. *Early Settler Children.* New York: Crabtree, 1982.

Kamerman, Sylvia, ed. *The Big Book of Christmas Plays: 21 Modern and Traditional One-Act Plays for the Celebration of Christmas.* Boston: Plays, 1988.

———. *Christmas Play Favorites for Young People.* Boston: Plays, 1982. pb.

Kamien, Janet. *What If You Couldn't?* A Book About Special Needs. Illus. by Signe Hanson. New York: Scribner, 1979.

Kandoian, Ellen. *Under the Sun.* New York: Dodd, 1987.

Kaplan, Chiam. *Scroll of Agony: The Warsaw Diary of Chiam A. Kaplan.* Trans. by Abraham Katsh. New York: Macmillan, 1965.

Kastner, Erich. *Emil and the Detectives.* Trans. by May Massee. Illus. by Walter Trier. New York: Scholastic, 1929, 1984.

Kasza, Keiko. *The Pig's Picnic.* Illus. by the author. New York: Putnam, 1988.

———. *Wolf's Chicken Stew.* Illus. by the author. New York: Putnam, 1987.

Kaufman, Curt and Gita Kaufman. *Rajesh.* Photos by Curt Kaufman. New York: Atheneum, 1985.

Kaula, Edna M. *African Village Folktales.* Cleveland: World, 1968.

Kaye, Marilyn. *Cassie.* San Diego: Gulliver/Harcourt, 1987.

———. *Daphne.* San Diego: Gulliver/Harcourt, 1987.

———. *A Friend Like Phoebe.* San Diego: Gulliver/Harcourt, 1989.

———. *Lydia.* San Diego: Gulliver/Harcourt, 1987.

———. *Phoebe.* San Diego: Gulliver/Harcourt, 1987.

Kaye, Mary Margaret. *The Ordinary Princess.* Illus. by the author. New York: Doubleday, 1984.

Keats, Ezra Jack. *Apt. 3.* Illus. by the author. New York: Macmillan, 1983. Aladdin pb. M72, M73, M74.

———. *Clementina's Cactus.* Illus. by the author. New York: Viking, 1982.

———. *Maggie and the Pirate.* Illus. by the author. New York: Four Winds/Macmillan, 1987.

———. *Peter's Chair.* Illus. by the author. New York: Harper, 1967. Trophy pb.

———. *The Snowy Day.* Illus. by the author. New York: Viking, 1962. Puffin pb.

Keeler, Stephen. *Louis Braille.* Illus. by Richard Hook. New York: Bookwright/Watts, 1986.

Keeton, Elizabeth. *Second-Best Friend.* New York: Atheneum, 1985.

Kehoe, Patricia. *Something Happened and I'm Scared to Tell: A Book for Young Children.* Seattle: Parenting Press, 1987. pb.

Keller, Charles. *Astronuts, Space Jokes and Riddles*. Illus. by Art Cumings. Englewood Cliffs, NJ: Prentice-Hall, 1985.

———. *Colossal Fossils, Dinosaur Riddles*. Illus. by Leonard Kessler. Englewood Cliffs, NJ: Prentice-Hall, 1987.

Keller, Helen. *The Story of My Life*. New York: Doubleday, 1954. Airmont pb., Scholastic pb., NAL/Signet pb. M1264.

Keller, Beverly. *A Small Elderly Dragon*. Illus. by Nola Langner. New York: Lothrop, 1984.

Keller, Holly. *Cromwell's Glasses*. Illus. by the author. New York: Greenwillow, 1982.

———. *Geraldine's Big Snow*. Illus. by the author. New York: Greenwillow, 1988.

———. *Goodbye, Max*. Illus. by the author. New York: Greenwillow, 1987.

———. *Henry's Fourth of July*. Illus. by the author. New York: Greenwillow, 1985.

Kelley, A. *Lenses, Spectacles, Eyeglasses and Contacts: The Story of Vision Aids*. New York: Elsevier/Nelson, 1979.

Kellogg, Steven. *Best Friends*. Illus. by the author. New York: Dial, 1986. M134.

———. *The Island of the Skog*. Illus. by the author. New York: Dial, 1973. Pied Piper pb. M653, M654, M655.

———. *The Mysterious Tadpole*. Illus. by the author. New York: Dial, 1977. Pied Piper pb. M936, M937, M938.

———. *The Mystery of the Stolen Blue Paint*. Illus. by the author. New York: Dial, 1982.

———. *Paul Bunyan*. Illus. by the author. New York: Morrow, 1984. pb. M1000. M10098.

———. *Pecos Bill*. Retold and illus. by S. Kellogg. New York: Morrow, 1986.

———. *Pinkerton, Behave!* Illus. by the author. New York: Dial, 1979. Pied Piper pb.

———. *Prehistoric Pinkerton*. Illus. by the author. New York: Dial, 1987.

———. *A Rose for Pinkerton*. Illus. by the author. New York: Dial, 1981. Pied Piper pb. M1130, M1131.

———. *Tallyho, Pinkerton!* Illus. by the author. New York: Dial, 1982. Pied Piper pb. M1311, M1312a.

Kendall, Carol. *The Gammage Cup*. Illus. by Erik Blegvad. San Diego: Harcourt, 1959. Voyager pb.

Kennedy. *Amy's Eyes*. Illus. by Richard Egielski. New York: Harper, 1985.

Kennedy, Richard. *Contests at Cowlick*. Illus. by Marc Simont. Boston: Little, 1975.

———. *The Parrot and the Thief*. Illus. by Marcia Sewall. Boston: Little, 1974. M996.

———. *The Rise and Fall of Ben Gizzard*. Illus. by M. Sewall. Boston: Little, 1978. M1117.

Kennedy, X. J. *The Forgetful Wishing Well*. Illus. by Monica Incisa. New York: McElderry/Macmillan, 1985.

Kent, Jack. *Joey*. Illus. by the author. Englewood Cliffs, NJ: Prentice Hall, 1984.

———. *Joey Runs Away*. Illus. by the author. Englewood Cliffs, NJ: Prentice Hall, 1985. M672, M673, M674.

———. *Little Peep*. Illus. by the author. Englewood Cliffs, NJ: Prentice Hall, 1981. Treehouse pb.

Kent, Zachary. *The Story of Admiral Peary at the North Pole*. Chicago: Childrens Press, 1988. pb.

———. *The Story of Ford's Theater and the Death of Lincoln*. Chicago: Childrens Press, 1987.

———. *The Story of the Surrender at Appomattox Court House*. Chicago: Childrens Press, 1987.

Kerr, Judith. *When Hitler Stole Pink Rabbit*. Illus. by the author. New York: Coward, 1972. Dell pb.

Kerr, M. E. *Gentlehands*. New York: Harper, 1978. Dell pb. M1093.

Kerr, Rita. *Texas Footprints*. Austin, TX: Eakin, 1988.

Kerrod, Robin. *See Inside a Space Station*. New York: Warwick, 1988.

Kessel, Joyce K. *Halloween*. Illus. by Nancy L. Carlson. Minneapolis: Carolrhoda, 1980. Lerner pb.

Kesseley, Deirdre. *A Child's Anne: Adapted from Lucy Maude Montgomery's Anne of Green Gables*. Illus. by Floyd Trainor. Charleston, PEI. Canada, 1983. M64, M65, M66, M67.

Kessler, Leonard. *Here Comes the Strikeout*. New York: Harper, 1965. Trophy pb. M573, M574.

Kettlekamp, Larry. *Bill Cosby: Family Funny Man*. New York: Messner, 1986.

———. *The Human Brain*. Hillside, NJ: Enslow, 1986.

Key, Alexander. *Escape to Witch Mountain*. Illus. by Leon Wisdom. Louisville, KY: Westminster, 1968. Archway pb. M415.

Khalsa, Dayal. *Julian*. Illus. by the author. New York: Potter/Crown, 1989.

———. *Tales of a Gambling Grandma*. Illus. by the author. New York: Potter/Crown, 1986.

Kherdian, David. *A Song for Uncle Harry*. Illus. by Nonny Hogrogian. New York: Philomel, 1989.

Khoury, Carol. *The Space Shuttle Mystery*. Illus. by Steve Myman. Hawthorne, NJ: January, 1986.

———. *The Philharmonic Gets Dressed.* Illus. by M. Simont. New York: Harper, 1982. Trophy pb. M1011.

Kuznet, Lois. *Kenneth Grahame.* Boston: Twayne, 1987.

Laird, Elizabeth. *The Road to Bethlehem: An Ethiopian Nativity.* Foreword by Terry Waite. New York: Holt, 1987.

Lamb, Charles and Mary Lamb. *Tales from Shakespeare.* Illus. by Elizabeth S. G. Elliott. New York: Crown, 1986. Penguin pb. NAL pb.

Lambert, David. *The Age of Dinosaurs.* Illus. by John Francis, et al. New York: Random, 1987. pb.

———. *A Field Guide to Dinosaurs.* New York: Diagram Group, 1983. Avon pb.

———. *A Field Guide to Prehistoric Life: A True Field Guide to Fossil Life from One-Celled Plants to Homo Sapiens.* New York: Facts on File, 1985.

Lamme, Linda and Literature in the Elementary Language Arts Committee. *Learning to Love Literature: Preschool Through Grade 3.* Urbana, IL: National Council of Teachers of English, 1981.

Lampman, Evelyn S. *Bargain Bride.* New York: Atheneum, 1977.

Lampton, Christopher. *New Theories on the Dinosaurs.* New York: Watts, 1989.

———. *Space Sciences.* Illus. by Anne C. Green. New York: Watts, 1983.

———. *Werner von Braun.* New York: Watts, 1988.

Landau, Elaine. *Alzheimer's Disease.* New York: Watts, 1987.

———. *Child Abuse, An American Epidemic.* New York: Messner, 1984.

Landes, Sonia and Edith Baxter. *Book Wise Literature Guide to Gardner's Stone Fox.* Cambridge, MA: Book Wise, 1988.

Landes, Sonia and Molly Flender. *Book Wise Literature Guide to Babbitt's Tuck Everlasting.* Cambridge, MA: Book Wise, 1987.

———. *Book Wise Literature Guide to de Paola's Charlie Needs a Cloak.* Cambridge, MA: Book Wise, 1989.

———. *Book Wise Literature Guide to Holman's Slake's Limbo.* Cambridge, MA: Book Wise, n.d.

———. *Book Wise Literature Guide to Leaf's The Story of Ferdinand.* Cambridge, MA: Book Wise, 1987.

———. *Book Wise Literature Guide to Lewis's The Magician's Nephew.* Cambridge, MA: Book Wise, 1987.

———. *Book Wise Literature Guide to Mac-Lachlan's Sarah Plain and Tall.* Cambridge, MA: Book Wise, 1987.

———. *Book Wise Literature Guide to Paterson's Bridge to Terabithia.* Cambridge, MA: Book Wise, 1989.

———. *Book Wise Literature Guide to White's Charlotte's Web.* Cambridge, MA: Book Wise, 1989.

Landes, Sonia and Barbara Moross. *Book Wise Literature Guide to Juster's The Phantom Tollbooth.* Cambridge, MA: Book Wise, 1989.

Landes, Sonia and Anita Moss. *Book Wise Literature Guide to Taylor's Roll of Thunder, Hear My Cry.* Cambridge, MA: Book Wise, 1990.

Landes, Sonia and Jon C. Stott. *Book Wise Literature Guide to George's Julie of the Wolves.* Cambridge, MA: Book Wise, 1989.

Landon, Lucinda. *Meg Mackintosh and the Case of the Missing Babe Ruth Baseball.* Boston: Joy Street/Little, 1986.

———. *Meg Mackintosh and the Case of the Curious Whale Watch.* Boston: Joy Street/Little, 1987.

———. *Meg Mackintosh and the Mystery at Camp Creepy.* Boston: Joy Street/Little, 1990.

———. *Meg Mackintosh and the Mystery at the Medieval Castle.* Boston: Joy Street/Little, 1989.

Landsman, Sandy. *Castaways on Chimp Island.* New York: Atheneum, 1986. Archway pb.

———. *The Gadget Factor.* New York: Atheneum, 1984. NAL pb.

Lane, Margaret. *Fox.* Illus. by Kenneth Lilly. New York: Dial, 1982.

———. *Frog.* Illus. by Grahame Corbett. New York: Dial, 1981.

Lane, Rose Wilder. *Let the Hurricane Roar.* New York: Longmans, 1933.

Lang, Andrew. *Arabian Nights Entertainments.* Magnolia, MA: Peter Smith, n.d. Dover pb.

Lang, Daniel. *A Backward Look: Germans Remember.* New York: McGraw, 1979. pb.

Lang, Denise. *Footsteps in the Ocean: Careers in Diving.* New York: Lodestar, 1987.

Langley, Andrew. *Spacecraft.* New York: Watts, 1987.

Langley, Noel. *The Wizard of Oz: The Screenplay.* Introduction by Michael Hearn. New York: Delacorte, 1989. M1475.

Langner, Nola. *Freddy My Grandfather.* Illus. by the author. New York: Four Winds, 1979.

Langstaff, John and Feodor Rojankovsky. *Over in the Meadow.* San Diego: Harcourt, 1973. Voyager pb. M924.

Levine, Edna S. *Lisa and Her Soundless World.* New York: Human Science Press, 1974. pb.

Levine, Ellen. *If You Traveled on the Underground Railroad.* Illus. by Richard Williams. New York: Scholastic, 1988.

———. *If You Traveled West in a Covered Wagon.* Illus. by Charles Shaw. New York: Scholastic pb., 1986.

———. *Secret Missions: Four True Life Stories.* New York: Scholastic, 1988.

Levinson, Nancy S. *Clara and the Bookwagon.* Illus. by Carolyn Croll. New York: Harper, 1988.

———. *I Lift My Lamp: Emma Lazarus and the Statue of Liberty.* New York: Lodestar/ Dutton, 1986.

Levinson, Riki. *I Go With My Family to Grandma's.* Illus. by Diane Goode. New York: Dutton, 1986. M617.

———. *Touch! Touch!* Illus. by True Kelley. New York: Dutton, 1987.

———. *Watch the Stars Come Out.* Illus. by D. Goode. New York: Dutton, 1985. Checkerboard pb. M1098, M1412.

Levitin, Sonia. *Journey to America.* Illus. by Charles Robinson. New York: Atheneum, 1970.

———. *The No-Return Trail.* San Diego: Harcourt, 1978.

Levoy, Myron. *Alan and Naomi.* New York: Harper, 1977. Trophy pb.

———. *The Magic Hat of Mortimer Wintergreen.* Illus. by Andrew Glass. New York: Harper, 1988.

———. *The Witch of Fourth Street and Other Stories.* Illus. by Gabriel Lisowski. New York: Harper, 1972. pb. M1473.

Levy, Elizabeth. *Bill Cosby's Fat Albert and the Cosby Kids: Take Two, They're Small.* New York: Dell Yearling, 1981.

———. *Dracula Is a Pain in the Neck.* New York: Harper, 1984. Trophy pb.

———. *If You Were There When They Signed the Constitution.* Illus. by Richard Rosenblum. New York: Scholastic, 1987.

———. *Running Out of Magic with Houdini.* New York: Knopf, 1981. pb.

———. *Running Out of Time.* New York: Knopf, 1980. pb.

———. *Something Queer at the Ball Park.* Illus. by Mordicai Gerstein. Magnolia, MA: Peter Smith, n.d. Dell pb.

———. *Something Queer at the Haunted School.* Illus. by M. Gerstein. New York: Delacorte, 1982. Dell pb. M1220.

———. *Something Queer at the Lemonade Stand.* Illus. by M. Gerstein. New York: Delacorte, 1982. Dell pb.

———. *Something Queer at the Library.* Illus. by M. Gerstein. New York: Delacorte, 1977. Dell pb.

———. *Something Queer in Rock and Roll.* Illus. by M. Gerstein. New York: Delacorte, 1987. Dell pb.

———. *Something Queer Is Going On.* Illus. by M. Gerstein. Magnolia, MA: Peter Smith, n.d. Dell pb. M1221.

———. *Something Queer on Vacation.* Illus. by M. Gerstein. New York: Delacorte, 1980. Dell pb.

Lewin, Hugh. *Jafta.* Illus. by Lisa Kopper. Minneapolis: Carolrhoda, 1981.

———. *Jafta and the Wedding.* Illus. by L. Kopper. Minneapolis: Carolrhoda, 1983.

———. *Jafta: The Journey.* Illus. by L. Kopper. Minneapolis: Carolrhoda, 1984.

———. *Jafta: The Town.* Illus. by L. Kopper. Minneapolis: Carolrhoda, 1984.

———. *Jafta's Father.* Illus. by L. Kopper. Minneapolis: Carolrhoda, 1983.

———. *Jafta's Mother.* Illus. by L. Kopper. Minneapolis: Carolrhoda, 1983.

Lewis, C. S. *The Horse and His Boy.* New York: Macmillan, 1969. Collier pb. M432.

———. *The Horse and His Boy.* Large print edition. Boston: G. K. Hall, 1986. M432.

———. *The Last Battle.* New York: Macmillan, 1956. M432.

———. *The Last Battle.* Large print edition. Boston: G. K. Hall, 1986. M432.

———. *The Lion, the Witch and the Wardrobe.* New York: Macmillan, 1968. Collier pb. M432, M722a, M722b.

———. *The Lion, the Witch and the Wardrobe.* Illus. by Michael Hague. New York: Macmillan, 1983. M432, M722a, M722b.

———. *The Lion, the Witch and the Wardrobe.* Large print edition. Boston: G. K. Hall, 1986. M432, M722a, M722b.

———. *The Magician's Nephew.* New York: Macmillan, 1969. Collier pb. M432.

———. *Prince Caspian. The Return to Narnia.* New York: Macmillan, 1969. Collier pb. M432.

———. *Prince Caspian. The Return to Narnia.* Large print edition. Boston: G. K. Hall, 1986. M432.

———. *The Silver Chair.* New York: Macmillan, 1977. Collier pb. M432.

———. *The Silver Chair.* Large print edition. Boston: G. K. Hall, 1986. M432.

———. *The Voyage of the Dawn Treader.* New York: Macmillan, 1970. Collier pb. M432.

———. *The Voyage of the Dawn Treader.* Large print edition. Boston: G. K. Hall, 1986. M432.

Lippman, Peter. *Trucks, Trucks, Trucks.* New York: Doubleday, 1984.

Lipson, Eden Ross. *The New York Times Parents' Guide to the Best Books for Children.* New York: Random, 1988, 1991.

Lisle, Janet Taylor. *Afternoon of the Elves.* New York: Orchard, 1989.

———. *The Great Dimpole Oak.* Illus. by Stephen Gammell. New York: Orchard, 1987.

———. *Sirens and Spies.* New York: Bradbury, 1985. Collier pb.

Litchfield, Ada Bassett. *Making Room for Uncle Joe.* Illus. by Gail Owens. Niles, IL: Whitman, 1984.

———. *Words in Our Hands.* Illus. by Helen Cogancherry. Niles, IL: Whitman, 1980.

Litterick, Ian. *Robots and Intelligent Machines.* Illus. by David Arstey. New York: Bookwright, 1984.

Little, Emily. *David and the Giant.* Illus. by Hans Wilhelm. New York: Random, 1987. pb.

Little, Jean. *Different Dragons.* Illus. by Laura Fernandez. New York: Viking, 1987. M347, M833.

———. *From Anna.* Illus. by Joan Sandin. New York: Harper, 1972. Trophy pb. M833.

———. *Kate.* New York: Harper, 1971. Trophy pb. M833.

———. *Listen for the Singing.* New York: Dutton, 1977. M833.

———. *Little by Little: A Writer's Education.* New York: Viking, 1987. Penguin pb. M833.

———. *Look Through My Window.* Illus. by J. Sandin. New York: Harper, 1970. M833.

———. *Lost and Found.* Illus. by L. O'Young. New York: Viking, 1986. Puffin pb. M833.

———. *Mama's Going to Buy You a Mocking Bird.* New York: Viking, 1984. Puffin pb. M808, M833.

———. *Mine for Keeps.* New York: Little, 1962. Archway pb. M833.

———. *One to Grow On.* Illus. by Jerry Lazare. Boston: Little, 1969. M833.

———. *Spring Begins in March.* Illus. by Lewis Parker. Boston: Little, 1966. M833.

———. *Stand in the Wind.* New York: Harper, 1975. M833.

———. *Take Wing.* Illus. by J. Lazare. Boston: Little, 1968. M833.

Little, Leslie. *Children of Long Ago: Poems.* Illus. by Jan Spivey Gilchrist. New York: Philomel, 1988.

Lively, Penelope. *The Ghost of Thomas Kempe.* New York: Dutton, 1973. Berkley pb. M493.

———. *The Ghost of Thomas Kempe.* Large print edition. Boston: G. K. Hall, n.d. M493.

———. *The House in Norham Gardens.* New York: Dutton, 1974.

———. *Uninvited Ghosts, and Other Stories.* Illus. by John Lawrence. New York: Dutton, 1985.

———. *The Revenge of Samuel Stokes.* New York: Dutton, 1981.

Livingston, Myra C. *Birthday Poems.* Illus. by Margot Tomes. New York: Holiday, 1989.

———. *Celebrations.* Illus. by Leonard Everett Fisher. New York: Holiday, 1985. pb.

———. *Poems for Fathers.* Illus. by Robert Casilla. New York: Holiday, 1989.

———. *Space Songs.* Illus. by Leonard Everett Fisher. New York: Holiday, 1988.

———. *Worlds I Know and Other Poems.* Illus. by Tim Arnold. New York: Atheneum, 1985.

Livo, Norma and Sandie Reitz. *Storytelling: Process and Practice.* Englewood, CO: Libraries Unlimited, 1986.

Lloyd, David. *Duck.* Illus. by Charlotte Voake. New York: Lippincott, 1988.

———. *Hello, Goodbye.* New York: Lothrop, 1988. Little Simon pb.

Lobel, Anita. *The Pancake.* Illus. by the author. New York: Greenwillow, 1978.

Lobel, Arnold. *Book of Pigericks.* Illus. by the author. New York: Harper, 1983. Trophy pb. M158, M836, M1094.

———. *Days with Frog and Toad.* Illus. by the author. New York: Harper, 1979. Trophy pb. M836. M1094.

———. *Fables.* Illus. by the author. New York: Harper, 1980. Trophy pb. M80, M421, M422, M836, M1094.

———. *Frog and Toad All Year.* Illus. by the author. New York: Harper, 1976. Trophy pb. M836, M1094.

———. *Frog and Toad Are Friends.* Illus. by the author. New York: Harper, 1970. Trophy pb. M80, M482, M483, M484, M485, M486, M836, M1094.

———. *The Frog and Toad Coloring Book.* Illus. by the author. New York: Harper, 1986. M836, M1094.

———. *Frog and Toad Pop-Up Book.* Illus. by the author. New York: Harper, 1986. M836, M1094.

———. *Frog and Toad Together.* Illus. by the author. New York: Harper, 1972. Trophy pb. M80, M484, M836, M1094.

———. *Mouse Soup.* Illus. by the author. Harper, 1977. Trophy pb. M80, M836, M907, M1094.

———. *Mouse Tales.* Illus. by the author. New York: Harper, 1978. Trophy pb. M836, M908, M1094.

———. *Owl at Home.* Illus. by the author. New York: Harper, 1975. Trophy pb. M836, M985, M1094.

———. *The Shadow in Hawthorn Bay*. New York: Scribner, 1987. Puffin pb.

Lydccker, Laura. *The Country Mouse and the City Mouse*. Retold and illus. by L. Lydccker. New York: Knopf, 1987.

Lynn, Ruth N. *Fantasy Literature for Children and Young Adults*. 3rd ed. New York: Bowker, 1989.

Lynn, Sara. *Clothes*. Illus. by the author. New York: Macmillan, 1986. Aladdin pb.

Lyon, David. *The Biggest Truck*. New York: Lothrop, 1988.

———. *The Runaway Duck*. New York: Lothrop, 1985. Mulberry pb. M1098, M1134.

Mabery, D. L. *This Is Michael Jackson*. Minneapolis: Lerner, 1984.

Mabie, Margot. *Constitution: Reflection of a Changing Nation*. New York: Holt, 1987.

McAfee, Annalena. *Kirsty Knows Best*. Illus. by Anthony Browne. New York: Knopf, 1988.

McCaffrey, Anne. *Dragondrums*. New York: Atheneum, 1979. Bantam pb.

———. *Dragonsinger*. New York: Atheneum, 1977. Bantam pb.

———. *Dragonsong*. New York: Atheneum, 1976. Bantam pb. M383.

McCarter, James. *Space Shuttle Disaster*. New York: Bookwright/Watts, 1988.

McCaslin, Mary. "Whole Language: Theory, Instruction, and Future Implementations." *Elementary School Journal*. Vol. 90, #2. November 1989. Pages 223–29.

McCaslin, Nellie. *Creative Drama in the Classroom*. 4th edition. New York: Longman, 1984.

———. *Creative Drama in the Primary Grades*. New York: Longman, 1987.

Macaulay, David. *Castle*. Illus. by the author. Boston: Houghton, 1977. pb. M236, M237, M238, M332.

———. *Cathedral*. Illus. by the author. Boston: Houghton, 1973. pb. M332.

———. *City*. Illus. by the author. Boston: Houghton, 1983. M332.

———. *Mill*. Illus. by the author. Boston: Houghton, 1983. pb. M332.

———. *Pyramid*. Illus. by the author. Boston: Houghton, 1975. pb. M332, M582, M1066.

———. *Unbuilding*. Illus. by the author. Boston: Houghton, 1980. Sandpiper pb. M332.

———. *Underground*. Illus. by the author. Boston: Houghton, 1976. pb. M332.

———. *Why the Chicken Crossed the Road*. Illus. by the author. Boston: Houghton, 1987. M332.

McCleery, William. *Wolf Story*. Illus. by Warren Chappell. Hamden, CT: Linnet, 1988.

McCloskey, Robert. *Make Way for Ducklings*. Illus. by the author. New York: Viking, 1941, 1963. Puffin pb. M802.

McClung, Robert. *Thor, Last of the Sperm Whales*. Hamden, CT: Linnct, 1988

McConaghy, June. *Children Learning Through Literature: A Teacher Researcher Study*. Portsmouth, NH: Heinemann, 1990.

McCracken, Robert A. and Marlene J. McCracken. *Stories, Songs, and Poetry to Teach Reading and Writing: Literacy Through Language*. Chicago: American Library Association, 1986.

McCully, Emily A. *Christmas Gift*. Illus. by E. A. McCully. New York: Harper, 1988.

———. *First Snow*. Illus. by E. A. McCully. New York: Harper, 1985. Trophy pb.

———. *The Grandma Mix-Up*. Illus. by the author. New York: Harper, 1988.

———. *The New Baby*. Illus. by E. A. McCully. New York: Harper, 1988.

———. *Picnic*. New York: Harper, 1984. Illus. by E. A. McCully. Trophy pb. M1013, M1014.

———. *School*. Illus. by E. A. McCully. New York: Harper, 1987.

McCutcheon, Elsie. *Summer of the Zeppelin*. New York: Farrar, 1985.

McDearman, K. *Foxes*. New York: Dodd, 1981.

McDermott, Gerald. *Anansi the Spider*. Retold and illus. by G. McDermott. New York: Holt, 1982. pb. M42, M42, M43, M44, M45, M457.

MacDonald, Margaret Read. *Booksharing: 101 Programs to Use with Preschoolers*. Hamden, CT: Library Professional Publications, 1988, 1991. pb.

MacDonald, Ruth. *Dr. Seuss*. Boston: Twayne, 1988.

MacDonald, Suse. *Alphabatics*. Illus. by the author. New York: Bradbury, 1986. M30, M31, M32.

Macdonald, Kate. *Anne of Green Gables Cookbook*. New York: Oxford, 1987. Bantam pb.

McDonald, Reby Edmond. *The Ghosts of Austwick Manor*. New York: Atheneum, 1982.

McDonnell, Christine. *Just for the Summer*. New York: Viking, 1987. Puffin pb.

———. *Lucky Charms and Birthday Wishes*. Illus. by Diane de Groat. New York: Viking, 1984. Puffin pb.

McElmeel, Sharron. *An Author a Month, for Pennies*. Englewood, CO: Libraries Unlimited, 1988.

McFarlan, Donald and Norris McWhirter. *The Guiness Book of World Records*. New York: Sterling, 1989.

Miquel, Pierre. *Days of Knights and Castles.* Needham Heights, MA: Silver Burdett, 1985. pb.

Mitchell, Barbara. *Click! A Story About George Eastman.* Illus. by Jan Hosking Smith. Minneapolis: Carolrhoda, 1986.

———. *"Good Morning, Mr. President."* A *Story About Carl Sandburg.* Minneapolis: Carolrhoda, 1988.

Mitchell, John H. *A Field Guide to Your Own Back Yard.* New York: Norton, 1985. pb.

Mitchell, William O. *Who Has Seen the Wind.* New York: Macmillan, 1947, 1974.

Moak, Allan. *A Big City ABC.* Illus. by the author. Plattsburgh, NY: Tundra, 1984.

Moche, Dinah. *If You Were an Astronaut.* Racine, WI: Western, 1985.

Modell, Frank. *Ice Cream Soup.* New York: Greenwillow, 1988.

Mohr, Carolyn, Dorothy Nixon, and Shirley Vickers. *Thinking Activities for Books Children Love: A Whole Language Approach.* Illus. by Kenda Kirby. Englewood, CO: Teacher Ideas Press, 1988.

Mohr, Joseph. *Silent Night.* Illus. by Susan Jeffers. New York: Dutton, 1984. Unicorn pb.

Mohr, Nicholas. *Going Home.* New York: Dial, 1986. Bantam Skylark pb. M503.

Monchieri, Lino. *Christopher Columbus.* Trans. by Mary Lee Grisanti. Morristown, NJ: Silver Burdett, 1985.

Montgomery County Public Library Staff. *A Teacher's Guide to Book Bird.* Illus. by Rachel Owings. Springfield, VA: CTI (Children's Television International), 1979. M156.

Montgomery, Elizabeth R. *Walt Disney: Master of Make-Believe.* Champaign, IL: Garrard, 1971.

Montgomery, Lucy Maud. *The Golden Road.* New York: Bantam, 1989.

———. *Anne of Avonlea.* Airmont pb., Bantam pb., Signet pb. M63, M68.

———. *Anne of Green Gables.* Airmont pb., Bantam pb., Signet pb. M64, M65, M66, M67, M68.

———. *Anne of Green Gables.* Boston: Godine, 1989. M64, M65, M66, M67, M68.

———. *Anne of Green Gables.* Illus. by Jody Lee. New York: Putam, 1984. M64, M65, M66, M67, M68.

———. *Anne of Ingleside.* New York: Bantam, 1987.

———. *Anne of the Island.* New York: Bantam, 1987.

———. *Anne of Windy Poplars.* New York: Bantam, 1987.

———. *Anne's House of Dreams.* New York: Bantam, 1987.

———. *Chronicles of Avonlea.* New York: Bantam, 1988.

———. *Emily Climbs.* New York: Bantam, 1983.

———. *Emily of the New Moon.* New York: Bantam, 1983.

———. *Emily's Quest.* New York: Bantam, 1983.

———. *Rainbow Valley.* New York: Bantam, 1985.

———. *Rilla of Ingleside.* New York: Bantam, 1985.

———. *Story Girl.* New York: Grosset, 1911.

Moon Buggy. Crystal Lake, IL: Rigby, n.d.

Mooney, Bel. *The Stove Haunting.* Boston: Houghton, 1988.

Moore, Ruth N. *The Ghost Town Mystery.* Scottsdale, PA: Herald Press, 1987. pb.

Moore, Lillian. *I'll Meet You at Cucumbers.* Illus. by Sharon Wooding. New York: Atheneum, 1988.

More Books from Cover to Cover, Teacher's Guide. Washington, DC: WETA-TV, n.d. M897.

Morey, Walter. *Gentle Ben.* New York: Dutton, 1965. Avon Camelot pb.

———. *Kavik the Wolf Dog.* New York: Dutton, 1968.

———. *Scrub Dog of Alaska.* New York: Dutton, 1971. Hillsboro, OR: Blue Heron pb., 1987.

———. *Year of the Black Pony.* Blue Heron, 1989.

Morgan, Gwyneth. *Life in a Medieval Village.* Minneapolis: Cambridge Univ./Lerner, 1975, 1982.

Morimato, Junko. *Inch Boy.* New York: Viking, 1986.

———. *Mouse's Marriage.* Illus. by the author. New York: Viking, 1986. Puffin pb.

Moritz, Charles, ed. *"Ballard, Robert D."* *Current Biography Yearbook, 1986.* Bronx, NY: Wilson, 1987. Pages 27–31.

Morris, Ann. *Hats, Hats, Hats.* Photos by Ken Heyman. New York: Lothrop, 1989.

Morris, Willie. *Good Old Boy: A Delta Boyhood.* New York: Oxford, MS: Uoknapatawpha, 1980. pb.

Morrison, Dorothy Nafus. *Somebody's Horse.* New York: Atheneum, 1986. Troll pb.

———. *Whisper Again.* New York: Atheneum, 1987.

———. *Whisper Goodbye.* New York: Atheneum, 1985.

Mosel, Arlene. *The Funny Little Woman.* Illus. by Blair Lent. New York: Dutton, 1972. pb.

Moseley, Keith. *Dinosaurs: A Lost World.* Illus. by Robert Cremins. New York: Putnam, 1984.

Moskin, Marietta. *I Am Rosemarie*. New York: Day, 1972. Dell pb.

Moskowitz, Rochelle. *A Teacher's Guide to Readit!* Bloomington, IN: AIT (Agency for Instructional Technology), 1982. M1003.

———. *A Teacher's Guide to Storybound.* Springfield, VA: CTI (Children's Television International), 1980. M1269.

Moss, Joy F. *Focus Units in Literature: A Handbook for Elementary School Teachers.* Urbana, IL: National Council of Teachers of English, 1984.

Most, Bernard. *Dinosaur's Cousins*. Illus. by the author. San Diego: Harcourt, 1987.

———. *If the Dinosaurs Came Back*. Illus. by the author. San Diego: Harcourt, 1978. Voyager pb.

———. *Whatever Happened to the Dinosaurs?* Illus. by the author. San Diego: Harcourt, 1984. Voyager pb.

Motyka, Sally M. *An Ordinary Day*. New York: Simon and Schuster, 1989. pb.

Mowat, Farley. *Lost in the Barrens*. Illus. by Charles Green. Boston: Joy Street/Little, 1956. Bantam Starfire. M759.

———. *Owls in the Family*. Illus. by Robert Frankenberg. Boston: Little, 1961. Bantam Skylark pb.

———. "The Voice of the Whale," in Durr, W. *Triumphs*. Boston: Houghton, 1986. Pages 434–48.

Muffs, Judith H. and Dennis B. Klein. *The Holocaust in Books and Films: A Selected Annotated List*. New York: Hippocrene, 1986.

Muller, Jorg. *The Changing City*. Illus. by the author. New York: McElderry/Macmillan, 1977.

———. *The Changing Countryside*. Illus. by the author. New York: McElderry/Macmillan, 1977.

Muncy, Patricia T. *Springboard to Creative Thinking*. Englewood Cliffs, NJ: Center for Applied Research, 1985.

Munro, Roxie. *Blimps*. Illus. by the author. New York: Dutton, 1988.

———. *Christmastime in New York City*. Illus. by the author. New York: Dodd, 1987.

———. *The Inside-Outside Book of London*. Illus. by the author. New York: Dutton, 1989.

———. *The Inside-Outside Book of New York City*. Illus. by the author. New York: Dodd, 1985.

———. *The Inside-Outside Book of Washington, D.C.* Illus. by the author. New York: Dutton, 1987.

Munsch, Robert. *Thomas' Snowsuit*. Illus. by Michael Martchenko. Toronto: Annick, 1985. Firefly pb.

Murphy, Jill. *Five Minutes' Peace*. Illus. by the author. New York: Putnam, 1986.

Murphy, Jim. *The Last Dinosaur*. Illus. by Mark Alan Weatherby. New York: Scholastic, 1988.

Murphy, Shirley Rousseau. *Dragonbards*. New York: Harper, 1988. pb.

———. *The Ivory Lyre*. New York: Harper, 1987. Starwanderer pb., Trophy pb.

———. *Nightpool*. New York: Harper, 1985. Starwanderer pb. Trophy pb.

———. *Valentine for a Dragon*. Illus. by Kay Chorao. New York: Atheneum, 1984.

Murray, Michele. *The Crystal Nights*. New York: Seabury, 1973.

Murray, John. *Mystery Plays for Young Actors*. Boston: Plays, 1984.

Murrow, Liza K. *West Against the Wind*. New York: Holiday, 1987.

Musgrove, Margaret. *Ashanti to Zulu*. Illus. by Leo and Diane Dillon. New York: Dial, 1976. Pied Piper pb. M97, M98.

Mwenye. See Hadithi, Mwenye.

Myers, Walter Dean. *Ambush in the Amazon*. New York: Puffin, 1986.

———. *Adventure in Granada*. New York: Puffin pb., 1985.

———. *Duel in the Desert*. New York: Penguin, 1986. Puffin pb.

———. *The Hidden Shrine*. New York: Penguin, 1985. Puffin pb.

———. *Me, Mop, and the Moondance Kid*. Illus. by Rodney Pate. New York: Delacorte, 1988.

———. *Mojo and the Russians*. New York: Viking, 1977. M892.

———. *The Scorpions*. New York: Harper, 1988.

———. *Won't Know Till I Get There*. New York: Viking, 1982. Puffin pb. M1483.

Nanus, Susan and Marc Kornblatt. *Mission to World War II*. New York: Bantam, 1986.

Nathanson, Laura. *The Trouble with Wednesdays*. New York: Putnam, 1986. Bantam pb.

National Council for the Social Studies. "Notable 1989 Children's Trade Books in the Field of Social Studies." *Social Education*. Vol. 54, #4. April/May 1990. Annual.

National Council of Teachers of English. *Adventuring with Books: A Booklist for Pre-K–Grade 6*, 9th ed. Urbana, IL: National Council of Teachers of English, 1989.

———. "Teacher's Choices." *Language Arts*. April issues, 1981–1986. M704.

National Geographic Society. *The National Geographic Index: 1888–1988*. Washington, DC: National Geographic, 1988.

Page, Michael. *The Great Bullocky Race*. Illus. by Robert Ingpen. New York: Dodd, 1988.

Palin, Michael. *The Mirrorstone: A Ghost Story with Holograms*. New York: Knopf, 1986.

Parish, Peggy. *Amelia Bedelia*. Illus. by Fritz Siebel. New York: Harper, 1963. Trophy pb. M35, M36.

———. *Amelia Bedelia and the Baby*. Illus. by Lynn Sweat. New York: Greenwillow, 1981. Avon Camelot pb.

———. *Amelia Bedelia and the Surprise Shower*. Illus. by F. Siebel. New York: Harper, 1966. Trophy pb. M36, M37.

———. *Amelia Bedelia Goes Camping*. Illus. by L. Sweat. New York: Greenwillow, 1986. Avon Camelot pb.

———. *Amelia Bedelia Helps Out*. Illus. by L. Sweat. New York: Greenwillow, 1979.

———. *Amelia Bedelia's Family Album*. Illus. by L. Sweat. New York: Greenwillow, 1988.

———. *Come Back: Amelia Bedelia*. Illus. by Wallace Tripp. New York: Harper, 1978. Trophy pb. M36, M286.

———. *Dinosaur Time*. Illus. by Arnold Lobel. New York: Harper, 1974. Trophy pb. Scholastic pb.

———. *Good Work, Amelia Bedelia*. Illus. by L. Sweat. New York: Greenwillow, 1976. Avon Camelot pb.

———. *Merry Christmas, Amelia Bedelia*. Illus. by L. Sweat. New York: Greenwillow, 1986. Avon Camelot pb. M36, M848.

———. *Play Ball, Amelia Bedelia*. Illus. by W. Tripp. New York: Harper, 1972. Trophy pb. Scholastic pb. M36, M1048.

———. *Scruffy*. Illus. by Kelly Oechsli. New York: Harper, 1988.

———. *Teach Us, Amelia Bedelia*. Illus. by L. Sweat. New York: Greenwillow, 1977. Scholastic pb.

———. *Thank You, Amelia Bedelia*. Illus. by F. Siebel. New York: Harper, 1964. Trophy pb.

Park, Barbara. *Almost Starring Skinnybones*. New York: Knopf, 1988.

———. *Beanpole*. New York: Knopf, 1983. Avon Flare pb.

———. *The Kid in the Red Jacket*. New York: Knopf, 1987. pb. M691.

———. *Operation: Dump the Chump*. New York: Knopf, 1982. Avon Camelot pb.

———. *Skinnybones*. New York: Knopf, 1982.

Park, Ruth. *Playing Beatie Bow*. New York: Atheneum, 1982. Puffin pb.

Parker, Cam. *Camp Off-The-Wall*. New York: Avon Camelot, 1987. pb.

Parker, Nancy Winslow. *Love from Aunt Betty*. Illus. by the author. New York: Dodd, 1983.

———. *The United Nations from A to Z*. New York: Dodd, 1985.

Parker, Nancy Winslow and Joan Richards Wright. *Bugs*. Illus. by N. W. Parker. New York: Greenwillow, 1987. M189, 1098.

Parker, Steve. *Dinosaurs and Their World*. New York: Putnam, 1988.

———. *Living with Blindness*. New York: Watts, 1989.

Parkinson, Kathy. *The Farmer in the Dell*. Illus. by N. Parkinson. Niles, IL: Whitman, 1988.

Parnall, Peter. *The Apple Tree*. Illus. by the author. New York: Macmillan, 1988.

———. *Winter Barn*. Illus. by the author. New York: Macmillan, 1986.

Parramon, J. M. and J. J. Puig. *Touch*. Illus. by Maria Rius. New York: Barrons, 1985. pb.

Pascal, Francine. *The Hand-Me-Down Kid*. New York: Viking, 1980. Dell pb. M530.

———. *Hangin' Out with Cici*. New York: Viking, 1977. Dell pb. M928.

Patent, Dorothy H. *All About Whales*. New York: Holiday, 1987.

———. *Appaloosa Horses*. Photos by William Munoz. New York: Holiday, 1988.

———. *Arabian Horses*. New York: Holiday, 1982.

———. *Christmas Trees*. Photos by W. Munoz. New York: Dodd, 1987.

———. *Dolphins and Porpoises*. New York: Holiday, 1987.

———. *Draft Horses*. Photos by W. Munoz. New York: Holiday, 1986.

———. *A Horse of a Different Color*. Photos by W. Munoz. New York: Putnam, 1988.

———. *Humpback Whales*. Illus. by Mark Farrari and D. Glockner-Farrari. New York: Holiday, 1989.

———. *Quarter Horses*. Photos by W. Munoz. New York: Holiday, 1985.

———. *Spider Magic*. New York: Holiday, 1982.

———. *Whales: Giants of the Deep*. New York: Holiday, 1984.

———. *Wheat: The Golden Harvest*. Photos by W. Munoz. New York: Dodd, 1987.

———. *Where the Wild Horses Roam*. Photos by W. Munoz. New York: Clarion, 1989.

Paterson, Katherine. *Bridge to Terabithia*. Illus. by Donna Diamond. New York: Crowell, 1977. Avon Camelot pb., Trophy pb., Scholastic pb. M180, M181, M182, M183, M250a, M491, M843.

———. *Bridge to Terabithia*. Large print edition. Santa Barbara: ABC-CLIO, 1987. M180, M181, M182, M183, M250, M491, M843.

Peck, Richard. *Blossom Culp and the Sleep of Death.* New York: Delacorte, 1986. Dell pb. M1093.

———. *The Dreadful Future of Blossom Culp.* New York: Delacorte, 1983. Dell pb. M1093.

———. *The Ghost Belonged to Me.* New York: Viking, 1975. Dell pb. M492, M1093.

———. *The Ghost Belonged to Me.* Large print edition. Santa Barbara: ABC-CLIO, n.d. M492, M1093.

———. *Ghosts I Have Been.* New York: Viking, 1977. Dell pb. M495, M1093.

Peck, Robert Newton. *Jo Silver.* Englewood, FL: Pineapple Pr., 1985.

———. *Soup.* Illus. by Charles Gehm. New York: Knopf, 1974. Dell pb.

———. *Soup and Me.* Illus. by Charles Lilly. New York: Knopf, 1975. Dell pb. M1231.

———. *Soup and Me.* Large Print edition. Santa Barbara: ABC-CLIO, 1990. M1231.

———. *Soup for President.* Illus. by Ted Lewin. New York: Knopf, 1978. Dell pb. M1232.

———. *Soup in the Saddle.* Illus. by Charles Robinson. New York: Knopf, 1983. Dell pb.

———. *Soup on Fire.* Illus. by C. Robinson. New York: Knopf, 1987. Dell pb.

———. *Soup on Ice.* Illus. by C. Robinson. New York: Knopf, 1985. Dell pb.

———. *Soup on Wheels.* Illus. by C. Robinson. New York: Knopf, 1981. Dell pb.

———. *Soup's Drum.* Illus. by C. Robinson. New York: Knopf, 1980. Dell pb.

———. *Soup's Goat.* Illus. by C. Robinson. New York: Knopf, 1984. Dell pb.

———. *Soup's Hoop.* Illus. by C. Robinson. New York: Doubleday, 1990.

———. *Soup's Uncle.* New York: Delacorte, 1988.

Pedersen, Stella. *The Tiny Patient.* New York: Knopf, 1989.

Peek, Merle. *The Balancing Act: A Counting Song.* Illus. by the author. New York: Clarion, 1987.

———. *Farewell to Shady Glade.* Boston: Houghton, 1966.

———. *Mary Wore Her Red Dress and Henry Wore His Green Sneakers.* Illus. by the author. New York: Clarion, 1985.

Peet, Bill. *Big Bad Bruce.* Illus. by the author. Boston: Houghton, 1977. pb. M139, M143.

———. *Bill Peet: An Autobiography.* Illus. by the author. Boston: Houghton, 1989. M143.

———. *Buford, the Little Bighorn.* Illus. by the author. Boston: Houghton, 1983. pb. M143.

———. *The Caboose Who Got Loose.* Illus. by the author. Boston: Houghton, 1971. pb. M143.

———. *Capyboppy.* Illus. by the author. Boston: Houghton, 1966. pb. M143.

———. *Chester the Worldly Pig.* Illus. by the author. Boston: Houghton, 1965. Voyager pb. M143.

———. *Cowardly Clyde.* Illus. by the author. Boston: Houghton, 1979. M143.

———. *Cyrus the Unsinkable Sea Serpent.* Illus. by the author. Boston: Houghton, 1975. M143.

———. *Eli.* Illus. by the author. Boston: Houghton, 1978. pb. M143.

———. *Ella.* Illus. by the author. Boston: Houghton, 1964. pb. M143.

———. *Encore for Eleanor.* Illus. by the author. Boston: Houghton, 1981. M143.

———. *Fly Homer Fly.* Illus. by the author. Boston: Houghton, 1976. M143.

———. *The Gnats of Knotty Pine.* Illus. by the author. Boston: Houghton, 1975. M143.

———. *How Droofus the Dragon Lost His Head.* Illus. by the author. Boston: Houghton, 1971. M143.

———. *Hubert's Hair-Raising Adventure.* Illus. by the author. Boston: Houghton, 1959. pb. M143.

———. *Huge Harold.* Illus. by the author. Boston: Houghton, 1961. pb.

———. *The Kweeks of Kookatumdee.* Illus. by the author. Boston: Houghton, 1985. Sandpiper pb. M143.

———. *The Luckiest One of All.* Illus. by the author. Boston: Houghton, 1982. M143.

———. *Merle the High Flying Squirrel.* Illus. by the author. Boston: Houghton, 1974. pb. M143.

———. *No Such Things.* Illus. by the author. Boston: Houghton, 1983. M143.

———. *Pamela Camel.* Illus. by the author. Boston: Houghton, 1984. Sandpiper pb. M143.

———. *The Pinkish, Purplish, Bluish Egg.* Illus. by the author. Boston: Houghton, 1963. M143.

———. *Randy's Dandy Lions.* Illus. by the author. Boston: Houghton, 1964. M143.

———. *Smokey.* Illus. by the author. Boston: Houghton, 1962. pb. M143.

———. *The Spooky Tail of Prewitt Peacock.* Illus. by the author. Boston: Houghton, 1979. pb. M143.

———. *Whingdingdilly.* Illus. by the author. Boston: Houghton, 1970. M143.

———. *Wump World.* Illus. by the author. Boston: Houghton, 1970. M143.

Pelgram, Els. *The Winter When Time Was Frozen.* Trans. by Maryka and Raphael Rudnik. New York: Morrow, 1980.

————. *More Creative Encounters: Activities to Expand Children's Responses to Literature.* Illus. by L. Welker. Littleton, CO: Libraries Unlimited, 1988.

Pollack, Penny. *Stall Buddies.* Illus. by Gail Owens. New York: Putnam, 1984.

Polushkin, Maria. *Baby Brother Blues.* Illus. by Ellen Weiss. New York: Bradbury, 1987.

Pomerantz, Barbara. *Who Will Lead Kiddush.* Illus. by Donna Ruff. New York: Union of American Congregations, 1985. pb.

Pomerantz, Charlotte. *The Half-Birthday Party.* Illus. by DyAnne DiSalvo-Ryan. New York: Clarion, 1984.

————. *How Many Trucks Can a Tow Truck Tow?* Illus. by R. W. Alley. New York: Random, 1987.

————. *One Duck, Another Duck.* Illus. by Jose Aruego and Ariane Dewey. New York: Greenwillow, 1984.

Pope, Joyce. *Taking Care of Your Rats and Mice.* New York: Watts, 1988.

Porte, Barbara. *Harry in Trouble.* Illus. by Yossi Abolafia. New York: Greenwillow, 1989. Dell pb.

————. *Harry's Dog.* Illus. by Y. Abolafia. New York: Greenwillow, 1983. Scholastic pb.

————. *Harry's Mom.* Illus. by Y. Abolafia. New York: Greenwillow, 1985.

————. *Harry's Visit.* Illus. by Y. Abolafia. New York: Greenwillow, 1983.

————. *Ruthann and Her Pig.* Illus. by Sucie Stevenson. New York: Orchard, 1989.

Porter, Gene Stratton. *Girl of the Limberlost.* New York: Grosset and Dunlap, 1909. Dell pb.

Posell, Elsa Z. *Homecoming.* San Diego: Harcourt, 1987.

Posner, Marcia. *Jewish Children's Books: How to Choose Them, How to Use Them.* New York: Jewish Education Hadassah and the Women's Zionist Organization of America, 1986.

Potter, Beatrix. *Sly Old Cat.* Illus. by the author. New York: Warne, 1971.

————. *The Story of a Fierce Bad Rabbit.* Illus. by the author. New York: Warne, 1906. M1297.

————. *The Story of Miss Moppet.* Illus. by the author. New York: Warne, 1906. M1297.

————. *The Tailor of Gloucester.* Illus. by the author. New York: Warne, 1903.

————. *The Tale of Benjamin Bunny.* Illus. by the author. New York: Warne, 1904. pb. M1005.

————. *The Tale of Jemima Puddleduck.* Illus. by the author. New York: Warne, 1908. pb. M1005, M1297.

————. *The Tale of Johnny Town Mouse.* Illus. by the author. New York: Warne, 1918. pb.

————. *The Tale of Mrs. Tittlemouse.* Illus. by the author. New York: Warne, 1910. pb. M1297.

————. *The Tale of Mr. Jeremy Fisher.* Illus. by the author. New York: Warne, 1906. pb. M1005, M1298, M1299.

————. *The Tale of Peter Rabbit.* Illus. by the author. New York: Warne, 1902. pb. M124, M125, M1005.

————. *The Tale of Squirrel Nutkin.* Illus. by the author. New York: Warne, 1903. pb.

————. *The Tale of Tom Kitten.* Illus. by the author. New York: Warne, 1907. pb. M1005, M1297.

————. *The Tale of Two Bad Mice.* Illus. by the author. New York: Warne, 1904. pb. M1005, M1300, M1301.

————. *Two Bad Mice.* New York: Warne, 1986. M1005, M1300, M1301.

————. *The World of Peter Rabbit.* Illus. by the author. New York: Warne, 1988. M1005, M1297.

Poulin, Stephane. *Ah! Belle Cite/A Beautiful City.* Plattsburgh, NY: Tundra, 1985.

————. *Can You Catch Josephine?* Plattsburgh, NY: Tundra, 1987.

————. *Could You Stop Josephine?* Plattsburgh, NY: Tundra, 1988.

————. *Have You Seen Josephine?* Plattsburgh, NY: Tundra, 1986. pb.

————. *Peux-Tu Attraper Joséphine?* Plattsburgh, NY: Tundra, 1987. pb.

————. *Pourrais-Tu Arrêter Joséphine?* Plattsburgh, NY: Tundra, 1988.

Powzyk, Joyce. *Tracking the Wild Chimpanzees in Kiriba National Park.* New York: Lothrop, 1988.

Praeger, Arthur and Emily Praeger. *World War II Resistance Stories.* Illus. by Steven Assel. New York: Watts, 1979.

Prall, J. *My Sister's Special.* Photos by Linda Gray. Chicago: Children's Press, 1985.

Prater, John. *The Perfect Day.* New York: Dutton, 1987.

Prelutsky, Jack, ed. *Read-Aloud Rhymes for the Very Young.* Illus. by Marc Brown. New York: Knopf, 1986. pb.

————. *Tyrannosaurus Was a Beast.* Illus. by Arnold Lobel. New York: Greenwillow, 1988.

Price, Margaret. *A Child's Book of Myths and Enchantment Tales.* Illus. by the author. New York: Macmillan, 1986.

Provenzo, Eugene and Asterie B. Provenzo. *Pursuing the Past: A Teacher's Handbook.* Menlo Park, CA: Addison-Wesley, 1984.

Provensen, Alice and Martin Provensen. *The Glorious Flight: Across the Channel with Louis Bleriot*. Illus. by the authors. New York: Viking, 1983. Penguin pb. M500, M501, M502.

———. *Leonardo da Vinci: The Artist, Inventor, Scientist in Three-Dimensional Movable Pictures*. Illus. by the authors. New York: Viking, 1984.

———. *Shaker Lane*. Illus. by the authors. New York: Viking, 1987.

———. *Town and Country*. Illus. by the authors. New York: Crown, 1984.

Provost, Gary and Gail Levine-Provost. *David and Max*. Philadelphia: Jewish Publication Society, 1988.

Pryor, Bonnie. *The House on Maple Street*. Illus. by Beth Peck. New York: Morrow, 1987.

———. *Porcupine Mouse*. Illus. by Maryjane Begin. New York: Morrow, 1988.

Purdy, Carol. *Iva Dunnit and the Big Wind*. Illus. by Steven Kellogg. New York: Dial, 1985. Pied Piper pb.

———. *Least of All*. Illus. by Tim Arnold. New York: McElderry/Macmillan, 1987.

Pyle, Howard. *The Merry Adventures of Robin Hood of Great Reknown in Nottinghamshire*. New York: Scribner, 1976. Dover pb. M4, M5, M409.

———. *The Story of King Arthur and His Knights*. Illus. by the author. New York: Scribner, 1984. M409, M1303, M1304.

Quackenbush, Robert. *City Trucks*. Illus. by the author. Chicago: Whitman, 1981.

———. *Danger in Tibet*. Illus. by the author. New York: Pippin, 1989.

———. *Detective Mole*. Illus. by the author. New York: Lothrop, 1976.

———. *Detective Mole and the Haunted Castle Mystery*. Illus. by the author. New York: Lothrop, 1985.

———. *Detective Mole and the Halloween Mystery*. Illus. by the author. New York: Lothrop, 1981.

———. *Dig to Disaster*. Illus. by the author. Englewood Cliffs, NJ: Prentice Hall, 1982.

———. *Dogsled to Dread: A Miss Mallard Mystery*. Illus. by the author. Englewood Cliffs, NJ: Prentice Hall, 1987.

———. *Express Train to Trouble*. Illus. by the author. Englewood Cliffs, NJ: Prentice Hall, 1981.

———. *Gondola to Danger*. Illus. by the author. Englewood Cliffs, NJ: Prentice Hall, 1983.

———. *Mark Twain? What Kind of Name Is That?* Illus. by the author. Englewood Cliffs, NJ: Prentice Hall, 1984. M817, M835.

———. *Mr. Snow Bunting's Secret*. Illus. by the author. New York. Lothrop, 1978.

———. *Once Upon a Time: A Story of the Brothers Grimm*. Illus. by the author. Englewood Cliffs, NJ: Prentice Hall, 1985.

———. *Rickshaw to Horror*. Illus. by the author. Englewood Cliffs, NJ: Prentice Hall, 1984.

———. *Sherlock Chick and the Peekaboo Mystery*. Illus. by the author. New York: Parents, 1987.

———. *Sherlock Chick's First Case*. Illus. by the author. New York: Parents, 1986.

———. *Stairway to Doom*. Illus. by the author. Englewood Cliffs, NJ: Prentice Hall, 1983.

———. *Surfboard to Peril*. Illus. by the author. Englewood Cliffs, NJ: Prentice Hall, 1986.

———. *Taxi to Intrigue*. Illus. by the author. Englewood Cliffs, NJ: Prentice Hall, 1984.

———. *Who Said There's No Man on the Moon? A Story of Jules Verne*. Illus. by the author. Englewood Cliffs, NJ: Prentice Hall, 1985. M680.

Quicke, Kenneth. *Let's Look at Horses*. Illus. by Wendy Meadway. New York: Bookwright/Watts, 1988.

Rabe, Bernice. *Margaret's Moves*. Illus. by Julie Downing. New York: Dutton, 1987. Apple pb.

———. *A Smooth Move*. Illus. by Linda Shute. Niles, IL: Whitman, 1987.

———. *Where's Chimpy?* Photos by Diane Schmidt. Niles, IL: Whitman, 1988.

Rabinowitz, Ann. *Knight on Horseback*. New York: Macmillan, 1987.

Raboff, Ernest. *Paul Klee*. New York: Harper, 1968. Trophy pb.

Radin, Ruth. *High in the Mountains*. New York: Macmillan, 1989.

———. *Raffi's Singable Songbook*. Illus. by Joyce Yamamoto. New York: Crown, 1987. M1200.

Radlauer, Ed and R. S. Radlauer. *Gymnastics School*. Photos by the author. New York: Watts, 1976.

Rahn, Joan. *Animals That Changed History*. Illus. by the author. New York: Atheneum, 1986.

———. *Eyes and Seeing*. New York: Atheneum, 1981.

Raines, Shirley C. and Robert J. Canady. *Story S-t-r-e-t-c-h-e-r-s: Activities to Expand Children's Favorite Books*. Mount Rainier, MD: Gryphon, 1989.

——. *My Brother Louis Measures Worms*. New York: Harper, 1988.

Robinson, Charles A. *Ancient Egypt, Second Edition*. Revised by Lorna Greenberg. New York: Watts, 1984.

Roche, P. K. *Webster and Arnold Go Camping*. Illus. by the author. New York: Viking, 1989. pb.

Rochman, Hazel. *Tales of Love and Terror: Booktalking the Classics, Old and New*. Chicago: American Library Association, 1987. pb. M1305.

Rockwell, Anne. *Big Wheels*. New York: Dutton, 1986.

——. *Bikes*. New York: Dutton, 1987.

——. *Cars*. New York: Dutton, 1984.

——. *Come to Town*. New York: Crowell, 1987.

——. *Fire Engines*. New York: Dutton, 1986.

——. *First Comes Spring*. New York: Crowell, 1985.

——. *Hugo at the Window*. New York: Macmillan, 1988.

——. *The Night We Slept Outside*. New York: Macmillan, 1983. pb.

——. *Planes*. New York: Dutton, 1985.

——. *Trains*. New York: Dutton, 1988.

——. *Trucks*. New York: Dutton, 1984. Unicorn pb.

Rockwell, Anne and Harlow. *At the Beach*. New York: Macmillan, 1987.

——. *Happy Birthday to Me*. New York: Macmillan, 1982.

Rockwell, Thomas. *How to Eat Fried Worms*. Illus. by Emily McCully. New York: Watts, 1973. Dell pb. M601, M602, M603, M604, M1052.

——. *How to Eat Fried Worms*. Large print edition. Santa Barbara: ABC-CLIO, 1988. M601, M602, M603, M604, M1052.

——. *How to Eat Fried Worms and Other Plays*. New York: Delacorte, 1980. M601, M602, M603, M604, M1052.

——. *How to Fight a Girl*. Illus. by Gioia Fiammenghi. New York: Watts, 1987. Dell pb.

Rockwood, Joyce. *Groundhog's Horse*. Illus. by Victor Kalin. New York: Holt, 1978. M521a.

Rodda, Emily. *The Pigs Are Flying!* Illus. by Noela Young. New York: Greenwillow, 1988.

Roe, Eileen. *Staying with Grandma*. Illus. by Jacqueline Rogers. New York: Bradbury, 1989.

Roennfeldt, Robert. *A Day on the Avenue*. New York: Viking, 1983.

Rofes, Eric. *The Kids' Book About Death and Dying*. Boston: Little, 1985.

——. *The Kids' Book About Parents by Students at Fayerweather Street School*. Boston: Houghton, 1984. Pocket Books pb.

——. *The Kids' Book of Divorce*. Lexington, MA: Lewis Pubs., 1981. Random pb.

Rogasky, Barbara. *Smoke and Ashes: The Story of the Holocaust*. New York: Holiday, 1988.

Rogers, Fred. *Daniel Striped Tiger Gets Ready For Bed*. New York: Random, 1988. M886, M887.

——. *First Experiences: Going on an Airplane*. Photos by Jim Judkis. New York: Putnam, 1989. pb.

——. *First Experiences: Going to Day Care*. Illus. by J. Judkis. New York: Putnam, 1985. pb. M886, M887.

——. *First Experiences: Going to the Doctor*. New York: Putnam, 1986. pb. M886, M887.

——. *First Experiences: Going to the Hospital*. Photos by J. Judkis. New York: Putnam, 1988. pb. M886, M887.

——. *First Experiences: Going to the Potty*. Photos by J. Judkis. New York: Putnam, 1986. pb. M886, M887.

——. *First Experiences: Making Friends*. Photos by J. Judkis. New York: Putnam, 1987. pb. M886, M887.

——. *First Experiences: Moving*. Photos by J. Judkis. New York: Putnam, 1987. pb. M886, M887.

——. *First Experiences: The New Baby*. Photos by J. Judkis. New York: Putnam, 1985. pb. M886, M887.

——. *First Experiences: When a Pet Dies*. Photos by J. Judkis. New York: Putnam, 1988. pb. M886, M887.

——. *Mr. Rogers' Playbook: Insights and Activities for Parents and Children*. New York: Berkley, 1986. M886, M887.

——. *Mr. Rogers Talks With Families About Divorce*. New York: Berkley, 1987. M886, M887.

——. *Mr. Rogers Talks With Parents*. New York: Berkley, 1985. M886, M887.

——. *Mr. Rogers' Songbook*. Illus. by Steven Kellogg. Music by John Costa. New York: Random, 1970. M886, M887.

——. *No One Can Ever Take Your Place*. New York: Random, 1988. pb. M886, M887.

——. *A Trolley Visit to Make-Believe*. Illus. by Pat Sustendal. New York: Random, 1987.

——. *When Monsters Seem Real*. New York: Random, 1988. pb. M886, M887.

——. *Wishes Don't Make Things Come True*. New York: Random, 1988. pb. M886, M887.

——. *You Can Never Go Down the Drain*. New York: Random, 1988. M886, M887.

Rogers, Fred and Barry Head. *Mr. Rogers: How Families Grow.* New York: Berkley, 1988. M886, M887.

Rogers, Fred and Pat Sustendal. *If We Were All the Same.* New York: Random, 1988. pb. M886, M887.

Rogers, Jean. *Runaway Mittens.* Illus. by Rie Munoz. New York: Greenwillow, 1988.

Rogers, Paul. *From Me to You.* Illus. by Jane Johnson. New York: Orchard, 1987. M886, M887.

Rogers, Richard and Oscar Hammerstein II. *The Sound of Music: A New Musical Play.* New York: Random, 1960. M1228.

Rollock, Barbara T. *Public Library Services for Children.* Hamden, CT: Library Professional Publications, 1988.

Roop, Peter and Connie Roop. *Dinosaurs: Opposing Viewpoints.* St. Paul, MN: Greenhaven, 1988.

———. *Keep the Lights Burning, Abbie.* Illus. by Peter Hanson. Minneapolis: Carolrhoda, 1985. Lerner pb. M688, M689, M1184.

———. *Space Out! Jokes About Outer Space.* Illus. by Joan Hanson. Minneapolis: Lerner, 1984.

Roos, Stephen. *My Horrible Secret.* Illus. by Carol Newson. New York: Delacorte, 1983. Dell pb.

Roos, Jean Carolyn. *Patterns of Reading: An Annotated Book List for Young Adults.* Chicago: American Library Association, 1961.

Rose, Anne. *Refugee.* New York: Dial, 1977.

Rosenberg, Maxine B. *Being Adopted.* Photos by George Ancona. New York: Lothrop, 1984.

———. *Finding a Way: Living With Exceptional Brothers and Sisters.* Photos by G. Ancona. New York: Lothrop, 1988.

———. *Growing Up Adopted.* New York: Bradbury, 1989.

———. *Making a New Home in America.* Photos by G. Ancona. New York: Lothrop, 1986.

———. *My Friend Leslie: The Story of a Handicapped Child.* Photos by G. Ancona. New York: Lothrop, 1983.

Rosenbloom, Joseph. *The Funniest Dinosaur Book Ever.* Illus. by Hans Willhelm. New York: Sterling, 1987.

———. *Wild West Riddles.* Illus. by Sanford Hoffman. New York: Sterling, 1983, 1985.

Rosenblum, Richard. *Airplane ABC.* New York: Atheneum, 1986.

———. *The Golden Age of Aviation.* New York: Atheneum, 1984. pb.

Ross, Pat. *Hannah's Fancy Notions.* Illus. by Bert Dodson. New York: Viking, 1988.

Ross, Tony. *Foxy Fables.* New York: Dial, 1986.

———. *Oscar Got the Blame.* New York: Dial, 1988.

Rossell, Seymour. *The Holocaust: The Fire that Raged.* New York: Watts, 1989.

Roth, Arthur. *Iceberg Hermit.* New York: Four Winds, 1974. Scholastic pb.

———. *Two for Survival.* New York: Scribner, 1976. Avon pb.

Roth, Susan and Ruth Phang. *Patchwork Tales.* New York: Atheneum, 1984.

Roth-Hana, Renee. *Touch Wood: A Girlhood in Occupied France.* New York: Four Winds, 1988. Puffin pb.

Rounds, Glen. *Blind Colt.* Illus. by the author. New York: Holiday, 1941, 1969. pb.

———. *Blind Outlaw.* Illus. by the author. New York: Holiday, 1980.

———. "The Prairie Schooner," in Smith, C. and V. Arnold, *Echoes of Time.* New York: Macmillan, 1986. Pages 500–11.

Roy, Ron. *Move Over, Wheelchairs Coming Through!* Photos by Rosemarie Hausherr. New York: Clarion, 1985.

Roy, Ron. *Whose Shoes Are These?* Photos by R. Hausherr. New York: Clarion, 1988.

Royds, Caroline, ed. *Poems for Young Children.* Illus. by Inga Moore. New York: Doubleday, 1986.

Rubenstein, Joshua. *Adolf Hitler.* New York: Watts, 1982.

Rubinstein, Erna F. *The Survivor in Us All: Four Young Sisters in the Holocaust.* Hamden, CT: Archon, 1983. pb.

Rubin, Arnold. *Hitler and the Nazis.* New York: Messner, 1977.

Rubinowicz, David. *The Diary of David Rubinowicz.* Trans. by Derek Bowman. Bellevue, WA: Creative Options, 1982.

Ruby, Lois. *The Pig-Out Inn.* Boston: Houghton, 1987.

Ruckman, Ivy. *Night of the Twisters.* New York: Crowell, 1984. Trophy pb.

Rudman, Marcia, ed. *Children's Literature: Resources for the Classroom.* Needham Heights, MA: Christopher Gordon, 1989.

Russell, William F. *Classic Myths to Read Aloud.* New York: Crown, 1989.

———. *More Classics to Read Aloud to Your Children.* New York: Crown, 1986.

Russo, Marisabina. *Why Do Grownups Have All the Fun?* New York: Greenwillow, 1987.

Rutland, Jonathan. *Planets.* Illus. by Ron Jobson. New York: Random, 1987. pb.

———. *See Inside an Airport.* New York: Watts, 1988.

Rutledge, Paul. *The Vietnamese in America.* Minneapolis: Lerner, 1987. pb.

———. *The Luttrell Village: Country Life in the Middle Ages.* New York: Crowell, 1983.

Sandak, Cass R. and Richard B. Morris. *Benjamin Franklin.* New York: Watts, 1986.

Sandburg, Carl. *Rootabaga Stories: Part One.* Illus. by Michael Hague. San Diego: Harcourt, 1988. pb.

———. *Rootabaga Stories: Part Two.* Illus. by M. Hague. San Diego: Harcourt, 1988. pb.

Sandin, Joan. *The Long Way to a New Land.* New York: Harper, 1981. Trophy pb.

———. *The Long Way Westward.* New York: Harper, 1989.

Santrey, Laurence. *Louisa May Alcott, Young Writer.* Illus. by Sandra Speidel. Mahwah, NJ: Troll, 1986. M772, M835.

Sargent, Pamela. *Earthseed.* New York: Starwanderer, 1987.

Sargent, Sarah. *Weird Henry Berg.* New York: Crown, 1980. Dell pb.

Sarnoff, Jane and Reynold Ruffins. *If You Were Really Superstitious.* New York: Scribner, 1980.

———. *Take Warning: A Book of Superstitions.* New York: Scribner, 1978.

Sasek, Miroslav. *This Is Historic Britain.* Illus. by the author. New York: Macmillan, 1974.

———. *This Is Hong Kong.* Illus. by the author. New York: Macmillan, 1965.

———. *This Is Paris.* Illus. by the author. New York: Macmillan, 1959.

Sattler, Helen. *Baby Dinosaurs.* Illus. by Jean Zallinger. New York: Lothrop, 1984.

———. *Dinosaurs of North America.* Illus. by Anthony Rao. New York: Lothrop, 1981.

———. *The Illustrated Dinosaur Dictionary.* Illus. by Pamela Carroll. New York: Lothrop, 1983.

———. *Peterosaurs: The Flying Reptiles.* Illus. by Christopher Santoro. New York: Lothrop, 1985.

———. *Sharks: The Super Fish.* Illus. by Jean Day Zallinger. New York: Lothrop, 1986.

———. *Train Whistles: Language in Code.* Illus. by Giulio Maestro. New York: Lothrop, 1977, 1985.

———. *Tyrannosaurus Rex and Its Kin: The Mesozoic Monsters.* New York: Lothrop, 1989.

———. *Whales: The Nomads of the Sea.* Illus. by J. D. Zallinger. New York: Morrow, 1987.

Sauer, Julia L. *Fog Magic.* Magnolia, MA: Peter Smith, n.d. Puffin pb.

Saunders, Scott. *Aurora Means Dawn.* Illus. by Jill Kastner. New York: Bradbury, 1989.

Saunders, Susan. *Stop the Presses!* New York: Minstrel, 1987.

Saville, Lynn. *Horses in the Circus Ring.* Photos by the author. New York: Dutton, 1989.

Savitt, Sam. *Horse to Remember.* New York: Viking, 1984. Puffin pb.

Sawicki, Norma J. *Something for Mom.* Illus. by Martha Weston. New York: Lothrop, 1987.

Say, Allen. *Lost Lake.* Illus. by the author. Boston: Houghton, 1989.

Scarry, Huck. *Aboard a Steam Locomotive: A Sketchbook.* Illus. by the author. Englewood Cliffs, NJ: Prentice Hall, 1987.

———. *Looking Into the Middle Ages: A Pop Up Book.* New York: Harper, 1985.

Scarry, Richard. *Pig Will and Pig Won't: A Book of Manners.* Illus. by the author. New York: Random, 1984.

Schatz, Dennis. *Dinosaurs: A Journey Through Time.* Seattle, WA: Pacific Science Center, 1987. pb.

Schlissel, Lillian. *Women's Diaries of the Westward Journey.* New York: Schocken, 1982. pb.

Schnieper, Claudia. *Amazing Spiders.* Minneapolis: Carolrhoda, 1989. Lerner pb.

———. *On the Trail of the Fox.* Trans. by Elise Scherer. Minneapolis: Carolrhoda, 1986.

Schoch, Tim. *Flash Fry, Private Eye.* Illus. by Wally Neibart. New York: Avon Camelot pb., 1986.

Schnurnberger, Lynne E. *Kings, Queens, Knights, and Jesters: Making Medieval Costumes.* Illus. by Alan Robert Showe. Photos by Barbara Brooks and P. Hort. New York: Harper, 1978.

Schotter, Roni. *Captain Snap and the Children of Vinegar Street.* Illus. by Marcia Sewall. New York: Orchard, 1989.

———. *Rhoda, Straight and True.* New York: Lothrop, 1986.

Schultz, Charles M. *Snoopy's Facts and Fun Book About Trucks.* New York: Random, n.d.

Schur, Maxine. *Hannah Szenes: A Song of Light.* Philadelphia: Jewish Publication Society, 1986.

Schwartz, Alvin. *In a Dark, Dark Room and Other Scary Stories.* Illus. by Dirk Zimmer. New York: Harper, 1984. Trophy pb. M630.

———. *Scary Stories to Tell in the Dark.* Illus. by Stephen Gammell. New York: Lippincott, 1981. Trophy pb. M1149.

———. *More Scary Stories to Tell in the Dark.* Illus. by S. Gammell. New York: Lippincott, 1984. Trophy pb. M899.

Schwartz, Amy. *Bea and Mr. Jones.* Illus. by the author. New York: Bradbury, 1983. Puffin pb.

———. *Oma and Bobo.* Illus. by the author. New York: Bradbury, 1987. Trophy pb.

Sierra, Judy. *The Flannel Board Storytelling Book*. Bronx, NY: Wilson, 1987.

Silverberg, Robert, ed. *Voyages in Time: Twelve Stories of Science Fiction*. New York: Meredith, 1967.

Silverman, Maida. *Dinosaur Babies*. New York: Simon and Schuster, 1988. Little Simon pb.

Silverstein, Alvin and Virginia Silverstein. *Heart Disease: America's #1 Killer*. New York: Lippincott, 1985.

———. *Mice: All About Them*. Photos by Robert Silverstein. New York: Lippincott, 1980.

———. *The Robots Are Here*. Illus. with photos. Englewood Cliffs, NJ: Prentice Hall, 1983.

———. *So You're Getting Braces: A Guide to Orthodontics*. Photos by the author. New York: Lippincott, 1978. pb.

Silverstein, Shel. *A Light in the Attic*. Illus. by the author. New York: Harper, 1981. M719.

———. *Where the Sidewalk Ends*. Illus. by the author. New York: Harper, 1974. M1447.

Silvey, Anita. "An Interview with Cynthia Rylant." *Horn Book*. Vol. 63, #6. November/December, 1987. Pages 695–702.

Simon, Norma. *All Kinds of Families*. Illus. by Joe Lasker. Niles, IL: Whitman, 1976.

Simon, Seymour. *Chip Rogers, Computer Whiz*. Illus. by Steve Miller. New York: Morrow, 1984.

———. *Earth: Our Planet in Space*. New York: Four Winds, 1984.

———. *Einstein Anderson Goes to Bat*. Illus. by Fred Winkowski. New York: Viking, 1982. Puffin pb.

———. *Einstein Anderson Lights Up the Sky*. Illus. by F. Winkowski. New York: Viking, 1982. Penguin pb.

———. *Einstein Anderson Makes Up for Lost Time*. New York: Viking, 1981. Puffin pb.

———. *Einstein Anderson, Science Sleuth*. Illus. by F. Winkowski. New York: Viking, 1980. Puffin pb.

———. *Einstein Anderson Sees Through the Invisible Man*. Illus. by F. Winkowski. New York: Viking, 1983. Penguin pb.

———. *Einstein Anderson Shocks His Friends*. Illus. by F. Winkowski. New York: Viking, 1980. Puffin pb.

———. *Einstein Anderson Tells a Comet's Tale*. Illus. by F. Winkowski. New York: Viking, 1981. Puffin pb.

———. *Icebergs and Glaciers*. Illus. with photos. New York: Morrow, 1987.

———. *Jupiter*. New York: Morrow, 1985.

———. *Killer Whales*. Illus. with photos. New York: Lippincott, 1978.

———. *The Largest Dinosaurs*. Illus. by Pam Carroll. New York: Macmillan, 1986.

———. *The Long Journey from Space*. Illus. with photos. New York: Crown, 1982.

———. *Mars*. New York: Morrow, 1987.

———. *Moon*. New York: Four Winds/Macmillan, 1984.

———. *Optical Illusion*. New York: Morrow, 1984. pb.

———. *Poisonous Snakes*. Illus. by William R. Downey. New York: Four Winds/Macmillan, 1981.

———. *Saturn*. New York: Morrow, 1985.

———. *The Smallest Dinosaurs*. Illus. by Anthony Rao. New York: Crown, 1982. pb.

———. *Stars*. New York: Morrow, 1986. Greenwillow pb.

———. *Storms*. New York: Morrow, 1989.

———. *Sun*. New York: Morrow, 1986. Greenwillow pb.

———. *Uranus*. New York: Morrow. 1987. Greenwillow pb.

———. *Whales*. New York: Crowell, 1989.

Simon, Sidney B. *Henry the Uncatchable Mouse*. Illus. by Nola Langner. New York: Norton, 1964.

Sims, Rudine. *Shadow and Substance: Afro-American Experiences in Contemporary Children's Fiction*. Urbana, IL: NCTE, 1982.

Singer, Isaac B. *Day of Pleasure: Stories of a Boy Growing Up in Warsaw*. Photos by Roman Vishniac. New York: Harper, 1978. Sunburst pb. M550, M842.

———. *Zlateh the Goat*. Illus. by Maurice Sendak. Trans. by Elizabeth Shub and I. B. Singer. New York: Harper, 1966. Trophy pb. M550, M842.

Singer, Marilyn. *It Can't Hurt Forever*. Illus. by Leigh Grant. New York: Harper, 1978.

———. *Turtle in July*. Illus. by Jerry Pinkney. New York: Macmillan, 1989.

Sis, Peter. *Going Up! A Color Counting Book*. Illus. by the author. New York: Greenwillow, 1989.

Skolsky, Mindy W. *The Whistling Teakettle and Other Stories About Hannah*. Illus. by Karen Ann Weinhaus. New York: Harper, 1977. M1456.

Skoofield, James. *Snow Country*. Illus. by Laura Jean Allen. New York: Harper, 1983.

Skurzynski, Gloria. *Lost in the Devil's Desert*. Illus. by Joseph Scrofani. New York: Lothrop, 1982.

———. *Trapped in the Slickrock Canyon*. Illus. by Daniel San Souci. New York: Lothrop, 1984.

———. *What Happened in Hamelin?* New York: Four Winds/Macmillan, 1979.

Murdocca. New York: Delacorte, 1979. Dell pb. M230.

———. *Encyclopedia Brown's Second Record Book of Weird and Wonderful Facts.* New York: Delacorte, 1981. M230.

———. *Encyclopedia Brown's Third Record Book of Weird and Wonderful Facts.* New York: Morrow, 1985. M230.

———. *More Two-Minute Mysteries.* New York: Scholastic, 1986. M230, M402.

———. *Still More Two-Minute Mysteries.* New York: Scholastic, 1986. M230, M402.

———. *Two-Minute Mysteries.* New York: Scholastic, 1987. M230, M402.

Sobol, Donald and Glenn Andrews. *Encyclopedia Brown Takes the Cake: A Cook and Case Book.* Illus. by Ib Ohlsson. New York: Four Winds/Macmillan, 1983. M230, M934.

Sobol, Harriet. *My Other Mother, My Other Father.* Photos by Patricia Agre. New York: Macmillan, 1979.

———. *We Don't Look Like Our Mom and Dad.* Photos by P. Agre. New York: Coward, 1984.

Somers, Albert B. and Janet Evans Worthington. *Response Guides for Teaching Children's Books.* Urbana, IL: National Council of Teachers of English, 1979.

Somme, Lauritz and Sybille Kalas. *The Penguin Family Book.* Trans. by Patricia Crompton. Saxonville, MA: Picture Book Studio, 1988.

Sommer-Bodenburg, Angela. *My Friend the Vampire.* Illus. by Amelie Glienke. New York: Dial, 1984. Minstrel pb.

———. *The Vampire Moves In.* New York: Dial, 1985. Pocket Book pb.

———. *The Vampire on the Farm.* New York: Dial, 1989. Minstrel pb.

———. *The Vampire Takes a Trip.* Illus. by A. Glienke. New York: Dial, 1985. Minstrel pb.

Sommerfeldt, Aimee. *Miriam.* Trans. by Pat Shaw Iversen. New York: Criterion, 1963. Scholastic pb.

Sonneborn, Ruth. *Friday Night Is Papa Night.* Illus. by Emily McCully. New York: Viking, 1970. Puffin pb.

Soule, Gardner. *Christopher Columbus: On the Green Sea of Darkness.* New York: Watts, 1988.

Space Shuttle. Crystal Lake, IL: Rigby, n.d.

Spaeth, Janet. *Laura Ingalls Wilder.* Boston: Twayne, 1987.

Speare, Elizabeth. *The Bronze Bow.* Boston: Houghton, 1961. Sandpiper pb. M187.

———. *Calico Captive.* Illus. by W. T. Mars. Boston: Houghton, 1957. Dell pb.

———. *Sara Bishop.* Boston: Houghton, 1980. Scholastic pb. M1406.

———. *The Sign of the Beaver.* Boston: Houghton, 1983. Dell pb. M957, M1190, M1191.

———. *The Sign of the Beaver.* Large print edition. Santa Barbara: ABC-CLIO, 1988. M1190, M1191.

———. "The Survival Story." *Horn Book Magazine.* Vol. 64, #2. March/April 1988. Pages 163–72.

———. *The Witch of Blackbird Pond.* Boston: Houghton, 1958. Dell pb. M1402, M1472.

———. *The Witch of Blackbird Pond.* Large print edition. Santa Barbara: ABC-CLIO, 1989. M1406.

Spenser, Edmund. *The Faerie Queene.* New York: Longmans, 1977.

Spencer, Scott. *The Magic Room.* Illus. by Coco Dupy. New York: Harmony/Crown, 1987.

Sperry, Armstrong. *Call It Courage.* Illus. by the author. New York: Macmillan, 1940. Collier pb. M205, M206, M207, M208, M209.

Spier, Peter. *The Fox Went Out on a Chilly Night.* Illus. by the author. New York: Doubleday, 1961. Zephyr pb. M470, M471, M472, M924.

———. *We the People: The Constitution of the United States of America.* Illus. by the author. New York: Doubleday, 1987. pb.

Spirn, Michele. *Gift of Fire.* Illus. by Gene Feller. Fairlawn, NJ: January, 1984.

———. *In Search of the Ruby Sword.* Fairlawn, NJ: January, n.d.

———. *In the Time of the Pharoahs.* Fairlawn, NJ: January, n.d.

———. *Liberty for All.* Illus. by G. Feller. Fairlawn, NJ: January, 1984.

Spirt, Diana L. *Introducing Bookplots 3: A Book Talk Guide for Use with Readers Ages 8–12.* New York: Wilson, 1988.

———. *Introducing More Books: A Guide for the Middle Grades.* New York: Wilson, 1978.

Spohn, Kate. *Clementine's Winter Wardrobe.* New York: Orchard, 1989.

Spyri, Johanna. *Heidi.* New York: Crown, 1986. M562, M563, M1006.

———. *Heidi.* Trans. by Helen B. Dole. Illus. by Judith Cheng. Racine, WI: Golden, 1986. M562, M563, M1006.

———. *Heidi.* New York: Illus. by Ruth Sanderson. Knopf, 1984. M562, M563, M1006.

———. *Heidi.* Airmont pb., Dell pb., Puffin pb., Scholastic pb. M562, M563, M1006.

Square One Television Teacher's Guide. New York: Children's Television Workshop, n.d. M1246.

Staden, Wendelgard von. *Darkness Over the Valley.* Trans. by Mollie Comerford Peters. New York: Ticknor and Fields, 1981.

——. *Grandpa's Too-Good Garden*. Illus. by the author. New York: Greenwillow, 1989.

——. *The Great Big Especially Beautiful Easter Egg*. Illus. by the author. New York: Greenwillow, 1983. Scholastic pb. M509.

——. *Grandpa's Great City Tour: An Alphabet Book*. Illus. by the author. New York: Greenwillow, 1983.

——. *Higher on the Door*. Illus. by the author. New York: Greenwillow, 1987.

——. *Howard*. Illus. by the author. New York: Greenwillow, 1980.

——. *Monty*. Illus. by the author. New York: Greenwillow, 1979.

——. *No Friends*. Illus. by the author. New York: Greenwillow, 1986.

——. *No Need for Monty*. Illus. by the author. New York: Greenwillow, 1987.

——, *That Dreadful Day*. Illus. by the author. New York: Greenwillow, 1985.

——. *That Terrible Halloween Night*. Illus. by the author. New York: Greenwillow, 1980. pb., Scholastic pb.

——. *There's Nothing to Do!* Illus. by the author. New York: Greenwillow, 1986.

——. *We Can't Sleep*. Illus. by the author. New York: Greenwillow, 1982. M1416.

——. *We Hate Rain*. Illus. by the author. New York: Greenwillow, 1988.

——. *What's Under My Bed?* Illus. by the author. New York: Greenwillow, 1983. Puffin pb. M1436, M1437.

——. *When I Was Nine*. Illus. by the author. New York: Greenwillow, 1986.

——. *Will You Please Feed Our Cat?* Illus. by the author. New York: Greenwillow, 1987.

——. *The Wish Card*. Illus. by the author. New York: Greenwillow, 1981.

——. *Worse Than Willie*. Illus. by the author. New York: Greenwillow, 1984.

Stevenson, Robert Louis. *Treasure Island*. New York: Crown, 1988. M344, M834, M1124.

——. *Treasure Island*. Illus. by N. C. Wyeth. New York: Scribner, 1911, 1981. M344, M834, M1124.

——. *Treasure Island*. Airmont, Bantam pb., Puffin pb., Signet pb. M344, M834, M1124.

Stevenson, Robin and Bruce Stevenson. *Sword of Caesar*. Illus. by Richard Hescox. New York: Bantam, 1987.

Stevenson, Sucie. *Do I Have to Take Violet?* Illus. by the author. New York: Putnam, 1987.

Stewart, Mary. *Walk in Wolf Wood: A Tale of Fantasy and Magic*. Illus. by Emanuel Schongut. New York: Morrow, 1980. Fawcett pb.

Stewig, John Warren. *Children and Literature*. Boston: Houghton, 1980, 1987.

Stewig, John Warren and Sam Sebesta. *Using Literature in the Elementary Classroom*. Urbana, IL: National Council of Teachers of English, 1989.

Stiles, Norman. *I'll Miss You, Mr. Hooper*. Illus. by Joe Mathieu. New York: Random and Children's Television Workshop, 1984. pb. M1167, M1168.

Stock, Catherine. *Emma's Dragon Hunt*. Illus. by the author. New York: Lothrop, 1984.

Stoll, Donald R. *Magazines for Children*. Glassboro, NJ: Educational Press Association of America, and Newark, DE: International Reading Association, 1990.

Stolz, Mary. *The Bully of Barkham Street*. Illus. by Leonard Shortall. New York: Harper, 1963. Trophy pb.

—— ——. *The Cat in the Mirror*. New York: Harper, 1975. Dell pb.

——. *The Cuckoo Clock*. Illus. by Pamela Johnson. Boston: Godine, 1986.

——. *The Dog on Barkham Street*. Illus. by L. Shortall. New York: Harper, 1960. Trophy pb.

——. *The Explorer of Barkham Street*. Illus. by Emily A. McCully. New York: Harper, 1985.

——. *Ivy Larkin*. San Diego: Harcourt, 1986. Dell pb.

——. *Quentin Corn*. Illus. by P. Johnson. Boston: Godine, 1985. Dell pb.

——. *Zekmet, The Stone Carver: A Tale of Ancient Egypt*. Illus. by Deborah Nourse. San Diego: Harcourt, 1988.

Stone, Jan. *Christmas Eve on Sesame Street*. New York: Random and Children's Television Workshop, 1981. pb.

Stone, L. *Prairies*. Vero Beach, FL: Rourke, 1989.

Stone, Lynn M. *Alligators and Crocodiles*. Chicago: Children's Press, 1989. pb.

——. *Marshes and Swamps*. Chicago: Childrens Press, 1983. pb.

Strachan, Elizabeth. *Whales and Dolphins*. Illus. by Norman Weaver. New York: Gloucester/Watts, 1986.

Strand, Mark. *Rembrandt Takes a Walk*. Illus. by Red Grooms. New York: Potter/Crown, 1986.

Strange, Ian J. *Penguin World*. Photos by the author. New York: Putnam, 1981.

Stratton, Joanne L. *Pioneer Women: Voices from the Kansas Frontier*. New York: Simon and Schuster, 1980. Touchstone pb. M1036.

Streich, Corrine. *Grandparents' Houses*. Illus. by Lillian Hoban. New York: Greenwillow, 1984.

Index to Multimedia (Nonbook) Materials

Included here are all nonbook materials noted in the text, plus a few that are relevant but were not discussed. Each is preceded by a number beginning with "M," which will permit cross-referencing from the *Index to Books*.

The term used for video cassettes or video recordings is "video;" the terms used for audio recordings are "cassette" or "phonograph record." "Motion picture" is the term used for full feature movies shown in theaters while "16mm" is the term used for 16mm films used in educational settings. All multimedia materials are in color unless black and white (b & w) is indicated.

M1a. *ABC After School Specials.* New York: ABC-TV, n.d.

M1b. *Abel's Island.* (TV program or video) A program from *Long Ago and Far Away.* Boston: WGBH-TV. New York: Italtoons, 1988. 30 min. Animated. Based on a book by William Steig.

M2. *Abel's Island.* (video) Hightstown, NJ: American School Publishers, 1988. 30 min. Based on a book by W. Steig.

M3a. *Abiyoyo.* (TV program or video) Program #35 of *Reading Rainbow.* 30 min. Buffalo: WNED-TV and Lincoln, NE: GPN, 1986. VHS or 3/4" Retold and sung by Pete Seeger.

M3b. *Action in Stories* (TV Program) A program of *Word Shop.* Washington, DC: WETA-TV, 1976. 15 min. 3/4".

M4. *Adventure.* (filmstrip with cassette) Costa Mesa, CA: Pied Piper, 1971. 12 min. (Literature for Children, Series 3) Introduces *Call It Courage* by Armstrong Sperry.

M5. *Adventures of Robin Hood.* (4 cassettes) New York: Harper/Caedmon, n.d. Read by Anthony Quayle. Includes: *How Robin Became an Outlaw; Outlaw Band of Sherwood Forest; Robin and His Merry Men; Robin's Adventures with Little John..*

M6. *Adventures of Robin Hood.* (2 cassettes) Niagara Falls, NY: Listen for Pleasure, 1986. 2 hrs. Read by Keith Barron.

M7. *AIT Newsletter.* Bloomington, IN: AIT (Agency for Instructional Technology) Quarterly.

M8. *The Agony of Alice.* (TV program or video) Program #4 of *More Books from Cover*

to Cover. Washington, DC: WETA-TV and Alexandria, VA: PBS, n.d. 15 min. VHS or 3/4". Based on a book by Phyllis Naylor.

M9. *Aircraft.* (TV program) Program #22 of *Draw Along.* Bloomington, IN: AIT and the Oklahoma Educational TV Authority, 1986. 15 min. Beta, VHS, or 3/4".

M10. *Alaskan Sled Dog.* (16mm film) Buena Vista, CA: Disney, 1966. Deerfield, IL: Coronet/MTI. 19 min.

M11. *Alexander and the Car with a Missing Headlight.* (16mm film or video) Weston, CT: Weston Woods, 1969. Animated. 13 min. Based on a book by Peter Fleischmann.

M12. *Alexander and the Car with a Missing Headlight.* (filmstrip with cassette; cassette) Weston Woods, 1969. 48 fr. 9 min. Based on a book by Peter Fleischmann.

M13a. *Alexander and the Terrible, Horrible, No Good, Very Bad Day.* (16mm film or video) Van Nuys, CA: Bernard Wilets/Aims, 1988. Based on a book by Judith Viorst.

M13b. *Alexander Who Used to Be Rich Last Sunday.* (16mm film or video) Aims, 1989. 14 min. Based on a book by J. Viorst.

M14. *Alice in Wonderland.* (motion picture or video) Los Angeles: Paramount and Bloomington, IN: IU-AV Center, 1941. 40 min. Excerpt from 1933 motion picture. Based on a book by Lewis Carroll.

M15. *Alice in Wonderland.* (motion picture or video) Los Angeles: Video Craft, Intl. and Prism Entertainment, 1951. 72 min. Based on a book by L. Carroll.

M16. *Alice in Wonderland*. (motion picture or video) Burbank, CA: Disney, and Buena Vista, CA: Disney Home Video, 1951. 75 min. Based on a book by L. Carroll.

M17. *Alice in Wonderland*. (4 cassettes) New York: Harper/Caedmon, 1985. 161 min. Based on a book by L. Carroll. Read by Christopher Plummer.

M18. *Alistair in Outer Space*. (TV program or video) Program #27 of *Reading Rainbow.* Buffalo: WNED-TV: Lincoln, NE: GPN, 1986. 30 min. VHS, or 3/4″. Based on a book by Marilyn Sadler.

M19. *All About Dinosaurs*. (4 filmstrips and 4 cassettes) Niles, IL: United Learning, 1988. 44–53 fr. each. Includes: *Dinosaurs: What Were They?*; *How Dinosaurs Lived*; *Digging Up Bones*; and *What Happened to the Dinosaurs?*

M20. *All About Ears*. (TV program) Program #3 of *Zoo Zoo Zoo*. Cincinnati: WCET-TV and the Greater Cincinnati Television Educational Foundation, 1981. 15 min. Beta, VHS, or 3/4″.

M21. *All About Eyes*. (TV program) Program #1 of *Zoo Zoo Zoo*. WCET-TV and the Greater Cincinnati Television Educational Foundation, 1981. 15 min. Beta, VHS, or 3/4″.

M22. *All About Feet*. (TV program) Program #2 of *Zoo Zoo Zoo*. WCET-TV and the Greater Cincinnati Television Educational Foundation, 1981. 15 min. Beta, VHS, or 3/4″.

M23. *All About Tails*. (TV program) Program #4 of *Zoo Zoo Zoo*. WCET-TV and the Greater Cincinnati Television Educational Foundation, 1981. 15 min.

M24. *All Fit With Slim Goodbody*. (TV series) 15 programs; 15 min each. Bloomington, IN: AIT (Agency for Instructional Technology) Beta, VHS, or 3/4″.

M25a. *All Kinds of Houses*. (TV program, 16mm, or video) Program #202 of *Images and Things*. AIT, 1971. 20 min. Beta, VHS, or 3/4″.

M25b. *All Summer in a Day*. (16 mm film or video). Deerfield, IL: Learning Corp. of America, 1982. 28 min. VHS or 3/4″.

M26. *Alligators All Around*. (16mm film or video) Weston, CT: Weston Woods, 1978. 2 min. Animated. Beta or VHS. Based on a book by Maurice Sendak.

M27. *Alligators All Around*. (filmstrip with cassette) Weston Woods, 1978. 30 fr., 4 min. Based on a book by M. Sendak.

M28. *Alligators All Around*. (hardcover book with cassette; cassette) Weston Woods, 1978. 4 min. Based on a book by M. Sendak.

M29. *Along Came a Dog*. (TV program) Program #6 of *Book Bird*. Springfield, VA: Children's Television International, 1979. 3/4″. Based on a book by Meindert De Jong.

M30. *Alphabatics*. (video) Hightstown, NJ: American School Publishers, n.d. 16 min. Based on a book by Suse MacDonald. VHS.

M31. *Alphabatics*. (filmstrip with cassette) American School Publishers, 1988. 142 fr., 15:43 min. Based on a book by S. MacDonald.

M32. *Alphabatics*. (hardback with cassette) American School Publishers, 1988. 15 min. Based on a book by S. MacDonald.

M33. *Amahl and the Night Visitors*. (video) New York: Video Artists, 1978. 120 min. Live action. Beta or VHS. Based on an opera by Gian Carlo Menotti.

M34a. *Amanda Pig and Her Big Brother Oliver*. (hardback or paperback with cassette) Old Greenwich, CT: Listening Library, 1982. 20 min. Based on a book by Jean Van Leeuwen.

M34b. *Amateur Naturalist*. (TV program or video) Falls Church, VA: Landmark Films, 1983. 24 min. VHS.

M35. *Amelia Bedelia*. (TV program or video) A program of *Tilson's Book Shop*. Cleveland: WVIZ-TV and Lincoln, NE: GPN, 1975. 15 min. VHS. Based on a book by Peggy Parish.

M36. *Amelia Bedelia*. (2 cassettes) Old Greenwich, CT: Listening Library, 1989. Includes: *Come Back, Amelia Bedelia*; *Play Ball, Amelia Bedelia*; *Amelia Bedelia*; *Amelia Bedelia and the Surprise Shower*; and *Merry Christmas, Amelia Bedelia*. Based on books by P. Parish.

M37. *Amelia Bedelia and the Surprise Shower*. (paperback with cassette) Listening Library, 1986. Based on a book by P. Parish.

M38. *America Moves West*. (computer program) Pound Ridge, NY: Orange Cherry Software, 1988. 2 disks, guide, backup disks. Apple II series, Commodore 64, TRS 80.

M39. *Among the Wild Chimpanzees*. (TV program or video) Washington, DC: National Geographic, 1987. 59 min. Live action. Beta or VHS.

M40. *Anansi of the Golden Box*. (TV program or video) Program #5 of *Sixteen Tales*. Bloomington, IN: AIT and Los Angeles: KLCS-TV, 1984. 15 min. Beta, VHS, or 3/4″. Based on an African folktale.

M41. *Anansi—Story and Song*. (video) Ann Arbor: Univ. of Michigan-TV, 1979. 30 min. 3/4″. Based on an African folktale.

M42. *Anansi the Spider.* (16mm film) Mc-Dermott, 1969. Chicago: Films Inc., Skokie, IL: Texture Films. 10 min. Animated. Based on a book by Gerald McDermott.

M43. *Anansi the Spider.* (filmstrip with cassette) Weston, CT: Weston Woods, 1974. 43 fr. 10 min. Based on a book by G. Mc-Dermott.

M44. *Anansi the Spider.* (hardback or paperback with cassette, cassette) Weston Woods, 1974. 10 min. Based on a book by G. Mc-Dermott.

M45. *Anansi the Spider Man.* (TV program or video) Program #3 of *Through the Pages.* Cleveland: WVIZ-TV and Lincoln, NE: GPN, 1982. 15 min. Beta, VHS, or 3/4″. Based on an African folktale.

M46a. *Anastasia at Your Service.* (paperback with cassette) Old Greenwich, CT: Listening Library, 1984. 83 min. (Soundways to Reading Series, Cliffhanger Read-along) Based on a book by Lois Lowry.

M46b. *And the Band Played Off.* (TV program) A program of *Shining Time Station.* New York: WNET-TV, 1989. 30 min.

M47a. *And Then What Happened, Paul Revere?* (TV program or video) A program of *Best of Cover to Cover, 1-A.* Washington, DC: WETA-TV and Alexandria, VA: PBS Video, n.d. 15 min. Based on a book by Jean Fritz.

M47b. *And Then What Happened, Paul Revere?* (cassette) Weston, CT: Weston Woods, 1977. 13 min. Based on a book by J. Fritz.

M47c. *Angelina Ballerina and Other Stories.* (cassette) New York: Harper/Caedmon, 1986. 27 min. Includes: *Angelina Ballerina* (5 min.); *Angelina and the Princess* (5 min.); *Angelina at the Fair* (5 min.); *Angelina's Christmas* (6 min); *Angelina on Stage* (6 min.) Based on books by Katharine Holabird. Performed by Sally Struthers.

M48. *Angus and the Cat.* (filmstrip with cassette) Weston, CT: Weston Woods, 1973. 34 fr. 6 min. Based on a book by Marjorie Flack.

M49. *Angus and the Ducks.* (filmstrip with cassette) Weston Woods, 1973. 35 fr. 6 min. Based on a book by M. Flack.

M50. *Angus Lost.* (16mm film or video) New York: Phoenix, 1982. 11 min. Live action. Based on a book by M. Flack.

M51. *Animal Cafe.* (TV program or video) Program #26 of *Reading Rainbow.* Buffalo: WNED-TV and Lincoln, NE: GPN, 1986. 30 min. VHS or 3/4″. Based on a book by John Stadler. Narrated by Marvin Short.

M52. *Animal Costumes.* (TV program) Program #5 of *Zoo Zoo Zoo.* Cincinnati: WCET-TV and the Greater Cincinnati Television Educational Foundation; Bloomington, IN: AIT, 1981. 15 min. Beta, VHS, or 3/4″.

M53. *Animal Defenses.* (TV program) Program #6 of *Zoo Zoo Zoo.* WCET-TV and the Greater Cincinnati Television Educational Foundation and AIT, 1981. 15 min. Beta, VHS, or 3/4″.

M54. *Animal Groups.* (TV program) Program #14 of *Zoo Zoo Zoo.* WCET-TV and the Greater Cincinnati Educational Foundation and AIT, 1981. 15 min. Beta, VHS, or 3/4″.

M55a. *Animal Homes.* (TV program) Program #13 of *Zoo Zoo Zoo.* WCET-TV and the Greater Cincinnati Educational Foundation, and AIT, 1981. 15 min. Beta, VHS, or 3/4″.

M55b. *Animal Kingdom.* (2 filmstrips with cassette) New York: Random, 1977. *Lions* 11 min.; *Sharks* 12 min.

M56. *The Animals.* (filmstrip) Falls Church, VA: Enjoy Communicating, 1982. 62 fr. 10 min. A Companion to *Environment and Research..*

M57. *Animals.* (filmstrip with cassette) Costa Mesa: Pied Piper, 1970. 24 min. Features: *King of the Wind* by Marguerite Henry; *The Biggest Bear* by Lynd Ward; and *The Incredible Journey* by Sheila Burnford. Introduces: *Big Red* by Jim Kjelgaard and *Follow My Leader* by J. Garfield.

M58a. *Animals Magazine.* (periodical) Boston: Massachusetts Society for the Prevention of Cruelty to Animals. Bi-monthly.

M58b. *Animals of the Past (Dinos).* (TV program or video) A Program of *Draw Along.* Bloomington, IN: Agency for Instructional Television, 1979. 15 min. VHS.

M59. *Anna Banana and Me.* (hardback or paperback with cassette; Reading Chest with 4 pbs and cassette) Ancramdale, NY: Live Oak Media, 1988. 9 min. Based on a book by Lenore Blegvad.

M60. *Anne Frank: A Legacy for Our Time.* (video) Chicago: SVE (Society for Visual Education), 1988. 39 min. VHS.

M61. *Anne Frank: A Legacy for Our Time.* (2 filmstrips with 2 cassettes; 16 skill sheets) SVE, 1985. Includes: *The Story of Anne Frank.* 65 fr. 20 min. *The Lesson of Anne Frank.* 65 fr. 20 min.

M62. *Anne Frank: The Diary of a Young Girl.* (paperback with cassette) Old Greenwich, CT: Listening Library, 1985. 64 min. (Young Cliffhangers Series) Based on a book by Anne Frank.

M63. *Anne of Avonlea: The Continuing Story of Anne of Green Gables.* (video) Burbank, CA: Walt Disney, 1988. 114 min. Live action.

Beta or VHS. Based on a book by Lucy Montgomery.

M64. *Anne of Green Gables.* (2 videos) Walt Disney, 1987. 224 min. Live action. Beta or VHS. Based on a book by L. Montgomery.

M65. *Anne of Green Gables.* (TV program, 16mm, or video) A program of *WonderWorks.* Los Angeles: Direct Cinema/Sullivan, 1986. 192 min. Live action. VHS. Based on a book by L. Montgomery.

M66. *Anne of Green Gables: The Charlottetown Festival Productions.* (cassette) Ontario, Canada: Arctic Records and Charlottetown, Prince Edward Island, Canada: Jack Richardson JAR Productions, 1984.

M67. *Anne of Green Gables.* (8 cassettes) Washington, DC: Audio Book Contractors, 1986. 630 min. Based on a book by L. Montgomery. Read by Flo Gibson.

M68. *Anne of Green Gables: The Sequel.* (TV program, 16mm film, or video) A program of *WonderWorks.* Pittsburgh: WQED-TV and Los Angeles: Direct Cinema/Sullivan, 1986. 235 min. VHS. Based on a book by L. Montgomery.

M69. *Annie and the Old One.* (cassette) Hightstown, NJ: American School Publishers, 1979. 18 min. Based on a book by Miska Miles.

M70. *Antarctica.* (2 filmstrips with cassettes) Falls Church, VA: Enjoy Communicating, 1982. Includes: *The Environment and Research,* 67 fr. 11 min. and *The Animals,* 62 fr. 10 min.

M71. *Antarctica.* (TV program) A program from *3-2-1-Contact.* New York: Children's Television Workshop, n.d. 30 min.

M72. *Apt. 3.* (16mm film or video) Weston, CT: Weston Woods, 1977. 10 min. Iconographic. Beta or VHS. Based on a book by Ezra Jack Keats.

M73. *Apt. 3.* (filmstrip with cassette) Weston Woods, 1977. 37 fr. 8 min. Based on a book by E. Keats.

M74. *Apt. 3.* (paperback with cassette; cassette) Weston Woods, 1977. 8 min. Based on a book by E. Keats.

M75. *Arch of Coal.* (TV program or video) Program #5 of *Explorers Unlimited.* Cleveland: WVIZ-TV and Bloomington, IN: AIT, 1971. 15 min. Beta, VHS, or 3/4″.

M76. *Architecture.* (TV program) Program #12 of *Pass It On.* Memphis, TN: WKNO-TV, 1983. 15 min. VHS or 3/4″.

M77. *Architecture.* (TV program) A program of *3-2-1-Contact.* New York: Children's Television Workshop, n.d. 30 min.

M78a. *Are You There, God? It's Me, Margaret.* (filmstrip with cassette) Costa Mesa, CA: Pied Piper Media, 1984. 17 min. Based on a book by Judy Blume.

M78b. *Are You There, God? It's Me, Margaret.* (hardback or paperback with cassette) Old Greenwich, CT: Listening Library, 1985. (Soundways to Reading, Cliffhanger Readalong) 83 min. Based on a book by J. Blume.

M79. *Are You There, God? It's Me, Margaret.* (3 cassettes) Listening Library, 1988. 3 hrs. 17 min. Based on a book by J. Blume.

M80. *Arnold Lobel Video Showcase.* (video) Includes: *Frog and Toad Are Friends, Frog and Toad Together, Fables, Mouse Soup,* and *Meet the Newbery Author.* Hightstown, NJ: American School Publishers, n.d. 60 min. VIIS. Based on books by Arnold Lobel.

M81. *Art and Music.* (filmstrip with cassette) Costa Mesa, CA: Pied Piper, 1980. 10 min. Introduces: *The First Book of Jazz* by Langston Hughes and *Art of the . . .* series by Shirley Glubok.

M82. *Arthur Celebrates the Holidays.* (video) Hightstown, NJ: American School Publishers, 1985. 8 min. each. Beta or VHS. Transferred from filmstrips. Includes: *Arthur's April Fool, Arthur's Christmas, Arthur's Halloween, Arthur's Thanksgiving,* and *Arthur's Valentine.* Based on books by Marc Brown.

M83. *Arthur Goes to Camp.* (filmstrip with cassette) American School Publishers, 1983. 76 fr. 9:30 min. Based on a book by M. Brown.

M84. *Arthur's April Fool.* (filmstrip with cassette) American School Publishers, 1983. 71 fr. 8 min. Based on a book by M. Brown.

M85. *Arthur's Baby.* (filmstrip with cassette) American School Publishers, 1988. 62 fr. 7:15 min. Based on a book by M. Brown.

M86. *Arthur's Christmas Cookies.* (paperback with cassette) New York: Harper, 1986. 15 min. Based on a book by Lillian Hoban.

M87. *Arthur's Eyes.* (TV program or video) Program #13 of *Reading Rainbow.* Buffalo: WNED-TV and Lincoln, NE: GPN, 1983. 30 min. Beta, VHS, or 3/4″. Based on a book by Marc Brown. Narrated by Bill Cosby.

M88. *Arthur's Eyes.* (filmstrip with cassette) Hightstown, NJ: American School Publishers, 1988. 51 fr. 6:10 min. Based on a book by M. Brown.

M89. *Arthur's Funny Money.* (paperback with cassette) New York: Harper, 1986. 15 min. Based on a book by Lillian Hoban.

M90. *Arthur's Halloween Costume.* (filmstrip with cassette) Chicago: Encyclopedia Britannica, 1987. 50 fr. 5 min. (Holidays series) Based on a book by L. Hoban.

M91. *Arthur's Honey Bear.* (paperback and cassette) Harper, 1986. 15 min. Based on a book by L. Hoban.

M92. *Arthur's Teacher Trouble.* (filmstrip with cassette) Hightstown, NJ: American School Publishers, 1988. 75 fr. 9:50 min. Based on a book by M. Brown.

M93. *Arthur's Teacher Trouble/Arthur Goes to Camp.* (video) New Rochelle, NY: Spoken Arts, 1988. 30 min. VHS. Based on books by M. Brown.

M94. *Arthur's Thanksgiving.* (filmstrip with cassette) Hightstown, NJ: American School Publishers, 1983. 73 fr. 9 min. Based on a book by M. Brown.

M95. *Arthur's Tooth.* (filmstrip with cassette) American School Publishers, 1983. 67 fr. 7:30 min. Based on a book by M. Brown.

M96a. *As Long As He Can Count the Cows.* (TV program) A program of *Long Ago and Far Away.* Denmark: Danmarks Radio, n.d. Boston: WGBH-TV. 30 min. Host: James Earl Jones.

M96b. *As Long As He Can Count the Cows.* (16mm film or video) Deerfield, IL: Coronet, 1989. 30 min.

M97. *Ashanti to Zulu.* (filmstrip with cassette) Weston CT: Weston Woods, 1977. 32 fr. 17 min. Based on a book by Margaret Musgrove.

M98. *Ashanti to Zulu.* (hardback with cassette; cassette) Weston Woods, 1977. 17 min. Based on a book by M. Musgrove.

M99. *Ask Mr. Bear.* (TV program or video) A program from the Brown Module of *Picture Book Park.* Cleveland: WVIZ-TV and Bloomington, IN: AIT, 1972/73. 15 min. Beta, VHS, or 3/4″. Based on a book by Marjorie Flack.

M100. *Ask Mr. Bear.* (hardback or paperback with cassette; Reading Chest with 4 pbs and cassette) Ancramdale, NY: Live Oak Media, 1990. 5 min. Based on a book by M. Flack.

M101. *Aunt Nina and Her Nephews and Nieces.* (filmstrip with cassette) Weston, CT: Weston Woods, 1984. 28 fr. 6 min. Based on a book by Franz Brandenberg.

M102. *Aunt Nina and Her Nephews and Nieces.* (hardcover with cassette; cassette) Weston Woods, 1984. 6 min. Based on a book by F. Brandenberg.

M103. *Australia.* (TV program) A program of *3-2-1-Contact.* New York: Children's Television Workshop, n.d. 30 min.

M104. *Autumn Field.* (TV program) Program #509 of *Naturescene.* Columbia: South Carolina Educational Television, n.d. 30 min.

M105. *Babar.* (doll) 10″ doll. Based on a book by Jean de Brunhoff. Book Mates; Storyteller.

M106. *Babar and Father Christmas.* (16mm film or video) Santa Monica: Hi Tops, Ottata Productions, and Thomas Horne, Ltd., 1986. 30 min. Based on a book by J. de Brunhoff.

M107. *Babar the King.* (2 filmstrips and 2 cassettes) Spectra Films, 1977. Based on a book by J. de Brunhoff.

M108. *Babar, the Movie.* (motion picture or video) Van Nuys, CA: Family Home Entertainment/Nelvanna Ellipse, 1989. 79 min. Animated. Beta or VHS. Based on a book by Laurent de Brunhoff.

M109. *Baby Panda.* (TV program) Seattle: KCTS-TV, n.d. Documentary.

M110. *Baby-Sitting Is a Dangerous Job.* (TV program or video) Program #9 of *More Books from Cover to Cover.* Washington, DC: WETA-TV and Alexandria, VA: PBS Video, 1987. 15 min. VHS or 3/4″. Based on a book by Willo D. Roberts.

M111. *Back Yard Angel.* (TV program or video) Program #11 of *Books from Cover to Cover.* WETA-TV and PBS Video, n.d. 15 min. VHS or 3/4″. Based on a book by Judy Delton.

M113. *Banner in the Sky.* (phonograph record or cassette) Hightstown, NJ: American School Publishers, n.d. 43 min. Adapted from a book by James Ullman.

M114. *The Bargain.* (TV program) Program #6 of *Teletales.* Bloomington, IN: AIT, 1984. 15 min. Beta, VHS, or 3/4″. Based on an Irish folktale.

M115. *A Bargain for Frances.* (TV program or video) A program of *Tilson's Book Shop.* Cleveland: WVIZ-TV and Lincoln, NE: GPN, 1975. 15 min. VHS. Based on a book by Russell Hoban.

M116. *Barn Dance!* (TV program or video) Program #51 of *Reading Rainbow.* WNED-TV and Lincoln, NE: GPN, 1989. 30 min. VHS, or 3/4″. Based on a book by Bill Martin, Jr. and John Archambault.

M117. *The Bassoon-Piano Show.* (TV program or video) Program #2 of *Musical Encounter.* LA: KLCS-TV and Lincoln, NE: GPN, 1983. VHS or 3/4″.

M118. *Battle of the Leaves.* (TV program) A program of *Nature.* New York: WNET-TV, 1984.

M119. *Be a Perfect Person in Just Three Days!* (TV program or video) Program #12 of *Books from Cover to Cover.* Alexandria, VA: PBS Video, n.d. 15 min. VHS or 3/4″. Based on a book by Steven Manes.

M120. *Be a Perfect Person in Just Three Days!* (TV program) A program on *Wonder-Works.* 60 min. Based on a book by S. Manes.

M121. *Bea and Mr. Jones.* (TV program and video) Program #3 of *Reading Rainbow.* Buffalo: WNED-TV and Lincoln, NE: GPN, 1983. 30 min. VHS, or 3/4″. Based on a book by Amy Schwartz.

M122. *A Bear Called Paddington.* (TV program or video) Program #3 of *Book Bird.* Springfield, VA: Children's Television International, 1979. 3/4″. Based on a book by Michael Bond.

M123. *A Bear Called Paddington.* (filmstrip with cassette) Englewood, CO: Learning Tree, 1983. 40 fr. Based on a book by M. Bond.

M124. *The Beast of Monsieur Racine.* (16mm film or video) Weston, CT: Weston Woods, 1974. 9 min. Animated. Beta or VHS. Based on a book by Tomi Ungerer.

M125. *The Beast of Monsieur Racine.* (filmstrip with cassette) Weston Woods, 1974. 52 fr. 14 min. Based on a book by T. Ungerer.

M126. *The Beast of Monsieur Racine.* (paperback with cassette; cassette) Weston Woods, 1974. 14 min. Based on a book by T. Ungerer.

M127. *Beatrix Potter Had a Pet Named Peter.* (video) Hightstown, NJ: American School Publishers, 1985. 14 min. B & W and color. Beta or VHS. Introduces *Peter Rabbit.*.

M128. *Beatrix Potter Had a Pet Named Peter.* (filmstrip with cassette) American School Publishers, 1984. 117 fr. 14 min. B & W and color. Introduces *Peter Rabbit.*.

M129. *Bedtime for Frances.* (TV program or video) A program from the Blue Module of *Picture Book Park.* Cleveland: WVIZ-TV and AIT, 1872/73. 15 min. Beta, VHS, or 3/4″. Based on a book by Russell Hoban.

M130. *Bella Arabella.* (TV program; video) Program #15 of *Books from Cover to Cover.* Alexandria, VA: PBS Video, n.d. 15 min. VHS or 3/4″. Based on a book by Liza Fosburgh.

M131. *Ben and Me.* (TV or video) Program #16 of *Readit!* Bloomington, IN: AIT, 1982. 15 min. Beta, VHS, or 3/4″. Based on a book by Robert Lawson.

M132. *Benjamin Franklin.* (filmstrip) New Rochelle, NY: Spoken Arts, 1982. 50 fr. 11 min. Based on a book by Ingri and Edgar d'Aulaire.

M133. *Benjamin Franklin.* (paperback with cassette) Spoken Arts, 1982. Based on a book by I. and E. d'Aulaire.

M134. *Best Friends.* (TV program or video) Program #43 of *Reading Rainbow.* Buffalo: WNED-TV and Lincoln, NE: GPN, 1987. 30 min. VHS, or 3/4″. Based on a book by Steven Kellogg.

M135. *Best Loved Poems of Longfellow.* (cassette) New York: Harper/Caedmon, n.d. Includes: "Paul Revere's Ride"; "The Village

Blacksmith"; "Hiawatha: His Childhood"; "The Children's Hour"; etc.

M136. *Best of Cover to Cover, 1-A.* (TV series or videos) Washington, DC: WETA-TV and Alexandria, VA: PBS Video, n.d. 15 programs, 15 min. each. Host: John Robbins.

M137. *Best of Cover to Cover, 2-A.* (TV series or videos) WETA-TV and PBS Video, n.d. 15 programs, 15 min. each. Host: John Robbins.

M138. *Bianchinetta.* (TV program or video) Program #10 of *Teletales.* Bloomington, IN: AIT, 1984. 15 min. Beta, VHS, or 3/4″. Based on a folk tale from Italy.

M139. *Big Bad Bruce.* (paperback with cassette) Boston: Houghton Mifflin, 1987. 32 min. Based on a book by Bill Peet.

M140a. *Big Bird in China.* (TV program or video) New York: Random, 1987. 75 min. VHS. From a Sesame Street special.

M140b. *Big Bird in Japan.* (TV program or video) New York: Children's Television Workshop/Random House, 1991. 60 min. VHS.

M141a. *Les Bikes.* (film and video) Falls Church, VA: Landmark, 1987. 22 min. Beta, VHS, or 3/4″.

M141b. *Bill Cosby's Picture Pages.* (4 videos) Burbank, CA: Walt Disney Media, 1985. 55 min. each. A component of Captain Kangaroo.

M142. *Bill Martin Junior's Treasure Chest of Poetry.* (poetry cards) DLM Teaching Resources, 1986. Prepared by B. Martin, John Archambault, and Peggy Brogan.

M143. *Bill Peet in His Studio.* (video) Burlington, MA: Houghton Mifflin, 1983. 14 min. Live action. Beta, VHS, or 3/4″.

M144. *Binky Brothers, Detectives.* (cassette) New York: Harper, 1984. 16 min. Based on a book by James Lawrence.

M145. *Biography.* (filmstrip with cassette) Costa Mesa, CA: Pied Piper, 1970. 12 min. (Literature for Children, Series 1) Introduces *Benjamin Franklin* by Ingri and Edgar d'Aulaire.

M146. *The Bionic Bunny Show.* (TV or video) Program #46 of *Reading Rainbow.* Buffalo: WNED-TV and Lincoln, NE: GPN, 1988. 30 min. VHS or 3/4″. Based on a book by Marc and Lauren Brown.

M147a. *Black Beauty.* (motion picture or video) Los Angeles: Paramount, 1971. 105 min. Live action. Beta or VHS. Based on a book by Anna Sewell.

M147b. *Black Holes in Space.* (filmstrip and cassette) Madison, WI: Educational Industries, 1982. 180 min.

M148. *The Black Stallion.* (motion picture or video) New York: United Artists/CBS/Fox Video, 1979. 118 min. Live action. Based on a book by Walter Farley.

M149. *Blackberries in the Dark.* (16mm film or video) Deerfield, IL: Coronet/MTI, 1988. 26 min. Based on a book by Mavis Jukes.

M150. *Blubber.* (filmstrip with cassette) Costa Mesa, CA: Pied Piper, 1984. 108 fr. 17 min. Based on a book by Judy Blume.

M151. *Blubber.* (paperback and cassette) Old Greenwich, CT: Listening Library, 1985. 50 min. (Soundways to Reading, Cliffhanger Read-along) Based on a book by Judy Blume.

M152. *Blue Moose/Return of Blue Moose.* (TV program or video) Program #1 of *Readit!* Bloomington, IN: AIT, 1982. 15 min. Beta, VHS, or 3/4″. Based on books by Daniel Pinkwater.

M153. *The Blue Sword.* (2 cassettes) Hightstown, NJ: American School Publishers, 1984. 90 min. each. Abridged from a book by Robin McKinley.

M154. *Boats and Water.* (TV program or video) Program #29 of *Draw Along.* Bloomington, IN: AIT and the Oklahoma Educational TV Authority, 1986. 15 min. Beta, VHS, or 3/4″.

M155. *The Body Symphony: The Inside Story of Your Whole Body.* (TV program) Program #8 of *The Inside Story with Slim Goodbody.* Bloomington, IN: AIT and Green Bay, WI: UW-GB Telecommunications Center, 1981. 15 min. Beta, VHS, or 3/4″.

M156. *Book Bird.* (TV series and video) Springfield, VA: Children's Television International, 1979. 16 programs 15 min. each. 3/4″. Host: John Robbins.

M158. *Book of Pigericks.* (hardcover with cassette) Hightstown, NJ: American School Publishers, 1985. 20 min. Based on a book by Arnold Lobel.

M159. *BookBrain 4–6.* (computer database) Phoenix, AZ: Oryx Press, 1987, 1988, 1990. 7 disks, manual. Apple II family, 64K.

M160. *BookBrain 7–9.* (computer database) Oryx, 1988, 1990. Apple II family, 64K.

M161. *Booklist.* (periodical) Chicago: American Library Association. 22 times a year.

M162. *Books About Animals.* (TV program) A program of *The Word Shop.* Washington, DC: WETA-TV, 1976. 15 min. Beta, VHS, or 3/4″.

M163. *Books About Fantasy.* (TV program) A program of *The Word Shop.* WETA-TV, 1976. 15 min. Beta, VHS, or 3/4″.

M164. *Books About People.* (TV program) A program of *The Word Shop.* WETA-TV, 1976. 15 min. Beta, VHS, or 3/4″.

M165. *Books About Places.* (TV program) A program of *The Word Shop.* WETA-TV, 1976. 15 min. Beta, VHS, or 3/4″.

M166. *Books from Cover to Cover.* (TV series) Washington, DC: WETA-TV and Alexandria, VA: PBS Video, n.d. 16 programs 15 min. each. Host: John Robbins. VHS or 3/4″.

M167. *Books Kids Love.* (video) Amherst, NY: Winward, 1989. 42 min.

M168. *Books That Answer Questions.* (TV program) A program of *The Word Shop.* Washington, DC: WETA-TV, 1976. 15 min. Beta, VHS, or 3/4″.

M169. "The Booktalker." (newsletter) Appears 5 times per year in the *Wilson Library Bulletin.* Edited by Joni Bodart.

M170. *Booktalking with Joni Bodart.* (video) New York: Wilson, 1986. 29 min. VHS.

M171. *The Borrowers.* (3 cassettes) Boston: G K Hall Audio Books, 1986. 3 hr. 30 min. Based on a book by Mary Norton. Read by Rowena Cooper.

M172. *The Boxcar Children.* (TV program or video) Program #5 of *Readit!* Bloomington, IN: AIT, 1982. 15 min. Beta, VHS, or 3/4″. Based on a book by Gertrude Warner.

M173. *The Boy Who Loved Mammoths and Other Tales.* (cassette) Weston, CT: Weston Woods, 1987. 55 min. Title story based on a story by Martin Wills. Performed by Rafe Martin.

M174. *The Boy Who Loved Trolls.* (TV program) A program from *WonderWorks.* Pittsburgh, PA: WQED-TV, 1985. Based on the play, "Ofoeti" by Wheater.

M175. *Boys' Life.* (periodical) Irving, TX: Boy Scouts of America. Monthly.

M176. *Brave Irene.* (filmstrip with cassette) Weston Woods, CT: Weston Woods, 1988. 75 fr. 14 min. Based on a book by William Steig.

M177. *Brave Irene.* (hardcover or paperback with cassette; cassette) Weston Woods, 1988. 14 min. Based on a book by W. Steig.

M178. *The Breath of Life: The Inside Story of Respiration.* (TV program) Program #2 of *The Inside Story with Slim Goodbody.* Bloomington, IN: AIT and Green Bay, WI: UW-GB Telecommunications Center, 1981. 15 min. Beta, VHS, or 3/4″.

M179. *The Bridge on the River Kwai.* (motion picture or video) Burbank, CA: RCA/Columbia, 1957. 161 min. Beta or VHS. Based on a book by Pierre Boulle.

M180. *Bridge to Terabithia.* (TV program or video) A program from *WonderWorks.* Pittsburgh, PA: WQED-TV, 1985. Based on a book by Katherine Paterson.

M181. *Bridge to Terabithia.* (TV program or video) Program #2 of *Storybound*. Lincoln, NE: GPN, 1981. 15 min. VHS or 3/4″. Based on a book by K. Paterson.

M182. *Bridge to Terabithia.* (2 filmstrips with 2 cassettes) Hightstown, NJ: American School Publishers, n.d. Based on a book by K. Paterson.

M183. *Bridge to Terabithia.* (cassette) American School Publishers, 1979. Based on a book by K. Paterson.

M184. *Brighty of the Grand Canyon.* (video) Los Angeles: Active Home Video, n.d. Live action. 92 min. Beta, VHS, or 3/4″. Based on a book by Marguerite Henry.

M185. *Brighty of the Grand Canyon.* (filmstrip with cassette) Costa Mesa, CA: Pied Piper, 1974. 38 min. Based on a book by M. Henry. Includes: author interview.

M186. *Bringing the Rain to Kapiti Plain.* (TV program or video) Program #3 of *Reading Rainbow*. Buffalo: WNED-TV and Lincoln NE: GPN, 1983. 30 min. VHS or 3/4″. Based on a book by Verna Aardema. Narrated by James Earl Jones.

M187. *The Bronze Bow.* (cassette) Hightstown, NJ: American School Publishers, 1972. Based on a book by Elizabeth Speare.

M188. *Brush.* (TV program or video) Program #49 of *Reading Rainbow*. Buffalo: WNED-TV and Lincoln, NE: GPN, 1988. 30 min. VHS or 3/4″. Based on a book by Pere Calders.

M189. *Bugs.* (TV program or video) Program #47 of *Reading Rainbow*. WNED-TV and GPN, 1988. 30 min. VHS or 3/4″. Based on a book by Nancy Winslow Parker and Joan Richards Wright.

M190. *Building a Conflict.* (filmstrip with cassette) (Narrative Writing, 5) Costa Mesa, CA: Pied Piper, 1975. 12 min. Introduces *Dick Whittington and His Cat* by Marcia Brown.

M191. *Buildings for Work and Play.* (TV program, 16mm film, or video) Program #203 of *Images and Things*. Bloomington, IN: AIT, 1971. 20 min. Beta, VHS, or 3/4″.

M192. *Bunnicula; A Rabbit-Tale of Mystery.* (cassette) New York: Harper/Caedmon, 1982. 60 min. Based on a book by Deborah and James Howe. Performed by Lou Jacobi.

M193. *The Butter Battle Book.* (filmstrip with cassette) Hightstown, NJ: American School Publishers, 1984. 119 fr. 14:30 min. Based on a book by Dr. Seuss.

M194. *By the Sea.* (filmstrip with cassette) Costa Mesa, CA: Pied Piper, 1984. 11 min. (Literature for Children, 7C) Introduces: *The Lighthouse Keeper's Lunch* by Ronda Armi-

tage and *Mr. Gumpy's Outing* by John Burningham.

M195. *Byrd Baylor Audio Tapes.* (3 cassettes) Tucson, AZ: Southwest Series, Inc., n.d. *The Desert Is Theirs* and *Everybody Needs a Rock*. Narrated by Will Rogers, Jr., Based on books by Byrd Baylor. *Moon Song*. Written and narrated by Byrd Baylor.

M196. *Byrd Baylor: Storyteller.* (3 cassettes or 3 videos) Southwest Series, Inc., 1989. Includes: *I'm in Charge of Celebrations*, 10:30; *Amigo*, 16:25; and *The Best Town in the World*, 11:08. Written and narrated by Byrd Baylor.

M197. *Byrd Baylor Video Series, Vol. 1.* (3 cassettes or 3 videos) Southwest Series, Inc., 1988. Includes: *The Way to Start a Day*, 10 min; *Hawk, I'm Your Brother*, 15 min; and *The Other Way to Listen*, 16 min. Based on books by Byrd Baylor. Narrated by Will Rogers, Jr.

M198. *CBS Storybreak.* (TV series) New York: CBS, n.d.

M199a. *The Cabin Faced West.* (TV program or video) Program #3 of *Books from Cover to Cover*. Alexandria, VA: PBS Video, n.d. 15 min. VHS or 3/4″. Based on a book by Jean Fritz.

M199b. *Cable in the Classroom.* (periodical) Alexandria, VA: PBS. Monthly except July and August.

M200. *Caddie Woodlawn.* (16mm film or video) Los Angeles: Churchill Films, 1989. 48 min. Based on a book by C. Brink.

M201. *Caddie Woodlawn.* (TV program or video) Program #15 of *Book Bird*. Springfield, VA: Children's Television International, 1979. 15 min. Beta, VHS, or 3/4″. Based on a book by C. Brink.

M202. *Caddie Woodlawn.* (2 filmstrips with 2 cassettes) Hightstown, NJ: American School Publishers 1972. 193 fr. 40 min. Based on a book by C. Brink.

M203. *Caddie Woodlawn.* (cassette) American School Publishers, 1972. 40 min. Based on a book by C. Brink.

M204. *Caliph Stork.* (TV program or video) Program #13 of *Teletales*. Bloomington, IN: AIT, 1984. 15 min. Beta, VHS, or 3/4″. Based on a folk tale from Iraq.

M205. *Call It Courage.* (motion picture, 16mm film, or video) Burbank, CA: Walt Disney Educational Media, 1980. 14 min. Beta, VHS, or 3/4″. Based on a book by Armstrong Sperry.

M206. *Call It Courage.* (TV program or video) Program #5 of *Storybound*. Lincoln, NE:

GPB, 1981. 15 min. VHS or 3/4″. Based on a book by A. Sperry.

M207. *Call It Courage.* (video) Hightstown, NJ: American School Publishers, n.d. 50 min. VHS. Based on a book by A. Sperry.

M208. *Call It Courage.* (2 filmstrips and 2 cassettes) American School Publishers, 1970. 201 fr. 40 min. Based on a book by A. Sperry.

M210. *Cam Jansen and the Mystery of the Babe Ruth Baseball.* (hardback or paperback with cassette) Old Greenwich, CT: Listening Library, 1984. 43 min. Based on a book by David Adler.

M211a. *Cam Jansen and the Mystery of the Dinosaur Bones.* (hardback or paperback with cassette) Listening Library, 1984. 45 min. Based on a book by D. Adler.

M211b. *The Campout.* (TV program) Program #5839 of *Lassie and Timmy.* New York: CBS-TV, 1954–71. Syndication 1971–. 28 min.

M212. *Can the Next President Win the Space Race?* (TV program or video) A program of NOVA. Deerfield, IL: Coronet, 1988. 58 min. VHS.

M213. *Canadian Children's Literature/Littérature Canadienne pour la Jeunesse.* (periodical) Guelph, Ontario: Canadian Children's Press/University of Guelph. Quarterly.

M215. *Can't Live With "Em."* (TV program) A program of *DeGrassi Jr. High.* Boston: WGBH-TV, n.d. 30 min.

M216. *Can't You Make Them Behave, King George?* (cassette) Weston, CT: Weston Woods, 1977. 28 fr. Based on a book by Jean Fritz.

M217. *Caps for Sale.* (16mm film or video) Weston, CT: Weston Woods, n.d. Based on a book by Esphyr Slobodkina.

M218. *Caps for Sale.* (filmstrip with cassette) Weston Woods, 1958. 34 fr. 5 min. Iconographic. Based on a book by E. Slobodkina.

M219. *Caps for Sale.* (hardback with cassette; cassette) Weston Woods, 1958. 5 min. Based on a book by E. Slobodkina.

M220a. *Caps for Sale.* (hardback or paperback with cassette; Reading Chest with 4 pbs and cassette) Ancramdale, NY: Live Oak Media, n.d. 8:34 min. Based on a book by E. Slobodkina.

M220b. *Captain Kangaroo.* (TV series) New York: CBS Network Television, 1955–1964. Host: Robert Keeshan.

M220c. *Car and Driver.* (periodical) New York: Ziff-Davis, monthly.

M221. *Carol Channing Sings "The Pooh Song Book."* (phonograph record or cassette) Harper/Caedmon, 1983. 49:02 min. Based on a book by A. A. Milne. Performed by C. Channing.

M222. *The Case of Bugs Meany's Revenge.* (paperback with cassette) Hightstown, NJ: American School Publishers, n.d. (The Best of Encyclopedia Brown) Based on a story by Donald Sobol.

M223. *The Case of Sir Biscuit-Shooter.* (paperback with cassette) American School Publishers, 1979. 7 min. Based on a story from *Encyclopedia Brown Solves Them All* by D. Sobol.

M224. *The Case of the Elevator Duck.* (16mm film or video) Deerfield, IL: LCA, 1974. 16 min. Live action. VHS. Based on a book by Polly Berends.

M225. *The Case of the Elevator Duck.* (TV program or video) Program #4 of *Books from Cover to Cover.* Washington, D.C.: WETA-TV and Alexandria, VA: PBS Video, n.d. 15 min. Based on a book by P. Berends.

M226. *The Case of the Hidden Penny.* (paperback with cassette). Hightstown, NJ: American School Publishers, n.d. (The Best of Encyclopedia Brown) Based on a story by Donald Sobol.

M227. *The Case of the Hungry Hitchhiker.* (paperback with cassette) American School Publishers, n.d. (The Best of Encyclopedia Brown) Based on a story by D. Sobol.

M228. *The Case of the Hungry Stranger.* (paperback with cassette) New York: Harper, 1985. 17 min. Based on a book by Crosby Bonsall.

M229. *The Case of the Missing Clues.* (paperback with cassette). American School Publishers, 1979. 10 min. Based on a story from *Encyclopedia Brown Solves Them All* by D. Sobol.

M230. *The Case of the Model-A Ford and the Man in the Snorkel Under the Hand: Donald J. Sobol.* (filmstrip with cassette) American School Publishers, 1981. 149 fr. 16 min.

M231. *The Case of the Muscle Maker.* (paperback with cassette). American School Publishers, 1979. 8 min. Based on a story from *Encyclopedia Brown Solves Them All* by D. Sobol.

M232. *The Case of the Mysterious Tramp.* (paperback with cassette) American School Publishers, n.d. (The Best of Encyclopedia Brown) Based on a story by D. Sobol.

M233. *The Case of the Super-Secret Hold.* (paperback with cassette) American School Publishers, 1979. 8 min. Based on a story from *Encyclopedia Brown Solves Them All* by D. Sobol.

M234. *The Case of the Whistling Ghost.* (paperback with cassette) American School Publishers, n.d. (The Best of Encyclopedia Brown) Based on a story by D. Sobol.

M235. *The Case of the World Traveler.* (paperback with cassette) American School Publishers, n.d. (The Best of Encyclopedia Brown) Based on a story by D. Sobol.

M236. *Castle.* (video) London: BBC; Skokie, IL: Texture Film Collection, and Alexandria, VA: PBS Video, 1985. 25 min. Live action and animated. Beta or VHS.

M237. *Castle.* (16mm film or video) Morris Plains, NJ: Lucerne and Unicorn Productions; Alexandria, VA: PBS Videos, 1983. 58 min. Beta, VHS, or 3/4". Includes drawings from David Macaulay's *Castle.*.

M238. *Castle.* (2 filmstrips and 2 cassettes) Costa Mesa, CA: Pied Piper, 1984. 35 min. Based on a book by David Macaulay.

M239. *Castle in the Attic.* (TV program or video) Program #8 of *More Books From Cover to Cover.* Alexandria, VA: PBS Video, n.d. 15 min. VHS or 3/4". Based on a book by Elizabeth Winthrop.

M240. *Cathedral.* (Video) Alexandria, VA: PBS Video, 1985. 60 min. Beta, VHS, or 3/4". Based on a book by David Macaulay.

M241. *The Celery Stalks at Midnight.* (cassette) New York: Harper/Caedmon, 1987. 60 min. Based on a book by James Howe. Performed by George Irving.

M243. *A Chair for My Mother.* (TV program or video) Program #20 of *Reading Rainbow.* Buffalo: WNED-TV and Lincoln, NE: GPN, 1985. 30 min. VHS or 3/4". Based on a book by Vera Williams.

M244. *A Chair for My Mother.* (video) Hightstown, NJ: American School Publishers, n.d. 8:30 min. VHS. Based on a book by V. Williams.

M245. *A Chair for My Mother.* (filmstrip with cassette) Hightstown, NJ: American School Publishers, 1985. 81 fr. 8 min. Based on a book by V. Williams.

M246. *A Chair for My Mother.* (paperback with cassette) American School Publishers, 1983. 8 min. Based on a book by V. Williams.

M247. *A Chair for My Mother.* (paperback with cassette) New York: Mulberry/Morrow, 1988. 15:30 min. Based on a book by V. Williams.

M248. *The Chalk Box Kid.* (paperback with cassette) New York: Random, 1989. 32 min. Based on a book by Clyde Bulla.

M248a. *Challenge.* (TV series) Nashville, TN: WDCN-TV and Lincoln, NE: GPN, 1983. 16 programs, 15 min. each. VHS or 3/4".

M249. *Chanticleer and the Fox.* (filmstrip with cassette) Weston, CT: Weston Woods, 1986. 47 fr. 10 min. Based on a tale in the *Canterbury Tales* by Geoffrey Chaucer, illustrated by Barbara Cooney.

M250a. *Character.* (filmstrip with cassette) Costa Mesa, CA: Pied Piper, 1985. 108 fr. 21 min. (Components of Fiction, Literature for Children, Series 9) Features: *Anastasia Krupnik* by Lois Lowry and *Jennifer, Hecate, Macbeth, William McKinley, and Me, Elizabeth* by E. L. Konigsburg. Introduces: *The Great Brain* by John Fitzgerald; *Bridge to Terahithia* by Katherine Paterson; and *The Loner* by Ester Wier.

M250b. *Character.* (filmstrip with cassette) (Components of Fiction: Literature for Children, Series 9). Costa Mesa, CA: Pied Piper, 1985. Introduces *Anastasia Krupnik* by Lois Lowry and *Jennifer, Hecate, Macbeth, William McKinley, and Me, Elizabeth* by E. L. Konigsburg.

M251. *Character Playing.* (TV program or video) A program of *The Word Shop.* Washington, DC: WNET-TV, 1976. 15 min. Beta, VHS, or 3/4".

M252. *Characters in Stories.* (TV program or video) A program of *The Word Shop.* WNET-TV, 1976. 15 min. Beta, VHS, or 3/4".

M253. *Charles Russell: An American Artist.* (16mm film or video) Pasadena: Barr Films, n.d. 19 min.

M254. *Charlie Needs a Cloak.* (16mm film or video) Weston, CT: Weston Woods, 1977. 8 min. Animated. Beta or VHS. Based on a book by Tomie de Paola.

M255. *Charlie Needs a Cloak.* (filmstrip with cassette) Weston Woods, 1977. 32 fr. 6 min. Based on a book by T. de Paola.

M256. *Charlie Needs a Cloak.* (hardback or paperback and cassette; cassette) Weston Woods, 1977. 6 min. Based on a book by T. dePaola.

M257. *Charlotte's Web.* (motion picture or video) Los Angeles: Paramount, 1973. 90 min. animated. VHS. Based on a book by E. B. White.

M258. *The Charmed Ring.* (TV program and video) Program #1 of *Teletales.* Bloomington, IN: AIT, 1984. 15 min. Beta, VHS, or 3/4". Based on a folk tale from India.

M259. *Chart Your Course!* (periodical) Mobile, AL: G/C/T Publishing. 8 issues per year.

M260. *The Chenoo.* (TV program and video) Program #7 of *Teletales.* Bloomington, IN:

M289. *Comic Strips.* (TV program) A program of *The Word Shop.* Washington, DC: WETA-TV, 1976. 15 min. Beta, VHS, or 3/4".

M290. *Commander Toad in Space.* (hardback or paperback with cassette) Old Greenwich, CT: Listening Library, n.d. 21 min. Based on a book by Jane Yolen.

M291. *Commodore Perry in the Land of the Shogun.* (filmstrip with cassette) Hightstown, NJ: American School Publishers, 1986. 150 fr. 27:45 min. Based on a book by Rhonda Blumberg.

M292. *The Complete Alice in Wonderland.* (4 phonograph records or 4 cassettes) New York: Harper/Caedmon, 1985. 163 min. Based on a book by Lewis Carroll. Read by Christopher Plummer.

M293. *Condor.* (TV program) A program in *The World of Audubon* series. Washington, DC: WETA-TV, 1987. 55 min.

M294. *Connect.* (periodical) Boston: Custom Magazines. Available from local cable companies. Monthly except July/Aug.

M295. *Conrad.* (TV series) Bloomington, IN: AIT and the Office of Instructional Television and Radio; Columbia: South Carolina State Department of Education, 1977. 24 programs, 15 min. each. Beta, VHS, or 3/4".

M296. *The Corner Grocery Store and Other Singable Songs.* (recording) Long Branch, NJ: Kimbo Educational, 1979. 29 min. Sung by Raffi.

M297. *The Cosby Show.* (TV series) New York: CBS-TV, 1984–. Situation comedy starring Bill Cosby and Phylicia Rashad. Weekly. 60 min each.

M298. *The Courage of Sarah Noble.* (video) Hightstown, NJ: American School Publishers, n.d. 48:30 min. Based on a book by Alice Dalgliesh.

M299. *The Courage of Sarah Noble.* (2 filmstrips with 2 cassettes) American School Publishers, n.d. Based on a book by A. Dalgliesh.

M300. *The Courage of Sarah Noble.* (cassette) American School Publishers, 1978. 48:47 min. Based on a book by A. Dalgliesh.

M301. *Creating a Beginning.* (filmstrip with cassette) Costa Mesa, CA: Pied Piper, 1975. 12 min. (Narrative Writing, 5) Introduces: "The Secret Life of Walter Mitty" by James Thurber, "The Ugly Duckling" by Hans C. Andersen, and "Little Red Riding Hood" by the Brothers Grimm.

M302. *Cricket.* (periodical) LaSalle, IL: Open Court Publishing Co. 12 issues per year.

M303. *The Cricket in Times Square.* (TV program or video) Program #1 of *Book Bird.* Springfield, VA: Childrens Television Interna-

tional, 1979. 15 min. 3/4". Based on a book by George Selden.

M304. *Crictor.* (filmstrip with cassette) Weston, CT: Weston Woods, 1981. 31 fr. 6 min. Based on a book by Tomi Ungerer.

M305. *Crictor.* (hardback or paperback and cassette) Weston Woods, 1981. 6 min. Based on a book by T. Ungerer.

M306. *Crocket's Victory Garden.* (TV series) See *The Victory Garden..*

M307. *Curious George.* (16mm film or video) Los Angeles: Churchill, 1985. 14 min. Puppet animation. Based on a book by H. A. Rey.

M308. *Curious George and the Dump Truck.* (16mm film or video) Morris Plains, NJ: Lucerne Films and Milktrain Productions, n.d. Beta, VHS, or 3/4". A companion to a book by Margret Rey and Alan Shalleck.

M309. *Curious George and the Pizza.* (paperback with cassette) Boston: Houghton Mifflin, 1988. 5:06 min. A companion to a book by M. Rey and A. Shalleck.

M310. *Curious George at the Airport.* (16mm film or video). Morris Plains, NJ: Lucerne Films, and Milktrain Productions, 1988. 5:32 min. A companion to a book by M. Rey and A. Shalleck.

M311a. *Curious George at the Fire Station.* (paperback with cassette) Boston: Houghton Mifflin, 1988. 10:33 min. A companion to a book by M. Rey and A. Shalleck.

M311b. *Curious George Gets a Pizza.* (16mm film or video) Lucerne Films, 1984. 5 min. Based on a book by M. Rey and A. Shalleck.

M311c. *Curious George Goes to an Amusement Park.* (16mm film or video) Lucerne Films, 1984. 5 min. Based on a book by M. Rey and A. Shalleck.

M312a. *Curious George Goes to the Hospital.* (16mm film or video) Los Angeles: Churchill Films, 1984. 15 min. Puppet animation. VHS. Based on a book by H. A. Rey.

M312b. *Curious George Goes to the Zoo.* (16mm film or video) Morris Plains, NJ: Lucerne Films, 1984. 5 min. Based on a book by M. Rey and A. Shlleck.

M313. *Curious George Learns the Alphabet.* (2 filmstrips and 2 cassettes, duplicating masters, chart) Hightstown, NJ: American School Publishers, 1977. Based on a book by H. A. Rey.

M314. *Curious George Rides a Bike.* (16mm film or video) Weston CT: Weston Woods, 1959. 10 min. Iconographic. VHS and Beta. Based on a book by H. A. Rey.

M315. *Curious George Rides a Bike.* (filmstrip with cassette). Weston Woods, 1959. 58 fr. 10

min. Iconographic. Based on a book by H. A. Rey.

M316. *Curious George Rides a Bike.* (hardback or paperback and cassette; cassette) Weston Woods, 1959. 10 min. Based on a book by H. A. Rey.

M317. *Curious George Visits the Zoo.* (paperback and cassette) Boston: Houghton Mifflin, n.d. A companion to a book by M. Rey and A. Shalleck.

M318. *Current Events Magazine.* (periodical) Columbus, OH: Xerox Educational Publications. 26 issues per year.

M319. *Current Health.* (periodical) Highland Park, IL: Curriculum Innovations. 9 issues per year.

M320. *Current Index to Journals in Education.* (periodical) Phoenix, AZ. Monthly.

M321. *Current Science.* (periodical) Middletown, CT: Field Publications. 18 issues per year.

M322. *Dad's House, Mom's House.* (16mm film or video) New York: National Film Board of Canada, 1987. 48 min.

M323. *The Dallas Titans Get Ready for Bed.* (hardback or paperback with cassette) Old Greenwich, CT: Listening Library, n.d. 15 min. Based on a book by Karla Kuskin.

M324. *The Dancing Granny and Other African Stories.* (phonograph record or cassette) New York: Harper/Caedmon, 1985. 46 min. Includes: "The Dancing Granny"; "Elephant and Frog Go Courting"; "Hen and Frog"; and "Frog and Two Wives." Written and performed by Ashley Bryan.

M325. *Dandelion.* (filmstrip with cassette) Ancramdale, NY: Live Oak Media, 1985. 5:15 min. Based on a book by Don Freeman.

M326. *Dandelion.* (hardbook or paperback with cassette; Reading Chest with 4 paperbacks and cassette) Live Oak Media, 1985. 4 min. Based on a book by D. Freeman.

M327. *Danny and the Dinosaur.* (paperback with cassette) New York: Harper, 1985. 15 min. Based on a book by Syd Hoff.

M328. *A Dark Dark Tale.* (16mm film or video) Weston, CT: Weston Woods, 1983. 4 min. Iconographic. Beta or VHS. Based on a book by Ruth Brown.

M329. *A Dark Dark Tale.* (filmstrip with cassette) Weston Woods, 1983. 27 fr. 5 min. Based on a book by R. Brown.

M330. *A Dark Dark Tale.* (hardcover or paperback with cassette) Weston Woods, 1983. 5 min. Based on a book by R. Brown.

M331. *The Dark is Rising.* (TV program or video) Program #16 of *More Books from Cover*

to Cover. Washington, DC: WETA-TV and Alexandria, VA: PBS, n.d. Beta or VHS. Based on a book by Susan Cooper.

M332. *David Macaulay in His Studio.* (video) Burlington, MA: Houghton Mifflin, 1983. 25 min. Live action. Beta, VHS, or 3/4″.

M333. *The Day Jimmy's Boa Ate the Wash.* (TV program or video) Program #14 of *Reading Rainbow.* Buffalo: WNED-TV and Lincoln, NE: Great Plains National, 1983. VHS or 3/4″. Based on a book by Trina Nobel. Narrated by Kaleena Kiff.

M334. *The Day Jimmy's Boa Ate the Wash.* (filmstrip with cassette) Weston, CT: Weston Woods, 1985. 35 fr. 5 min. Based on a book by T. Nobel.

M335. *The Day Jimmy's Boa Ate the Wash.* (hardcover or paperback with cassette) Weston Woods, 1985. 5 min. Based on a book by T. Nobel.

M336. *The Day Jimmy's Boa Ate the Wash and Other Stories.* (phonograph record or cassette) New York: Harper/Caedmon, 1985. 30 min. Includes: *The Day Jimmy's Boa Ate the Wash*; *Jimmy's Boa Bounces Back*; *A King's Tale*; *Apple Tree Christmas*; and *Hansy's Mermaid.* Based on books by Trina Noble. Read by Sandy Duncan.

M337. *Deadwood City.* (TV program; video) Program #6 of *Readit!.* Bloomington, IN: AIT, 1982. 15 min. Beta, VHS, or 3/4″. Based on a book by Edward Packard. Also includes: *The Third Planet from Altair* by E. Packard.

M338. *Dear Mr. Henshaw.* (2 filmstrips and 2 cassettes) Hightstown, NJ: American School Publishers, 1985. 85 and 95 fr. 16:30 min. each. Based on a book by Beverly Cleary.

M339. *Dear Mr. Henshaw.* (cassette) American School Publishers, 1984. 34 min. Based on a book by B. Cleary. Read by Gregory Premmer.

M340. *DeGrassi Jr. High.* (TV series, 16mm films, or videos) Los Angeles: Direct Cinema and Taylor Productions, 1987. 26 programs, 30 min. each. VHS.

M341. *Desert Giant: The World of the Saguaro Cactus.* (TV program or video) Program #62 of *Reading Rainbow.* Buffalo: WNED-TV and Lincoln, NE: GPN, 1990. Beta, VHS, or 3/4″. Based on a book by Barbara Bash.

M342. *Designasaurus.* (computer program) Designerware/Britannica Software, 1988. 3 disks and guide. Apple II family. IBM PC.

M343. *Detectives.* (TV program) A program of *3-2-1-Contact.* New York: Children's Television Workshop, n.d. 30 min.

M344. *Developing a Character*. (filmstrip with cassette) (Narrative Writing) Costa Mesa, CA: Pied Piper, 1975. 12 min. Introduces: *Treasure Island* by Robert Louis Stevenson; *Little Women* by Louisa May Alcott; and *Roosevelt Grady* by Louise Shotwell.

M345. *The Devil and Daniel Webster*. (phonograph record or cassette) New York: Harper/Caedmon, n.d. 39 and 58 min. Based on a story by Stephen Vincent Benet. Read by Pat Hingle.

M346. *Diary-Journal: Realistic Fiction*. (filmstrip with cassette) (Literature to Enjoy and Write About, Series 1) Costa Mesa, CA: Pied Piper, 1989. 22 fr. Includes: *Dear Mr. Henshaw* by Beverly Cleary; *Where the Red Fern Grows*, by Wilson Rawls; and *In the Year of the Boar and Jackie Robinson* by Bette Lord.

M347. *Different Dragons*. (TV program or video) Program #6 of *Books from Cover to Cover*. Alexandria, VA: PBS Video, n.d. 15 min. VHS or 3/4″. Based on a book by Jean Little.

M348. *Digging Up Dinosaurs*. (TV program) Program #6 of *Reading Rainbow*. Buffalo: WNED-TV and Lincoln, NE: GPN, 1983. 30 min. VHS or 3/4″. Based on a book by Aliki.

M349. *Digging Up Dinosaurs*. (hardback or paperback with cassette) Old Greenwich, CT: Listening Library, n.d. 11 min. Based on a book by Aliki.

M350. *Dinosaur*. (16mm film or video) Santa Monica, CA: Pyramid, 1980. 14 min. Beta, VHS, or 3/4″.

M351. *Dinosaur Bob and His Adventures with the Family Lizardo*. (TV program or video) Program #60 of *Reading Rainbow*. Buffalo: WNED-TV and Lincoln, NE: GPN, 1989. 30 min. VHS or 3/4″. Based on a book by William Joyce. Narrated by Ed Asner.

M352. *Dinosaur Poster Book*. (16 posters) Philadelphia: Running Press, 1988.

M353. *Dinosaur Rock*. (cassette) New York: Harper/Caedmon, 1983. 45 min. Performed by Michele Valeri and Michael Stein.

M354. *Dinosaur Year 1989 Calendar*. New York: Knopf, 1989. 17″ x 15″.

M355. *Dinosaurs*. (video) Santa Monica, CA: Pyramid Films/Golden Book Video, 1987. 30 min. Animated. VHS.

M356. *Dinosaurs*. (poster, booklet, and cassette) San Francisco: California Academy of Sciences, 1987. 20 min.

M357. *Dinosaurs*. (hardback or paperback with cassette) Old Greenwich, CT: Listening Library, 1989. 18 min. Based on a book by Gail Gibbons.

M358. *Dinosaurs Beware!* (filmstrip with cassette) Hightstown, NJ: American School Publishers, 1984. 86 fr. 11 min. Based on a book by Marc Brown and Stephen Krensky.

M359. *Dinosaurs Divorce: A Guide for Changing Families*. (filmstrip with cassette) American School Publishers, 1987. 122 fr. 11:10 min. Based on a book by Laurene and Marc Brown.

M360. *Dinosaurs: Giant Reptiles*. (30 booklets with cassette; activity sheets) Washington, DC: National Geographic, 1986. 30 min. VHS or 3/4″.

M361. *Dinosaurs: Puzzles from the Past*. (16mm film or video) National Geographic, 1981. 20 min. VHS or 3/4″.

M362a. *Dinosaurs: The Terrible Lizards*, 2nd ed. (16mm film or video) Van Nuys, CA: AIMS, 1986. 9:30 min.

M362b. *The Discovery Network's Educators' Guide*. (newsletter/poster) Bethesda, MD: The Discovery Channel. monthly.

M363. *Dive to the Coral Reefs*. (TV program or video) Program #61 of *Reading Rainbow*. Buffalo: WNED-TV and Lincoln, NE: GPN, 1990. Beta, VHS, or 3/4. Based on a book by Elizabeth Tayntor, Paul Erichson, and Les Kaufman.

M364. *Divorce Can Happen to the Nicest People*. (video) Los Angeles: LCA/New World Video, 1987. 30 min. Animated. Beta, VHS, or 3/4″.

M365. *The Divorce Express*. (3 filmstrips and 3 cassettes) Cleveland: Cheshire Corp., n.d. 57–78 fr. each, 12–15 min. each. Based on a book by Paula Danziger.

M366. *The Divorce Express*. (hardback or paperback with cassette) Old Greenwich, CT: Listening Library, 1985. 81 min. (Young Adult Cliffhangers) Based on a book by P. Danziger.

M367. *Do Animals Talk?* (TV program) Program #8 of *Zoo Zoo Zoo*. Cincinnati: WCET-TV and the Greater Cincinnati Television Educational Foundation, n.d. 15 min.

M368. *Do Children Also Divorce?* (video) New York: Filmmakers Library, 1988. 30 min. VHS or 3/4″.

M369. *Doctor De Soto*. (16mm film or video) Weston, CT: Weston Woods, 1984. 10 min. Animated. VHS or Beta. Based on a book by William Steig.

M370. *Doctor De Soto*. (filmstrip with cassette) Weston Woods, 1984. 47 fr. 9 min. Based on a book by W. Steig.

M371. *Doctor De Soto*. (hardback or paperback with cassette) Weston Woods, 1984. 9 min. Based on a book by W. Steig. Read by Ian Thompson.

M372. *Doctor De Soto and Other Stories.* (cassette) New York: Harper/Caedmon, 1984. 40 min. Based on books by William Steig. Read by Pat Carroll.

M373. *Dr. Seuss's Caldecotts.* (video) Hightstown, NJ: American School Publishers, 1985. 56 min. VHS. Includes: *McElligot's Pool,* 9 min.; *Bartholomew and the Oobleck,* 26 min.; and *If I Ran the Zoo,* 17 min. Based on books by Dr. Seuss.

M374. *Does It Bite?* (TV program) A program of *Shining Time Station.* New York: WNET-TV, 1989. 30 min. Host: Ringo Starr.

M375. *Dogs.* (16mm film or video) Washington, DC: National Geographic, 1985. 16 min. Live action. VHS or 3/4″.

M376. *Dogsong.* (video) Hightstown, NJ: American School Publishers, 1988. 40 min. VHS. Based on a book by Gary Paulsen. Read by Jamake Highwater.

M377. *Dogsong.* (2 filmstrips with cassettes) American School Publishers, 1988. 134 and 147 fr. 19:36 and 20:42 min. Based on a book by G. Paulsen. Read by J. Highwater.

M378. *Dogsong.* (cassette) American School Publishers, 1988. 40 min. Based on a book by G. Paulsen. Read by J. Highwater.

M379. *Dolphin Adventure.* (video) Stamford, CT: Vestron, 1986. 59 min. Live action. Beta or VHS.

M380. *Dolphins.* (16mm film or video) Washington, DC: National Geographic, 1983. 15 min. Live action. VHS or 3/4″.

M381. *Down, Down, Down: The Inside Story of Your Bones and Muscles.* (TV program or video) A program of *The Inside Story with Slim Goodbody.* Bloomington, IN: AIT and Green Bay, WI: UW-GB Telecommunications Center, 1981. 15 min. Beta, VHS, or 3/4″.

M382. *Dragon Slayer: The Story of Beowulf.* (2 cassettes) Boston: G. K. Hall and Chivers Productions, 1986. 2 hours.

M383. *Dragonsong.* (cassette) Taos, NM: Performing Arts Press, 1985. 30 min. Written and read by Anne McCaffrey.

M384. *Draw Along.* (TV series or videos) Bloomington, IN: AIT (Agency for Instructional Technology) and the Oklahoma Educational TV Authority, 1986. 25 min. each. Beta, VHS, or 3/4″. Host: Paul Ringler.

M385. *The Draw Man.* (TV series or videos) Bloomington, IN: AIT, (Agency for Instructional Technology) and Oklahoma City: KOKH-TV, 1975. 32 programs. 15 min. each. VHS or 3/4″.

M386. *Ducks Under Siege.* (TV program) A program from *The World of Audubon.* Washington, DC: WETA-TV and the National Audubon Society, n.d. 60 min.

M387. *Duncan and Dolores.* (TV program or video) Program #52 of *Reading Rainbow.* Buffalo: WNED-TV and Lincoln, NE: GPN, 1989. 30 min. VHS or 3/4″. Based on a book by Barbara Samuels. Read by Jane Curtin.

M388a. *Early Instruments, Part 1 and Part 2.* (TV programs or videos) Programs #9 and #10 of *Musical Instruments.* Lincoln, NE: GPN, 1979. 20 min. VHS or 3/4″.

M388b. *Early Frontier Life.* (filmstrip with cassette) Westward Movement Series. Niles, IL: United Learning, 1985. 11 min.

M389. *The Earth.* (TV program) A program of *Challenge.* Nashville: WDCN-TV, n.d. 15 min.

M390. *East African Instruments Part 1 and Part 2.* (TV programs or videos) Programs #14 and #15 of *Musical Instruments.* Lincoln, NE: GPN, 1979. 17 min each. VHS or 3/4″.

M391. *Eating.* (TV program) A program of *3-2-1-Contact.* New York: Children's Television Workshop, n.d. 30 min.

M392. *Ebony, Jr.* (periodical) Chicago: Johnson Publishing Co. 10 issues per year.

M394. *The Eighteenth Emergency.* (TV program or video) A program of *Best of Cover to Cover, 1-A.* Washington, DC: WETA-TV and Alexandria, VA: PBS, n.d. 15 min. Based on a book by Betsy Byars.

M395. *Electricity.* (TV program) A program of *Challenge.* Nashville: WDCN-TV, n.d. 15 min.

M396. *Elementary English.* (periodical) Urbana, IL: National Council of Teachers of English. Replaced in 1975 by *Language Arts.*.

M397. *Elementary School Journal.* (periodical) Chicago: University of Chicago Press. Bimonthly, Sept. to May.

M398. *Elements of a Story.* (filmstrip with cassette) (Narrative Writing, 5) Costa Mesa, CA: Pied Piper, 1975. 12 min. Introduces *The Wizard of Oz* by L. Frank Baum.

M399a. *The Emergency Librarian.* (periodical) Vancouver, BC: Dyad Services. 5 issues per year.

M399b. *Emma's Pet.* (filmstrip with cassette) Ancramdale, NY: Live Oak Media, 1986. 30 fr. 4 min. Based on a book by David McPhail.

M400. *Encyclopedia Brown: The Boy Detective in Five E. B. Mysteries.* (video) Culver City, CA: Deutsch Productions and Santa Monica, CA: High-Tops Video, 1989. 30 min. VHS. Includes 5 cases based on books by Donald Sobol.

M401. *Encyclopedia Brown: The Boy Detective in the Case of the Missing Time Capsule.* (video) Santa Monica, CA: Hi-Tops Video, 1989. 5 min. Live action. Based on a book by D. Sobol.

M402. *Encyclopedia Brown: One-Minute Mysteries.* (video) Hi-Tops Video/Media Home Entertainment, 1989. Based on books by D. Sobol.

M403. *Encyclopedia Brown's Reading Adventures.* (4 filmstrips with cassettes and skill sheets) Chicago: SVE, 1983. Includes: *The Case of the Secret Pitch,* 27 fr. 9 min.; *The Case of the Blueberry Pies,* 31 fr. 9 min.; *The Case of the Flying Boy,* 29 fr. 9 min.; *The Case of the Silver Fruit Bowl,* 29 fr. 8 min.; *The Case of the Junk Sculptor,* 29 fr. 8 min.; *The Case of the Smelly Nellie,* 29 fr. 8 min.; *The Case of the Headless Runner,* 28 fr. 7 min.; *The Case of the Barefoot Thieves,* 29 fr. 8 min.

M404. *English Composition for Children, 1: Organizing Ideas.* (4 filmstrips and 4 cassettes) Costa Mesa, CA: Pied Piper, 1973. 9 min each. Includes: *Kinds of Sentences; Paragraphs; More Than a Paragraph;* and *Outlines..*

M405. *English Composition for Children, 2: Building Word Power.* (4 filmstrips with 4 cassettes) Pied Piper, 1973. 9 min. each. Includes: *Picture Words; Figures of Speech; Action Words;* and *Sensory Description..*

M406. *English Composition for Children, 5: Narrative Writing.* (4 filmstrips with cassettes) Pied Piper, 1975. 12 min each. Includes: *Developing Character; Building a Conflict;* and *Elements of a Story..*

M407. *The Enormous Egg.* (hardback or paperback with cassette) Old Greenwich, CT: Listening Library, 1985. 45 min. (Soundways to Reading, Cliffhanger Read-along) Based on a book by Oliver Butterworth.

M408. *The Environment and Research.* (filmstrip with cassette) (Antarctica Series). Falls Church, VA: Enjoying Communicating, 1982. 67 fr. 11 min.

M409. *Epics and Legends.* (filmstrip with cassette) (Literature for Children, Series 6). Costa Mesa, CA: Pied Piper, 1980. 13 min. Includes: "The Trojan Horse," "King Arthur," and "Robin Hood."

M409a. *ERIC*—Educational Resources Information Center (database). Washington, DC: Office of Educational Research, Department of Education. Indexes: *Resources in Education* and *Current Index to Journals in Education..*

M410. *Ernest and Celestine.* (filmstrip with cassette) Weston, CT: Weston Woods, 1984. 27 fr. 5 min. Based on a book by Gabrielle Vincent.

M411. *Ernest and Celestine.* (hardcover or paperback and cassette) Weston Woods, 1984. 5 min. Based on a book by G. Vincent.

M412. *Ernest and Celestine's Picnic.* (filmstrip with cassette) Weston Woods, 1984. 31 fr. 7 min. Based on a book by G. Vincent.

M413. *Ernest and Celestine's Picnic.* (hardcover or paperback and cassette) Weston Woods, 1984. 7 min. Based on a book by G. Vincent.

M414. *Escape from Warsaw.* (TV program) Program #16 of *Storybound.* Lincoln, NE: GPN, 1981. 15 min. VHS or 3/4″. Based on a book by Ian Serraillier. Alternate title is *The Silver Sword..*

M415. *Escape to Witch Mountain.* (motion picture and video) Burbank, CA: Disney, 1975. Walt Disney Home Video, 1980. 27 min. Beta, VHS, or 3/4″. Based on a book by Alexander Key.

M416. *Everglades.* (TV program or video) Washington, DC: National Geographic, 1986. 12 min. VHS and 3/4″.

M417. *Everglades National Parks: Everglades, Big Cypress, Biscayne, and Fort Jefferson.* (video) Whittier, CA: Finley-Holiday Home Video, 1989. 56 min.

M418. *Every Dog's Guide to Complete Home Safety.* (16mm film or video) New York: National Film Board of Canada, n.d. 10 min.

M419. *Explorers Unlimited.* (TV series) Cleveland: WVIZ-TV, Educational Association of Metropolitan Cleveland, and Bloomington, IN: AIT, 1971. 33 programs, 15 min. each. Beta, VHS, or 3/4″.

M420. *Exploring New Places.* (filmstrip with cassette) (Literature for Children, Series 7B) Costa Mesa, CA: Pied Piper, 1982. 10 min. Introduces: *Henry Explores the Mountains* by Mark Taylor and *Madeline* by Ludwig Bemelmans.

M421. *Fables.* (filmstrip with cassette) Hightstown, NJ: American School Publishers, 1981. 18 min. Based on a book by Arnold Lobel.

M422. *Fables.* (paperback with cassette) American School Publishers, 1981. 18 min. Based on a book by A. Lobel.

M423. *Fables of Harry Allard.* (16mm film or video) Deerfield, IL: Learning Corp. of America, 1986. 30 min. Beta or VHS. Includes: *Miss Nelson Is Missing* and *It's So Nice to Have a Wolf Around the House.* Based on books by Harry Allard.

M424. *Faces.* (periodical) Peterborough, NH: Cobblestone Publications. 10 issues per year.

M425. *The Fairy Tale.* (filmstrip with cassette) Peoria, IL: Thomas Klise, 1981. 82 fr.

M426. *Families.* (2 filmstrips with cassettes) Baldwin, NY: Activity Records, Educational Activities, 1985. 60 and 68 fr. 9 and 11 min.

M427. *Families.* (2 filmstrips with 2 cassettes) Freeport, NY: Aschoff Associates and Educational Activities, 1985. 65 fr. 8 min. 54 fr. 8 min.

M428. *Families Are Different and Alike.* (16mm film or video) Deerfield, IL: Coronet, 1989. 13 min. Beta, VHS, or 3/4".

M429. *The Fantastic Mr. Fox.* (cassette) New York: Harper/Caedmon, 1978. 54:08 min. Written and read by Roald Dahl.

M430. *Fantastic Series.* (5 filmstrips and cassettes) Peoria, IL: Thomas Klise, 1981. Includes: *The Folktale; The Fairy Tale; Horror/ Ghost Stories,* and *Science Fiction.*.

M431. *The Fantastic Voyage.* (motion picture or video) New York: CBS/Fox, 1966. 100 min. Beta or VHS. Based on a book by Isaac Asimov.

M432. *Fantasy.* (filmstrip with cassette) (Literature for Children, Series 1) Costa Mesa, CA: Pied Piper, 1970. 12 min. Features: *The Cricket in Times Square* by George Selden and *Doctor Dolittle* by Hugh Lofting. Introduces fantasy by C. S. Lewis; Mary Norton; Astrid Lindgren; Eleanor Cameron; and W. E. B. DuBois.

M433. *Fantasy Literature.* (filmstrip with cassette) Peoria, IL: Thomas Klise, 1981. 73 fr.

M434. *Fantasy Stories.* (TV program) A program of *The Word Shop.* Washington, DC: WETA-TV, 1976. 15 min. Beta, VHS, or 3/4".

M435. *Farms.* (TV program) A program of 3-2-1-Contact. New York: Children's Television Workshop, n.d. 30 min.

M436. *Father Bear Comes Home.* (paperback with cassette) Old Greenwich, CT: Listening Library, 1982. Based on a book by Elsie Minarik.

M437. *Father Fox's Feast of Songs and Three Stories.* (cassette) Hanover, NH: Sassafras, 1986. 50 min. Based on a book by Clyde Watson.

M438. *Feelings.* (TV program or video) Program #28 of *Reading Rainbow.* Buffalo: WNED-TV and Lincoln, NE: GPN, 1986. 30 min. VHS or 3/4". Host: LeVar Burton.

M439. *Fiddy Wow Wow.* (TV program or video) Program #14 of *Teletales.* Bloomington, IN: AIT, 1984. 15 min. Beta, VHS, or 3/4". Based on a folk tale from Denmark.

M440. *Field and Stream.* (periodical) New York: Times Mirror. Monthly.

M441. *The Fig Tree.* (TV program) A program on *WonderWorks.* Pittsburgh: WQED-TV and the Children's Family Consortium, n.d. 60 min. Based on a short story by K. A. Porter.

M442. *Fight.* (TV program) A program of *DeGrassi Jr. High.* Boston: WGBH-TV, n.d. 30 min.

M443. *Fins, Feathers, and Fur.* (TV series) Rochester, NY: WXXI-TV and Bloomington, IN: AIT (Agency for Instructional Technology), 1986. 15 programs, 15 min. each. Beta, VHS, or 3/4".

M444. *First Dinosaur Reader.* (computer program) Pound Ridge, NY: Orange Cherry Software, 1988. 2 disks, guide, backup disks. Apple II family, Commodore 64/228.

M445. *The First Frontier.* (filmstrip with cassette) Niles: IL: United Learning, 1985. 51 min.

M446. *Five Lionni Classics* (video) Westminster, MD: Random, 1988. 30 min. VHS. Includes: *Frederick, Cornelius, It's Mine!, Fish Is Fish,* and *Swimmy.* Based on books by Leo Lionni.

M447. *Five Senses.* (four filmstrips and cassettes) New York: Children's Television Workshop, Guidance Associates, and 3-2-1 Contact, 1985. Includes *Hearing* (16 min.); *Smell and Taste* (13 min.); *Touch* (9 min.); and *Vision* (10 min.).

M448. *Flight of the Whooping Crane.* (TV program or video) Washington, DC: National Geographic, n.d. 59 min. Beta or VHS.

M449. *Flip.* (hardback or paperback with cassette; Reading Chest with 4 paperbacks and cassette) Ancramdale, NY: Live Oak Media, 1977. 9 min. Based on a book by Wesley Dennis.

M450. *Flip and the Morning.* (hardback or paperback with cassette; Reading Chest with 4 paperbacks and cassette) Live Oak Media, 1979. 9:15 min. Based on a book by W. Dennis.

M451. *Flossie and the Fox.* (filmstrip with cassette) Weston, CT: Weston Woods, 1988. 61 fr. 13 min. Based on a book by Patricia McKissack.

M452. *Flossie and the Fox.* (hardcover with cassette) Weston Woods, 1988. 13 min. Based on a book by P. McKissack.

M453. *The Folk Book.* (TV series) Bloomington, IN: AIT (Agency for Instructional Technology), Green Bay, WI: University of Wisconsin, 1980. 15 programs 20 min. each. Beta, VHS, or 3/4".

M454. *Folk Tales.* (TV program) A program of *The Word Shop.* Springfield, VA: Children's Television International, 1976. 15 min. Beta, VHS, or 3/4".

M455. *Folktale Characters.* (filmstrip with cassette) (Literature for Children, Series 8). Costa Mesa, CA: Pied Piper, 1983. Includes: "Jorinda and Joringel" and "The Donkey Prince." Based on folk tales from Germany.

M456. *Folktales.* (filmstrip with cassette) Peoria, IL: Thomas Klise, 1981. 83 fr. 20 min.

M457. *Folktales from Afar.* (filmstrip with cassette) (Literature for Children, Series 8) Costa Mesa, CA: Pied Piper, 1983. 15 min. Includes: "The Tale of the Gentle People," "Anansi the Spider," and "The Crane Maiden." Based on folktales from South America, Africa, and Japan.

M458. *Follow My Leader.* (16mm film or video) Van Nuys, CA: AIMS Media, 1988. Classroom version: 29 min. Live action. Based on a book by James Garfield.

M459. *Follow My Leader.* (filmstrip with cassette) Costa Mesa, CA: Pied Piper, 1976. Based on a book by J. Garfield.

M460a *Food and Digestion.* (TV program).

M460b. *Food for Tomorrow.* (TV program) A program of *Challenge.* Nashville: WDCN-TV, n.d. 15 min.

M461. *Fossils! Fossils!* (16mm film or video) Irwindale, CA: Centre Productions/Barr, 1989. 18 min.

M462. *Four-B Goes Wild.* (TV program) Program #2 of *Books from Cover to Cover.* Alexandria, VA: PBS Video, n.d. 15 min. VHS or 3/4". Based on a book by Jamie Gilson.

M463. *The Fourth Grade Celebrity.* (hardback or paperback with cassette) Old Greenwich, CT: Listening Library, 1985. 77 min. (Soundways to Reading, Cliffhanger Read-along) Based on a book by Patricia Giff.

M464. *Fox.* (2 cassettes) Old Greenwich, CT: Listening Library, 1989. 60 min. Includes: *Fox in Love, Fox at School, Fox and His Friends,* and *Fox on Wheels.* Based on books by Edward Marshall.

M465. *Fox and His Friends.* (paperback with cassette) Listening Library, 1985. 15 min. Based on a book by E. Marshall.

M466. *Fox at School.* (paperback with cassette) Listening Library, 1985. 14 min. Based on a book by E. Marshall.

M467. *Fox Busters.* (2 cassettes) Boston: G. K. Hall, 1987. 80 min. Based on a book by Dick King-Smith.

M468. *Fox in Love.* (paperback with cassette) Listening Library, 1985. 12 min. Based on a book by E. Marshall.

M469. *Fox on Wheels.* (paperback with cassette) Listening Library, 1985. 13 min. Based on a book by E. Marshall.

M470. *The Fox Went Out on a Chilly Night.* (16mm or video) Weston, CT: Weston Woods, 1969. 8 min. Iconographic. Beta or VHS. Based on a book by Peter Spier.

M471. *The Fox Went Out on a Chilly Night.* (filmstrip with cassette) Weston Woods, 1969. 40 fr. 8 min. Based on a book by P. Spier.

M472. *The Fox Went Out on a Chilly Night.* (hardback with cassette; cassette) Weston Woods, 1969. 8 min. Based on a book by P. Spier.

M473. *Fox's Dream.* (filmstrip with cassette) Hightstown, NJ: American School Publishers, 1989. 57 fr. 6 min. Based on a book by Keizaburo Tejima.

M475. *Freckle Juice.* (TV program or video) A program of *Best of Cover to Cover, 1-A.* Washington, DC: WETA-TV and Alexandria, VA: PBS, n.d. 15 min. Based on a book by Judy Blume.

M476. *Freckle Juice.* (filmstrip with 2 cassettes) Costa Mesa, CA: Pied Piper, 1984. 113 fr. 26 min. Based on a book by J. Blume.

M477. *Freckle Juice.* (hardback or paperback with cassette) Old Greenwich, CT: Listening Library, 1982. 31 min. Based on a book by J. Blume.

M478. *Frederick.* (TV program or video) A program from the Green Module of *Picture Book Park.* Cleveland: WVIZ-TV and AIT, 1972/73. 15 min. Beta, VHS, or 3/4". Based on a book by Leo Lionni.

M479. *Free to Be . . . A Family.* (phonograph record or cassette) Hollywood, CA: A & M Records, 1988. 57 min. Hostess: Marlo Thomas.

M480. *Free to Be . . . You and Me.* (video) Del Mar, CA: CRM/McGraw-Hill, 1974. Stamford, CT: Vestron, 1983. 44 min. Beta, VHS. Hostess: M. Thomas.

M480a. *Freight Train.* (filmstrip with cassette) Hightstown, NJ: American School Publishers, 1980. 5 min. Based on a book by Donald Crews.

M481. *Friendly Letter: Realistic Fiction.* (filmstrip with cassette) (Literature to Enjoy and Write About, Series 2) Costa Mesa, CA: Pied Piper, 1989. 22 min. Includes: *Summer of the Swans* by Betsy Byars; *Arthur for the Very First Time* by Patricia MacLachlan; *On My Honor* by Marion Bauer; and *The One-Eyed Cat* by Paula Fox.

M482. *Frog and Toad Are Friends.* (TV program or video) A program of *Tilson's Book Shop.* Cleveland: WVIZ-TV and Lincoln, NE:

GPN, 1975. 15 min. VHS. Based on a book by Arnold Lobel.

M483. *Frog and Toad Are Friends.* (16mm or video) Los Angeles: Churchill Films, 1985. 17 min. Based on a book by A. Lobel.

M484. *Frog and Toad Are Friends; Frog and Toad Together; Frog and Toad: Behind the Scenes.* (TV program or video) A program of *Long Ago and Far Away.* Boston: WGBH-TV, 1986. Los Angeles: Churchill Films, 1987. 60 min. Puppet animation. Based on books by A. Lobel.

M485. *Frog and Toad Are Friends/Some Frogs Have Their Own Rocks.* (TV program or video) A program of *Tilson's Book Shop.* Cleveland: WVIZ-TV and Lincoln, NE: GPN, 1975. 15 min.

M486. *Frog and Toad: Behind the Scenes.* (TV program, 16mm film, or video) Churchill Films, 1987. 9:30 min. Based on a TV show about books by A. Lobel.

M487. *Frozen Fire.* (TV program; video) Program #5 of *Book Bird.* Springfield, VA: Children's Television Institute, 1979. 15 min. 3/4″. Based on a book by James Houston.

M488. *George and Martha.* (paperback with cassette) Boston: Houghton Mifflin, 1987. 15 min. Based on a book by James Marshall.

M489. *Germs Make Me Sick.* (TV program or video) Program #34 of *Reading Rainbow.* Buffalo: WNED-TV and Lincoln, NE: GPN, 1986. 15 min. VHS or 3/4″. Based on a book by Melvin Berger.

M490. *Getting Hooked on Books: Challenges.* (2 filmstrips with cassettes) Mt. Kisco, NY: Guidance Associates, 1986. 39 and 40 frs. 6:02 and 5:15 min. Booktalks introduce: *Summer of the Swans* by Betsy Byars; *The Sword in the Stone* by Theodore White; *Anne Frank: The Diary of a Young Girl* by Anne Frank; *Dicey's Song* by Cynthia Voigt; *The Westing Game* by Ellen Raskin; *The Great Gilly Hopkins* by Katherine Paterson; *The Mixed-Up Files of Mrs. Basil E. Frankweiler* by E. L. Konigsburg; *Dear Mr. Henshaw* by Beverly Cleary; *Homesick: My Own Story* by Jean Fritz; and *My Brother Sam Is Dead* by James and Christopher Collier.

M491. *Getting Hooked on Books: Friendships.* (2 filmstrips with cassettes) Guidance Associates, 1986. Booktalks introduce: *Little Women* by Louisa May Alcott; *The One-Eyed Cat* by Paula Fox; *Bridge to Terabithia* by Katherine Paterson, and others.

GPN Newsletter. See *Great Plains National Newsletter.*

M492. *The Ghost Belonged to Me.* (hardback or paperback with cassette) Ancramdale, NY: Live Oak Media, 1976. 54:67 min. Based on a book by Richard Peck.

M493. *The Ghost of Thomas Kempe.* (TV program or video) A program of *Best of Cover to Cover, 2-A.* Washington, DC: WETA-TV and Alexandria, VA: PBS Video, n.d. 15 min. Based on a book by Penelope Lively.

M494. *The Ghost Squad.* (TV program or video) Program #7 of *More Books from Cover to Cover.* Washington, DC: WETA-TV and Alexandria, VA: PBS, n.d. 15 min. VHS or 3/4″. Based on a book by E. W. Hildick.

M495. *Ghosts I Have Been.* (TV program or video) Program #4 of *Storybound.* 15 min. Springfield, VA: Children's Television International, 1981. Beta, VHS, or 3/4″. Based on a book by Richard Peck.

M496. *Gift of the Sacred Dog.* (TV program or video) Program #10 of *Reading Rainbow.* Buffalo: WNED-TV and Lincoln, NE: GPN, 1983. 15 min. VHS or 3/4″. Based on a book by Paul Goble. Narrated by Michael Ansara.

M497. *Gila Monsters Meet You at the Airport.* (TV program or video) Program #8 of *Reading Rainbow.* WNED-TV and GPN, 1983. 15 min. Beta or VHS. Based on a book by Marjorie Sharmat.

M498. *A Girl Called Al.* (hardback or paperback with cassette) Old Greenwich, CT: Listening Library, 1985. 45 min. (Soundways to Reading, Cliffhanger Read-along) Based on a book by Constance Greene.

M499. *Give Us a Great Big Smile, Rosy Cole.* (TV program or video) Program #11 of *Readit!* 15 min. Bloomington, IN: AIT, 1982. Beta, VHS, or 3/4″. Based on a book by Sheila Greenwald.

M500. *The Glorious Flight: Across the Channel with Louis Bleriot.* (video) Hightstown, NJ: American School Publishers, n.d. 10 min. VHS. Based on a book by Alice and Martin Provensen.

M501. *The Glorious Flight: Across the Channel with Louis Bleriot.* (video) Ancramdale, NY: Live Oak Media, 1987. 11 min. VHS. Based on a book by A. and M. Provensen.

M502. *The Glorious Flight: Across the Channel with Louis Bleriot.* (filmstrip with cassette) Live Oak Media, 1984. 52 fr. 10 min. Based on a book by A. and M. Provensen.

M503. *Going Home.* (TV program or video) Program #12 of *Books from Cover to Cover.* Washington, DC: WETA-TV and Alexandria, VA: PBS Video, n.d. 15 min. Based on a book by Nicholas Mohr.

M504. *Good Manners.* (2 filmstrips with cassettes) Stamford, CT: Educational Dimensions, 1986. Includes: *Communications and Manners,* 63 fr. 16:30 min. and *Manners at Home, In School, and In Public Places.* 59 fr. 14 min.

M506. *Gorilla.* (video) Washington, DC: National Geographic, WQED-TV, and Vestron, 1981. 59 min. Live action. Beta or VHS.

M507. *A Grandmother for the Orphelines.* (TV program or video) Program #13 of *Readit!* Bloomington, IN: AIT, 1982. 15 min. Beta, VHS, or 3/4″. Based on a book by Natalie Carlson.

M508. *Graven Images.* (filmstrip with cassette) Hightstown, NJ: American School Publishers, 1983. 163 fr. 27:30 min. Based on a book by Paul Fleischman.

M509. *The Great Big Especially Beautiful Easter Egg.* (filmstrip with cassette) American School Publishers, 1985. 89 fr. 8:27 min. Based on a book by James Stevenson.

M510. *The Great Brain.* (hardback or paperback with cassette) Old Greenwich, CT: Listening Library, 1986. 78 min. (Soundways to Reading, Cliffhanger Read-along) Based on a book by John Fitzgerald.

M511. *The Great Brain.* (5 cassettes) Salt Lake City, UT: The Great Brain Enterprise, 1987. 5 hours. Based on a book by J. Fitzgerald.

M512. *The Great Brain Does It Again.* (4 cassettes) The Great Brain Enterprise, 1987. 4 hrs. Based on a book by John Fitzgerald.

M513. *The Great Brain Reforms.* (filmstrip with cassette) Costa Mesa, CA: Pied Piper, 1981. 17 min. Based on a book by J. Fitzgerald.

M514a. *The Great Circus Parade.* (TV program and video) Milwaukee: WITI-TV, 1987. 90 min. 3/4″.

M514b. *The Great Gilly Hopkins.* (2 cassettes) Hightstown, NJ: American School Publishers, 1980. 16 min. each. Based on a book by Katherine Paterson.

M515. *Great Plains National Newsletter.* Lincoln, NE: Great Plains National Instructional Television. Quarterly.

M516. *The Great Whales.* (video) Washington, DC and Stamford, CT: Vestron, n.d. 59 min. Beta or VHS.

M517. *Greece.* (TV program) A program of *3-2-1-Contact.* New York: Children's Television Workshop, n.d. 30 min.

M518. *The Green Book.* (TV program or video) Program #16 of *Books from Cover to Cover.* Washington, DC: WETA-TV and Alexandria, VA: PBS, n.d. 15 min. Beta, VHS, or 3/4″. Based on a book by Jill P. Walsh.

M519. *Gregory the Terrible Eater.* (TV program or video) Program #11 of *Reading Rainbow.* Buffalo: WNED-TV and Lincoln, NE: GPN, 1983. 15 min. VHS or 3/4″. Based on a book by Mitchell Sharmat. Narrated by Marilyn Michaels.

M520a. *Grinch Grinches the Cat in the Hat.* (TV program or video) New York: De Patre-Frelong Playhouse Video, 1981. 49 min. Beta or VHS. Based on books by Dr. Seuss.

M520b. *Grizzley and Man.* (TV program and video) World of Audubon series. Washington, DC: WETA-TV, 1988. 59 min.

M521a. *Groundhog's Horse.* (TV program or video) Program #12 of *Readit!* Bloomington, IN: AIT, 1982. 15 min. Beta, VHS, or 3/4″. Based on a book by Joyce Rockwood.

M521b. *Gryphon.* (TV program) WonderWorks series. Chicago: Public Media Video, 1988. 58 min. VHS.

M522. *Gulliver's Travels.* (16mm or video) Morris Plains, NJ: Lucerne, 1981. 81 min. Based on a book by Jonathan Swift. Starring Richard Harris.

M523. *Hairy Maclary.* (filmstrip with cassette) Milwaukee: Gareth Stevens, 1987. 2:25 min. Based on a book by Lynley Dodd.

M524. *Hairy Maclary—Scattercat.* (filmstrip with cassette) Gareth Stevens, 1987. 2:27 min. Based on a book by L. Dodd.

M525. *Hairy Maclary's Bones.* (filmstrip with cassette) Gareth Stevens, 1987. 2:02 min. Based on a book by L. Dodd.

M526. *Half-Chick.* (TV program or video) Program #4 of *Teletales.* Bloomington, IN: AIT, 1984. 16 min. Beta, VHS, or 3/4″. Based on a folk tale from Germany.

M527. *Half Magic.* (TV program or video) Program #14 of *Book Bird.* Springfield, VA: Children's Television International, 1979. 15 min. 3/4″. Based on a book by Edward Eager.

M528. *Halley's Comet.* (filmstrip with cassette) Buena Vista, CA: Disney, 1986.

M529. *Halley's Comet.* (TV program or video) A program of NOVA. Alexandria, VA: PBS Video, 1986. 60 min.

M530. *The Hand-Me-Down Kid.* (TV program, 16mm film, or video) An ABC After School Special. Deerfield, IL: Learning Corporation of America, 1983. 31 min. VHS. Based on a book by Francine Pascal.

M531. *Hansel and Gretel.* (TV program or video) Program #4 of *Teletales.* Bloomington, IN: AIT, 1984. 15 min. Beta, VHS, or 3/4″. Based on a folk tale from Germany.

M532. *Happy Birthday.* (phonograph record or cassette) Hollywood, CA: Elephant Records/ A & M, 1988. 43 min. Sung by Sharon, Lois, and Bram.

M533. *Happy Birthday, Moon.* (16mm film or video) Weston, CT: Weston Woods, 1986. 7 min. Animated. VHS or Beta. Based on a book by Frank Asch.

M534. *Happy Birthday, Moon.* (filmstrip with cassette) Weston Woods, 1986. 33 fr. 6 min. Based on a book by F. Asch.

M535. *Happy Birthday, Moon.* (hardback or paperback with cassette; cassette) Weston Woods, 1986. 6 min. Based on a book by F. Asch.

M536. *Happy Birthday, Moon.* (paperback with cassette) New York: Simon and Schuster, 1988. 20 min. Based on a book by F. Asch.

M537. *Happy Birthday, Ronald Morgan.* (filmstrip with cassette) Ancramdale, NY: Live Oak Media, 1988. 10 min. Based on a book by Patricia Giff.

M538. *Happy Birthday, Ronald Morgan.* (hardback or paperback with cassette; Reading Chest with 4 paperbacks and cassette) Live Oak Media, 1989. 11 min. Based on a book by P. Giff.

M539. *The Happy Circus.* (TV program or video) A program of *Long Ago and Far Away.* Grenoble, France: Maison du Cinema, n.d. Boston: WGBH-TV, 1989. 30 min. Animated.

M540. *The Happy Owls.* (16mm film or video) Weston, CT: Weston Woods, 1969. 7 min. Animated. Beta or VHS. Based on a book by Celestino Piatti.

M541. *The Happy Owls.* (filmstrip with cassette) Weston Woods, 1969. 21 fr. 4 min. Based on a book by C. Piatti.

M542. *The Happy Owls.* (paperback with cassette; cassette) Weston Woods, 1969. 4 min. Based on a book by C. Piatti.

M543. *Harriet and the Garden.* (hardback or paperback with cassette; Reading Chest with 4 paperbacks and cassette) Ancramdale, NY: Live Oak Media, 1985. 6 min. Based on a book by Nancy Carlson.

M544. *Harriet and the Roller Coaster.* (hardback or paperback with cassette; Reading Chest with 4 paperbacks and cassette) Live Oak Media, 1984. 6 min. Based on a book by N. Carlson.

M545. *Harriet and Walt.* (hardback or paperback with cassette; Reading Chest with 4 paperbacks and cassette) Live Oak Media, 1984. 6:50 min. Based on a book by N. Carlson.

M546. *Harriet Tubman/Thomas Jefferson.* (paperbacks with cassette) Mahwah, NJ: Troll Associates, 1982. 10 min.

M547. *Harriet's Halloween Candy.* (filmstrip with cassette) Live Oak Media, 1989. 5:40 min. Based on a book by N. Carlson.

M548. *Harriet's Halloween Candy.* (hardback or paperback with cassette; Reading Chest with 4 paperbacks and cassette) Live Oak Media, n.d. 5:40 min. Based on a book by N. Carlson.

M549. *Harriet's Recital.* (hardback or paperback with cassette; Reading Chest with 4 paperbacks and cassette) Live Oak Media, 1985. 4:55 min. Based on a book by N. Carlson.

M550. *Harry and the Lady Next Door.* (16mm film or video) Irwindale, CA: Barr Films, 1989. 20 min. VHS. Based on a book by Gene Zion.

M551. *Harry, the Dirty Dog.* (16mm film or video) Barr Films, 1987. 18 min. VHS or 3/4". Based on a book by G. Zion.

M552. *Hatchet.* (video) Hightstown, NJ: American School Publishers, 1990. 49 min. VHS. Based on a book by Gary Paulsen.

M553. *Hatchet.* (2 filmstrips with 2 cassettes) American School Publishers, 1989. 28 fr. 53:16 min. Based on a book by G. Paulsen.

M554. *Hatchet.* (cassette) American School Publishers, 1989. Based on a book by G. Paulsen.

M555. *Have You Seen Hyacinth Macaw?* (TV program or video) Program #3 of *Readit!* Bloomington, IN: AIT, 1982. 15 min. Beta, VHS, or 3/4". Based on a book by Patricia Giff.

M556. *The Headless Cupid.* (TV program or video) A program of *Best of Cover to Cover,* 2-A. Washington, DC: WETA-TV and Alexandria, VA: PBS Video, 1975. 15 min. Based on a book by Zilpha Snyder.

M557. *The Headless Cupid.* (filmstrip with cassette) Costa Mesa, CA: Pied Piper, 1980. 19 min. Based on a book by Z. Snyder.

Hearing. See *Five Senses.*

M558. *Hearing.* (TV program or video) Princeton, NJ: Films for the Humanities and Sciences, 1987. 19 min.

M559. *The Heart.* (TV program) A program of *Challenge.* Nashville: WDCN-TV, n.d. 15 min.

M560. *A Healthy Day.* (filmstrip with cassette) (Slim Goodbody's Health Series). Chicago: SVE, 1982. 48 fr. 6 min.

M561. *Heckedy Peg.* (filmstrip with cassette) Hightstown, NJ: American School Publishers, 1988. 90 fr. 10 min. Based on a book by Audrey Wood.

M562. *Heidi.* (Motion picture or video) Stamford, CT: NBC/Vestron, 1967, 1989. 100 min.

Beta or VHS. Based on a book by Johanna Spyri. Starring Shirley Temple.

M563. *Heidi.* (2 cassettes) Lewiston, NY: Listen for Pleasure, 1982. 180 min. Based on a book by J. Spyri. Read by Petula Clark.

M564. *Henry and Mudge in Puddle Trouble.* (filmstrip with cassette) Hightstown, NJ: American School Publishers, 1988. 90 fr. 11:35 min. Based on a book by Cynthia Rylant.

M565. *Henry and Mudge in Puddle Trouble.* (hardback with cassette) American School Publishers, 1988. 11 min. Based on a book by C. Rylant.

M566. *Henry and Mudge in the Green Time.* (filmstrip with cassette) American School Publishers, 1988. 71 fr. 8 min. Based on a book by C. Rylant.

M567. *Henry and Mudge in the Green Time.* (hardcover with cassette) American School Publishers, 1988. 8 min. Based on a book by C. Rylant.

M568. *Henry and Mudge in the Sparkle Days.* (filmstrip with cassette) American School Publishers, n.d. Based on a book by C. Rylant.

M569. *Henry and Mudge in the Sparkle Days.* (hardcover with cassette) American School Publishers, n.d. Based on a book by C. Rylant.

M570. *Henry and Mudge: The First Book of Their Adventures.* (filmstrip with cassette) American School Publishers, 1988. 70 fr. 8:50 min. Based on a book by C. Rylant.

M571. *Henry and Mudge: The First Book.* (hardcover with cassette) American School Publishers, 1988. 8 min. Based on a book by C. Rylant.

M572. *Henry Reed, Inc.* (hardback or paperback with cassette) Ancramdale, NY: Live Oak Media, 1973. 51:52 min. Based on a book by Keith Robertson.

M573. *Here Comes the Strikeout.* (filmstrip with cassette) Costa Mesa, CA: Pied Piper, 1984. 14 min. Based on a book by Leonard Kessler.

M574. *Here Comes the Strikeout.* (paperback with cassette) New York: Harper, 1987. 15 min. Based on a book by L. Kessler.

M575. *Here to There.* (TV program or video) Program #205 of *Images and Things.* Bloomington, IN: AIT, 1971. 20 min. Beta, VHS, or 3/4".

M576. *The Hero and the Crown.* (2 cassettes) Hightstown, NJ: American School Publishers, 1985. 60 min. each. Based on a book by Robin McKinley.

M577. *Hiawatha's Childhood.* (filmstrip with cassette) Hightstown, NJ: American School

Publishers, 1986. 55 fr. 7:30 min. Abridged from a poem by Henry Wadsworth Longfellow. Read by Jamake Highwater.

M578. *Highlights for Children.* (periodical) Honesdale, PA: Highlights for Children. 11 issues per year.

M579. *Hill of Fire.* (TV program or video) Program #23 of *Reading Rainbow.* Buffalo: WNED-TV and Lincoln, NE: GPN, 1985. 30 min. VHS or 3/4". Based on a book by Thomas Lewis.

M580. *Hill of Fire.* (paperback with cassette) New York: Harper, 1987. 15 min. Based on a book by T. Lewis.

M581. *Historical Fiction.* (filmstrip with cassette) (Literature for Children, Series 3) Costa Mesa, CA: Pied Pier, 1971. 12 min. Includes: *The Perilous Road* by William O. Steele and *Island of the Blue Dolphins* by Scott O'Dell.

M582. *History Books: Nonfiction Too Good to Miss.* (filmstrip with cassette) (Literature for Children, Series 5) Pied Piper, 1980. 10 min. Introduces: *Pyramid* by David Macaulay.

M583. *The Holocaust.* (2 filmstrips with 2 cassettes) Westminster, MD: Contemporary Media Productions/Random, 1988. 17:10 min. 20:30 min. Documentary.

M585. *Homesick, My Own Story.* (2 filmstrips with cassettes) Hightstown, NJ: American School Publications, 1985. Based on a book by Jean Fritz.

M586. *Honey, I Shrunk the Kids.* (motion picture) Buena Vista, CA: Disney, 1989. 86 min.

M587. *The Horn Book Magazine.* (periodical) Boston: Horn Book, Inc. 6 issues per year.

M588a. *Horror/Ghost Stories.* (filmstrip with cassette) (Fantasy Literature series). Peoria, IL: Thomas Klise, 1981.

M588b. *The Horse Without a Head* (video) Burbank, CA: Walt Disney Home Video, 1963. 89 min. Beta or VHS.

M589. *Hot-Air Henry.* (TV program or video) Program #16 of *Reading Rainbow.* Lincoln, NE: GPN, 1984. 30 min. Beta or VHS. Based on a book by Mary Calhoun. Read by William Windom.

M590. *Hot Hippo.* (filmstrip with cassette) Weston, CT: Weston Woods, 1987. 28 fr. 5 min. Based on a book by Mwenye Hadithi.

M591. *Hot Hippo.* (hardcover book with cassette) Weston Woods, 1987. 5 min. Based on a book by M. Hadithi.

M592. *The House of Dies Drear.* (TV program) A program of *WonderWorks.* Pittsburgh, PA: WQED-TV, 1984. 58 min. Based on a book by Virginia Hamilton.

M593. *The House of Dies Drear.* (filmstrip with cassette) Costa Mesa, CA: Pied Piper,

1978. 16 min. Based on a book by V. Hamilton.

M594. *A House Is a House for Me.* (paperback with cassette; Reading Chest with 4 paperbacks and cassette) Ancramdale, NY: Live Oak Media, 1984. 8 min. Based on a book by Ann Hoberman.

M595. *The House on East Eighty-Eighth Street.* (paperback with cassette) Boston: Houghton Mifflin, 1988. 24:81 min. Based on a book by Bernard Waber.

M596. *The House with a Clock on Its Walls.* (hardback or paperback with cassette) Old Greenwich, CT: Listening Library, 1985. 55 min. (Soundways to Reading, Cliffhanger Read-along) Based on a book by John Bellairs.

M597. *How and What Animals Eat.* (TV program) Program #9 of *Zoo Zoo Zoo.* Cincinnati: WCET-TV and the Greater Cincinnati Television Educational Foundation, 1981. 15 min. Beta, VHS, or 3/4".

M598. *How Animals Help Each Other.* (TV program) Program #11 of *Zoo Zoo Zoo.* WCET-TV, 1981. 15 min. Beta, VHS, or 3/4".

M599a. *How Animals Move.* (TV program) Program #10 of *Zoo Zoo Zoo.* WCET-TV, 1981. 15 min. Beta, VHS, or 3/4".

M599b. *How the Camel Got His Hump and How the Rhinoceros Got His Skin.* (video) Los Angeles: Sony, 1987. 30 min. Based on stories by Rudyard Kipling.

M600. *How to Be a Perfect Person in Just Three Days.* (16mm film or video) Deerfield, IL: Learning Corp. of America, 1984. 31 min. Based on *Be a Perfect Person in Just Three Days* by Stephen Manes.

M601. *How to Eat Fried Worms.* (TV program or video) A program of *Best of Cover to Cover, 2-A.* Washington, DC: WETA-TV and Alexandria, VA: PBS Video, n.d. VHS or 3/4". Based on a book by Thomas Rockwell.

M602. *How to Eat Fried Worms.* (3 filmstrips with 3 cassettes) Hightstown, NJ: American School Publishers, n.d. 17 min. each. Based on a book by T. Rockwell.

M603. *How to Eat Fried Worms.* (3 filmstrips with 3 cassettes) Engelwood, CO: Reis and Associates, Cheshire, 1985. 60 fr. and 10 min. each. Based on a book by T. Rockwell.

M604. *How to Eat Fried Worms.* (hardback or paperback with cassette) Old Greenwich, CT: Listening Library, 1985. 39 min. (Soundways to Reading, Cliffhanger Read-along) Based on a book by T. Rockwell.

M605. *Howliday Inn.* (cassette) New York: Harper/Caedmon, 1984. 57 fr. Based on a book by James Howe. Performed by Lou Jacobi.

M606. *Human Body: An Overview.* (computer program) New York: BrainBank, 1982. 8 programs on 2 disks. Apple II Plus or IIe, 16K. DOS 3.3. Commodore 64.

M607. *Humor.* (filmstrip with cassette) (Literature for Children, Series 3). Costa Mesa, CA: Pied Piper, 1970. 12:26 min. Includes: *Mr. Popper's Penguins* by Richard and Florence Atwater; *Ribsy* by Beverly Cleary; and *The Duchess Bakes a Cake* by Virginia Kahl.

M608. *Humphrey the Lost Whale: A True Story.* (TV program or video) Program #56 of *Reading Rainbow.* Buffalo: WNED-TV and Lincoln, NE: GPN, 1989. 30 min. VHS or 3/4". Based on a book by Wendy Takuda and Richard Hall.

M609. *Humpty Dumpty's Magazine.* (periodical) Des Moines, IA: Children's Better Health Institute, Benjamin Franklin Literary and Medical Society. 8 issues per year.

M610. *The Hundred Penny Box.* (2 filmstrips with cassettes) Hightstown, NJ: American School Publishers, 1979. 100 fr. and 24 min. each. Based on a book by Sharon Bell Mathis.

M611. *The Hundred Penny Box.* (cassette) American School Publishers, 1977. 50 min. Based on a book by S. B. Mathis.

M615. *Hungarian Folk Tales.* (TV program) A program of *Long Ago and Far Away.* Boston: WGBH-TV, 1989. Hungary: MTV Enterprises, n.d. 30 min. Animated. Includes "The Hedgehog" and "Pinko."

M616. *The Hunters of Chubut: The Killer Whale.* (video) Toronto: New Wilderness Productions, n.d. 23 min. Beta, VHS, or 3/4".

M617. *I Go With My Family to Grandma's.* (filmstrip with cassette) Hightstown, NJ: American School Publishers, 1988. 86 fr. 6:50 min. Based on a book by Riki Levinson.

M618. *I Like Me.* (filmstrip with cassette) Weston, CT: Weston Woods, 1988. 15 fr. 4 min. Based on a book by Nancy Carlson.

M619. *I Like Me.* (hardcover book with cassette) Weston Woods, 1988. 4 min. Based on a book by N. Carlson.

M620. *I Was a Second Grade Werewolf.* (filmstrip with cassette) Ancramdale, NY: Live Oak Media, 1986. 6 min. Based on a book by Daniel Pinkwater.

M621. *I Was a Second Grade Werewolf.* (hardcover or paperback with cassette, Reading Chest with 4 paperbacks and cassette) Live Oak Media, 1986. 6:30 min. Based on a book by D. Pinkwater.

M622. *If I Ran the Zoo.* (video) Hightstown, NJ: American School Publishers, n.d. 18 min. VHS. Based on a book by Dr. Seuss.

M623. *If I Ran the Zoo.* (filmstrip with cassette) American School Publishers, 1977. Based on a book by Dr. Seuss.

M624. *If I Ran the Zoo.* (hardcover book with cassette) American School Publishers, n.d. Based on a book by Dr. Seuss.

M625. *If You Didn't Have Me.* (TV program or video) Program #7 of *Books from Cover to Cover.* Washington, DC: WETA-TV and Alexandria, VA: PBS, n.d. 15 min. Beta, VHS, or 3/4″. Based on a book by Ulf Nilsson.

M626. *Images and Things.* (TV series or videos) Bloomington, IN: AIT (Agency for Instructional Television); Louisville: Kentucky Authority for ETV; and St. Louis: KETC-TV, 1971. 30 programs, 20 Min. each. Beta, VHS, or 3/4″.

M627. *Imogene's Antlers.* (TV program or video) Program #33 of *Reading Rainbow.* Buffalo: WNED-TV and Lincoln, NE: GPN, 1986. 30 min. VHS or 3/4″. Based on a book by David Small.

M628. *The Importance of Predators.* (TV program or video) A program of *Zoo, Zoo, Zoo.* Washington, DC: WETA-TV and Bloomington, IN: AIT, 1981. 15 min. Beta, VHS, or 3/4″.

M629. *Impractical Jokes.* (TV program) A program of *Shining Time Station.* New York: WNET-TV, n.d. 30 min.

M630. *In a Dark, Dark Room.* (paperback with cassette) New York: Harper, 1986. 5 min. Based on a book by Alvin Schwartz.

M631. *In Coal Country.* (filmstrip with cassette) Hightstown, NJ: American School Publishers, 1989. Based on a book by Judith Hendershot.

M632. *In Coal Country.* (hardback with cassette) American School Publishers, 1989. 11 min. Based on a book by J. Hendershot.

M633. *In Love with Paris.* (video) San Ramon, CA: International Video Network, 1986. VHS.

M634. *In the Air.* (TV program) A program of *3-2-1-Contact.* New York: Children's Television Workshop, n.d. 30 min.

M635. *In the Land of Polar Bears.* (TV program or video) Program #1204 of *NOVA.* Boston: WGBH-TV and Deerfield, IL: Coronet, 1988. 58 min.

M636. *Incognito Mosquito, Private Insective.* (cassette) New York: Harper/Caedmon, 1984. 55 min. Based on a book by E. A. Hass.

M637. *The Inside Story with Slim Goodbody.* (TV series or video) Bloomington, IN: AIT and Green Bay, WI: University of Wisconsin-Green Bay Telecommunications Center, 1981. 8 programs, 15 min. each. Beta, VHS, or 3/4″.

M638. *Interstellar Pig.* (hardback or paperback with cassette) Old Greenwich, CT: Listening Library, 1985. 55 min. (Young Adult Cliffhangers) Based on a book by William Sleator.

M639. *Instructor.* (periodical) Cleveland, OH. Monthly. Incorporating *Teacher* since 1981.

M640. *Interviewing Biographies.* (filmstrip with cassette) (Literature to Enjoy and Write About, Series 1) Costa Mesa, CA: Pied Piper, 1989. 22 min. Introduces: *The Double Life of Pocahontas* by Jean Fritz; *Lincoln: A Photobiography* by Russell Freedman; and *Martin Luther King* by Pat McKissack.

M641. *Introduction to Chimpanzee Behavior.* (16mm film or video) Washington, DC: National Geographic, 1977. 23 min. VHS or 3/4″.

M642. *Ira Says Goodbye.* (video) Ancramdale, NY: Live Oak Media, 1989. 18 min. VHS. Based on a book by Bernard Waber.

M643. *Ira Says Goodbye.* (filmstrip with cassette) Live Oak Media, 1990. 16:30 min. Based on a book by B. Waber.

M644. *Ira Sleeps Over.* (TV program or video) A program of *Tilson's Book Shop.* Cleveland: WVIZ-TV and Lincoln, NE: GPN, 1974. 15 min. VHS. Based on a book by B. Waber.

M645. *Ira Sleeps Over.* (16mm film or video) NY: Phoenix/BFA, 1977. 17 min. Beta, VHS, or 3/4″. Based on a book by B. Waber.

M646. *Ira Sleeps Over.* (video) Ancramdale, NY: Live Oak Media, 1987. 14 min. Based on a book by B. Waber.

M647. *Ira Sleeps Over.* (filmstrip with cassette) Live Oak Media, 1984. 57 fr. 13:30 min. Based on a book by B. Waber.

M648. *Ira Sleeps Over.* (hardback or paperback with cassette; Reading Chest with 4 paperbacks and cassette) Live Oak Media, n.d. 14 min. Based on a book by B. Waber.

M649. *Ira Sleeps Over.* (paperback with cassette) Boston: Houghton Mifflin, 1987. 22:44 min. Based on a book by B. Waber. Read by Jim Trelease.

M650. *Isaac in America.* (16mm or video) Los Angeles: Direct Cinema, Ltd. and Amran Nowah Assoc., 1986. 58 min. Documentary. VHS.

M651. *Island.* (TV program) A program of *3-2-1-Contact.* NY: Children's Television Workshop, n.d. 30 min.

M652. *Island of the Blue Dolphins.* (TV program or video) Program #13 of *Storybound.* 15 min. Springfield, VA: Children's Television International, 1981. Beta, VHS, or 3/4″. Based on a book by Scott O'Dell.

M653. *The Island of the Skog.* (16mm film or video) Weston, CT: Weston Woods, 1980. 13

min. Iconographic. Beta or VHS. Based on a book by Steven Kellogg.

M654. *The Island of the Skog.* (filmstrip with cassette) Weston Woods, 1980. 50 fr. 11 min. Based on a book by S. Kellogg.

M655. *The Island of the Skog.* (hardcover or paperback with cassette) Weston Woods, 1980. 11 min. Based on a book by S. Kellogg.

M656. *It's Mine.* (filmstrip with cassette) Hightstown, NJ: American School Publishers, 1988. 39 fr. 4:14 min. Based on a book by Leo Lionni.

M657. *It's Not the End of the World.* (TV program or video) Program #6 of *Storybound.* Springfield, VA: Children's Television International, 1981. 15 min. Beta, VHS or 3/4″. Based on a book by Judy Blume.

M658. *It's Not the End of the World.* (paperback with cassette) Old Greenwich, CT: Listening Library, 1985. 82 min. (Young Adult Cliffhangers Series) Based on a book by Judy Blume.

M659. *It's the Truth.* (phonograph record or cassette) Brattleboro, VT: RS Records, 1984. 37 min. Includes "House at Pooh Corner" based on a book by A. A. Milne and "Somewhere Over the Rainbow" from the motion picture *The Wizard of Oz* based on a book by L. F. Baum.

M660. *Jack and Jill.* (periodical) Des Moines, IA: Children's Better Health Institute, Benjamin Franklin Literary and Medical Society. 8 issues per year.

M661. *Jack London.* (filmstrip with cassette) Hawthorne, NJ: January Productions, 1983. 54 fr. 18 min.

M662a. *Jacob Have I Loved.* (TV program) A program of *WonderWorks.* Los Angeles: KCET-TV, 1989. 60 min. Based on a book by Katherine Paterson.

M662b. *Jacob Have I Loved.* (16mm film or video) Chicago: Films Inc., 1989. Based on a book by K. Paterson.

M663. *Jacob Have I Loved.* (2 filmstrips with 2 cassettes) Hightstown, NJ: American School Publishers, 1983. Based on a book by K. Paterson.

M664. *Jamberry.* (hardback or paperback with cassette; Reading Chest with 4 paperbacks and cassette) Ancramdale, NY: Live Oak Media, 1986. 3:40 min. Based on a book by Bruce Degan.

M665. *James Marshall in His Studio.* (video) Burlington, MA: Houghton Mifflin, n.d. Live action. 17 min. Beta, VHS, or 3/4″. Includes information about Miss Nelson, the Stupids, and George and Martha.

M666. *Jane Goodall: Studies of the Chimpanzee.* (16mm film or video) Washington, DC: National Geographic, 1977. 23 min. VHS or 3/4″.

M667. *Japan.* (TV program) A program of *3-2-1-Contact.* NY: Children's Television Workshop, n.d. 30 min.

M668. *Jean Fritz Reads Homesick, My Own Story.* (3 cassettes) Weston, CT: Weston Woods, 1983. 4 hrs. 20 min. Based on a book by Jean Fritz.

M669. *Jean Fritz: Six Revolutionary War Figures.* (filmstrip with cassette) Weston, CT: Weston Woods, 1983. 68 fr. and 13 min. each.

M670. *Jelly Belly.* (hardback or paperback with cassette) Old Greenwich, CT: Listening Library, 1984. 85 min. (Soundways to Reading, Cliffhanger Read-along) Based on a book by Robert Kimmel Smith.

M671. *Jerusalem, Shining Still.* (cassette) New York: Harper/Caedmon, 1988. 39 min. Based on a book by Karla Kuskin. Read by Theodore Bikel.

M672. *Joey Runs Away.* (16mm or video) Weston, CT: Weston Woods, 1988. 8 min. Animated. Based on a book by Jack Kent.

M673. *Joey Runs Away.* (filmstrip with cassette) Weston Woods, 1986. 39 fr. 5 min. Based on a book by J. Kent.

M674. *Joey Runs Away.* (hardback with cassette) Weston Woods, 1988. 5 min. Based on a book by J. Kent.

M675. *John Glenn and the Lunar Astronauts.* (video) Princeton, NJ: Films for the Humanities and Sciences, n.d. 27 min. VHS or 3/4″.

M676. *Johnny Crow's Garden.* (filmstrip with cassette) Weston, CT: Weston Woods, 1986. 28 fr. 4 min. Based on a book by L. Leslie Brooke.

M677. *The Journal of Youth Services in Libraries (JOYS).* (periodical) Chicago: American Library Association's Association for Library Service to Children and the Young Adult Services Division. Quarterly. Formerly *Top of the News..*

M678. *The Journey Back.* (16mm film or video) Los Angeles: Direct Cinema, 1987. 60 min. Beta or VHS. Based on a book by Johanna Reiss.

M679a. *Journey into Space.* (TV program) A program of *Challenge.* Nashville: WDCN-TV, n.d. 15 min.

M679b. *Joyful Noise.* (16mm film or video) Hightstown, NJ: American School Publishers, 1989. 18 min. Based on a book by Paul Fleischman.

M679c. *Joyful Noise.* (2 filmstrips with cassettes) American School Publishers, 1989. 18 min. Based on a book by P. Fleischman.

M680. *Jules Verne.* (filmstrip with cassette) Hawthorne, NJ: January Productions, 1985. 52 fr. 13 min.

M681. *Julian's Glorious Summer.* (paperback with cassette) Hightstown, NJ: American School Publisers, 1989. 40 min. Based on a book by Ann Cameron.

M682. *Julie of the Wolves.* (2 filmstrips with 2 cassettes) Hightstown, NJ: American School Publishers, n.d. Based on a book by Jean Craighead George.

M683. *Julie of the Wolves.* (cassette) New York: Caedmon, 1977. 60:24 min. Based on a book by J. George. Read by Irene Worth.

M684. *Junior Scholastic.* (periodical) New York: Scholastic, Inc. 18 issues per year, September to May.

M685. *Just So Stories.* (cassette) Waterbury, VT: Kids Records, Silo/Alcazar, 1987. 45 min. Based on a book by Rudyard Kipking. Includes: "The Elephant's Child"; "The Sing-Song of Old Man Kangaroo"; "The Cat That Walked by Himself"; and "How the Camel Got His Hump."

M686. *Katy and the Big Snow.* (paperback with cassette) Boston: Houghton Mifflin, 1989. 19 min. Based on a book by Virginia Burton.

M687. *Katy No-Pocket.* (paperback with cassette) Houghton Mifflin, 1989. 25:38 min. Based on a book by Emmy Payne.

M688. *Keep the Lights Burning, Abbie.* (TV program or video) Program #37 of *Reading Rainbow.* Buffalo: WNED-TV and Lincoln, NE: GPN, 1987. 30 min. VHS or 3/4″. Based on a book by Peter and Connie Roop.

M689. *Keep the Lights Burning, Abbie.* (hardback or paperback with cassette; Reading Chest with 4 paperbacks and cassette) Ancramdale, NY: Live Oak Media, 1989. 10 min. Based on a book by P. and C. Roop.

M690. *Kid City.* (periodical) Boulder, CO: Formerly *Electric Co. Magazine.* 10 issues per year.

M691. *The Kid in the Red Jacket.* (TV program or video) Program #8 of *Books from Cover to Cover.* Washington, DC: WETA-TV and Alexandria, VA: PBS Video, n.d. 15 min. VHS or 3/4″. Based on a book by Barbara Park.

M692a. *Kidstamps.* (rubber stamps) Cleveland Heights, OH: 1980–. Based on book characters.

M692b. *King Arthur and His Knights.* (cassette) Benicia, CA: Greathall Productions, 1989. 60 min. Based on a legendary character.

M693. *King of the Cats.* (filmstrip with cassette) Weston, CT: Weston Woods, 1984. 35 fr. 6 min. Based on a book by Paul Galdone.

M694. *King of the Cats.* (hardcover or paperback with cassette) Weston Woods, 1984. 6 min. Based on a book by P. Galdone.

M695. *Kirsten.* (doll) 18″. Middleton, WI: Pleasant Company. Based on a book character by Janet Shaw.

M696. *Kirsten Learns a Lesson: A School Story.* (paperback with cassette) Pleasant Company, 1986. Based on a book by J. Shaw.

M697. *A Kiss for Little Bear.* (filmstrip with cassette) Weston, CT: Weston Woods, 1973. 35 fr. 4 min. Based on a book by Else Minarik.

M698. *A Kiss for Little Bear.* (hardback or paperback with cassette) Weston Woods, 1973. 4 min. Based on a book by E. Minarik.

M699. *Knots on a Counting Rope.* (TV program or video) Program #53 of *Reading Rainbow.* Buffalo: WNED-TV and Lincoln, NE: GPN, 1989. 30 min. VHS or 3/4″. Based on a book by Bill Martin, Jr. and John Archambault.

M700. *Knots on a Counting Rope.* (video) New Rochelle, NY: Spoken Arts Video, n.d. Based on a book by B. Martin, Jr. and J. Archambault.

M701. *Koko's Kitten.* (16mm film or video) Los Angeles: Churchill, 1989. 16 min. Based on a book by Patterson.

M702. *.Konrad.* (TV program or video) Program #3 of *Storybound.* Springfield, VA: Children's Television International, 1981. 15 min. Beta, VHS, or 3/4″. Based on a book by Christine Nostlinger.

M703. *Land of the Tiger.* (TV program or video) Pittsburgh: WQED-TV/National Geographic Society; Stamford, CT: Vestron, 1986. 58 min. Beta or VHS.

M704. *Language Arts.* (periodical) Urbana, IL: NCTE (National Council of Teachers of English) Formerly *Elementary English.* Issued 8 times per year, September-April.

M705. *Lassie.* (TV series) New York: CBS, 1954–1971. 30 min. each. Based on a book by Eric Knight.

M706. *Lassie Come Home.* (motion picture or video) Culver City, CA: MGM/UA, 1943, 1990. 88 min. Based on a book by E. Knight. Starring Roddy McDowall and Elizabeth Taylor.

M707a. *Lassie Come Home.* (2 filmstrips with 2 cassettes) Wilmette, IL: Films, Inc., 1976. 33 min. Based on a book by E. Knight and taken from the MGM motion picture.

M707b. *Lassie's Decision.* (TV program) #5807 of *Lassie and Timmy.* New York: CBS-TV, 1954–71. Syndication 1971–. 28 min.

M708. *Laura* or *Mary* (dolls) 7 1/2″. Based on the "Little House" books by Laura Ingalls Wilder.

M709. *Laura Ingalls Wilder: Up Close and Real.* (video) Albuquerque: Sagas Unlimited, 1986. 47 min. Performed by Kathy Carlson.

M709a. *Laurent de Brunhoff: Daydreamer.* (filmstrip with cassette) (Famous Authors and Illustrators series). New York: Random, 1983. 131 fr. 15 min. Introduces *Babar.*.

M710. *Learning.* (periodical) Springhouse, PA: Springhouse Corp. Issued 9 times per year, August–May.

M711. *Leo Lionni's Caldecotts.* (video) Hightstown, NJ: American School Publishers, 1985. VHS or Beta. Taken from filmstrips. Includes: *Swimmy,* 3 min.; *Frederick,* 4 min.; and *Alexander and the Wind-up Mouse,* 7 min. Based on books by Leo Lionni.

M712. *The Lesson of Anne Frank.* (filmstrip with cassette) Chicago: SVE, 1985. 65 fr. 20 min. Companion to *The Story of Anne Frank.*.

M713. *Liang and the Magic Paintbrush.* (TV program or video) Program #7 of *Reading Rainbow.* Buffalo: WNED-TV and Lincoln, NE: GPN, 1983. 30 min. VHS or 3/4″. Based on a book by Demi.

M715. *The Life of Anne Frank.* (video) Princeton, NJ: Films for the Humanities and Sciences, 1988.

M716. *The Life Cycle of the Honeybee.* (TV program or video) Program #36 of *Reading Rainbow.* Lincoln, NE: GPN, 1987. 30 min. VHS or 3/4″. Based on a book by Paula Hogan.

M717. *Light.* (TV program) A program of *Challenge.* Nashville: WDCN-TV, n.d. 15 min.

M718. *Light.* (TV program) A program of *3-2-1-Contact.* New York: Children's Television Workshop, n.d. 30 min.

M719. *A Light in the Attic.* (phonograph record or cassette) New York: Harper and Columbia Records, 1985. 36 min. Poetry written and read by Shel Silverstein.

M720. *Like Jake and Me.* (16mm film or video) Deerfield, IL: Coronet/MTI, 1989. 13:50. Based on a book by Mavis Jukes.

M721. *Lincoln: A Photobiography.* (video) Hightstown, NJ: American School Publishers,

1989. 65 min. VHS. Based on a book by Russell Freedman.

M722a. *The Lion, the Witch, and the Wardrobe.* (TV programs) A program of *WonderWorks.* Pittsburgh: WQED-TV, 1989. 95 min. Based on a book by C. S. Lewis.

M722b. *The Lion, the Witch, and the Wardrobe.* (16mm film or video) Stamford, CT: Vestron, 1985. 95 min. Beta or VHS. Based on a book by C. S. Lewis.

M723. *Literature for Children, Series 1.* (4 filmstrips with 4 cassettes) Costa Mesa, CA: Pied Piper, 1970. 12 min. each. Includes: *Fantasy*; *Tall Tales*; *Story of a Book*; and *Biography.*.

M724. *Literature for Children, Series 3.* (4 filmstrips with 4 cassettes) Pied Piper, 1971. 12 min. each. Includes: *Enjoying Illustrations*; *Historical Fiction*; *Myths*; and *Adventure.*.

M725. *Literature for Children, Series 5.* (4 filmstrips with 4 cassettes) Pied Piper, 1980. 10 min each. Includes: *History*; *Science*; *Sports and Hobbies*; and *Art and Music.*.

M726. *Literature for Children, Series 6.* (4 filmstrips with 4 cassettes) Pied Piper, 1980. 13 min each. Includes: *Mysteries*; *Epics and Legends*; *Realistic Fiction*; and *Science Fiction.*.

M727. *Literature for Children, Series 7A.* (4 filmstrips with 4 cassettes) Pied Piper, 1982. 11 min each. Includes: *Imagine That!*; *Just Like Me*; *Books About Real Things*; and *Stories Without Words.*.

M728. *Literature for Children, Series 7B.* (4 filmstrips with 4 cassettes) Pied Piper, 1982. 10 min each. Includes: *Animal Stories*; *What's So Funny?*; *Exploring New Places*; and *Stories about Friends.*.

M729. *Literature for Children, Series 7C.* (5 filmstrips with 5 cassettes) Pied Piper, 1984. 11 min each. Includes: *Scary Stories*; *Yummy Stories About Food*; *Nature Stories and Poems*; *Stories About Pets*; and *By the Sea.*.

M730. *Literature for Children, Series 8; Folktales.* (3 videos) Pied Piper, 1988. 90 min. Includes: *Folktales Then and Now*; *Folktale Characters*; *Folktale Wisdom*; *Folktales from Afar*; *Funny Folktales*, and *The Magical World of Folktales.*.

M731. *Literature for Children, Series 8; Folktales.* (4 filmstrips with 4 cassettes) Pied Piper, 1983. 15 min each. Includes: *Folktales Then and Now*; *Folktale Characters*; *Folktale Wisdom*; *Folktales from Afar*; *Funny Folktales*, and *The Magical World of Folktales.*.

M732. *Literature for Children, Series 9; Components of Fiction.* (2 videos) Pied Piper,

1985. 102 min. Includes: *Character*; *Plot*; *Setting*; *Style*; and *Theme.*.

M733. *Literature for Children, Series 9; Components of Fiction.* (5 filmstrips with 5 cassettes) Pied Piper, 1985. 19 min each. Includes: *Character*; *Plot*; *Setting*; *Style*; and *Theme.*.

M734. *Literature, Literacy, and Learning: Classroom Teacher.* (video) Chicago: Encyclopedia Britannica, 1989. 23 min. Live action. Beta or VHS.

M735. *Literature to Enjoy and Write About, Series l.* (5 filmstrips with 5 cassettes) Costa Mesa, CA: Pied Piper, 1989. 22 min each. Includes: *Diary-Journal, Realistic Fiction*; *New Endings, Adventure*; *Problem Solving, Humorous Stories*; *Mapping, Mysteries*; and *Interviewing Biographies.*.

M736. *Literature to Enjoy and Write About Series 2.* (5 filmstrips with 5 cassettes) Pied Piper, 1989. 22 min each. Includes: *Friendly Letter: Realistic Fiction*; *Persuasive Writing: Non-Fiction*; *TV Book Review: Fantasy*; *Sequel: Animal Stories*; and *Radio Program: Historical Fiction.*.

M737. *Little Bear.* (2 cassettes) Old Greenwich, CT: Listening Library, n.d. Includes: *Little Bear*; *Father Bear Comes Home*; *Little Bear's Friend*; and *Little Bear's Visit.* Based on books by Else Minarik.

M738. *Little Bear's Friend.* (paperback with cassette) New York: Harper/Caedmon, 1985. 15 min. Based on a book by E. Minarik.

M739. *Little Bear's Visit.* (filmstrip with cassette) Weston, CT: Weston Woods, 1967. 62 fr. 14 min. Based on a book by E. Minarik.

M740. *Little Bear's Visit.* (hardback or paperback with cassette) Weston Woods, 1967. 14 min. Based on a book by E. Minarik.

M741. *The Little Giants: The Inside Story of Your Glands.* (TV program or video) Program #7 of *The Inside Story with Slim Goodbody.* Bloomington, IN: AIT and Green Bay, WI: UW-GB Telecommunications Center, 1981. 15 min. Beta, VHS, or 3/4″.

M742. *The Little House.* (filmstrip with cassette) Weston, CT: Weston Woods, 1973. 55 fr. 13 min. Based on a book by Virginia Burton.

M743. *The Little House.* (hardback or paperback with cassette) Weston Woods, 1973. 13 min. Based on a book by V. Burton.

M744. *The Little House.* (paperback with cassette) Boston: Houghton Mifflin, 1988. 13:13 min. Based on a book by V. Burton.

M745. *The Little House in the Big Woods.* (TV program or video) Program #2 of *Book Bird.* Springfield, VA: Children's Television International, 1979. 15 min. 3/4″. Based on a book by Laura Ingalls Wilder.

M746. *The Little House on the Prairie.* (TV series) New York: NBC, 1976–1983. Based on a book by L. I. Wilder. Starring Michael Landon and Melissa Gilbert.

M747. *Little Nino's Pizzeria.* (TV program or video) Program #58 of *Reading Rainbow.* Buffalo: WNED-TV and Lincoln, NE: GPN, 1989. 30 min. Beta or VHS. Based on a book by Karen Barbour.

M748. *The Little Prince.* (16mm film or video) New York: Billy Budd Films, 1979. 27 min. Clay animation. Based on a book by Antoine de Saint-Exupéry.

M749. *The Little Prince.* (motion picture or video) Los Angeles: Paramount Home Video, n.d. Musical. 88 min. Beta or VHS. Based on a book by A. Saint-Exupéry.

M750. *The Little Prince.* (phonograph record or cassette) New York: Harper/Caedmon, n.d. 60 min. Abridged from a book by A. Saint-Exupéry. Read by Louis Jordan.

M751. *The Little Riders.* (TV program or video) Program #5 of *Books from Cover to Cover.* Washington, DC: WETA-TV and Alexandria, VA: PBS Video, n.d. 15 min. VHS or 3/4″. Based on a book by Margaret Shemin.

M752. *Little Women.* (filmstrip with cassette) Chicago: SVE, 1983. 66 fr. 15 min. Based on a book by Louisa May Alcott.

M753. *Live and Learn.* (cassette) Weston, CT: Weston Woods, 1984. 54 min. Read by Donald Davis.

M754. *Living and Working in Space.* (filmstrip with cassette) (Today and Tomorrow in Space: The Space Shuttle and Beyond) Washington, DC: National Geographic, 1983. 50 fr. 16 min.

M755. *The Living Smithsonian.* (TV program) A program of *Smithsonian World.* Washington, DC: WETA-TV and the Smithsonian Institution, n.d.

M756a. *Lizard Music.* (TV program or video) Program #7 of *Storybound.* Lincoln, NE: GPN, 1981. 15 min. VHS and 3/4″. Based on a book by D. Manus Pinkwater.

M756b. *The L. L. Bean Catalog.* Freeport, ME: L. L. Bean. Semi-annual.

M757. *Long Ago and Far Away.* (TV series) Boston: WGBH-TV, 1989–. 16 programs per year; 30 min. each. Host: James Earl Jones.

M758. *Long Nose.* (TV program or video) Program #9 of *Teletales.* Bloomington, IN: AIT, 1984. 15 min. Beta, VHS, and 3/4″. Based on a folk tale from Germany.

M759. *Lost in the Barrens.* (TV program or video) Program #16 of *Book Bird.* Springfield, VA: Children's Television International,

1979. 15 min. 3/4″. Based on a book by Farley Mowat.

M760. *Louanne Pig in Making the Team.* (hardback or paperback with cassette; Reading Chest with 4 paperbacks and cassette) Ancramdale, NY: Live Oak Media, 1987. 4:45 min. Based on a book by Nancy Carlson.

M761. *Louanne Pig in the Mysterious Valentine.* (filmstrip with cassette) Live Oak Media, n.d. 5:47 min. Based on a book by N. Carlson.

M762. *Louanne Pig in the Mysterious Valentine.* (hardback or paperback with cassette; Reading Chest with 4 paperbacks and cassette) Live Oak Media, 1986. 5:47 min. Based on a book by N. Carlson.

M763. *Louanne Pig in the Perfect Family.* (hardback or paperback with cassette; Reading Chest with 4 paperbacks and cassette) Live Oak Media, 1987. 7:30 min. Based on a book by N. Carlson.

M764. *Louanne Pig in the Talent Show.* (hardback or paperback with cassette; Reading Chest with 4 paperbacks and cassette) Live Oak Media, 1987. 5:32 min. Based on a book by N. Carlson.

M765. *Louanne Pig in Witch Lady.* (hardcover or paperback with cassette; Reading Chest with 4 paperbacks and cassette) Live Oak Media, 1988. 6:48 min. Based on a book by N. Carlson.

M766. *Loudmouth George and the Big Race.* (hardback or paperback with cassette; Reading Chest with 4 paperbacks and cassette) Live Oak Media, 1986. 7:20 min. Based on a book by N. Carlson.

M767. *Loudmouth George and the Coronet.* (hardback or paperback with cassette; Reading Chest with 4 paperbacks and cassette) Live Oak Media, 1986. 7:48 min. Based on a book by N. Carlson.

M768. *Loudmouth George and the Fishing Trip.* (hardback or paperback with cassette; Reading Chest with 4 paperbacks and cassette) Live Oak Media, 1986. 6:08 min. Based on a book by N. Carlson.

M769. *Loudmouth George and the New Neighbors.* (hardback or paperback with cassette; Reading Chest with 4 paperbacks and cassette) Live Oak Media, 1986. 5:09 min. Based on a book by N. Carlson.

M770. *Loudmouth George and the Sixth Grade Bully.* (hardback or paperback with cassette; Reading Chest with 4 paperbacks and cassette) Live Oak Media, 1986. 7:16 min. Based on a book by N. Carlson.

M771. *Louis the Fish.* (TV program or video) Program #5 of *Reading Rainbow.* Buffalo: WNED-TV and Lincoln, NE: GPN, 1983. 30 min. VHS or 3/4″. Based on a book by Arthur Yorinks. Narrated by Vincent Gardenia.

M772. *Louisa May Alcott.* (filmstrip with cassette) Hawthorne, NJ: January Productions, 1985. 54 fr. 15 min. Introduces *Little Women..*

M773. *Lovable Lyle.* (TV program or video) A program from the Red Module of *Picture Book Park.* Cleveland: WVIZ-TV and Bloomington, IN: AIT, 1973. 15 min. Beta, VHS, or 3/4″. Based on a book by Bernard Waber.

M774. *Lubba Dubba: The Inside Story of Your Heart and Blood.* (TV program or video) Program #1 of *The Inside Story with Slim Goodbody.* Green Bay, WI: UW-GB Telecommunications Center, 1981. 15 min. Beta, VHS, or 3/4″.

M775. *The Lucky Stone.* (TV program or video) Program #7 of *Readit!* Bloomington, IN: AIT, 1982. 15 min. Beta, VHS, or 3/4″. Based on a book by Lucille Clifton. Also includes: *Who's in Charge of Lincoln?* by Dale Fife.

M776. *Ludlow Laughs.* (TV program or video) Program #59 of *Reading Rainbow.* Buffalo: WNED-TV and Lincoln, NE: GPN, 1989. 30 min. VHS or 3/4″. Based on a book by Jon Agee. Narrated by Phyllis Diller.

M777. *Lyle, Lyle, Crocodile: The Musical.* (video) New York: Ambrose Video, 1989. 24 min. Animated. Based on Bernard Waber's *House on East Eighty-Eighth Street..*

M778. *Lyle, Lyle Crocodile.* (paperback with cassette) Boston: Houghton Mifflin, 1987. 14:19 min. Based on a book by B. Waber.

M779. *McBroom's Ghost.* (filmstrip with cassette) Costa Mesa, CA: Pied Piper, 1988. 22 min. Based on a book by Sid Fleischman.

M780. *McBroom's Zoo.* (TV program or video) A program of *Best of Cover to Cover, 1-A.* Washington, DC: WETA-TV and Alexandria, VA: PBS Video, n.d. VHS or 3/4″. 15 min. Based on a book by S. Fleischman.

M781. *McElligot's Pool.* (video) Hightstown, NJ: American School Publications, 1986. 12:30 min. VHS. Based on a book by Dr. Seuss.

M782. *McElligot's Pool.* (filmstrip with cassette) American School Publications, 1981. 79 fr. 10 min. Based on a book by Dr. Seuss.

M783. *McElligot's Pool.* (hardback with cassette) American School Publications, 1981. Based on a book by Dr. Seuss.

M784. *Madeline.* (video) Santa Monica, CA: Hi-Tops, Heron Communications, and Media Home Entertainment, 1989. 30 min. VHS. Based on a book by Ludwig Bemelmans.

M785. *Madeline.* (filmstrip with cassette) Hightstown, NJ: American School Publishers, 1985. 80 fr. 6:38 min. Based on a book by L. Bemelmans.

M786. *Madeline.* (paperback with cassette) American School Publishers, 1985. 6 min. Based on a book by L. Bemelmans.

M787. *Madeline.* (hardback or paperback with cassette; Reading Chest with 4 paperbacks and cassette) Ancramdale, NY: Live Oak Media, 1975. 8:15 min. Based on a book by L. Bemelmans.

M788. *Madeline and the Bad Hat.* (hardback or paperback with cassette; Reading Chest with 4 paperbacks and cassette) Live Oak Media, 1979. 11:50 min. Based on a book by L. Bemelmans.

M789. *Madeline and the Gypsies.* (hardback or paperback with cassette; Reading Chest with 4 paperbacks and cassette) Live Oak Media, 1980. 14:40 min. Based on a book by L. Bemelmans.

M790. *Madeline in London.* (hardback or paperback with cassette; Reading Chest with 4 paperbacks and cassette) Live Oak Media, 1977. 12:36 min. Based on a book by L. Bemelmans.

M791. *Madeleine L'Engle: Star Gazer.* (video) Patterson, NY: Ishtar Films, 1989. 30 min. Beta, VHS, or 3/4″. Includes information about *A Wrinkle in Time.*.

M792. *Madeline: The Musical.* (video) New York: Ambrose Video, 1989. 30 min. Based on a character of Ludwig Bemelmans.

M793. *Madeline's Rescue.* (filmstrip with cassette) Weston CT: Weston Woods, 1961. 53 fr. 6 min. Based on a book by L. Bemelmans.

M794. *Madeline's Rescue.* (hardback or paperback with cassette; Reading Chest with 4 paperbacks and cassette) Live Oak Media, 1977. 10:08 min. Based on a book by L. Bemelmans.

M795. *Madeline's Rescue.* (paperback with cassette) Hightstown, NJ: American School Publishers, n.d. Based on a book by L. Bemelmans.

M797. *The Magic Broom.* (video) Mahwah, NJ: Troll, 1987. 13 min. Animated. Based on a book by Michael Pellowski.

M798. *The Magic Carpet.* (TV series or videos) San Diego, CA: San Diego County Dept. of Education and Lincoln, NE: GPN, 1976. 13 programs, 15 min each. VHS or 3/4″.

M799. *The Magic of Lassie.* (video) New York: McGraw/UA Home Video, 1986. 100 min. Based on the 1977 motion picture. Based on a book character by E. Knight. Starring Mickey Rooney.

M800. *The Magic Schoolbus Inside the Earth.* (TV program or video) Program #66 of *Reading Rainbow.* Lincoln, NE: GPN, 1990. 30 min. Based on a book by Joanna Cole.

M801. *The Magnificent Dinosaurs.* (4 filmstrips with 4 cassettes) Niles, IL: United Learning, 1987. 48–54 fr. each. 7–9 min. each.

M801a. *Majestic Brass, Part 1 and Part 2.* (TV programs or videos). Programs #3 and #4 of *Musical Instruments.* Lincoln, NE: GPN, 1979. 15 min. VHS or 3/4″.

M802. *Make Way for Ducklings.* (filmstrip with cassette) Weston Woods, CT: Weston Woods, 1958. 47 fr. 11 min. Based on a book by Robert McCloskey.

M803. *Making a Book.* (TV program) A program of *The Word Shop.* Washington, DC: WETA-TV, 1976. 15 min. Beta, VHS, or 3/4″.

M804. *Mama Don't Allow.* (TV program or video) Program #30 of *Reading Rainbow.* Buffalo: WNED-TV and Lincoln, NE: GPN, 1986. 29 min. VHS or 3/4″. Based on a book by Thatcher Hurd.

M805. *Mama Don't Allow.* (filmstrip with cassette) Hightstown, NJ: American School Publications, 1986. 90 fr. 9 min. Based on a book by T. Hurd.

M806. *Mama Don't Allow.* (hardback with cassette) American School Publications, 1986. 9 min. Based on a book by T. Hurd.

M807. *Mama One, Mama Two and Other Stories.* (cassette) New York: Harper/Caedmon, 1986. 31 min. Includes *Mama One, Mama Two* and *Through Grandpa's Eyes.* Based on books by Patricia McLachlan. Read by Glenn Close.

M808. *Mama's Going to Buy You a Mocking Bird.* (TV program) Program #6 of *More Books From Cover to Cover.* Washington, DC: WETA-TV and Alexandria, VA: PBS Video, n.d. 15 min. Beta, VHS, or 3/4″. Based on a book by Jean Little.

M809. *Mammals.* (TV program) A program of *3-2-1-Contact.* New York: Children's Television Workshop, n.d. 30 min.

M810. *The Man Who Planted Trees.* (hardback and cassette) Post Mills, VT: Earth Music Productions/Chelsea Green, 1990. 40 min. Based on a story by Jean Giono.

M811. *The Man Who Planted Trees.* (TV program, 16mm film, or video) A program of *Long Ago and Far Away.* Boston: WGBH-TV, Canada: Société Radio-Canada, 1987. Animated. 30 min. Based on a story by J. Giono.

M812. *The Man Who Planted Trees.* (16mm film or video) Los Angeles: Direct Cinema,

1987. Animated. 30 min. Based on a story by J. Giono.

M813. *Maple Sugaring Story.* (video) Charlotte, VT: Perceptions, 1988. 28:27 min.

M814. *Maple Sugaring Story.* (filmstrip with cassette) Charlotte, VT: Perceptions, 1988. 18:27 min.

M815. *Mapping Mysteries.* (filmstrip with cassette) Costa Mesa, CA: Pied Piper, 1989. 22 min. (Literature to Enjoy and Write About, Series 1) Features: *The House With a Clock in Its Walls* by John Bellairs and *Bunnicula* by Barbara and James Howe. Introduces: *The Westing Game* by Ellen Raskin.

M816. *The Mare on the Hill.* (filmstrip with cassette) Hightstown, NJ: American School Publishers, 1987. 39 fr. 1:25 min. Based on a book by Thomas Locker.

M817. *Mark Twain.* (filmstrip with cassette) Hawthorne, NJ: January Productions, 1983. 52 fr. 15 min.

M818. *Mathnet.* (TV programs) A feature of the TV program, *Square One.* New York: Children's Television Workshop.

M819. *Matter and Its Properties.* (TV program) A program of *Challenge.* Nashville: WDCN-TV, n.d. 15 min.

M820. *Maude Hart Lovelace, 1892–1980: A Minnesota Childhood.* (filmstrip with cassette) Minneapolis, MN: Heritage Productions, 1984. 87 fr. 14 min.

M821. *Maurice Sendak—1965.* (16mm film or video) Weston, CT: Weston Woods, 1965. 24 min. Beta or VHS. Introduces *Where the Wild Things Are* by M. Sendak.

M822. *Max's Christmas.* (16mm film or video) Weston, CT: Weston Woods, 1988. 5 min. Animated. Based on a book by Rosemary Wells.

M823. *Max's Christmas.* (filmstrip with cassette) Weston Woods, 1987. 26 fr. 5 min. Based on a book by R. Wells.

M824. *Max's Christmas.* (hardcover book and cassette) Weston Woods, 1987. 5 min. Based on a book by R. Wells.

M825. *May I Bring a Friend?* (TV program or video) A program in the Brown Module of *Picture Book Park.* Cleveland: WVIZ-TV and Bloomington, IN: AIT, 1972/73. 15 min. Beta, VHS, or 3/4". Based on a book by Beatrice S. De Regniers.

M826. *Meanwhile Back at the Ranch.* (TV program or video) Program #44 of *Reading Rainbow.* Buffalo: WNED-TV and Lincoln, NE: GPN, 1987. 30 min. VHS or 3/4". Based on a book by Trinka Noble.

M827. *A Medieval Feast.* (filmstrip with cassette) Hightstown, NJ: American School Pub-

lishers, 1984. 82 fr. 10:30 min. Based on a book by Aliki.

M828. *A Medieval Feast.* (hardcover with cassette) American School Publishers, 1984. Based on a book by Aliki.

M829. *Meet Kirsten: An American Girl* (paperback with cassette) Middleton, WI: Pleasant Co., 1986. 55 min. Based on a book by Janet Shaw.

M830. *Meet Sid Fleischman: The Newbery Author.* (video) Costa Mesa, CA: Pied Piper, 1987. 20:10 min. Includes information about *Humbug Mountain* and *The Whipping Boy* by Fleischman.

M831. *Meet Sid Fleischman: The Newbery Author.* (filmstrip with cassette. Pied Piper, 1987. 75 fr. 15 min. Includes information about *Humbug Mountain* and *The Whipping Boy* by Fleischman.

M832. *Meet the Author: A. A. Milne and the Pooh.* (filmstrip and cassette) Hightstown, NJ: American School Publishers, 1986. 119 fr. 13 min. Introduces: *Winnie the Pooh..*

M833. *Meet the Author: Jean Little.* (filmstrip with cassette) Toronto: Mead Sound Filmstrips and the Canadian Children's Centre, 1985. 99 fr. 20 min.

M834. *Meet the Author: Robert Louis Stevenson.* American School Publishers, 1989. 138 fr. 18:15 min.

M835. *Meet the Classic Author, #2.* (video) New Rochelle, NY: Spoken Arts, 1988. 30 min. Includes: Mark Twain, Louisa May Alcott, and Herman Melville.

M836. *Meet the Newbery Author: Arnold Lobel.* Revised edition. (filmstrip with cassette) Hightstown, NJ: American School Publishers, 1987. 106 fr. 11 min.

M837. *Meet the Newbery Author: Betsy Byars.* (filmstrip with cassette) American School Publishers, 1978. 95 fr. 12 min.

M838. *Meet the Newbery Author: Betty Miles.* (filmstrip with cassette) American School Publishers, 1988. 100 fr. 11 min. Includes information about *The Real Me..*

M839. *Meet the Newbery Author: Beverly Cleary.* (filmstrip with cassette) American School Publishers, 1979. Includes selections from *A Girl from Yamhill: A Memoir* by Cleary.

M840a. *Meet the Newbery Author: Carol Ryrie Brink.* (filmstrip with cassette) American School Publishers, 1976. 83 fr. 15 min. Introduces *Caddie Woodlawn..*

M840b. *Meet the Newbery Author: Cynthia Rylant.* (video) American School Publishers, 1989. 17 min.

M841. *Meet the Newbery Author: E. B. White.* (filmstrip with cassette) American School Publishers, 1987. Introduces: *Stuart Little, Trumpet of the Swan,* and *Charlotte's Web.*.

M842. *Meet the Newbery Author: Isaac Bashevis Singer.* (filmstrip with cassette) American School Publishers, 1976. 89 fr. 19 min. Includes a selection from *Zlateh the Goat.*.

M843. *Meet the Newbery Author: Katherine Paterson.* (filmstrip with cassette) American School Publishers, 1983. 145 fr. 10 min.

M844. *Meet the Newbery Author: Laura Ingalls Wilder.* (filmstrip with cassette) American School Publishers, 1980. 11 fr. 17 min. Introduces "The Little House" books.

M845. *Meet the Newbery Author: Laurence Yep.* (filmstrip with cassette) American School Publishers, 1981. 84 fr. 12 min. Includes *Dragonwings.*.

M846. Meet the Newbery Author: Nancy Willard. (filmstrip with cassette) American School Publishers, 1983. 155 fr. 19 min. Includes information about *A Visit to William Blake's Inn.*.

M847. *Meet the Newbery Author: Scott O'Dell.* (filmstrip with cassette) American School Publishers, 1974. 83 fr.

M848. *Merry Christmas, Amelia Bedelia.* (paperback with cassette) Old Greenwich, CT: Listening Library, 1988. 18 min. Based on a book by Peggy Parish.

M849. *Merry Christmas, Space Case.* (filmstrip with cassette) (Holiday with Humor series) New Rochelle, NY: Spoken Arts, 1986. 40 fr. 5 min. Based on a book by Edward Marshall.

M850. *Merry Christmas, Strega Nona.* (filmstrip with cassette) Old Greenwich, CT: Listening Library, 1988. 16 min. Based on a book by Tomie dePaola. Narrated by Celeste Holm.

M851. *Merry Christmas, Strega Nona.* (hardback or paperback with cassette) Listening Library, 1988. Based on a book by T. de Paola. Narrated by Celeste Holm.

M852a. *Merry Ever After: The Story of Two Medieval Weddings.* (video) Ancramdale, NY: Live Oak Media, 1977. 70 fr. 18:09 min. Based on a book by Joe Lasker.

M852b. *Messages from the Birds.* (TV program and video) World of Audubon series. Washington, D.C.: WETA-TV, 1989. 59 min. VHS.

M852c. *Messengers to the Brain.* (TV program) Washington, D.C.: National Geographic, 1984.

M853. *Maia: A Dinosaur Grows Up.* (video) West Coast Video, 1987. 30 min. Based on a book by John Horner and Doug Henderson.

M854. *Mickey's Birthday Party.* (16mm film or video) Deerfield, IL: Walt Disney, Coronet/MTI, 1988. 8 min.

M855. *The Middle Ages.* (filmstrip with cassette) (Music: Medieval to Modern). Chicago: Encyclopedia Britannica, 1982. 71 fr. 14 min.

M856. *The Midnight Fox.* (hardback or paperback with cassette) Ancramdale, NY: Live Oak Media, 1973. 54:42 min. Based on a book by Betsy Byars.

M857. *Midnight Is a Place.* (TV program or video) Program #13 of *More Books from Cover to Cover.* Washington, DC: WETA-TV and Alexandria, VA: PBS Video, n.d. 15 min. VHS or 3/4". Based on a book by Joan Aiken.

M858. *Mike Mulligan and His Steam Shovel.* (16mm film or video) Weston, CT: Weston Woods, 1956. 11 min. Iconographic. Based on a book by Virginia Lee Burton.

M859. *Mike Mulligan and His Steam Shovel.* (filmstrip with cassette) Weston Woods, 1957. 59 fr. 11 min. Based on a book by V. Burton.

M860. *Mike Mulligan and His Steam Shovel.* (hardback or paperback with cassette) Weston Woods, 1957. 11 min. Based on a book by V. Burton.

M861. *Mike Mulligan and His Steam Shovel.* (paperback with cassette) Boston: Houghton Mifflin, 1987. 14:56 min. Based on a book by V. Burton.

M862. *Milk Makers.* (TV program or video) Program #32 of *Reading Rainbow.* Buffalo: WNED-TV and Lincoln, NE: GPN, 1986. 30 min. VHS or 3/4". Based on a book by Gail Gibbons.

M863. *Miracle at Mreaux.* (TV program) A program of *WonderWorks.* Pittsburgh, PA: WQED-TV, 1986. Based on *Twenty and Ten* by Claire Bishop.

M864. *The Miracle of Flight.* (2 filmstrips and 2 cassettes) Pomfret, CT: Focal Point, 1984. *The Wright Brothers.* 56 fr. 12 min. *How Do Jets Fly?* 59 fr. 12 min.

M865. *Miss Goodall and the Wild Chimpanzees.* (video) Washington, DC: National Geographic, 1966. 52 min. VHS or 3/4".

M866. *Miss Nelson Has a Field Day.* (paperback with cassette) Boston: Houghton Mifflin, 1989. 19 min. Based on a book by Harry Allard.

M867. *Miss Nelson Is Back.* (TV program or video) Program #2 of *Reading Rainbow.* Buffalo: WNED-TV and Lincoln, NE: GPN, 1983. 30 min. VHS or 3/4". Based on a book by H. Allard.

M868. *Miss Nelson Is Back.* (paperback with cassette) Boston: Houghton Mifflin, 1988. 19:50 min. Based on a book by H. Allard.

M869. *Miss Nelson Is Missing.* (video) Deerfield, IL: Learning Corp., 1979. 15 min. Beta, VHS, or 3/4". Based on a book by H. Allard.

M870. *Miss Nelson Is Missing.* (filmstrip with cassette) Weston, CT: Weston Woods, 1984. 43 fr. 7 min. Based on a book by H. Allard.

M871. *Miss Nelson Is Missing.* (hardcover or paperback with cassette) Weston Woods, 1984. 7 min. Based on a book by H. Allard.

M872. *Miss Nelson Is Missing.* (paperback with cassette) Boston: Houghton Mifflin, 1987. 7 min. Based on a book by H. Allard.

M873. *Mrs. Frisby and the Rats of NIMH.* (video) Hightstown, NJ: American School Publishers, n.d. 29 min. VHS. Based on a book by Robert O'Brien.

M874. *Mrs. Frisby and the Rats of NIMH.* (filmstrip with cassette) American School Publishers, 1972. Based on a book by R. O'Brien.

M875. *Mrs. Frisby and the Rats of NIMH.* (cassette) American School Publishers, 1972. Based on a book by R. O'Brien.

M876. *Mr. and Mrs. Pig's Evening Out.* (filmstrip with cassette) Weston, CT: Weston Woods, 1984. 49 fr. 9 min. Based on a book by Mary Rayner.

M877. *Mr. and Mrs. Pig's Evening Out.* (hardcover book with cassette) Weston Woods, 1984. 9 min. Based on a book by M. Rayner.

M878. *Mr. Frog Went A-Courting.* (16mm film or video) New York: National Film Board of Canada, 1973. 5 min. VHS or 3/4".

M879. *Mr. Popper's Penguins.* (video) Hightstown, NJ: American School Publishers, 1985. 42 min. Live action. VHS. Based on a book by Richard and Florence Atwater.

M880. *Mr. Popper's Penguins.* (2 filmstrips with 2 cassettes) American School Publishers, 1975. Based on a book by R. and F. Atwater.

M881. *Mr. Popper's Penguins.* (cassette) American School Publishers, 1975. Abridged from a book by R. and F. Atwater.

M882. *Mr. Popper's Penguins.* (2 cassettes) American School Publishers, n.d. Word for word from a book by R. and F. Atwater. Narrated by Jim Backus.

M883. *Mr. Rabbit and the Lovely Present.* (TV program or video) A program in the Brown Module of *Picture Book Park.* Cleveland: WVIZ-TV and Bloomington, IN: AIT, 1972. 15 min. Beta, VHS, or 3/4". Based on a book by Charlotte Zolotow.

M884. *Mr. Rabbit and the Lovely Present.* (filmstrip with cassette) Weston, CT: Weston Woods, 1967. 26 fr. 7 min. Based on a book

by C. Zolotow. Includes *Charlotte and the White Horse* by Ruth Krauss.

M885. *Mr. Rabbit and the Lovely Present.* (hardback or paperback with cassette; Reading Chest with 4 paperbacks and cassette) Ancramdale, NY: Live Oak Media, 1987. 10 min. Based on a book by C. Zolotow.

M886. *Mr. Rogers' Neighborhood.* (TV series) Pittsburgh, PA: WQED-TV, 1967–. 30 min. each.

M887. *Mr. Rogers' Neighborhood: Music and Feelings.* (video). Pittsburgh, PA: Family Communications, 1986. 65 min.

M888. *Misty of Chincoteague.* (TV program or video) Program #13 of *Book Bird.* Springfield, VA: Children's Television International, 1979. 15 min. Beta, VHS or 3/4". Based on a book by Marguerite Henry.

M889. *Misty of Chincoteague.* (video) Hightstown, NJ: American School Publishers, 1988. 26:30 min. Based on a book by M. Henry.

M890. *Misty of Chincoteague.* (filmstrip with cassette) American School Publishers, 1988. 16 min. Based on a book by M. Henry.

M891. *Modeling.* (TV program) A program of *3-2-1-Contact.* New York: Children's Television Workshop, n.d. 30 min.

M892. *Mojo and the Russians.* (TV program or video) Program #15 of *Storybound.* Springfield, VA: Children's Television International, 1981. 15 min. VHS or 3/4". Based on a book by Walter Dean Myers.

M893. *Molly O'Mally.* (TV program or video) Program #8 of *Teletales.* Bloomington, IN: AIT, 1984. Beta, VHS, or 3/4". Based on a folk tale from England and Wales.

M894. *Molly's Pilgrim.* (16mm film or video) New York: Phoenix Films, 1986. 24 min. Live action. Based on a book by Barbara Cohen.

M895. *Moon Man.* (16mm film or video) Weston, CT: Weston Woods, 1981. 8 min. Animated. Beta or VHS. Based on a book by Tomi Ungerer.

M896. *Moon Man.* (filmstrip with cassette) Weston Woods, 1981. 36 fr. 8 min. Based on a book by T. Ungerer.

M897. *More Books from Cover to Cover.* (TV series or videos) Washington, D.C.: WETA-TV and the Greater Washington Educational Telecommunications Association; Alexandria, VA: PBS Video, n.d. 16 programs, 15 min. each. VHS or 3/4". Host: John Robbins.

M898. *More Dinosaurs.* (video) Studio City, CA: Twin Towers, 1987. 30 min. Animated. Narrated by Gary Owens.

M899. *More Scary Stories to Tell in the Dark.* (hardback or paperback with cassette) Old Greenwich, CT: Listening Library, 1986. 55

min. (Soundways to Reading, Cliffhangers Read-along) Based on a book by Alvin Schwartz.

M900.   *More Tales of Oliver Pig.* (hardback or paperback with cassette) (Follow the Reader) Old Greenwich, CT: Listening Library, 1984. 15 min. Based on a book by Jean Van Leeuwen.

M901.   *Morris and Boris Stories.* (paperback with cassette) Old Greenwich, CT: Listening Library, 1982. Based on books by Bernard Wiseman.

M902.   *Morris Goes to School.* (16mm film or video) Los Angeles: Churchill Films, 1989. 14:50 min. Clay animation. Based on a book by B. Wiseman.

M903.   *Mother's Day Mice.* (paperback with cassette) Boston: Houghton Mifflin, 1989. Based on a book by Eve Bunting.

M904a.   *Motion.* (TV program) A program of 3-2-1-Contact. New York: Children's Television Workshop, n.d. 30 min.

M904b.   *Motor Trend* (periodical). Los Angeles: Petersen, monthly.

M905.   *The Mouse and the Motorcycle.* (TV program or video) Program #7 of *Book Bird.* Springfield, VA: Children's Television International, 1979. 3/4″. Based on a book by Beverly Cleary.

M906.   *The Mouse and the Motorcycle* (16mm film or video) Los Angeles: Churchill Films, 1986. 41 min. Live action. VHS. Based on a book by B. Cleary.

M907.   *Mouse Soup.* (filmstrip with cassette) Hightstown, NJ: American School Publishers, 1983. 133 fr. 11 min. Based on a book by Arnold Lobel.

M908.   *Mouse Tales.* (paperback with cassette) New York: Harper, 1985. 15 min. Based on a book by A. Lobel.

M909.   *Mousekin's Thanksgiving.* (filmstrip with cassette) (Holidays, Holidays, series) Chicago: Encyclopedia Britannica and Westport Communications, 1987. Based on a book by Edna Miller.

M910a.   *Movie Maker.* (computer program) New York: Prentice-Hall, 1984. 48K, disk drive, joystick. Apple family, Commodore 64, Atari 800, 1200, 1400XL, and 1450XLD.

M910b.   *Moving Deep into the Interior.* (filmstrip and cassette) Westward Movement series. Niles, IL: United Learning, 1985. 11 min.

M911.   *Mufaro's Beautiful Daughters.* (TV program or video) Program #55 of *Reading Rainbow.* Buffalo: WNED-TV and Lincoln, NE: GPN, 1989. 30 min. VHS or 3/4″. Based

on a book by John Steptoe. Read by Phylicia Rashad.

M912.   *Mufaro's Beautiful Daughters.* (16mm film or video) Weston, CT: Weston Woods, 1989. 14 min. Iconographic. Beta or VHS. Based on a book by J. Steptoe.

M913.   *Mufaro's Beautiful Daughters.* (filmstrip with cassette) Weston Woods, 1988. 39 fr. 9 min. Based on a book by J. Steptoe.

M914.   *Mufaro's Beautiful Daughters.* (hardcover book with cassette) Weston Woods, 1988. 9 min. Based on a book by J. Steptoe.

M915.   *Mummies Made in Egypt.* (TV program or video) Program #54 of *Reading Rainbow.* Buffalo: WNED-TV and Lincoln, NE: GPN, 1989. 30 min. VHS or 3/4″. Based on a book by Aliki.

M916.   *Mummies Made in Egypt.* (TV program or video) Program #5 of *Through the Pages.* Cleveland: WVIZ-TV and Lincoln, NE: GPN, 1982. 15 min. Beta, VHS, or 3/4″.

M917.   *Muppet Magazine.* (periodical) New York: Telepictures, Inc. Quarterly.

M918a.   *The Muppet Movie.* (motion picture or video) ITC, n.d. Farmington Hills, MI: CBS/Fox, 1979. 96 min. VHS.

M918b.   *The Muppet Show.* (TV and video series) Farmington Hills, MI: Playhouse Video, 1984. 55 min. VHS.

M919.   *Music Is Magic.* (cassette) Salem, OR: Resources for Creative Teaching/Nellie Edge, 1988.

M920.   *Music: Medieval to Modern.* (5 filmstrips) Chicago: Encyclopedia Britannica, 1982. Includes: *The Middle Ages*; *The Renaissance and the Baroque*; *Classical Age*; *Romantic Age*; *The Twentieth Century*; and *Origins of American Popular Music.* 70 fr. each 15 min. each.

M921.   *Musical Encounter.* (TV series or videos) 21 programs, 30 min. each. Cooperatively produced by several Public Broadcasting Service stations between 1983–88 and distributed by Lincoln, NE: Great Plains National (GPN). VHS or 3/4″.

M922.   *Musical Families.* (TV program) Program #5 of *Musical Encounter.* GPN, n.d. 30 min. VHS or 3/4″.

M923.   *Musical Instruments.* (TV series or videos) 15 programs, 20 min. each. Morgantown, WV: WNPB-TV and Lincoln, NE: GPN, 1979. VHS or 3/4″.

M924.   *Musical Stories from the Picture Book Parade.* (phonograph record or cassette) Weston, CT: Weston Woods, 1981. 48 min. Includes: *The Star-Spangled Banner* by Key and Spier; *She'll Be Comin' Round the Mountain* by Quackenbush; *Yankee Doodle* by

Shackburg; *Clementine* by Quackenbush; *The Fox Went Out on a Chilly Night* by Spier; *London Bridge Is Falling Down* by Emberley; *I Know an Old Lady* by Bonne; *The Erie Canal* by Spier; *Waltzing Matilda* by Paterson; and *Over in the Meadow* by Langstaff.

M925. *My Brother's Keeper: The Holocaust Through the Eyes of an Artist.* (filmstrip with cassette) Chicago: SVE, 1988. 72 fr. 16 min. Based on a book by Israel Bernbaum.

M926. *My Father's Dragon.* (TV program or video) Program #4 of *Readit!* Bloomington, IN: AIT, 1982. 15 min. Beta, VHS, or 3/4″. Based on a book by Ruth Gannett.

M927. *My Little Island.* (TV program or video) Program #45 of *Reading Rainbow.* Buffalo: WNED-TV and Lincoln, NE: GPN, 1987. 30 min. VHS or 3/4″. Based on a book by Frane Lessac.

M928. *My Mother Never Was a Kid.* (16mm film or video) Deerfield, IL: Learning Corp. of America, 1981. 30 or 46 min. editions. Beta, VHS, or 3/4″. Based on *Hangin' Out with Cici* by Francine Pascal.

M929. *My Robot Buddy.* (TV program or video) Program #2 of *Readit!* Bloomington, IN: AIT, 1982. 15 min. Beta, VHS, or 3/4″. Based on a book by Alfred Slote. Also includes: *My Trip to Alpha 1.*.

M930. *My Side of the Mountain.* (video) Los Angeles: Paramount Home Video, 1985. Live action. 100 min. Based on a book by Jean George.

M931. *My Trip to Alpha 1.* (TV program or video) Program #2 of *Readit!* AIT, 1982. 15 min. Beta, VHS, or 3/4″. Based on a book by A. Slote. Also includes: *My Robot Buddy.*.

M932. *My Trip to Alpha 1.* (hardback or paperback with cassette) Old Greenwich, CT: Listening Library, 1985. 41 min. (Soundways to Reading, Cliffhanger Read-along) Based on a book by A. Slote.

M933. *My Visit to the Dinosaurs.* (paperback with cassette) New York: Harper, 1987. Based on a book by Aliki.

M934. *Mysteries.* (filmstrip with cassette) Costa Mesa, CA: Pied Piper, 1980. (Literature for Children, Series 6) Features: *The Egypt Game* by Zilpha Snyder; *Encyclopedia Brown* by Donald Sobol; and *The House of Dies Drear* by Virginia Hamilton. Introduces: *The Westing Game* by Ellen Raskin and *The House with a Clock on Its Walls* by John Bellairs.

M935. *The Mysterious Black-footed Ferret.* (TV program or video) A program of *The World of Audubon.* Stamford, CT: Vestron

and National Audubon Society, 1989. 60 min. Beta or VHS.

M936. *The Mysterious Tadpole.* (16mm film or video) Weston, CT: Weston Woods, 1986. 9 min. Animated. Beta or VHS. Based on a book by Steven Kellogg.

M937. *The Mysterious Tadpole.* (filmstrip with cassette) Weston Woods, 1980. 41 fr. 9 min. Based on a book by S. Kellogg.

M938. *The Mysterious Tadpole.* (hardcover or paperback with cassette) Weston Woods, 1980. 9 min. Based on a book by S. Kellogg.

M939. *Mystery Books.* (TV program) A program of *The Word Shop.* Washington, DC: WETA-TV, 1976. 15 min. Beta, VHS, or 3/4″.

M940. *Mystery Meal.* (TV program or video) Los Angeles: Churchill Films, Atlantis Films, Lancit Media, and Revcom TV, 1987. 30 min. Beta or VHS. Based on a book about Ramona by Beverly Cleary.

M941. *Mystery Stories.* (TV program) A program of *The Word Shop.* Washington, DC: WETA-TV, 1976. 15 min. Beta, VHS, or 3/4″.

M942. *Nags Head Woods.* (TV program) Program #312 of *Naturescene.* Columbia: South Carolina Educational Television, n.d. 30 min.

M943. *Narrative Writing.* (4 filmstrips with 4 cassettes) Costa Mesa, CA: Pied Piper, 1975. Includes: *Creating a Beginning*; *Developing a Character*; *Building a Conflict*; and *Elements of a Story.*.

M944. *Nate the Great.* (hardback or paperback with cassette) (Follow the Reader) Old Greenwich, CT: Listening Library, 1985. 17:30 min. Based on a book by Marjorie Sharmat.

M945. *Nate the Great and the Missing Key.* (hardback or paperback with cassette) (Follow the Reader) Listening Library, 1982. 19 min. Based on a book by M. Sharmat.

M946. *Nate the Great and the Sticky Case.* (16mm film or video) Chicago: Encyclopedia Britannica, 1983. 19 min. Beta, VHS, or 3/4″. Based on a book by M. Sharmat.

M947. *Nate the Great Goes Undercover.* (16mm film or video) Santa Monica: Bosustow Entertainment and Los Angeles: Churchill Films, 1978. Based on a book by M. Sharmat.

National Audubon Specials. (TV series). See *The World of Audubon.*.

M948. *National Geographic.* (periodical) Washington, DC: National Geographic Society. Monthly.

M949. *National Geographic Specials.* (TV series or videos) Washington, DC: National Geographic Society. Four new programs annually on PBS. VHS or 3/4″.

M950. *National Geographic World.* (periodical) Washington, DC: National Geographic Society. Monthly.

M951. *National Wildlife.* (periodical) Washington, DC: National Wildlife Federation. Bimonthly.

M952. *Natural World.* (TV series or videos) London: BBC-TV and Chicago: Films, Inc. 50 min. each.

M953. *Nature.* (TV series or videos) New York: WNET-TV; Chicago: Films, Inc. 1984–.

M954. *Naturescene.* (TV series) Columbia, SC: South Carolina ETV and CPB, 1980. 52 programs, 30 min. each.

M955. *A New Coat for Anna.* (filmstrip with cassette) Hightstown, NJ: American School Publishers, 1988. 86 fr. 9:50 min. Based on a book by Harriet Ziefert.

M956. *A New Coat for Anna.* (paperback with cassette) American School Publishers, 1988. 10 min. Based on a book by H. Ziefert.

M957. *New Endings: Adventure.* (filmstrip with cassette) (Literature to Enjoy and Write About, Series 1) Costa Mesa, CA: Pied Piper, 1989. 19 min. Features: *Hatchet* by Gary Paulsen and *Julie of the Wolves* by Jean George. Introduces: *Sign of the Beaver* by Elizabeth Speare and *The Cay* by Theodore Taylor.

M958. *New England Autumn.* (TV program) Program #313 of *Naturescene*. Columbia, SC: South Carolina Educational Television, n.d. 30 min.

M959. *New Pajamas.* (TV program, 16mm film, or video) Los Angeles: Churchill Films, Atlantis Films, Lancit Media, and Revcom Television, 1988. Based on *Ramona and Her Mother* by Beverly Cleary.

M961. *News Stories.* (TV program) A program of *The Word Shop*. Washington, DC: WETA-TV, 1976. 15 min. Beta, VHS, or 3/4″.

M962. *Nighty-Nightmare.* (cassette) New York: Harper/Caedmon, 1988. 1 hr. 30 min. Based on a book by James Howe.

M964. *Nonsense and Made-Up Words in Poetry.* (TV program) A program of *The Word Shop*. Washington, DC: WETA-TV, 1976. 15 min. Beta, VHS, or 3/4″.

M965. *The Not-Just-Anybody Family.* (TV program or video) Program #11 of *More Books from Cover to Cover*. Washington, DC: WETA-TV and Alexandria, VA: PBS Video, 1987. 15 min. VHS or 3/4″. Based on a book by Betsy Byars.

M966. *The Not-Just-Anybody Family.* (paperback with 3 cassettes) Old Greenwich, CT: Listening Library, 1988. 3 hrs. 19 min. Based on a book by B. Byars.

M967. *Nothing's Fair in Fifth Grade.* (hardback or paperback with cassette) Listening Library, 1985. 81 min. (Soundways to Reading, Cliffhanger Read-along) Based on a book by Barthe DeClements.

M968. *NOVA.* (TV series or videos) Boston: WGBH-TV, Deerfield IL: Coronet, or New York: Time-Life Videos. 60 min. each.

M969. *The Nutcracker.* (video) Mount Kisco, NY: Guidance Associates, n.d. 78 min. Performed by the American Ballet Theatre and Mikhail Baryshnikov.

M970. *The Nutshell Library from the Picture Book Parade.* (video) Weston, CT: Weston Woods, n.d. 16 min. Includes books by Maurice Sendak: *Alligators All Around, One Was Johnny, Pierre*, and *Chicken Soup With Rice*..

M971. *Obadiah the Bold.* (filmstrip with cassette) Ancramdale, NY: Live Oak Media, 1970. 5:47 min. Based on a book by Brinton Turkle.

M972. *Oceans.* (TV program) A program of *3-2-1-Contact*. New York: Children's Television Workshop, n.d. 30 min.

M973. *Odyssey: The Young People's Magazine of Astronomy and Outer Space.* (periodical) Milwaukee, WI: Kalmbach Publishing Co. Monthly.

M974. *Oh, Kojo! How Could You?* (filmstrip with cassette) Hightstown, NJ: American School Publishers, 1987. 110 fr. 17:30 min. Based on a book by Verna Aardema.

M975. *Oh, Kojo! How Could You?* (cassette) American School Publishers, 1986. 18 min. Based on a book by V. Aardema.

M976. *Old Henry.* (filmstrip with cassette) Hightstown, NJ: American School Publishers, 1989. 74 fr. 7:22 min. Based on a book by Joan Blos.

M977. *On the Edge of Extinction: Panthers and Cheetahs.* (TV program) A program of *The World of Audubon*. Washington, DC: WETA-TV and the National Audubon Society, n.d. 48 min.

M977a. *101 Dalmatians.* (motion picture or video) Burbank, CA: Walt Disney, Films, Inc., and MGM/UA, Twayne Films, 1961. Animated. 80 min. Based on a book by Dodie Smith.

M977b. *101 Dalmatians.* (2 cassettes) Lewiston, NY: Listen for Pleasure, 1984. 2 hrs. Based on a book by D. Smith. Read by Joanna Lumley.

M977c. *101 Things for Kids to Do.* (video) New York: Random Home Video, 1987. 60 min. Beta or VHS. Based on the book *Shari*

Lewis Presents One Hundred and One Things for Kids to Do. Hostess: Shari Lewis.

M978.   *One Was Johnny.* (16mm film or video) Weston, CT: Weston Woods, 1975. 3 min. Animated. Beta or VHS. Based on a book by Maurice Sendak.

M979.   *One Was Johnny.* (filmstrip with cassette) Weston Woods, 1976. 26 fr. 3 min. Based on a book by M. Sendak.

M980.   *One Was Johnny.* (hardback or paperback with cassette) Weston Woods, 1976. 3 min. Based on a book by M. Sendak.

M981.   *The Orchestra.* (TV program) Program #5 of *Musical Encounter.* Lincoln, NE: GPN, 1983. 30 min. VHS or 3/4″.

M982.   *Oregon Trail.* (computer program) St. Paul, MN: MECC (Minnesota Educational Computing Corporation), 1985. Apple family, 64K, MS-Dos, 156K.

M983.   *Otherwise Known as Sheila the Great.* (16mm film or video) Irwindale, CA: Barr Films and Calico Films, 1989. 24 min. Based on a book by Judy Blume.

M984.   *Outer Space.* (TV program or video) Program #23 of *Draw Along.* Bloomington, IN: AIT, 1986. 15 min. Beta, VHS, or 3/4″. Host: Paul Ringler.

M985a.   *The Owl.* (TV program and video) Olney, PA: Bullfrog Films, National Audubon Society, *Owl Magazine*, WNET-TV, and Canadian Broadcasting Corporation, 1988–. 30 min.

M985b.   *Owl at Home.* (paperback and cassette) New York: Harper, 1986. 15 min. Based on a book by Arnold Lobel.

M986.   *Owl Moon.* (16mm film or video) Weston, CT: Weston Woods and LA: Churchill Films, 1989. 8 min. Based on a book by Jane Yolen.

M987a.   *Owl Moon.* (filmstrip with cassette) Weston, CT: Weston Woods, 1988. 43 fr. 8 min. Based on a book by J. Yolen.

M987b.   *Owl Moon.* (hardback or paperback with cassette) Weston Woods, 1988. 8:30 min. Based on a book by J. Yolen.

M988.   *The Owl Who Was Afraid of the Dark.* (cassette) Atlanta: Cover to Cover Cassettes, 1986. 70 min. Based on a book by Jill Tomlinson. Narrated by Maureen Lipman.

M989.   *The Ox-Cart Man.* (TV program or video) Program #18 of *Reading Rainbow.* Buffalo: WNED-TV and Lincoln, NE: GPN, 1984. 30 min. VHS and 3/4″. Based on a book by Donald Hall. Narrated by Lorne Greene.

M990.   *The Ox-Cart Man.* (video) Ancramdale, NY: Live Oak Media, 1987. 8 min. Based on a book by D. Hall.

M991.   *The Ox-Cart Man.* (hardback with cassette or Reading Chest with 4 paperbacks). Live Oak, 1984. 7 min. Based on a book by D. Hall.

M992.   *Padre Island.* (TV program) Program #508 of *Naturescene.* Columbia: Carolina Educational Television, n.d. 30 min.

M993.   *A Pair of Red Clogs.* (TV program or video) A program from the Green Module of *Picture Book Park.* Cleveland: WVIZ-TV and Bloomington, IN: AIT, 1972/73. 15 min. Beta, VHS, or 3/4″. Based on a book by Masako Matsuno.

M994.   *Paka'a.* (TV program or video) Program #15 of *Teletales.* Bloomington, IN: AIT, 1984. 15 min. Based on a Hawaiian legend.

M995.   *The Paper Crane.* (TV program or video) Program #39 of *Reading Rainbow.* Buffalo: WNED-TV and Lincoln, NE: GPN, 1987. 30 min. VHS or 3/4″. Based on a book by Molly Bang.

M996.   *The Parrot and the Thief.* (TV program or video) Program #8 of *Readit!* Bloomington, IN: AIT, 1982. 15 min. Beta, VHS, or 3/4″. Based on a book by Richard Kennedy. Includes: *The Rise and Fall of Ben Gizzard* and *Contests at Cowlick* by Kennedy.

M997.   *Pass It On.* (TV series) Memphis, TN: WKNO-TV and Lincoln, NE: GPN, 1983. 30 programs, 15 min. each. VHS and 3/4″.

M998.   *The Patchwork Quilt.* (TV program or video) Program #22 of *Reading Rainbow.* Buffalo: WNED-TV and Lincoln, NE: GPN, 1985. 30 min. VHS or 3/4″. Based on a book by Valerie Flourney. Narrated by Isabel Sanford.

M999.   *Patrick's Dinosaur.* (paperback with cassette) Boston: Houghton Mifflin, 1987. Based on a book by Carol and Don Carrick.

M1000.   *Paul Bunyan.* (TV program or video) Program #21 of *Reading Rainbow.* Buffalo: WNED-TV and Lincoln, NE: GPN, 1985. 30 min. Beta or VHS. Based on a book by Steven Kellogg. Narrated by Buddy Ebsen.

M1001.   *Perfect the Pig.* (TV program or video) Program #25 of *Reading Rainbow.* WNED-TV and GPN, 1985. 30 min. VHS or 3/4″. Based on a book by Susan Jeschke.

M1002.   *Persuasive Writing: Non-fiction.* (filmstrip with cassette) (Literature to Enjoy and Write About, Series 2) Costa Mesa, CA: Pied Piper, 1989. 22 min. Introduces: *Koko's Kitten* by Francine Patterson.

M1003.   *Peter Pan.* (4 cassettes) Washington, DC: Audio Book Contractors, 1987. 60–90 min. each. Based on a book by James Barrie. Read by Flo Gibson.

M1004. *Peter Pan.* (4 cassettes) West Chester, PA: Dercm Pr., 1986. 75 min. each. Based on a book by J. Barrie. Read by Carol Noone.

M1005. *Peter Rabbit and Friends from the Picture Book Parade.* (cassette) Weston, CT: Weston Woods, 1986. 39 min. Includes: *The Tale of Peter Rabbit*; *The Tale of Mr. Jeremy Fisher*; *The Tale of Tom Kitten*; *The Tale of Benjamin Bunny*; and *The Tale of Two Bad Mice.* Based on books by Beatrix Potter.

M1006. *Petula Clark Reads Heidi.* (2 cassettes) Lewiston, NY: Listen for Pleasure, 1984. 180 min. Based on a book by Joanna Spyri.

M1007. *Petunia.* (TV program or video) A program of *Tilson's Book Shop.* Cleveland: WVIZ-TV and Lincoln, NE: GPN, 1975. 15 min. VHS. Based on a book by Roger Duvoisin.

M1008. *The Phantom Tollbooth.* (TV program or video) NY: MGM/UA Home Video, 1969, 1989. 89 min. Beta or VHS. Based on a book by Norton Juster.

M1009. *The Phantom Tollbooth.* (cassette) New York: Harper/Caedmon, 1982. 51 min. Based on a book by N. Juster.

M1010. *The Phantom Tollbooth.* (hardback or paperback with cassette) Old Greenwich, CT: Listening Library, 1985. 61 min. Based on a book by N. Juster.

M1011. *The Philharmonic Gets Dressed.* (16mm film) Northbrook, IL: MTI Film and Video, 1988. 17 min. Based on a book by Karla Kuskin.

M1012. *The Piano Show.* (TV program or video) Program #4 of *Musical Encounter.* Lincoln, NE: GPN, 1979. 30 min. VHS or 3/4".

M1013. *Picnic.* (filmstrip with cassette) Weston, CT: Weston Woods, 1985. 34 fr. 4 min. Based on a book by Emily McCully.

M1014. *Picnic.* (hardcover book with cassette) Weston Woods, 1985. 4 min. Based on a book by E. McCully.

M1015. *Picture Book Park.* (TV series or videos) Cleveland: WVIZ-TV and Bloomington, IN: AIT, 1972–73. 16 programs, 15 min. each.

M1016. *Picture Pages.* (TV program or videos) Part of the *Captain Kangaroo* TV series. 5–6 min. each. Narrated by Bill Cosby. Burbank, CA: Walt Disney Home Video, 1985.

M1017. *Picture This.* (TV program or video) Program #6 of *Writer's Realm.* Bloomington, IN: AIT and Maryland Instructional Television, 1986. 14 min. Beta, VHS, or 3/4".

M1018. *The Pied Piper of Hamelin.* (TV program) A program of *Long Ago and Far Away.*

London: Cosgrove Hall, 1982. Boston: WGBH-TV, 1989. 30 min.

M1019. *Pierre.* (16mm film or video) Weston, CT: Weston Woods, 1978. 6 min. Animated. Based on a book by Maurice Sendak.

M1020. *Pierre.* (filmstrip with cassette) Weston Woods, 1976. 33 fr. 6 min. Based on a book by M. Sendak.

M1021. *Pierre.* (hardcover book with cassette) Weston Woods, 1976. 6 min. Based on a book by M. Sendak.

M1022. *Pig Pig Grows Up.* (filmstrip with cassette) Weston, CT: Weston Woods, 1981. 30 fr. 6 min. Based on a book by David McPhail.

M1023. *Pig Pig Grows Up.* (hardcover or paperback with cassette) Weston Woods, 1981. 6 min. Based on a book by D. McPhail.

M1024. *Pig Pig Grows Up.* (hardcover or paperback with cassette; Reading Chest with 4 paperbacks and cassette) Ancramdale, NY: Live Oak Media, 1985. 8:20 min. Based on a book by D. McPhail.

M1025. *Pig Pig Rides.* (hardcover or paperback with cassette; Reading Chest with 4 paperbacks and cassette) Live Oak Media, n.d. 3:15 min. Based on a book by D. McPhail.

M1026. *Piggins and Picnic with Piggins.* (cassette) New York: Harper/Caedmon, 1988. 26 min. Based on books by Jane Yolen.

M1027. *The Pigs' Wedding.* (filmstrip with cassette) Weston, CT: Weston Woods, 1987. 43 fr. 8 min. Based on a book by Helme Heine.

M1028. *The Pigs' Wedding.* (hardcover book with cassette) Weston Woods, 1987. 8 min. Based on a book by H. Heine.

M1029. *Pilot Down, Presumed Dead.* (TV program or video) Program #1 of *Storybound.* Springfield, VA: Children's Television International, 1971. 15 min. Beta, VHS, or 3/4". Based on a book by Marjorie Phleger.

M1030. *Pilot Down, Presumed Dead.* (hardback or paperback with cassette) Old Greenwich, CT: Listening Library, 1985. 26 min. (Soundways to Reading, Cliffhanger Read-along) Based on a book by M. Phleger.

M1031. *Pinballs.* (TV program or video) Program #8 of *Storybound.* Springfield, VA: Children's Television International, 1981. 15 min. Beta, VHS, or 3/4". Based on a book by Betsy Byars.

M1032. *Pinballs.* (hardback or paperback with cassette) Old Greenwich, CT: Listening Library, 1985. 84 min. (Young Adult Cliffhangers) Based on a book by B. Byars.

M1033. *Pinballs.* (2 cassettes) Old Greenwich, CT: Listening Library and ABC-CLIO, 1988. 2 hrs. 46 min. (Large Print Read-Alongs).

M1034. *Pinch.* (TV program or video) Program #14 of *Storybound.* Springfield, VA: Children's Television International, 1981. 15 min. Beta, VHS, or 3/4″. Based on a book by Larry Callen.

M1035. *Pioneer Women.* (video) Emporia, KS: Emporia State Univ. Instructional TV, 1982. Interview with Joanna Stratton.

M1036. *Pioneer Women: Selections from Their Journals.* (2 cassettes) New York: Harper/Caedmon, 1974. 120 min. Based on the writings of: Elenore Plaisted; Martha Summerhayes; Elinore Pruitt; and Mary Richardson Walker. Read by Sandy Dennis and Eileen Heckart.

M1037. *Pippi Goes on Board.* (video) Los Angeles: Video Gems, 1981. 84 min. Based on a book by Astrid Lindgren.

M1038. *Pippi Goes on Board.* (hardback or paperback with cassette) Old Greenwich, CT: Listening Library, 1985. 27 min. (Soundways to Reading, Cliffhanger Read-along) Based on a book by A. Lindgren.

M1039. *Pippi in the South Seas.* (hardback or paperback with cassette) Listening Library, 1985. 16 min. (Soundways to Reading, Cliffhanger Read-along) Based on a book by A. Lindgren.

M1040. *Pippi Longstocking.* (motion picture or video) Los Angeles: Video Gems, NW Russo, GG Communications, 1973, 1981. 99 min. Based on a book by A. Lindgren.

M1041. *Pippi Longstocking.* (16mm film or video) Chicago: Films Inc., n.d. 99 min. Based on a book by A. Lindgren.

M1042. *Pippi Longstocking.* (hardback or paperback with cassette) Ancramdale, NY: Live Oak Media, n.d. 52:10 min. Based on a book by A. Lindgren.

M1043. *The Pirate Hero of New Orleans.* (filmstrip with cassette) Live Oak Media, n.d. 5:02 min. Based on a book by Carl Carmer.

M1044. *Planet Earth.* (TV series or videos) Wilmette, IL: Annenberg/CPB Collection and Chicago: Films, Inc., n.d. 7 programs, 60 min. each.

M1045. *Planet of the Apes.* (motion picture or video) New York: 20th Century Fox, 1968. 112 min. Based on a book by Pierre Boulle.

M1046. *Plants.* (TV program) A program of *Challenge.* Nashville: WDCN, n.d. 15 min.

M1047. *Plants and Animals in the City.* (2 filmstrips with cassettes) Washington, DC: National Geographic, 1981. Includes: *Plants in the City,* 44 fr. 17 min. and *Animals in the City.* 43 fr. 17 min.

M1048. *Play Ball, Amelia Bedelia.* (paperback with cassette) New York: Harper, 1985. 15 min. Based on a book by Peggy Parish.

M1049. *Plays: The Drama Magazine for Young People.* (periodical). Boston: Plays, Inc. Issued 7 times a year, October–May.

M1050. *Playwrights.* (TV program) A program of *The Word Shop.* Washington, DC: WETA-TV, 1976. 15 min. Beta, VHS, or 3/4″.

M1051. *Plazas, Malls and Squares.* (TV program or video) Program #204 of *Images and Things.* Bloomington, IN: AIT, 1973. 20 min. Beta, VHS, or 3/4″.

M1052. *Plot.* (filmstrip with cassette) Costa Mesa, CA: Pied Piper, 1985. 113 fr. 21 min. (Components of Fiction—Literature for Children, Series 9) Features: *Get Out of Here, Philip Hall* by Bette Greene and *How to Eat Fried Worms* by Thomas Rockwell. Introduces: *Kneeknock Rise* by Natalie Babbitt; *Who Really Killed Cock Robin* by Jean George; and *Mrs. Frisby and the Rats of NIMH* by Robert O'Brien.

M1053. *Poems as Descriptions.* (TV program) A program of *The Word Shop.* Washington, DC: WETA-TV, 1976. 15 min. Beta, VHS, or 3/4″.

M1054. *Poems as Rhythm.* (TV program) A program of *The Word Shop.* WETA-TV, 1976. 15 min. Beta, VHS, or 3/4″.

M1055. *Poems as Sounds.* (TV program) A program of *The Word Shop.* WETA-TV, 1976. 15 min. BETA, VHS, or 3/4″.

M1056. *Poems as Stories.* (TV program) A program of *The Word Shop.* WETA-TV, 1976. 15 min. Beta, VHS, or 3/4″.

M1057. *Poets.* (TV program) A program of *The Word Shop.* WETA-TV, 1976. 15 min. Beta, VHS, or 3/4″.

M1058. *Polar Express.* (filmstrip with cassette) Hightstown, NJ: American School Publishers, 1986. 70 fr. 11:33 min. Based on a book by Chris Van Allsburg.

M1059. *The Pop Show.* (TV program or video) Santa Monica: Pyramid or Easton, IL: Viewfinders, n.d. 8 min.

M1060. *Portrait of a Coal Miner.* (16mm film or video) Washington, DC: National Geographic, 1980. 15 min. VHS or 3/4″.

M1061. *Power to Do Work.* (TV program) A program of *Challenge.* Nashville: WDCN-TV, n.d. 15 min.

M1062. *The Prince and the Pauper.* (4 filmstrips with 4 cassettes) Hawthorne, NJ: January Productions, 1984. 63 fr. each. 15 min. each. Based on a book by Mark Twain.

M1063. *Problem Solving: Humorous Stories.* (filmstrip with cassette) (Literature to Enjoy and Write About, Series 1) Costa Mesa, CA: Pied Piper, 1989. 22 min. Introduces: *Superfudge* by Judy Blume; *Return of the Great Brain* by John Fitzgerald; and *Be a Perfect Person in Just Three Days* by Stephen Manes.

M1064.   *Protecting Endangered Animals.* (16mm film or video) Washington, DC: National Geographic, 1984. 15 min. VHS or 3/4".

M1065.   *The Purple Coat.* (TV program or video) Program #50 of *Reading Rainbow.* Buffalo: WNED-TV and Lincoln, NE: GPN, 1988. 30 min. VHS or 3/4". Based on a book by Amy Hest. Narrated by Jack Gilford.

M1066.   *Pyramid.* (2 filmstrips with 2 cassettes) Costa Mesa, CA: Pied Piper, 1984. 27 min. Based on a book by David Macaulay.

M1067.   *Race Against Death.* (TV program or video) Program #12 of *Book Bird.* Springfield, VA: Children's Television International, 1979. 15 min. 3/4". Based on a book by Seymour Reit.

M1068.   *Rachel and Obadiah.* (filmstrip with cassette) Ancramdale, NY: Live Oak Media, 1978. 9:53 min. Based on a book by Brinton Turkle.

M1069.   *Radio Program: Historical Fiction.* (filmstrip with cassette) (Literature to Enjoy and Write About) Costa Mesa, CA: Pied Piper, 1989. 22 min. Introduces: *Sarah Plain and Tall* by Patricia MacLachlan; *Zia* by Scott O'Dell; *Charley Skedaddle* by Patricia Beatty; and *Dragonwings* by Laurence Yep.

M1070.   *Rainy Sunday* (16mm film or video) Los Angeles: Churchill Films, 1988. 27 min. Beta or VHS. Based on a book about Ramona by Beverly Cleary.

M1071.   *Ralph S. Mouse.* (16mm film or video) Churchill Films, 1989. 40 min. Based on a book by B. Cleary.

M1072.   *Ralph S. Mouse.* (cassette) Hightstown, NJ: American School Publishers, 1983. 34 min. Based on a book by B. Cleary.

M1073.   *Ramona.* (doll) Book Mates.

M1074.   *Ramona and Her Father.* (2 filmstrips and 2 cassettes) American School Publishers, n.d. Based on a book by B. Cleary.

M1075.   *Ramona and Her Father.* (cassette) American School Publishers, 1978. Based on a book by B. Cleary.

M1076.   *Ramona and Her Mother.* (cassette) American School Publishers, n.d. 36 min. Based on a book by B. Cleary.

M1077.   *Ramona and Her Mother.* (paperback with 2 cassettes) Old Greenwich, CT: Listening Library, 1989. Based on a book by B. Cleary.

M1078.   *Ramona Forever.* (2 filmstrips with cassettes) Hightstown, NJ: American School Publishers, 1987. 114 and 125 fr. 17 and 19 min. Based on a book by B. Cleary.

M1079.   *Ramona Forever.* (cassette) American School Publishers, n.d. Based on a book by B. Cleary.

M1080.   *Ramona Forever.* (paperback with 2 cassettes) Old Greenwich, CT: Listening Library, 1989. Based on a book by B. Cleary.

M1081.   *Ramona Quimby, Age 8.* (cassette) Hightstown, HJ: American School Publishers, 1981. 26 min. Based on a book by B. Cleary.

M1082.   *Ramona Quimby, Age 8.* (paperback with 2 cassettes) Old Greenwich, CT: Listening Library, 1989. Based on a book by B. Cleary.

M1083.   *Ramona Series.* (TV series, 16mm film or video) Los Angeles: Churchill Films, Atlantis Films, Lancit Media, Revcom Television, 1988. 10 programs, 27 min. each. Beta or VHS.

M1083a.   *Ramona: Bad Day.* (16mm, TV program, video) Los Angeles: Churchill Films, 1988. Atlantis Films, Lancit Media, Revcom TV, 1988. 27 min. Beta or VHS. Based on a book about Ramona by B. Cleary.

M1083b.   *Ramona: Goodbye-Hello.* (16mm, TV program, video) Churchill Films, 1988. Atlantis Films, Lancit Media, Revcom TV, 1988. 27 min. Beta or VHS. Based on a book about Ramona by B. Cleary.

M1083c.   *Ramona: Mystery Meal.* (16mm, TV program, video) Churchill Films, 1988. Atlantis Films, Lancit Media, Revcom TV, 1988. 27 min. Beta or VHS. Based on a book about Ramona by B. Cleary.

M1083d.   *Ramona: New Pajamas.* (16mm, TV program, video) Churchill Films, 1989. Atlantis Films, Lancit Media, Revcom TV, 1988. 27 min. Beta or VHS. Based on *Ramona and Her Mother* by B. Cleary.

M1083e.   *Ramona: Perfect Day.* (16mm, TV program, video) Churchill Films, 1988. Atlantis Films, Lancit Media, Revcom TV, 1988. 27 min. Beta or VHS. Based on a book by B. Cleary.

M1083f.   *Ramona: Rainy Sunday.* (16mm, TV program, video) Churchill Films, 1988. Atlantis Films, Lancit Media, Revcom TV, 1988. 27 min. Beta or VHS. Based on a book about Ramona by B. Cleary.

M1083g.   *Ramona: Siblingitis.* (16mm, TV program, video) Churchill Films, 1989. Atlantis Films, Lancit Media, Revcom TV, 1988. 27 min. Beta or VHS. Based on a book about Ramona by B. Cleary.

M1083h.   *Ramona: Squeakerfoot.* (16mm, TV program, video) Churchill Films, 1989. Atlantis Films, Lancit Media, Revcom TV, 1988. 27 min. Beta or VHS. Based on a book about Ramona by B. Cleary.

M1083i.   *Ramona: The Great Hair Argument.* (16mm, TV program, video) Churchill Films, 1989. Atlantis Films, Lancit Media, Revcom TV, 1988. 27 min. Beta or VHS. Based on a book about Ramona by B. Cleary.

M1084.   *Ramona the Brave.* (filmstrip with cassette) Hightstown, NJ: American School Publishers, n.d. Based on a book by B. Cleary.

M1085.   *Ramona the Brave.* (cassette) American School Publishers, 1980. 21:20 min. Based on a book by B. Cleary.

M1086.   *Ramona the Patient.* (TV program, 16mm film or video) Los Angeles: Churchill Films, Atlantis Films, Lancit Media, Revcom TV, 1989. 27 min. Beta or VHS. Based on a book by B. Cleary.

M1087.   *Ramona: Mystery Meal/Rainy Sunday.* (TV programs, 16mm film, or video) Churchill Films, Atlantis Films, Lancit Media, Revcom TV, 1987. 54 min. Beta or VHS. Based on books by B. Cleary.

M1088.   *Ramona: Perfect Day/Bad Day.* (TV programs, 16mm film or video) Churchill Films, Atlantis Films, Lancit Media, Revcom TV, 1987. 54 min. Beta or VHS. Based on a book by B. Cleary.

M1089.   *Ramona: Squeakerfoot/Goodbye, Hello.* (TV programs, 16mm film or video) Churchill Films, Atlantis Films, Lancit Media, Revcom TV, 1987. 54 min. Beta or VHS. Based on a book by B. Cleary.

M1090.   *Randolph Caldecott: The Man Behind the Medal.* (filmstrip with cassette) Weston, CT: Weston Woods, 1983. 57 fr. 15 min.

M1091a.   *Ranger Rick.* (periodical) Washington, DC: National Wildlife Federation. Monthly.

M1091b.   *Read All About It!* (TV series) Chapel Hill, N.C. and Ontario, Canada: TV Ontario, 1987. Series of 10 videos. 30 min. each.

M1092.   *Read Aloud: Questions and Answers.* (cassette) Springfield, MA: Reading Tree Productions, 1986. 90 min. Companion to *Turning on the Turned-off Reader.* Based on *The Read-Aloud Handbook* by Jim Trelease.

M1093.   *Readers as Writers, #1.* (packet) Chicago: American Library Association, 1988. Authors included: Nina Bawden, Betsy Byars, Jean Fritz, Marguerite Henry, M. E. Kerr, Evaline Ness, Ed Radlauer, Judith St. George, and Yoshika Uchida.

M1094.   *Readers as Writers, #2.* (packet) American Library Association, 1989. Authors included: Ashley Bryan, Mary Calhoun, Paul Goble, Beverly Cleary, Lois Duncan, Arnold Lobel, Richard Peck, Marilyn Sachs, and Jane Yolen.

M1095.   *Reading Aloud.* (16mm film) Springfield, MA: Reading Tree Productions, 1989. 80 min. Based on *The New Read-Aloud Handbook* by Jim Trelease.

M1096.   *Reading Aloud: Motivating Children to Make Books into Friends, Not Enemies.* (cassette) Springfield, MA: Reading Tree Productions, 1983. 90 min. Based on *The New Read-Aloud Handbook* by Jim Trelease.

M1097.   *Reading Improvement.* (periodical) Mobile, AL: Project Innovation of Mobile. Quarterly.

M1098.   *Reading Rainbow.* (TV series or videos) Buffalo: WNED-TV; Lincoln, NE: Great Plains National, the Nebraska Educational TV Network, and the University of Nebraska; NY: Lancit Media Productions, 1983–. 65 programs, 30 min. each. Beta or VHS.

M1099.   *Reading Rainbow Gazette: An Activity Magazine for Kids.* (periodical) New York: Reading Rainbow Gazette. Issue #3—Programs 1–20; Issue #4—Programs 21–25; Issue #5—Programs 26–35; Issue #6—Programs 36–45; Issue #7—Programs 46–55, Issue #8—Programs 56–65.

M1100.   *Reading Rainbow Songs.* (phonograph record or cassette) New York: Harper/Caedmon, 1984. 37 min. Music from the TV series.

M1101.   *The Reading Teacher.* (periodical) Newark, DE.: International Reading Association. Issued 9 times a year, October–May.

M1102.   *Reading Together—A Wrinkle in Time; A Wind in the Door; A Swiftly Tilting Planet.* (cassette) San Diego: Luramedia, 1987. Interviews with Madeleine L'Engle and her husband, Hugh Franklin. Introduces: *A Wrinkle in Time; A Wind in the Door;* and *A Swiftly Tilting Planet.*

M1103.   *Readit!* (TV series or videos) Bloomington, IN: AIT (Agency for Instructional Technology), 1982. 16 programs, 15 min. each. Beta, VHS, or 3/4". Host: John Robbins.

M1104.   *The Real, the True, the Gen-u-ine Wizard of Oz: L. Frank Baum.* (filmstrip with cassette) Hightstown, NJ: American School Publishers, 1987. 123 fr. 15:55 min. Introduces: *The Wizard of Oz..*

M1105.   *Realistic Fiction.* (filmstrip with cassette) (Literature for Children, Series 6) Costa Mesa, CA: Pied Piper, 1980. Introduces: *Queenie Peavy* by Robert Burch; *Harriet the*

Spy by Louise Fitzhugh; and *Summer of the Swans* by Betsy Byars.

M1106. *Really Rosie.* (16mm film or video) Weston, CT: Weston Woods, 1976. 26 min. Animated. Includes: *One Was Johnny; Pierre; Alligators All Around;* and *Chicken Soup With Rice.* Based on the Nutshell Library books by Maurice Sendak.

M1107. *Really Rosie.* (cassette) New York: CBS Records, 1981. 59 min. Sung by Carole King. Based on the Nutshell Library books by M. Sendak.

M1108. *Rebecca of Sunnybrook Farm.* (cassette) New York: Harper/Caedmon, 1980. 40 min. Abridged from a book by Kate Wiggin. Narrated by Julie Harris.

M1109. *A Record Show.* (TV program or video) Program #3 of *Musical Encounter.* Lincoln, NE: GPN, 1985. 30 min. VHS and 3/4″.

M1110. *The Relatives Came.* (filmstrip with cassette) Hightstown, NJ: American School Publishers, 1987. 70 fr. 7:50 min. Written and narrated by Cynthia Rylant.

M1111. *The Reluctant Dragon.* (TV program) A program of *Long Ago and Far Away.* London: Cosgrove Hall, 1988. Boston: WGBH-TV, 1989. Based on a book by Kenneth Grahame.

M1112. *Renewable Energy.* (TV program) A program of *Challenge.* Nashville: WDCN-TV, n.d. 15 min.

M1113. *Reptiles and How They Grow.* (cassette with 30 booklets) Washington, DC: National Geographic, 1986. 13:50 min.

M1114. *Resources in Education.* (serial) Washington, DC: Department of Education, Office of Educational Research and Improvement. Annual.

M1115. *Return of the Moose/Blue Moose.* (TV program or video) Program #1 of *Readit!* Bloomington, IN: AIT, 1982. 15 min. Beta, VHS, or 3/4″. Based on books by Daniel Pinkwater.

M1116. *Ring of Endless Light.* (2 filmstrips and 2 cassettes) Hightstown, NJ: American School Publishers, 1984. 158 and 161 fr. 27 min. each. Based on a book by Madeleine L'Engle.

M1117. *The Rise and Fall of Ben Gizzard.* (TV program or video) Program #8 of *Readit!* Bloomington, IN: AIT, 1982. 15 min. Beta, VHS, or 3/4″. Based on a book by Richard Kennedy. Also includes: *Parrot and the Thief* and *Contests at Cowlick* by Kennedy.

M1118. *The Rise of Nazism: Terror and Tragedy.* (2 filmstrips with 2 cassettes) Bedford Hills, NY: Educational Enrichment, 1982. 87 fr. and 108 fr.

M1119. *Rich Mitch.* (TV program or video) Program #1 of *Books from Cover to Cover.* Washington, DC: WETA-TV and Alexandria, VA: PBS Video, n.d. 15 min. VHS or 3/4″. Based on a book by Marjorie Sharmat.

M1120. *Robbery at the Diamond Dog Diner.* (TV program or video) Program #48 of *Reading Rainbow.* Buffalo: WNED-TV and Lincoln, NE: GPN, 1988. 30 min. VHS or 3/4″. Based on a book by Eileen Christelow. Narrated by Peter Falk.

M1121. *Robbery at the Diamond Dog Diner.* (paperback with cassette) (Information Age series). Boston: Houghton Mifflin, 1989. 11 min. Based on a book by E. Christelow.

M1122. *Robots and Artificial Intelligence.* (filmstrip with cassette) Westminster, MD: Random, 1984. 107 fr. 12 min.

M1123. *Robots and Computers.* (TV program) A program of *Challenge.* Nashville: WDCN-TV, n.d. 15 min.

M1124. *Robert Louis Stevenson.* (filmstrip with cassette) Hawthorne, NJ: January Productions, 1985. 55 fr. 13 min.

M1125. *Rocks, Fossils, and Minerals.* (TV program) A program of *Challenge.* Nashville: WDCN-TV, n.d. 15 min.

M1126. *Rocks to Rings.* (TV program) A program of *Challenge.* WDCN-TV, n.d. 15 min.

M1127. *Roll of Thunder, Hear My Cry.* (cassette) Hightstown, NJ: American School Publishers, 1981. 22–23 min. Based on a book by Mildred Taylor.

M1128. *Romping.* (cassette) Montval, NJ: Cloudstone, 1985–. 52 min. Story by Diane Wolkstein.

M1129. *The Root Cellar.* (TV program or video) Program #14 of *More Books from Cover to Cover.* Washington, DC: WETA-TV and Alexandria, VA: PBS Video, n.d. 15 min. VHS or 3/4″. Based on a book by Janet Lunn.

M1130. *A Rose for Pinkerton.* (filmstrip with cassette) Weston, CT: Weston Woods, 1983. 42 fr. 7 min. Based on a book by Steven Kellogg.

M1131. *A Rose for Pinkerton.* (hardback or paperback with cassette) Weston Woods, 1983. 7 min. Based on a book by S. Kellogg.

M1132. *Rotten Ralph.* (paperback with cassette) Boston: Houghton Mifflin, 1988. 15 min. Based on a book by Jack Gantos.

M1133. *Rudyard Kipling.* (filmstrip with cassette) Hawthorne, NJ: January Productions, 1986. 15 min.

M1134. *Rumplestiltskin.* (TV program or video) Program #42 of *Reading Rainbow.* Buffalo: WNED-TV and Lincoln, NE: GPN,

1987. 30 min. VHS or 3/4″. Based on a book by Paul Zelinsky.

M1135. *Runaway Duck.* (TV program or video) Program #40 of *Reading Rainbow.* Buffalo: WNED-TV and Lincoln, NE: GPN, 1987. 30 min. VHS or 3/4″. Based on a book by David Lyon.

M1136. *Runaway Ralph.* (16mm film or video) Los Angeles: Churchill Films, 1987. Live action. 40 min. Based on a book by Beverly Cleary.

M1137. *Runaway Ralph.* (hardback or paperback with cassette) Old Greenwich, CT: Listening Library, 1985. 48 min. (Soundways to Reading, Cliffhanger Read-along) Based on a book by B. Cleary.

M1138. *Sacajawea.* (phonograph record or cassette) Amawalk, NY: Golden Owl, n.d. 25 min.

M1139. *Saint George and the Dragon.* (video) Hightstown, NJ: American School Publishers, n.d. 12 min. VHS. Based on a book by Margaret Hodges.

M1140. *Saint George and the Dragon.* (filmstrip with cassette) American School Publishers, 1986. 89 fr. 12 min. Based on a book by M. Hodges.

M1141. *Saint George and the Dragon.* (hardback with cassette) American School Publishers, 1984. 12 min. Based on a book by M. Hodges.

M1142. *Sarah, Plain and Tall.* (video) Hightstown, NJ: American School Publishers, n.d. 29:30 min. Based on a book by Patricia MacLachlan.

M1143. *Sarah, Plain and Tall.* (2 filmstrips with 2 cassettes). American School Publishers, 1986. 108 and 113 frs. 14:30 and 15:15 min. Based on a book by P. MacLachlan.

M1144. *Sarah, Plain and Tall.* (cassette) American School Publishers, 1986. Based on a book by P. MacLachlan.

M1145. *Sarah, Plain and Tall.* (cassette) New York: Harper/Caedmon, 1986. 61 min. Based on a book by P. MacLachlan. Read by Glenn Close.

M1146. *Satellites and How They Help Us.* (filmstrip with cassette) (Today and Tomorrow in Space: The Space Shuttle and Beyond). Washington, DC: National Geographic, 1983. 50 fr. 16 min.

M1147. *The Saturday Evening Post.* (periodical) Indianapolis, IN: Benjamin Franklin Literacy and Medical Society. Monthly except February, June, and August.

M1148. *Scary Stories.* (filmstrip with cassette) Costa Mesa, CA: Pied Piper, 1984. 73 fr. 11 min. Features *The Terrible Troll* by Mayer and *King of the Cats* by Galdone.

M1149. *Scary Stories to Tell in the Dark.* (cassette) New York: Harper/Caedmon, 1986. 58 min. Based on a book by Alvin Schwartz. Read by George S. Irving.

M1150. *Scene Playing.* (TV program) A program of *The Word Shop.* Washington, DC: WETA-TV, 1976. 15 min. Beta, VHS, or 3/4″.

M1151. *School Library Journal.* (periodical) New York: Bowker. Monthly.

M1152. *Science and Children.* (periodical) Washington, DC: National Science Teachers Association. 8 issues per year.

M1153. *Science.* (filmstrip with cassette) (Literature for Children, Series 5) Costa Mesa, CA: Pied Piper, 1980. 13 min. Introduces *Octopus* by Carol Carrick.

M1154. *Science Books and Films.* (periodical) Danville, NJ: American Association for the Advancement of Science. 5 issues per year, September to May.

M1155. *Science Fiction.* (filmstrip with cassette) (Literature for Children, Series 6) Costa Mesa, CA: Pied Piper, 1980. 12 min. Includes *City of Gold and Lead* by John Christopher and *A Wrinkle in Time* by Madeleine L'Engle.

M1156. *Science World.* (periodical) New York: Scholastic. 18 times per year, September to May.

M1157. *The Search for Grissi.* (TV program or video) Program #14 of *Books Cover to Cover.* Alexandria, VA: PBS Video, n.d. 15 min. VHS and 3/4″. Based on a book by Mary Francis Shura.

M1158. *The Secret Garden.* (video) London: BBC-TV and New York: CBS/Fox Video, 1988. 107 min. VHS. Based on a book by Frances Burnett.

M1159. *The Secret Garden.* (hardback or paperback with cassette) Old Greenwich, CT: Listening Library, 1985. 77:30 min. (Soundways to Reading, Cliffhanger Read-along) Based on a book by F. Burnett.

M1160. *The Secret Garden.* (cassette) New York: Harper/Caedmon, 1976. 64:29 min. Based on a book by F. Burnett.

M1161. *The Secret Garden.* (6 cassettes) New Rochelle, NY: Spoken Arts, 1987. 7 hours 53 min. Based on a book by F. Burnett. Read by Susan Fitzgerald.

M1162. *The Secret Garden.* (6 cassettes) Washington, DC. Audio Book Contractors, 1987. 8 hours. Based on a book by F. Burnett. Read by Flo Gibson.

M1163. *The Secret Garden.* (cassettes) Niagara Falls, NY: Listen for Pleasure, n.d. Based on a book by F. Burnett. Read by Gwen Watford.

M1164. *Secrets of the Titanic.* (video) Washington, DC: National Geographic and Vestron Video, 1986. 60 min. Beta or VHS.

M1165. *Sendak.* (16mm film or video) Weston, CT: Weston Woods, 1986. 27 min. Live action. Beta or VHS. Scenes from the following books written and illustrated by Sendak: *In the Night Kitchen, Where the Wild Things Are, Outside Over There*; also Hoffman's *The Nutcracker,* illustrated by Sendak.

M1166. *The Sensational Five: The Inside Story of Your Senses.* (TV program or video) Program #6 of *The Inside Story with Slim Goodbody.* Bloomington, IN: AIT and Green Bay, WI: UW-GB Telecommunications Center, 1981. 15 min. Beta, VHS, or 3/4″.

M1167. *Sequel: Animal Stories.* (filmstrip with cassette) Costa Mesa, CA: Pied Piper, 1989. 22 min. Introduces *Misty of Chincoteague* by Marguerite Henry.

M1168a. *Sesame Street.* (TV series or videos) New York: Children's Television Workshop, and Washington, DC: Corporation for Public Broadcasting, 1969– . 130 programs 60 min. each.

M1168b. *Sesame Street: Don't Eat the Pictures* (TV program and video) New York: Children's Television Workshop and Random House, 1990. 60 mins. VHS.

M1168c. *Sesame Street in Puerto Rico.* (TV program) New York: Children's Television Workshop, 1979. 60 min. VHS.

M1169. *Sesame Street Magazine* (periodical) Boulder, CO: The Children's Television Workshop. 10 issues per year. English and Spanish editions.

M1170. *Setting* (filmstrip with cassette) (Components of Fiction, Literature for Children, Series 9) Costa Mesa, CA: Pied Piper, 1985. 115 fr. 22 min. Features: *The Children of Green Knowe* by Lucy Boston and *The Midnight Fox* by Betsy Byars. Introduces: *Homesick* by Jean Fritz; *Julie of the Wolves* by Jean George, and *It's Like This, Cat* by Emily Neville.

M1171. *Setting in Stories* (TV program) A program of *The Word Shop.* Washington, DC: WETA-TV, 1976. 15 min. Beta, VHS, or 3/4″.

M1172. *Shadow.* (filmstrip with cassette) Weston, CT: Weston Woods, 1984. 33 fr. 9 min. Based on a book by Blaise Cendrars.

M1173. *Shadow.* (cassette) Weston Woods, 1983. 9 min. Based on a book by B. Cendrars. Read by Marcia Brown.

M1174. *Sharks.* (TV program) A program of *The World of Audubon.* Washington, DC: WETA-TV and the National Audubon Society, n.d.

M1175. *Sharks.* (16mm film or video) Washington, DC: National Geographic, 1982. 59 min. VHS or 3/4″.

M1176. *Sharks.* (filmstrip with cassette) National Geographic, 1977. 12 min.

Shari Lewis Presents 101 Things for Kids to Do. See M977c.

M1177. *Sharon, Lois and Bram: The Elephant Show.* (video) Waterbury, CT: Silo/Alacazar, Golden Book Video and Columbia Film and Video. 1984. 30 min.

M1178. *Sharon, Lois and Bram at the Young People's Theatre.* (16mm film or video) Northwood, MA: Beacon and Cambium Film Productions, 1983. 30 min. Beta, VHS, or 3/4″.

M1179. *Sharon, Lois and Bram's Elephant Show.* (TV series or videos) Olney, PA: Bullfrog Films and Cambium Film Productions. 13 programs, 27 min. each.

M1180. *The Sheep-Pig.* (2 cassettes) Atlanta: Cover to Cover Cassettes, 1987. 1 hr. 50 min. Unabridged reading of *Babe, the Gallant Pig* (alternate title) by Dick King-Smith.

M1181. *Shh! We're Writing the Constitution.* (filmstrip with cassette) Weston, CT: Weston Woods, 1987. 90 fr. 31 min. Based on a book by Jean Fritz.

M1182. *Shh! We're Writing the Constitution.* (hardback or paperback with cassette) Weston Woods, 1987. 60 min. Based on a book by J. Fritz.

M1183. *Shining Time Station* (TV series) New York: WNET-TV and Quality Family Entertainment, 1989–. 20 programs, 30 min. each. Live action and animation. Host: Ringo Starr.

M1184. *Shipwrecks and Lighthouses.* (TV program) Program #301 of *Naturescene.* Columbia: South Carolina Educational Television, n.d. 30 min.

M1185. *Shoah: An Oral History of the Holocaust.* (TV program or 5 videos) New York: WNET-TV and PBS; Hollywood, CA: Paramount Home Video and New York: New York Films, 1985. 570 min. Based on a book by Claude Lanzmann.

M1186. *Shoes.* (hardback or paperback with cassette; Reading Chest with 4 paperbacks and cassette) Ancramdale, NY: Live Oak Media, 1988. 3:50 min. Based on a book by Elizabeth Winthrop.

M1187. *Shoeshine Girl.* (16mm film or video) Deerfield, IL: LCA, 1980. 25 min. Based on a book by Clyde Bulla.

M1188. *Show and Yell.* (TV program) A program of *Shining Time Station.* New York: WNET-TV, 1989. 30 min.

M1189a. *Siblingitis.* (TV program, 16mm film, or video) Los Angeles: Churchill Films, Atlantis Films, Lancit Media, and Revcom Television, 1989. 27 min. Beta or VHS. Based on a book about Ramona by Beverly Cleary.

M1189b. *Sierra Club: Whales.* (video) San Francisco: Sierra Club, n.d. 60 min. Beta or VHS.

M1189c. *Sight.* (filmstrip and cassette) Five Senses series. New York: Children's Television Workshop, Guidance Associates, and 3-2-1 Contact, 1985.

M1190. *The Sign of the Beaver.* (2 filmstrips with cassettes) Hightstown, NJ: American School Publishers, 1985. Based on a book by Elizabeth Speare.

M1191. *The Sign of the Beaver.* (cassette) American School Publishers, 1985. Based on a book by E. Speare.

M1192. *Signals.* (TV program) A program of 3-2-1-Contact. New York: Children's Television Workshop, 1976. 30 min. Beta, VHS, or 3/4″.

M1193. *Signs.* (TV program) A program of *The Word Shop.* Washington, DC: WETA-TV, 1976. 15 min. Beta, VHS, or 3/4″.

M1194. *The Silver Coronet.* (TV program) A program of *Long Ago and Far Away.* Boston: WGBH-TV; Washington, DC, PBS; England: Yorkshire TV; the European Broadcasting Union, 1989. 30 min.

M1195. *The Silver Coronet.* (16mm film or video) Deerfield, IL: Coronet, 1989. 30 min. VHS or 3/4″.

M1196. *Simon's Book.* (TV program or video) Program #17 of *Reading Rainbow.* Buffalo: WNED-TV and Lincoln, NE: GPN, 1984. 30 min. VHS or 3/4″. Based on a book by Henrik Drescher. Narrated by Ruby Dee.

M1197. *Simon's Book.* (filmstrip with cassette) Hightstown, NJ: American School Publishers, 1985. 63 fr. 6:32 min. Based on a book by H. Drescher.

M1198. *Simple Machines.* (TV program) A program of *Challenge.* Nashville: WDCN-TV, n.d. 15 min.

M1199. *Simple Machines.* (TV program) A program of *3-2-1-Contact.* New York: Children's Television Workshop, n.d. 30 min.

M1200. *Singable Songs for the Very Young.* (cassette) Long Branch, NJ: Kimbo Educational, 1976. 27 min. Performed by Raffi.

Six Revolutionary War Figures. See *Jean Fritz: Six Revolutionary War Figures.*.

M1201. *The Skates of Uncle Richard.* Program #10 of *Book Bird.* Springfield, VA: Children's Television International, 1979. 15 min. 3/4″. Based on a book by Carol Fenner.

M1202. *Skyscraper.* (TV or video) A program of *Explorers Unlimited.* Cleveland: WVIZ-TV

and Bloominton, IN: AIT, 1971. 15 min. Beta, VHS, or 3/4″.

M1203. *The Sleeping Princess* (TV program) A program of *Long Ago and Far Away.* Boston: WGBH-TV and London: BBC, n.d. 30 min. Based on a version of "Sleeping Beauty" by the Brothers Grimm. Host: James Earl Jones.

M1204. *Slim Goodbody—Inside Out.* (phonograph record or cassette with poster) New York: Caedmon, 1982. 90 min. 14 and 57 min.

M1205. *Slim Goodbody's Daily Desk'ercises.* (video) Chicago: SVE (Society for Visual Education), 1986. 30 min. Live action. VHS.

M1206. *Slim Goodbody's Health Series.* (4 filmstrips with 4 cassettes) SVE, 1982. 5–7 min. each. Includes: *A Healthy Day, A Visit to the Dentist; A Visit to the Doctor*; and *A Visit to the Hospital.*.

M1207. *Smart Parts: The Inside Story of Your Brain and Nervous System.* (TV program or video) Bloomington, IN: AIT and Green Bay, WI: UW-GB Telecommunications Center, 1981. 15 min. Beta, VHS, or 3/4″.

M1208. *Smart Pics: The Learning Channel's Programming Quarterly.* (newsletter) Quarterly.

Smell and Taste. See *Five Senses.*

M1209. *Smithsonian.* (periodical) Washington, DC: Smithsonian Institution. Monthly.

M1210. *Smithsonian World.* (TV program) Washington, DC: WETA-TV and the Smithsonian Institution, 1985–. 60 min. each. Host: David McCullough.

M1211. *Snakes.* (filmstrip with cassette) (Animal Kingdom series). Chicago: Encyclopedia Britannica, n.d.

M1212. *Snakes.* (TV program or video) Program #7 of *Up Close and Natural.* Washington, DC: WETA-TV, 1975. 15 min.

M1213. *Snakes,* revised ed. (16mm film or video) Deerfield, IL: Coronet, 1983. 15 min.

M1214. *Snowbound.* (TV program, 16mm film, or video) A program of NBC Specials Treat. Deerfield, IL: Learning Corp. of America, 1978. 32 min. VHS. Based on a book by Harry Mazer.

M1215. *Snow Bound.* (hardback or paperback with cassette) Old Greenwich, CT: Listening Library, 1985. 86 min. Based on a book by Harry Mazer.

M1216. *The Snow Spider.* (3 cassettes) Boston: G. K. Hall and Chivers Sound and Vision, 1988. 3 hours. Based on a book by Jenny Nimmo.

M1217. *Social Education.* (periodical) Washington, DC. National Council for the Social Studies. 7 issues per year.

M1218. *Sodbusters, Cowboys, and Indians.* (filmstrip with cassette) (Westward Movement: A Unit of Study) Niles, IL: United Learning, 1985. 12 min.

M1219. *Some Secrets Should Be Told.* (video) Deerfield, IL: MTI Teleprograms, 1982. 12 min. Beta or VHS.

M1220. *Something Queer at the Haunted School.* (cassette) Old Greenwich, CT: Listening Library, 1985. 19 min. Based on a book by Elizabeth Levy.

M1221. *Something Queer is Going On.* (cassette) Listening Library, 1983. 17 min. Based on a book by E. Levy.

M1222. *Son of Dinosaurs.* (video) Studio City, CA: Twin Towers, 1989. 60 min. Live action and animated. VHS. Gary Owens and Eric Boardman.

M1223a. *The Song and Dance Man.* (filmstrip with cassette) Hightstown, NJ: American School Publishers, 1989. 80 fr. 8 min. Based on a book by Karen Ackerman.

M1223b. *Song of the Trees.* (TV program or video) Program #10 of *Book Bird.* Springfield, VA: Children's Television International, 1979. 3/4″. Based on a book by Mildred Taylor. Includes *Skates for Uncle Richard* by Fenner.

M1224. *Songs for Sleepyheads and Out-of-Beds!* (cassette) Scarborough, Ontario: A & M Records and Lullaby Lady Productions, 1985. 45 min. Sung by Pat Carfra.

M1225. *Songspinner: Folktales and Fables Sung and Told.* (cassette) Weston, CT: Weston Woods, 1982. 41:39 min. Performed by Heather Forest.

M1226. *Soongoora and Simba.* (TV program or video) Program #5 of *Teletales.* Bloomington, IN: AIT, 1984. 15 min. Based on a folk tale from Africa.

M1227. *The Sorcerer's Boy.* (TV program or video) Program #11 of *Teletales.* Bloomington, IN: AIT, 1984. 15 min. Based on a folk tale from Russia.

M1228. *The Sound of Music.* (motion picture or video) New York: CBS/Fox, 1965. 145 min. Beta or VHS. Based on the life of Maria von Trapp. Starring Julie Andrews and Christopher Plummer.

M1229. *The Sound of Sunshine, Sound of Rain.* (16mm film or video) Studio City, CA: FilmFair, 1984. 14 min. Animated. VHS.

M1230. *Sounder.* (TV program or video) Program #9 of *Storybound.* Springfield, VA: Children's Television International, 1981. 15 min. Beta, VHS, or 3/4″. Based on a book by William Armstrong.

M1231. *Soup and Me.* (TV program, 16mm film or video) (ABC Weekend Special) Deerfield, IL: MTI, 1977. 24 min. Based on a book by Robert Newton Peck.

M1232. *Soup for President.* (TV program, 16mm film or video) (ABC Weekend Special) Deerfield, IL: MTI, 1978. 24 min. Based on a book by R. N. Peck.

M1233. *South American Instruments, Part 1 and Part 2.* (TV programs and videos) Programs #11 and #12 of *Musical Instruments.* Lincoln, NE: GPN, 1979. 20 min. each. VHS or 3/4″.

M1234. *Space Camp.* (4 filmstrips with cassettes) New Rochelle, NY: Spoken Arts, 1987. 41 fr. each, 8 min. each.

M1235. *Space Camp.* (TV program) Program #11 of *Challenge.* Nashville: WDCN-TV, n.d. 15 min.

M1236. *Space Case.* (TV program) Program #31 of *Reading Rainbow.* Lincoln, NE: GPN, 1984. 30 min. Beta, VHS or 3/4″. Based on a book by Edward Marshall.

M1237. *Space Case.* (filmstrip with cassette) (Holiday with Humor series) New Rochelle, NY: Spoken Arts, 1986. 40 fr. 5 min. Based on a book by E. Marshall.

M1238. *Space Shuttle.* (filmstrip with cassette) (Today and Tomorrow in Space: The Space Shuttle and Beyond). Washington, DC: National Geographic, 1983. 55 fr. 16 min.

M1239. *Space Women.* (TV program or video) A program of NOVA. New York: Time Life, 1984. 57 min.

M1240. *Spaceborne.* (film or video) Santa Monica, CA: Pyramid, 1977. 14 min. Beta, VHS, or 3/4″.

M1241. *Spaces to Live In.* (TV program or video) Program #201 of *Images and Things.* Bloomington, IN: AIT, 1971. 20 min. Beta, VHS, or 3/4″.

M1242. *Speaking Without Words.* (TV program) A program of *Smithsonian World.* Washington, DC: WETA-TV and the Smithsonian Insititution, n.d. 50 min.

M1243. *Spider.* (16mm film or video) Evanston, IL: Beacon, 1984. 3 min. Beta, VHS, or 3/4″.

M1244. *Spiders.* (filmstrip with cassette) Washington, DC: National Geographic, 1981. 15 min.

M1245. *Sports and Hobbies.* (filmstrip with cassette) (Non-fiction, Literature for Children, Series 5) Costa Mesa, CA: Pied Piper, 1980. 10 min. Introduces *Mr. Mysterious's Secrets of Magic* by Sid Fleischman.

M1246. *Square One.* (TV series) New York: Children's Television Workshop, National Science Foundation, and Washington, DC: Corporation for Public Broadcasting, 1987–. 140 programs, 60 min. each.

M1247. *The Squire's Bride.* (TV program or video) Program #12 of *Teletales.* Bloomington, IN: AIT, 1984. 15 min. Beta, VHS, or 3/4″. Based on a folk tale from Norway.

M1248. *Stan Bolovan.* (TV program) Program #3 of *Teletales.* Bloomington, IN: AIT, 1984. 15 min. Beta, VHS, or 3/4″. Based on a folk tale from Russia.

M1249. *Stanley and the Dinosaurs* (16mm film or video) Los Angeles: Churchill, 1989. 15:30 min. Based on a book by Sid Hoff.

M1250. *Stay Away from the Junkyard.* (TV program or video) Program #57 of *Reading Rainbow.* Buffalo: WNED-TV and Lincoln, NE: GPN, 1989. 30 min. VHS and 3/4″. Based on a book by Tricia Tusa.

M1251. *Stepdancing: Portrait of a Remarried Family.* (16mm film or video) Santa Monica, CA: Pyramid Films and Kensington Communications, 1987. 27 min. Beta or VHS.

M1252. *Stone Fox.* (TV program or video) Program #5 of *More Books Cover to Cover.* Washington, DC: WETA-TV; Alexandria, VA: PBS, n.d. 15 min. VHS or 3/4″. Based on a book by John Gardiner.

M1253. *Stone Fox.* (hardback or paperback with cassette) Old Greenwich, CT: Listening Library, n.d. 60 min. Based on a book by J. Gardiner.

M1254. *Stone Soup.* (periodical) Santa Cruz, CA: Children's Art Foundation. 5 issues per year.

M1255. *The Storm.* (TV program or video) Burbank, CA: Groundstar and Warner Home Video, 1986, 1989. 100 min.

M1256. *Storm Boy.* (16mm film or video) South Australia Film Commission, 1980. 30 min. Based on a book by Colin Thiele.

M1257. *Story Maker.* (TV program) A program of *Word Shop.* Washington, DC: WETA-TV, 1976. 15 min. Beta, VHS, and 3/4″.

M1258. *A Story, A Story.* (16mm film or video) Weston, CT: Weston Woods, 1973. 10 min. Animated. Based on a book by Gail Haley.

M1259a. *A Story, A Story.* (filmstrip with cassette) Weston Woods, 1972. 40 fr. 10 min. Based on a book by G. Haley.

M1259b. *A Story, A Story.* (hardback or paperback with cassette) Weston Woods, 1972. 10 min. Based on a book by G. Haley.

M1260. *Story About Ping.* (filmstrip with cassette) Weston, CT: Weston Woods, n.d. 45 fr. 10 min. Based on a book by Marjorie Flack.

M1261. *Story of a Book.* (video) Costa Mesa, CA: Pied Piper, 1980. 16 min. Beta, VHS or 3/4″. Introduces *San Domingo: The Medicine Hat Stallion* by Marguerite Henry.

M1262. *Story of a Book, Second Edition: With Marguerite Henry.* (filmstrip with cassette) Pied Piper, 1982. 16 min. Introduces *San Domingo: The Medicine Hat Stallion* by M. Henry.

M1263. *The Story of Anne Frank.* (filmstrip with cassette) Chicago: SVE, 1985. 65 fr. 19:30 min. Companion to *The Lesson of Anne Frank..*

M1264. *The Story of My Life.* (3 cassettes) Washington, DC: Audio Book Contractors, 1987. 90 min. Narrated by Flo Gibson.

M1265. *Story of the Everglades.* (2 filmstrips and 2 cassettes) Mount Kisco, NY: Prentice Hall Media, n.d. 93 and 100 fr. 16 and 17 min.

M1267. *Story Playing.* (TV program) A program of *The Word Shop.* WETA-TV, 1976. 15 min. Beta, VHS, or 3/4″.

M1268. *Story Telling.* (TV program) A program of *The Word Shop.* WETA-TV, 1976. 15 min. Beta, VHS, or 3/4″.

M1269a. *Storybound.* (TV series and videos) Springhill, VA: Children's Television International, 1981. 18 programs, 15 min. each. Beta, VHS, or 3/4″.

M1270. *Stranger at Greene Knowe.* (TV program or video) A program of *Best of Cover to Cover, 2-A.* Washington, D.C.: WETA-TV and Alexandria, VA: PBS Video, n.d. 15 min. Based on a book by Lucy Boston.

M1271. *Stranger With My Face.* (hardback or paperback with cassette) Old Greenwich, CT: Listening Library, 1985. 91 min. (Young Adult Cliffhanger) Based on a book by Lois Duncan.

M1272. *Strega Nona.* (doll) 13″. Weston, CT: Weston Woods, Boulder, CO: The Storyteller. ·

M1273. *Strega Nona.* (16mm film or video) Weston, CT: Weston Woods, 1978. 9 min. Animated. Beta or VHS. Based on a book by Tomie dePaola.

M1274. *Strega Nona.* (filmstrip with cassette) Weston Woods, 1978. 55 fr. 12 min. Based on a book by T. dePaola.

M1275. *Strega Nona.* (hardcover or paperback with cassette) Weston Woods, 1978. 12 min. Based on a book by T. dePaola. Read by Peter Hawkins.

M1276. *Strega Nona's Magic Lessons and Other Stories.* (cassette) New York: Harper/Caedmon, 1984. 60 min. Includes: *Big Anthony and the Magic Ring; Nana Upstairs and Nana Downstairs, Now One Foot and the Other*; and *Oliver Button is a Sissy.* Based on books by T. de Paola. Read by Tammy Grimes.

M1277. *Striped Ice Cream.* (TV program or video) Program #11 of *Book Bird.* Springfield, VA: Children's Television International, 1979. 3/4″. Based on a book by Joan Lexau.

M1278. *Structure in Stories.* (TV program or video) A program of *The Word Shop.* Washington, DC: WETA-TV, 1976. 15 min. Beta, VHS, or 3/4″.

M1279. *Structures.* (TV program) A program of *3-2-1-Contact.* New York: Children's Television Workshop, n.d. 30 min.

M1280. *Stuff.* (TV program) A program of *3-2-1-Contact.* Children's Television Workshop, n.d. 30 min.

M1281. *Style.* (filmstrip with cassette) Costa Mesa, CA: Pied Piper, 1985. 93 fr. 20 min. (Components of Fiction—Literature for Children, Series 9) Features: *Humbug Mountain* by Sid Fleischman and *The White Archer* by James Houston. Introduces: *Beat the Turtle Drum* by Constance Greene; *Sing Down the Moon* by Scott O'Dell; and *The Witches of Worm* by Zilpha Snyder.

M1282. *Sugar Bush.* (TV program) Program #9 of *Explorers Unlimited.* Cleveland: WVIX-TV and Bloomington, IN: AIT, 1971. 15 min. Beta, VHS, or 3/4″.

M1283. *Sugaring Time.* (filmstrip with cassette) Hightstown, NJ: American School Publishers, 1985. 137 fr. 22 min. b & w. Based on a book by Katherine Lasky.

M1284. *Sugaring Time.* (cassette) American School Publishers, 1985. 23 min. Based on a book by K. Laksy.

M1285. *The Summer Birds.* (TV program or video) Program #2 of *Books from Cover to Cover.* Washington, DC: WETA-TV and Alexandria, VA: PBS Video, n.d. 15 min. VHS or 3/4″. Based on a book by Penelope Farmer.

M1286. *Summer of Fear.* (hardback or paperback with cassette) Old Greenwich, CT: Listening Library, 1985. 72 min. (Young Adult Cliffhangers) Based on a book by Lois Duncan.

M1287. *Summer of the Swans.* (TV program or video) A program of *Best of Cover to Cover, 2-A.* Washington, DC: WETA-TV and Alexandria, VA: PBS Video, n.d. 15 min. Based on a book by Betsy Byars.

M1288. *Summer of the Swans.* (hardback or paperback with cassette) Ancramdale, NY: Live Oak Media, 1972. 51:04 min. Based on a book by B. Byars.

M1289. *Sundays at Grandma's.* (cassette) Charlottesville, VA: Michael Parent, 1988. 48 min.

M1290. *A Sunny Song.* (paperback and cassette) Cosgrove, Shaerie Ideals, n.d. 20 min.

M1291. *Superfudge.* (filmstrip with cassette) Costa Mesa, CA: Pied Piper, 1984. 97 fr. 16 min. Based on a book by Judy Blume.

M1292. *The Surprise Party.* (filmstrip with cassette) Weston, CT: Weston Woods, 1972. 30 fr. 6 min. Based on a book by Pat Hutchins.

M1293. *Svatohor (Saint Mountain).* (TV program) A program on *Long Ago and Far Away.* Boston: WGBH-TV, 1989. Czechoslovak TV, n.d. 30 min. Puppet animation. Based on a Russian folktale.

M1294. *Sylvester and the Magic Pebble.* (TV program or video) A program from the Blue Module of *Picture Book Park.* Cleveland: WVIZ-TV and Bloomington, IN: AIT, 1972/73. 15 min. Beta, VHS, or 3/4″. Based on a book by William Steig.

M1295. *Sylvester and the Magic Pebble.* (paperback with cassette) New York: Simon and Schuster, 1988. 15 min. Based on a book by W. Steig.

M1296. *Tadpoles and Frogs.* (video) Washington, DC: National Geographic, 1979, 1986. 12 min. VHS or 3/4″.

M1297. *The Tale of Flopsy Bunnies and Five Other Stories by Beatrix Potter.* (cassette) New York: Harper/Caedmon, 1985. 38 min. Includes: *The Tale of Jemima Puddleduck; The Tale of Tom Kitten; The Tale of Miss Moppet; The Tale of Mrs. Tittlemouse;* and *The Story of a Fierce Bad Rabbit.* Based on books by Beatrix Potter. Read by Claire Bloom.

M1298. *The Tale of Mr. Jeremy Fisher.* (filmstrip with cassette) Weston, CT: Weston Woods, 1968. 30 fr. 6 min. Based on a book by B. Potter.

M1299. *The Tale of Mr. Jeremy Fisher.* (hardback or paperback with cassette) Weston Woods, 1968. 6 min. Based on a book by B. Potter.

M1300. *The Tale of Two Bad Mice.* (filmstrip with cassette) 30 fr. 6 min. Weston Woods, 1968. Based on a book by B. Potter.

M1301. *The Tale of Two Bad Mice.* (hardback or paperback with cassette) Weston Woods, 1968. 6 min. Based on a book by B. Potter.

M1302. *Tales of a Fourth Grade Nothing.* (filmstrip with cassette) Costa Mesa, CA: Pied Piper, 1980. 13 min. Based on a book by Judy Blume.

M1303. *Tales of King Arthur and His Knights: Excalibur.* (cassette) New York: Caedmon, 1975. 63 min. Based on a book by Howard Pyle. Read by Ian Richardson.

M1304. *Tales of King Arthur and His Knights: Story of Sir Galahad.* (cassette) Caedmon, 1978. 60 min. Based on a book by Howard Pyle. Read by Ian Richardson.

M1305. *Tales of Love and Terror, Booktalking the Classics, Old and New.* (video) Chicago: American Library Association, 1987. 25 min. Live action. 15 booktalks by Hazel Rochman. Includes *The Fantastic Voyage* by Isaac Asimov and *Animal Farm* by George Orwell.

M1306. *Tales of Oliver Pig.* (hardback or paperback with cassette) Old Greenwich, CT: Listening Library, 1982. 24 min. Based on a book by Jean Van Leeuwen.

M1307. *Tales of the Southwest.* (cassette) Weston, CT: Weston Woods, 1984. 41 min. 6 stories told by Joe Hayes.

M1308. *Talk to Me.* (paperback and cassette) Crystal Lake, IL: Rigby, n.d. Based on a book by Clyde Bellanger.

M1309. *The Talking Parcel.* (TV program, 16mm film, or video) San Diego: Media Guild, 1978. London: Cosgrove Hall and Thames TV, 1984. 40 min. Animated. Beta, VHS, or 3/4″. Based on a book by Gerald Durell.

M1310. *Tall Tales.* (TV program) A program of *The Word Shop.* Washington, DC: WETA-TV, 1976. 15 min. Beta, VHS, or 3/4″.

M1311. *Tallyho, Pinkerton!* (filmstrip with cassette) Weston, CT: Weston Woods, 1984. 43 fr. 6 min. Based on a book by Steven Kellogg.

M1312a. *Tallyho, Pinkerton!* (hardcover or paperback with cassette) Weston Woods, 1984. 6 min. Based on a book by S. Kellogg.

M1312b. *TDC: The Discovery Channel Magazine.* (periodical) Marion, OH: The Discovery Channel/Cable Educational Network. Monthly.

M1313. *A Taste of Blackberries.* (paperback with cassette) Old Greenwich, CT: Listening Library, 1982. 75 min. Based on a book by Doris Buchanan Smith.

M1314. *A Team Show.* (TV program or video) A program of *Musical Encounters.* Los Angeles: KLCS-TV and Lincoln, NE: GPN, 1983. 30 min. VHS or 3/4″.

M1315. *The Team That Hustles: The Inside Story of Your Bones and Muscles.* (TV program or video) Bloomington, IN: AIT and Green Bay, WI: UW-GB Telecommunications Center, 1981. 15 min. Beta, VHS, or 3/4″.

M1316. *Teletales.* (TV series or videos) Bloomington, IN: AIT (Agency for Instructional Technology) and Positive Image Productions, 1984. 15 programs, 15 min. each. Beta, VHS, or 3/4″.

M1317. *TV Book Review: Fantasy.* (filmstrip with cassette) Costa Mesa, CA: Pied Piper, 1989. 22 min. (Literature to Enjoy and Write About, Series 2) Introduces: *The Return of the Indian* by Lynne Reid Banks; *The Black Cauldron* by Lloyd Alexander; and *Tuck Everlasting* by Natalie Babbitt.

M1318. *TV Entertainment Monthly.* (periodical) Boston: TV Entertainment Monthly. Monthly.

M1319. *The TV Kid.* (TV program or video) Program #8 of *Book Bird.* Springfield, VA: Children's Television International, 1979. 15 min. 3/4″. Based on a book by Betsy Byars.

M1320. *The TV Kid.* (hardback or paperback with cassette) Ancramdale, NY: Live Oak Media, 1976. 53:19 min. Based on a book by B. Byars.

M1321. *Tender Places.* (16mm film or video) Deerfield, Il: MTI, 1985. 24 min.

M1322. *Text Extenders.* (book packages) 60 paperback books including 6 copies of 5 books. Englewood Cliffs, NJ: Scholastic, 1986.

M1323. *Theme.* (filmstrip with cassette) Costa Mesa, CA: Pied Piper, 1985. 88 fr. 18 min. (Components of Fiction—Literature for Children, Series 9) Features: *Annie and the Old One* by Miska Miles and *The Pushcart War* by Jean Merrill. Introduces: *Sounder* by William Armstrong; *The Great Gilly Hopkins* by Katherine Paterson; and *Shadow of a Bull* by Mia Wojciechowska.

M1326. *There's a Bat in Bunk Five.* (3 filmstrips and 3 cassettes) Denver: Cheshire, 1989. 75 fr. each. 15 min. each. Based on a book by Paula Danziger.

M1327. *There's a Bat in Bunk Five.* (paperback with cassette) Old Greenwich, CT: Listening Library, 1985. 81 min. (Young Adult Cliffhangers) Based on a book by P. Danziger.

M1328. *Third Planet from Altair.* (TV program or video) Program #6 of *Readit!* Bloomington, IN: AIT, 1982. 15 min. Beta, VHS, or 3/4″. Based on a book by Edward Packard. Also includes: *Deadwood City* by Packard.

M1329. *Thirteen Ways to Sink a Sub.* (paperback with cassette) Old Greenwich, CT: Listening Library, 1985. 41 min. (Soundways to Reading, Cliffhanger Read-along) Based on a book by Jamie Gilson.

M1330. *Thirteen Ways to Sink a Sub.* (hardcover and 3 cassettes) Santa Barbara: ABC-CLIO and Old Greenwich, CT: Listening Library, 1988. 3 hours. (Large Print Read-Along series). Based on a book by J. Gilson.

M1331. *Three by the Sea*. (TV program or video) Program #12 of *Reading Rainbow*. Buffalo: WNED-TV and Lincoln, NE: GPN, 1983. 30 min. VHS or 3/4″. Based on a book by Edward Marshall.

M1332. *Three by the Sea*. (paperback with cassette) Old Greenwich, CT: Listening Library, 1985. 12 min. Based on a book by E. Marshall.

M1333. *Three Days on a River in a Red Canoe*. (TV program or video) Program #9 of *Reading Rainbow*. WNED-TV and GPN, 1983. VHS or 3/4″. Based on a book by Vera Williams.

M1334. *Three Fox Fables*. (16mm film) Chicago: Encyclopedia Britannica, 1984. 11 min. Animated. Based on fables by Aesop.

M1335. *The Three Hat Day*. (TV program or video) Program #41 of *Reading Rainbow*. Buffalo: WNED-TV and Lincoln, NE: GPN, 1987. 30 min. VHS or 3/4″. Based on a book by Laura Geringer.

M1336. *3-2-1-Contact*. (periodical) Boulder, CO: Children's Television Workshop. 10 times per year.

M1337. *3-2-1-Contact*. (TV series and videos) New York: Children's Television Workshop; Washington, DC: Corporation for Public Broadcasting; and Mt. Kisco, NY: Guidance Associates, 1984–. 17 programs per season.

M1338. *3-2-1-Contact*. (database) Children's Television Workshop, 1989. Apple IIc/e, IBM PC. Correlated to the following textbooks: Addison-Wesley; Harcourt Brace Jovanovich; Holt, Reinhart, and Winston; Laidlaw; Merrill; Scott Foresman; and Silver Burdett/Ginn.

M1339. *Through Grandpa's Eyes*. (16mm film or video) Irwindale, CA: Grey Haven Films/Barr Films, 1987. VHS or 3/4″. 20 min. Based on a book by Patricia MacLachlan.

M1340. *Through the Looking Glass and What Alice Found There*. (3 cassettes) New York: Harper/Caedmon, 1986. 3 hours. Based on a book by Lewis Carroll. Read by Christopher Plummer.

M1341. *Thy Friend, Obadiah*. (filmstrip with cassette) Ancramdale, NY: Live Oak Media, 1971. 28 fr. 6:11 min. Based on a book by Brinton Turkle. Narrated by the author.

M1342. *Tight Times*. (TV program or video) Program #1 of *Reading Rainbow*. Buffalo: WNED-TV and Lincoln, NE: GPN, 1983. 30 min. VHS or 3/4″. Based on a book by Barbara Hazen.

M1343. *Tilson's Book Shop*. (TV series or videos) Cleveland: WVIZ-TV, The Eductional Television Association of Metropolitan Cleveland, and Lincoln, NE: GPN, Great Plains National, 1975. 23 programs, 15 min. each. VHS.

M1344. *Time Can Be So Magic: Songs from Captain Kangaroo*. (phonograph record or cassette) Providence, RI: North Star Records, 1988.

M1345. *The Time Machine*. (16mm film or video) Morris Plains, NJ: Lucerne, 1978. 44 min. Beta or VHS. Based on a book by H. G. Wells.

M1346. *The Time Machine*. (2 cassettes) Washington, DC: Audio Book Contractors, 1987. 90 min. Based on a book by H. G. Wells.

M1347. *Timmy and Lassie*. (TV series) Syndicated title for *Lassie*. 60 min. each. Based on a book character by Eric Knight.

M1348. *The Titanic: Lost and Found*. (paperback with cassette) Westminster, MD: Random, 1988. 16 min. Based on a book by Judy Donnelly.

M1349. *A Toad for Tuesday*. (paperback with cassette) Old Greenwich, CT: Listening Library, 1982. 62 min. Based on a book by Russell Erickson.

M1350. *Today and Tomorrow in Space: The Space Shuttle and Beyond*. (3 filmstrips with 3 cassettes) Washington, DC: National Geographic, 1983. Includes: *Space Shuttle*, 60 fr. 18 min; *Living and Working in Space*, 62 fr. 18 min; and *Satellites and How they Help Us*, 55 fr. 17 min.

M1351. *Today Was a Terrible Day*. (filmstrip with cassette) Ancramdale, NY: Live Oak Media, n.d. 8:07. Based on a book by Patricia Giff.

M1352. *Tomi Ungerer, Storyteller*. (video) Weston, CT: Weston Woods, 1981. 21 min. Live action. Beta or VHS. Introduces: *The Three Robbers*; *Moon Man*; and *The Beast of Monsieur Racine*..

M1353. *Tom's Midnight Garden*. (TV program or video) Program #12 of *More Books Cover to Cover*. Washington, DC: WETA-TV and Alexandria, VA: PBS Video, 1987. 15 min. VHS or 3/4″. Based on a book by Philippa Pearce.

M1354. *Top of the News*. (periodical) Chicago: American Library Association (Association for Library Service to Children and Young Adult Services Division) After 1987 became *The Journal of Youth Services in Libraries (JYS)*..

M1355. *Top Secret*. (TV program or video) Program #9 of *Books from Cover to Cover*. Alexandria, VA: PBS, n.d. 15 min. VHS or 3/4″. Based on a book by John Gardiner.

M1356. *The Tortoise and the Hare*. (TV program or video) Program #24 of *Reading Rainbow*. Buffalo: WNED-TV and Lincoln, NE:

M1383. *The Upstairs Room.* (2 filmstrips with 2 cassettes) American School Publishers, 1976. 212 fr. 33 min. Based on a book by J. Reiss.

M1384. *The Upstairs Room.* (cassette) American School Publishers, 1974. Based on a book by J. Reiss.

M1385. *The Velveteen Rabbit.* (video) Hightstown, NJ: American School Publishers, 1986. 26:30 min. VHS. Based on a book by Margery Williams.

M1386. *The Velveteen Rabbit.* (phonograph record or cassette) NY: Knopf, 1985. 30 min. Based on a book by M. Williams. Read by Meryl Streep.

M1387. *The Velveteen Rabbit.* (cassette) New York: Harper/Caedmon, 1984. 55 min. Based on a book by M. Williams. Read by Gwen Verdon.

M1388. *The Velveteen Rabbit.* (hardback or paperback with cassette) Old Greenwich, CT: Listening Library, 1985. 24:20 min. (Follow the Reader series) Based on a book by M. Williams.

M1389. *The Velveteen Rabbit.* (paperback with cassette) NY: Platt and Munk, 1987. 10 min. Based on a book by M. Williams. Read by Florence Graham.

M1390. *Vertebrates.* (TV program) A program of *Challenge.* Nashville: WDCN-TV, n.d. 15 min.

M1391. *Vibrant Strings, Part 1 and Part 2.* (TV programs or videos) Programs #5 and #6 of *Musical Instruments.* Lincoln, NE: GPN, 1979. 20 min. VHS or 3/4″.

M1392. *The Victory Garden.* (TV series) Boston: WGBH-TV, n.d. Hosts: Bob Thompson, Jim Wilson, and Peter Seabrook.

M1393. *The Village of Round and Square Houses.* (16mm film or video) Weston, CT: Weston Woods, 1990. 12 min. Based on a book by Ann Grifalconi.

M1394. *The Village of Round and Square Houses.* (filmstrip with cassette) Weston Woods, 1987. 90 fr. 12 min. Based on a book by A. Grifalconi.

M1395. *The Village of Round and Square Houses.* (hardcover book with cassette) Weston Woods, 1987. 12 min. Based on a book by A. Grifalconi.

M1396. *A Visit to the Dentist.* (filmstrip with cassette) Chicago: SVE, 1982. 50 fr. 5:30 min. (Slim Goodbody's Health Series).

M1397. *A Visit to the Doctor.* (filmstrip with cassette) SVE, 1982. 50 fr. 5:30 min. (Slim Goodbody's Health Series).

M1398. *A Visit to the Hospital.* (filmstrip with cassette) SVE, 1982. 58 fr. 7:30 min. (Slim Goodbody's Health Series).

M1399. *A Visit to William Blake's Inn: Poems for Innocent and Experienced Travelers.* (video) Hightstown, NJ: American School Publishers, n.d. 17:30 min. VHS. Based on a book by Nancy Willard.

M1400. *A Visit to William Blake's Inn: Poems for Innocent and Experienced Travelers.* (filmstrip with cassette) American School Publishers, 1982. 17 min. Based on a book by N. Willard.

M1401. *A Visit to William Blake's Inn: Poems for Innocent and Experienced Travelers.* (paperback with cassette) American School Publishers, 1982. 17 min. Based on a book by N. Willard.

M1402. *A Visit with Elizabeth George Speare.* (video) Burlington, MA: Houghton Mifflin, n.d. 13 min. Live action. Beta, VHS, or 3/4″. Introduces: *The Witch of Blackbird Pond..*

M1403. *A Visit with Jean Fritz.* (video) New York: Putnam, 1986. 11 min. Beta, VHS, or 3/4″.

M1404. *A Visit with Lois Duncan.* (video) Albuquerque: R.A.D., 1986. 18 min.

M1405. *A Visit with Lois Lowry.* (video) Burlington, MA: Houghton Mifflin, n.d. 19 min. Live action. Beta, VHS, or 3/4″. Introduces: *Anastasia Krupnik; Anastasia Ask Your Analyst;* and *Anastasia Has the Answers..*

M1406. *A Visit with Scott O'Dell.* (video) Burlington, MA: Houghton Mifflin, 1983. 15 min. Beta, VHS, or 3/4″. Includes information about *Sarah Bishop. .*

M1407. *Voyage of the Ludgate Hill: Travels with Robert Louis Stevenson.* (filmstrip with cassette) Hightstown, NJ: American School Publishers, 1988. 73 fr. Adapted from a poem by Nancy Willard.

M1408. *Wagon's West.* (computer program) Garden City, NY: Focus Media. Apple family. 5 disks, 5 guides, and 2 posters.

M1409a. *Walkabout.* (16mm film) Wilmette, IL: Films, Inc, 1971. 96 min. Based on a book by James Marshall.

M1409b. *Walking on Air.* (video) A program of *WonderWorks.* Los Angeles, CA: KCET-TV and Public Media Video, 1986. 58 min. VHS.

M1410. *Wanda Gag 1883–1946: A Minnesota Childhood.* (filmstrip with cassette) Minneapolis, MN: Heritage Productions, 1984. 86 fr. 16 min. Introduces *Millions of Cats..*

M1411a. *War and Remembrance.* (7 videos) Oak Forest, IL: MPI, 1988. 120 min. each.

Beta, VHS. Based on a book by Herman Wouk.

M1411b. *The War with Grandpa.* (paperback with cassette) Old Greenwich, CT: Listening Library, 1985. 70 min. (Soundways to Reading, Cliffhangers Read-along) Based on a book by Robert Kimmel Smith.

M1412. *Watch the Stars Come Out.* (TV program or video) Program #29 of *Reading Rainbow.* Buffalo: WNED-TV and Lincoln, NE: GPN, 1986. 30 min. VHS or 3/4″. Based on a book by Riki Levinson.

M1413. *Watership Down.* (4 cassettes) San Francisco: Mind's Eye, 1986. 4 hours. Based on a book by Richard Adams.

M1414a. *The Way It Is: After the Divorce.* (16mm film or video) Los Angeles: Churchill Films and New York: National Film Board of Canada, 1983. 24 min. Beta, VHS, or 3/4″.

M1414b. *The Way-Out Cassette for Children.* (cassette) Salt Lake City, UT: Dimension 5, 1987. 43 min.

M1415. *The Way We Wear.* (TV program) A program of *Smithsonian World.* Washington, DC: WETA-TV and the Smithsonian Institution, n.d. 60 min.

M1416. *We Can't Sleep.* (filmstrip with cassette) Hightstown, NJ: American School Publishers, 1985. 77 fr. 8 min. Based on a book by James Stevenson.

M1417. *The Web: Wonderfully Exciting Books.* (newsletter) Columbus, OH: Center for Language, Literature and Reading; College of Education; Ohio State University. Quarterly.

M1418. *Webbing Your Idea.* (TV program or video) Program #3 of *Fins, Feathers and Fur.* Bloomington, IN: AIT, 1986. 15 min. Beta, VHS, or 3/4″.

M1419. *Wee TV.* (video) Great Neck, NY: Best Films and Video and Cynthia Cherbock Productions, 1988. 30 min.

M1420a. *Welcome Home, Jellybean.* (16mm film or video) Deerfield, IL: MTI, 1986. 30 min. VHS. Based on a book by Marlene Shyer.

M1420b. *Welcome to Pooh Corner.* (video) Burbank, CA: Walt Disney, 1983. 111 min. Based on books by A. A. Milne.

1420c. *Well, Well, Well with Slim Goodbody.* (TV programs or videos) Bloomington, IN: AIT (Agency for Instructional Technology), 1985. 15 programs, 15 min. each.

M1420d. *West African Instruments.* (TV program) Program #13 of *Musical Instruments.* Morgantown, WVA: WNPB-TV and Lincoln, NE: GPN, 1979. 20 min. VHS or 3/4″.

M1421a. *The Westing Game.* (2 filmstrips and 2 cassettes) Costa Mesa, CA: Pied Piper, 1986.

86 and 80 frs. 15:30 min. each. Based on a book by Ellen Raskin.

M1421b. *The Westward Movement: A Unit of Study* (5 filmstrips and 5 cassettes) Niles, IL: United Learning, 1985. Includes *The First Frontier; Early Frontier Life; Moving Deep into the Interior; Settling Westward Lands; Sodbusters, Cowboys, and Indians.*

M1422a. *Whale Rescue.* (TV program, 16mm film or video) A program of NOVA. Deerfield, IL: Coronet, 1988. 52 min.

M1422b. *Whales.* (filmstrip) Washington, DC: National Geographic, 1979. 14 min.

M1423. *Whales.* (TV program and video) A *World of Audubon* program. Washington, DC: WETA-TV and the National Audubon Society, n.d. 60 min.

M1424. *Whales.* (video) Los Angeles: Churchill, 1970. 23 min. Beta, VHS, or 3/4″.

M1425. *Whales.* (16mm film or video) Washington, DC: National Geographic, 1984. VHS or 3/4″.

M1426. *Whales.* (cassette and 30 booklets) National Geographic, 1984.

M1427. *Whalesong.* (16mm film or video) Olay, PA: Bullfrog Films, 1986. 17:47 min.

M1428. *Wharton and the Castaways.* (TV program or video) Program #4 of *Books from Cover to Cover.* Washington, DC: WETA-TV and Alexandria, VA: PBS, n.d. 15 min. Based on a book by Russell Erickson.

M1429. *What Do You Do, Dear?* (filmstrip with cassette) Weston, CT: Weston Woods, 1970. 5 min. 27 fr. Based on a book by Sesyle Joslin.

M1430. *What Do You Do, Dear?* (cassette) Weston Woods, 1970. 5 min. Based on a book by S. Joslin.

M1431. *What Do You Say, Dear?* (filmstrip with cassette) Weston Woods, 1964. 27 fr. 5 min. Based on a book by S. Joslin.

M1432. *What Do You Say, Dear?* (hardcover or paperback with cassette) Weston Woods, 1964. 5 min. Based on a book by S. Joslin.

M1433a. *What Happened to Patrick's Dinosaurs?* (paperback with cassette) Boston: Houghton Mifflin, 1988. Based on a book by Donald Carrick.

M1433b. *What's a Good Book? Selecting Books for Children.* (film or video) Weston, CT: Weston Woods, 1982. 26 min. Beta or VHS.

M1434. *What's the Big Idea, Ben Franklin?* (TV program or video) Program #7 of *Through the Pages.* Cleveland: WVIZ-TV and Bloomington, IN: AIT, 1982. 15 min. Beta, VHS, or 3/4″. Based on a book by Jean Fritz.

M1435. *What's the Big Idea, Ben Franklin?* (paperback with cassette) Weston, CT: Weston Woods, n.d. 30 min. Based on a book by J. Fritz.

M1436. *What's Under My Bed?* (filmstrip with cassette) Weston Woods, 1984. 61 fr. 10 min. Based on a book by James Stevenson.

M1437. *What's Under My Bed?* (hardcover or paperback with cassette) Weston Woods, 1984. 10 min. Based on a book by J. Stevenson.

M1438. *When I Was Young in the Mountains.* (filmstrip with cassette) Hightstown, NJ: American School Publishers, 1984. 68 fr. 6 min. Based on a book by Cynthia Rylant.

M1439a. *When I Was Young in the Mountains.* (cassette) American School Publishers, 1984. 6 min. Based on a book by C. Rylant.

M1439b. *When the Rain Came Down.* (cassette) C. and P. Potluck Records, 1984.

M1440. *Where Animals Live.* (TV program) Program #16 of *Zoo Zoo Zoo.* Cincinnati: WCET-TV and the Greater Cincinnati Television Educational Foundation, 1981. 15 min.

M1441. *Where Did They Go? A Dinosaur Update.* (video) Bohemia, NY: Rainbow Educational Video, 1988. 19 min. VHS.

M1442. *Where Do You Think You're Going, Christopher Columbus?* (hardback or paperback with cassette) Weston, CT: Weston Woods, 1982. 17 min. Based on a book by Jean Fritz.

M1443. *Where the Red Fern Grows.* (paperback with cassette) Old Greenwich, CT: Listening Library, 1984. 80 min. (Young Adult Cliffhangers) Based on a book by Wilson Rawles.

M1444. *Where the Red Fern Grows.* (cassette) New York: Bantam Audio, 1989. 180 min. Based on a book by W. Rawles. Read by Richard Thomas.

M1445. *Where the River Begins.* (filmstrip with cassette) MD: Random, 1986. 40 fr. 5 min. Based on a book by Thomas Locker.

M1446. *Where the River Begins.* (hardcover with cassette) Westminster, MD: Random, 1986. 5 min. Based on a book by T. Locker.

M1447. *Where the Sidewalk Ends.* (phonograph record or cassette) NY: Harper, 1984. 40 min. Abridged from a book by Shel Silverstein.

M1448. *Where Was Patrick Henry on the 29th of May?* (hardback or paperback with cassette) Weston, CT: Weston Woods, 1977. 36 min. Based on a book by Jean Fritz.

M1449. *Where the Wild Things Are.* (16mm film or video) Weston, CT: Weston Woods, 1974, 1989. 8 min. Animated. Based on a book by Maurice Sendak.

M1450. *Where the Wild Things Are.* (filmstrip with cassette) Weston Woods, 1967. 38 fr. 5 min. Based on a book by M. Sendak.

M1451. *Where the Wild Things Are.* (hardback or paperback with cassette) Weston Woods, 1967. 5 min. Based on a book by M. Sendak.

M1452. *Where the Wild Things Are: A Fantasy Opera.* (video) Chicago: Home Vision, n.d. 40 min. VHS. Based on a book by M. Sendak.

M1453. *The Whipping Boy.* (TV program or video) Program #15 of *More Books from Cover to Cover.* Washington, DC: WETA-TV and Alexandria, VA: PBS Video, 1987. 15 min. VHS or 3/4″. Based on a book by Sid Fleischman.

M1454. *The Whipping Boy.* (2 filmstrips with 2 cassettes) Costa Mesa, CA: Pied Piper, 1988. 38 min. Based on a book by S. Fleischman.

M1455. *Whistle While You Work.* (TV program) A program of *Shining Time Station.* New York: WNET-TV, 1989. 30 min. Host: Ringo Starr.

M1456. *The Whistling Teakettle.* (TV program or video) Program #15 of *Readit!* Bloomington, IN: AIT, 1982. 15 min. Beta, VHS, or 3/4″. Based on a book by Mindy Skolsky.

M1457. *Who's Dr. Seuss? Meet Ted Geisel.* (filmstrip with cassette) Hightstown, NJ: American School Publisher, 1981. 122 fr. 13:30 min.

M1458. *Who's in Charge of Lincoln?* (TV program or video) Program #7 of *Readit!* Bloomington, IN: AIT, 1982. 15 min. Beta, VHS, or 3/4″. Based on a book by D. Fife. Also includes *The Lucky Stone* by L. Clifton.

M1459. *Who's That Stepping on Plymouth Rock?* (hardback or paperback with cassette) Weston, CT: Weston Woods, 1982. 23 min. Based on a book by Jean Fritz.

M1460. *Who Works at the Zoo?* (TV program or video) Program #15 of *Zoo, Zoo, Zoo.* Cincinnati: WCET-TV and the Greater Cincinnati Television Educational Foundation, 1981. 15 min.

M1461a. *Why Don't You Get a Horse, Sam Adams?* (hardback or paperback with cassette) Weston, CT: Weston Woods, 1977. 19 min. Based on a book by Jean Fritz.

M1461b. *Why Spiders Hide in Dark Corners.* (TV program and video) *Magic Carpet* series. Lincoln, NE: Great Plains Instructional TV Library, 1977. 15 min. 3/4″.

M1461c. *The Wild Pony.* (TV program and video) Van Nuys, CA: Vestron, 1983. 87 min. VHS.

M1462. *Wild Things.* (4 dolls) 11″. each. Weston CT: Weston Woods. Boulder, CO: The Storyteller. Based on a book by Maurice Sendak.

M1463. *Wilfrid Gordon McDonald Partridge.* (filmstrip with cassette) Weston, CT: Weston Woods, 1986. 38 fr. 7 min. Based on a book by Mem Fox.

M1464. *Wilfrid Gordon McDonald Partridge.* (hardback book with cassette) Weston Woods, 1986. 7 min. Based on a book by M. Fox.

M1465. *Will You Sign Here, John Hancock?* (hardback or paperback with cassette) Weston, CT: Weston Woods, 1977. 34 min. Based on a book by Jean Fritz.

M1466. *The Willow Tree.* (TV program or video) Program #2 of *Teletales.* Bloomington, IN: AIT, 1984. 15 min. Beta, VHS, or 3/4″. Based on a folk tale from England and China.

M1467. *Wilson Library Bulletin.* (periodical) Bronx, NY: H W Wilson Co. Monthly, September–June.

M1468. *The Wind in the Willows.* (video) New York: Thorne EMI; HBO, n.d. 78 min. Based on a book by Kenneth Grahame.

M1469a. *The Wind in the Willows: The Further Adventures of Toad.* (TV program) New York: Thorne EMI; HBO, 1984. 60 min. Based on a book by K. Grahame.

M1469b. *Winnie-the-Pooh and the Honey Tree.* (video) Burbank, CA: Walt Disney Home Video, 1965. 25 min. 1/2″. Based on a book by A. A. Milne.

M1469c. *Winnie-the-Pooh and Tigger Too.* (video) Walt Disney Home Video, n.d. 25 min. 1/2″. Based on a book by A. A. Milne.

M1470. *The Wish Giver.* (TV program or video) Program #1 of *More Books from Cover to Cover.* Washington, DC: WETA-TV and Alexandria, VA: PBS Video, n.d. 15 min. VHS or 3/4″. Based on a book by Bill Brittain.

M1471. *The Wish Giver.* (2 filmstrips with cassettes) Hightstown, NJ: American School Publishers, 1985. 147 and 148 fr. 10:50 and 19:50 min. Based on a book by B. Brittain.

M1472. *The Witch of Blackbird Pond.* (TV program or video) Program #11 of *Storybound.* Springfield, VA: Childrens Television International, 1981. 15 min. Beta, VHS, or 3/4″. Based on a book by Elizabeth Speare.

M1473. *The Witch of Fourth Street.* (TV program or video) Program #15 of *Readit!* Bloomington, In: AIT, 1982. 15 min. Beta, VHS, or 3/4″. Based on a book by Myron Levoy.

M1474. *The Wizard of Earthsea.* (TV program or video) A program of *Best of Cover to Cover, 2-A.* Washington, DC: WETA-TV and Alexandria, VA: PBS Video, n.d. 15 min. Based on a book by Ursula Le Guin.

M1475. *The Wizard of Oz.* (motion picture or video) Culver City, CA: MGM/UA Home Video, 1939, 1987. 101 min. b & w and color. Beta, VHS. Based on a book by Frank Baum. Starring Judy Garland.

M1476. *The Wolves of Willoughby Chase.* (TV program or video) A program of *Best of Cover to Cover, 2-A.* Washington, DC: WETA-TV and Alexandria, VA: PBS Video, n.d. 15 min. Based on a book by Joan Aiken.

M1477. *The Wolves of Willoughby Chase.* (2 cassettes) New York: Bantam Audio, 1989. 180 min. Based on a book by J. Aiken.

M1478. *Women of Courage: Ida Lewis.* (phonograph record or cassette) St. Paul, MN: Eclectic, 1985. 11 min.

M1479. *Women of Courage: Libby Riddles.* (phonograph record or cassette) Eclectic, 1985. 7:21 min.

M1480. *Women of Courage: Sally Ride.* (phonograph record or cassette) Eclectic, 1985. 7 min.

M1481. *The Wonderful Flight to the Mushroom Planet.* (TV program or video) Program #9 of *Book Bird.* Springfield, VA: Children's Television International, 1979. 15 min. 3/4″. Based on a book by Eleanor Cameron.

M1482. *WonderWorks.* (TV series) Pittsburgh: WQED-TV and the Children's and Family Consortium; Los Angeles: KCET-TV; Minneapolis: KTCA-TV; Columbia: South Carolina Educational TV; and Washington, DC: WETA-TV. 60 min. each.

M1483. *Won't Know Till I Get There.* (TV program or video) Program #3 of *More Books from Cover to Cover.* Washington, DC: WETA-TV and Alexandria, VA: PBS Video, n.d. 15 min. VHS or 3/4″. Based on a book by Walter Dean Myers.

M1484. *Woodstorks, Barometers of the Everglades.* (TV program and video) (World of Audubon) New York: National Audubon Society, and Washington, D.C.: WETA-TV, 1987. 58 min.

M1485. *Word Shop.* (TV series) WETA-TV and the Greater Washington Educational Telecommunication Association and Springfield, VA: Children's Television International, 1976. 30 programs, 15 min. each. 3/4″. Host: John Robbins.

M1486. *Words by Heart, Parts 1 and 2.* (TV program) A program of *WonderWorks.* Philadelphia: WQED-TV and the Children's and

Family Consortium, 1985. 50 min. each. Based on a book by Ouida Sebestyen.

M1487. *The World of Audubon.* (TV series) Washington, DC: WETA-TV and the National Audubon Society, 1986–.

M1488. *A Wrinkle in Time.* (TV program or video) Program #10 of *Storybound.* Springfield, VA: Children's Television International, 1981. 15 min. Beta, VHS, or 3/4″. Based on a book by Madeleine L'Engle.

M1489a. *You Don't Have to Die: Jason's Story.* (TV program or video) New York: Ambrose Video, 1988. 30 min. VHS or 3/4″. Based on the book *My Book for Kids with Cansur: A Child's Autobiography of Hope* by Jason Gaes.

M1489b. *The Young Fliers.* (TV program) Program 5823 of *Lassie and Timmy.* New York: CBS-TV, 1954–1971. Syndicated 1971. 28 min.

M1490. *Your Body.* (TV program) A program of *3-2-1-Contact.* New York: Children's Television Workshop, n.d. 30 min.

M1491. *Zoo.* (filmstrip with cassette) Ancramdale, NY: Live Oak Media, 1989. 7:45 min. Based on a book by Gail Gibbons.

M1492. *Zoo Babies.* (TV program or video) Program #12 of *Zoo Zoo Zoo.* Cincinnati: WCET-TV and the Greater Cincinnati Television Educational Foundation, 1981. 15 min.

M1493. *Zoo Zoo Zoo.* (TV series or videos) Cincinnati: WCET-TV and the Greater Cincinnati Television Educational Foundation, 1981. 16 programs, 15 min. each.

Title Index

This is a fully-integrated index to titles of all items—books, multimedia materials, stories, and so forth—that are cited in the text. Author name is given to facilitate cross-indexing to the *Index to Books*. All main page references are to books; otherwise, the type of material (TV program, video, filmstrip, recording, and so forth) is indicated.

Subject Index

About the Author

Born on a farm near Bay Port, Michigan, Mary Ann Strieter Paulin began sharing books while she was a student librarian in high school and a summer helper at the small local library. She has been sharing books ever since.

A graduate of Western Michigan University, where she received the B.A., M.L.S., and Ed.S., Ms. Paulin is a library media specialist in the Negaunee, Michigan public schools. Her first book, *Creative Uses of Children's Literature,* was published in 1982 to outstanding reviews, and the techniques of sharing books with children she pioneered there are now used routinely in many schools and libraries. Mary Ann Paulin is active professionally too in the school library, media, and reading associations of her state; the American Library Association and its youth divisions; and is currently the chairperson of the 1994 Newbery Award Committee of the Association of Library Services to Children (ALSC) of the ALA.

A frequent conference speaker in the U.S. and abroad, Ms. Paulin has presented sessions for the American Association of School Librarians (AASL), the International Reading Association (IRA), and the National Council of Teachers of English (NCTE), among others. She also conducts workshops for teachers, librarians, media specialists and other people concerned with children and books, and has taught college courses via television as well.

Mary Ann Paulin is married to Dr. Kenneth C. Paulin, a professor in the speech department at Northern Michigan University.